Web Development with JavaServer Pages

Web Development with
JavaServer Pages

SECOND EDITION

DUANE K. FIELDS
MARK A. KOLB
SHAWN BAYERN

MANNING
Greenwich
(74° w. long.)

For online information and ordering of this and other Manning books, go to www.manning.com. The publisher offers discounts on this book when ordered in quantity. For more information, please contact:

Special Sales Department
Manning Publications Co.
209 Bruce Park Avenue
Greenwich, CT 06830

Fax: (203) 661-9018
email: orders@manning.com

♾ Recognizing the importance of preserving what has been written, it is Manning's policy to have the books we publish printed on acid-free paper, and we exert our best efforts to that end.

Manning Publications Co.
209 Bruce Park Avenue
Greenwich, CT 06830

Copyeditor: Elizabeth Martin
Typesetter: Tony Roberts
Cover designer: Leslie Haimes

Printed in the United States of America
1 2 3 4 5 6 7 8 9 10 – VHG – 04 03 02 01

To Kris—
for her patience, encouragement
and good humor that made this project possible
D.K.F.

For Megan, Andrew, and Jean—
your presence is my strength, and your love my inspiration
M.A.K.

To my parents—
For teaching me everything I know (except JSP)
S.B.

brief contents

1 ▪ Introduction 1

2 ▪ HTTP and servlets 17

3 ▪ First steps 30

4 ▪ How JSP works 46

5 ▪ Programming JSP scripts 65

6 ▪ Actions and implicit objects 101

7 ▪ Using JSP components 129

8 ▪ Developing JSP components 165

9 ▪ Working with databases 198

10 ▪ Architecting JSP applications 229

11 ▪ An example JSP project 272

12 ▪ Introducing filters and listeners 318

13 ▪ Applying filters and listeners 334

14 ▪ Deploying JSP applications 384

15 ▪ Performing common JSP tasks 418

16 ▪ Generating non-HTML content 470

17 ▪ JSP by example 493

18 ▪ Creating custom tags 529

19 ▪ Implementing advanced custom tags 582

20 ▪ Validating custom tag libraries 621

A ▪ Changes in the JSP 1.2 API 669

B ▪ Running the reference implementation 676

C ▪ Incorporating Java applets 683

D ▪ JSP resources 697

E ▪ JSP syntax reference 702

F ▪ JSP API reference 718

contents

preface to the second edition *xxv*

preface to the first edition *xxix*

acknowledgments *xxxi*

about this book *xxxiii*

about the authors *xxxviii*

authors online *xxxix*

about the cover illustration *xl*

1 *Introduction* *1*

1.1 What is JSP? *2*

1.2 Dynamic content on the web *2*

Why dynamic content? *3* ▪ *Common Gateway Interface* *4* ▪ *Template systems* *5* ▪ *Java on the Web* *8* ▪ *How XML fits in* *11*

1.3 The role of JSP *13*

The JavaBeans component architecture *13*
JSP and Java 2 Platform Enterprise Edition *15*

2 *HTTP and servlets* 17

2.1 The Hypertext Transfer Protocol (HTTP) *18*

HTTP basics 18 ▪ GET versus POST 21

2.2 Java servlets *23*

How a web server uses servlets 24 ▪ The anatomy of a servlet 24 ▪ A servlet example 26

3 *First steps* 30

3.1 Simple text *31*

3.2 Dynamic content *32*

Conditional logic 33 ▪ Iteration 34
Non-HTML output 37

3.3 Processing requests and managing sessions *38*

Accessing request parameters 38 ▪ Using sessions 39

3.4 Separating logic from presentation *41*

Reusing logic with JavaBeans 42
Abstracting logic with custom tags 44

3.5 Review of examples *45*

4 *How JSP works* 46

4.1 The structure of JSP pages *47*

Directives and scripting elements 47
Standard and custom actions 48

4.2 Behind the scenes *52*

Translation to servlets 52 ▪ Translation versus execution 54

4.3 What the environment provides *56*

Automatic servlet generation 56 ▪ Buffered output 57
Session management 59 ▪ Exception handling 63
Implicit objects 64 ▪ Support for JavaBeans and HTML forms 64

5 *Programming JSP scripts* 65
5.1 Scripting languages *66*
5.2 JSP tags *68*
5.3 JSP directives *68*
Page directive 68 ▪ Include directive 80
Tag library directive 82
5.4 Scripting elements *83*
Declarations 84 ▪ Expressions 88 ▪ Scriptlets 91
5.5 Flow of control *93*
Conditionalization 93 ▪ Iteration 94
Exception handling 94 ▪ A word of caution 97
5.6 Comments *97*
Content comments 98 ▪ JSP comments 98
Scripting language comments 99

6 *Actions and implicit objects* 101
6.1 Implicit objects *102*
Servlet-related objects 104 ▪ Input/Output 105
Contextual objects 112 ▪ Error handling 120
6.2 Actions *121*
Forward 122 ▪ Include 125 ▪ Plug-in 128
Bean tags 128

7 *Using JSP components* 129
7.1 The JSP component model *130*
Component architectures 130 ▪ Benefits of a component architecture 131 ▪ Component design for web projects 132 ▪ Building applications from components 133

7.2 JavaBean fundamentals *135*
The different types of JavaBeans 138

7.3 JSP bean tags *140*
Tag-based component programming 140 ▪ Accessing JSP components 142 ▪ Initializing beans 150
Controlling a bean's scope 157

8 *Developing JSP components 165*

8.1 What makes a bean a bean? *166*
Bean conventions 166 ▪ The bean constructor 167
Defining a bean's properties 168 ▪ Indexed properties 172 ▪ Implementing bean properties as cursors 176 ▪ Boolean properties 178 ▪ JSP type conversion 179 ▪ Configuring beans 181

8.2 Some examples *182*
Example: a TimerBean 182
A bean that calculates interest 184

8.3 Bean interfaces *189*
The BeanInfo interface 189 ▪ The Serializable interface 190 ▪ The HttpSessionBindingListener interface 190
Other features of the Bean API 191

8.4 Mixing scriptlets and bean tags *192*
Accessing beans through scriptlets 192
Accessing scriptlet created objects 193

9 *Working with databases 198*

9.1 JSP and JDBC *199*
JNDI and data sources 200 ▪ Prepared statements 201

9.2 Database driven JSPs *202*

Creating JSP components from table data 202
JSPs and JDBC data types 205 ▪ Maintaining persistent connections 208 ▪ Handling large sets of results 211
Transaction processing 216

9.3 Example: JSP conference booking tool *217*

Project overview 217 ▪ Our database 218
Design overview 218

10 ***Architecting JSP applications 229***

10.1 Web applications *230*

Web application flow 232
Architectural approaches 233

10.2 Page-centric design *233*

Role-based pages 233 ▪ Managing page flow with action targets 236 ▪ Building composite pages 238
Limitations of the page-centric approach 241

10.3 Servlet-centric design *242*

Hello, World—with servlets 243 ▪ JSP and the servlet API 244 ▪ Servlets for application control 247
Servlets for handling application logic 248 ▪ Servlets as single entry points 249 ▪ Handling errors in the servlet 252 ▪ Example: servlet-centric employee browser 253 ▪ EmployeeBean 255
FetchEmployeeServlet 258 ▪ JSP employee list 261
JSP page viewer 262

10.4 Enterprise JavaBeans *263*

What are Enterprise JavaBeans? 263 ▪ JavaBeans vs. EJBs 264 ▪ Application servers and EJB containers 264
Application design with EJBs 265

10.5 Choosing an appropriate architecture *266*
Application environment 267 ▪ Enterprise software requirements 268 ▪ Performance, scalability, and availability 269 ▪ Technical considerations 269
Organizational considerations 270

11 ***An example JSP project 272***
11.1 An FAQ system *273*
Project motivations 273 ▪ Application requirements 273
Application modules 275
Building an FAQ component 276
11.2 The storage module *278*
Database schema 279 ▪ The FaqRepository class 279
Storage module exceptions 285
11.3 The administration module *286*
The administration servlet 287 ▪ The main menu 293
Adding an FAQ 297 ▪ Deleting an FAQ 300
Updating an FAQ 306
11.4 The web access module *311*
The FaqServlet 312 ▪ Viewing a single FAQ 313
Viewing all the FAQs 314 ▪ A table of contents view 315
Plain text view 317

12 ***Introducing filters and listeners 318***
12.1 Life-cycle event listeners *319*
Session listeners 319 ▪ Application listeners 324
12.2 Filters *326*
How filters work 327 ▪ Filter classes 330
Wrapper classes 332
12.3 Using filters and listeners *333*

13 *Applying filters and listeners 334*

13.1 Application description *335*

13.2 User authentication *337*

User account representation 337 ▪ User management interface 338 ▪ User management implementation 339

13.3 Web authentication *341*

Session interactions 341 ▪ Login servlet 344
Login pages 350 ▪ Content pages 353
Logout servlet 357 ▪ Logout pages 358

13.4 Access control filters *360*

Authentication filter 361 ▪ Role filter 364

13.5 Logging listener *368*

HttpSessionListener methods 369
HttpSessionAttributeListener methods 369

13.6 Content filter *372*

Filter methods 373 ▪ Response wrapper inner class 375
Output stream inner class 376 ▪ More filter methods 377
Filter results 380 ▪ Other content filters 381

14 *Deploying JSP applications 384*

14.1 This means WAR *385*

WAR is XML 386 ▪ Waging WAR 389

14.2 The art of WAR *390*

WAR materiel 390 ▪ Drafting deployment descriptors 396

14.3 Maintaining a WAR footing *415*

15 ***Performing common JSP tasks 418***

15.1 Handling cookies *419*

Managing cookies 419 ▪ The Cookie class 420

Example 1: setting a cookie 421

Example 2: retrieving a cookie 422

15.2 Creating error pages *425*

An erroneous page 426 ▪ Data collection methods 427

Sending electronic mail 432 ▪ The error page 433

15.3 Mixing JSP and JavaScript *437*

15.4 Building interactive interfaces *441*

Sticky widgets 441 ▪ Utility methods 442

The example form 443 ▪ Setting up the form 445

Text and hidden fields 446 ▪ Text areas 447

Radio buttons 447 ▪ Select boxes 448

Check boxes 448 ▪ Form source 449

15.5 Validating form data *451*

Client- and server-side validation 451

Example: server-side validation 452

15.6 Building a shopping cart *458*

Overview 459 ▪ The catalog page 460

ShoppingCartItem and InventoryManager 460

The ShoppingCart bean 464

Displaying the shopping cart 466

15.7 Miscellaneous tasks *467*

Determining the last modification date 467

Executing system commands 468

16 *Generating non-HTML content 470*

16.1 Working with non-HTML content 471

The importance of MIME 471 ▪ Controlling the content type 472 ▪ Detecting your client 472 Designing multiformat applications 473 Controlling the file extension 474

16.2 Text content formats 475

Plain text output 475 ▪ WYGIWYG output (what you generate is what you get) 476

16.3 XML documents 477

Creating voice XML documents 479

16.4 External content 482

JSP style sheets 483 ▪ JavaScript 485

16.5 Advanced content formats 487

Excel spreadsheets 488 ▪ Code generation 489

17 *JSP by example 493*

17.1 A rotating banner ad 494

The BannerBean 494 ▪ Using the bean 495

17.2 A random quote generator 497

The QuoteBean 497 ▪ Using the bean 498

17.3 The Tell a Friend! sticker 499

The sticker 500 ▪ The MailForm page 502 Sending the mail 503

17.4 A JSP Whois client 505

The Whois protocol 505 ▪ Requirements and design considerations 507 ▪ The WhoisBean 507 Building the front end 515

17.5 An index generator *517*

A basic implementation 518 ▪ An improved version 520
Going further 525

17.6 A button to view JSP source *525*

Displaying the source 525 ▪ Limitations of the view source program 527 ▪ Adding a view source button \to a page 527 ▪ Viewing source through a bookmark 528

18 *Creating custom tags 529*

18.1 Role of custom tags *530*

18.2 How tag libraries work *531*

18.3 Tag library descriptors *535*

Library elements 535 ▪ Validator elements 537
Listener elements 538 ▪ Tag elements 538
Variable elements 540 ▪ Attribute elements 541
Example element 543

18.4 API overview *544*

Tag handlers 544 ▪ Tag handler life-cycle 550
Helper classes 556 ▪ Auxiliary classes 559

18.5 Example tag library *559*

18.6 Content substitution *560*

18.7 Tag attributes *563*

18.8 Content translation *567*

URL rewriting 568 ▪ HTML encoding 572

18.9 Exception handling *575*

18.10 To be continued *580*

19 *Implementing advanced custom tags 582*

19.1 Tag scripting variables *583*

Example tag 583 ▪ Scripting variable JavaBean 585

19.2 Flow of control *587*

Conditionalization 588 ▪ Iteration 595

19.3 Interacting tags *613*

Interaction mechanisms 614 ▪ Index tag 616

19.4 The final ingredient *619*

20 *Validating custom tag libraries 621*

20.1 Two representations of JSP *622*

20.2 JSP pages as XML documents *624*

The root element 625 ▪ Template text 626

Scripting elements 627 ▪ Request-time attribute values 627

Directives and actions 629 ▪ Sample page 629

20.3 Tag library validation *631*

20.4 Example validators *634*

Copying validator 635 ▪ Script-prohibiting validator 638

Error handling 642 ▪ Content handler 645

Nesting validator 651

20.5 Packaging the tag library *660*

Packaging a single library 661

Packaging multiple libraries 662

20.6 For further information *666*

A *Changes in the JSP 1.2 API 669*

A.1 Introduction *669*

A.2 Changes to the API *670*

Java 2, Version 1.2 now a requirement 670

Servlet API 2.3 required 670 ▪ XML syntax now fully supported 670 ▪ Determining the real path 671 Redirects are not relative to the servlet context 671 Restricted names 671 ▪ Page encoding attribute 671 Flush on include no longer required 671

A.3 Web application changes *672*

New 2.3 web application DTD 672 ▪ Handling of white space 672 ▪ Resolving path names in the web.xml file 672 Request mappings 672 ▪ Dependency on installed extensions 672

A.4 Custom tag improvements *673*

Translation time validation 673 ▪ New tag interfaces 673 ▪ Changes to the TLD 673

A.5 JavaBean changes *674*

Bean tags cannot implicitly access scriptlet objects 674 Fully qualified class names required 674

A.6 New servlet features *674*

Servlet filters 675 ▪ Application events 675

B ***Running the reference implementation 676***

B.1 Prerequisites *677*

B.2 Downloading and installing Tomcat *677*

B.3 Web applications and Tomcat *681*

C ***Incorporating Java applets 683***

C.1 Browser support for Java *683*

C.2 The plug-in action *685*

Required attributes 685 ▪ Optional attributes 687 Parameters 688 ▪ Fallback text 689

C.3 Example: applet configuration *690*

D *JSP resources 697*

D.1 Java implementations *697*
D.2 JSP-related web sites *697*
D.3 JSP FAQs and tutorials *698*
D.4 JSP containers *698*
D.5 Java application servers with JSP support *699*
D.6 JSP development tools *700*
D.7 Tools for performance testing *700*
D.8 Mailing lists and newsgroups *700*

E *JSP syntax reference 702*

E.1 Content comments *702*
E.2 JSP comments *703*
E.3 <jsp:declaration> *704*
E.4 <jsp:directive.include> *705*
E.5 <jsp:directive.page> *706*
E.6 <jsp:directive.taglib> *707*
E.7 <jsp:expression> *708*
E.8 <jsp:forward> *709*
E.9 <jsp:getProperty> *710*
E.10 <jsp:include> *711*
E.11 <jsp:plugin> *712*
E.12 <jsp:scriptlet> *713*
E.13 <jsp:setProperty> *714*
E.14 <jsp:useBean> *715*

F ***JSP API reference 718***

F.1 JSP implicit objects *719*

F.2 Package javax.servlet *719*

Interface Filter† 719 ▪ *Interface FilterChain† 719*
Interface FilterConfig† 720 ▪ *Class GenericServlet 720*
Interface RequestDispatcher 720 ▪ *Interface servlet 721*
Interface ServletConfig 721 ▪ *Interface ServletContext 721*
Interface ServletContextAttributeEvent† 722
Interface ServletContextAttributeListener† 722
Interface ServletContextEvent† 722
Interface ServletContextListener† 723
Class ServletException 723 ▪ *Class ServletInputStream 723*
Class ServletOutputStream 724
Interface ServletRequest 724
Class ServletRequestWrapper† 725
Interface ServletResponse 726
Class ServletResponseWrapper† 726
Interface SingleThreadModel 727
Class UnavailableException 727

F.3 Package javax.servlet.http *727*

Class cookie 727 ▪ *Class HttpServlet 728*
Interface HttpServletRequest 729
Class HttpServletRequestWrapper† 730
Interface HttpServletResponse 730
Class HttpServletResponseWrapper† 732
Interface HttpSession 733
Interface HttpSessionActivationListener† 733
Interface HttpSessionAttributeListener† 733
Class HttpSessionBindingEvent 734

Interface HttpSessionBindingListener 734
Class HttpSessionEvent† *734*
Interface HttpSessionListener† *735* ▪ *Class HttpUtils 735*

F.4 Package javax.servlet.jsp *735*
Interface HttpJspPage 735 ▪ *Class JspEngineInfo 736*
Class JspException 736 ▪ *Class JspFactory 736*
Interface JspPage 737 ▪ *Class JspTagException 737*
Class JspWriter 737 ▪ *Class PageContext 738*

F.5 Package javax.servlet.jsp.tagext *740*
Class BodyContent 740 ▪ *Interface BodyTag 740*
Class BodyTagSupport 740 ▪ *Interface IterationTag*† *741*
Class PageData† *741* ▪ *Interface Tag 741*
Class TagAttributeInfo 742 ▪ *Class TagData 742*
Class TagExtraInfo 743 ▪ *Class TagInfo 743*
Class TagLibraryInfo 744
Class TagLibraryValidator† *744*
Class TagSupport 744 ▪ *Class TagVariableInfo*† *745*
Interface TryCatchFinally† *745* ▪ *Class VariableInfo 745*

index *747*

preface to the second edition

When the first edition of *Web Development with JavaServer Pages* was published some eighteen months ago, URLs ending with a .jsp file extension were a novelty. Today, this is a commonplace occurrence for millions of web surfers. JSP has been widely adopted, and we are very pleased to have played a supporting role in its popularization.

We are likewise very pleased with the reception of the first edition. As one of the first JSP books on the market, we knew we were taking a risk. It's clear from the response, however, that JSP addresses a serious need in the development community, resulting in an equally serious need for good reference material. By presenting such reference material from the practitioner's point of view, we appear to have struck a nerve. The first edition received both critical and popular acclaim as one of the leading books on the subject, and our thanks go out to all of the readers who contributed to its success.

Of course, the book's success is due in no small part to the success of JSP itself. JavaServer Pages technology has experienced a rapid adoption in the past year or so, anxiously embraced by the "teeming millions" of Java and web developers who had been clamoring for a standard mechanism for generating dynamic web content. At the time the first edition was published, there were only a handful of application servers supporting JSP 1.0, and even fewer supporting version 1.1. As a required component of the J2EE (Java 2 Enterprise Edition) platform, however, there are now dozens of commercial application servers with full JSP support. Tool support is another area that has thankfully experienced significant growth. Today, web developers can take advantage of a wide array of editors, IDEs, and code generators with built-in support for JSP.

As with any Internet technology though, JSP continues to evolve.

In September 2001 Sun released the JavaServer Pages 1.2 and the Java Servlets 2.3 specifications. These APIs were updated to provide several new features, clarify some outstanding issues from the previous specifications, and pave the way for improved tool support. Among those new features are full XML support, servlet filters and life-cycle event handlers, and enhanced validation of custom tag libraries. Readers interested in a quick overview of the new APIs are directed to Appendix A.

Given these changes to the specifications, as well as our desire to fix a few gaffes from the first edition, we felt an obligation to our readers—both past and future—to start work on a second edition.

As was true of the first edition, our goals for this new edition are twofold. In addition to updating the text to address the changes and enhancements introduced in JSP 1.2, we have also revised and expanded the opening chapters to provide a gentler introduction to JSP and the underlying technologies (such as HTTP and servlets) for those who are new to web development. At the turn of the millennium, it was safe to assume that anyone brave enough to be dabbling with JSP already knew their way around the underlying protocols. JSP is now an established platform in its own right, and it was felt that providing a bit more context for understanding the inherent properties of that platform was more than justified.

We've also added more examples, including the much-requested shopping cart, as well as an entire chapter on creating non-HTML content. JSP was always intended as a general-purpose mechanism for generating dynamic content of all kinds, not just HTML. With the recent excitement revolving around XML and other text-based document formats, full coverage of this topic was a given for the second edition.

A pair of new chapters focus on servlet filters and life-cycle event listeners, two new features of the Servlet 2.3 API that are equally applicable to JSP applications. Filters enable developers to layer new functionality—such as on-the-fly encryption, compression, translation, or authentication—atop existing servlets and JSP pages, without having to change the original code. Event listeners provide applications with the ability to monitor (and therefore take advantage of) the activity of the underlying servlet or JSP container more closely. A chapter-length example demonstrates how both of these features may be leveraged to simplify the implementation of key application behaviors.

As we continue to gain experience in real-world web development projects, we are often exposed to new techniques for architecting JSP applications. In the interest of keeping readers abreast of such alternatives, new material in chapter 10 introduces the concept of action targets, an extension to the page-centric design approach presented in the first edition.

In keeping with the industry's growing interest in custom tag libraries, we've expanded our coverage of this topic, as well. There are now three chapters dedicated to using, developing, validating, and deploying custom tags. New examples are included to demonstrate JSP 1.2 enhancements, and new custom tag libraries are available from our companion web site, http://www.taglib.com/.

Observant readers will notice an additional name on the cover of this second edition, Shawn Bayern. Shawn, an active member of the Java Community Process, is the reference-implementation lead for the JSP Standard Tag Library, a collection of general-purpose custom tags that will ultimately be supported by all JSP containers. He lends us his unique insight into JSP's place in the technology spectrum, and we are confident that readers will value his contributions to this book as much as we do.

Welcome then, to readers both new and returning. We hope that this second edition will prove itself a worthy successor to the original *Web Development with JavaServer Pages*. And we look forward to uncovering even more .jsp file extensions as we surf the web, hunting for the next generation of killer web applications.

preface to the first edition

In late 1998 we were asked to develop the architecture for a new web site. Our employer, a vendor of enterprise software for system and network management, had an unconventional set of requirements: that the site be able to provide product support data customized for each customer; and that the support data be tailored to the software the customer had already purchased, as well as the configurations already selected.

Of course, the web site needed to look sharp and be easy to navigate. Management software, which of necessity must be flexible and support a wide range of operating conditions, tends to be very complex. This particular software was targeted at Internet and electronic commerce applications, so using the web as a major component of product support was a natural fit. By personalizing web-based support for each customer, this inherent complexity would be reduced, and the customer experience improved. But how to accomplish that ... and how to do it within the time constraints the project required?

What we needed was an architecture that would give everyone on the team, both the designers and the programmers, as much freedom as possible to work unhindered in the limited time available. The ability of these two groups to progress independently, without costly rework, was crucial. A solution that could provide dynamic content as an add-on to otherwise conventional HTML files clearly was the best approach. We briefly considered, then just as quickly dismissed, the notion of building our own dynamic context system. There just wasn't enough time to deliver both a publishing system and a web site.

At the time we were already familiar with Java servlets. Indeed, servlets were a key element of the architecture of the product to which this site would be devoted. We mulled over using servlets for the site itself but were concerned with how this would affect those responsible for the content, graphics, and layout of the site.

As we researched the problem further we were reminded of an ongoing initiative at Sun Microsystems called JavaServer Pages (JSP). JSP was still being refined, and Version 1.0 was months away. However, it was intended to become a standard Java technology, and it used Java servlets as its foundation. It also allowed us to implement dynamic content on top of standard HTML files. Best of all, it worked! As we became more familiar with JSP, we found that it worked very well indeed.

As is often the case, there were some rough spots as the JSP specification went through major changes along the way. Hair was pulled, teeth were gnashed, lessons were learned. Fortunately, we obtained a great deal of help from the JSP community—the developers at Sun and the other JSP vendors, as well as our fellow early adopters.

This book thus serves a twofold purpose. First, we hope to help future users of JSP by sharing the hard-earned lessons of our experience. We offer them what we hope is a helpful guide to the current JSP feature set: JavaServer Pages is now at version 1.1 and the need for published reference material has long been recognized.

Second, we offer this book as an expression of gratitude to the current community of JSP developers in return for the assistance they provided when we needed it. Thanks to all.

acknowledgments

We recognize the support and understanding of the many people who helped make this book possible. We acknowledge:

T. Preston Gregg, the former development manager of Duane and Mark, for allowing them to make the early leap to a JSP architecture, before the technology was considered ready for prime time. This head start was painful at times, but ultimately proved a boon to their web development projects. It also gave them the experience necessary to develop this text, for which they are equally grateful. Other colleagues who advised them during the writing of the this book include Kirk Drummond and Ward Harold.

Pierre Delisle for encouraging and guiding Shawn's efforts in the Java community. *Merci pour tout, mon ami.* Shawn also wishes to thank his colleagues at Yale, especially Andy Newman and Nicholas Rawlings.

The JSP design team at Sun Microsystems, especially Eduardo Pelegrí-Llopart. His assistance and attentiveness to our queries was critical to the success of this effort.

The teeming millions of Java and JSP developers who continue to offer their insights and expertise to the development community through their unselfish participation in mailing lists, newsgroups, and the web. Double thanks to everyone participating in the Jakarta and Apache projects for their outstanding work in the Open Source arena. You are all instrumental to the continuing success of Java and establishing it as a *lingua franca* for Internet development.

Our publisher, Marjan Bace, for giving us this opportunity; our editor, Elizabeth Martin, for her yeoman's effort in polishing this manuscript; and our typesetter,

Tony Roberts. Their insights, guidance, and expertise were invaluable to the completion of this book.

Our reviewers, whose comments, criticisms, and commendations advised, corrected and encouraged us. Our deep appreciation is extended to Michael Andreano, Dennis Hoer, Vimal Kansal, Chris Lamprecht, Max Loukianov, James McGovern, Dave Miller, Dr. Chang-Shyh Peng, Anthony Smith, and Jason Zhang. Special thanks to Lance Lavandowska for his technical edit of the final manuscript.

Our friends, families, and coworkers for their unfailing support, assistance, and tolerance throughout the writing process. Without them this book could not have been possible.

about this book

JavaServer Pages is a technology that serves two different communities of developers. Page designers use JSP technology to add powerful dynamic content capabilities to web sites and online applications. Java programmers write the code that implements those capabilities behind the scenes.

Web Development with JavaServer Pages is intended to present this technology to both groups. It is impossible in a book of this length to provide all the background information required by this subject, and, for this reason, we do not attempt to describe the HTML markup language. It is assumed that the reader is sufficiently familiar with HTML to follow the examples presented. It is likewise assumed that the reader is familiar with URLs, document hierarchies, and other concepts related to creating and publishing web pages.

We also do not include a primer on the Java programming language. As with HTML, there is a wealth of reference information available on the language itself. Programmers reading this book are assumed to be familiar with Java syntax, the development cycle, and object-oriented design concepts. A basic understanding of relational database technology in general, and JDBC in particular, is recommended but not required.

Our focus here, then, is strictly on JavaServer Pages. The interaction between JSP and the technologies already mentioned—HTML, Java, and databases—will of course be covered in depth. For the benefit of readers not so well versed in the enabling technologies upon which JSP depends, however, this second edition features new coverage of HTTP, the protocol that web browsers and web servers use to communicate with one another, and Java servlets, the foundational technology for server-side Java applications.

The topics covered are as follows:

Chapter 1 introduces JavaServer Pages (JSP) and presents a brief history of web development. JSP is contrasted with past and present web technologies. Since this chapter provides historical context and a broad introduction, it is intended for a general audience.

Chapter 2 discusses core technologies on which JSP depends. The Hypertext Transfer Protocol (HTTP) and the Java Servlet platform, both of which help define how JSP operates, are introduced. A simple Java Servlet example is discussed. This chapter focuses on technical details that are important for programmers, but page designers can read it to learn how the web works.

Chapter 3 presents a tutorial introduction to JSP. Examples designed to demonstrate JSP's capabilities—from simple iteration and conditionalization to session management and non-HTML content generation—are discussed in a gradual progression. This chapter's examples are intended for a general audience.

Chapter 4 provides more information for programmers and page designers about how JSP operates behind the scenes. The chapter focuses on how JSP works and introduces some of the core, time-saving features that JSP provides. The core elements of a JSP page are also introduced more formally than in chapter 3.

Chapters 5 and 6 introduce the four basic categories of JSP tags: directives, scripting elements, comments, and actions. The use and syntax of all standard JSP tags is presented, with the exception of those specific to JavaBeans. The first three categories are covered in chapter 5. Chapter 6 introduces action tags, and describes the implicit Java objects accessible from all JSP pages. In both of these chapters, particular emphasis is placed on the application of these tags and objects to dynamic content generation via scripting. The scripting examples use the Java programming language, and may be of secondary interest to page designers. Because this chapter introduces most of the major functionality provided by JavaServer Pages, it is intended for a general audience.

Chapters 7 and 8 cover JSP's component-centric approach to dynamic page design through the use of JavaBeans and JSP bean tags. The JSP tags covered in chapter 7 allow page designers to interact with Java components through HTML-like tags, rather than through Java code. Chapter 8 will explain the JavaBeans API and teach you to develop your own JSP components.

Chapter 9 covers techniques for working with databases through JSP. Nowadays, most large-scale web sites employ databases for at least some portion of their content, and JSP fits in nicely. By combining the power of a relational database with the flexibility of JSP for content presentation and front-end design, it is practical to build rich, interactive interfaces.

In chapter 10, we discuss several architectural models useful for developing JSP applications. We examine the various architectural options available when we combine JSP pages with servlets, Enterprise JavaBeans, HTML, and other software elements to create web-based applications.

In chapter 11 we apply the JSP programming techniques we covered in previous chapters to the development of a real world, enterprise web application. In a chapter-length example, we will be developing a system for managing and presenting lists of frequently asked questions (FAQs). This chapter is based on a project the authors recently completed for a major software company's customer support site. The presentation aspect of this chapter should be of interest to page designers, while the implementation aspects should be of interest to programmers.

Chapters 12 and 13 introduce two new features of the JSP 1.2 and Servlet 2.3 specifications—filters and listeners. Filters can be used to layer new functionality onto JSP and servlet-based applications in a modular fashion, such as encryption, compression, and authentication. Listeners enable developers to monitor various activities and events occurring over the life cycle of a web application. Chapter 12 covers the basics, while chapter 13 presents a chapter-length intranet example which demonstrates the use of filters and listeners to add enhanced capabilities to an existing application.

Issues surrounding the deployment of web-based applications are the focus of chapter 14. Web Application Archives provide a portable format for the packaging of related servlets and JSP pages into a single, easily-deployed file, called a WAR file. The practical aspects of this approach to web deployment are demonstrated through coverage of the configuration and construction of a WAR file for the example application presented in chapter 13. Since both code and pages are stored together in a WAR file, this chapter should be of interest to all JSP developers.

Chapter 15 explains how to perform common tasks with JSP. A multitude of examples and mini-projects address issues such as cookies, form processing, and error handling. If you learn best by example, you will find this chapter particularly helpful.

In chapter 16 we examine a newer application of JSP programming, creating content other than HTML. The chapter explores this new area with coverage of plain text, XML, JavaScript, and even dynamic spreadsheets.

We return to the topic of JSP examples in chapter 17. Here, the emphasis is on full-fledged applications that illustrate the various techniques and practices presented in previous chapters.

Chapter 18 covers the development, deployment, and application of custom tag libraries. This material focuses primarily on the implementation of custom tags by Java programmers. From the perspective of jointly designing a set of application-specific tags, page designers may find some benefit in reviewing the introductory sections of this chapter, which discuss the types of functionality that can be provided by custom tags.

In chapter 19, we expand upon the topic of custom tags with additional examples that take advantage of more advanced features of Java and JSP.

Coverage of JSP custom tags concludes in chapter 20 with a discussion of tag library validators, a new feature introduced in JSP 1.2. Using validators, custom tag developers can enforce constraints and manage dependencies within all JSP pages that make use of their tags. Furthermore, because tag library validation occurs during page translation and compilation, rather than in response to a request, it enables custom tag errors to be detected earlier in the development process.

There are six appendices in the book. Appendix A is provided for the benefit of readers of the first edition, the terminally impatient, and those wanting a quick look at what's new. In it we hit the highlights of recent advances in JSP technology, notably JSP 1.2 and the Servlet 2.3 API.

Appendix B describes how to download, install, and run Tomcat, the JSP reference implementation. This appendix is aimed at readers who don't already have a JSP container to use; setting up Tomcat will help these readers experiment with the book's examples.

Java applets are small applications that run within the context of a web browser. Appendix C describes the <jsp:plugin> action, a cross-platform tag for specifying applets which use Sun Microsystems's Java Plug-in technology in order to take advantage of the Java 2 platform within the browser. This appendix is directed at Java programmers.

As is the case with any major software technology in use today, there is a wealth of information on JSP and related topics available online. Appendix D provides a collection of mailing lists, newsgroups, and web sites of relevance to all categories of JSP developers, accompanied by brief descriptions of the content available from each.

Appendix E, serving as a quick reference, summarizes the use and syntax of all of the standard (i.e., built-in) JSP tags available to page designers.

Appendix F, geared toward Java programmers, lists all of the Java classes introduced by the JSP and servlet specifications to supplement the standard Java class library for web-based application development. Summary descriptions of these classes and their methods are provided, as is a table of the JSP implicit objects.

In summary, the second edition brings new content and updated coverage of JSP. Chapters 1 through 4 offer a broader, completely rewritten introduction to JSP and web development. Entirely new for the second edition, chapters 12 and 13 introduce servlet filters and listeners and include a thorough example of these new features in action. Also brand new, chapter 16 discusses a new class of applications for JSP, and chapter 20 discusses an advanced custom tag feature. The rest of the book is updated with new examples and information, including full coverage of JSP 1.2.

Source code

The source code for all of the examples called out as listings in the book is freely available from our publisher's web site, www.manning.com/fields2, and from the book's companion web site, www.taglib.com. The listings are organized by chapter and topic and include the source for both Java classes and JSP pages used in the examples. If any errors are discovered updates will be made available on the web.

Code conventions

`Courier` typeface is used to denote code (JSP, Java, and HTML) as well as file names, variables, Java class names, and other identifiers. When JSP is interspersed with HTML, we have used a bold Courier font for JSP elements in order to improve the readability of the code. Italics are used to indicate definitions and user specified values in syntax listings.

about the authors

DUANE K. FIELDS, web applications developer and Internet technologist, has an extensive background in the design and development of leading edge Internet applications for companies such as IBM and Netscape Communications. Duane lives in Austin, Texas, where he consults, does Java applications development, and tries to find more time to fish. He frequently speaks at industry conferences and other events and has published numerous articles on all aspects of web application development from Java to relational databases. He is a Sun Certified Java Programmer, an IBM Master Inventor, and holds an engineering degree from Texas A&M University. He can be reached at his web site at www.deepmagic.com.

MARK A. KOLB, Ph.D., is a reformed rocket scientist with graduate and undergraduate degrees from MIT. A pioneer in the application of object-oriented modeling to aerospace preliminary design, his contributions in that field were recently recognized with a NASA Space Act Award. With over 15 years' experience in software design, Mark's current focus is on Internet applications, ranging from applet-based HTML editors to server-side systems for unified messaging and residential security monitoring. Mark resides in Round Rock, Texas, with his family and a large stack of unread books he's hoping to get to now that this one is done. His home on the web is at www.taglib.com.

SHAWN BAYERN is a research programmer at Yale University. An active participant in the Java Community Process, he serves as the reference-implementation lead for the JSP Standard Tag Library (JSPTL). He is a committer for the Jakarta Taglibs Project and has written articles for a number of popular industry journals. Shawn holds a computer-science degree from Yale University and lives in New Haven, Connecticut. He can be found on the web at www.jsptl.com.

authors online

Purchase of *Web Development with Java Server Pages* includes free access to a private web forum run by Manning Publications where you can make comments about the book, ask technical questions, and receive help from the author and from other users. To access the forum and subscribe to it, point your web browser to www.manning.com/fields2 This page provides information on how to get on the forum once you are registered, what kind of help is available, and the rules of conduct on the forum.

Manning's commitment to our readers is to provide a venue where a meaningful dialog between individual readers and between readers and the authors can take place. It is not a commitment to any specific amount of participation on the part of the authors, whose contribution to the AO remains voluntary (and unpaid). We suggest you try asking the authors some challenging questions lest their interest stray!

The Author Online forum and the archives of previous discussions will be accessible from the publisher's web site as long as the book is in print.

about the cover illustration

The cover illustration of this book is from the 1805 edition of Sylvain Maréchal's four-volume compendium of regional dress customs. This book was first published in Paris in 1788, one year before the French Revolution. Its title alone required no fewer than 30 words.

> *"Costumes Civils actuels de tous les peuples connus dessinés d'après nature gravés et coloriés, accompagnés d'une notice historique sur leurs coutumes, moeurs, religions, etc., etc., redigés par M. Sylvain Maréchal"*

The four volumes include an annotation on the illustrations: "gravé à la manière noire par Mixelle d'après Desrais et colorié." Clearly, the engraver and illustrator deserved no more than to be listed by their last names—after all they were mere technicians. The workers who colored each illustration by hand remain nameless.

The remarkable diversity of this collection reminds us vividly of how distant and isolated the world's towns and regions were just 200 years ago. Dress codes have changed everywhere and the diversity by region, so rich at the time, has melted away. It is now hard to tell the inhabitant of one continent from another. Perhaps we have traded cultural diversity for a more varied personal life—certainly a more varied and interesting technological environment.

At a time when it is hard to tell one computer book from another, Manning celebrates the inventiveness and initiative of the computer business with book covers based on the rich diversity of regional life of two centuries ago, brought back to life by Maréchal's pictures. Just think, Maréchal's was a world so different from ours people would take the time to read a book title 30 words long.

1 Introduction

This chapter covers

- An introduction to JSP technology
- The evolution of dynamic content on the Web
- How JSP interacts with other Java code
- How to separate presentation and implementation

Welcome to *Web Development with JavaServer Pages*. This book has been written to address the needs of a wide audience of web developers. You might just be starting out as a web programmer, or perhaps you're moving to JavaServer Pages (JSP) from another language such as Microsoft Active Server Pages (ASP) or ColdFusion. You could be a Hypertext Markup Language (HTML) designer with little or no background in programming—or a seasoned Java architect! In any case, this book will show you how to use JSP to improve the look and maintainability of web sites, and it will help you design and develop web-based applications. Without further ado, let's begin our look at JavaServer Pages.

1.1 What is JSP?

JavaServer Pages—JSP, for short—is a Java-based technology that simplifies the process of developing dynamic web sites. With JSP, designers and developers can quickly incorporate dynamic content into web sites using Java and simple markup tags. The JSP platform lets the developer access data and Java business logic without having to master the complexities of Java application development.

In short, JSP gives you a way to define how dynamic content should be introduced into an otherwise static page, such as an unchanging HTML file. When a JSP page is requested by a web browser, the page causes code to run and decide, on the fly, what content to send back to the browser. Such dynamic content allows for the construction of large and complex web applications that interact with users.

JSP is flexible: it adapts to the needs of developers and organizations. For some, JSP is a simple way to mix Java code and HTML text to produce dynamic web pages. For others, it helps separate Java code from presentation text, giving nonprogrammers a way to produce functional and dynamic web pages. JSP is not even limited to the production of dynamic HTML-based content. For instance, it can be used in wireless and voice-driven applications.

Because JSP is based on widely accepted standards, products from numerous vendors support it. Like Java itself, JSP isn't dependent on a particular platform. When you learn JSP, you can be confident that your new skills will be applicable outside the individual environment in which you learned them.

1.2 Dynamic content on the web

The simplest application of the web involves the transmission of static, unchanging data (figure 1.1). When discussing computer systems, however, it's important to keep in mind that *static* is a relative term. Compared with traditional forms of data storage—file cabinets and stone carvings, for instance—all computer files are transient. When we discuss content on the Web, we draw a conventional distinction between URLs that refer to simple files and those that refer to the output of a program.

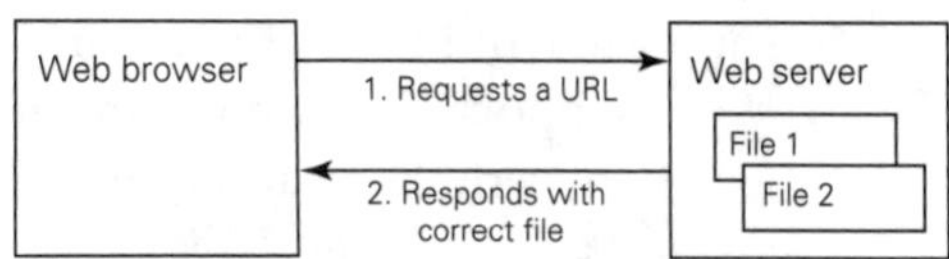

Figure 1.1 Static web sites transmit only simple, static files

---

DEFINITION *Static* content on the Web comes directly from text or data files, such as HTML or JPEG files. These files might be changed, but they are not altered automatically when requested by a web browser. *Dynamic* content, on the other hand, is generated on the fly, typically in response to an individual request from a browser.

1.2.1 Why dynamic content?

By our definition, dynamic content is typically generated upon individual requests for data over the Web. This is not the only way that an ever-changing web site might be produced. A typical computer system that runs a web server might easily run other software that can modify files in the server's file systems. If the web server then sends these automatically processed files to web browsers, the server achieves a primitive style of dynamic content generation.

For example, suppose that a program running in the background on a web server updates an HTML file every five minutes, adding a randomly selected quotation at the bottom. Or suppose that a news organization has a program that accepts manual entry of breaking-news stories from journalists, formats these into HTML, and saves them in a file accessible by a web server. In both cases, a web site provides relatively dynamic data without requiring specific web programming (figure 1.2).

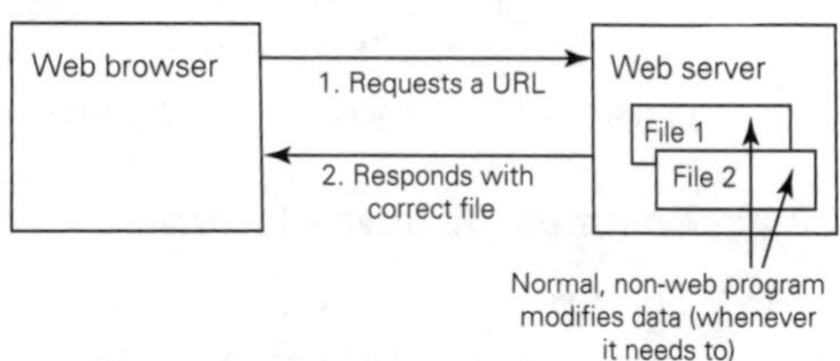

Figure 1.2 A simple way to achieve dynamic content is to modify files behind the scenes programmatically.

However, such web sites don't easily support interaction with web users. Suppose there were a search engine that operated using this type of behind-the-scenes approach. Theoretically, such an engine could figure out all of the search terms it supported and then create—and store—individual HTML pages corresponding to every supported combination of terms. Then, it could produce a gigantic list of HTML hyperlinks to all of them, in a file that looked like the following:

```
...
<a href="aardvark-and-lizard.html">Search for "aardvark and lizard"</a>
<a href="aardvark-and-mouse.html">Search for "aardvark and mouse"</a>
<a href="aardvark-and-octopus.html">Search for "aardvark and octopus"</a>
...
```

Such a scheme, of course, would rapidly become unworkable in practice. Not only would the user interface be tedious, but the search engine would have to store redundant copies of formatted search results across trillions of HTML files. Imagine how long it would take to generate these files when new search terms were added, and consider how much disk space would be required.

Moreover, many sites need to be able to respond to arbitrary, unpredictable input from the user. An online email application certainly couldn't predict every message a user might write. And often, a web site needs to do more than simply send HTML or other data when a request is issued; it also needs to take programmatic, behind-the-scenes action in responce to a request. For example, an online store might need to save users' orders into a database, and an email application would actually have to send email messages. In many cases, simply displaying prefabricated HTML isn't enough.

For all of these reasons, several web-specific technologies have been designed to allow programmers to design sites that respond dynamically to requests for URLs from browsers. JSP is one such technology, and we can get a better sense of how JSP is useful if we look at a few of its predecessors and competitors.

1.2.2 Common Gateway Interface

The first widely used standard for producing dynamic web content was the Common Gateway Interface, or CGI, which defined a way for web servers and external programs to communicate. Under typical operating systems, there are only a few ways that a program can communicate with another one that it starts: it might specify particular text on the target program's command line, set up environment variables, or use a handful of other strategies. CGI takes advantage of these approaches to allow a web server to communicate with other programs. As shown in figure 1.3, when a web server receives a request that's intended for a CGI program, it runs that program and provides it with information associated with the particular incoming request. The CGI program runs and sends its output back to the server, which in turn relays it to the browser.

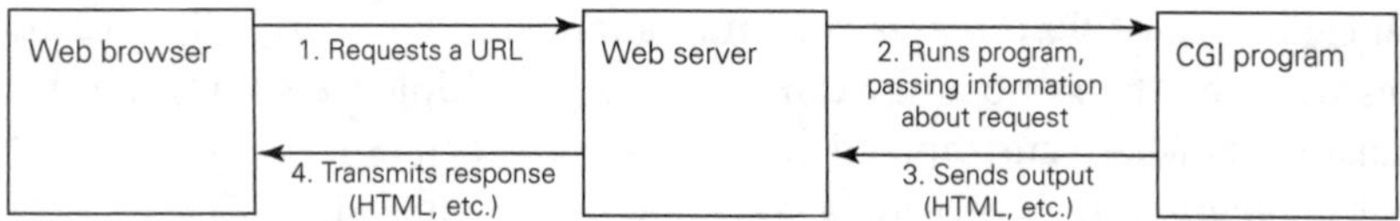

Figure 1.3 To respond dynamically, a web server can spawn a CGI program to handle a web request.

CGI is not an application programming interface (API) for any particular language. In fact, CGI is almost completely language-neutral. Many CGI programs have been written in Perl, but nothing prevents you from writing one in C, LISP, or even Java. The CGI standard simply defines a series of conventions which, when followed, let programs communicate with CGI-aware web servers and thus respond to web requests.

Because it imposes few constraints, CGI is quite flexible. However, the CGI model has an important drawback: a web server that wants to use a CGI program must call a new copy in response to every incoming web request.

DEFINITION In operating-system parlance, a running instance of a program is known as a *process*. In slightly more formal terms, then, CGI requires that a new process be created, or *spawned*, for every new incoming web request.

CGI doesn't provide for any mechanism to establish an ongoing relationship between a server process and the external CGI processes it runs. This limitation leads to a relatively large cost of initialization upon each new request, for creating a process on a server is a relatively expensive operation. This cost isn't immediately obvious when a server runs only a handful of programs, but for large web sites that deal with thousands of requests every minute, CGI becomes an unattractive solution, no matter how efficient an individual CGI program might be.

1.2.3 Template systems

The CGI model has another drawback: it requires programs to produce HTML files and other content, meaning that program code often needs to contain embedded fragments of static text and data (figure 1.4). Many newer technologies have taken a different approach. Systems such as Macromedia ColdFusion, Microsoft ASP, and the open-source PHP (a hypertext preprocessor) all permit the integration of scripting code directly into an otherwise static file. In such a file, the static text—typically HTML—can be thought of as a template around which the dynamic content, generated by the scripting code, is inserted (figure 1.5). The mechanism is similar to the now-ancient idea of *mail merge*, a feature supported by nearly all word-processing systems whereby the same letter can be printed multiple times, varying only in the particular spots where customized content is necessary.

Such *template systems* provide a convenient way for web designers to insert dynamic content into their web pages. Unlike CGI, template systems don't require developers to write stand-alone, executable programs that print HTML. In fact, a template system usually doesn't require an in-depth understanding of programming in the first place. Instead, designers need only learn a scripting language supported by the template system they use. Even the procedure for debugging and testing pages developed under such systems is similar to that of HTML: reload a page in the browser, and changes to both scripting code and template HTML take effect.

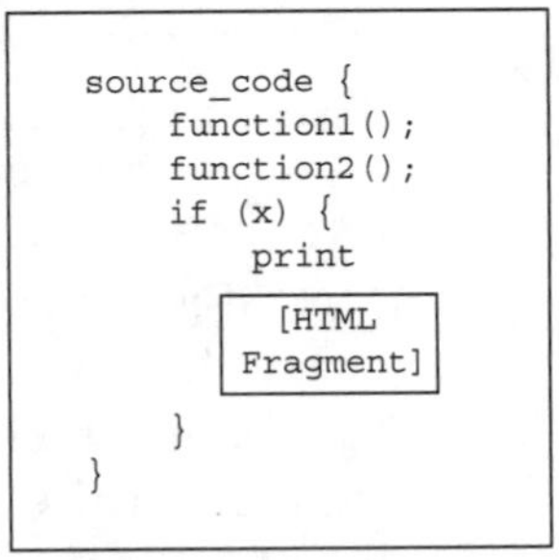

```
source_code {
    function1();
    function2();
    if (x) {
        print
          [HTML
          Fragment]
    }
}
```

Figure 1.4 CGI often requires that HTML fragments appear within program code, making both harder to maintain.

Conceptually, template languages are all fairly similar. The most visible differences among these systems involve the particular scripting languages they support, the syntax used for accessing such languages, and the way that they provide access to back-end logic.

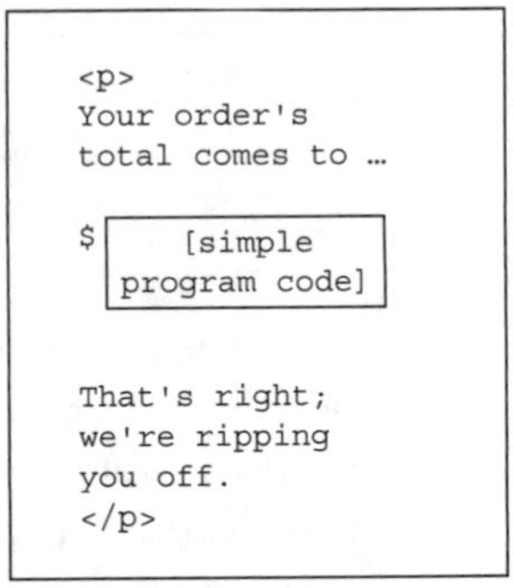

```
<p>
Your order's
total comes to …

$ [simple
  program code]

That's right;
we're ripping
you off.
</p>
```

Figure 1.5 Template systems let HTML designers embed simple program code within HTML documents.

ColdFusion

ColdFusion provides a set of HTML-like tags that can be used to produce dynamic content. Instead of writing more traditional types of code, ColdFusion developers can build applications using a combination of HTML tags and ColdFusion-specific tags. Using tag-based syntax has the advantage of consistency: pages that consist only of HTML-like tags are more accessible to HTML designers who do not have experience with programming languages.

ColdFusion is available for Microsoft Windows and a variety of UNIX platforms, and it allows developers to write extensions to its core tag set in C++ and Java. Furthermore, ColdFusion code can access reusuable components such as CORBA objects and Enterprise JavaBeans (EJBs)—as well as COM objects when it runs on Windows. Work on ColdFusion also gave birth to a technology known as Web-Distributed Data Exchange (WDDX), which helps transfer data from one platform to another. ColdFusion supports WDDX and can communicate with other services that use it.

Active Server Pages

ASP technology supports multiple scripting languages, which can be embedded in HTML documents between the delimiters `<%` and `%>`. (As we will see, JSP uses these same delimiters.) ASP is a core feature of the Microsoft Internet Information Server (IIS), and it provides access to reusable Windows-based objects known as *ActiveX components*. Traditional ASP supports two scripting languages by default—Visual Basic Scripting Edition, based on Visual Basic, and JScript, based on JavaScript.

More recently, Microsoft has introduced ASP.NET as part of its .NET framework. While classic ASP offers an interpreted scripting environment where code is executed directly out of a text file every time a page is loaded, ASP.NET logic is compiled, yielding greater performance. ASP.NET offers access to any programming language supported in the .NET environment, including Visual Basic (in contrast with simple VBScript on ASP) and C#, which is pronounced "C sharp" and represents a new language offering from Microsoft. The new ASP.NET environment, like Java, supports type-safe programming, which can improve code maintainability. Furthermore, ASP.NET introduces the concept of an *ASP.NET server control*, which lets ASP.NET code authors access logic using a simple, HTML-like tag interface, just like ColdFusion—and, as we will see later, JSP.

The greatest drawback of the ASP and ASP.NET environments is that they are centered primarily on a single platform—Windows. Some vendors, such as Chili!Soft, have introduced products that support ASP in other environments. And the more recent .NET framework promotes certain kinds of integration with non-Microsoft platforms. Nonetheless, ASP and ASP.NET have not typically been regarded as attractive solutions for organizations that are not committed to Microsoft technology.

PHP and other alternatives

PHP is an open source template system. As with other open source projects, such as the Linux operating system and the Apache HTTP Server, PHP is not a commercial product. Instead, it is the result of contributions from a community of developers who freely build and support its code base. Open source products are typically available on a variety of operating systems, and PHP is no exception.

Like ASP, PHP was once based on purely interpreted scripting, but it has moved closer to compilation over time. PHP 4 provides improved efficiency over PHP 3 by compiling scripts before executing them. PHP 4 comes with a rich function library that includes support for accessing mail services, directories, and databases. Like ColdFusion, it supports WDDX, which provides for interoperability with other languages. Furthermore, it can interact with Java code, and it provides an API that allows programmers to insert custom modules.

PHP isn't the only open source platform for generating dynamic content on the Web. For instance, like PHP, a system called Velocity falls under the umbrella of the Apache Software Foundation. Velocity is a template engine that is geared toward providing access to Java objects using a simple, custom template language.

Open source template systems are flexible and free. Because their source code is available, experienced developers can debug nearly any problem they run into while using open source systems. In contrast, when a bug is encountered in a proprietary system, developers might need to wait for new releases to see it addressed. Some developers, however, see the sheer number of solutions offered by the open source community as a drawback. With dozens of competing alternatives that change frequently, the community can appear fragmentary, and some organizations might find it hard to settle with confidence on a solution they trust to be stable.

1.2.4 Java on the Web

So far, we have mentioned little about how Java and JSP fit into the larger picture. Java, as you probably know, is a language that was developed by Sun Microsystems. Java programs run inside a Java Virtual Machine (JVM), which provides a platform-independent level of processing for Java *bytecodes*, into which Java source files are compiled. Java thus avoids tying itself to a particular hardware platform, operating-system vendor, or web server. Furthermore, because Java has gained wide industry acceptance, and because the Java Community Process provides a well-defined mechanism for introducing changes into the platform when enough industry support exists, Java users can be confident that they develop applications on a standard and flexible platform. Let's take a quick look at how Java is used on the Web.

Java applets

All of the technologies discussed so far involve dynamic content generation on the web server's end. However, the Web can also be used to deliver software that acts dynamically once it reaches the client machine.

Determining the appropriate mixture of client-side and server-side code to use in an application is a complex problem, and the industry historically seems to swing between the two alternatives. At the client-side end of the spectrum, a web site could offer fully functional, downloadable programs that users can run; at the server-side end, servers handle almost all of the processing of an application, merely asking clients to render screens of HTML or other markup languages.

Java *applets*, an early use of Java technology that remains popular in some environments, are examples of client-side code. Applets are typically small programs that can be downloaded and run inside web browsers. Applets can access the network and perform a variety of other functions, offering a rich user interface from within a simple web browser. But applets have drawbacks and are not suitable for all applications. For instance, not all web browsers support Java applets identically; in fact, not all web browsers support Java applets in the first place. Furthermore, in many situations, server-side code is easier to maintain and support.

Java servlets

A Java servlet relates to a server, roughly, as a Java applet does to a web browser. A *servlet* is a program that plugs into a web server and allows it to respond to web requests according to instructions provided as Java code. As we mentioned, the CGI standard allows developers to write code in Java. Why, then, would a separate standard for Java servlets be necessary?

Foremost, servlets offer a great performance advantage over CGI programs. This may seem counterintuitive to those who realize that code that runs inside a JVM is typically slower than code that runs natively on a particular platform. Even though the performance difference between Java and native code diminishes as research improves, the gap is still noticeable. Thus, if CGI supports native code but Java requires a JVM, how could servlets be faster than CGI programs?

The major difference lies in the limitation of CGI that we discussed earlier: CGI processes need to be run individually in response to web requests. The Java Servlet platform offers a different model that allows a Java program within a single JVM process to direct requests to the right Java classes. Since no new operating-system processes—only lighter-weight threads of execution within the JVM—need to be created for incoming requests, servlets end up scaling better than CGI programs do.

Servlets also offer Java programmers more convenience than the base CGI specification. CGI does not provide language-specific APIs, nor does it provide standard libraries to facilitate programming. The Java Servlet standard, in contrast, provides an API that supports abstraction and convenience. In order to access information about incoming requests, for example, servlet programmers can use objects from a particular class hierarchy defined in the Servlet specification. Moreover, servlets have access to all of the benefits of the Java platform itself, including reusable class libraries and platform independence. Since a servlet is just a Java class, it can naturally access other Java code.

NOTE We'll look more at servlets in the next chapter. Appendix F provides a reference to the servlet API.

Servlets first appeared as part of the Sun Java web server product, which was an HTTP server written in Java. Versions 2.1 and 2.2 of the Servlet standard appeared in 1999, and version 2.3 was released in 2001. The evolution of the Servlet platform continues under the Java Community Process.

Even with the services provided by the Java Servlet API, however, the platform has a drawback in terms of convenience and maintainability when it is used to produce dynamic web pages. Servlets offer all of the tools necessary to build web sites, but just like the CGI standard, they require developers to write code that prints entire HTML files—or other data—on demand. Code that looks like

```
out.println("<p>One line of HTML.</p>");
out.println("<p>Another line of HTML.</p>");
```

is common. The ease of template systems, where code can simply be embedded in static text, is not present.

Libraries and toolkits help orient the servlet environment toward the creation of HTML pages (and other types of data). For instance, the Element Construction Set (ECS), another open source project under the Apache Software Foundation's umbrella, offers an approach that should be familiar to object-oriented programmers. ECS supports the creation of HTML and Extensible Markup Language (XML) pages using a class hierarchy representing textual elements. This approach facilitates the construction and maintenance of textual documents, but it has a potential drawback: all document content, both static and dynamic, still exists inside source code. To edit the layout of a page, a developer must modify Java code; an HTML designer cannot simply edit a straightforward text file.

JavaServer Pages (JSP)

Ideally, then, it seems that web designers and developers who use the Java platform would want a standards-based template system built on top of the Servlet platform. As we discussed, servlets provide performance benefits and can take advantage of existing Java code. But template systems let dynamic web pages be created and maintained easily.

JSP was the natural result of this need. JSP works like a template system, but it also extends the Servlet platform and provides most of the advantages of servlets. Like servlets, JSP pages have access to the full range of Java code's capabilities. JSP pages can include Java as embedded scripting code between `<%` and `%>` delimiters, the same as those used in ASP. But like ColdFusion, JSP also provides several standard HTML-like tags to access back-end logic, and it lets developers design new tags.

In short, JSP is a standards-based template system that extends the Java Servlet framework. The first draft of the JSP specification appeared in 1998, followed by versions 1.0 and 1.1 in 1999. The newest version of the standard—JSP 1.2—was released in 2001; this version is the one covered by this book.

In addition to the underlying technical specifics, servlets and JSP differ from most other technologies in another important respect: they are supported by a wide variety of vendors. Dozens of server-side platforms and development tools support servlets and JSP.

1.2.5 How XML fits in

What implications does XML have for web developers? XML is not a development language; it does not serve a function coordinate with that of template systems, CGI, or anything else we've discussed so far. XML is, at heart, a format for representing data. A quick primer on XML's syntax and how it relates to HTML is given in chapter 4, but for now, think of an XML document as a way to represent tree-structured data in textual form. XML is not tied to any particular programming language, so it is sometimes called "portable data." (For example, the WDDX technology mentioned in section 1.2.3 is based on XML.)

A quick tour of XML technologies

Several technologies support XML and make it useful as a mechanism for storing, transmitting, and manipulating data for web applications. For instance, document type definitions (DTDs) ensure a certain level of structure in XML documents. XML Schema is a technology that goes far beyond DTDs in ensuring that an XML document meets more complex constraints.

TIP Here's a relatively lighthearted but instructional way to look at XML basics. Suppose you want to store a list of jokes on your computer. You could easily store such a list in a simple text file. XML lets you impose structure: for example, you can mark off sections of the jokes into set-ups and punchlines. Given such a structured file, DTDs let you make sure that every joke has a punchline. And XML Schema, one might say, comes close to ensuring that the punchlines are funny!

Of course, such a claim about XML Schema is not literally true. But XML Schema can be used to define details about how data needs to appear in a document.

Several APIs and languages exist for manipulating XML. The Document Object Model (DOM) provides programmatic, well-defined access to an in-memory copy of an XML document. The Simple API for XML (SAX), by contrast, supports an event-driven model that allows programmers to handle XML without keeping an entire document in memory at once.

Extensible Stylesheet Language Transformations (XSLT) provides a mechanism for manipulating XML documents—that is, for extracting pieces of them, rearranging these pieces, and so on. XSLT uses the XML Path Language (XPath) for referencing portions of the XML document. An XPath expression, as an example, can refer to "all `<punchline>` elements under all `<joke>` elements" within a document. An XSLT transformation would let you format an XML document containing data into HTML for presentation on web browsers—and also into the Wireless Markup Language (WML) for use on cell phones and other wireless devices.

Some web-specific technologies have focused specifically on XML. One such technology is Cocoon, yet another product of the Apache Software Foundation. Cocoon supports *pipelines* of XSLT transformations and other operations, so that a single XML document gets massaged through a series of steps before being sent to its final destination. Cocoon uses this model to support presentation of data in HTML and other formats. The Cocoon framework also introduces the idea of eXtensible Server Pages (XSP), which works like an XML-based template system; XSP can be used to generate XML documents dynamically, using markup that references either embedded or external instructions.

XML and JSP

JSP touches on XML technology at a number of points. Most simply, JSP can easily be used to create dynamic XML documents, just as it can create dynamic HTML documents. Java code used by JSP pages can, moreover, easily manipulate XML documents using any of the Java APIs for XML, such as the Java API for XML Processing (JAXP). JSP pages can even be written as XML documents; most of JSP syntax is compatible with XML, and the syntactic constructs that aren't compatible have analogous representations that are.

Behind the scenes, the JSP 1.2 specification uses XML to let developers validate pages. Just as JSP pages can be authored in XML, every JSP page is represented, internally by the JSP processor, as an XML document. JSP 1.2 lets developers use this view of the page to verify the document as it is being processed—that is, to ensure that the page meets custom constraints the developer can specify. This might be useful in environments where back-end developers want to ensure that HTML designers using the developers' code follow certain conventions appropriately.

Future versions of JSP might use this internal XML representation to let developers execute automatic XSL transformations, or other modifications, on JSP pages before they execute.

1.3 The role of JSP

When we presented individual template systems, we discussed how they provided access to back-end libraries and custom logic. For instance, ASP supports ActiveX controls and ColdFusion can be extended with C++ or Java, thus providing access to back-end C++ or Java objects. We now look at how JSP pages fit into Java frameworks—that is, how they access reusable Java classes, and what role they play in large, distributed Java applications.

1.3.1 The JavaBeans component architecture

JavaBeans is a component architecture for Java. To software developers, the term *component* refers to reusable logic that can be plugged into multiple applications with ease. The goals of component architectures include abstraction and reusability. That is, new applications don't need to know the details of how a particular component works, and the same component can be used in a variety of applications. Because of this reusability, component architectures increase productivity; code performing the same task does not need to be written, debugged, and tested repeatedly.

Think of JavaBeans as Java classes that follow particular conventions designed to promote reusability. JavaBeans can encapsulate data and behaviors. For instance, you might design JavaBeans that represent your customers or products, or you might write a bean that handles a particular type of network call. Because JavaBeans automatically provide information to their environments about how their data can be accessed, they are ideally suited for use by development tools and scripting languages. For example, a scripting language might let you recover the last name of a customer whose data is stored in a JavaBean just by referring to the bean's `lastName` property. Because of JavaBeans' conventions, the scripting language can automatically determine, on the fly, the appropriate methods of the JavaBean to call in order to access such a property (as well as the Java data type of the property). JavaBeans can also, because of their generality, be connected and combined to support more sophisticated, application-specific functionality.

NOTE We'll discuss more about the technical details of JavaBeans in chapter 8. For now, our intent is to explore high-level advantages that JavaBeans provide to JSP applications.

Just as JavaBeans can be used by scripting languages, they can also be used inside JSP pages. Of course, the Java code that is embedded in a JSP page can access JavaBeans directly. In addition, though, JSP provides several standard HTML-like tags to support access to properties within JavaBeans. For instance, if you wanted to print the `lastName` property of a `customer` bean, you might use a tag that looks like this:

```
<jsp:getProperty name="customer" property="lastName"/>
```

In addition to the typical reusability that the JavaBeans' architecture offers (figure 1.6), beans thus serve another role in the JSP environment. Specifically, they promote the separation of presentation instructions and implementation logic. A `customer` bean referenced by a JSP page might have an arbitrarily complex implementation; for instance, it might use the JDBC Data Access API to retrieve customer information or process demographic data related to the customer. Regardless of what goes on behind the scenes, however, the single line of JSP code above still retrieves the `lastName` property out of the `customer` bean. The Java code is thus abstracted out of the JSP page itself, so that an HTML designer editing the page would not even need to see it—much less be given a chance to modify it accidentally.

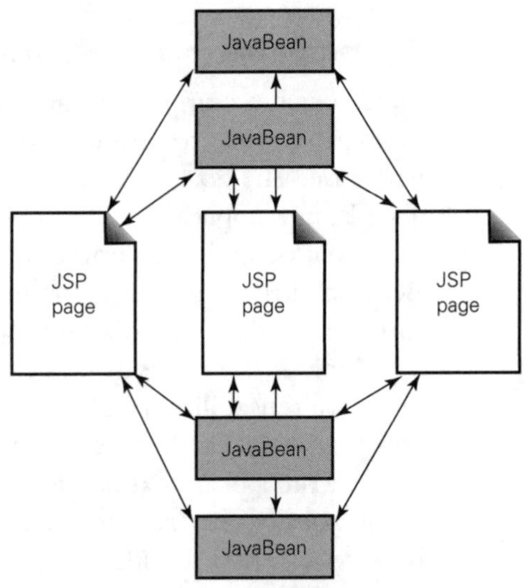

Figure 1.6 The same JavaBeans component can be used in multiple JSP pages.

Note that JavaBeans, while greatly assisting the separation of presentation instructions from back-end program logic, do not provide this separation automatically. JavaBeans' properties can contain arbitrary data, and you could easily construct an application that stores HTML tags as data inside JavaBeans. For instance, instead of a `lastName` property that might store the name `Jones`, you might instead store a `formattedLastName` property that looked more like this:

```
<p><font color="red">Jones</font></p>
```

Doing this would compromise the separation of HTML from logic, however. Including this HTML inside a JavaBean would limit the bean's reusability. Suppose you wanted to start using the bean in a wireless, WML-based application, or in an applet. In such a case, storing HTML inside the bean would not be desirable. Instead, it would be more productive to surround the JSP tag that refers to the bean with HTML formatting.

Similarly, JavaBean logic itself should not produce HTML tags. You might be tempted to use a JavaBean to construct an HTML table automatically as the result of a database query, but in most situations, it would be better, instead, to use JSP to construct the table and the JavaBean only to access the database.

The separation between logic and presentation that JSP promotes can, as we've hinted, assist with division of labor within development teams. The more Java code that is removed from JSP pages, the more those pages should feel familiar to web designers. When programmers focus their work on Java code and designers manage HTML pages, the need for coordination among team members is reduced, and the team can become more productive. Even on relatively small projects, using JavaBeans might save you work and make your code more maintainable. It is typically easier to debug standalone JavaBeans than Java code embedded in a JSP page—and, as we've discussed, encapsulating code in a bean will let you easily use it in multiple pages.

NOTE JavaBeans are not the only way to abstract logic out of JSP pages. Custom tags, described in more detail in chapters 17–19, provide another means of referencing Java logic within JSP pages without embedding it in the page itself. Chapter 18 covers design considerations that will help you choose between JavaBeans and custom tags.

1.3.2 JSP and Java 2 Platform Enterprise Edition

JSP technology is integral to the Java 2 Platform, Enterprise Edition (J2EE). Because it focuses on tasks related to presentation and flexibly supports access to back-end functionality, JSP is a natural choice for the *web tier* of multi-layer applications.

J2EE in contrast with the Standard Edition (J2SE) and the Micro Edition (J2ME), supports the development of enterprise applications. J2EE includes technologies targeted at designing robust, scalable applications. At J2EE's core is the Enterprise JavaBeans (EJB) specification, which aids developers of enterprise components by managing such things as security, transactions, and component life cycle considerations.

The J2EE BluePrints, a set of documents and examples from Sun Microsystems that describe recommendations for building enterprise applications, prominently feature JSP technology. In many enterprise environments, JSP provides an effective mechanism for handling the presentation of data, irrespective of the data's source, the use of EJB, and other considerations.

JSP is also being used as the basis for emerging standards. For example, the JavaServer Faces initiative, operating under the Java Community Process, had recently begun investigations into a standard mechanism for simplifying the development of graphical web applications using servlets and JSP.

Because JSP is regarded as enterprise-quality technology, JSP developers can depend on backwards compatibility from future versions of the JSP specification. While JSP actively continues to evolve, its days as an experimental platform are over. Instead, users of JSP can rely on its platform independence, its status as an enterprise technology, and its basis on standards accepted by the industry.

2 HTTP and servlets

This chapter covers

- HTTP basics
- HTTP GET versus HTTP POST
- Java servlet basics
- An example servlet

Like most web applications, JSP pages require a style of programming different from that of traditional desktop applications. For one thing, you cannot choose how and when your JSP application interacts with its users; JSP pages are limited by the protocols and technologies on which they rest. In this chapter, we look at the Hypertext Transfer Protocol (HTTP) and Java servlets, both of which help define how JSP functions.

2.1 The Hypertext Transfer Protocol (HTTP)

HTTP is the default protocol for JSP, which means that JSP applications typically receive requests and send responses over this protocol. HTTP is also the basic protocol of the World Wide Web, and you've almost certainly used it already if you've accessed a web page.

For computers on a network to communicate, they need a set of rules—that is, a *protocol*—for sending and receiving data. HTTP is one such protocol, and it's the one that has been adopted by the web. All web browsers support HTTP, as do the web servers they connect to. HTTP supports both static content, such as HTML files, and dynamic content, including data generated by the technologies we discussed in chapter 1.

DEFINITION *Web server* is a general term that can be used to describe both the hardware and the software of a machine that answers requests from web browsers. In this discussion, we usually refer to the software—that is, to HTTP-server software running on a networked machine. Examples of HTTP servers include the Apache Server and Microsoft IIS.

2.1.1 HTTP basics

As it turns out, HTTP is simpler than many other protocols. It defines a relatively straightforward model of interaction between a web browser and a server. Specifically, HTTP is oriented around requests and responses. Under HTTP, a browser sends a request for data to a server, and the server responds to that request by providing HTML or some other content.

By contrast, some application protocols are bidirectional. For example, when you establish a terminal connection to a host using Telnet, either your client program or the server may arbitrarily decide that it is time to send a message to the other party. As suggested in figure 2.1, web servers do not have this flexibility. For a web server to send data to a web browser, it must wait until it receives a request from that browser. While a Windows application like Microsoft Word, or even a terminal application running on top of Telnet, can simply decide to display a message on the user's screen when it needs new input, an HTTP-based application must follow the request/response model.

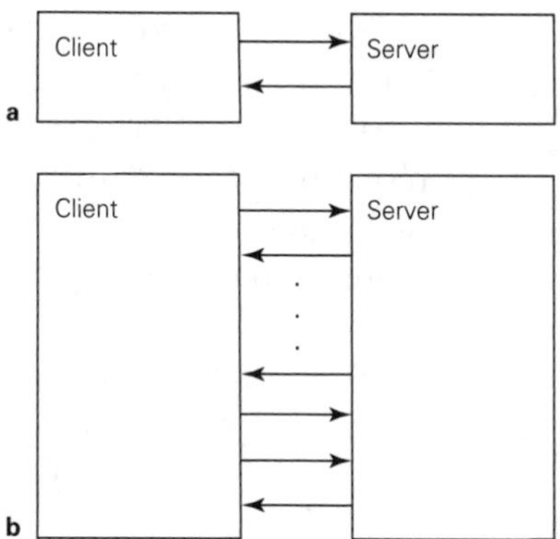

Figure 2.1 a. A request-response protocol such as HTTP. b. A bidirectional protocol such as Telnet. Note that the server can initiate a message once the protocol is established.

NOTE To get around some of HTTP's constraints on application flow, web applications can send JavaScript code—or even full programs like Java applets—as part of their responses to browsers. (See chapter 15 for an example of using JavaScript, and see appendix C for more information about applets.)

Applets and scripting code are not appropriate for all web applications. For example, not every browser supports JavaScript and Java applets. Furthermore, underneath such code, the requests and responses of HTTP are still present, and you will need to keep them in mind when designing your web applications.

HTTP is also *stateless*, meaning that once a web server answers a request, it doesn't remember anything about it. Instead, the web server simply moves to the next request, forgetting tasks as it finishes them. You will occasionally need to keep this statelessness of HTTP in mind as you develop web applications. For example, suppose you want to design an application that ties together successive requests; perhaps you want to remember that a user added a product to a shopping cart, or you need to assemble the results of several pages' worth of HTML forms. By itself, HTTP does not join together such logically connected requests—a task often referred to as *session management*. As we will see in chapter 4, the JSP environment provides support for session management, but you should keep in mind that you have some control over how your application manages sessions; HTTP does not solve, or even address, this issue for you.

Because HTTP is stateless, a web browser must build two separate, complete requests if it needs two pages from a server. In fact, for pages that contain embedded images, music, or other data, the browser might have to send numerous requests to the server in order to load a single page completely.

NOTE If you have experimented with HTTP, you may have realized that it supports *persistent connections*, meaning that a browser can keep a single network connection open if it has many requests it needs to send to a server. This ability is just an implementation detail, however: it represents only a low-level performance improvement. As far as web applications are concerned, persistence does not change the way HTTP functions; the protocol is still stateless and oriented around individual requests and their responses.

Although HTML is clearly one of the most popular formats for data on the web, HTTP is a general-purpose protocol and is not limited to serving HTML. For example, HTTP also frequently carries images, sound files, and other multimedia—and it can be used for just about anything else. HTTP responses are typically tagged with a *content type*; that is, they include information about the data's format. This extra information is encoded as part of an HTTP message's *headers*.

A typical HTTP response has a status line, headers, and a body (figure 2.2). The body contains the response's payload—an HTML file, for example—while the header and status line provide information that the browser uses to figure out how to handle the response. Although the web server typically manages some response headers itself, JSP pages have access to set the headers for the responses they generate. For example, your JSP page can set the content type of its response; we'll see how to take advantage of this ability in chapter 15.

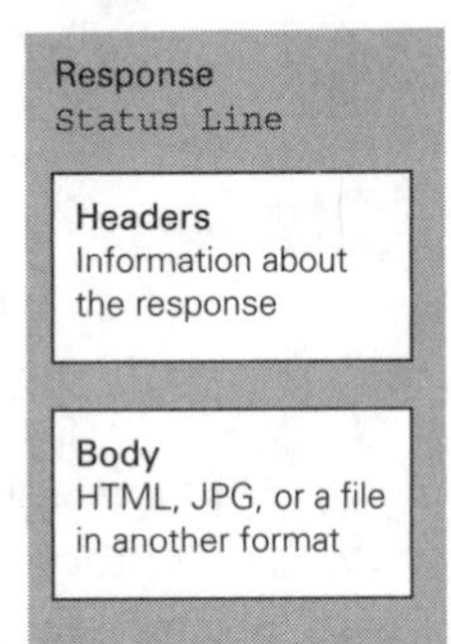

Figure 2.2 The typical structure of an HTTP response.

As described, HTTP is a reasonably simple protocol. Many users of the web think that HTTP does more than it really does. An important point to keep in mind is that HTTP doesn't care what content it carries or how that content was generated. Neither, in fact, do web browsers: a browser does not need to know whether the HTML it renders was transmitted from a static file, a CGI script, an ASP page, or a JSP application. As suggested by figure 2.3, the flow of a typical web application is not very different, as far as a web browser is concerned, from aimless browsing of static pages by a user: the browser transmits a request and gets a response, the user reads the page and takes some action, and the cycle repeats.

As an example of HTTP's simplicity, consider a web-server feature you might be familiar with. When a browser asks for a URL that corresponds to a directory of files instead of a particular file name, many servers generate a listing of the files in that directory. It is important to realize that the server generates this listing; it automatically fabricates an HTML message that represents a directory listing, and the browser renders this HTML message just as it would render a static file. (In other words, the browser has no idea that it just requested a list of files.) The very correspondence between the URL and a directory is idiosyncratic to the web server's configuration; the web server, on its own, establishes this mapping. Likewise, it's up to web servers to decide whether a particular request will be served from a simple file or dispatched to a JSP page.

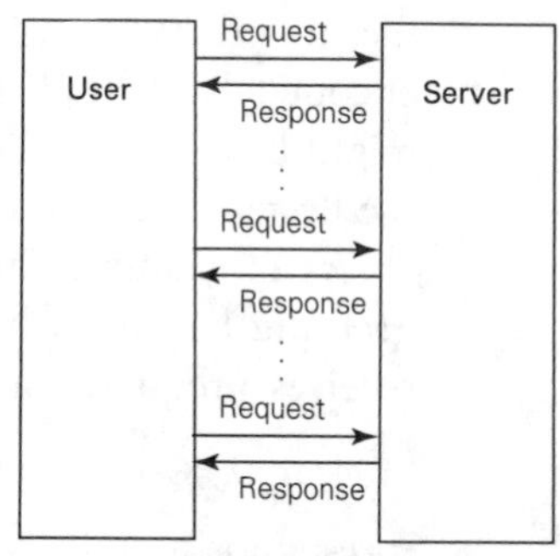

Figure 2.3 The flow of a typical web application is not substantially different from that of aimless browsing by a web user. Broadly speaking, the web is made up of requests and responses.

2.1.2 *GET versus POST*

As we discussed earlier, HTTP servers need to wait for requests from web browsers. These requests can come in a variety of forms, but the two request types—formally called *methods*—that are most important to web developers are called *GET* and *POST.*

Just like HTTP responses, HTTP requests can be broken up into headers and bodies. However, while most HTTP response messages contain a body, many HTTP requests do not. A simple type of HTTP request just asks for information identified by a URL. (To be more specific, browsers don't send the entire URL to servers; they send only the portion of the URL relative to the server's root. When we discuss URLs in HTTP requests, we refer to this type of relative URL.) This kind of request usually consists of a line of text indicating the desired URL, along with some headers (figure 2.4). Because such requests support simple information retrieval, they are called GET requests.

Figure 2.4 The typical structure of a GET request.

Handling GET requests is relatively simple: the server reads and parses the requested URL and sends an appropriate response. GET methods are often used to retrieve simple files, such as static HTML or images. However, they are not limited to this simple functionality. URLs come in many shapes and sizes, and as we've discussed, servers have discretion in processing them: URLs don't necessarily map to files in a filesystem, JSP pages, or anything else. Furthermore, information can be encoded dynamically into a URL. For example, a value you type into an HTML form might be added to the end of a URL. A web server can process this information on the fly, taking customized action depending on the information that a URL contains.

As an example, suppose a web server is configured to respond with a custom greeting based on information that it parses out of the URL. When the server receives a request corresponding to a URL such as

```
http://example.taglib.com/hello?name=Name
```

it responds with HTML output of the form

```
<html><body><p> Hello, Name </p></body></html>
```

The server is well within its rights to respond to a request in this manner; again, a URL doesn't necessarily correspond to a particular file on the server, so no file called `hello` or `hello?name=` or anything similar needs to exist on the `example.taglib.com` server. The server can simply make an arbitrary decision to respond to the request in this way.

As it turns out, many real-life web applications handle GET requests in a very similar fashion when responding to HTML forms. Web browsers have a standard format for submitting the information that users enter through such forms. (Therefore, when servers parse this information, they can know what to expect.) One way that browsers submit this kind of encoded information is by appending it to the URL in a GET request.

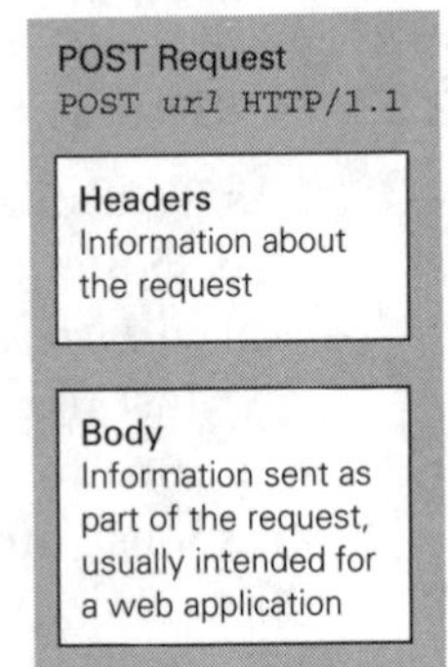

Figure 2.5 The typical structure of a POST request.

POST requests are similar to GET requests. However, in addition to transmitting information as part of the structure of the URL, POST requests send data as part of the request's body (figure 2.5). As with GET requests, this information might be in any format, but web browsers and server-side applications generally use standard encoding rules.

When requesting URLs as the result of an `<a>`, `<img>`, or similar HTML element, web browsers use GET requests. When submitting the result of an HTML `<form>`, browsers use GET by default but can be told to use POST by specifying the `method` attribute of `<form>` as `POST`, as follows:

```
<form method="POST">
```

Why is there a need for both GET and POST, considering how similarly they function? For one thing, many web applications require the browser to transmit a large volume of data back to the server, and long URLs can get unwieldy. Although there is no formal length limitation on URLs, some software—such as HTTP proxies—has historically failed to function properly when URLs are greater than 255 characters. POST is therefore useful to get around this limitation.

The HTTP standard also draws a logical difference between the two types of requests. The standard suggests that GET methods, by convention, should not cause side effects. For example, a properly functioning web application should not store information in a database in response to a GET request; actions that cause side effects should be designed, instead, to use POST requests. In practice, this guideline is not always followed, and in most cases, it does not have many practical ramifications.

A more important consideration raised by the HTTP standard is that software engaged in the processing of URLs—including web browsers, proxies, and web servers—often stores these URLs as they are processed. For instance, browsers often keep histories of visited URLs, and servers often maintain logs of URLs that have been requested. Therefore, if your web application passes sensitive data, such as a user's password, using an HTML form, it should POST the data instead of sending it as part of the URL in a GET request. Data sent as the body of a POST is not typically logged by browsers, proxies, or servers.

TIP As you develop web applications, you'll probably find that you use POST requests more frequently than GET requests for submitting web forms, given the volume and sensitivity of the data you'll need to transfer. GET requests are useful, however, if you want to access dynamic content from an `<a>` or `<img>` tag; these tags cause browsers to use the GET method. We'll see an example of this use of `<a>` in the servlet example.

2.2 Java servlets

A Java servlet is a special type of web-based Java program. As we saw in chapter 1, JSP pages depend intricately on servlets. In fact, every JSP page ultimately becomes a servlet before it's used. Therefore, before jumping into JSP, you might want to familiarize yourself with how servlets work.

2.2.1 How a web server uses servlets

A web server, as we have seen, has fairly wide discretion in how it decides to respond to HTTP requests. It might serve files from a disk, or it might call a program and produce a response based on that program's output. More sophisticated servers, such as the Apache Server, have rich configuration mechanisms that allow modules to be installed and run from within the web server's process. One such program might be a servlet container.

DEFINITION A program that manages servlets is called a *servlet container*, or a *servlet engine*. If a web server is configured to respond to certain types of requests by running a servlet, a servlet container is responsible in part for handling these requests. For example, the container sets up and shuts down servlets as necessary and provides information to servlets to facilitate their processing. The servlet container also calls the appropriate methods on servlet objects in order to cause specific servlets' logic to run.

A servlet container might be implemented as a separate operating-system process from the web server it communicates with, or it might be configured to run inside the web server's process (figure 2.6). The model of communication between web servers and servlet containers is fairly general; as long as the container can manage servlets appropriately, hand them requests, and deliver their responses, servlet and JSP developers can be shielded from the details of the back-end interaction between servlet containers and the generic web-server logic that drives them.

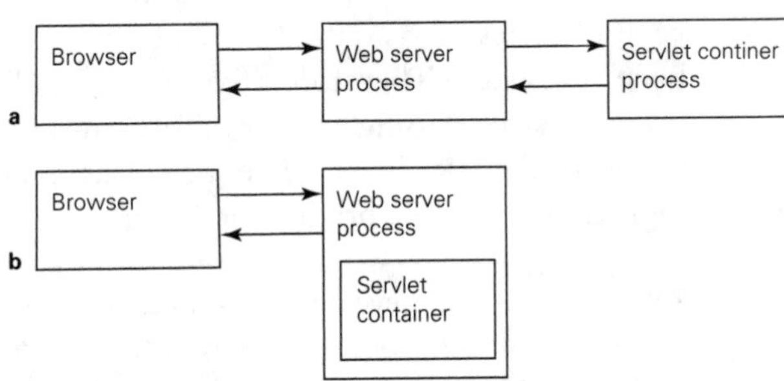

Figure 2.6 A servlet container may run in a separate operating-system process from the web server logic that depends on it (a). A servlet container may also run inside a web server's process (b).

2.2.2 The anatomy of a servlet

Like HTTP, servlets are based on the request/response model. In fact, a servlet is essentially a Java class that implements a particular, formal interface for producing responses based on requests. The Java interface `javax.servlet.Servlet`, which defines how servlets function, has a method that looks like

```
public void service(ServletRequest req, ServletResponse res)
```

The `ServletRequest` and `ServletResponse` interfaces, both in the `javax.servlet` package, represent the requests that a servlet processes and the responses that a servlet generates.

Because all servlets implement the `javax.servlet.Servlet` interface, each provides an implementation of the `service()` method. (Implementing a Java interface requires that a class provide implementations of all of the methods declared in that interface.) Therefore, all servlets have logic for processing a request and producing a response.

The `Servlet` interface has other methods that servlets must implement. JSP developers do not typically need to deal with these methods directly, but it may be useful to know that servlets can provide logic to handle initialization in an `init()` method and cleanup in a `destroy()` method.

The most common type of servlet is tied specifically to HTTP, which the Servlet specification requires every servlet container to support. The servlet standard defines a class, `javax.servlet.http.HttpServlet`, that represents HTTP-capable servlets and contains some convenience logic for their programmers. Specifically, authors of HTTP servlets do not usually need to write a `service()` method manually; instead, they can extend the `HttpServlet` class and override one or more of the higher-level methods it provides. Since `HttpServlet` is aware of HTTP, it has Java methods that correspond to HTTP methods: for instance, it specifies a `doGet()` method to handle GET requests and a `doPost()` method to handle POST requests. As figure 2.7 suggests, the `service()` method of `HttpServlet` calls these methods when the servlet receives GET or POST requests. Because `service()` provides this switching mechanism to differentiate among different types of HTTP requests, the developer of an HTTP servlet does not need to analyze each request, determine its type, and decide how to handle it. Instead, HTTP servlet authors can simply plug in logic to respond to GET or POST requests, as appropriate to their applications.

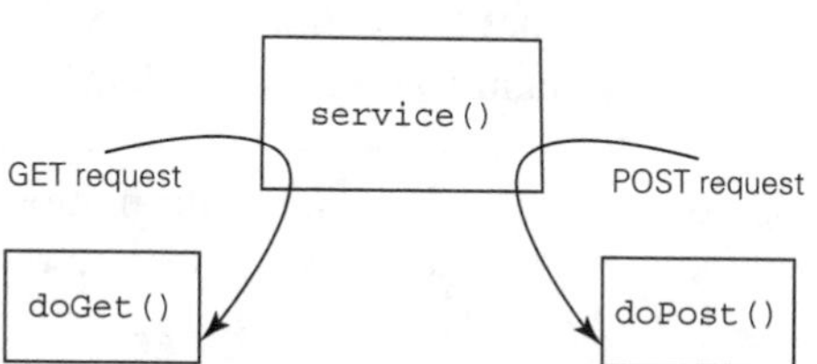

Figure 2.7 The mapping of GET and POST requests within an HttpServlet implementation.

The `doGet()` and `doPost()` methods accept arguments of type `HttpServletRequest` and `HttpServletResponse`, both of which are located in the `javax.servlet.http` package. These two interfaces extend their more generic equivalents and provide HTTP-specific request information and response directives. For example, because the type of message headers we discussed earlier are an HTTP concept and might not be present in another protocol, the method `getHeaders()` is defined in `HttpServletRequest`, not in the base `ServletRequest` interface. That is, the general interface does not need to have any concept of HTTP headers, but HTTP-specific request objects do. Similarly, the `HttpServletResponse` interface lets a servlet set HTTP cookies, which are described in more detail in chapters 4 and 14; cookie functionality would not be appropriate in the generic interface.

Consider another use of the `ServletRequest` interface. As we discussed earlier, browsers have a standard mechanism for encoding the data that users enter on HTML forms. In the servlet environment, it is the job of the servlet container to understand this encoding and represent it to the servlet. It does this through a `ServletRequest` object, which has methods like `getParameter()` that let the servlet easily recover the information entered by the user. Servlet authors therefore don't need to parse the encoded form data themselves; they can use the simple Java API that the container provides. `HttpServletRequest` objects will resurface when we begin to discuss the details of JSP functionality.

NOTE For more information on the servlet and JSP APIs, including the classes and interfaces shown in this chapter, see appendix F.

2.2.3 A servlet example

Even though detailed knowledge of servlets is not necessary for JSP developers—in fact, one of JSP's great advantages is that it lets developers create Java-based web applications without having to write servlets by hand—a simple servlet example might help you understand how servlets function. As we discussed, the servlet container does a lot of work behind the scenes, so a simple servlet is actually fairly straightforward to write. A basic HTTP servlet just needs to provide logic to respond to GET or POST request, which it can do by overriding the `doGet()` or `doPost()` methods in `HttpServlet`. The source code to a basic servlet that greets the user and prints extra information is shown in listing 2.1.

Listing 2.1 A servlet that greets and prints

```
import java.io.*;
import javax.servlet.*;
import javax.servlet.http.*;

public class BasicServlet extends HttpServlet {

  public void doGet(HttpServletRequest req, HttpServletResponse res)
      throws IOException {
```

```
    // output to the browser via the "response" object's Writer
    PrintWriter out = res.getWriter();

    // print out some unchanging template "header" text
    out.println("<html>");
    out.println("<body>");
    out.println("<p>");

    // print some dynamic information based on the request
    String name = req.getParameter("name");
    if (name != null)
      out.println("Hello, " + name + ".");
    else
      out.println("Welcome, anonymous user.");
    out.println("You're accessing this servlet from "
      + req.getRemoteAddr() + ".");

    // print out some unchanging template "footer" text
    out.println("</p>");
    out.println("</body>");
    out.println("</html>");
  }
}
```

This servlet implements only the `doGet()` method; it does not concern itself with POST requests. From `doGet()`, the servlet prints unchanging information, often called *template* data, to a `java.io.PrintWriter` object it has retrieved from the `HttpServletResponse` object it was passed. Then, it greets the user by retrieving a particular parameter from the HTTP request, much as the web server in our prior discussion did. It also prints the IP address from which the request originated. (Some applications use this information for gathering statistics or auditing users.)

TIP It is relatively easy to install a servlet container and run the servlet from listing 2.1. See appendix B for more information on Jakarta Tomcat, a free servlet and JSP container that provides the official reference implementation for the Java servlets and JSP platforms.

Notice how the servlet makes multiple calls of the form `out.println()` in order to display HTML and other miscellaneous text. Servlets that print HTML become unwieldy quickly because they output a large amount of text from within program logic. As we saw in chapter 1, this awkward use of servlets is one of the motivating factors behind JSP.

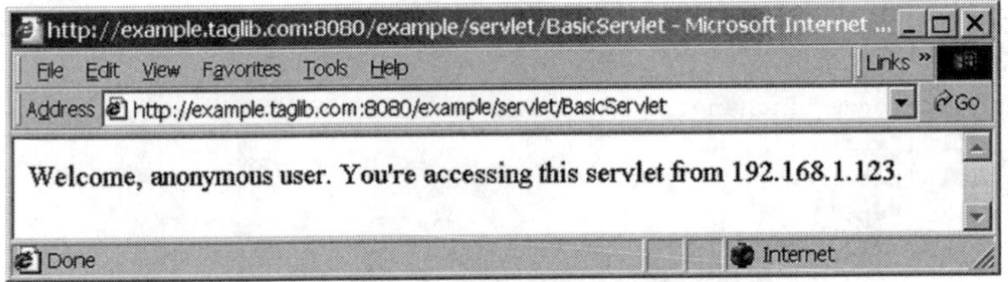

Figure 2.8 Output of the basic servlet when no name is specified.

Figures 2.8 and 2.9 show the servlet responding to two different requests. Note the differences between the two trial runs of the servlet. In figure 2.8, no `name` parameter is specified, so the test against such a parameter in the code causes an anonymous greeting to be displayed; figure 2.9 greets the user by name. Note also that the IP addresses shown in the two windows are different; the servlet detects the IP address of each new request as it's processed.

The servlet determines the `name` parameter from the HTTP request by parsing it according to the standard rules we mentioned before; the details of these rules are not important for now, but as you can probably see from the example, strings of the form

```
name=value
```

following a question mark (`?`) in the URL are interpreted as request parameters.

URLs containing such parameters can also be constructed manually—for example, as references from an <a> element. A file containing the following HTML might allow a user to click two different links and be greeted by two different names:

```
<a href="BasicServlet?name=Justin"> Say hello to Justin. </a>
<a href="BasicServlet?name=Melissa"> Say hello to Melissa. </a>
```

More dynamically, an HTML form containing the element

```
<input type="text" name="name" />
```

could allow the user to enter his or her name and be greeted appropriately.

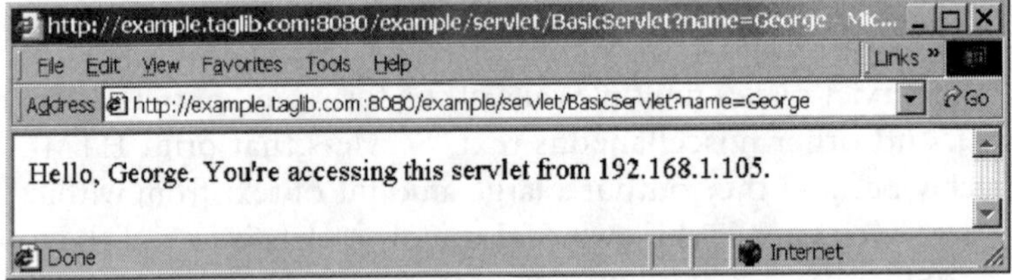

Figure 2.9 Output of the basic servlet when a name is specified.

This crash course in servlets was not designed to turn you into a servlet programmer overnight. As we've discussed, JSP makes it easy to develop dynamic web pages without having to use servlets. But many JSP programmers find a basic understanding of servlets useful as they approach more complex problems. Some applications, as we will see in chapter 10, can be built using both JSP and servlets. In other situations, having experimented with servlets will give you a deeper understanding of the JSP environment; we'll discuss more about how JSP pages and servlets interrelate in chapter 4.

3 First steps

This chapter covers

- Writing your first JSP page
- Simple dynamic content with JSP
- Basic session management
- Abstracting logic behind JSP pages

Now we're ready to see what JSP looks like. This chapter explores some of JSP's capabilities, giving you a quick tour of its basic functionality. The goal isn't to swamp you with technical details; we'll begin to consider those in the next two chapters, when we introduce the syntax and back-end implementation of JSP. The examples in this chapter should familiarize you with JSP pages' look and feel, which will be helpful when we discuss the syntax more formally.

About the examples

As indicated in chapter 1, a strength of JSP is that it lets you produce dynamic content using a familiar, HTML-like syntax. At the same time, however, the mixture of JSP elements and static text can make it difficult to look at a file and quickly find the JSP elements. To help remedy this problem for the examples in this book that mix JSP elements with static text, we have adopted the convention of marking JSP tags in such examples in **boldface**.

All of the examples presented in this chapter (except for one) are real, usable JSP, and you're encouraged to experiment with them yourself before moving forward. If you do not yet have a JSP environment in which to experiment, appendix B contains a quick installation guide for Tomcat, a free JSP container that provides the reference implementation for the JSP platform.

DEFINITION A *JSP container* is similar to a servlet container, except that it also provides support for JSP pages.

3.1 Simple text

No programming book would be complete without an example that prints "Hello, world!" This simple task serves as an excellent starting point for experimentation. Once you can use a language to print a text string of your choice, you're well on your way to becoming a programmer in that language.

For the web, it makes sense to print "Hello, world!" inside an HTML file. Here's a JSP page that does this:

```
<html>
<body>
<p>
Hello, world!
</p>
</body>
</html>
```

At this point, you're probably thinking, "Wait! That's nothing but a plain HTML file." And you're exactly right; this example is almost disappointingly simple. But it emphasizes an important point about JSP pages: they can contain unchanging text, just as normal HTML files do. Typically, a JSP page contains more than simple static content, but this static—or *template*—text is perfectly valid inside JSP pages.

If a JSP container were to use the JSP page in the example code to respond to an HTTP request, the simple HTML content would be included in the generated HTTP response unchanged. This would be a roundabout way of delivering simple, static HTML to a web browser, but it would certainly work.

Unfortunately, this example didn't show us much about what JSP really looks like. Here's a JSP page that prints the same "Hello, world!" string using slightly more of JSP's syntax:

```
<html>
<hody>
<p>
<%= "Hello, world!" %>
</p>
</body>
</html>
```

This example differs from the previous one because it includes a tag, or element, that has special meaning in JSP. In this case, the tag represents a *scripting element*. Scripting elements are marked off by `<%` and `%>`, and they let you include Java code on the same page as static text. While static text simply gets included in the JSP page's output, scripting elements let Java code decide what gets printed. In this case, the Java code is trivial: it's simply a literal string, and it never changes. Still, the processing of this page differs from that of the prior example: the JSP container notices the scripting element and ends up using our Java code when it responds to a request.

3.2 Dynamic content

If JSP pages could only print unchanging text, they wouldn't be very useful. JSP supports the full range of Java's functionality, however. For instance, although the scripting element in the last example contained only a simple Java string, it might have contained any valid Java expression, as in

```
<%= customer.getAddress() %>
```

or

```
<%= 17 * n %>
```

NOTE As we'll see in chapter 5, JSP is not strictly limited to Java code. The JSP standard provides for the possibility that code from other languages might be included between <% and %>. However, Java is by far the most common and important case, and we'll stick with it for now.

Let's take a closer look at some examples of JSP pages that produce content dynamically.

3.2.1 Conditional logic

One of the simplest tasks for a Java program, and thus for a JSP page, is to differentiate among potential courses of action. That is, a program can make a decision about what should happen next. You are probably familiar with basic conditional logic in Java, which might look like this:

```
if (Math.random() < 0.5)
    System.out.println("Your virtual coin has landed on heads.");
else
    System.out.println("Your virtual coin has landed on tails.");
```

This Java code, which simulates the flip of a coin, can transfer to a JSP page with only small modifications:

```
<html>
<body>
<p>Your virtual coin has landed on
<% if (Math.random() < 0.5) { %>
heads.
<% } else { %>
tails.
<% } %>
</p>
</body>
</html>
```

This example is similar to the Java code, except that JSP takes care of the output for us automatically. That is, we don't need to call `System.out.println()` manually. Instead, we simply include template text and let the JSP container print it under the right conditions.

So what, exactly, does this latest example do? Up until the first `<%`, the page is very similar to our first example: it contains just static text. This text will be printed for every response. However, the template text is interrupted by the Java code between the `<%` and `%>` markers. In this case, the Java code uses `Math.random()` to generate a pseudorandom number, which it uses to simulate the flip of a coin. If this number is less than 0.5, the block of JSP between the first two { and } braces gets evaluated. This block consists of static text (`heads.`), so this text simply gets included if the conditional check succeeds. Otherwise, the value `tails.` will be printed. Finally, the template text after the final `%>` marker gets included, unconditionally, into the output.

Therefore, this JSP page can result in two different potential outputs. Ignoring white space, one response looks like this:

```
<html>
<body>
<p>Your virtual coin has landed on
heads.
</p>
</body>
</html>
```

The other potential response is identical, except that the line containing the word "heads" is replaced with one containing "tails." In either case, the browser renders the resulting HTML. Recall from chapter 2 that browsers do not need to know how the HTML was generated; they simply receive a file and process it.

3.2.2 Iteration

Another fundamental task for programs is *iteration*—that is, looping. Like conditional logic, iterative code can be moved into JSP pages as well. Let's take the previous example and turn it into a page that flips five coins instead of one:

```
<html>
<body>
<% for (int i = 0; i < 5; i++) { %>
  <p>
  Your virtual coin has landed on
  <% if (Math.random() < 0.5) { %>
    heads.
  <% } else { %>
    tails.
  <% } %>
  </p>
<% } %>
</body>
</html>
```

How have we modified the example from the conditional logic section (other than by indenting it for clarity)? We've simply added a Java `for()` loop around part of it, embedded between the same `<%` and `%>` markers that we used earlier. As shown in figure 3.1, this loop causes its body to be executed five times.

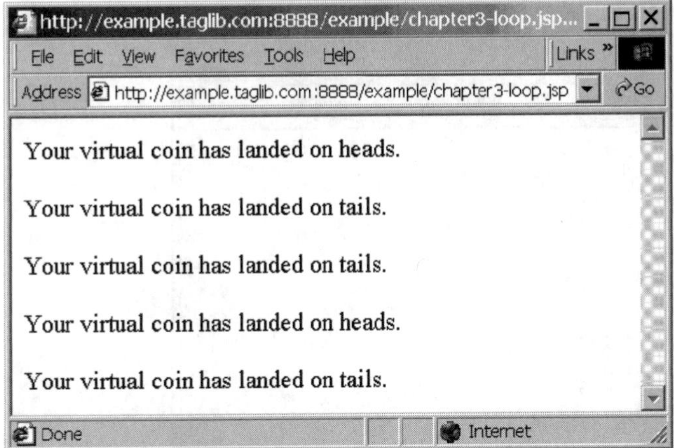

Figure 3.1 A sample run of our iteration example.

To get more of a feel for iteration, let's look at a simple JSP page that prints a traditional multiplication table in HTML (figure 3.2). This table would be tedious to type by hand, even for the most capable mathematicians. JSP turns the problem into a simple programming task that can be solved using two loops, one nested inside the other:

```
<table border="1">
<% for (int row = 1; row < 11; row++) { %>
   <tr>
   <% for (int column = 1; column < 11; column++) { %>
       <td><tt><%= row * column %></tt></td>
   <% } %>
   </tr>
<% } %>
</table>
```

How does this example work? First, we set up an HTML table with the `<table>` element. Then, for each number in the outer loop, we start a new row with the `<tr>` element. Within each row, we create columns for each number in the inner loop using the HTML `<td>` element. We close all elements appropriately and, finally, close the table.

Figure 3.3 shows the HTML source (from our browser's `View Source` command) for the HTTP response sent when the multiplication-table page runs. Note how, as we've emphasized before, the browser plays no part in the generation of this HTML. It does not multiply our numbers, for instance. It simply renders the HTML that the JSP engine generates.

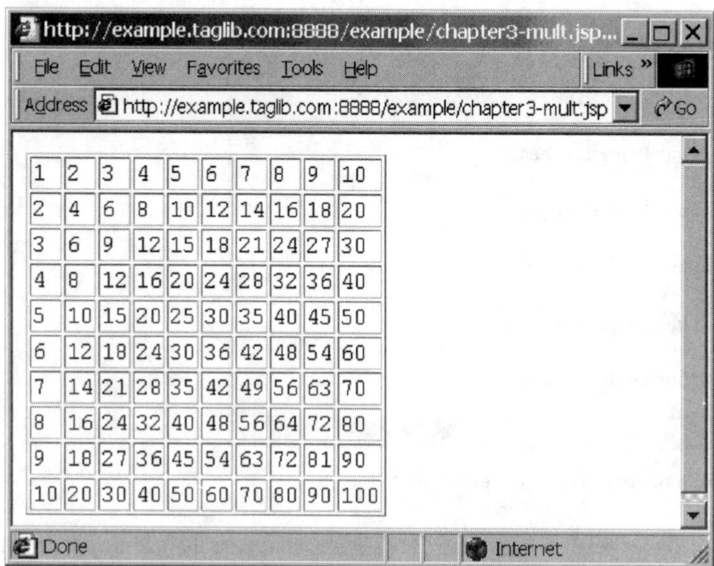

Figure 3.2 A multiplication table printed in a web browser

WARNING You might not have expected JSP processing to add some of the white space that appears in figure 3.3. JSP processing preserves the spaces in the source JSP file. For example, the body of the inner loop in our multiple-table example begins by starting a new line, for a line starts immediately after the inner `for()` loop's closing `%>` tag. In the majority of cases, you won't need to worry about the spacing of your output, but on rare occasions, you may need to eliminate extra white space in your source file.

This is the first example we've shown that mixes the simple `<%` marker with the `<%=` marker. As in the ASP environment, the `<%` marker introduces code that will simply be executed. By contrast, `<%=` introduces an expression whose result is converted to a string and printed. In the JSP code in the multiplication table example, the `for()` loops are structural and thus appear in blocks beginning with `<%`. When it comes time to print our `row * column` value, however, we include the Java code inside a block that starts with `<%=`.

NOTE We'll cover the details of these special markup tags—and describe more about iteration and conditional logic—in chapter 5.

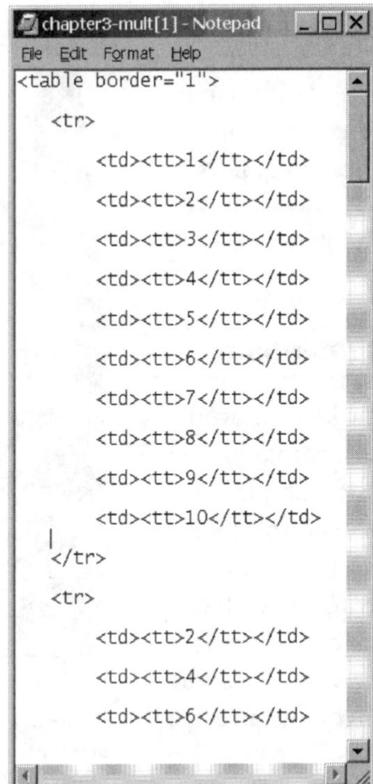

Figure 3.3
Output of the multiplication-table JSP page

3.2.3 *Non-HTML output*

JSP doesn't care about the form of static, template text. To demonstrate that JSP isn't tied to HTML exclusively, here's a simple JSP page that can be used as a time service for cell phones. It outputs WML, a form of XML that's used by some wireless devices:

```
<%@ page contentType="text/vnd.wap.wml;charset=UTF-8"
         import="java.text.*, java.util.*"
%><?xml version="1.0"?>
<%
  SimpleDateFormat df =
    new SimpleDateFormat("hh:mm a");
%>
<!DOCTYPE wml PUBLIC "-//WAPFORUM//DTD WML 1.1//EN"
 "http://www.wapforum.org/DTD/wml_1.1.xml">
<wml>
 <card id="time" title="Time">
   <p>It's <%= df.format(new Date()) %>.</p>
   <p>(Do you know where your laptop is?)</p>
 </card>
</wml>
```

Don't worry about the details of WML. JSP doesn't, and WML specifics are beyond the scope of this book. This example just demonstrates an application of JSP beyond the traditional, HTML-based web. Figure 3.4 shows sample output on an emulator for a particular wireless device, the Ericsson R320s.

Figure 3.4 Output of a WML emulator receiving input from a sample JSP page

NOTE For further details on the generation of non-HTML content, see chapter 15.

3.3 Processing requests and managing sessions

So far, our examples have performed simple tasks that aren't inherently web based. That is, you could write a command-line or Windows program analogous to each of the JSP examples presented so far. Let's move on to JSP pages that are web specific.

In JSP, several Java objects are exposed automatically to scripting code. When you write scripting code, you can refer to these objects without having to declare them by hand. Known as *implicit objects*, these variables—with names such as `request`, `session`, and `response`—give you a simple mechanism to access requests, manage sessions, and configure responses, among other tasks. The next few examples rely on features that the JSP container exposes through implicit objects. They make sense only in environments that are, like the Web, based on the request/response model described in chapter 2.

We'll go into further detail about implicit objects in chapter 6. For now, we introduce them just to demonstrate some more of JSP's functionality.

3.3.1 Accessing request parameters

In chapter 2, we saw how the Java Servlets API gives servlets access to information sent as part of the request. We also saw an example of a servlet that uses this information to greet the user by name. Compared to the servlet in listing 2.1, the JSP code to perform the same task is even simpler. Here's a JSP page that works just like the servlet in the last chapter:

```
<% String name = request.getParameter("name"); %>
<html>
<body>
<p>
<% if (name != null) { %>
```

```
  Hello, <%= name %>.
<% } else { %>
  Welcome, anonymous user.
<% } %>
You're accessing this servlet
from <%= request.getRemoteAddr() %>.
</p>
</body>
</html>
```

This example pulls out two pieces of information from the request: the value of the `name` parameter and the IP address of the machine that sent the request. (The calls work just as they did in listing 2.1.) Notice that we didn't need to declare the `request` variable; the environment has done so for us. The call to `request.getRemoteAddr()` means, "Get the IP address of the current request"; every time the JSP page runs, the value of the `request` object automatically represents the then-current request.

Accessing requests is very common in JSP, for access to requests lets JSP pages retrieve information from users. The `request` object is, by default, an instance of the same `HttpServletRequest` interface that we saw in chapter 2. All of the functionality of `HttpServletRequest` is thus available through the request object. For example, you can access the data entered into an HTML form by calling `request.getParameter()`, just as our example does.

3.3.2 Using sessions

Recall that HTTP is stateless, meaning that a web server starts with a blank slate as it processes each new request it receives. If you need to tie different requests—for example, all requests from the same user—into a *session*, you need either to program this yourself or to use a platform that handles the task for you.

Fortunately, JSP is one such platform. We'll see how JSP actually manages sessions later, in chapters 4 and beyond, but let's take a look now at how sessions might be used. As we mentioned, scripting elements in JSP pages have access to an implicit `session` object. You can store and retrieve session-related data by using methods this object provides.

As an example, imagine that during the processing of a request, you have built up an object called `userData` for a particular user. Suppose you wish to remember this object for subsequent requests that come from the same user. The session object lets you make this association. First, you would write a call like `session.setAttribute("login", userData)` to tie the `userData` object to the session. Then, for the rest of the session, even for different requests, you would be able to call `session.getAttribute("login")` to recover the same `userData` object. The `session` object keys data under particular names, much as a typical hash table, or an implementation of `java.util.Map`, does. In this case, the `userData` object is keyed under the name `login`.

Let's see how sessions work in practice by converting our virtual coin-flip page from before into one that keeps track of how many times "heads" and "tails" have been chosen. Listing 3.1 shows the source code for such a page.

Listing 3.1 A small application that uses sessions

```
<%
   // determine the winner
   String winner;
   if (Math.random() < 0.50)
     winner = "heads";
   else
     winner = "tails";

   synchronized (session) {
     // initialize the session if appropriate
     if (session.isNew()) {
       session.setAttribute("heads", new Integer(0));
       session.setAttribute("tails", new Integer(0));
     }
     // increment the winner
     int oldValue =
       ((Integer) session.getAttribute(winner)).intValue();
     session.setAttribute(winner, new Integer(oldValue + 1));
   }
%>
<html>
<body>
<h1>Current standings:</h1>
<table border="1">
<tr>
  <th>Heads</th>
  <th>Tails</th>
</tr>
<tr>
  <td><%= session.getAttribute("heads") %></td>
  <td><%= session.getAttribute("tails") %></td>
</tr>
</table>
</body>
</html>
```

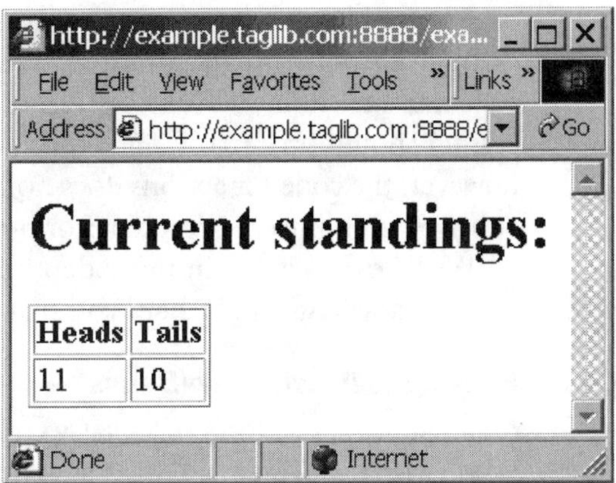

Figure 3.5 A stateful tally of prior events, made possible by session management.

At its heart, this page is similar to the one from before that emulates a coin flip. However, the page contains extra logic to keep a tally of prior coin flips in the `session` object. Without getting too caught up in the details, the page initializes the session if it's new—that is, if `session.isNew()` returns `true`—and then it keeps track of the tally for "heads" and "tails," keying the data, imaginatively enough, under the names `heads` and `tails`. Every time you reload the page, it updates the tallies and displays them for you in an HTML table (figure 3.5). If you reload the page, the tallies change. If your friend, however, begins accessing the application from a different computer, the `session` object for your friend's requests would refer to a new session, not yours. When different users access the page, they will all receive their own, individual tallies of heads and tails. Behind the scenes, the JSP container makes sure to differentiate among the various users' sessions.

3.4 Separating logic from presentation

In the examples so far, Java code has been mixed right in with HTML and other static text. A single JSP file might contain some HTML, then some Java code, and finally some more HTML. While this mixture is a convenient way to generate dynamic content, it might be difficult for a large software-development team to maintain. For instance, programmers and HTML designers would need to manage the same combined JSP files. If problems are encountered, they might not be immediately clear whether they come from HTML problems or logic errors.

To help address these issues and provide for greater maintainability, JSP provides another mechanism for generating on-the-fly content. In addition to the simple scripting elements we've shown, JSP allows special, XML-based tags called *actions* to abstract Java code away from the JSP page itself.

Many actions look just like HTML tags, but they work like a signal to the JSP container to indicate that some processing needs to occur. When processing of a JSP page hits a block of static HTML text, like `<p>Hello!</p>`, such text is simply passed through to the JSP page's output. Processing for actions is different: when the JSP page hits an action, such as `<jsp:include>`, it runs extra code to figure out how processing should proceed. Unlike the Java between scripting elements `<%` and `%>` tags, however, the code for actions does not appear directly on the JSP page. Instead, it can either be built into the container or provided as a custom add-on by developers.

We'll cover actions in more depth in chapters 4 and 6. For now, let's take a look at how these tags might help you manage your JSP applications.

3.4.1 Reusing logic with JavaBeans

One common use of the special XML-based tags we've mentioned is to communicate with JavaBeans. In fact, JSP provides several standard action tags to help you communicate with these beans. As we discussed in chapter 1, JavaBeans are reusable Java components: they are Java classes that follow conventions, defined in the JavaBeans standard, that promote modularity and reusability. The details of this standard, as it relates to JSP pages, will be covered in chapter 8. For now, let's look at a simple JavaBean class so that we can present a JSP page that uses it:

```
package com.taglib.wdjsp.firststeps;
public class HelloBean implements java.io.Serializable {
  String name = "world";
  public String getName() {
    return name;
  }

  public void setName(String name) {
    this.name = name;
  }
}
```

Indeed, this is a very simple Java class. It contains a single instance variable, `name`, which refers to a string. By default, this string has the value `world`, but it can be changed using the method `setName()`, which takes an instance of the Java `String` class as its parameter. Code outside the bean can retrieve the name by using `getName()`. These methods have names that the JavaBeans framework will look for, by default, when it needs to modify or retrieve the `name` variable, which in bean terms is called a *property*.

A JSP page may use this bean as follows:

```
<html>
<body>
<p>
<jsp:useBean id="hello"
  class="com.taglib.wdjsp.firststeps.HelloBean"/>
```

```
<jsp:setProperty name="hello" property="name"/>
Hello, <jsp:getProperty name="hello" property="name"/>!
</p>
</body>
</html>
```

The first action tag that appears is the `<jsp:useBean>` tag. As its name suggests, this tag lets the JSP page begin using a bean, specified by a particular class name and page-specific ID. In this case, we have indicated that we wish to use an instance of the `HelloBean` class and, for the purposes of the page, to call it `hello`. The appearance of the `<jsp:setProperty>` tag in the code causes the request parameter called `name`—if it exists and isn't an empty string—to be passed as the `String` parameter in a call to the bean's `setName()` method. We could have written

```
<% if (request.getParameter("name") != null
       && !request.getParameter("name").equals(""))
     hello.setName(request.getParameter("name"));
%>
```

and it would have had a similar effect, but `<jsp:setProperty>` is both easier to use and provides us with a level of abstraction. If we needed to set multiple properties in the `HelloBean`, `<jsp:setProperty>` would make our page substantially easier to read and less prone to errors.

The final action tag that appears in the example is `<jsp:getProperty>`, which retrieves the `name` property from the `HelloBean` and includes it in the JSP page's output. Therefore, the example prints a personalized greeting if it can retrieve the user's name from the request; if not, it simply prints `Hello, world!`, just like our first example.

The bean-centered approach gives our page several advantages in readability and maintainability. As we just mentioned, the tags beginning with `<jsp:` take care of various operations for us behind the scenes. This way, we don't have to write Java code that manually sets and retrieves information out of the bean.

Suppose that `HelloBean` were a little more complex. Instead of a bean that simply stores a name, imagine one that capitalizes names correctly or that uses the name as part of a database query that retrieves more information about the user. Even if `HelloBean` performed these extra tasks, its interface with the JSP page would be the same: `<jsp:getProperty>` and `<jsp:setProperty>` would still work just as they do in the example we just saw. If multiple pages in your application—or even multiple applications—need to use the logic contained inside the bean, they can all simply use different copies of the bean—or even the same copy—via the `<jsp:useBean>` tag. Beans therefore let you move more of your own Java code outside the JSP page itself, and they let you reuse this code among multiple pages. By contrast, Java logic that appears between `<%` and `%>` might need to be replicated in a number of different pages.

NOTE We cover JavaBeans and bean-based design strategies in detail, beginning with chapter 7.

3.4.2 Abstracting logic with custom tags

Action tags thus have some of the benefits as do functions in a language like Java; they let you hide and reuse logic. Tags have an additional benefit, too: their syntax, being XML-based, is similar to that of HTML. Therefore, if you are working as a developer on part of a team that also includes nonprogramming HTML designers, you might decide that you want to expose your back-end functionality through tags instead of through simple function calls.

As we'll discuss further in the next chapter, JSP lets you write your own new actions and expose them in *tag libraries*. Writing new tags is an advanced JSP topic that we leave until chapters 17–19, but let's briefly look, for now, at how we might use one of the tags we demonstrate in those later chapters. One such tag is `<mut:ifProperty>`, which, in its simplest usage, conditionally includes the text contained between it and its ending `</mut:ifProperty>` tag if the specified property of a JavaBean is `true` instead of `false`.

Once we import the appropriate tag library—a procedure we'll learn more about in chapter 5—we can use the `<mut:ifProperty>` tag in a JSP page as follows:

```
<mut:ifProperty name="user" property="important">
Welcome!  Thanks for visiting again.
</mut:ifProperty>

<mut:ifProperty name="user" property="unimportant">
Oh, it's you again.  Sigh.
</mut:ifProperty>
```

WARNING As we mentioned, this JSP fragment depends on advanced JSP features. You won't be able to run it just as it appears. See chapters 17–19 for more information on custom tag libraries.

As with `<jsp:setProperty>`, we could have written functionally similar code by using Java inside `<%` and `%>` delimiters, but these tags give us a level of abstraction and allow us to reuse logic.

3.5 Review of examples

The goal in this chapter wasn't to cover any syntactic specifics or to explain behind-the-scenes operation; we'll have ample time for that later. For now, our progression of examples has given you a first look at JSP. You've seen that JSP pages can contain

- static HTML text
- static non-HTML text
- embedded Java code that supports iteration, conditionalization, and other abstract logic
- standard tags that, among other benefits, hide logic and let you access JavaBeans
- custom tags that you've written yourself, or that other developers have written

Now, we're ready to look more formally at how JSP pages are composed and how they get processed before they execute.

4 How JSP works

This chapter covers

- JSP directives and scripting elements
- JSP action elements
- Phases in processing a JSP page
- Advantages of the JSP environment

In chapter 3, we jumped into JSP by looking at some of its capabilities. Let's now take a closer look at the structure of JSP pages, studying the building blocks of JSP pages in more detail. Full syntax and functionality will be covered in chapter 5 and beyond; our goal for now is to discuss how JSP works, what happens to JSP pages behind the scenes before and while they run, and how the JSP container provides services on which you will rely as you learn more about JSP.

4.1 The structure of JSP pages

As we saw in chapter 3, JSP pages are a combination of text and special markup tags (figure 4.1). Template text is static text that's passed through to the output, while the special JSP markup tags allow JSP pages to be dynamic. For example, a markup tag might cause on-the-fly HTML to get generated, or it might decide whether static text will be displayed. A markup tag might also take some behind-the-scenes action, such as sending an email or checking a database.

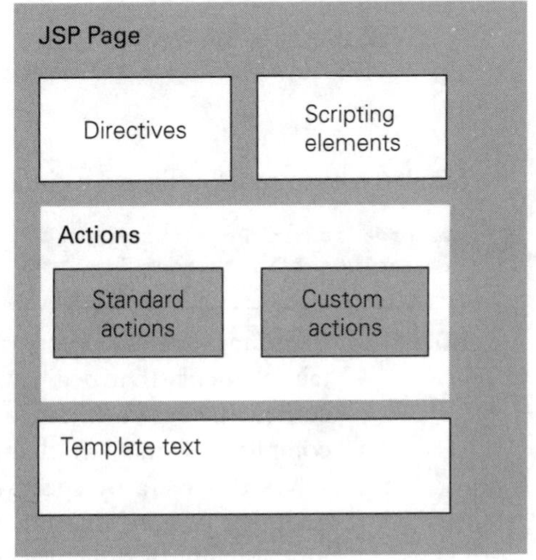

Figure 4.1 Elements that can appear, in any order, in a JSP page

One group of such dynamic JSP tags is reminiscent of ASP's syntax; this variety of tags supports configuration and scripting. Another class of tags is based on the syntax of the XML and lets JSP developers produce dynamic content without including Java code directly on a JSP page.

4.1.1 Directives and scripting elements

Some JSP tags begin with the characters `<%` and end with `%>`, the same delimiters used in the ASP environment. In JSP, an additional character may appear after the leading `<%` to further describe the purpose of the tag.

Tags of this style have one of two purposes: either they include Java code in the JSP page, or they contain instructions for the JSP container.

DEFINITION If a tag introduces Java code into a JSP page, it is called a *scripting element*. A JSP *directive*, by contrast, provides instructions to the JSP container; it either requests action on the part of the container, or it specifies information about the JSP page.

The following tags are examples of scripting elements:

```
<%! int count = 0; %>
<%= 2 * Math.PI * radius %>
<%
  if (radius > 10.0) {
    out.println("Exceeds recommended maximum.  Stress analysis advised.");
  }
%>
```

Similarly, examples of directives include:

```
<%@ page isErrorPage="true" %>
<%@ include file="header.html" %>
```

NOTE These tags are not compatible with XML; an XML document could not contain elements that begin with `<%` and end with `%>`, with somewhat arbitrary content in between. Since JSP 1.2 allows authorship of JSP pages in XML-compliant syntax, as chapter 1 described, these tags pose a problem. JSP solves this issue by specifying a corresponding XML-compliant element for each type of non-XML tag. Chapter 5, in addition to covering the full use and functionality of directives and scripting elements, will go into further detail about the dual, XML-compliant elements.

4.1.2 Standard and custom actions

The rest of the JSP special markup tags are based on XML syntax. That is, they follow the style and conventions of XML. Before going into too much detail about how these tags work, let's first describe some of the basics of XML syntax, in case it is new to you.

Basic XML syntax

XML looks a lot like HTML, but it is specified a more strictly. For example, XML tags are case sensitive, while HTML tags are not. When designing a page in HTML, you might choose to write either `<p>` or `<P>`, and it doesn't much matter which one you pick. In XML, these two tags are entirely different elements.

XML also requires that all attribute values be placed within quote marks. HTML is often written without quote characters surrounding attributes, as in

```
<a href=http://www.taglib.com/>
```

This tag would be illegal in XML; instead, the URL specified for the `href` attribute would need to be surrounded with either single or double quotes. XML also requires that every nonempty tag—that is, any tag that contains text or other tags—have an appropriate closing counterpart. It is common to see HTML that looks like this:

```
<ul>
  <li> First list item
  <li> Second list item
</ul>
```

This fragment could not be part of a legal XML document. For use in XML, closing tags would need to be provided. For example:

```
<ul>
  <li> First list item </li>
  <li> Second list item </li>
</ul>
```

Not every tag contains text or other tags, however. For instance, the HTML `<br>` tag stands alone and can't sensibly contain anything else. To differentiate such tags from those that do require a closing counterpart, XML uses `/>` as the ending delimiter for the tag. For instance, a standalone tag like HTML's `<br>` would be written as `<br/>` in XML. (Technically, you could also write `<br></br>`, but there is generally little reason not to use the `/>` shortcut.)

While HTML has a fixed set of tags, you can extend XML in application-specific ways by defining sets of tags that have meaning in a particular context. For instance, if you wanted to store a database of jokes in an XML file, you might define tags such as `<joke>`, `<setup>`, `<punchline>`, and so on, and then include them in a file as follows:

```
<joke quality="poor">
  <setup>
    ...
  </setup>
  <punchline>.
     ... and she said, "No, silly, it's a servlet container!"
  </punchline>
</joke>
```

To allow tags defined for different applications to appear unambiguously in the same file, XML uses *namespaces*, which are essentially collections of tag and attribute names. An XML file can refer to a namespace by attaching the namespace identifier, followed by a colon (`:`), to the beginning of a tag's name. In this manner, a single XML file can use two different tags with the same name, as long as they are part of different namespaces. For example, if our joke-oriented tags were qualified with the namespace identifier `joke`, and a separate namespace identified by the name `configuration` had a `<setup>` element, namespaces would allow a single document to use both elements by specifying them as `<joke:setup>` and `<configuration:setup>`. (We leave it to your imagination to concoct a file that would appropriately contain both configuration directives and jokes.)

JSP action elements

JSP *actions* are XML-style tags that cause special processing to occur at a specific point in the run-time execution of a JSP page. This processing might involve the text contained by the action tag, or it might simply involve calling some stand-alone Java code that performs a task.

JSP action tags come in two varieties, standard and custom. First, JSP defines several tags known as standard actions.

DEFINITION A *standard action* is an action tag that has been defined by the JSP standard. For JSP, standard actions are associated with the namespace `jsp`, and standard actions appear in JSP pages with a prefix of `jsp:`, even for JSP pages that are not written using the XML-compliant syntax mentioned earlier.

JSP defines actions that cover several commonly used features, like forwarding a request to a new page. Standard actions, however, are not the only actions supported in JSP pages. A powerful feature of JSP is the ability to program new actions.

DEFINITION A *custom action* is an action tag whose behavior is added to the environment through an API provided by the JSP standard. Collections of custom actions are usually called *tag libraries.*

Tag libraries are incorporated into JSP pages using the JSP `<%@ taglib %>` directive. This directive associates a prefix with each tag library imported into a page. As with namespaces, these prefixes prevent clashes between two tags with the same name but from different tag libraries. (In fact, in the XML view of a JSP page, tag libraries are imported using the actual XML namespace mechanism.)

NOTE In some organizations that use JSP to develop large applications, custom tag libraries provide a means of abstracting logic away from JSP pages—and even for eliminating Java code from them, if this is desired. A complex operation, such as a database update, might be hidden behind a custom tag. In some cases, this abstraction can simplify maintenance of JSP pages. Some organizations have adopted the approach of separating JSP developers from tag developers: the former group is familiar with HTML and JSP tags, and the latter group programs in Java and exposes all custom application logic through tags. The premise, in short, is that HTML developers can easily learn how to use custom JSP tag libraries because the syntax of JSP tags is so similar to that of HTML.

This organizational style is just one of many options for developing web applications, but it might help you envision one benefit of JSP's ability to expose Java logic through XML-like tags. We discuss several architectures and organizational models for JSP pages in chapter 10.

Although JSP actions are, as we've discussed, based primarily on XML syntax, JSP departs from XML syntax by allowing tags to be embedded within one another. This can happen in two different ways. First, any JSP tag—including directives or scripting expressions—can appear arbitrarily inside an HTML tag, supplying dynamic content to fill in the HTML tag's attributes (or even part of its name). For example, the following is legal JSP:

```
<a href="<%= sourceVariable %>">
```

This is not a major issue, though; the JSP container can regard HTML merely as arbitrary text. Since JSP doesn't process HTML tags, it can treat them as plain text. And since JSP tags can clearly be embedded in plain text, it is not problematic to embed them in HTML or other tag-based content.

Second, more interesting use of JSP tags occurs inside other JSP tags. Specifically, a JSP scripting expression can specify the value of a JSP action's attribute. For example, the following can be legal JSP:

```
<myTagLibrary:customAction attribute="<%= value %>" />
```

As a real-life example of this feature, consider the following use of a standard action tag:

```
<jsp:setProperty name="login" property="visits"
                 value="<%= previousVisits + 1 %>"/>
```

Such embedded tags are referred to as *request-time attribute expressions* or *request-time attribute values*, for the attribute's value is determined when the page is run in response to a request, not when the page is initially processed. These embedded expression tags may look strange, but they are very useful in practice. We'll see more about request-time attribute values, including the restrictions placed on their use, in the next three chapters.

The syntax we've shown here for request-time attribute values is not valid in XML. But like other constructs valid in JSP but not in XML, the JSP standard defines an XML-attribute equivalent that can be used when authoring pages in XML syntax. The particulars of this mechanism are not important for now, however.

NOTE Details on most JSP actions will be presented in chapters 5 and 6. A few action tags, however, are specific to JSP's built-in support for the JavaBeans component programming model. Descriptions of these tags will be covered in chapter 7.

4.2 Behind the scenes

Once a JSP container has been installed and configured, using it is relatively straightforward. JSP files that are added to the appropriate directory hierarchy—or otherwise marked off in a manner agreed upon by the web server and the JSP server, such as by using a file extension of .jsp or another configured value—are simply handled by the JSP container when appropriate. (Chapter 13 describes the process of deploying JSP applications in more detail.)

Although you can rely on this process and ignore the details of how the JSP container works most of the time, some knowledge of its operation will help you get more out of the JSP environment.

4.2.1 Translation to servlets

Like most source code, JSP pages start life as text files and end up being compiled. A JSP file, though, takes a somewhat more circuitous route through this process than does a typical Java program. Before being run, JSP pages are translated to servlets. This translation involves conversion of JSP source code into servlet source code by the JSP container. (This step is sometimes referred to as *compilation* of a JSP page into a servlet, but it should be differentiated from compilation of Java code into bytecodes.) After this translation, the servlet class is, itself, compiled.

Because JSP pages are translated to servlets, they inherit servlets' dependence on the request/response model. JSP pages, like servlets, are called in response to requests, and they produce responses. When the JSP container translates the body of a JSP page into a servlet, it produces a new class that implements the `javax.servlet.Servlet` interface. This class has a method called `_jspService()` that is built from the body of the JSP page. Furthermore, unless the page author specifically requests greater control via the `extends` attribute of the `<%@ page %>` directive—which is extremely rare—the container bases the generated class on a class whose `service()` calls `_jspService()`. In short, a JSP page is translated into a method that maps requests to responses based on the contents of the JSP page.

How do the contents get translated? The easiest part of the JSP source file to translate is the template text—that is, the part of the page that isn't a directive, a scripting element, an action, or anything else specific to JSP (such as JSP comments, which will be introduced in chapter 5). This template text might be HTML, or it could be XML or text in an arbitrary format. The JSP container doesn't care what it is; it simply outputs it as part of the response. For example, the following text:

```
<p>Template text</p>
```

might be converted into a call that looks like

```
out.println("<p>Template text</p>");
```

Scripting expressions are also easy to translate and incorporate into the servlet, for the Java code embedded in them is passed through as is. The Java code will be included at the right place in the servlet, and it will be run as appropriate when the servlet is run.

WARNING As we will see again in chapter 5, JSP technically allows scripting languages other than Java to be included in scripting expressions. However, the JSP 1.2 standard doesn't provide formal rules for what happens when a JSP page uses a language other than Java for scripting elements. The discussion here applies only to cases where Java is used as the scripting language—which is, for now, the vast majority.

Action elements are somewhat more complicated to transfer, but the end result is that the JSP container writes calls to appropriate Java code at the correct spots in the generated servlet's source code. If the action is a custom action you've written yourself, the translation will involve creating calls to your custom code.

Once the translation from the JSP page into a servlet is complete, the behind-the-scenes servlet is compiled into Java bytecodes.

4.2.2 Translation versus execution

JSP defines two stages of processing for JSP pages: the *translation phase* and the *execution phase.* (It is common to speak of the execution phase as the *request phase* or simply as *run time*). We've just discussed what occurs during translation: the JSP page is converted into a servlet. Subsequently, when a request is received by the container, this servlet is run. The distinction between the purposes of the two phases is clear, but there are still some differences worth emphasizing.

Performance implications

The translation phase occurs only when necessary, not as a response to every request. As you can imagine, the process of parsing a JSP page, translating it to a servlet, and then compiling that servlet can be time-consuming. Fortunately, the JSP container does not need to repeat the process of translation for each request that it handles. As long as the underlying JSP page hasn't been changed, there's no reason to generate a new servlet. A typical JSP container, therefore, will check the last modification time on a JSP file, and it will translate the file only if necessary. This extra check does not reduce the amount of time necessary for translation upon the first request for a JSP page; however, all subsequent requests will proceed much more quickly, for these requests can simply be served from a compiled servlet. (This process is summarized in figure 4.2.)

TIP JSP also supports *precompilation* of JSP pages into servlets to avoid the performance hit associated with compiling a JSP page the first time it is requested. If the JSP page is compiled before any user requests it, the first request will proceed smoothly. For details, see chapter 13.

The separation of translation and request phases gives JSP a performance edge over many other web-based development environments. In many scripting environments, script code needs to be interpreted for every request. Since JSP can take care of expensive parsing and compilation operations before requests are processed, the JSP container's delay during a response is greatly reduced. Furthermore, since JSP pages depend on servlets, the JSP environment automatically yields the benefits of servlets' performance improvements. Recall from chapter 1 that servlets are multithreaded, which makes them substantially faster than environments such as CGI that depend on spawning new processes at request time.

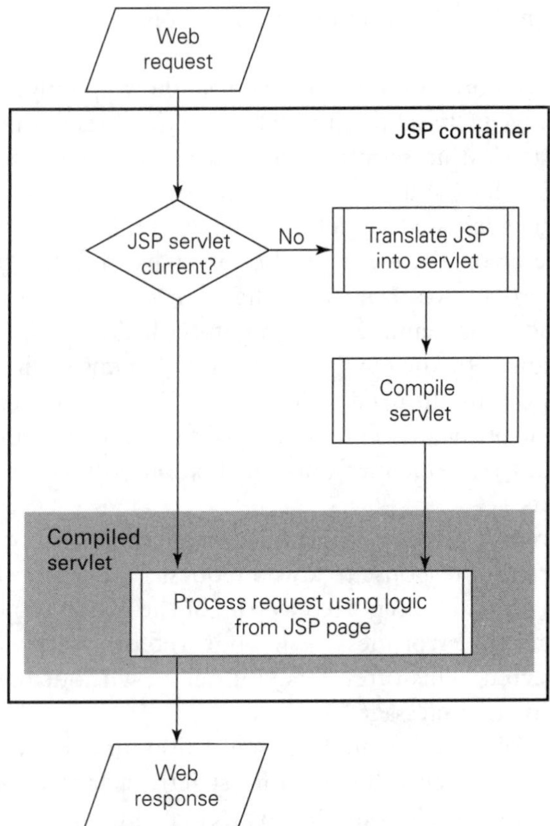

Figure 4.2 The typical process for translating and running JSP pages

Error handling

Another difference between the translation and request phases concerns how errors are handled. Translation-time errors in JSP are analogous to compile-time errors in traditional Java programming: some, but not all, errors can be caught before the program even runs, but the rest must, unfortunately, show up at run time.

Broadly speaking, there are two sorts of translation-time errors a container might encounter. First, there are errors in the structure of the JSP page. For instance, a scripting expression might not contain its closing `%>`, or a directive's name might be misspelled. In cases like this, the container might be able to pinpoint the error's location in the JSP file and return a reasonably useful message to help you fix the problem.

The second class of errors is more insidious; these errors show up only once the JSP page is translated into a servlet. Recall that the JSP container does not necessarily process Java code embedded within scripting elements; it merely includes this code directly as part of the servlet's source code. Therefore, errors in such code only show up as a failure of the generated servlet to compile. If this embedded Java code leads to a compile-time error, the error can be somewhat difficult to track down. The container might provide you with only the error's line number in the offending servlet's source code, for example. You might get lucky and be able to correlate a misspelling highlighted by the compiler's error with a misspelling in the original JSP code, but if not, you might need to look through the generated servlet's source code to identify the problem. (The location of the servlet's source code is container-specific; check your JSP container's documentation to find out what it does with its generated servlets.)

The way that containers report errors is implementation dependent, but if the problematic translation occurred in response to a web request for a newly changed JSP file, it is likely that the error will be reported as part of the HTTP response to that request. That is, you'll get the error message in your web browser, instead of getting the output you expected. This often lets you debug without having to search through log files to find error messages.

As we mentioned, not all errors can be caught at translation time. Request-time errors occur by virtue of a Java exception (or, more strictly, a Java `Throwable` object) being thrown as the JSP page's compiled servlet is run in response to a request. JSP provides a mechanism to let developers catch request-time errors gracefully; we'll discuss the advantages of this mechanism in the next section and detail its operation in chapter 14.

4.3 What the environment provides

JSP inherits convenience features from servlets, and it provides features of its own. Let's take a look at some of these advantages and go into detail about how JSP containers provide them. These services are some of the features you'll come to rely on as you design and write JSP applications.

4.3.1 Automatic servlet generation

As we've seen, an obvious difference between writing servlets and JSP pages is that JSP authors don't need to write servlets manually. Instead, the JSP container creates servlets automatically. In fact, JSP might be looked at—or even used—as a convenient platform for developing stand-alone servlets rapidly. (In practice, though, most JSP authors think of servlets as a behind-the-scenes detail.)

Besides the simple convenience of not having to write `doGet()` and `doPost()` methods by hand, the automatic creation of servlets has another important advantage: it supports an organizational model that separates presentation tasks from back-end implementation tasks. That is, JSP provides for a productive division of labor for web-application development. Because the JSP environment takes care of the compilation process automatically and hides the details of the Java methods that need to be written, JSP pages become more accessible to nonprogrammers or novice programmers. JSP authors do not need to know the detailed structure of a Java class or the syntax for declaring methods; instead, they can write Java code as if it were simple scripting code. Furthermore, as we noted earlier, some uses of JSP that rely heavily on tag libraries can even push Java code entirely out of JSP pages.

NOTE Engineers working under the Java Community Process are striving to provide a standard tag library for JSP with some of these goals in mind. Automatic servlet generation made JSP pages accessible to novice programmers, and a standard tag library would continue the trend by providing new standard tags for common operations within JSP page. These tags could help minimize the use of Java code in JSP pages. For example, instead of writing a simple conditional block using Java code inside scripting expressions, a JSP author could use a standard conditional tag to provide for control flow.

Even advanced Java programmers can appreciate the convenience that comes with automatic generation of a servlet. If a programmer needs to add dynamic content to a web page, adding a simple scripting element is much easier than manually writing a servlet that prints out a large block of HTML with calls like `out.println()`.

4.3.2 Buffered output

As we saw in chapter 2, HTTP places constraints on the way that web applications can interact with web browsers. In that discussion, we saw that HTTP responses typically contain a status line, followed by headers, followed by a body. This sequence is not negotiable; that is, once the body of an HTTP response begins transmission on the network, the web server has lost its opportunity to specify headers or the status line.

Because the pre-body structures support error reporting (among many other features), this constraint might have been a problem for fault-tolerant JSP

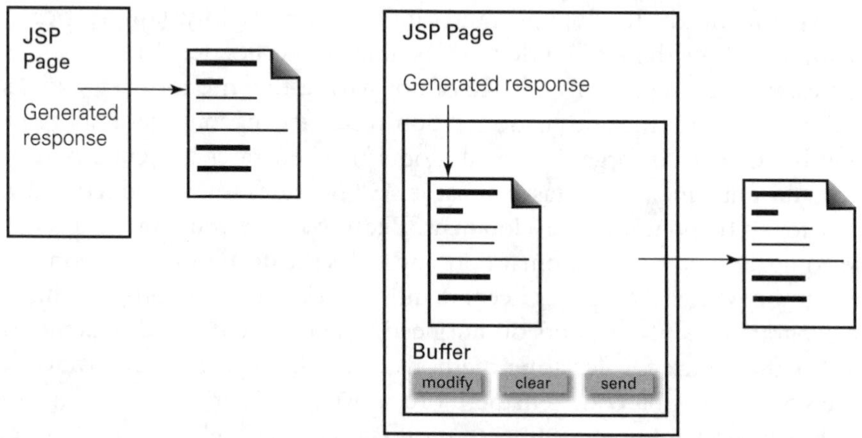

Figure 4.3 Unbuffered versus buffered output. When output is unbuffered, it leaves the JSP page's control immediately and cannot be retracted.

applications. Suppose that halfway through the code that generates a response, an error occurs, and the JSP page decides that it needs to set a status code to describe the error or a header to forward the user to a new page. If the web server has already sent part of the response's body, it will not be able to go back and edit the headers or status line.

JSP solves this problem by *buffering* the output of JSP pages.

DEFINITION A *buffer* is a temporary space for storing information. *Buffering* involves using such temporary space to hold data before sending it on to its ultimate destination.

Instead of sending the output generated by a JSP page directly to web browsers, the JSP container first buffers the output. This buffering gives the JSP page leeway if it needs to add or modify a header after generation of the page's output has begun. That is, the JSP page can simply modify the buffer before sending it on the network. If the JSP page decides to forward the request to another page, it can simply clear the buffer (figure 4.3).

WARNING JSP output buffers do not grow automatically; that is, they have a fixed size. We will see in the next chapter how to configure this size, but it is important to understand how the buffer size might affect the functionality of a JSP page. By default, when the buffer fills up, its contents are sent to the browser. Therefore, once the initial buffer for a response has filled up and is sent, the JSP page no longer has an opportunity to set headers.

If seamless error reporting or header handling is essential to an application, the JSP container can be configured to throw an exception when the buffer becomes full. This prevents a partial response from being sent to the web browser, and it ensures that a JSP page will never run into a situation where it unexpectedly finds it can't set a header. In practice, however, it is rare for an output buffer to be filled by a JSP application; the default size must be at least 8 kilobytes (KB) on any container, and this is enough for a typical JSP page. For details, see chapter 5.

Because the JSP container, by default, automatically builds output buffering into the servlets it generates for JSP pages, JSP authors can simply forget about the issue in most cases. For example, you can use the mechanisms we'll discuss in chapter 6 to modify the response's headers, and you will not typically need to remember how HTTP response messages are structured. The container takes care of the ugly details for you.

4.3.3 Session management

As we saw in chapter 2, HTTP is stateless, meaning in part that HTTP servers do not remember requests once they've processed them. If a server gets three requests in a row from the same web browser, it sees these as three separate requests; nothing binds them together.

Cookies

One common way to connect requests together is through HTTP *cookies*, which work specifically to bind requests together. Cookies work as follows: in response to a request, a web server decides to send a cookie to a browser. It does this by adding a particular header to its response. If the browser supports cookies, it processes the header and finds the cookie, which it stores for later use. For all subsequent requests the browser sends, the browser checks its lists of cookies and finds the ones whose properties indicate that the cookie is appropriate for the request. Keep in mind that the server does not subsequently request cookies it has sent. Instead, the server relies on the browser to send cookies automatically once the browser receives them. (This process is depicted in figure 4.4.)

If a server wants to link requests together into a session, it is easy to see how it might accomplish this via cookies. Suppose a server stores a unique session

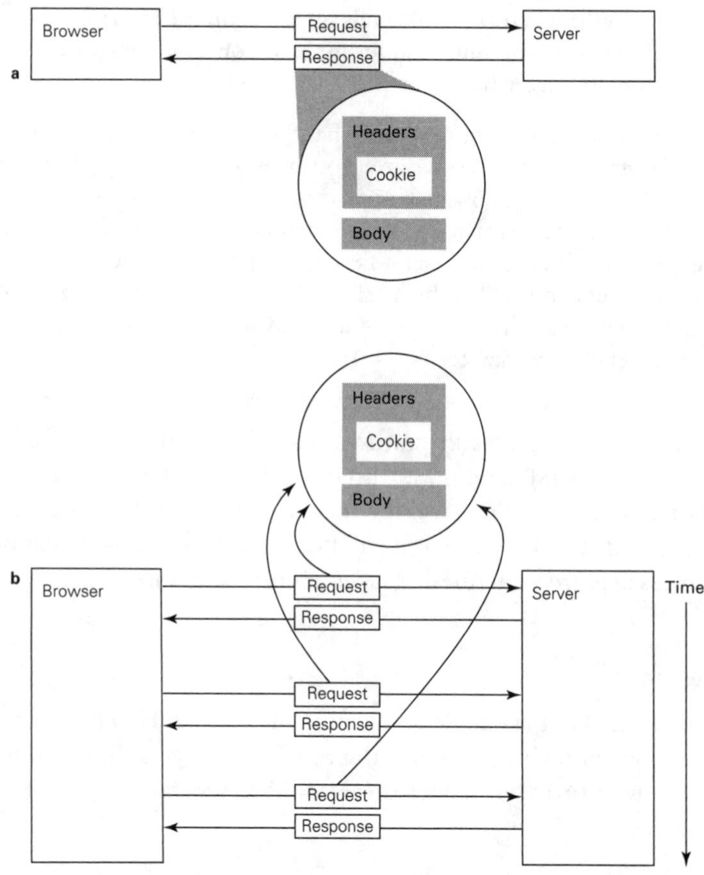

Figure 4.4 Setting and using an HTTP cookie. Step 1, a cookie is sent to the browser as part of the response headers (a). Step 2, once the cookie is sent, it is sent back by the browser automatically for all requests in the cookie's scope. The server does not subsequently request the cookie; it gets it automatically (b).

identifier in the cookie that it sends to a browser. When the server processes subsequent requests and notices this session ID in a cookie sent back to it, it knows that the request came from the same user to whom the server sent the cookie in the past.

NOTE Because not every browser supports cookies, other mechanisms have been devised for handling session management. A session ID can be sent back to the server as part of the URL (a practice generally known as *URL rewriting*), or for form-based applications, it can be included in HTML forms as an `<input type="hidden">` element. Since environments such as JSP can dynamically generate HTML, including the URLs and forms it contains, web developers can add the appropriate session IDs to HTML output as part of their applications' responses.

Sessions are extremely popular in web applications, since they allow an application to remember previous actions of the user and provide a level of continuity in the user interface. For instance, any e-commerce web site that lets a user browse products and store them in a shopping cart needs some way to manage sessions. Applications that support data entry across multiple HTML forms also require some way to associate the various forms with one another. Portal sites may allow a user to receive a customized view of an application without having to repeatedly enter their preferences; to do so, they needs sessions.

Fortunately, the JSP environment supports sessions automatically, for it inherits the session support that comes with the servlet platform. By default, a JSP page has access to an implicit object called `session` that represents the session for the current request. The author of the JSP page can store data in this session and retrieve it later, during a different request. The JSP container takes care of session-management automatically; individual JSP pages do not typically need to handle session IDs or decode session cookies automatically. There is a small caveat: if an alternative to cookies is used, more work may need to be handled manually by the JSP page; for instance, if URL rewriting is used, URLs need to be generated dynamically and can't appear simply as static text in the page.

Session pitfalls

JSP's session management facilities usually let JSP developers ignore the underlying mechanism; for the most part, JSP pages can assume that session management is handled properly by the container. However, two issues related to session management might complicate the design and deployment of web applications.

First, a session-based web application that serves a large base of users should consider how much storage each session requires. Even if you store data as small as 5 KB in the session, supporting 1,000 simultaneous users takes up 5 megabytes (MB) of storage. For a million active sessions, the requirement becomes 5 gigabytes (GB). There is no need for all of this storage to be physical memory, of course; typical operating systems support virtual memory as well. Still, an application that has a large base of users requires careful planning and an understanding of storage requirements imposed by sessions; the size of the data stored in a session has a direct impact on the number of simultaneous users that can be practically supported on a particular hardware configuration.

TIP Java has no analog of the `sizeof` operator in C or C++, but you can estimate the storage requirements of a Java object in several ways. In some cases, you can make this estimate by writing a stand-alone program that calls the `freeMemory()` method of `java.lang.Runtime` before and after instantiating the object. Another strategy is to use Java's serialization facility. If the object you are measuring implements the `java.io.Serializable` interface, you can write it out to disk using the `writeObject()` method of `java.io.ObjectOutputStream`. The size of the resulting file will provide a conservative estimate of the object's memory footprint.

We've discussed active or simultaneous users, but this concept is somewhat vague. Because HTTP is stateless, JSP containers have no way of knowing or not whether a session is still in use. A user might simply be taking a long time to fill in a form, or that user might have exited the web browser and walked away from the computer. JSP and servlets base session expiration on time-outs. After a configurable period of inactivity, the session and its contents will be removed from memory. Applications can also provide an explicit mechanism to let a user log out; for example, an application can display a link labeled `Log Out` and clear out a session in response to that link. (Of course, there is no guarantee that users will click such a link before leaving the application, so the inactivity time-out is useful in these cases as well.)

A second issue is that sessions have an effect on the scalability of your application. Suppose an application has too many users to run with acceptable performance on a single server. A common response might be to spread the application out among many servers. This strategy is known as *load balancing* or *load distribution*. However, session management complicates such a solution, for the session object represents an actual, in-memory Java object on a particular computer.

This object is not automatically available on every server that might need to take part in the processing of the application.

One way around this is to make sure the user's browser always communicates with the server that happens to store that particular user's session. For instance, the application might have a front page that chooses one of several load-balancing servers randomly and then redirects the user to that server. All of the user's subsequent interactions will be with that server, and the application will therefore be able to recover the user's session state easily, for it exists as a simple object on that server.

In some cases, this approach is not good enough. For example, if a high degree of fault tolerance is required, it might not be acceptable to associate a particular server with a user; if this server goes down, the user may be left stranded. In other situations, a higher granularity of load-balancing might be necessary; an application or container might need to decide to pass off a user to a new machine in the middle of that user's session. In some cases, it may therefore be necessary to make sure that all servers that take part in an application are able to recover a user's session. This is handled by a mechanism known as *session migration*, which involves copying a user's session object from one server to another as needed.

NOTE Web applications in a servlet environment may be marked as *distributable* using a feature defined in the servlet standard. When an application is marked in this manner, objects stored in the session should implement the same `java.io.Serializable` interface that we noted earlier. Keep this in mind when using sessions from within JSP pages that are part of a distributable application. Making sure that the objects you store in your sessions are serializable is good practice in general, since it also allows sessions to be stored on server shutdown under JSP containers that support this behavior.

4.3.4 Exception handling

JSP uses Java's exception-handling mechanism, which helps keep code readable by letting developers focus on the tasks they're trying to solve, instead of on handling errors manually. A key principle of Java's exception support is that it lets errors propagate up to the code that's appropriate to handle them. For instance, a library function might be able to deal with some errors, but it should pass any errors it can't handle up to its caller.

A JSP page works similarly: if a JSP page wants to handle certain types of unexpected events, it certainly can do so. But a JSP page can also ignore certain errors and let them be handled by code that gets built into the servlets that the JSP container generates. Specifically, JSP allows you to specify an error page that handles unexpected errors that occur during its processing. Suppose you write a JSP page that connects to a database, but the database is down. You don't need to catch this unexpected event by writing code in your JSP page. Instead, you can use the `errorPage` mechanism to let the environment catch the error for you, thus giving you less to worry about for each new JSP page you write.

NOTE The `errorPage` mechanism is described further in chapters 5 and 14.

4.3.5 Implicit objects

The Servlet API specifies a Java mapping to functionality that is useful for web applications. For example, through the `HttpServletRequest` and `HttpServletResponse` interfaces introduced in chapter 2, Java web applications can easily access requests and configure responses.

Since JSP inherits functionality from the servlet API, JSP applications can take advantage of the convenient Java mappings provided by the servlet environment. JSP takes things a step further, too, by giving simple names to commonly used objects. These names can be accessed from within scripting elements to give Java code within JSP pages easy access to its environment. For instance, in a JSP page operating over HTTP, the name `request` is given to the `HttpServletRequest object`, and request parameters can be accessed simply through calls to `request.getParameter()`. This explains the convenient syntax we demonstrated in chapter 2.

NOTE There are implicit objects for accessing the request, the response, the session, and other useful functionality, including the exception-handling features we just mentioned. Implicit objects will be covered in detail in chapter 6.

4.3.6 Support for JavaBeans and HTML forms

Recall that JavaBeans are reusable Java components that can simplify application development. JSP includes built-in support for JavaBeans through standard actions that let you easily set and retrieve properties from JavaBeans without having to write Java code to do so. Recall also that the servlet environment, and hence JSP, also supports automatic parsing of request parameters—for example, data from HTML forms. Servlets and JSP pages have simple access to request parameters through an object of type `HttpServletRequest`.

Using these two features together can simplify one of the most common tasks that web developers need to implement: reading and storing information from HTML forms. JSP provides a standard action, `<jsp:setProperty>`, that has a mode that causes data from an entire form to be stored in an appropriately constructed JavaBean. This means that in many cases, you can process an HTML form without writing more than a single line of code.

NOTE `<jsp:setProperty>` and other features of JSP's JavaBean support are discussed in detail in chapter 7.

---

5 Programming JSP scripts

This chapter covers

- Using JSP directives
- JSP scripting elements
- Flow of control via scriptlets
- Comments in JSP pages

In chapter 1, emphasis was placed on leveraging component-centric design to promote the separation of presentation and implementation. By taking advantage of JSP's built-in support for server-side JavaBeans, it is possible to write JSP pages that contain only HTML and HTML-like tags. Doing so yields considerable benefits with respect to code reuse, application maintainability, and division of labor. This "purist" approach to JSP development is not always the most practical solution, however. Circumstances may dictate the use of an alternative approach: JSP pages with embedded scripts, typically referred to as *scripting elements.*

For example, when developing an application prototype, the schedule may not provide developers with sufficient time for a full-scale component design effort. Of course, if the design is not based on JavaBeans, then the JSP bean tags (see chapter 7) will be of little use. The scripting tags, however, can apply the full expressive power of the underlying Java language, and are, therefore, fully compatible with whatever data model you select, JavaBeans or otherwise.

Furthermore, even if you are using JavaBeans, the capabilities of the built-in JSP bean tags are somewhat limited. If your needs go beyond the creation of server-side JavaBeans and the access and modification of their properties, you will either need to use (and perhaps even write) a custom tag library, or take advantage of the existing scripting tags. Like JavaBeans component design, creating a custom tag library requires a considered approach that your development schedule may not permit. Designing a custom tag library is only justified when you know you will be using its custom tags over and over again. Reusability is a key element of tag library design, and a key reason that good library design tends to be difficult and time-consuming. If such an effort is infeasible, the scripting tags are available to supply any required functionality not provided by the standard bean tags.

What scripts lack in abstraction, then, they more than make up for in power. This power results, of course, from the ability of scripts to express arbitrary computations in the associated scripting language. With the full strength of a programming language at their disposal, scripts are the ultimate tool of last resort when developing JSP: if you can't find another way to do something, you can always write a script. And, as suggested earlier, there are also times when scripts are the first tool of choice.

5.1 Scripting languages

The default scripting language for JSP is, naturally enough, Java. Unless otherwise specified, the JSP parser assumes that all scripting elements on a page are written in

Java. Given that JSP pages are compiled into Java servlets, this assumption makes the translation of scripts into servlet code very straightforward.

The JSP specification, however, allows JSP implementers to support alternative scripting languages as well. To be acceptable for use with JSP, a scripting language must meet three requirements:

- It must support the manipulation of Java objects. This includes creating objects and, in the case of JavaBeans, accessing and modifying their properties.
- It must be able to invoke methods on Java objects.
- It must include the ability to catch Java exceptions, and specify exception handlers.

More succinctly, for a scripting language to be compatible with JSP, it needs to have sufficient expressive power to take advantage of the capabilities provided by the JSP platform. For example, if a scripting language cannot access Java objects and call their methods, it cannot read request parameters, participate in session management, or set cookies. The core functionality of JSP is made accessible to web developers via Java objects, so a scripting language that cannot use these objects is of limited utility.

If a scripting language is able to interact with Java objects, or can be extended to interact with Java objects, then it is a good candidate for integration with a JSP container. Caucho Technology, for example, has developed a JSP container called Resin, which is integrated with the company's Java-based implementation of JavaScript. As a result, Resin supports both Java and JavaScript as its scripting languages. Support for alternative scripting languages makes JSP accessible to a larger development community by giving developers who are uncomfortable with Java syntax the option to use a different programming language in their JSP pages.

Unfortunately, while alternative languages for JSP scripting are supported by the JSP specification, portable mechanisms for integrating scripting languages with JSP containers are not. Such a mechanism is under consideration for a future version of JSP, but the only JSP scripting language that is universally available is Java. For this reason, we will use Java as the scripting language for all of the examples in this book. If you are using a JSP container that supports scripting languages other than Java, please consult your software documentation for further details on the use of those alternatives.

5.2 JSP tags

JSP provides four major categories of markup tags. The first, *directives*, is a set of tags for providing the JSP container with page-specific instructions for how the document containing the directives is to be processed. Directives do not affect the handling of individual requests, but instead affect global properties of the JSP page that influence its translation into a servlet.

Scripting elements are used to embed programming instructions, written in the designated scripting language for the page, which are to be executed each time the page is processed for a request. Some scripting elements are evaluated purely for their side effects, but they may also be used to generate dynamic content that appears in the output of the page.

Comments are used for adding documentation strings to a JSP page. JSP supports multiple comment styles, including one which enables documentation to appear in the output from the page. Other JSP comments can only be viewed in the original JSP file, or in the source code for the servlet into which the page is translated.

Actions support several different behaviors. Like scripting elements, actions are processed for each request received by a page. Actions can transfer control between pages, specify applets, and interact with server-side JavaBeans components. Like scripting elements, actions may or may not generate dynamic content. All custom tags incorporated via extended tag libraries take the form of actions.

The remaining sections of this chapter cover the first three categories of JSP tags, while the fourth will be presented in chapters 6 and 7. The individual tags included in these categories are introduced, and their use is described.

5.3 JSP directives

Directives are used to convey special processing information about the page to the JSP container. For example, directives may be used to specify the scripting language for the page, to include the contents of another page, or to indicate that the page uses a custom tag library. Directives do not directly produce any output that is visible to end users when the page is requested; instead, they generate side effects that change the way the JSP container processes the page.

5.3.1 Page directive

The `page` directive is the most complicated JSP directive, primarily because it supports such a wide range of attributes and associated functionality. The basic syntax of the page directive is as follows:

```
<%@ page attribute1="value1" attribute2="value2" attribute3=... %>
```

White space after the opening `<%@` and before the closing `%>` is optional, but recommended to improve readability. Like all JSP tag elements, the `page` directive has an XML-based form, as well:

```
<jsp:directive.page attribute1="value1"
                    attribute2="value2" attribute3=... />
```

Attribute specifications are identical for the two tag styles, and there are twelve different attributes recognized for the page directive. In the examples to follow, we will use the first style, which is much more amenable to manual page creation. To use the XML format, the entire JSP page must be specified as an XML document, such as is produced when a page using the first style is parsed by the page compiler (see chapter 20 for further details).

Table 5.1 Attributes supported by the `page` directive

Attribute	Value	Default	Examples
`info`	Text string	None	`info="Registration form."`
`language`	Scripting language name	`"java"`	`language="java"`
`contentType`	MIME type, character set	See first example	`contentType="text/html; charset=ISO-8859-1"` `contentType="text/xml"`
`pageEncoding`	Character set	`"ISO-8859-1"`	`pageEncoding="ISO-8859-1"`
`extends`	Class name	None	`extends="com.taglib.wdjsp.MyJspPage"`
`import`	Class and/or package names	None	`import="java.net.URL"` `import="java.util.*, java.text.*"`
`session`	Boolean flag	`"true"`	`session="true"`
`buffer`	Buffer size, or `false`	`"8kb"`	`buffer="12kb"` `buffer="false"`
`autoFlush`	Boolean flag	`"true"`	`autoFlush="false"`
`isThreadSafe`	Boolean flag	`"true"`	`isThreadSafe="true"`
`errorPage`	Local URL	None	`errorPage="results/failed.jsp"`
`isErrorPage`	Boolean flag	`"false"`	`isErrorPage="false"`

A summary of the twelve attributes supported by the `page` directive is presented in table 5.1, and individual discussions of each attribute follow. In view of this large number of attributes, you will likely find it very convenient that JSP allows you to specify multiple `page` directives on a single page. With the exception of the `import` attribute, however, no individual page directive attribute may be specified multiple times on the same page. This means an attribute cannot appear multiple times within the same directive, nor can it appear in multiple directives on the same page. For example, the following sequence of page directives is valid, since the only attribute that is repeated is import:

```
<%@ page info="This is a valid set of page directives." %>
<%@ page language="java" import="java.net.*" %>
<%@ page import="java.util.List, java.util.ArrayList" %>
```

The following page directive, however, is not valid, because the session attribute occurs twice:

```
<%@ page info="This is an invalid page directive" session="false"
         buffer="16k" autoFlush="false" session="false" %>
```

Similarly, this sequence of page directives is invalid because the info attribute is repeated:

```
<%@ page info="This is not a valid set of page directives." %>
<%@ page extends="com.taglib.wdjsp.MyJspPage"
         info="Use my superclass." %>
```

Unrecognized attributes are also invalid. If a JSP page contains any invalid page directives, a translation-time error will result when the JSP container attempts to generate the source code for the corresponding servlet.

Info attribute

The info attribute allows the author to add a documentation string to the page that summarizes its functionality. This string will then be available for use by the JSP container or other tools in a programmatic manner for displaying the summary information. There are no restrictions on the length or contents of the documentation string, but author, version, and copyright information are commonly included, as in the following example:

```
<%@ page info="The CLU homepage, Copyright 1982 by Kevin Flynn." %>
```

The default value for the info attribute is the empty string.

Language attribute

The language attribute specifies the language to be used in all scripting elements on the page. All JSP containers are required to support Java as a scripting language, and this is the default if the language attribute is not explicitly specified. As indicated earlier in the chapter, support for other scripting languages is optional, and varies among JSP implementations. Here is how the `language` attribute is used to specify Java as the scripting language:

```
<%@ page language="java" %>
```

Note that if the `include` directive is employed, scripting elements in the included page must use the same scripting language as the current page.

ContentType attribute

This attribute is used to indicate the MIME type of the response being generated by the JSP page. Although MIME stands for Multipurpose Internet Mail Extensions, MIME types are also used to indicate the type of information contained in an HTTP response, and this is the context in which they are used in JSP. The most common MIME types for JSP are `"text/html"`, `"text/xml"`, and `"text/plain"`, indicating responses in HTML, XML, and plain text formats, respectively. To specify that a JSP document is generating XML content, for example, this attribute is specified as follows:

```
<%@ page contentType="text/xml" %>
```

The default MIME type for JSP pages is `"text/html"`.

The `contentType` attribute can also be used to specify an alternate character set for the JSP page. This enables page authors to deliver localized content using the language encoding most appropriate for that content. The character set is specified via the `contentType` attribute by appending a semicolon, the string `charset=`, and the name of the desired character set to the end of the attribute value. (An optional space is permitted between the semicolon and `charset=`.) For example, to specify an HTML response using the (default) ISO-8859-1 character set, the following directive would be used:

```
<%@ page contentType="text/html; charset=ISO-8859-1" %>
```

Note that if the response to be generated by a JSP uses an alternate character set, the JSP page must itself be written in that character set. Of course, the JSP container can't know a page is using an alternate character set until it reads the `page` directive that specifies the character set, so only character sets that allow specification of this directive are valid for use in a JSP page. Once the directive has been read by the JSP container (i.e., using the default character set), it can switch to the indicated character set for the remainder of the page. All the characters read before switching character sets, however, must be compatible with the final character set.

The official registrar for both MIME types and character sets is the Internet Assigned Numbers Authority (IANA). This standards body maintains lists of all valid MIME types and character set names.

PageEncoding attribute

The `pageEncoding` attribute, introduced in JSP 1.2, provides an alternate means for specifying the character set used by the JSP page. Instead of supplying the character set as part of the `contentType` attribute's value, it can be declared independently via the `pageEncoding` attribute, as in:

```
<%@ page pageEncoding="ISO-8859-1" %>
```

The default character set for JSP pages is ISO-8859-1, also known as latin-1. The various caveats regarding alternate character sets presented in the discussion of the `contentType` attribute apply to the `pageEncoding` attribute, as well.

Extends attribute

The `extends` attribute identifies the superclass to be used by the JSP container when it is translating the JSP page into a Java servlet, and is specified as follows:

```
<%@ page extends="com.taglib.wdjsp.myJspPage" %>
```

There is no default value for this attribute. If this attribute is not specified, the JSP container is free to make its own choice of JSP servlet class to use as the superclass for the page. Note that if you specify this attribute, JSP imposes certain restrictions on the specified superclass. If, as is typically the case, the JSP page is being delivered via the HTTP protocol, then the specified superclass must implement the `javax.servlet.jsp.HttpJspPage` interface. If an alternate protocol is being used, then the specified superclass must implement the `javax.servlet.jsp.JspPage` interface. (The API documentation for these classes is available from Sun Microsystems, and is included with the JSP reference implementation described in appendix B.)

In practice, this attribute is very rarely used because the default behavior, letting the JSP container select the superclass for the page, typically yields the best performance. The vendors of JSP containers devote considerable resources to tuning their implementations, including optimization of their default page superclasses. Except when you have very specific needs not anticipated by your JSP vendor, it is unlikely that writing and optimizing your own page superclass will be worth the effort.

Import attribute

Unlike the `extends` attribute, use of the `import` attribute is quite common, because it extends the set of Java classes which may be referenced in a JSP page without having to explicitly specify class package names (in other words, because it saves typing). All Java classes and interfaces are associated with a package name; to completely specify a class, the package name must be prepended to the class name. For example, the discussion of the `extends` attribute makes mention of the interface `javax.servlet.jsp.HttpJspPage`. This is actually a reference to an interface named `HttpJspPage`, which resides in the `javax.servlet.jsp` package.

NOTE Java programmers will notice from the discussion that follows that the `import` attribute of the `page` directive has an analogous role to Java's `import` statement, used when writing Java class files. This is, of course, no coincidence. When a JSP page is compiled into a servlet, any `import` attributes are translated directly into the corresponding `import` statements.

The advantages of packages are twofold. First, packages make it easy to keep track of classes that are related in functionality and origin, since these are typically used as the criterion for grouping a set of classes into a package. Second, they make it possible to avoid class naming collisions between different developers (or groups of developers). As long as the developers put their classes into separate packages, there will not be any conflicts if some of the classes share the same name. For example, the J2SE platform includes two classes (actually, one class and one interface) named `List`. One resides in the `java.awt` package, and represents a user interface component for selecting one or more items from a scrolling list. The second resides in the `java.util` package, and represents an ordered collection of objects. Users of these classes distinguish between the two via their package names.

It can become very tedious, however, to always have to refer to classes using their package names. The `import` attribute can be used to identify classes and/or packages that will be frequently used on a given page, so that it is no longer necessary to use package names when referring to them. This is referred to as *importing* a class or package into the JSP page. To import a specific class, simply specify its name (including the package) as the value of the `import` attribute, as in:

```
<%@ page import="java.util.List" %>
```

If this directive is present in a JSP page, the `java.util.List` class can be referred to on that page by simply using the unqualified class name, `List`, also called its *base name*. This will hold true anywhere on the page a class name might appear in a JSP element—including both scripting elements and Bean tags—except in the `<jsp:plugin>` tag (appendix C).

It is also possible to import an entire package into a JSP page, in cases where multiple classes from the same package are being used. This is accomplished by specifying the name of the package, followed by a period and an asterisk, as the value of the `import` attribute:

```
<%@ page import="java.util.*" %>
```

This example directive has the effect of importing all of the classes in the `java.util` package into the current JSP page, such that any class in the `java.util` package may now be referred to using only its base name.

As mentioned previously in this chapter, `import` is the only attribute of the `page` directive that may occur multiple times within a single JSP page. This allows JSP developers to import multiple classes and/or packages into the same page, via multiple `page` directives with `import` attributes, or multiple `import` attributes within the same `page` directive, or a combination. In addition, the `import` attribute itself supports importing multiple classes and/or packages via a single attribute value, by separating the items to be imported using commas. For example, the following directive imports an interface, a class, and a package using a single `import` attribute:

```
<%@ page import="java.util.List, java.util.ArrayList, java.text.*" %>
```

The space character following the comma is optional, but recommended for improved readability.

You may be wondering what would happen if you tried to import two classes that have the same base name, as in the following:

```
<%@ page import="java.util.List, java.awt.List" %>
```

The JSP container considers this to be an illegal statement, and will refuse to process a JSP page that includes such an ambiguity. You might instead try to import these two classes using their packages, as follows:

```
<%@ page import="java.util.*, java.awt.*" %>
```

In this case, however, the conflict is resolved by allowing neither of the two `List` classes to be referred to by its base name. Instead, both must use their fully qualified class names, which include their package names. In order to be able to refer to one of the two classes by its base name, you will have to explicitly import that class, as in the following:

```
<%@ page import="java.util.*, java.awt.List" %>
```

Using this last directive, the `List` class from the `java.awt` package can be referred to via its base name, but the `List` class from the `java.util` package must be referred to using its full name, `java.util.List`.

Finally, note that, as a convenience for JSP developers, every page for which Java is selected as the scripting language automatically imports all of the classes from the following four packages: `java.lang`, `javax.servlet`, `javax.servlet.http`, and `javax.servlet.jsp`.

Session attribute

The `session` attribute is used to indicate whether or not a JSP page participates in session management (as described in chapter 4). The value for this attribute is a simple boolean indicator, either `true` or `false`. For example, to specify that a page is not part of a session, the following form is used:

```
<%@ page session="false" %>
```

The default value for this attribute is `true`; by default then, all pages participate in session management. If a JSP does not interact with the session, then a slight performance gain can be obtained by setting this attribute to `false`. Note, however, that the `session` implicit object, described in chapter 6, is available only on pages for which the `session` attribute is set to `true`.

Buffer attribute

The `buffer` attribute controls the use of buffered output for a JSP page. To turn off buffered output, so that all JSP content is passed immediately to the HTTP response, this attribute should be set to `none`, as follows:

```
<%@ page buffer="none" %>
```

Alternatively, this attribute can be used to set the size of the output buffer in kilobytes, by specifying the attribute value as an integer, followed by the character string "`kb`". For example:

```
<%@ page buffer="12kb" %>
```

The default value for this attribute is `"8kb"`. Note that the JSP container is allowed to use an output buffer larger than the requested size, if it so chooses; the specified value can therefore be thought of as the minimum buffer size for the page. This allows the JSP container to optimize performance by creating a pool of output buffers and using them as needed, instead of creating a new output buffer for every JSP page request.

Buffering the output of JSP pages is generally a good practice to follow, primarily because it enables transferring control from one page to another (e.g., via the `<jsp:forward>` action, described in chapter 6). This enables you to retract all of the output generated so far by a page, including headers and cookies, for replacement with the contents of another page.

In particular, output buffering allows you to make full use of the `errorPage` attribute of the `page` directive, discussed later, to forward control to a user-friendly error page when exceptions arise in the course of JSP processing. Such custom error pages are greatly preferred over the output of JVM error messages in the middle of what otherwise appears to be normal output. In addition, error pages can be scripted to notify the webmaster or the development team when a run-time error occurs, yielding a dual benefit: the end user sees an unintimidating and perhaps apologetic message that there was a problem in responding to their request, while the implementers receive a full report detailing the context and circumstances of the error. (For further details, see the error-handling example in chapter 15.)

If, as recommended, you elect to use buffered output, it is key that you select an appropriate buffer size. This is because, as indicated in chapter 4, if the output from the page is able to fill the buffer, most of the benefits of buffering—including the ability to forward to an alternate page—will be lost. Fortunately, estimating the size of your output is a rather straightforward, if tedious, exercise. If your output is primarily English text, then one character of output will consume 1 byte of data in your output buffer. Other encodings use multiple bytes of data for representing individual characters. Once you know the size of the characters you will be using, the next step is to estimate the number of characters that will be generated by the page.

Each character of static text in the original JSP page will of course translate into one character's worth of data in the final output. For dynamically generated content, a conservative approach is to estimate the maximum number of characters corresponding to each JSP element which generates output. After summing all of these character counts, multiply by the number of bytes per character to compute the required buffer size, dividing by 1,024 to convert bytes into kilobytes. You will likely find that the default value of 8 KB is sufficient for most JSP pages, but pages which generate significant amounts of dynamic content may need correspondingly larger output buffers.

AutoFlush attribute

This attribute is also used for controlling buffered output. In particular, this attribute controls the behavior of the JSP container when the page's output buffer becomes full. If this attribute is set to `true` (the default), the output buffer will automatically be flushed, and its current contents sent to the HTTP server for transmission to the requesting web browser. Page processing then resumes, with any and all new content being buffered until the buffer once again becomes full, or the end of the page is reached. This attribute is set as follows:

```
<%@ page autoFlush="true" %>
```

As mentioned in chapter 4, note that once the buffer has been flushed and its initial contents sent to the browser, it is no longer possible for the JSP page to set response headers or forward processing to a different JSP page.

If `autoFlush` is set to `false`, the JSP container will not automatically flush the buffer when it becomes full. Instead, it will raise an exception, which will have the effect of halting processing of the JSP page and displaying an error page in the browser that originally requested the page. The class of the exception raised under these circumstances is implementation-specific. Also, keep in mind that it is illegal to set the `autoflush` attribute to `false` when the `buffer` attribute is set to `none`. In other words, the JSP container cannot be set to signal an exception when the output buffer becomes full if there is no output buffer in the first place.

The best setting for this attribute will vary from page to page. If the amount of output that might be generated by a page is unpredictable, the `autoFlush` attribute should be set to `true`. Under such circumstances, overflowing the output buffer is a very real possibility, so you need to ensure that the page's contents will be delivered to the browser, rather than an error message. If you also might need to set response headers on this page, or conditionally forward to another page, the decision to do so should be made near the beginning of the page, in order to guarantee that these actions will take place before the buffer might be flushed and the opportunity for taking these actions is lost.

If, however, you need to keep your options open as long as possible with respect to setting response headers or forwarding to another page, then setting `autoFlush` to `false` is the appropriate choice. In this case, it is critical that the page's output buffer be large enough for any conceivable output that might be generated by the page. If not, you again risk the possibility that, if it turns out the output buffer must be flushed, the end user will see an error message rather than your page contents.

IsThreadSafe attribute

The `isThreadSafe` attribute is used to indicate whether your JSP page, once it is compiled into a servlet, is capable of responding to multiple simultaneous requests. If not, this attribute should be set to `false`, as in the following:

```
<%@ page isThreadSafe="false" %>
```

When this attribute is set to `false`, the JSP container will dispatch outstanding requests for the page sequentially, in the order they were received, waiting for the current request to finish processing before starting the next. When this attribute is set to `true` (the default), a thread is created to handle each request for the page, such that multiple requests for the page are handled simultaneously.

This attribute should be set to its default value of `true`. If not, performance will suffer dramatically whenever multiple users try to access the JSP page at the same time, since each subsequent user will have to wait until all previously submitted requests have been handled before processing of their request can begin. If the page is heavily trafficked, or its content generation is at all computationally intensive, this delay will likely not be acceptable to users.

Whether or not this attribute can be set to `true`, however, is usually dependent upon its use of resources. For example, if your JSP page creates and stores a database connection that can be used by only one end user at a time, then, unless special measures are taken to control the use of that connection, the page cannot safely be accessed by multiple threads simultaneously. In this case, the `isThreadSafe` attribute should be set to `false`, or else your users are likely to encounter run-time errors when accessing the page. If, however, your JSP page accesses a pool of database connections and waits for a free connection before it begins processing, then the `isThreadSafe` attribute can probably be set to `true`.

Setting `isThreadSafe` to `false` is certainly the more conservative approach. However, this yields a significant performance penalty. Fortunately, the thread safety of a JSP page is typically dependent more upon *how* resources are used, rather than *what* resources are used. If you are not a Java developer and are concerned about whether or not your page is safe for multithreading, the best approach is to consult an experienced programmer; if the page is not thread-safe as is, it can usually be made so.

TIP Judicious use of Java's `synchronized` keyword is the best approach to ensuring thread safety. All access to objects that are shared across multiple JSP pages, or across multiple invocations of the same JSP page, should be synchronized if there is the potential for inconsistency or deadlocks should those objects be simultaneously accessed and/or modified by multiple threads. In this vein, you should carefully examine all static variables, and all objects used by JSP pages whose scope is either `session` or `application` (as discussed in chapter 6), for potential thread safety issues.

Finally, you also need to be aware that, even if a JSP page sets the `isThreadSafe` attribute to `false`, JSP implementations are still permitted to create multiple instances of the corresponding servlet in order to provide improved performance. In this way, the individual instances handle only one request at a time, but by creating a pool of servlet instances, the JSP container can still handle some limited number of simultaneous requests. For this reason, you still must consider the resource usage even of pages that are not marked thread-safe, to make sure there are no potential conflicts between these multiple instances. Given this harsh reality, you are usually better off biting the bullet and making sure that your page is fully thread-safe. This discussion of the `isThreadSafe` attribute is presented here in the interest of completeness, but the bottom line is that if you're tempted to set this attribute's value to `false`, you will be doing both yourself and your users a favor if you reconsider.

ErrorPage attribute

This attribute is used to specify an alternate page to display if an (uncaught) error occurs while the JSP container is processing the page. This alternate page is indicated by specifying a local URL as the value for this attribute, as in the following:

```
<%@ page errorPage="/misc/error.jsp" %>
```

The error page URL must specify a JSP page from within the same web application (see chapter 14) as the original page. As in this example, it may be an absolute URL, which includes a full directory specification. Such URLs are resolved within the context of that web application; typically, this means a top-level directory—corresponding to the name under which the web application was deployed—will be appended to the beginning of the URL. Alternatively, a relative URL may be specified, in which case any directory information included in the URL is appended to the directory information associated with the current page, in order to form a new URL. In the context of the `errorPage` attribute, absolute URLs start with a forward slash, while relative URLs do not.

The default value for this attribute is implementation-dependent. Also, note that if the output of the JSP page is not buffered and any output has been generated before the error occurs, it will not be possible to forward to the error page. If the output is buffered and the `autoFlush` attribute is set to `true`, once the buffer becomes full and is flushed for the first time, it will likewise become impossible to forward to the error page. As you might expect, if `autoFlush` is `false`, then the exception raised when the buffer is filled will cause the JSP container to forward control to the page specified using the `errorPage` attribute.

IsErrorPage attribute

The `isErrorPage` attribute is used to mark a JSP page that serves as the error page for one or more other JSP pages. This is done by specifying a simple boolean attribute value, as follows:

```
<%@ page isErrorPage="true" %>
```

When this attribute is set to `true`, it indicates that the current page is intended for use as a JSP error page. As a result, this page will be able to access the `exception` implicit object, described in chapter 6, which will be bound to the Java exception object (i.e., an instance of the `java.lang.Throwable` class) which caused control to be forwarded to the current page.

Since most JSP pages do not serve as error pages, the default value for this attribute is `false`.

5.3.2 Include directive

The second JSP directive enables page authors to include the contents of one file in another. The file to be included is identified via a local URL, and the directive has the effect of replacing itself with the contents of the indicated file. The syntax of the `include` directive is as follows:

```
<%@ include file="localURL" %>
```

Like all JSP tags, an XML translation of this directive is also available. Its syntax is as follows:

```
<jsp:directive.include file="localURL" />
```

There are no restrictions on the number of `include` directives that may appear in a single JSP page. There are also no restrictions on nesting; it is completely valid for a JSP page to include another JSP page, which itself includes one or more other JSP pages. As mentioned earlier, however, all included pages must use the same scripting language as the original page.

As in the URL specification for the `errorPage` attribute of the `page` directive, the value of the `include` directive's `file` attribute can be specified as an absolute path within the current web application (chapter 14), or relative to the current page, depending upon whether or not it starts with a forward slash character. For example, to include a file in a subdirectory of the directory that the current JSP page is in, a directive of the following form would be used:

```
<%@ include file="includes/navigation.jspf" %>
```

To include a file using an absolute path within a web application, the following form would be used:

```
<%@ include file="/shared/epilogue/copyright.html" %>
```

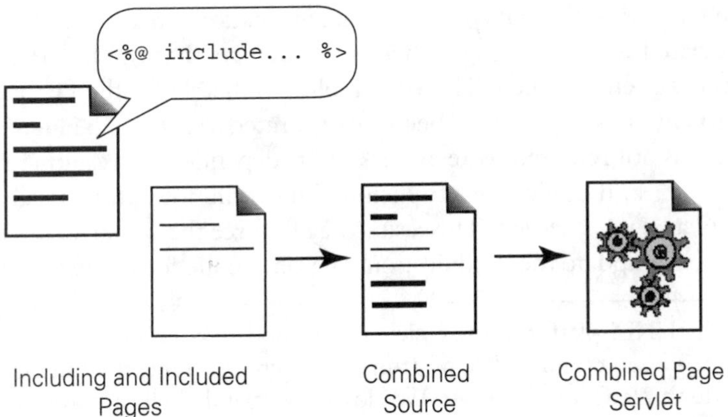

Figure 5.1 Effect of the include directive on page compilation

The decision whether to use a common top-level directory for shared content, versus directory-specific files, depends upon the overall design of your web site or application hierarchy. A combination of both approaches may also be appropriate.

It is recommended that the .jsp file extension be reserved for JSP pages that will be viewed as top-level documents (i.e., pages that are expected to be referenced explicitly in URLs requested by an end user). An alternate extension, such as .jspf or .jsf, is preferred for JSP fragments meant to be included as elements of other JSP pages. As indicated in figure 5.1, the `include` directive has the effect of substituting the contents of the included file before the page is translated into source code and compiled into a servlet. The contents of the included file may be either static text (e.g., HTML) or additional JSP elements that will be processed as if they were part of the original JSP page. This means that it is possible to make reference in the included page to variables that are local to the original page, and vice versa, since the included page effectively becomes part of that original page. In practice, this approach can lead to software maintenance problems, since it breaks the modularity of the individual files. If used in a disciplined manner, though, it can be helpful to isolate code that appears repeatedly across a set of JSP pages into a single file, and use the `include` directive to share this common code.

NOTE For C and C++ developers, the JSP `include` directive is a direct analog of the `#include` directive provided by the preprocessor for those two languages.

As described in chapter 4, the JSP container will automatically rebuild and recompile the servlet associated with a JSP page whenever it detects that the file defining the page's contents has been modified. This only applies to the file for the JSP page itself, however, not to any files which have been incorporated via the `include` directive. The JSP container is not required to keep track of file dependencies resulting from the use of this directive, so modifications to included files will not automatically trigger the generation of a new JSP servlet. The easiest way to force the construction of a new servlet is to manually update the modification date on the file for the including page.

TIP On the UNIX platform, the easiest way to update a file's modification date is via the `touch` command. Unfortunately, there is no direct equivalent on the Windows platform. Alternate Windows command shells are available which provide this functionality, or you can simply open the file in an editor and save its contents, unchanged.

JSP also provides an alternative means for including the contents of one JSP file within another, via the `<jsp:include>` action, described in chapter 6. Unlike the `include` directive, which treats the contents of the file to be included as if it were part of the original page, the `<jsp:include>` action obtains the contents of the file to be included at the time the request for the original page is being handled, by forwarding the request to the included page and then inserting the results of processing this secondary request into the results of the original page.

5.3.3 *Tag library directive*

This directive is used to notify the JSP container that a page relies on one or more custom tag libraries. A tag library is a collection of custom tags that can be used to extend the functionality of JSP on a page-by-page basis. Once this directive has been used to indicate the reliance of a page on a specific tag library, all of the custom tags defined in that library become available for use on that page. The syntax of this directive is as follows:

```
<%@ taglib uri="tagLibraryURI" prefix="tagPrefix" %>.
```

Here, the value of the `uri` attribute indicates the location of the Tag Library Descriptor (TLD) file for the library, and the prefix attribute specifies the XML namespace identifier that will be prepended to all occurrences of the library's tags on the page. For example, the following directive loads in a tag library whose TLD is accessible via the local URL `/EncomTags`:

```
<%@ taglib uri="/EncomTags" prefix="mcp" %>
```

Within the page in which this directive appears, the tags defined by this library are accessed using the prefix `mcp`. A tag from this library named `endProgram`, then, would be referenced within the page as `<mcp:endProgram/>`. Note that all custom tags follow XML syntax conventions. In addition, the prefix names `jsp`, `jspx`, `java`, `javax`, `servlet`, `sun`, and `sunw` are reserved by the JSP specification; you may not provide them as the value for the `prefix` attribute of the `taglib` directive within your own JSP pages.

NOTE Unlike the other directives introduced in this chapter, there is no direct XML version of the `taglib` directive. Instead, when constructing a JSP page as an XML document, the use of a custom tag library is specified as an attribute of the document's root element. For further details, see chapter 20.

Because the custom tag prefix is specified external to the library itself, and on a page-specific basis, multiple libraries can be loaded by a single page without the risk of conflicts between tag names. If two libraries both define tags with the same name, a JSP page would still be able to load and use both libraries since it can distinguish those tags via their prefixes. As such, there are no restrictions on how many tag library directives may appear on a page, as long as each is assigned a unique prefix. If, however, the JSP container cannot find the TLD at the indicated location, or the page references a tag that is not actually defined in the library (based on the contents of the TLD), an error will result when the JSP container tries to compile the page.

The construction of custom tag libraries and their associated TLDs is described in chapter 18. The deployment of custom tag libraries is presented in chapter 14.

WARNING For security reasons, the JSP specification mandates that the Java classes implementing a library's custom tags must be stored locally, as part of the deployed web application which uses them (see chapter 13). Some JSP containers, however, allow page authors to specify URLs referencing complete tag library JAR files in the `uri` attribute of the `taglib` directive, including JAR files stored on remote servers. Support for this behavior is intended to ease development, but keep in mind that downloading arbitrary Java code from a remote URL and running that code on your web server is a rather risky proposition.

5.4 Scripting elements

Whereas the JSP directives influence how the page is processed by the JSP container, scripting elements enable developers to directly embed code in a JSP page, including code that generates output to appear in the results sent back to the user. JSP provides three types of scripting elements: *declarations*, *scriptlets*, and *expressions*. Declarations allow the developer to define variables and methods for a page, which may be accessed by other scripting elements. Scriptlets are blocks of code to be executed each time the JSP page is processed for a request. Expressions are individual lines of code. Like scriptlets, they are executed for every request. The results of evaluating an expression, however, are automatically inserted into the page output in place of the original expression tag.

All scripting elements in a page are written in the scripting language designated for the page via the `language` attribute of the `page` directive. In the absence of an explicit specification of the scripting language, it is assumed by the JSP container that the scripting language is Java. Recall, as well, that if the `include` directive is used to incorporate the contents of one JSP page into another, both pages must use the same scripting language. Finally, none of the tags for the JSP scripting elements supports attributes.

5.4.1 Declarations

Declarations are used to define variables and methods specific to a JSP page. Declared variables and methods can then be referenced by other scripting elements on the same page. The syntax for declarations is:

```
<%! declaration(s) %>
```

Note that multiple declarations may appear within a single tag, but each declaration must be a complete declarative statement in the designated scripting language. Also note that white space after the opening delimiter and before the closing delimiter is optional, but recommended to improve readability. For JSP pages specified as XML documents, the corresponding syntax is:

```
<jsp:declaration> declaration(s) </jsp:declaration>
```

The two forms are identical in effect.

Variable declarations

Variables defined as declarations become instance variables of the servlet class into which the JSP page is translated and compiled. Consider the following declaration of three variables:

```
<%! private int x = 0, y = 0; private String units = "ft"; %>
```

This declaration will have the effect of creating three instance variables in the servlet created for the JSP page, named `x`, `y`, and `units`. These variables can be referenced by any and all other scripting elements on the page, including those scripting elements that appear earlier in the page than the declaration itself.

When declaring JSP instance variables, it is important to keep in mind the potential that multiple threads will be accessing a JSP simultaneously, representing multiple simultaneous page requests. If a scripting element on the page modifies the value of an instance variable, all subsequent references to that instance variable will use the new value, including references in other threads. If you wish to create a variable whose value is local to the processing of a single request, this may be done in a scriptlet. Declared variables are associated with the page itself (through the servlet class), not with individual requests.

Since variables specified via JSP declarations are directly translated into variables of the corresponding servlet class, they may also be used to declare class variables. Class, or static, variables, are those whose values are shared among all instances of a class, rather than being specific to an individual instance. When the scripting language is Java, class variables are defined using the `static` keyword, as in the following example:

```
<%! static public int counter = 0; %>
```

The effect of this declaration is to create an integer variable named `counter` that is shared by all instances of the page's servlet class. If any one instance changes the value of this variable, all instances see the new value.

In practice, because the JSP container typically creates only one instance of the servlet class representing a particular JSP page, there is little difference between declaring instance variables and declaring class variables. As explained earlier, the major exception to this rule is when a JSP page sets the `isThreadSafe` attribute of the `page` directive to `false`, indicating that the page is not thread-safe. In this case, the JSP container may create multiple instances of the page's servlet class, in order to handle multiple simultaneous requests, one request per instance. To share a variable's value across multiple requests under these circumstances, the variable must be declared as a class variable, rather than an instance variable.

When the `isThreadSafe` attribute is `true`, however, it makes little practical difference whether a variable is declared as an instance variable or a class variable. Declaring instance variables saves a little bit of typing, since you don't have to include the `static` keyword. Class variables, though, do a somewhat better job of conveying the typical usage of declared JSP variables, and are appropriate regardless of the setting of the `isThreadSafe` attribute.

Method declarations

Methods defined via declarations become methods of the servlet class into which the JSP page is compiled. For example, the following declaration defines a method for computing factorials:

```
<%! public long fact (long x) {
        if (x == 0) return 1;
        else return x * fact(x-1);
    } %>
```

As with variable declarations, declared methods can be accessed by any and all scripting elements on the page, regardless of the order in which the method declaration occurs relative to other scripting elements.

DEFINITION The factorial of a number is the product of all of the integers between that number and 1. The factorial function is only valid for non-negative integers, and the factorial of zero is defined to be one. The standard mathematical notation for the factorial of a variable x is $x!$ Thus, $x! = x * (x - 1) * (x - 2) * ... * 1$. For example, $5! = 5 * 4 * 3 * 2 * 1 = 120$. The method definition provided here implements this definition in a recursive manner, by taking advantage of the fact that $0! = 1$, and the observation that, for $x > 0$, it is true that $x! = x * (x\text{-}1)!$

In addition, multiple method definitions can appear within a single declaration tag, as can combinations of both variable and method declarations, as in the following:

```
<%! static private char[] vowels =
      { 'a', 'e', 'i', 'o', 'u', 'A', 'E', 'I', 'O', 'U' };
    public boolean startsWithVowel (String word) {
      char first = word.charAt(0);
      for (int i = 0; i < vowels.length; ++i) {
        if (first == vowels[i]) return true;
      }
      return false;
    }
    static private String[] articles = { "a ", "an " };
    public String withArticle (String noun) {
      if (startsWithVowel(noun)) return articles[1] + noun;
      else return articles[0] + noun;
    }
%>
```

This declaration introduces two methods and two class variables. The `withArticle()` method, which relies upon the other variables and methods included in the declaration, can be used to prepend the appropriate indefinite article to whatever character string is provided as its argument.

As with class variables, class methods may be specified using JSP declarations. Class methods, also known as static methods, are methods associated with the class itself, rather than individual instances, and may be called without requiring access to an instance of the class. In fact, class methods are typically called simply by prepending the name of the class to the name of the method. Class methods may reference only class variables, not instance variables. In practice, because it is generally not possible to obtain (or predict) the name of the servlet class corresponding to a particular JSP page, class methods have little utility in the context of JSP.

Handling life-cycle events

One particularly important use for method declarations is the handling of events related to the initialization and destruction of JSP pages. The initialization event occurs the first time the JSP container receives a request for a JSP page. The destruction event occurs when the JSP container unloads the servlet class, either because the JSP container is being shut down, or because the page has not been requested recently and the JSP container needs to reclaim the resources (e.g., system memory) associated with its servlet class.

These events are handled by declaring special life-cycle methods that will automatically be called by the JSP container when the corresponding event occurs. The initialization event is handled by `jspInit()`, and the destruction event is handled by `jspDestroy()`. Neither method returns a value nor takes any arguments, so the general format for declaring them is:

```
<%! public void jspInit () {
      // Initialization code goes here...
    }
    public void jspDestroy () {
      // Destruction code goes here...
    }
%>
```

Both methods are optional. If a JSP life-cycle method is not declared for a JSP page, the corresponding event is simply ignored.

If `jspInit()` is defined, the JSP container is guaranteed to call it after the servlet class has been instantiated, but before the first request is processed. For example, consider a JSP page that relies upon a pool of database connections in order to collect the data used to generate its contents. Before the page can handle any requests, it needs to ensure that the connection pool has been created, and is available for use. The initialization event is the standard JSP mechanism for enforcing such requirements, as in:

```
<%! static private DbConnectionPool pool = null;
    public void jspInit () {
      if (pool == null) {
        String username = "sark", password = "mcpr00lz";
        pool = DbConnectionPool.getPool(this, username, password);
      }
    } %>
```

Here, a class variable is declared for storing a reference to the connection pool, an instance of some hypothetical `DbConnectionPool` class. The `jspInit()` method calls a static method of this class named `getPool()`, which takes the `page` instance as well as a `username` and `password` for the database as its arguments, and returns an appropriate connection pool, presumably either reusing an existing connection pool or, if necessary, creating one.

In a similar manner, if `jspDestroy()` is defined, it will be called after all pending requests have been processed, but just before the JSP container removes the corresponding servlet class from service. To continue the example introduced above, imagine the following method declaration for the page destruction event:

```
<%! public void jspDestroy () {
      pool.maybeReclaim(this);
    } %>
```

Here, the connection pool is given a chance to reclaim its resources by calling its `maybeReclaim()` method with the page instance as its sole argument. The implication here is that if this page is the only consumer of connection pools that is still using this particular pool, the pool can reclaim its resources because this page no longer needs them.

5.4.2 Expressions

Declarations are used to add variables and methods to a JSP page, but are not able to directly contribute to the page's output, which is, after all, the objective of dynamic content generation. The JSP expression element, however, is explicitly intended for output generation. The syntax for this scripting element is as follows:

```
<%= expression %>
```

An XML version is also provided:

```
<jsp:expression> expression </jsp:expression>
```

In both cases, the *expression* should be a valid and complete scripting language expression, in whatever scripting language has been specified for the page. The effect of this element is to evaluate the specified expression and substitute the resulting value into the output of the page, in place of the element itself.

JSP expressions can be used to print out individual variables, or the result of some calculation. For example, the following expression, which uses Java as the scripting language, will insert the value of π into the page's output, courtesy of a static variable provided by the `java.lang.Math` class:

```
<%= Math.PI %>
```

Assuming a variable named `radius` has been introduced elsewhere on the page, the following expression can be used to print the area of the corresponding circle:

```
<%= Math.PI * Math.pow(radius, 2) %>
```

Again, any valid scripting language expression is allowed, so calls to methods are likewise permitted. For example, a page including the declaration of the `fact()` method could then insert factorial values into its output using expressions of the following form:

```
<%= fact(12) %>
```

This particular expression would have the effect of substituting the value `479001600` into the contents of the page.

These three expressions all return numeric values, but there are no restrictions on the types of values that may be returned by JSP expressions. Expressions can return Java primitive values, such as numbers, characters, and booleans, or full-fledged Java objects, such as strings and JavaBeans. All expression results are converted to character strings before they are added to the page's output. As indicated in table 5.2, various static `toString()` methods are used to convert primitive values into strings, while objects are expected to provide their own `toString()` methods (or rely on the default implementation provided by the `java.lang.Object` class).

Table 5.2 Methods used to convert expression values into strings

Value Type	Conversion to String
boolean	`java.lang.Boolean.toString(boolean)`
byte	`java.lang.Byte.toString(byte)`
char	`new java.lang.Character(char).toString()`
double	`java.lang.Double.toString(double)`
int	`java.lang.Integer.toString(int)`

Table 5.2 Methods used to convert expression values into strings (continued)

Value Type	Conversion to String
float	`java.lang.Float.toString(float)`
long	`java.lang.Long.toString(long)`
object	`toString()` method of object's class

Notice that no semicolon was provided at the end of the Java code used in the example JSP expressions. This is because Java's semicolon is a statement delimiter. A semicolon has the effect of transforming a Java language expression into a program statement. In Java, statements are evaluated purely for their side effects; they do not return values. Thus, leaving out the semicolon in JSP expressions is the right thing to do, because the JSP container is interested in the value of the enclosed code, not its side effects.

Given that this scripting element produces output only from expressions, not statements, you may be wondering if there is a convenient way to do conditional output in a JSP page. Java's standard `if/then` construct, after all, is a statement, not an expression: its clauses are evaluated purely for side effects, not value. Fortunately, Java supports the oft-forgotten ternary conditional operator, which does return a value based on the result of a conditional test. The syntax of Java's ternary operator is as follows:

```
test_expr ? true_expr : false_expr
```

Each operand of the ternary operator is itself an expression. The `test_expr` expression should evaluate to a boolean value. If the value of `test_expr` expression is `true`, then the `true_expr` expression will be evaluated and its result returned as the result of the ternary operator. Alternatively, if the value of `test_expr` expression is `false`, then the `false_expr` expression is evaluated and its result will be returned.

The ternary operator can thus be used in a JSP expression as in the following:

```
<%= (hours < 12) ? "AM" : "PM" %>
```

In this particular example, the value of the `hours` variable is checked to determine whether it is less than twelve. If so, the ternary operator returns the string `"AM"`, which the JSP expression then inserts into the page. If not, the operator returns `"PM"` and, again, the JSP expression adds this result to the page output.

TIP The ternary operator is particularly convenient for use in JSP expressions not just for its functionality, but also for its brevity.

5.4.3 Scriptlets

Declarations and expressions are intentionally limited in the types of scripting code they support. For general purpose scripting, the appropriate JSP construct is the scriptlet. Scriptlets can contain arbitrary scripting language statements which, like declarations, are evaluated for side effects only. Scriptlets do not, however, automatically add content to a JSP page's output. The general syntax for scriptlets is:

```
<% scriptlet %>
```

Scriptlets can also be specified using XML notation, as follows:

```
<jsp:scriptlet> scriptlet </jsp:scriptlet>
```

For either tag style, the *scriptlet* should be one or more valid and complete statements in the JSP page's scripting language. Alternatively, a scriptlet can leave open one or more statement blocks, which must be closed by subsequent scriptlets in the same page. In the case where the JSP scripting language is Java, statement blocks are opened using the left brace character (i.e., {) and closed using the right brace character (i.e., }).

Here is an example of a scriptlet which contains only complete statements:

```
<% GameGrid grid = GameGrid.getGameGrid();
   Recognizer r1 = new Recognizer(new Coordinates(grid, 0, 0));
   Recognizer r2 = new Recognizer(new Coordinates(grid, 100, 100));
   r1.findProgram("Flynn");
   r2.findProgram("Flynn"); %>
```

This scriptlet fetches one object via a class method, which it then uses to instantiate two new objects. Methods are then called on these objects to initiate some computation.

Note that a page's scriptlets will be run for each request received by the page. For the previous example, this means that two instances of the `Recognizer` class are created every time the JSP page containing this scriptlet is requested. Furthermore, any variables introduced in a scriptlet are available for use in subsequent scriptlets and expressions on the same page (subject to variable scoping rules). The foregoing scriptlet, for example, could be followed by an expression such as the following:

```
<%= r1.statusReport() %>
```

This expression would then insert the results of the `statusReport()` method call for instance `r1` into the page's output. Later scriptlets or expressions could make additional references (such as method calls, or inclusion in argument lists) to this instance and the `r2` instance, as well the `grid` object.

If you wish to control the scoping of a variable introduced by a scriptlet, you can take advantage of JSP's support for leaving code blocks open across multiple scriptlets. Consider, for example, the following JSP page which reproduces the above scriptlet, with one small but important modification:

```
<html>
<body>
<h1>Intruder Alert</h1>
<p>Unauthorized entry, dispatching recognizers...</p>
<% GameGrid grid = GameGrid.getGameGrid();
   { Recognizer r1 = new Recognizer(new Coordinates(grid, 0, 0));
     Recognizer r2 = new Recognizer(new Coordinates(grid, 100, 100));
     r1.findProgram("Flynn");
     r2.findProgram("Flynn"); %>
<h2>Status</h2>
<ul>
<li>First Recognizer: <%= r1.statusReport() %>
<li>Second Recognizer: <%= r2.statusReport() %>
</ul>
<% } %>
Alert Level:     <%= grid.alertLevel() %>
</body>
</html>
```

In this case, the first scriptlet introduces a new program block before creating the two `Recognizer` instances. The second scriptlet, toward the end of the page, closes this block. Within that block, the `r1` and `r2` instances are said to be *in scope*, and may be referenced freely. After that block is closed, these objects are *out of scope*, and any references to them will cause a compile-time error when the page is compiled into a servlet by the JSP container. Note that because the `grid` variable is introduced before the block is opened, it is in the page's top-level scope, and can continue to be referenced after the second scriptlet closes the block opened by the first, as in the call to its `alertLevel()` method near the end of the page.

The reason this works has to do with the translation of the contents of a JSP page into source code for a servlet. Static content, such as HTML code, is translated into Java statements which print that text as output from the servlet. Similarly, expressions are translated into Java statements which evaluate the expression, convert the result to a string, and print that string value as output from the servlet. Scriptlets, however, undergo no translation at all, and are simply inserted into the source code of the servlet as is. If a scriptlet opens a new block without also closing it, then the Java statements corresponding to any subsequent static content or JSP elements simply become part of this new block. The block must ultimately be closed by another scriptlet, or else compilation will fail due to a Java syntax error.

NOTE Java statements corresponding to a JSP page's static content, expressions, and scriptlets are used to create the `_jspService()` method of the corresponding servlet. This method is responsible for generating the output of the JSP page. Directives and declarations are also translated into servlet code, but do not contribute to the `_jspService()` method and so are not affected by scoping due to scriptlets. On the other hand, the JSP Bean tags, discussed in chapter 7, are translated into Java statements for the `_jspService()` method and therefore are subject to scoping restrictions introduced via scriptlets.

5.5 Flow of control

This ability of scriptlets to introduce statement blocks without closing them can be put to good use in JSP pages to affect the flow of control through the various elements, static or dynamic, that govern page output. In particular, such scriptlets can be used to implement conditional or iterative content, or to add error handling to a sequence of operations.

5.5.1 Conditionalization

Java's `if` statement, with optional `else if` and `else` clauses, is used to control the execution of code based on logical true/false tests. Scriptlets can use the `if` statement (or the appropriate analog if the scripting language is not Java) to implement conditional content within a JSP page. The following page fragment, for example, uses the `fact()` method introduced earlier in this chapter to compute the factorial of a page variable named `x`, as long as it is within the appropriate range:

```
<% if (x < 0) { %>
   <p>Sorry, can't compute the factorial of a negative number.</p>
<% } else if (x > 20) { %>
   <p>Sorry, arguments greater than 20 cause an overflow error.</p>
<% } else { %>
   <p align=center><%= x %>! = <%= fact(x) %></p>
<% } %>
```

Three different blocks of statements are created by these scriptlets, only one of which will actually be executed. If the value of `x` is negative, then the first block will be executed, causing the indicated static HTML code to be displayed. If `x` is greater than `20`, the second block is executed, causing its static HTML to be displayed. Otherwise, the output from the page will contain the static and dynamic content specified by the third block, including the result of the desired call to the `fact()` method.

5.5.2 Iteration

Java has three different iteration constructs: the `for` loop, the `while` loop, and the `do/while` statement. They may all be used via scriptlets to add iterative content to a JSP page, and are particularly useful in the display of tabular data. Here, for example, is a page fragment which uses the `fact()` method defined earlier in this chapter to construct a table of factorial values:

```
<table>
<tr><th><i>x</i></th><th><I>x</I>! </th></tr>
<% for (long x = 01; x <= 201; ++x) { %>
  <tr><td><%= x %></td><td><%= fact(x) %></td></tr>
<% } %>
</table>
```

Static HTML is used to create the table and its headers, while a `for` loop is used to generate the contents of the table. Twenty-one rows of data are created in this manner (figure 5.2). The other iteration constructs may be used in a similar manner. In addition to generating row data for HTML tables, another common use for iteration scriptlets is looping through a set of results from a database query.

5.5.3 Exception handling

As described in chapter 4, the default behavior when an exception is thrown while processing a JSP page is to display an implementation-specific error message in the browser window. In this chapter, we have also seen how the `errorPage` attribute of the `page` directive can be used to specify an alternative page for handling any uncaught errors thrown by a JSP page. A third option allows even finer control over errors by incorporating the standard Java exception-handling mechanisms into a JSP page using scriptlets.

If a block of code on a JSP page has the potential of signaling an error, Java's exception handling construct, the `try` block, may be used in a set of scriptlets to catch the error locally and respond to it gracefully within the current page. By way of example, consider the following alternative declaration for the factorial method presented earlier:

```
<%! public long fact (long x) throws IllegalArgumentException {
       if ((x < 0) || (x > 20))
         throw new IllegalArgumentException("Out of range.");
       else if (x == 0) return 1;
       else return x * fact(x-1);
    } %>
```

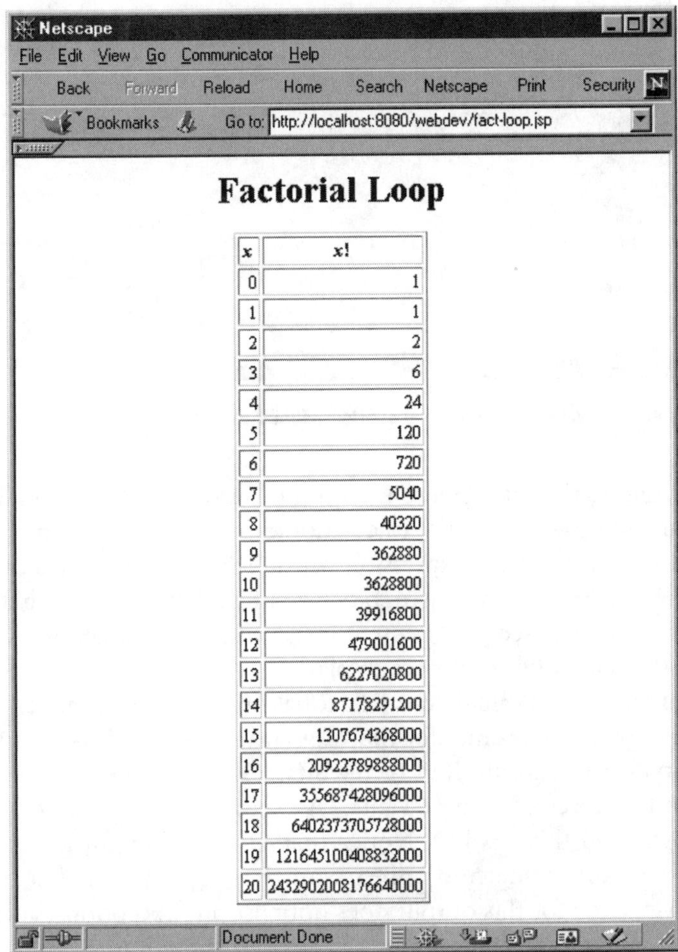

Factorial Loop

x	*x*!
0	1
1	1
2	2
3	6
4	24
5	120
6	720
7	5040
8	40320
9	362880
10	3628800
11	39916800
12	479001600
13	6227020800
14	87178291200
15	1307674368000
16	20922789888000
17	355687428096000
18	6402373705728000
19	121645100408832000
20	2432902008176640000

Figure 5.2 Tabular results generated by the iteration example

This version of the method verifies that the method's argument is within the valid range for this calculation, signaling an `IllegalArgumentException` if it is not.

Using this version of the method, we could consider an alternative implementation of the example presented in the foregoing section on conditionals, as follows:

```
<% try { %>
  <p align=center> <%= x %>! = <%= fact(x) %></p>
<% } catch (IllegalArgumentException e) { %>
  <p>Sorry, factorial argument is out of range.</p>
<% } %>
```

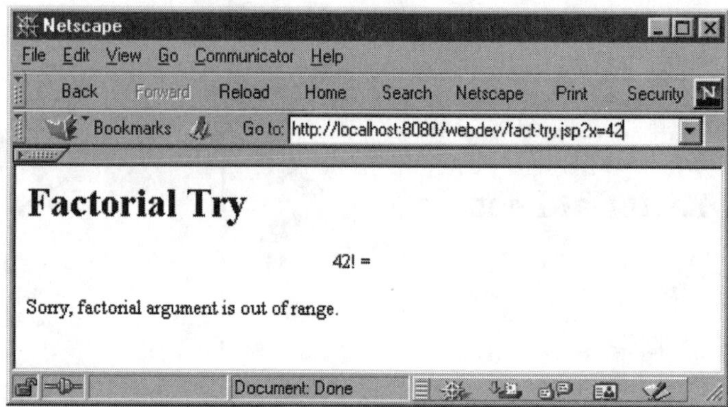

Figure 5.3 Failure results generated by the first exception handler example

Like the earlier example, the intent here is to print the result of a factorial calculation, or display an error message if the calculation cannot be made. In this case, a `try` block is established around the expression which calls `fact()`. If this call raises an `IllegalArgumentException` the `catch` block will handle it by printing an error message. If no exception is raised, the content enclosed by the `catch` block will be ignored, and only the successful results are displayed.

In figure 5.3 an attempt to calculate the factorial of 42 has been made, but this is out of the range of permitted values for the `fact()` method. (This is because Java integer values of type `long` are limited to 64 bits. Twenty is the largest integer whose factorial can be expressed using 64 bits.) As a result, the `IllegalArgumentException` is thrown, and then caught. Notice that all of the output generated up until the call to the `fact()` method appears on the page. This is because the corresponding servlet code for this output does not raise any exceptions, and therefore is executed when the page is processed. As soon as the call to `fact()` occurs, however, the exception is raised and control is transferred to the `catch` block, which then prints the error message.

In order to suppress the equation output altogether, the code on the JSP page must be rearranged to call the `fact()` method before any of that output is generated. One possible approach is to rewrite the first scriptlet:

```
<% try {
     long result = fact(x); %>
  <p align=center> <%= x %>! = <%= result %></p>
<% } catch (IllegalArgumentException e) { %>
  <p>Sorry, factorial argument is out of range.</p>
<% } %>
```

In this case, the factorial value is computed in the scriptlet itself, at the beginning of the `try` block, and stored in a new local variable named `result`. This variable is then used in the expression which displays the factorial value, rather than directly calling the method, as before. And because the method call now precedes any output, if an exception is thrown, control will be transferred to the `catch` block before the output in the `try` block begins.

5.5.4 A word of caution

As you can see from these examples, scriptlets that introduce enclosing blocks are very powerful. Short of using custom tag libraries, they are the only means available in JSP to implement conditional or iterative content, or to add custom exception handlers to a page. At the same time, excessive use of these scriptlets can lead to maintainability problems.

The primary reason for this is readability. The fact that Java delimiters (i.e., { and }) appear adjacent to the HTML-like scriptlet delimiters (i.e., `<%` and `%>`) introduces a syntax clash, which can make these tags difficult to follow. Adhering to an indentation convention, as the examples here do, can help address this issue, particularly when there are several lines of content interleaved between the scriptlet that opens a block and the scriptlet that closes it.

As discussed in chapter 1, maintenance of JSP pages is often shared by individuals skilled in Java programming and others who are skilled in page design and HTML. While it is certainly true that HTML has tags that must appear in pairs in order to have meaning, the notion that some scriptlets are stand-alone while others are mutually dependent is somewhat foreign to those familiar with HTML syntax but not Java syntax. As the preceding examples demonstrate, there are cases where three or more scriptlets are required to implement conditional logic or exception handling, a scenario that has no parallels in HTML.

As a result, modifying and debugging pages that make heavy use of scriptlets such as these can be complicated. If the web designers on a team are uncomfortable with the syntax issues, it is not unlikely that they will involve the programming staff when making even minor changes to a page. Likewise, if there is a problem with the display of a page, a joint effort may be required to resolve it.

5.6 Comments

If the number of ways comments can be expressed in a language is an indication of its power, then JSP must be the most powerful dynamic content system around: there are three different ways to insert comments into a JSP page. These three styles of comments themselves divide into two major types, comments that are transmitted back to the browser as part of the JSP response, and those that are only visible in the original JSP source file.

5.6.1 Content comments

Only one of the three comments styles falls into the first group. These are referred to as content comments, because they use the comment syntax associated with the type of content being generated by the JSP page. To write a comment that will be included in the output of a JSP page that is generating web content, the following syntax is used:

```
<!-- comment -->
```

Those familiar with HTML and XML will recognize that this is the standard comment syntax for those two markup languages. Thus, a JSP page that is generating either HTML or XML simply uses the native comment syntax for whichever form of content it is constructing. Such comments will then be sent back to the browser as part of the response. Since they are comments, they do not produce any visible output, but they may be viewed by the end user via the browser's View Source menu item.

Since these comments are part of the output from the page, you can, if you wish, include dynamic content in them. HTML and XML comments can, for example, include JSP expressions, and the output generated by these expressions will appear as part of the comment in the page's response. For example:

```
<!-- Java longs are 64 bits, so 20! = <%= fact(20) %> is
     the upper limit. -->
```

In this case, the computed value of the factorial expression will appear in the comment that is actually sent to the browser.

5.6.2 JSP comments

JSP comments are independent of the type of content being produced by the page. They are also independent of the scripting language used by the page. These comments can only be viewed by examining the original JSP file, and take the following form:

```
<%-- comment --%>
```

The body of this comment is ignored by the JSP container. When the page is compiled into a servlet, anything appearing between these two delimiters is skipped while translating the page into servlet source code.

For this reason, JSP comments such as this are very useful for commenting out portions of a JSP page, as when debugging. In the following page fragment, for example, only the first and last expressions, displaying the factorials of 5 and 9, will appear in the page output:

```
5! = <%= fact(5) %><br>
<%--
6! = <%= fact(6) %><br>
7! = <%= fact(7) %><br>
8! = <%= fact(8) %><br>
--%>
9! = <%= fact(9) %><br>
```

All of the other expressions have been commented out, and will not appear in the page's output. Keep in mind that these comments do not nest. Only the content between the opening comment delimiter, `<%--`, and the *first* occurrence of the closing delimiter, `--%>`, is ignored.

5.6.3 Scripting language comments

Finally, comments may also be introduced into a JSP page within scriptlets, using the native comment syntax of the scripting language. Java, for example, uses `/*` and `*/` as comment delimiters. With Java as the JSP scripting language, then, scripting language comments take the following form:

```
<% /* comment */%>
```

Like JSP comments, scripting language comments will not appear in the page's output. Unlike JSP comments, though, which are ignored by the JSP container, scripting language comments will appear in the source code generated for the servlet.

Scripting language comments can appear by themselves in scriptlets or may accompany actual scripting code, as in the following example:

```
<% long valid = fact(20);
   long overflow = fact(21); /* Exceeds 64-bit long! */
%>
```

In this case, the comment will again appear in the source code of the corresponding servlet.

Scripting language comments can also appear in JSP expressions, as long as they are also accompanied by, or part of, an expression. For example, all of the following JSP expressions are valid:

```
<%= /* Comment before expression */ fact(5) %>
<%= fact(7) /* Comment after expression */ %>
<%= fact(9 /* Comment inside expression */) %>
```

A JSP expression that contains only a comment, but not a scripting language expression, is not valid, and will result in a compilation error.

Java also supports a second comment syntax, in which the characters // are the opening delimiter, and the closing delimiter is the end of the line. This comment syntax can also be used in JSP pages, as long as the scriptlet or expression in which it is used is careful to include the end-of-line delimiter, as in the following examples:

```
<% long valid = fact(20);       // This one fits in a 64-bit long.
   long overflow = fact(21);        // This one doesn't.
%>

5! = <%= fact(5) // Getting tired of factorial examples yet?
%>
```

If the scriptlet or expression does not include the end-of-line delimiter, there is a danger that the content immediately following it may be commented out when the JSP page is translated into a servlet. Consider, for example, the following JSP page fragment:

```
Lora's brother is over <%= fact(3) // Strange ruler... %> feet tall!
```

Depending upon the implementation of the JSP container, it is possible that the code generated to print out the character string `"feet tall!"` may appear in the servlet source code on the same line as the code corresponding to the JSP expression. If so, this code will be commented out in the servlet source code and never appear in the output from the page. In fact, it is also possible that part of the code generated for the expression itself will be commented out, in which case a syntax error will result the first time the page is compiled. For this reason, the fully delimited Java comment syntax (i.e., `/* ... */`) is the preferred style for JSP usage, particularly in JSP expressions.

6 Actions and implicit objects

This chapter covers

- Types of JSP implicit objects
- Accessing and applying implicit objects
- Attributes and scopes
- Action tags for transfer of control

Three types of JSP tags were introduced in chapter 5: directives, scripting elements, and comments. The remaining type, actions, will be introduced here. Actions encapsulate common behavior into simple tags for use from any JSP page. Actions are the basis of the custom tag facility described in chapters 18–20, but a number of standard actions are also provided by the base JSP specification. These standard actions, presented later in this chapter, are supported by all JSP containers.

Before we look at the standard actions, however, we will first consider the set of Java objects that the JSP container makes available to developers from each page. Through their class APIs, these objects enable developers to tap into the inner workings of the JSP container and leverage its functionality. These objects can be accessed as built-in variables via scripting elements. They may also be accessed programmatically by JavaBeans (chapter 7), servlets (chapter 10) and JSP custom tags (chapters 18–20).

6.1 Implicit objects

As the examples presented in chapter 5 suggest, the JSP scripting elements provide a great deal of power for creating, modifying, and interacting with Java objects in order to generate dynamic content. Application-specific classes can be instantiated and values from method calls can be inserted into JSP output. Network resources and repositories, such as databases, can be accessed to store and retrieve data for use by JSP pages.

In addition to objects such as these, which are completely under the control of the developer, the JSP container also exposes a number of its internal objects to the page author. These are referred to as *implicit objects*, because their availability in a JSP page is automatic. The developer can assume that these objects are present and accessible via JSP scripting elements. More specifically, these objects will be automatically assigned to specific variable names in the page's scripting language. Furthermore, as summarized in table 6.1, each implicit object must adhere to a corresponding API, in the form of a specific Java class or interface definition. Thus, it will either be an instance of that class or interface, or of an implementation-specific subclass.

Table 6.1 JSP implicit objects and their APIs for HTTP applications

Object	Class or *Interface*	Description
`page`	*`javax.servlet.jsp.HttpJspPage`*	Page's servlet instance.
`config`	*`javax.servlet.ServletConfig`*	Servlet configuration data.
`request`	*`javax.servlet.http.HttpServletRequest`*	Request data, including parameters.

Table 6.1 JSP implicit objects and their APIs for HTTP applications (continued)

Object	Class or *Interface*	Description
response	*javax.servlet.http.HttpServletResponse*	Response data.
out	javax.servlet.jsp.JspWriter	Output stream for page content.
session	*javax.servlet.http.HttpSession*	User-specific session data.
application	*javax.servlet.ServletContext*	Data shared by all application pages.
pageContext	javax.servlet.jsp.PageContext	Context data for page execution.
exception	java.lang.Throwable	Uncaught error or exception.

The nine implicit objects provided by JSP fall naturally into four major categories: objects related to a JSP page's servlet, objects concerned with page input and output, objects providing information about the context within which a JSP page is being processed, and objects resulting from errors.

Beyond this functional categorization, four of the JSP implicit objects—`request`, `session`, `application`, and `pageContext`—have something else in common: the ability to store and retrieve arbitrary attribute values. By setting and getting attribute values, these objects are able to transfer information between and among JSP pages and servlets as a simple data-sharing mechanism.

The standard methods for attribute management provided by the classes and interfaces of these four objects are summarized in table 6.2. Note that attribute keys take the form of Java `String` objects, while their values are referenced as instances of `java.lang.Object`.

WARNING Note that attribute names beginning with the prefix `java` are reserved by the JSP specification, and should therefore not be used within your application. An example of this is the `javax.servlet.jsp.jspException` attribute associated with requests, as presented in chapter 10.

Table 6.2 Common methods for storing and retrieving attribute values

Method	Description
setAttribute(key, value)	Associates an attribute value with a key (i.e., a name).
getAttributeNames()	Retrieves the names of all attributes associated with the session.
getAttribute(key)	Retrieves the attribute value associated with the key.
removeAttribute(key)	Removes the attribute value associated with the key.

6.1.1 Servlet-related objects

The two JSP implicit objects in this category are based on the JSP page's implementation as a servlet. The `page` implicit object represents the servlet itself, while the `config` object stores the servlet's initialization parameters, if any.

Page object

The `page` object represents the JSP page itself or, more specifically, an instance of the servlet class into which the page has been translated. As such, it may be used to call any of the methods defined by that servlet class. As indicated in the previous chapter, the `extends` attribute of the `page` directive may be used to specify a servlet superclass explicitly, otherwise an implementation-specific class will be used by the JSP container when constructing the servlet. In either case, the servlet class is always required to implement the `javax.servlet.jsp.JspPage` interface. In the specific case of web-based JSP applications built on HTTP, the servlet class must implement the `javax.servlet.jsp.HttpJspPage` interface. The methods of this class are presented in appendix F.

In practice, the `page` object is rarely used when the JSP scripting language is Java, because the scripting elements will ultimately be incorporated as method code of the constructed servlet class, and will automatically have access to the class's other methods. (More specifically, when the scripting language is Java, the `page` object is the same as the `this` variable.) For other scripting languages, however, the scripting variable for this implicit object grants access to all of the methods provided by the `javax.servlet.jsp.JspPage` interface, as well as any methods that have been defined for the page via method declarations.

Here is an example page fragment that utilizes this implicit object:

```
<%@ page info="Page implicit object demonstration." %>
Page info:
<%= ((javax.servlet.jsp.HttpJspPage)page).getServletInfo() %>
```

This expression will insert the value of the page's documentation string into the output from the page. In this example, note that because the servlet class varies from one page to another, the standard type for the `page` implicit object is the default Java type for nonprimitive values, `java.lang.Object`. In order to access methods defined by the `javax.servlet.jsp.HttpJspPage` interface, the `page` object must first be cast to that interface.

Config object

The `config` object stores servlet configuration data—in the form of initialization parameters—for the servlet into which a JSP page is compiled. Because JSP pages are seldom written to interact with initialization parameters, this implicit object is rarely used in practice. This object is an instance of the `javax.servlet.ServletConfig` interface. The methods provided by that interface for retrieving servlet initialization parameters are listed in table 6.3.

Table 6.3 Methods of javax.servlet.ServletConfig interface for accessing initialization parameters

Method	Description
`getInitParameterNames()`	Retrieves the names of all initialization parameters.
`getInitParameter(name)`	Retrieves the value of the named initialization parameter.

Due to its role in servlet initialization, the `config` object tends to be most relevant in the initialization of a page's variables. Consider the following declaration and scriptlet, which provide similar functionality to the sample `jspInit()` method presented in the previous chapter:

```
<%! static private DbConnectionPool pool = null; %>
<%  if (pool == null) {
      String username = config.getInitParameter("username");
      String password = config.getInitParameter("password");
      pool = DbConnectionPool.getPool(this, username, password);
    } %>
```

In this case, rather than storing the `username` and `password` values directly in the JSP page, they have been provided as initialization parameters and are accessed via the `config` object.

Values for initialization parameters are specified via the deployment descriptor file of a web application. Deployment descriptor files are described in chapter 14.

6.1.2 Input/Output

These implicit objects are focused on the input and output of a JSP page. More specifically, the `request` object represents the data coming into the page, while the `response` object represents its result. The `out` implicit object represents the actual output stream associated with the `response`, to which the page's content is written.

Request object

The `request` object represents the request that triggered the processing of the current page. For HTTP requests, this object provides access to all of the information associated with a request, including its source, the requested URL, and any headers, cookies, or parameters associated with the request. The `request` object is required to implement the `javax.servlet.ServletRequest` interface. When the protocol is

HTTP, as is typically the case, it must implement a subclass of this interface, `javax.servlet.http.HttpServletRequest`.

The methods of this interface fall into four general categories. First, the `request` object is one of the four JSP implicit objects that support attributes, by means of the methods presented in table 6.2. The `HttpServletRequest` interface also includes methods for retrieving request parameters and HTTP headers, which are summarized in tables 6.4 and 6.5, respectively. The other frequently used methods of this interface are listed in table 6.6, and provide miscellaneous functionality such as access to the request URL and the session.

Among the most common uses for the `request` object are looking up parameter values and cookies. Here is a page fragment illustrating the use of the `request` object to access a parameter value:

```
<% String xStr = request.getParameter("num");
   try { long x = Long.parseLong(xStr); %>
     Factorial result: <%= x %>! = <%= fact(x) %>
<% } catch (NumberFormatException e) { %>
     Sorry, the <b>num</b> parameter does not specify an
     integer value.
<% } %>
```

In this example, the value of the `num` parameter is fetched from the request. Note that all parameter values are stored as character strings, so conversion is required before it may be used as a number. If the conversion succeeds, this value is used to demonstrate the factorial function. If not, an error message is displayed.

WARNING When naming your request parameters, keep in mind that parameter names beginning with the prefix `jsp` are reserved by the JSP specification. You must therefore avoid the temptation of using them in your own applications, since the container is likely to intercept them and may block access to them from your JSP pages. An example of this is the `jsp_precompile` request parameter, presented in chapter 14.

When utilizing the `<jsp:forward>` and `<jsp:include>` actions described at the end of this chapter, the `request` object is also often used for storing and retrieving attributes in order to transfer data between pages.

Table 6.4 Methods of the javax.servlet.http.HttpServletRequest interface for accessing request parameters

Method	Description
`getParameterNames()`	Returns the names of all request parameters
`getParameter(name)`	Returns the first (or primary) value of a single request parameter
`getParameterValues(name)`	Retrieves all of the values for a single request parameter.

Table 6.5 Methods of the javax.servlet.http.HttpServletRequest interface for retrieving request headers

Method	Description
`getHeaderNames()`	Retrieves the names of all headers associated with the request.
`getHeader(name)`	Returns the value of a single request header, as a string.
`getHeaders(name)`	Returns all of the values for a single request header.
`getIntHeader(name)`	Returns the value of a single request header, as an integer.
`getDateHeader(name)`	Returns the value of a single request header, as a date.
`getCookies()`	Retrieves all of the cookies associated with the request.

Table 6.6 Miscellaneous methods of the javax.servlet.http.HttpServletRequest interface

Method	Description
`getMethod()`	Returns the HTTP (e.g., GET, POST) method for the request.
`getRequestURI()`	Returns the path information (directories and file name) for the requested URL.
`getRequestURL()`	Returns the requested URL, up to, but not including any query string.
`getQueryString()`	Returns the query string that follows the request URL, if any.
`getRequestDispatcher(path)`	Creates a request dispatcher for the indicated local URL.
`getRemoteHost()`	Returns the fully qualified name of the host that sent the request.
`getRemoteAddr()`	Returns the network address of the host that sent the request.
`getRemoteUser()`	Returns the name of user that sent the request, if known.
`getSession(flag)`	Retrieves the session data for the request (i.e., the session implicit object), optionally creating it if it doesn't exist.

Response object

The `response` object represents the response that will be sent back to the user as a result of processing the JSP page. This object implements the `javax.servlet.ServletResponse` interface. If it represents an HTTP response, it will furthermore implement a subclass of this interface, the `javax.servlet.http.HttpServletResponse` interface.

The key methods of this latter interface are summarized in tables 6.7–6.10. Table 6.7 lists a pair of methods for specifying the content type and encoding of a response. Table 6.8 presents methods for setting response headers, while those in table 6.9 are for setting response codes. The two methods in table 6.10 provide support for URL rewriting, which is one of the techniques supported by JSP for session managment. For a full listing of all the methods associated with the `javax.servlet.http.HttpServletResponse` interface, consult appendix F.

Table 6.7 Methods of the `javax.servlet.http.HttpServletResponse` interface for specifying content

Method	Description
`setContentType()`	Sets the MIME type and, optionally, the character encoding of the response's contents.
`getCharacterEncoding()`	Returns the character encoding style set for the response's contents.

Table 6.8 Methods of the `javax.servlet.http.HttpServletResponse` interface for setting response headers

Method	Description
`addCookie(cookie)`	Adds the specified cookie to the response.
`containsHeader(name)`	Checks whether the response includes the named header.
`setHeader(name, value)`	Assigns the specified string value to the named header.
`setIntHeader(name, value)`	Assigns the specified integer value to the named header.
`setDateHeader(name, date)`	Assigns the specified date value to the named header.
`addHeader(name, value)`	Adds the specified string value as a value for the named header.
`addIntHeader(name, value)`	Adds the specified integer value as a value for the named header.
`addDateHeader(name, date)`	Adds the specified date value as a value for the named header.

Table 6.9 Response code methods of the `javax.servlet.http.HttpServletResponse` interface

Method	Description
`setStatus(code)`	Sets the status code for the response (for nonerror circumstances).
`sendError(status, msg)`	Sets the status code and error message for the response.
`sendRedirect(url)`	Sends a response to the browser indicating it should request an alternate (absolute) URL.

Table 6.10 Methods of the `javax.servlet.http.HttpServletResponse` interface for performing URL rewriting

Method	Description
`encodeRedirectURL(url)`	Encodes a URL for use with the `sendRedirect()` method to include session information.
`encodeURL(name)`	Encodes a URL used in a link to include session information.

Here, for example, is a scriptlet that uses the `response` object to set various headers for preventing the page from being cached by a browser:

```
<% response.setDateHeader("Expires", 0);
   response.setHeader("Pragma", "no-cache");
   if (request.getProtocol().equals("HTTP/1.1")) {
     response.setHeader("Cache-Control", "no-cache");
   }
%>
```

The scriptlet first sets the `Expires` header to a date in the past. This indicates to the recipient that the page's contents have already expired, as a hint that its contents should not be cached.

NOTE For the `java.util.Date` class, Java follows the tradition of the UNIX operating system in setting time zero to midnight, December 31, 1969 (GMT). That moment in time is commonly referred to as the UNIX epoch.

The `no-cache` value for the `Pragma` header is provided by version 1.0 of the HTTP protocol to further indicate that browsers and proxy servers should not cache a page. Version 1.1 of HTTP replaces this header with a more specific `Cache-Control` header, but recommends including the `Pragma` header as well for backward compatibility. Thus, if the request indicates that the browser (or its proxy server) supports HTTP 1.1, both headers are sent.

Out object

This implicit object represents the output stream for the page, the contents of which will be sent to the browser as the body of its response. The `out` object is an instance of the `javax.servlet.jsp.JspWriter` class. This is an abstract class that extends the standard `java.io.Writer` class, supplementing it with several of the methods provided by the `java.io.PrintWriter` class. In particular, it inherits all of the standard `write()` methods provided by `java.io.Writer`, and also implements all of the `print()` and `println()` methods defined by `java.io.PrintWriter`.

For example, the out object can be used within a scriptlet to add content to the generated page, as in the following page fragment:

```
<P>Counting eggs
<% int count = 0;
   while (carton.hasNext()) {
     count++;
     out.print(".");
   }
%>
<BR>
There are <%= count %> eggs.</P>
```

The scriptlet in this fragment, in addition to counting the elements in some hypothetical iterator named carton, also has the effect of printing a period for each counted element. If there are five elements in this iterator, this page fragment will produce the following output:

```
Counting eggs.....
There are 5 eggs.
```

By taking advantage of this implicit object, then, output can be generated from within the body of a scriptlet without having to temporarily close the scriptlet to insert static page content or JSP expressions.

In addition, the javax.servlet.jsp.JspWriter class defines a number of methods that support JSP-specific behavior. These additional methods are summarized in table 6.11, and are primarily used for controlling the output buffer and managing its relationship with the output stream that ultimately sends content back to the browser. The full set of methods for this class appears in appendix F.

Table 6.11 JSP-oriented methods of the javax.servlet.jsp.JspWriter interface

Method	Description
isAutoFlush()	Returns true if the output buffer is automatically flushed when it becomes full, false if an exception is thrown.
getBufferSize()	Returns the size (in bytes) of the output buffer.
getRemaining()	Returns the size (in bytes) of the unused portion of the output buffer.
clearBuffer()	Clears the contents of the output buffer, discarding them.
clear()	Clears the contents of the output buffer, signaling an error if the buffer has previously been flushed.
newLine()	Writes a (platform-specific) line separator to the output buffer.
flush()	Flushes the output buffer, then flushes the output stream.
close()	Closes the output stream, flushing any contents.

Here is a page fragment that uses the `out` object to display the buffering status:

```
<% int total = out.getBufferSize();
   int available = out.getRemaining();
   int used = total - available; %>
Buffering Status:
<%= used %>/<%= total %> = <%= (100.0 * used)/total %>%
```

Local variables are created to store the buffer size parameters, and expressions are used to display the values of these local variables. This page fragment is particularly useful when tuning the buffer size for a page, but note that the values it prints are only approximate, because the very act of displaying these values on the page uses up some of the output buffer. As written, the displayed values are accurate for all of the content that precedes this page fragment, but not for the fragment itself (or any content that follows it, of course). Given, however, that this code would most likely be used only during page development and debugging, this behavior is not only acceptable, but also preferable: the developer needs to know the buffer usage of the actual page content, not of the debugging message.

The methods provided for clearing the buffer are also particularly useful. In the discussion of exception handling, recall that it was necessary to rewrite our original example in order to make the output more user-friendly when an error condition arose. More specifically, it was necessary to introduce a local variable and pre-compute the result we were interested in. Consider, instead the following approach:

```
<% out.flush();
   try { %>
  <p align=center> <%= x %>! = <%= fact(x) %></p>
<% } catch (IllegalArgumentException e) {
         out.clearBuffer(); %>
  <p>Sorry, factorial argument is out of range.</p>
<% } %>
```

In this version, the `flush()` method is called on the `out` object to empty the buffer and make sure all of the content generated so far is displayed. Then the `try` block is opened and the call to the `fact()` method, which has the potential of throwing an `IllegalArgumentException`, is made. If this method call successfully completes, the code and content in the `catch` block will be ignored.

If the exception is thrown, however, then the `clearBuffer()` method is called on the `out` object. This will have the effect of discarding any content that has been generated since the last time the output buffer was flushed. In this particular case, the output buffer was flushed just before opening the `try` block. Therefore, only the content generated by the `try` block before the exception occurred would be in the output buffer, so only that content will be removed when the output buffer is cleared. The output buffer will then be overwritten with the error message indicating that the argument was out of range.

WARNING There is, of course, a down side to this approach. Recall from the discussion of buffered output in chapter 4, that once the output buffer has been flushed, it is no longer possible to change or add response headers, or forward to another page. The call to the `flush()` method at the beginning of this page fragment thus limits your options for processing the remainder of the page.

6.1.3 Contextual objects

The implicit objects in this category provide the JSP page with access to the context within which it is being processed. The `session` object, for example, provides the context for the request to which the page is responding. What data has already been associated with the individual user who is requesting the page? The `application` object provides the server-side context within which the page is running. What other resources are available, and how can they be accessed? In contrast, the `pageContext` object is focused on the context of the JSP page itself, providing programmatic access to all of the other JSP implicit objects which are available to the page, and managing their attributes.

Session object

This JSP implicit object represents an individual user's current session. As described in the section on session management in chapter 4, all of the requests made by a user that are part of a single series of interactions with the web server are considered to be part of a session. As long as new requests by that user continue to be received by the server, the session persists. If, however, a certain length of time passes without any new requests from the user, the session expires.

The `session` object, then, stores information about the session. Application-specific data is typically added to the session by means of attributes, using the methods in table 6.12. Information about the session itself is available through the other methods of the `javax.servlet.http.HttpSession` interface, of which the `session` object is an instance. The most commonly used methods of this interface are summarized in table 6.12, and the full API appears in appendix F.

Table 6.12 Relevant methods of the `javax.servlet.http.HttpSession` interface

Method	Description
`getId()`	Returns the session ID.
`getCreationTime()`	Returns the time at which the session was created.
`getLastAccessedTime()`	Returns the last time a request associated with the session was received.
`getMaxInactiveInterval()`	Returns the maximum time (in seconds) between requests for which the session will be maintained.
`setMaxInactiveInterval(t)`	Sets the maximum time (in seconds) between requests for which the session will be maintained.
`isNew()`	Returns `true` if user's browser has not yet confirmed the session ID.
`invalidate()`	Discards the session, releasing any objects stored as attributes.

One of the primary uses for the `session` object is the storing and retrieving of attribute values, in order to transmit user-specific information between pages. As an example, here is a scriptlet that stores data in the session in the form of a hypothetical `UserLogin` object:

```
<% UserLogin userData = new UserLogin(name, password);
   session.setAttribute("login", userData); %>
```

Once this scriptlet has been used to store the data via the `setAttribute()` method, another scripting element—either on the same JSP page or on another page later visited by the user—could access that same data using the `getAttribute()` method, as in the following:

```
<% UserLogin userData = (UserLogin) session.getAttribute("login");
   if (userData.isGroupMember("admin")) {
     session.setMaxInactiveInterval(60*60*8);
   } else {
     session.setMaxInactiveInterval(60*15);
   }
%>
```

Note that when this scriptlet retrieves the stored data, it must use the casting operator to restore its type. This is because the base type for attribute values is `java.lang.Object`, which is therefore the return type for the `getAttribute()` method. Casting the attribute value enables it to be treated as a full-fledged instance of the type to which it has been cast. In this case, a hypothetical `isGroupMember()` method is called to determine whether or not the user is a member of the administrator group. If so, the session time-out is set to eight hours. If not, the session is set to expire after fifteen minutes of inactivity. The implication is that administrators (who are presumably more responsible about restricting access to their computers) should not be required to log back in after short periods of inactivity during the workday, while access by other users requires stricter security.

Note that JSP provides a mechanism for objects to be notified when they are added to or removed from a user's session. In particular, if an object is stored in a session and its class implements the `javax.servlet.http.HttpSessionBindingListener` interface, then certain methods required by that interface will be called whenever session-related events occur. Details on the use of this interface are presented in chapter 8.

Unlike most of the other JSP implicit objects which can be accessed as needed from any JSP page, use of the `session` object is restricted to pages that participate in session management. This is indicated via the `session` attribute of the `page` directive, as described earlier in this chapter. The default is for all pages to participate in session management. If the session attribute of the `page` directive is set to `false`, however, any references to the session implicit object will result in a compilation error when the JSP container attempts to translate the page into a servlet.

Application object

This implicit object represents the application to which the JSP page belongs. It is an instance of the `javax.servlet.ServletContext` interface. JSP pages are deployed as a group (in combination with other web-based assets such as servlets, images, and HTML files) in the form of a web application. This grouping is then reflected by the JSP container in the URLs by which those assets are exposed. More specifically, JSP containers typically treat the first directory name in a URL as an application. For example, http://server/ games/index.jsp, http://server/games/matrixblaster.jsp, and http://server/ games/space/paranoids.jsp are all elements of the same games application. Specification of this grouping and other properties of the web application is accomplished via Web Application Descriptor files, as described in chapter 14.

The key methods of the `javax.servlet.ServletContext` interface can be grouped into five major categories. First, the methods in table 6.13 allow the developer to retrieve version information from the servlet container. Next, table 6.14 lists several methods for accessing server-side resources represented as file names and URLs. The `application` object also provides support for logging, via the methods summarized in table 6.15. The fourth set of methods supported by this interface are those for getting and setting attribute values, presented in table 6.2. A final pair of methods (identical to those in table 6.3) provides access to initialization parameters associated with the application as a whole (as opposed to the page-specific initialization parameters accessed via the `config` implicit object). For the full API of the `javax.servlet.ServletContext` interface, see appendix F.

Table 6.13 Container methods of the `javax.servlet.ServletContext` interface

Method	Description
`getServerInfo()`	Returns the name and version of the servlet container.
`getMajorVersion()`	Returns the major version of the Servlet API for the servlet container.
`getMinorVersion()`	Returns the minor version of the Servlet API for the servlet container.

Table 6.14 Methods of the `javax.servlet.ServletContext` interface for interacting with server-side paths and files

Method	Description
`getMimeType(y)`	Returns the MIME type for the indicated file, if known by the server.
`getResource(path)`	Translates a string specifying a URL into an object that accesses the URL's contents, either locally or over the network.
`getResourceAsStream(path)`	Translates a string specifying a URL into an input stream for reading its contents.
`getRealPath(path)`	Translates a local URL into a pathname in the local filesystem.
`getContext(path)`	Returns the application context for the specified local URL.
`getRequestDispatcher(path)`	Creates a request dispatcher for the indicated local URL.

Table 6.15 Methods of the `javax.servlet.ServletContext` interface for message logging

Method	Description
`log(message)`	Writes the message to the log file.
`log(message, exception)`	Writes the message to the log file, along with the stack trace for the specified exception.

As indicated in tables 6.13–6.15, the `application` object provides a number of methods for interacting with the HTTP server and the servlet container in an implementation-independent manner. From the point of view of JSP development, however, perhaps the most useful methods are those for associating attributes with an application. In particular, a group of JSP pages that reside in the same application can use application attributes to implement shared resources. Consider, for example, the following expression, which implements yet another variation on the construction and initialization of a database connection pool:

```
<% DbConnectionPool pool =
     (DbConnectionPool) application.getAttribute("dbPool");
   if (pool == null) {
     String username = application.getInitParameter("username");
     String password = application.getInitParameter("password");
     pool = DbConnectionPool.getPool(this, username, password);
     application.setAttribute("dbPool", pool);
   } %>
```

In this case, the connection pool is constructed in the same manner, but is stored in a local variable instead of a class variable. This is done because the long-term storage of the connection pool is handled via an application attribute. Before constructing the connection pool, the application attribute is first checked for a pool that has already been constructed.

If a pool is not available via this application attribute, a new connection pool must be constructed. In this case, construction proceeds as before, with the added step of assigning this pool to the application attribute. The other significant difference is that, in this version, the initialization parameters are retrieved from the `application` object, rather than from the `config` object. Initialization parameters associated with the application can be accessed by any of the application's JSP pages. Such parameters need only be specified once, using the Web Application Descriptor file (see chapter 14), whereas the initialization parameters associated with the `config` object must be specified on a page-by-page basis.

Reliance on application initialization parameters enables reuse of this code across multiple JSP pages within the application, without having to specify the initialization parameters multiple times. Such reuse can be facilitated by making use of the JSP `include` directive, and enables you to ensure that the connection pool will only be constructed once, and then shared among all of the pages.

TIP Like `session` attributes, the base type for application attributes is `java.lang.Object`. When attribute values are retrieved from an application, they must be cast back to their original type in order to access their full functionality. Initialization parameters take the form of `String` objects.

As indicated in table 6.13, the `application` implicit object also provides access to information about the environment in which the JSP page is running, through the `getServerInfo()`, `getMajorVersion()`, and `getMinorVersion()` methods. Keep in mind, however, that the data returned by these methods is with respect to the servlet container in which the JSP page is running. To obtain the corresponding information about the current JSP container, the JSP specification provides an abstract class named javax.servlet.jsp.JspEngineInfo that provides a method for retrieving the JSP version number. Since this is an abstract class, a somewhat convoluted path is necessary in order to access an actual instance. The required steps are implemented by the following JSP page fragment:

```
<%@ page import="javax.servlet.jsp.JspFactory" %>
<% JspFactory factory = JspFactory.getDefaultFactory(); %>
JSP v. <%= factory.getEngineInfo().getSpecificationVersion() %>
```

For further details on the JspEngineInfo and JspFactory classes, see appendix F.

PageContext object

The pageContext object provides programmatic access to all other implicit objects. For the implicit objects that support attributes, the pageContext object also provides methods for accessing those attributes. In addition, the pageContext object implements methods for transferring control from the current page to another, either temporarily to generate output to be included in the output of the current page or permanently to transfer control altogether.

The pageContext object is an instance of the javax.servlet.jsp.PageContext class. The full API for this class in presented in appendix F, but the important methods of this class fall into four major groups. First, there is a set of methods for programmatically accessing all of the other JSP implicit objects, as summarized in table 6.16. While these methods are not particularly useful from a scripting perspective (since these objects are already available as scripting variables), we will discover their utility in chapter 18 when we look at how JSP custom tags are implemented.

The second group of javax.servlet.jsp.PageContext methods enables the dispatching of requests from one JSP page to another. Using the methods listed in table 6.17, the handling of a request can be transferred from one page to another either temporarily or permanently. Further details on the application of this functionality will be provided when we look at the <jsp:forward> and <jsp:include> actions toward the end of this chapter.

Table 6.16 Methods of the javax.servlet.jsp.PageContext class for programatically retrieving the JSP implicit objects

Method	Description
getPage()	Returns the servlet instance for the current page (i.e., the page implicit object).
getRequest()	Returns the request that initiated the processing of the page (i.e., the request implicit object).
getResponse()	Returns the response for the page (i.e., the response implicit object).

Table 6.16 Methods of the `javax.servlet.jsp.PageContext` class for programatically retrieving the JSP implicit objects (continued)

Method	Description
`getOut()`	Returns the current output stream for the page (i.e., the out implicit object).
`getSession()`	Returns the session associated with the current page request, if any (i.e., the session implicit object).
`getServletConfig()`	Returns the servlet configuration object (i.e., the config implicit object).
`getServletContext()`	Returns the context in which the page's servlet runs (i.e., the application implicit object).
`getException()`	For error pages, returns the exception passed to the page (i.e., the exception implicit object).

Table 6.17 Request dispatch methods of the `javax.servlet.jsp.PageContext` class

Method	Description
`forward(path)`	Forwards processing to another local URL.
`include(path)`	Includes the output from processing another local URL.

The remaining two groups of methods supported by the `pageContext` object deal with attributes. This implicit object is among those capable of storing attributes. Its class therefore implements all of the attribute access methods listed in table 6.2. In keeping with its role as an avenue for programmatically accessing the other JSP implicit objects, however, the `javax.servlet.jsp.PageContext` class provides a set of methods for managing their attributes, as well. These methods are summarized in table 6.18.

Table 6.18 Methods of the `javax.servlet.jsp.PageContext` class for accessing attributes across multiple scopes

Method	Description
`setAttribute(key, value, scope)`	Associates an attribute value with a key in a specific scope.
`getAttributeNamesInScope(scope)`	Retrieves the names of all attributes in a specific scope.
`getAttribute(key, scope)`	Retrieves the attribute value associated with the key in a specific scope.
`removeAttribute(key, scope)`	Removes the attribute value associated with the key in a specific scope.
`findAttribute(name)`	Searches all scopes for the named attribute.
`getAttributesScope(name)`	Returns the scope in which the named attribute is stored.

As indicated earlier in this chapter, four different implicit objects are capable of storing attributes: the `pageContext` object, the `request` object, the `session` object, and the `application` object. As a result of this ability, these objects are also referred to as *scopes*, because the longevity of an attribute value is a direct result of the type of object in which it is stored. Page attributes, stored in the `pageContext` object, only last as long as the processing of a single page. Request attributes are also short-lived, but may be passed between pages as control is transferred during the handling of a single request. Session attributes persist as long as the user continues interacting with the web server. Application attributes are retained as long as the JSP container keeps one or more of an application's pages loaded in memory—conceivably, as long as the JSP container is running.

NOTE Only a single thread within the JSP container can access attributes stored with either page or request scope: the thread handling the processing of the associated request. Thread safety is more of a concern, then, with session and application attributes. Because multiple requests for an application's pages will be handled simultaneously, objects stored with application scope must be robust with respect to access by these multiple threads. Similarly, because a user may have multiple browser windows accessing a server's JSP pages at the same time, it must be assumed that objects stored with session scope may also be accessed by more than one thread at a time.

In conjunction with the methods listed in table 6.18 whose parameters include a scope specification, the `javax.servlet.jsp.PageContext` class provides static variables for representing these four different scopes. Behind the scenes, these are just symbolic names for four arbitrary integer values. Since the actual values are hidden, the symbolic names are the standard means for indicating attribute scopes, as in the following page fragment:

```
<%@ page import="javax.servlet.jsp.PageContext" %>
<% Enumeration atts =
     pageContext.getAttributeNamesInScope(PageContext.SESSION_SCOPE);
   while (atts.hasMoreElements()) { %>
  Session Attribute: <%= atts.nextElement() %><BR>
<% } %>
```

These variables are summarized in table 6.19.

Table 6.19 Class scope variables for the `javax.servlet.jsp.PageContext` class

Variable	Description
`PAGE_SCOPE`	Scope for attributes stored in the pageContext object.
`REQUEST_SCOPE`	Scope for attributes stored in the request object.
`SESSION_SCOPE`	Scope for attributes stored in the session object.
`APPLICATION_SCOPE`	Scope for attributes stored in the application object.

The last two methods listed in table 6.18 enable developers to search across all of the defined scopes for an attribute with a given name. In both cases, the `pageContext` object will search through the scopes in order—first page, then request, then session, and finally application—to either find the attribute's value or identify in which scope (if any) the attribute is defined.

WARNING The session scope is accessible only to `pageContext` methods on pages that actually participate in session management.

6.1.4 *Error handling*

This last category of JSP implicit objects has only one member, the `exception` object. As its name implies, this implicit object is provided for the purpose of error handling within JSP.

Exception object

The ninth and final JSP implicit object is the `exception` object. Like the `session` object, the `exception` object is not automatically available on every JSP page. Instead, this object is available only on pages that have been designated as error pages using the `isErrorPage` attribute of the `page` directive. On those JSP pages that are error pages, the `exception` object will be an instance of the `java.lang.Throwable` class corresponding to the uncaught error that caused control to be transferred to the error page. The methods of the `java.lang.Throwable` class that are particularly useful in the context of JSP are summarized in table 6.20.

Table 6.20 Relevant methods of the `java.lang.Throwable` class

Method	Description
`getMessage()`	Returns the descriptive error message associated with the exception when it was thrown.
`printStackTrace(output)`	Prints the execution stack in effect when the exception was thrown to the designated output stream.
`toString()`	Returns a string combining the class name of the exception with its error message (if any).

Here is an example page fragment demonstrating the use of the `exception` object:

```
<%@ page isErrorPage="true" %>
<H1>Warning!</H1>
The following error has been detected:<BR>
<B><%= exception %></B><BR>
<% exception.printStackTrace(new java.io.PrintWriter(out)); %>
```

In this example, the `exception` object is referenced in both an expression and a scriptlet. As you may recall, expression values are converted into strings for printing. The expression here will therefore call `exception` object's `toString()` method in order to perform this conversion, yielding the results described in table 6.20. The scriptlet is used to display the stack trace for the exception, by wrapping the `out` implicit object in an instance of `java.io.PrintWriter` and providing it as the argument to the `printStackTrace()` method.

6.2 Actions

In chapter 5 we examined three types of JSP tags, directives, scripting elements, and comments. Actions are the fourth and final major category of JSP tags, and themselves serve three major roles. First, JSP actions allow for the transfer of control between pages. Second, actions support the specification of Java applets in a browser-independent manner. Third, actions enable JSP pages to interact with JavaBeans component objects residing on the server.

In addition, all custom tags defined via tag libraries take the form of JSP actions. The creation and use of custom tags is described in chapter 18. Finally, note that unlike directives and scripting elements, actions employ only a single, XML-based syntax.

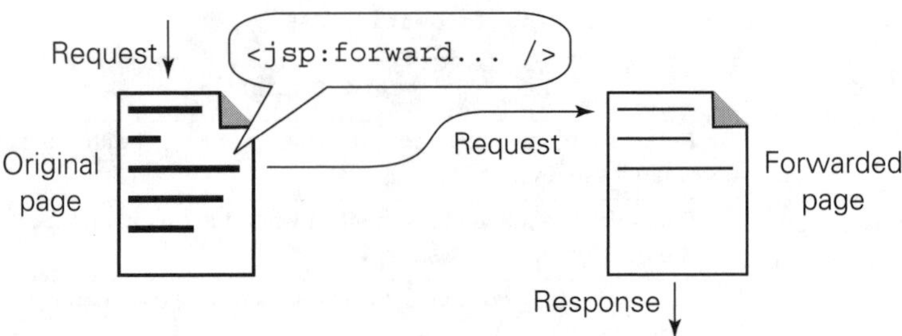

Figure 6.1 Effect of the <jsp:forward> action on the processing of a request

6.2.1 *Forward*

The `<jsp:forward>` action is used to permanently transfer control from a JSP page to another location within the same web application (see chapter 13) as the original page. Any content generated by the current page is discarded, and processing of the request begins anew at the alternate location. The basic syntax for this JSP action is as follows:

```
<jsp:forward page="localURL" />
```

The `page` attribute of the `<jsp:forward>` action is used to specify this alternate location to which control should be transferred, which may be a static document, a servlet, or another JSP page. Note that the browser from which the request was submitted is not notified when the request is transferred to this alternate URL. In particular, the location field at the top of the browser window will continue to display the URL that was originally requested. The behavior of the `<jsp:forward>` action is depicted in figure 6.1. As with the `include` directive described in the previous chapter, if the string value identifying the URL for the `page` attribute starts with a forward slash character, it is resolved relative to the top-level URL directory of the web application. If not, it is resolved relative to the URL of the JSP page containing the `<jsp:forward>` action.

For added flexibility, the `<jsp:forward>` action supports the use of request-time attribute values (as described in chapter 4) for the `page` attribute. Specifically, this means that a JSP expression can be used to specify the value of the `page` attribute, as in the following example:

```
<jsp:forward page='<%= "message" + statusCode + ".html" %>' />
```

Every time the page is processed for a request and the `<jsp:forward>` action is to be taken, this expression will be evaluated by the JSP container, and the resulting value will be interpreted as the URL to which the request should be forwarded. In this particular example, the URL value is constructed by concatenating two constant `String` values with the value of some local variable named `statusCode`. If, for example, the value of `statusCode` were 404, then this action would forward control to the relative URL, `message404.html`.

As mentioned, the `<jsp:forward>` action can be used to transfer control to any other document within the same web application. For the specific case when control is transferred to another JSP page, the JSP container will automatically assign a new `pageContext` object to the forwarded page. The `request` object, the `session` object, and the `application` object, though, will be the same for both the original page and the forwarded page. As a result, some but not all of the attribute values accessible from the original page will be accessible on the forwarded page, depending upon their scope: page attributes are not shared, but request, session, and application attributes are. If you need to transfer data as well as control from one page to another, the typical approach is to store this data either in the request, the session, or the application itself, depending upon how much longer the data will be needed, and whether it is user-specific. (Recall, however, that the `session` object is available only on pages which are marked as participating in session management.)

TIP All of the objects in which JSP pages can store attribute values, with the exception of the `pageContext`, are also accessible via the servlet API. As a result, this approach can also be used to transfer data when forwarding from a JSP page to a servlet.

Since the `request` object is common to both the original page and the forwarded page, any request parameters that were available on the original page will also be accessible from the forwarded page. It is also possible to specify additional request parameters to be sent to the forwarded page through use of the `<jsp:param>` tag within the body of the `<jsp:forward>` action. The syntax for this second form of the `<jsp:forward>` action is as follows:

```
<jsp:forward page="localURL">
  <jsp:param name="parameterName1"
             value="parameterValue1"/>
      …
  <jsp:param name="parameterNameN"
             value="parameterValueN"/>
</jsp:forward>
```

For each `<jsp:param>` tag, the `name` attribute identifies the request parameter to be set and the `value` attribute provides the corresponding value. This value can be either a static character string or a request-time attribute value (i.e., a JSP expression). There is no limit on the number of request parameters that may be specified in this manner. Note also that the passing of additional request parameters is independent of the type of document to which control is transferred; the `<jsp:param>` tag can thus be used to set request parameters for both JSP pages and servlets.

NOTE As you might infer from the inclusion of `getParameterValues()` among the methods of the `request` implicit object listed in table 6.4, HTTP request parameters can actually have multiple values. The effect of the `<jsp:param>` tag when used with the `<jsp:forward>` and `<jsp:include>` actions is to add a value to a particular parameter, rather than simply set its value.

This means that if a request parameter has already been assigned one or more values by some other mechanism, the `<jsp:param>` tag will simply add the specified value to those already present. Note, however, that this new value will be added as the first (or primary) value of the request parameter, so subsequent calls to the `getParameter()` method, which returns only one value, will in fact return the value added by the `<jsp:param>` tag.

If the `<jsp:param>` tag is applied to a request parameter that does not already have any values, then the value specified in the tag becomes the parameter's first and only value. Again, subsequent calls to `getParameter()` will return the value set by the tag.

Given that the `<jsp:forward>` action effectively terminates the processing of the current page in favor of the forwarded page, this tag is typically used in conditional code. Although the `<jsp:forward>` action could be used to create a page which generates no content of its own, but simply uses the `<jsp:param>` tag to set request parameters for some other page, scenarios such as the following are much more common:

```
<% if (! database.isAvailable()) { %>
  <%-- Notify the user about routine maintenance. --%>
  <jsp:forward page="db-maintenance.html"/>
<% } %>
<%-- Database is up, proceeed as usual... --%>
```

Here, a method is called to check whether or not a hypothetical database server is available. If not, control is forwarded to a static HTML page which informs the user that the database is currently down for routine maintenance. If the server is up and running, then processing of the page continues normally, as indicated in the comment following the conditional code.

One factor that you need to keep in mind when using this tag is its interaction with output buffering. When the processing of a page request encounters the `<jsp:forward>` tag, all of the output generated thus far must be discarded by clearing the output buffer. If the output buffer has been flushed at least once, however, some of the output from the page will already have been sent to the user's browser. In this case, it is impossible to discard that output. Therefore, if the output buffer associated with the current page request has ever been flushed prior to the `<jsp:forward>` action, the action will fail, and an `IllegalStateException` will be thrown.

As a result, any page that employs the `<jsp:forward>` action should be checked to make sure that its output buffer is large enough to ensure that it will not be flushed prior to any calls to this action. Alternatively, if output buffering is disabled for the page, then any code which might call the `<jsp:forward>` action must appear on the page before any static or dynamic elements that generate output.

The final consideration in the use of this tag is the issue of cleanup code. If a JSP page allocates request-specific resources, corresponding cleanup code may need to be run from the page once those resources are no longer needed. If such a page makes use of the `<jsp:forward>` tag, then processing of that page will end if and when this tag is reached. Any cleanup code that appears in the JSP file after the `<jsp:forward>` tag will therefore not be run if processing of the page causes this action to be taken. Dependent upon the logic in the page, then, it may be necessary to include a call to the cleanup code just before the `<jsp:forward>` tag, in order to make sure that resources are managed properly.

6.2.2 Include

The `<jsp:include>` action enables page authors to incorporate the content generated by another local document into the output of the current page. The output from the included document is inserted into the original page's output in place of the `<jsp:include>` tag, after which processing of the original page resumes. In contrast to the `<jsp:forward>` tag, then, this action is used to *temporarily* transfer control from a JSP page to another location on the local server.

The `<jsp:include>` action takes the following form:

```
<jsp:include page="localURL" flush="flushFlag" />
```

The `page` attribute of the `<jsp:include>` action, like that of the `<jsp:forward>` action, is used to identify the document whose output is to be inserted into the current page, and is specified as a URL within that page's web application (i.e., there is no host or protocol information in the URL, just directories and a file name). The included page can be a static document, a servlet, or another JSP page. As with the `<jsp:forward>` action, the `page` attribute of the `<jsp:include>` action supports request-time attribute values (i.e., specifying its value via a JSP expression).

The `flush` attribute of the `<jsp:include>` action controls whether or not the output buffer for the current page (if any) is flushed prior to including the content from the included page. In version 1.1 of the JSP specification, it was required that the `flush` attribute be set to `true`, indicating that the buffer is flushed before processing of the included page begins. This was a result of earlier limitations in the underlying servlet API. In JSP 1.2, which is based on version 2.3 of the servlet API, this limitation has been removed. In containers implementing JSP 1.2, then, the `flush` attribute of the `<jsp:include>` action can be set to either `true` or `false`; the default value is `false`.

When the value of the `flush` attribute is set to `true`, the first step of the JSP container in performing the `<jsp:include>` action is to flush the output buffer. Under these circumstsances, then, the standard restrictions on the behavior of JSP pages after the buffer has been flushed apply. In particular, forwarding to another page— including an error page—is not possible. Likewise, setting cookies or other HTTP headers will not succeed if attempted after processing the `<jsp:include>` tag. For similar reasons, attempting to forward requests or set headers or cookies in the included page will also fail (in fact, an exception will be thrown), although it is perfectly valid for an included page to itself include other pages via the `<jsp:include>` action. If the `flush` attribute is set to `false`, only the restrictions on setting headers and cookies still apply; forwarding, including to error pages, is supported.

As with pages accessed via the `<jsp:forward>` action, JSP pages processed via the `<jsp:include>` tag will be assigned a new `pageContext` object, but will share the same `request`, `session`, and `application` objects as the original page. As was also the case with the `<jsp:forward>` action, then, the best way to transfer information from the original page to an included JSP page (or servlet) is by storing the data as an attribute of either the `request` object, the `session` object, or the `application` object, depending upon its expected longevity.

Another element of functionality that the `<jsp:include>` action has in common with the `<jsp:forward>` action is the ability to specify additional request parameters for the included document. Again, this is accomplished via use of the `<jsp:param>` tag within the body of the `<jsp:include>` action, as follows:

```
<jsp:include page="localURL" flush="true">
  <jsp:param name="parameterName1"
             value="parameterValue1"/>
    …
```

```
  <jsp:param name="parameterNameN"
             value="parameterValueN"/>
</jsp:include>
```

As before, the `name` attribute of the `<jsp:param>` tag identifies the request parameter to be set and the `value` attribute provides the corresponding value (which may be a request-time attribute value), and there is no limit on the number of request parameters that may be specified in this manner, or on the type of document to which the request parameters will be passed.

As indicated in figure 6.2, the `<jsp:include>` action works by passing its request on to the included page, which is then handled by the JSP container as it would handle any other request. The output from the included page is then folded into the output of the original page, which resumes processing. This incorporation of content takes place at the time the request is handled. In addition, because the JSP container automatically generates and compiles new servlets for JSP pages that have changed, if the text in a JSP file included via the `<jsp:include>` action is changed, the changes will automatically be reflected in the output of the including file. When the request is directed from the original file to the included JSP page, the standard JSP mechanisms—that is, translation into a stand-alone servlet, with automatic recompilation of changed files—are employed to process the included page.

In contrast, the JSP `include` directive, described in the previous chapter, does not automatically update the including page when the included file is modified. This is because the `include` directive takes effect when the including page is translated into a servlet, effectively merging the base contents of the included page into those of the original. The `<jsp:include>` action takes effect when processing requests, and merges the output from the included page, rather than its original text.

There are a number of tradeoffs, then, that must be considered when deciding whether to use the action or the directive. The `<jsp:include>` action provides the benefits of automatic recompilation, smaller class sizes (since the code

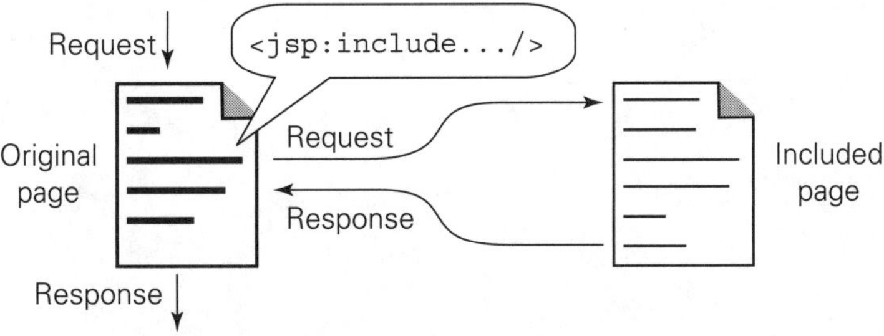

Figure 6.2 Effect of the `<jsp:include>` action on the processing of a request

corresponding to the included file is not repeated in the servlets for every including JSP page), and the option of specifying additional request parameters. The `<jsp:include>` action also supports the use of request-time attribute values for dynamically specifying the included page, which the directive does not. Furthermore, the `include` directive can only incorporate content from a static document (e.g., HTML) or another JSP page. The `<jsp:include>` action, since it includes the output from an included URL rather than the contents of an included source document, can be used to include dynamically generated output, such as from a servlet.

On the other hand, the `include` directive offers the option of sharing local variables, as well as slightly better run-time efficiency, since it avoids the overhead of dispatching the request to the included page and then incorporating the response into the output of the original page. In addition, because the `include` directive is processed during page translation and compilation, rather than during request handling, it does not impose any restrictions on output buffering. As long as the output buffer is sufficiently large, pages which utilize the `include` directive are not limited with respect to setting headers and cookies or forwarding requests.

6.2.3 *Plug-in*

The `<jsp:plugin>` action is used to generate browser-specific HTML for specifying Java applets which rely on the Sun Microsystems Java plug-in. As the primary focus of this book is the use of JSP for server-side Java applications rather than client-side applications, details on the use of this action may be found in appendix C.

6.2.4 *Bean tags*

JSP provides three different actions for interacting with server-side JavaBeans: `<jsp:useBean>`, `<jsp:setProperty>`, and `<jsp:getProperty>`. Because component-centric design provides key strengths with respect to separation of presentation and application logic, the next two chapters are devoted to the interaction between JSP and JavaBeans.

7 Using JSP components

This chapter covers

- The JSP component model
- JavaBean fundamentals
- Interacting with components through JSP

JSP scriptlets and expressions allow developers to add dynamic elements to web pages by interleaving their HTML pages with Java code. While this is a great way for Java programmers to create web-based applications and expressive sites, in general this approach lacks an elegant separation between presentation and implementation, and requires the content developer to be well versed in the Java programming language. Along with scripting, JSP provides an alternative, component-centric approach to dynamic page design. JSP allows content developers to interact with Java components not only though Java code, but through HTML-like tags as well. This approach allows for a cleaner division of labor between application and content developers.

7.1 The JSP component model

The JSP component model is centered on software components called JavaBeans. Before we can explain the specifics of JavaBeans and how they relate to JSP development we must first understand the role of software components in the development process. Once we have an understanding of component-based design principles we will learn how to apply these techniques to web page design in JSP.

7.1.1 Component architectures

Components are self-contained, reusable software elements that encapsulate application behavior or data into a discrete package. You can think of components as black box devices that perform specific operations without revealing the details of what's going on under the hood. Because they abstract their behavior from their implementation, they shield their user from messy details—providing added functionality without increased complexity. Components are stand-alone and not bound tightly to any single application or use. This allows them to be used as building blocks for multiple, potentially unrelated projects. These two principles, abstraction and reusability, are the cornerstones of component-centric design. Figure 7.1 illustrates how a collection of independent software components is assembled to form a complete solution.

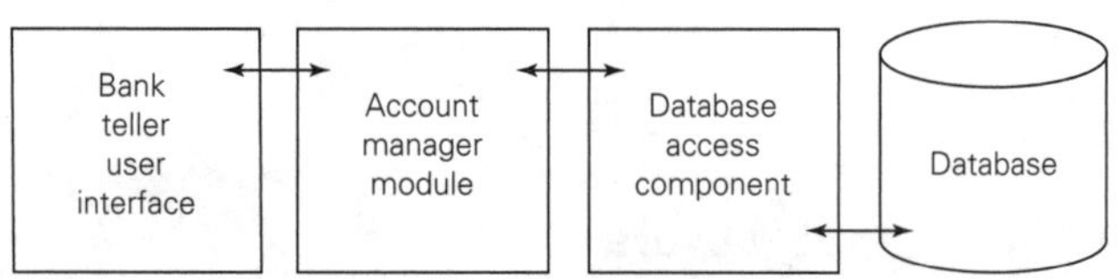

Figure 7.1 A component-based application

Think of components as reusable software elements that we can glue together to construct our applications. A good component model allows us to eliminate or greatly reduce the amount of glue code necessary to build our applications. Component architectures work by employing an interface that allows our components to work together in a more integrated fashion. It is this commonality that binds components together and allows them to be used by development tools that understand the interface to further simplify development.

7.1.2 Benefits of a component architecture

Let's look at an example of component-centric design that's more concrete. When an architect designs a new home he or she relies on components to save time, reduce complexity, and cut costs. Rather than design every wall unit, window frame, and electrical system from scratch he or she uses existing components to simplify the task. Architects don't design a custom air-conditioning system; they select an existing unit that will fit their requirements from the many models available on the market. There's a good chance that the architect doesn't have the skills or resources to design an air-conditioning system anyway. And conversely the designer of the air-conditioning system probably couldn't build a house. Because of this component-based approach the architect and contractor can concentrate on building what they know best—houses, and the air-conditioning company can build air-conditioners. Component architectures allow us to hide a component's complexity behind an interface that allows it to interact with its environment or other components. It isn't necessary to know the details of how a component works in order to access its functionality.

We can use this real world example to illustrate another important feature of component design—reusability. The construction company can select an off-the-shelf air-conditioner because it supports standard connectors, fastens with standard screws, and runs off a standard electric voltage. Later, if the homeowner decides to replace the unit with a new and improved model, there is no need to rebuild the house—simply swap out the old component for the new. Standardized environments and design specifications have allowed for a flexible system that is easily maintained. Software components are designed to operate in specific environments, and interact in predetermined ways. The fact that components must follow a certain set of rules allows us to design systems that can accept a wide array of components.

Component development

While it would be nice if we could design our entire application from pre-existing components, that's an approach that's rarely practical for real application design. Usually an application developed with a component approach involves a combination of general purpose and application specific components. The benefits of component reuse surface not only by sharing components among differing applications, but through reuse of components across several segments of the same or related applications.

A banking application, for example, might have several different customer interfaces, an employee access module, and an administrative screen. Each of these related applications could make use of a common component that contained all of the knowledge necessary to display the specifics of a particular bank account. With luck, and good forethought during component design, this banking component might be useful to anyone developing financial management applications.

Once a component has been designed, the component's author is relatively free to change its inner-workings without having to track down all of the component's users. The key to achieving this high level of abstractness is defining an interface that shields any application relying on the component from the details of its implementation.

7.1.3 Component design for web projects

A component-based approach is ideal for the design of web applications. JSP lets web designers employ the same component design principles that other software developers have been using for years. Rather than having to embed complex logic directly into pages through scripting code, or building page content into the programming logic, they can simply employ HTML layout around components. The component model's ability to reuse common components can reduce development time and project complexity.

Isolating application logic from presentation layout is a necessity for web development organizations that are built around teams whose members have a diverse set of complementary skill sets. In many enterprises the web team is composed of both application developers and web developers. Java application developers are skilled in tasks such as exchanging information with a database and optimizing back-end server code for performance, while web developers are good with the presentation aspects such as interface design and content layout. In a componentized JSP development project, application developers are free to concentrate on developing components that encapsulate program logic, while web developers build the application around these components, focusing their energies on its presentation. As illustrated in figure 7.2, clearly defined boundaries between an application's core functionality and its presentation to its user allow for a clearer separation of responsibilities between development teams.

In some cases a single person may handle both aspects of design, but as project complexity grows, splitting up the tasks of the development process can yield a number of benefits. Even for web projects being handled by a small, unified team of developers, a component-based architecture makes sense. The flexibility offered by

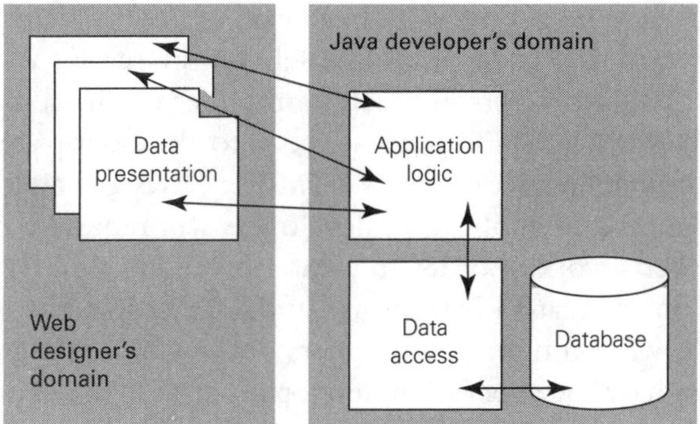

Figure 7.2 Division of labor in a web application's development

components allows a project to handle the sudden changes in requirements that often seem to accompany web projects.

7.1.4 *Building applications from components*

So how can we use these component design principles in the design of web applications? Let's look at how we might develop a web shopping application with such an approach. As is typical for an enterprise application, this example involves collecting information from a database based on user input, performing some calculations on the data, and displaying the results to the user. In this case we will display a catalog of items, allow the user to select some for purchase, and calculate tax and shipping costs, before sending the total back to the user.

What we want to end up with is an online form that allows us to enter the customer's purchases, and, upon submitting the form, returns a new page with a nicely formatted invoice that includes shipping fees and tax. Our page designers should have no problem creating an attractive input form and invoice page, and our developers can easily calculate shipping and tax costs. It is only the interaction between the two worlds that gets a little sticky. What technologies are best utilized in the design of such an application?

Since our product catalog is stored in a database, that portion of the application has to be tied to the server, but where should the tax and shipping calculations take place? We could use a client-side scripting approach with something like JavaScript. However, JavaScript isn't supported in every browser, and would reveal our calculations in the source of our page. Important calculations such as shipping and tax should be confined to the server for security purposes; we certainly don't want the client browser performing the task.

A server-side approach using JSP scripts would get around this problem. We can access back-end resources with the code running safely on the server. While this approach works well for smaller projects, it creates a number of difficulties for a project such as this one. Directly imbedding JSP scripts into all of our pages introduces a high degree of intermingling between our HTML page design and our business logic. Our web designers and application developers will require a detailed understanding of each other's work in order to create the application. We could choose to have the developers create a bare-bones implementation, then let our designers polish it up. Or, we could let the designers develop a nice page layout with no logic in it and then have the application developer punch in the code to calculate tax and shipping. Does that provide the division of labor we're looking for? Not quite.

A problem with this approach surfaces when we deploy and maintain our application. Consider, for example, what happens when our catalog sales application (originally developed for use by a single location of the company) becomes so wildly successful our bosses decide to deploy it companywide to all twenty-eight branches. Of course the sales tax is different at each branch so we make twenty-eight copies of our page and find an application developer familiar with the code to make the necessary changes to the JSP scripts. Then, we have to get our web developers to change the HTML of each page to correct any branch-specific design or branding issues. Over the course of the application's lifetime we will constantly have to fiddle with calculations, fix bugs, increase shipping rates, update the design, and add new features. All of this work must happen across twenty-eight different versions of the code. Why should we need two groups of people doing the same job twenty-eight times over?

A web application developed around components offers a better approach. With the ability to deploy components into our HTML pages we can allow our application developers to design tax and shipping calculating components that can be configured at run time with determining factors like the local tax rate. Our web page developers can then rely on these components without having to involve the application developers each time some HTML needs to be changed or a new version of the page created. On the application development side any bug fixes or updates would be isolated to the components themselves and would not affect our web page developer's duties. So how do components fit in with JSP? JSP leverages the JavaBeans component model, which we'll explore next.

7.2 JavaBean fundamentals

JavaBeans are software components written in Java. The components themselves are called *beans* and must adhere to specifications outlined in the JavaBeans API. The JavaBeans API was created by Sun with the cooperation of the industry and dictates the rules that software developers must follow in order to create stand-alone, reusable software components. Like many other software components, beans encapsulate both state and behavior. By using JSP's collection of bean-related tags in their web pages, content developers can leverage the power of Java to add dynamic elements to their pages without writing a single line of Java code. Before delving into the specifics of working with beans in JSP, we need to learn more about the beans themselves.

Bean containers

A *bean container* is an application, environment, or programming language that allows developers to call up beans, configure them, and access their information and behavior. Applications that use beans are composed purely of Java code, but bean containers allow developers to work with it at a higher conceptual level. This is possible because JavaBeans expose their features and behavior to the bean container, allowing the developer to work with the bean in a more intuitive fashion. The bean container defines its own way of presenting and interacting with the bean and writes the resulting Java code itself.

If you have used Sun's Bean Box, IBM's Visual Age for Java, Visual Café, or other Java development tools you've already had some experience with beans. These applications include bean containers that work with beans in a visual format. With these tools you can build an application by simply dragging bean icons into position and defining the specifics of their behavior and their connections to other beans. The application then generates all of the necessary Java code. Like these visual tools, JSP containers allow developers to create web-based Java applications without needing to write Java. In JSP we interact with beans through a collection of tags that we can embed inside our HTML.

Bean properties

Bean containers allow you to work with beans in terms of *properties*—named attributes of the bean that maintain its state and control its behavior. A bean is defined by its properties, and would be pretty much useless without them. Bean properties can be modified at run time by the bean container to control specifics of the bean's behavior. These property values are the sole mechanism the bean container uses to expose beans to the developer.

As an example, let's suppose we have a bean called `WeatherBean` that knows various things about the current weather conditions and forecasts. The bean could collect current weather information from the National Weather Service computers, or extract it from a database—the point being that as the bean's user we do not need to understand the specifics of how the bean gets its information. All we care about as developers is that the `WeatherBean` is able to give us information such as the current temperature, the projected high, or the chances for rain. Each of these bits of information is exposed to the bean container as a property of the bean whose value we can access for our web page or application.

Each bean will have a different set of properties depending on the type of information it contains. We can customize a bean by setting some of its property values ourselves. The bean's creator will impose restrictions on each property of the bean, controlling our access to it. A property can be read-only, write-only, or readable and writable. This concept of accessibility allows the bean designer to impose limits on how the beans can be used. In our `WeatherBean`, for example, it doesn't make any sense to allow developers to modify the value of the bean's property representing today's high temperature. That information is managed by the bean itself and should be left read-only. On the other hand, if the bean had a property controlling the ZIP code of the region in whose weather we are interested, it would certainly make sense to allow developers to specify it. Such a property would be writable, and probably readable as well.

NOTE As we'll learn in detail in chapter 8, behind the scenes JavaBeans are merely Java objects. A JavaBean's properties map to the methods of a Java object that manipulates its state. So when you set a property of a bean, it's like a shortcut for calling object methods through Java. Likewise, viewing the current value of a bean's property is essentially calling a method of an object and getting its results. We'll learn how a Java object's methods map into bean properties in the next chapter.

Trigger and linked properties

Some properties are used to trigger behavior as well as report information and are thus called *trigger properties.* Reading from or writing to a trigger property signals the bean to perform an activity on the back end. These triggers, once activated, can either update the values of other properties or cause something to happen on the back end. Changing the value of our ZIP code property for example might cause the bean to run off to the National Weather Service, request weather conditions in the new ZIP code, and update its other weather related properties accordingly. In that case the weather properties and the ZIP code property are considered *linked properties* because changing the value of one updates the values of others.

Indexed properties

It is also possible for a single property to store a collection of values. These properties are known as *indexed properties* because each value stored in the property is accessed through an index number, which specifies which particular value you want. For example you can request the first value in the list, the third, or the twenty-seventh. Our `WeatherBean` could have a property that holds forecasted temperatures for the next five days, for example. Not every bean container provides a simple mechanism for working with these multivalue properties directly, however. The JSP bean tags, for example, do not recognize indexed properties. Instead, you must use JSP scriptlets, JSP expressions, or custom JSP tags (discussed in chapters 18 and 19) to access them.

Property data types

Bean properties can be used to hold a wide array of information. `WeatherBean`'s properties would need to store everything from temperatures to rainfall odds, forecasts, ZIP codes, and more. Each property of a bean can hold only one specific type of data such as text or a number. bean property values are assigned a Java data type, which is used internally by the bean and in the Java code generated by the bean container. As you might expect, properties can hold any of the Java primitives like `int` or `double`, as well as Java objects like `Strings` and `Dates`. Properties can also store user-defined objects and even other beans. Indexed properties generally store an array of values, each of the same data type.

The bean container determines how we work with the property values of a bean. With JSP scriptlets and expressions we reference property values by their Java data type. If a property stores integer values we get integer values out of it and must put integer values into it. With bean tags, however, we treat every property as if it were stored text, or in Java parlance, a `String`. When you set the value of a bean property, you pass it text. Likewise, when you read the contents of a property you get back text, regardless of the internal data type used inside the bean. This text-only strategy keeps JSP bean tags simple to work with and fits in nicely with HTML.

The JSP container automatically performs all of the necessary type conversions. When you set an integer property, for example, it performs the necessary Java calls to convert the series of numeric characters you gave it into an actual integer value. Of course this conversion process requires you to pass in appropriate text values that Java can correctly convert into the native data type. If a property handles floating point values, for example, it would throw an error if you attempted to set the value to something like `banana bread`, `one hundred`, or `(3,9)`.

Clever bean designers can control property values themselves by accepting string values for nonstring properties and performing the conversions themselves. For any value which is neither a string nor a Java primitive type, this technique must be used. Therefore it might be perfectly legal to set an integer property to `one hundred`, provided the bean's designer had prepared it for such input.

Bean property sheets

A bean's capabilities are documented in a table called a property sheet which lists all of the properties available on the bean, their level of access afforded to the users, and their Java type. Property sheets may also specify example or valid values for each property of the bean. Table 7.1 shows the property sheet for the `WeatherBean` component that we have been using.

Table 7.1 Property sheet examples

Name	Access	Java Type	Example Value
`zipCode`	read/write	`String`	77630
`currentTemp`	read-only	`int`	87
`todaysHigh`	read-only	`int`	101
`todaysLow`	read-only	`int`	85
`rainOdds`	read-only	`float`	0.95
`forecasts`	read-only	`String[]`	Sunny, Rainy, Cloudy, Sunny, Hot
`iconURL`	read-only	`URL`	http://imageserver/weather/rainy.gif

Property sheets allow bean designers to describe the features of a bean to its users, such as JSP developers, servlet programmers, and the like. From the property sheet a developer can determine what type of information the bean can contain and what behavior it can provide. Of course, the property sheet alone may not be enough to adequately explain the behavior of a bean to the end user. In this case additional information can be communicated through the bean's documentation.

7.2.1 The different types of JavaBeans

For purposes of discussion we can think of beans as falling into three general categories: *visual component beans* used as elements of graphical user interfaces (GUI), *data beans* that provide access to a collection of information, and *service beans* (also known as *worker* beans) that can perform specific tasks or calculations. Of course some beans can be classified in more than one category.

Visual component beans

The development of visual components has been one of the most common uses of JavaBeans. Visual components are elements such as text fields, selectors, or other widgets useful for building user interfaces. By packaging GUI components into beans, Java development environments can take advantage of JavaBean's support for visual programming. This allows developers to create their interfaces by simply dragging the desired elements into position. Since visual beans have been designed to run as part of graphical Java applications, they are not compatible with JSP, which is intended for text-based applications such as HTML interface design.

Data beans

Data beans provide a convenient way to access data that a bean itself does not necessarily have the capability to collect or generate. The calculation or collection of the data stored inside data beans is the responsibility of some other, more complex component or service. Data beans are typically read-only, allowing you to fetch data from them but not allowing you to modify their values on your own.

However, some data beans allow you to set some of their properties in order to control how data is formatted or filtered before being returned through other properties. For example, an `AccountStatusBean` might also have a `currencyType` property that controls whether the balance property returned data in dollars, pounds, or Swiss francs. Because of their simplicity, data beans are useful to standardize access to information by providing a stable interface.

Service beans

Service beans, as you might expect, provide access to a behavior or particular service. For this reason they are sometimes referred to as worker beans. They can retrieve information from a database, perform calculations, or format information. Since the only way that we can interact with a bean is through its properties, this is how we will access a bean's services. In a typical design, we will set the value of certain properties that control the bean's behavior, and then read the results of the request through other properties. A bean designed to access a database of employee phone numbers, for example, might have a property called `employee`, which we could set to the name we wish to look up. Setting this property triggers the database search and sets the `phone` and `email` properties of the bean to reflect the information of the requested employee.

Not all service beans collect data from a back-end source. Some simply encapsulate the logic necessary to perform calculations, conversions, or operations. A `StatisticsBean` might know how to calculate averages, medians, and standard deviations, for example. A `UnitConversionBean` might allow the page designer to specify some distance in inches and get it back in feet, yards, miles, or furlongs.

Some service beans will not return any information. Their service may be to store information in a database or log file, for example. In this case, you might set a property's value not to get results of the service, but simply for its side-effect behavior—what happens on the back end. Service beans allow for a clear separation of responsibility and for teams to have separate knowledge domains. The web designer doesn't need to understand statistical calculations and the programmer doesn't need to understand subtleties of page layout. A change in either the presentation or the program logic will not affect the others, provided the bean's interface does not change.

7.3 JSP bean tags

Now that we have a good understanding of the principles of component architecture and JavaBeans we can get into the nitty-gritty of building web pages around them. JSP has a set of bean tags which can be used to place beans into a page, then access their properties. Unlike JSP scriptlets and expressions we explored in the previous chapter, you do not need to be a Java programmer in order to design pages around beans. In fact, you don't need to be any type of programmer at all because JSP does a pretty good job of eliminating the need for messy glue between our HTML and components.

7.3.1 Tag-based component programming

JSP needs only three simple tags to enable interaction with JavaBeans: `<jsp:useBean>`, `<jsp:setProperty>`, and `<jsp:getProperty>`. These tags allow you to place beans into the page as well as alter and access their properties. Some people complain about the simplicity of the JSP tag set, preferring an approach that embeds more functionality into the tags themselves similar to PHP or ColdFusion. It is important to understand that the limited set of functionality afforded to JSP bean tags is intentional. They are not meant to provide a full-featured programming language; programmers can use JSP scriptlets for that. Instead, the bean tags enable the use of component design strategies in HTML documents without the need for the page author to learn a programming language or to understand advanced programming concepts.

As always, there is a fine line in determining the trade-off between the power of a language and its complexity. As a good compromise, the JSP designers elected to keep the core functionality very simple, defining only a few tags for working with beans and establishing a specification that allows for the development of new, custom tags that solve specific problems. The standard tags allow you to create references to beans you need to use, set the values of any configurable properties they might have, and read information from the bean's properties. Custom tags with more complex levels of functionality can be developed by individuals and organizations and integrated into any JSP environment through an extension mechanism known as custom tag libraries. Through custom tags the JSP language can be extended to support additional programming constructs, like conditionals and loops, as well as provide additional functionality such as direct access to databases. We'll learn about custom tags and tag libraries in chapters 18 and 19.

An illustrative example

Let's whet our appetite by looking at JSP code built around components, rather than scriptlets. This example shows some of the things we can accomplish with the component-centric design model, and will serve as a kickoff to our discussion of JSP's component features.

```
<jsp:useBean id="user" class="RegisteredUser" scope="session"/>
<jsp:useBean id="news" class="NewsReports" scope="request">
  <jsp:setProperty name="news" property="category" value="financial"/>
  <jsp:setProperty name="news" property="maxItems" value="5"/>
</jsp:useBean>
<html>
<body>
Welcome back <jsp:getProperty name="user" property="fullName"/>,
your last visit was on
<jsp:getProperty name="user" property="lastVisitDate"/>.
Glad to see you again!
<P>
There are <jsp:getProperty name="news" property="newItems"/> new articles
available for your reading pleasure. Please enjoy your stay and come back soon.
</body>
</html>
```

Notice how straightforward the page design has become? We have used a few special JSP tags to eliminate all of the Java code from our page. Even though we have not yet discussed the specifics of any of the bean tags, you probably already have a good idea of what the code does just by looking at it. It uses two components, `user` and `news`. The first allows us to greet visitors personally, and the second stores news items in which they might be interested. JSP bean tags allow us to more clearly

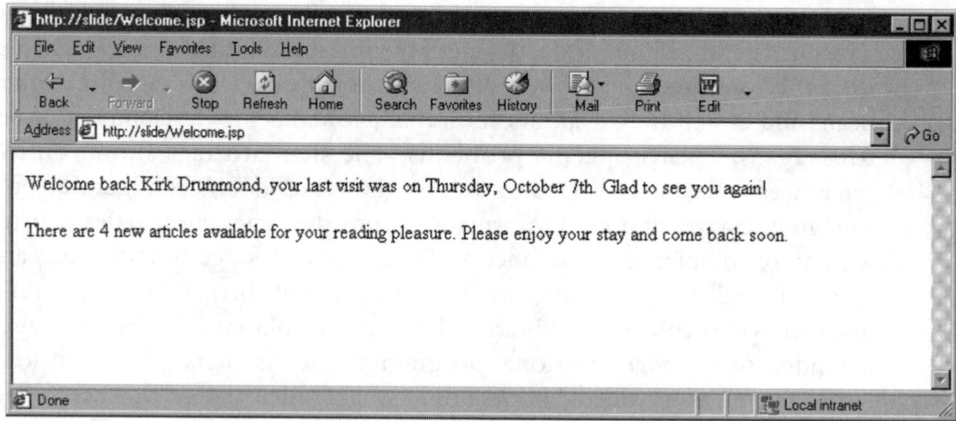

Figure 7.3 Dynamic content with JSP

understand the page's layout because we are writing HTML, not code. Figure 7.3 shows what the page looks like on the browser.

7.3.2 *Accessing JSP components*

To interact with a bean we first tell the page where to find the Java class file that defines the bean and assign it a name. We can then use this name to access the values stored in the bean's properties. By mastering just three simple JSP tags you can add component-based web page design to your repertoire. We will look at each of these tags in-depth.

The <jsp:useBean> tag

The `<jsp:useBean>` tag tells the page that we want to make a bean available to the page. The tag is used to create a bean or fetch an existing one from the server. Attributes of the tag specify the type of bean you wish to use and assign it a name we can use to refer to it. The `<jsp:useBean>` tag comes in two forms, a single empty tag and a matching pair of start and end tags that contain the body of the tag which can be used to specify additional configuration information. In its simplest and most straightforward form the `<jsp:useBean>` tag requires only two attributes, `id` and `class`. Like all of the JSP tags, you must enclose each attribute value in quotes. The basic syntax for the tag's two forms is:

```
<jsp:useBean id="bean name" class="class name"/>

<jsp:useBean id="bean name" class="class name">
  initialization code
</jsp:useBean>
```

Table 7.2 shows all of the possible attribute values supported by the `<jsp:useBean>` tag. We will discuss the purpose of each throughout the chapter, but for now we will concentrate on understanding the basic bean tag attributes.

Table 7.2 Attributes of the `<jsp:useBean>` tag

Attribute	Value	Default	Example Value
id	Java identifier	none	myBean
scope	page, request, session, application	page	session
class	Java class name	none	java.util.Date
type	Java class name	same as class	com.manning.jsp.AbstractPerson
beanName	Java class or serialized Bean	none	com.manning.jsp.USCurrency.ser

The ID attribute

The `id` attribute specifies a name for the bean—a unique value that will refer to this particular bean throughout the page and over the course of its lifetime (we'll learn how to extend the bean's life beyond the current page later). We can use multiple `<jsp:useBean>` tags to define more than one bean within a page, even multiple instances of the same bean class, as long as there is a unique identifier associated with each individual bean. The name we select for our bean is arbitrary, but it must follow some simple rules:

- It must be unique to the page
- It must be case sensitive
- The first character must be a letter
- Only letters, numbers, and the underscore character (_) are allowed (no spaces)

The class attribute

The value of the `class` attribute specifies the class name of the JavaBean itself. To help better organize code and avoid conflicts, Java classes are usually organized into *packages*. Packages are collections of individual Java class files organized inside a single directory. Package names are usually composed of multiple, period-separated names where each name is a directory in the package hierarchy. You must always specify the fully qualified name of the bean class. A fully qualified class name consists of the name of the class's package and the class name itself. By convention, packages begin with the Internet domain name of their creator, and usually include more levels of hierarchy to help better organize collections of classes into logical collections. The bean's developer will determine the actual package and class name of the bean. Some fully qualified bean class names might look something like the following:

```
com.manning.RegisteredUserBean
com.deepmagic.beans.database.logging.LogBean
com.blokware.MagicPizzaBean
com.taglib.wdjsp.arch.EmployeeBean
```

The actual bean class is the last part of the fully qualified name, so in the first example we are talking about a `RegisteredUserBean` inside the `com.manning` package. Unlike other Java code, which allows you to import packages and refer to the classname alone, JSP requires fully qualified class names inside the `<jsp:useBean>` tag. For example, the following does *not* work:

```
<%@page import="com.manning.*" %>
<jsp:useBean id="user" class="RegisteredUserBean" />
```

The correct way…

```
<jsp:useBean id="user" class="com.manning.RegisteredUserBean" />
```

Early implementations of the JSP specification sometimes allowed non-fully qualified class names in this tag, but as of version 1.2 these are no longer allowed. Even if your container supports this shortcut, you should always fully qualify your names to keep your code compatible with other containers or updates to yours. Note that for scripting variables, imported packages are supported and fully qualified class names are not required.

The type attribute

In practice you won't use this attribute too much. The `<jsp:useBean>` tag's `class` attribute determines which Java class is used to create our bean, but JSP offers a way of fine-tuning the JSP container's interpretation of the bean's type which is sometimes needed when beans exist on the server and are not being instantiated by the current page. By default, the bean is referenced by the class type corresponding directly to the underlying object's class. However, if you need to refer to the bean as another type, for example a base class or an interface that the bean implements, you can use the `type` attribute of the `<jsp:useBean>` tag to do so. The class type you specify is used to represent the bean object in the Java resulting from the JSP compilation phase. The bean's actual class must, of course, be assignable to the class type specified. If you specify both `class` and `type` attributes, the bean will be created using the given class, then cast to the given type. The `type` attribute can only be used alone (that is without a corresponding `class` attribute) in cases where the bean already exists on the server, a feature known as *scope* which we'll cover in the last section of this chapter. Like the class attribute, you must specify the fully qualified name of the class.

The beanName attribute

This attribute, which is not used too often, specifies the name of a bean which will be passed to the `instantiate()` method of the `java.beans.Beans` class. It will always take the format of "x.y.z", but can refer to either a fully qualified classname or a local serialized bean, located in the file path x/y/z.ser. If present, this class or resource will be instantiated and assigned to the reference specified by the `id` attribute. One unique feature of this attribute of the `<jsp:useBean>` tag is that it can be assigned through a run-time expression, allowing you to specify the name of the class or resource via a request parameter.

The tag body

The tag's optional body portion can be used to initialize any user configurable properties of the bean. This lets us configure a bean specifically for this page or our particular application. We will discuss bean initialization in detail later. For now, we'll look at beans that do not require any special initialization at the time they are created.

<jsp:useBean> in action

Let's get into using the bean tags. Here's an example of the `<jsp:useBean>` tag in action.

```
<jsp:useBean id="myclock" class="com.manning.jsp.ClockBean"/>
<html>
<body>
There is a Bean hiding in this page!
</body>
</html>
```

We've told the page that we will be using a bean that is defined in the Java class file `ClockBean` in the `com.manning.jsp` package and we've named the bean `myclock` for use in the page. In practice we like to put all of our `<jsp:useBean>` tags at the beginning of the HTML document, but syntactically it is valid to use the tag anywhere in the page. However, keep in mind that beans are only available to portions of the page following the `<jsp:useBean>` tag in which they were defined. Portions of the page before the `<jsp:useBean>` tag will have no reference to the bean, and attempting to access the bean will cause an error.

The `<jsp:useBean>` tag creates an instance of the bean and assigns its ID as specified by the `id` attribute. When the new bean is created it performs any tasks or data processing as designed by the bean's author. For example, the ClockBean sets its internal state to reflect the current time and date, while another bean might look up information in a database. This is part of the normal Java instantiation process and happens without any help from you. Once a bean has been given a name and been made available to the page we can begin using its properties. Depending on the bean design, the properties may simply provide information such as the time of day or the name of the current user, or they might also execute complex transactions or look up information in a database. Whichever the case, the results are accessible through the bean's properties.

It is important to understand the difference between a bean's class and its instance. The bean's class controls what type of bean will be created, its properties, and capabilities. It is used like an object template to create a unique instance of the bean with each call of the <jsp:useBean> tag. For example, consider the following tags:

```
<jsp:useBean id="clock1" class="com.manning.jsp.ClockBean" />
<jsp:useBean id="clock2" class="com.manning.jsp.ClockBean" />
```

This creates two independent, that is, completely separate, beans with their own names: clock1 and clock2. They are instances of the same class, but any changes made to one bean will have no effect on the other. Later in this chapter we will talk about how other attributes of the <jsp:useBean> tag can allow a bean to be reused between visits to a single page or across multiple pages throughout the site. In the examples above, our beans are there, but we aren't actually using them to do anything. The next bean tag, <jsp:getProperty> allows us to retrieve the information stored inside the bean.

Accessing bean properties with <jsp:getProperty>

The primary way to access a bean's properties in JSP is through the <jsp:getProperty> tag. Unlike the <jsp:useBean> tag which performs some work behind the scenes but doesn't produce any output, the <jsp:getProperty> tag actually produces content that we can see in the HTML generated by the page. The <jsp:getProperty> tag is empty with no body element and expects two attributes, name and property. Its syntax is:

```
<jsp:getProperty name="bean name" property="property name"/>
```

The name attribute specifies the bean we are evaluating, and should correspond to the name we selected for the bean in the <jsp:useBean> tag's id attribute. Don't forget that the <jsp:useBean> tag refers to the bean with the id attribute, and that other tags refer to the bean through a name attribute. It is a JSP convention that the id attribute is used to define a new object, while the name attribute is used to reference an existing object. Be careful, it can be easy to confuse the two.

In the resulting HTML that is displayed at run time, the tag is replaced with the value of the property of the bean you request. Of course, since we are creating an HTML document, the property is first converted into text by the JSP container. This tag is very easy to use. Let's look at the ClockBean example again, but this time we'll use the <jsp:getProperty> tag to ask the bean to tell us what time it is:

```
<jsp:useBean id="myclock" class="com.manning.jsp.ClockBean"/>
<html>
<body>
The Bean says that the time is now:
<jsp:getProperty name="myclock" property="time"/>
</body>
</html>
```

This should display HTML that looks something like:

```
<html>
<body>
The Bean says that the time is now: 12:33 pm
</body>
</html>
```

You'll use this tag a lot, as it's the key to component-based dynamic output with JSP. You can use as many <jsp:getProperty> tags in your page as you need. You can intersperse them with HTML to not only dynamically generate single values and blocks of text, but to control attributes of the HTML as well. It is perfectly legal to nest JSP tags inside HTML attributes. A bean's property could be used to control the page's background color, the width of a table, or the source of an image. For example, a bean reflecting a standardized corporate style might have a property that exposes the URL location of the latest version of the corporate logo and the corporate color scheme. We can display this image in our HTML as shown next without hard coding the URL value in each page.

```
<jsp:useBean id="style" class="beans.CorporateStyleBean"/>
<html>
<body bgcolor="<jsp:getProperty name="style" property="color"/>">
<center>
<img src="<jsp:getProperty name="style" property="logo"/>">
Welcome to Big Corp!
</center>
</body>
</html>
```

This would generate HTML like this:

```
<html>
<body bgcolor="pink">
<center>
<img src="http://imageserver/logo.gif">
Welcome to Big Corp!
</center>
</body>
</html>
```

If the logo changes next week when the company replaces the corporate branding director, or is acquired, all of your pages will instantly reflect the new value built into the `CorporateStyleBean`. Another advantage here is that application programmers might be relying on the same bean to brand their interfaces, and the change would be reflected there as well.

TIP According to the specifications, white space in a document is not significant to the JSP parser, but should be preserved by the JSP processor. In some implementations that we have encountered, however, the parser does not properly preserve white space characters between JSP bean tags when no other (non-white space) characters are present. For example, you would expect the following JSP code to display something like "Firstname Lastname", but instead you might get "FirstnameLastname":

```
<jsp:getProperty name="user" property="firstName"/>
<jsp:getProperty name="user" property="lastName"/>
```

This might happen because the JSP parser ignored the newline, which would normally be treated as a white space character. If this happens, adding blank lines probably won't help as the JSP parser would simply ignore them too, assuming that there was nothing relevant between the two bean tags.

If your JSP container suffers from this annoyance, you can work around it by placing meaningful, but empty content, such as an HTML comment, which should force it to preserve the newline character in the page output.

```
<jsp:getProperty name="user" property="firstName"/>
<!-- insert a space -->
<jsp:getProperty name="user" property="lastName"/>
```

The <jsp:setProperty> tag

We use `<jsp:setProperty>` to modify the properties of beans. The `<jsp:setProperty>` tag can be used anywhere within the page to modify a bean's properties, provided that the property has been made writable by the bean developer. We modify property values of a bean either to control specifics of the bean's operation or access its services. The exact behavior of changing a property's value is bean specific. The bean's author might, for example, provide a `query` property that specifies a database query whose results are reflected in other properties. In that case you might call `<jsp:setProperty>` several times in the page, reading the results properties again and again, since they would return new values after each change to the `query` property.

Most service beans will require some amount of run-time configuration to be useful, because they depend on user-configurable properties that control some aspect of their behavior. This allows the same bean to be used over and over again to encapsulate different sets of information. For example, if a developer needed a bean to provide information about a registered user it would not be necessary to create a different type of bean for each user—`BobBean`, `SueBean`, `JoeBean`, and so forth. The developer would instead design the bean's properties to abstractly refer to properties of any user, and then make one of the bean's properties control which user's information is stored in the bean

The `<jsp:setProperty>` tag is relatively straightforward. It requires three attributes: `name`, `property`, and `value`. Just as in the `<jsp:getProperty>` tag, the `name` attribute specifies the bean you are working with; the `property` attribute specifies which of the bean's properties you wish to set; the `value` attribute is text to which you want to set the property.

```
<jsp:setProperty name="bean name" property="property name"
                 value="property value"/>
```

The `<jsp:setProperty>` tag can be used anywhere inside the JSP document after the bean has been defined with the `<jsp:useBean>` tag. At run time JSP evaluates the tags in a page in the order they were defined, from top to bottom. Any property values that you set will only affect tags in the page that follow the `<jsp:setProperty>` tag. The `value` attribute can be specified as text or calculated at run time with JSP expressions. For example, here are a couple of ways that we can set the days since a user's last visit by setting the value of a property. Both examples are functionally equivalent, they set the `daysLeft` property to a value of `30`.

```
<jsp:setProperty name="user" property="daysLeft" value="30"/>
<jsp:setProperty name="user" property="daysLeft" value="<%= 15 * 2 %>"/>
```

Indexed properties

As we mentioned earlier, indexed properties contain a whole collection of values for the property. To access a value, you must pass the bean an index to indicate which value you are interested in. The standard JSP bean tags cannot deal with indexed properties; they can only be accessed through JSP scriptlets, expressions, and custom tags. For example, let's look at WeatherBean's forecasts property, which holds five String values, a forecast for each of the next five days. To view tomorrow's forecast we must specify the first element, which is referenced in array style notation as element 0, the next day's is element 1, and so forth. You access an indexed property through a JSP scriptlet or expression simply by calling the method behind the property and passing it an index value. To read from an indexed property, prefix it with the word get; to write to it use the prefix set. (We'll explain how properties are mapped to method names in detail in chapter 8.) To read from the forecasts property we would call the method getForecasts(). For example:

```
<B>Tomorrow's Forecast</B>: <%= weather.getForecasts(0) %> <BR>
<B>The Rest of the Week</B>
<UL>
<% for (int index=1; index < 5; index++) { %>
<LI><%= weather.getForecasts(index) %> (maybe)
<% } %>
</UL>
```

In the above example we use JSP scriptlets and expressions to access the indexed forecasts property of our WeatherBean, which has been loaded into the page with an id of weather. To display the forecast for tomorrow, we use a JSP expression to get the first element of the forecast's property by calling its access method, getForecasts(), with an argument of 0. We then use a scriptlet to loop through elements 1, 2, 3, and 4 to display a list of the forecasts for the rest of the week.

Beans with indexed properties can be designed to work more easily with JSPs so that the JSP developer doesn't have to resort to scriptlets in order to access them. A bean can include a convenience property that allows you to treat an indexed property as a single string value by separating each value with a comma or other delimiter.

7.3.3 Initializing beans

When a bean is first created it can be initialized by setting the value of its configurable properties. This initialization happens only the first time the bean is created. By default, this initialization phase will take place each time the page is accessed, since a bean is being created for each request. As we will see later when we discuss the bean life cycle, beans can also be stored in and retrieved from the environment of the web server, in which case they will not need to be reinitialized.

When a bean is first created it may be necessary to initialize it by setting the value of any properties that control its operation before we attempt to read any bean properties. We could simply use the <jsp:setProperty> tag in the page, but as we will learn later on, it is possible for beans to exist beyond the scope of a single page request, and thus it becomes important to define a separate block of initialization code for the bean.

Bean configuration

The body tag version of the `<jsp:useBean>` tag allows you to configure the bean before using it by setting any necessary properties with the `<jsp:setProperty>` tag. This form of the `<jsp:useBean>` has both start and end tags enclosing a body area as follows:

```
<jsp:useBean id="myBean" class="com.manning.jsp.MyBean">
<%-- This is the body area --%>
</jsp:useBean>
```

Any commands inside the body are processed immediately after the bean is instantiated and before it is made available to the rest of the page. For example:

```
<jsp:useBean id="clock" class="com.manning.jsp.ClockBean">
  <jsp:setProperty name="clock" property="timezone" value="CST"/>
</jsp:useBean>
```

You can think of the `<jsp:useBean>` tag's body elements as a run-once configuration phase. It is a useful way to configure the bean with page-specific configuration data or to prepare the bean for use later in the page. You can even set properties of other beans, as long as they have been created earlier in the page.

The body of the `<jsp:useBean>` tag can also contain JSP scriptlets and arbitrary HTML markup. This HTML will be displayed as part of the page only if the bean must be instantiated. (Be sure that you place such text after your opening HTML tag!) If the bean already exists in the environment, then subsequent page requests will not display this initialization HTML. For example:

```
<html>
<body>
<jsp:useBean id="clock" class="com.manning.jsp.ClockBean">
  The <b>ClockBean</b> is initializing...
</jsp:useBean>
The main page follows…
</body>
</html>
```

Initializing beans from the request

A key feature of the `<jsp:setProperty>` tag is its ability to set a bean's properties dynamically at run time using information retrieved from the page request. This allows us to dynamically configure our beans based on user input or other events by embedding the configuration information into the page request itself. The request information typically comes from an HTML form, or from request parameters hard coded into the URL. It can also be populated with values—and even entire beans—from a servlet. HTML forms provide a natural way to get input from users, fitting well into the name/value pairs associated with JavaBean properties. Like a CGI program, a JSP page can be used as a form handler by specifying its URL in the form tag's `action` attribute. Any data in the form will be accessible to the JSP page and can be used to provide information to the bean.

Example: a compound interest calculator

Listing 7.1 shows how to build a simple application that can calculate the value of compounded interest for an investment. We'll first create an HTML page with a form that will collect the necessary information to perform our calculation:

Listing 7.1 CompoundInterest.htm

```
<html>
<body>
<form action="CompoundInterestResults.jsp">
Principal: <input type="text" name="principal">
Interest Rate: <input type="text" name="interestRate">
Years: <input type="text" name="years">
<input type="submit" value="Calculate Future Value">
</form>
</body>
</html>
```

We can then create a handler for our form called `CompoundInterestResults.jsp`, which will use the values specified in the form fields to configure a bean that can calculate compounded interest. We'll actually create this bean in the next chapter, but for now let's concentrate on using this bean as a service for our page. Let's see the `CompoundInterestBean`'s property sheet, shown in table 7.3.

Table 7.3 `CompoundInterestBean` property sheet

Name	Access	Java Type	Example
`principal`	read/write	double	100.50
`interestRate`	read/write	double	.10
`years`	read/write	int	10
`futureValue`	read-only	String	155.21

The futureValue property is linked to the other properties. Its value is calculated using the values of the principal, interestRate, and years properties. To use this bean we must therefore first set the values of these three properties, then read the results from the futureValue property. Let's look at the JSP that will be the form's handler. First we must create a reference to the CompoundInterestBean.

```
<jsp:useBean id="calculator"
            class="com.taglib.wdjsp.components.CompoundInterestBean"/>
<jsp:useBean id="calculator" class="com.manning.jsp.CompoundInterestBean"/>
```

In the body of our <jsp:useBean> tag we need to map each of the bean's configuration properties to the appropriate data from the form field. The <jsp:setProperty> tag looks for an incoming request parameter matching the value specified in the param attribute of the tag. If it finds one, it tells the bean to set the corresponding property, specified via the property attribute, to that value, performing any necessary type conversion. We'll add the following three lines to the body of our <jsp:useBean> tag:

```
<jsp:setProperty name="calculator" property="principal" param="principal"/>
<jsp:setProperty name="calculator" property="interestRate"
  param="interestRate"/>
<jsp:setProperty name="calculator" property="years" param="years"/>
```

The param attribute of the <jsp:setProperty> tag is the equivalent of the JSP scriptlet <% request.getParameter("something") %>. So, the above block of code is functionally equivalent to the following, which uses scriptlets instead of the param attribute to initialize the bean's values:

```
<jsp:setProperty name="calculator" property="principal"
  value='<%= request.getParameter("principal") %>'/>
<jsp:setProperty name="calculator" property="interestRate"
  value='<%= request.getParameter("interestRate") %>'/>
<jsp:setProperty name="calculator" property="years"
  value='<%= request.getParameter("years") %>'/>
```

When the request comes in from the form, the bean's properties will be set to the form values specified by the user. Since this is such a common way of configuring beans in JSP, a shortcut has been provided. If a property name is the same as the name of the parameter passed in through the form, we can omit the param attribute. Therefore the body of our <jsp:useBean> tag could be simplified to:

```
<jsp:setProperty name="calculator" property="principal"/>
<jsp:setProperty name="calculator" property="interestRate"/>
<jsp:setProperty name="calculator" property="years"/>
```

When multiple form field names map directly to bean properties you can also use the special wild card character "*" in the place of a property name. Using a wild card indicates that you wish to set the value of any bean property whose name corresponds to the name of a request parameter. The names must match exactly as there is no way to map parameters to properties with different names when the wild card is used. For each property of the bean, a matching request parameter is looked for. Extra request parameters are ignored, though they can be accessed through scriptlets and the implicit `request` object. You can, of course, issue additional `<jsp:setProperty>` commands to pick up any request parameters whose names do not map directly to bean properties. There is no way to determine or specify the order in which the bean's properties are changed. If there are interdependencies, one property depending on another, you will want to explicitly set them by specifying a `<jsp:setProperty>` tag for each one. If we are careful to match up all of the form field names with our bean's property names, we can configure all of the bean's properties with a single statement. Using the wild card, our bean could be configured with a single line, like this:

```
<jsp:setProperty name="calculator" property="*"/>
```

Now that the bean has been configured, we can read the results of the bean's calculation in the `futureValue` property. We can also verify the input by reading the values of the properties that we just configured.

```
If you invest $<jsp:getProperty name="calculator" property="principal"/>
for <jsp:getProperty name="calculator" property="years"/> years
at an interest rate of
<jsp:getProperty name="calculator" property="interestRate"/>%
compounding monthly, you will have
$<jsp:getProperty name="calculator" property="futureValue"/>
```

The output of our JSP form handler will produce results like this:

```
If you invest $1000 for 30 years at an interest rate of 15% compounding
monthly, you will have $87,541.99
```

The JSP page is shown in its entirety in listing 7.2.

Listing 7.2 CompoundInterestResults.jsp

```
<jsp:useBean id="calculator"
            class="com.taglib.wdjsp.components.CompoundInterestBean"/>
<jsp:useBean id="calculator" class="CompoundInterestBean"/>
  <jsp:setProperty name="calculator" property="principal"/>
  <jsp:setProperty name="calculator" property="years"/>
  <jsp:setProperty name="calculator" property="interestRate"/>
```

```
</jsp:useBean>
<html>
<body>
If you invest $<jsp:getProperty name="calculator" property="principal"/>
for <jsp:getProperty name="calculator" property="years"/> years
at an interest rate of
<jsp:getProperty name="calculator" property="interestRate"/>%
compounding monthly, you will have
$<jsp:getProperty name="calculator" property="futureValue"/>

</body>
</html>
```

JSP does not care if you are using GET or POST requests for form submission. If desired, you can also use hidden form elements to add configuration information to a form without requiring the user to enter it. You can also encode directives into the request URL directly by following standard URL encoding conventions. For example the following URL will calculate interest for us, no form needed:

```
http://host/InterestCalculator.jsp?interestRate=0.10&years=15&principal=1000
```

The properties in the URL are exactly the same as if they came from a form using the GET method of data delivery. You will need to escape any special characters of course, but you will not need to decode them in the JSP, because the JSP container handles this automatically. A word of warning on form values: do not rely on hidden fields for the storage of sensitive information like database passwords. Any form data fields in your HTML, hidden or otherwise, can be viewed quite easily by anyone viewing the source of the HTML page that contains the form data. It is all right to store sensitive information inside your JSP however, provided it is part of a bean tag or JSP scriptlets, because this data will be processed on the server and will never be seen by the client code.

WARNING You cannot use request parameters that begin with `jsp`, `jsp_`, `java.`, `javax.`, `sun.` and `com.sun.` They are reserved for the JSP container's own use and may conflict with request parameters assigned to the request by the container itself. One example of a reserved request parameter is `jsp_precompile`, used to control compilation in JSP 1.2. You can read about this precompilation feature in chapter 14.

Specifying default initialization values

If you are attempting to initialize a bean property from a request parameter that does not exist or is defined as an empty value then the `<jsp:setProperty>`

command has no effect. The property does not get set to a `null` value, the `<jsp:setProperty>` tag is just ignored. You can provide a default value for a property by first setting it explicitly, then attempting to set it from the request as shown:

```
<jsp:setProperty name="calculator" property="interestRate" value="0.10"/>
<jsp:setProperty name="calculator" property="interestRate" param="interestRate"/>
```

In this example, the `interestRate` property is set to 10 percent, but can be overwritten by the value of the `interestRate` request parameter if it exists. This allows you to supply appropriate default values for critical properties and to create flexible pages that might be accessed through several means.

A security consideration

The wild card notation introduced earlier, `<jsp:setProperty property="*">`, is a very powerful shortcut for initializing bean properties from a request. It is particularly convenient for mapping the input values from a form into a set of bean properties that perform some computation. Because it is very easy for a user to construct his or her own requests, you need to be careful about using this shorthand notation when the properties of the bean control sensitive information.

For example, consider an online banking application that represents account information via a JavaBean class named `AccountBean`. The `AccountBean` class provides properties for accessing information about the account, such as `accountNumber` and `balance`, as well as properties corresponding to account transactions, such as `withdrawalAmount` and `transferAmount`. Given a form that allows a user to specify a withdrawal amount, this form might then point to a JSP page such as the following that actually performs the transaction (as a side effect of setting the property values) and reports the result:

```
<jsp:useBean id="myAccount" class="AccountBean">
  <jsp:setProperty name="myAccount" property="*"/>
</jsp:useBean>
<html>
<head><title>Cash Withdrawal</title></head>
<body>
<p>
$<jsp:getProperty name="myAccount" property="withdrawalAmount"/>
has been withdrawn from Account
#<jsp:getProperty name="myAccount" property="accountNumber"/>.
Your new balance is $<jsp:getProperty name="myAccount" property="balance"/>.
Thank you for patronizing us at the First Bank of Orange.
```

At first glance, the code seems benign. Assuming, however, that both getters and setters are available for the bean's properties, the potential is very real. If the URL for this page were withdraw.jsp, consider the effect of a user submitting a request for:

```
http://server/account/withdraw.jsp?accountNumber=PH1L31N&balance=1000000
```

Normally, this page would be accessed as the target of a form, but there is nothing to prevent a user from manually constructing his or her own request. No withdrawal amount is specified in this URL, which presumably is not a problem, but the presence of a request parameter named `balance` seems a bit troublesome. When processing the page's `<jsp:setProperty>` tag, the JSP container will map this parameter to the bean's like-named `balance` property, and attempt to set it to $1,000,000!

One must hope the Java developer responsible for the `AccountBean` implementation will have put safeguards in place to prevent this sort of tampering, but the bottom line is that care must be taken when using the `<jsp:setProperty>` wild card. If the bean whose properties are to be set contains properties whose access must be carefully controlled (such as a bank account balance), then the bean must enforce that access control itself. Otherwise, the bean will be subject to the sort of request spoofing described here if it is ever used in conjunction with a `<jsp:setProperty>` tag employing the wildcard shortcut.

7.3.4 Controlling a bean's scope

Up to now we've been talking about using beans as ways to encapsulate data or behavior over the life span of a single page. Each time the page is requested, a new instance of a bean is created and possibly modified via `<jsp:setProperty>` tags. However JSP has a very powerful feature that allows you to specify that a bean should continue to exist beyond the scope of a single page request. Such beans are stored in the server environment and reused on multiple pages, or across multiple requests for the same page. This allows us to create a bean once and then access it throughout a user's visit to our site. Any properties that we set will remain set throughout the lifetime of the bean.

Bean accessibility and life span

A bean's accessibility and life span are controlled through the `scope` attribute of the `<jsp:useBean>` tag. The `scope` attribute can have a value of `page`, `request`, `session`, or `application`. The accessibility of a bean determines which pages or parts of a web application can access the bean and its properties. A bean's life span determines how long a particular bean exists before it is no longer accessible to any page. A summary of how each scope value affects the accessibility and life span of a bean is shown in table 7.4.

Table 7.4 Possible bean scopes

Scope	Accessibility	Life span
`page`	current page only	until page is displayed or control is forwarded to a new page
`request`	current page and any included or forwarded pages	until the request has been completely processed and the response has been sent back to the user
`session`	the current request and any subsequent request from the same browser	life of the user's session
`application`	the current and any future request that is part of the same web application	life of the application

When a bean is created on the server for reuse between pages it is identified by the name specified by the `id` attribute of its `<jsp:useBean>` tag. Any time you attempt to create a bean with the `<jsp:useBean>` tag, the server searches for an existing instance of the bean with the same `id` as specified in the tag, in the scope specified by the tag. If one is found that instance of the bean is used instead of creating one. If any configuration commands have been specified in the body of the `<jsp:useBean>` tag, they will be ignored because the bean has already been initialized. The syntax of the `scope` attribute is shown below. A bean can have only one `scope` value. You cannot combine them in any fashion; they are by definition mutually exclusive.

```
<jsp:useBean id="beanName" class="class"
scope="page|request|session|application"/>
```

Page beans

If you do not specify a scope for a bean at the time it is created through the `<jsp:useBean>` tag, it is assigned the default scope value of `page`. A bean with a page-level scope is the least accessible and shortest lived of all JSP beans. Each time the page is requested, either from a new visitor or a return visitor, an instance of the bean is created. If there are any initialization tags or scriptlets in the body of the `<jsp:useBean>` tag, these will be executed each time.

Essentially, beans with a page-level scope are transient—they are not persistent between requests. For that matter, such beans are not accessible outside of the page itself. If you use the `<jsp:include>` or `<jsp:forward>` tags, any beans with only page-level scope will not be available within the new or included page. If a page referenced by one of these tags contains `<jsp:useBean>` tags specifying a bean with the same `id` as a bean created on the parent page, they will ignore the original bean because it is out of scope, and will be forced to create their own new instance of the bean instead. Since the default scope of the <jsp:useBean> tag is page-level, there is no difference between these two tags:

```
<jsp:useBean id="bean1" class="com.manning.jsp.ClockBean"/>
<jsp:useBean id="bean2" class="com.manning.jsp.ClockBean scope="page"/>
```

If a bean does not need to persist between requests, or its information is of no use after the request has been completed, it's probably a good candidate for page-level scope. For example, if our ClockBean is initialized to the current time and date the first time it is created then it probably doesn't do any good to keep it around for very long. If you are using the <jsp:include> or <jsp:forward> tags however, you may need to set the scope of your bean to request-level so it can be accessed from within these supplemental pages.

Request beans

If you specify a value of request for the scope attribute of a <jsp:useBean> tag the JSP container will attempt to retrieve the bean from the request itself. Since the HTTP protocol does not provide a mechanism that would allow a web browser to store anything other than simple name value pairs into the request, a bean can only be stored in the request by a servlet or another JSP page on the local server. Beans are stored in the request as request attributes, a feature added to Java Servlets in the 2.2 API which we cover in chapter 8. If the bean is not initially found in the request it will be created and placed there.

The life span for a bean with request-level scope is essentially the same as one with page scope except that the bean's accessibility will be extended to pages referenced with the <jsp:include> and <jsp:forward> tags. This gives the request scope a dual purpose. First, it allows you to use Java servlets to create a bean and forward it to your JSP page. Second, it gives you a way to extend the reach of bean to pages that are included in or forwarded from the original page.

For example, consider the situation where you include a footer at the bottom of each page via the <jsp:include> tag, and want to include page specific data. If you place the data into the page scope however, it will not be accessible by the included footer. The desired effect can be accomplished by storing your information in a bean with request scope, assuring that if present it will be seen by the footer, as well as the current page. In this example, we associate a contact name with each page, which appears in the footer.

```
<jsp:useBean id="contact" class="jsp.ContactBean" scope="request">
  <jsp:setProperty name="contact" property="name" value="Kris DeHart"/>
</jsp:useBean>
<html>
```

```
<body>
Welcome to our web site!
<jsp:include file="/footers/standardFooter.jsp" flush="true"/>
</body>
</html>
```

In this example, `contact` will be accessible from both the current page and `standardFooter.jsp`, which is an HTML excerpt which looks like this:

```
<HR>
To request changes to this page contact
<jsp:getProperty name="contact" property="name"/>
```

This example of building up a page by including smaller, component pages to build a larger composite one is a useful technique for designing complex pages. It will be discussed in detail in chapter 8.

Session beans

The session scope introduces component persistence to JSP, and is one of its most powerful constructs. Unlike the request and page scopes, a bean with a scope attribute value of `session` exists beyond the life of a single request because it is placed into the user's session object. Recall from our discussion of JSP session management in chapter 4 that the JSP container maintains a unique session object for each user visiting the site. Placing a bean into session scope stores it in this session object, using the value of the `id` attribute as its identifier.

A bean does not have to do anything special to support such persistence; the JSP container itself will handle the necessary state maintenance whenever you place a bean into the session through the `scope` attribute. Once the bean is stored in a user's session it will be available to any other JSP on the server. If you call up a bean with the `<jsp:useBean>` tag that already exists in the session, the identifier that you specify will refer to the existing instance of the bean, rather then creating a new one.

Since it is the JSP container that determines the length of time a session bean exists, its lifetime might be minutes, hours, or days. Some JSP containers, like IBM's WebSphere, can write session data to disk when the server is shut down, and restore the sessions upon restart. A container with such a capability effectively gives the beans an infinite life span. Not all containers exhibit this behavior so it's not currently a feature you can rely on. If you need to store information for an indefinite length of time, or the session will be used to store critical data, you should consider storing your information in a database instead. Typically, most containers will let session data expire after it hasn't been accessed for a few hours.

TIP If you have used the `<%@ page session="false" %>` to indicate that your page does not require session support you will be unable to add beans to or fetch them from the current session! The default value of the session attribute is `true`, enabling session support. If you have no need for session support however, you set this attribute to `false` to prevent the servlet container from creating needless, wasteful session objects in memory. The session implicit object will not be available to pages where the session attribute has been set to `false` and will result in a run-time exception.

Sessions are useful for storing information collected through a user's visit to the site and for caching information that is frequently needed at the page level. Sessions can be used to pass information from page to page without each one needing to include the logic or additional processing time required to access information stored in a database or external resource. A shopping cart is a good example of session-oriented data. A user would like a shopping cart's contents to be accessible throughout the JSP application, so we create a `ShoppingCartBean` and store it in the user's session. At each page we can include a reference to the shopping cart, allowing us to display a running total if we wish. There is an example of how to build your own JSP shopping cart in chapter 14.

As a simple example, let's look at how we would use a `TimerBean` to report to us how long a user's session has been active. We can use such a bean to log the person out after a period of inactivity or to record time-sensitive visits like completing an online survey or exam. Our `TimerBean` has one basic function: to report the difference between its creation time and the current time. This bean, which we'll develop in chapter 8, has the properties shown in its property sheet, table 7.5.

Table 7.5 TimerBean properties

Name	Access	Java Type	Example
`elapsedMillis`	read-only	long	180000
`elapsedSeconds`	read-only	long	180
`elapsedMinutes`	read-only	long	3
`startTime`	read/write	long	857374234

The `startTime` property is intended to provide a way to affect the bean's start time by either setting it to a particular time (expressed in milliseconds since the epoch), or the current time by passing it a zero or negative value.

Here's a simple use of the bean that on the first load will start the clock, and display the elapsed time every subsequent load—providing of course that the time between visits does not exceed the JSP container's session timeout value.

```
<jsp:useBean id="timer" class="com.manning.jsp.TimerBean" scope="session"/>
<html>
<body>
Elapsed Time:
<jsp:getProperty name="timer" property="elapsedMinutes"/> minutes
</body>
</html>
```

If we wanted to add this functionality to a whole series of pages, we could include the appropriate bean tags in their own file, which we then call with the `<jsp:include>` tag. This example, taken from a web-based quiz application, uses the `TimerBean` through an included file to display the elapsed time in the footer of each page:

```
<html>
<body>
<form action="/servlet/processQuestions/6">
<b>Question 6</b><br>
What is the airspeed velocity of an unlaiden European swallow?
<br> <input type="text" name="answer">
<br> <input type="submit" value="Submit Answer">
</form>
<jsp:include page="/footers/ElapsedTimeFooter.html" flush="true"/>
</body>
</html>
```

Here are the contents of the `ElapsedTimedFooter.html` file:

```
<jsp:useBean id="timer" class="com.manning.jsp.TimerBean" scope="session"/>
<hr>
Remember, speed is a factor in this exam!<BR>
Time Used: <jsp:getProperty name="timer" property="elapsedSeconds"/> seconds
```

We can even have several different instances of `TimerBean` running at once, as long as they have different identifiers. It is the `id` attribute of the `<jsp:useBean>` tag that is important in distinguishing between different instances of a bean, whether referencing it from within the page or searching for it in the session.

TIP The default lifetime of a session is determined by the JSP container (or more accurately, the servlet container). Beginning with the Servlet API 2.2, the `HttpSession` interfaces's `getMaxInactiveInterval()` and `setMax-InactiveInterval()` methods can be used to view or set the timeout variables. The `getLastAccessedTime()` method of this interface can tell you how long it has been since the data in the session was last accessed.

Application beans

A bean with a scope value of `application` has an even broader life cycle and further reaching availability than a session bean. Beans with `application` scope are associated with a given JSP application on the server. A JSP application is a collection of JSP pages, HTML pages, images, applets, and other resources that are bundled together under a particular URL hierarchy. Application beans exist throughout the life of the JSP container itself, meaning that they are not reclaimed until the server is shut down—they do not expire after a few hours or days. Unlike session beans that are available only to subsequent requests from a given user, application beans are shared by all users of the application with which they are associated. Any JSP page that is part of an application can access application beans created by other pages within that application. We will explain how to create the packaged JSP applications themselves in chapter 14.

The application scope is used to store information that is useful throughout the application and not specific to the individual page requesting access to the bean. Once a bean is placed into application scope it will be used by pages throughout the site. If the bean requires any configuration information it must be page independent. If you expect configuration information to change between page requests or between users, it is probably not a good candidate for application scope.

When a bean is stored in application scope there is only one instance of the bean per server. You should be very cautious about changing an application bean's property once it has been stored in the application because any changes you make to the properties will instantly affect all of the JSP pages which reference the bean.

Another good use of the `application` scope is the ability to cache application information that would be too computationally expensive to generate for each individual page request. For example, say that all of the pages of your online catalog needed access to a table of shipping rates. This information can be encapsulated into a bean and placed into the application scope. This would mean that the data would have to be collected from the database only once, conserving not only database access time but server memory as well. In each page you simply reference the bean as normal, if it has not yet been instantiated and placed into the application, the server will handle it:

```
<jsp:useBean id="ship" class="com.manning.ShipRateBean" scope="application"/>
<html>
<body>
Current shipping charges are:
<jsp:getProperty name="ship" property="baseCharge"/>
per shipment plus
<jsp:getProperty name="ship" property="perItemCharge"/>
per each item shipped.
</body>
</html>
```

If the bean requires any configuration you should use the body of the `<jsp:useBean>` tag to set your initial property values. Since you would have to do this on each and every page users might enter, you will probably want to seek alternatives in this situation. First, you could use application-specific beans which require no special configuration or whose constructor's collect configuration information from another source (such as a property file). Second, you could take steps to assure that the necessary bean is placed into the application scope prior to the time any of the dependent pages would need to access the bean. Or, you can serialize your preconfigured beans off to disk, and restore them as needed.

Scope and the type attribute

The `type` attribute of the `<jsp:useBean>` tag is generally only used when dealing with beans that are expected to be in scope and that are subclasses of some higher base class. If the bean exists in the current scope (say in the request or session), but you have no way of knowing its exact type, you can simply specify its base class through the type attribute. For example, a servlet or other JSP page placed a collection of objects into your session. You know that the objects are in some derivative of Java's `Collection` interface, but have no way of knowing if the other pages used a `List`, a `Set`, a `ListArray`, or anything else. In this case you simply reference the common `Collection` interface as the bean's type; there is no need to specify a class in this case. For example:

```
<jsp:useBean id="elements" type="java.util.Collection" scope="session"/>
```

8 Developing JSP components

This chapter covers

- The JavaBeans API
- Developing your own JSP components
- Mixing scriptlets and beans

This chapter will help developers create their own JavaBeans for use as JSP components, and teach web designers how they are implemented behind the scenes. Fortunately, it is not necessary to understand all of the details of JavaBeans development to work with JSP. As component architectures go, the interface between JavaServer Pages and JavaBeans is quite simple, as we will see.

8.1 What makes a bean a bean?

So what makes a bean so special? A bean is simply a Java class that follows a set of simple naming and design conventions outlined by the JavaBeans specification. Beans are not required to extend a specific base class or implement a particular interface. If a class follows these bean conventions, and you treat it like a bean—then it is a bean. A particularly good thing about the bean conventions is that they are rooted in sound programming practices that you may already be following to some extent.

8.1.1 Bean conventions

The JavaBean conventions are what enable us to develop beans because they allow a bean container to analyze a Java class file and interpret its methods as properties, designating the class as a JavaBean. The conventions dictate rules for defining a bean's constructor and the methods that will define its properties.

The JavaBeans API

Following the conventions specified by the JavaBeans API allows the JSP container to interact with beans at a programmatic level, even though the containing application has no real understanding of what the bean does or how it works. For JSP we are primarily concerned with the aspects of the API that dictate the method signatures for a bean's constructors and property access methods.

Beans are just objects

Like any other Java class, instances of bean classes are simply Java objects. As a result, you always have the option of referencing beans and their methods directly through Java code in other classes or through JSP scripting elements. Because they follow the JavaBeans conventions, we can work with them a lot easier than by writing Java code. Bean containers, such as a JSP container, can provide easy access to beans and their properties. Following the JavaBeans API coding conventions, as we will see, means creating methods that control access to each property we wish to define for our bean. Beans can also have regular methods like any other Java object. However,

JSP developers will have to use scriptlets, expressions, or custom tags to access them since a bean container can manipulate a bean only through its properties.

Class naming conventions

You might have noticed that in most of our examples bean classes often include the word bean in their name, such as `UserBean`, `AlarmClockBean`, `DataAccessBean`, and so forth. While this is a common approach that lets other developers immediately understand the intended role of the class, it is not a requirement for a bean to be used inside a JSP page or any other bean container. Beans follow the same class-naming rules as other Java classes: they must start with an alphabetic character, contain only alphanumeric and underscore characters, and be case sensitive. Additionally, like other Java classes it is common, but not required, to start the name of a bean class with a capital letter.

The magic of introspection

How can the JSP container interact with any bean object without the benefit of a common interface or base class to fall back on? Java manages this little miracle through a process called *introspection* that allows a class to expose its methods and capabilities on request. The introspection process happens at run time, and is controlled by the bean container. It is introspection that allows us to rely on conventions to establish properties.

Introspection occurs through a mechanism known as *reflection*, which allows the bean container to examine any class at run time to determine its method signatures. The bean container determines what properties a bean supports by analyzing its public methods for the presence of methods that meet criteria defined by the JavaBeans API. For a property to exist, its bean class must define an access method to return the value of the property, change the value of the property, or both. It is the presence of these specially named access methods alone that determine the properties of a bean class, as we will soon see.

8.1.2 The bean constructor

The first rule of JSP bean building is that you must implement a constructor that takes no arguments. It is this constructor that the JSP container will use to instantiate your bean through the `<jsp:useBean>` tag. Every Java class has a constructor method that is used to create instances of the class. If a class does not explicitly specify any constructors, then a default zero-argument constructor is assumed. Because of this default constructor rule the following Java class is perfectly valid, and technically satisfies the bean conventions:

```
public class DoNothingBean { }
```

This bean has no properties and can't do or report anything useful, but it is a bean nonetheless. We can create new instances of it, reference it from scriptlets, and control its scope. Here is a better example of a class suitable for bean usage, a bean which knows the time. This class has a zero-argument constructor that records the time of its instantiation:

```
package com.taglib.wdjsp.components;
import java.util.*;

public class CurrentTimeBean {
  private int hours;
  private int minutes;

  public CurrentTimeBean() {
    Calendar now = Calendar.getInstance();
    this.hours = now.get(Calendar.HOUR_OF_DAY);
    this.minutes = now.get(Calendar.MINUTE);
  }
}
```

We've used the constructor to initialize the bean's instance variables `hours` and `minutes` to reflect the current time at instantiation. The constructor of a bean is the appropriate place to initialize instance variables and prepare the instance of the class for use. Of course to be useful within a JSP page we will need to define some properties for the bean and create the appropriate access methods to control them.

8.1.3 Defining a bean's properties

As we've mentioned, a bean's properties are defined simply by creating appropriate access methods for them. Access methods are used either to retrieve a property's value or make changes to it. A method used to retrieve a property's value is called a *getter* method, while a method that modifies its value is called a *setter* method. Together these methods are generally referred to as *access methods*—they provide access to values stored in the bean's properties.

To define properties for a bean simply create a `public` method with the name of the property you wish to define, prefixed with the word `get` or `set` as appropriate. Getter methods should return the appropriate data type, while the corresponding setter method should be declared void and accept one argument of the appropriate type. It is the `get` or `set` prefix that is Java's clue that you are defining a property. The signature for property access methods, then, is:

```
public void setPropertyName(PropertyType value);
public PropertyType getPropertyName();
```

For example, to define a property called `rank`, which can be used to store text, and is both readable and writable, we would need to create methods with these signatures:

```
public void setRank(String rank);
public String getRank();
```

Likewise, to create a property called `age` that stores numbers:

```
public void setAge(int age);
public int getAge();
```

NOTE Making your property access methods `public` is more than a good idea, it's the law! Exposing your bean's access methods by declaring them `public` is the only way that JSP pages will be able to call them. The JSP container will not recognize properties without `public` access methods.

Conversely, if the actual data being reflected by the component's properties is stored in instance variables it should be purposely hidden from other classes. Such instance variables should be declared `private` or at least `protected`. This helps ensure that developers restrict their interaction with the class to its access methods and not its internal workings. Otherwise, a change to the implementation might negatively impact code dependent on the older version of the component.

Let's revisit our previous example and make it more useful. We will add a couple of properties to our `CurrentTimeBean` called `hours` and `minutes`, that will allow us to reference the current time in the page. These properties must meet the getter method signatures defined by the JavaBeans design patterns. They therefore should look like this:

```
public int getHours();
public int getMinutes();
```

In our constructor we store the current time's hours and minutes into instance variables. We can have our properties reference these variables and return their value where appropriate. The source for this bean is shown in listing 8.1.

Listing 8.1 CurrentTimeBean.java

```
package com.taglib.wdjsp.components;
import java.util.*;

public class CurrentTimeBean {
  private int hours;
```

```
  private int minutes;

  public CurrentTimeBean() {
    Calendar now = Calendar.getInstance();
    this.hours = now.get(Calendar.HOUR_OF_DAY);
    this.minutes = now.get(Calendar.MINUTE);
  }

  public int getHours() {
    return hours;
  }

  public int getMinutes() {
    return minutes;
  }
}
```

That's all there is to it. These two methods simply return the appropriate values as stored in the instance variables. Since they meet the JavaBean rules for naming access methods, we have just defined two properties that we can access through JSP Bean tags. For example:

```
<jsp:useBean id="time" class="CurrentTimeBean"/>
<html><body>
It is now <jsp:getProperty name="time" property="minutes"/>
minutes past the hour.
</body></html>
```

Properties should not be confused with instance variables, even though instance variables are often mapped directly to property names but properties of a bean are not required to correspond directly with instance variables. A bean's properties are defined by the method names themselves, not the variables or implementation behind them. This leaves the bean designer free to alter the inner workings of the bean without altering the interface and collection of properties that you expose to users of the bean.

As an example of dynamically generating property values, here is a bean that creates random numbers in its property access methods rather than simply returning a copy of an instance variable. Its code is shown in listing 8.2.

Listing 8.2 DiceBean.java

```
package com.taglib.wdjsp.components;
import java.util.*;

public class DiceBean {
  private Random rand;
  public DiceBean() {
```

```
    rand = new Random();
  }

  public int getDieRoll() {
    // return a number between 1 and 6
    return rand.nextInt(6) + 1;
  }

  public int getDiceRoll() {
    // return a number between 2 and 12
    return getDieRoll() + getDieRoll();
  }
}
```

In this example, our `dieRoll` and `diceRoll` properties are not managed by instance variables. Instead, we create a `java.util.Random` object in the constructor and call its random number generator from our access methods to dynamically generate property values. In fact, nowhere in the bean are any static values stored for these properties—their values are recomputed each time the properties are requested.

You are not required to create both getter and setter methods for each property you wish to provide for a bean. If you wish to make a property read-only then define a getter method without providing a corresponding setter method. Conversely creating only a setter method specifies a write-only property. The latter might be useful if the bean uses the property value internally to affect other properties but is not a property that you want clients manipulating directly.

Property name conventions

A common convention is that property names are mixed case, beginning with a lowercase letter and uppercasing the first letter of each word in the property name. For the properties `firstName` and `lastName` for example, the corresponding getter methods would be `getFirstName()` and `getLastName()`. Note the case difference between the property names and their access methods. Not to worry, the JSP container is smart enough to convert the first letter to uppercase when constructing the target getter method. If the first two or more letters of a property name are uppercased, for example `URL`, then the JSP container assumes that you really mean it, so its corresponding access methods would be `getURL()` and `setURL()`.

TIP **Naming Properties**—One situation that often leads to confusing property names is acronyms. For example consider a property representing an identification number. It could be `getId` or `getID`, making the bean property `id` or `ID`. This leads to more confusion (and ugly method names) when you combine acronyms with additional words using capatilization of their own.

For example something like an accessor for an XML document, is that `getXMLDocument` or `getXmlDocument`? Is the property name `xmlDocument`, `XMLDocument`, or `XmlDocument`? To keep down confusion and improve consistency, you should only capitalize the first letter of acronyms. Without this rule teams tend to end up with several variations for the same basic property throughout their code base. It is first and foremost consistent and predictable and also clearly deliniates multiple word property names through capitalization. So a property method representing a Social Security number is immediately understood to be `getUserSsn` with a property name of `userSsn`. It may look funny, but you'll be amazed how much confusion it avoids.

8.1.4 Indexed properties

Bean properties are not limited to single values. Beans can also contain multivalued properties. For example, you might have a property named `contacts` that is used to store a list of objects of type `Contact`, containing phone and address information. Such a property would be used in conjunction with scriptlets or a custom iteration tag to step through the individual values. Each value must be of the same type; a single indexed property cannot contain both string and integer elements, for example.

To define an indexed valued property you have two options. The first style is creating an access method that returns the entire set of properties as a single array. In this case, a JSP page author or iterative custom tag can determine the size of the set and iterate through it. For example:

```
public PropertyType[] getProperty()
```

In the second option, you can access elements of the set by using an index value. This allows you additional flexibility. For example you might want to access only particular contacts from the collection.

```
public PropertyType getProperty(int index)
```

While not specifically required by JavaBean conventions, it is useful to implement both styles for a multivalued property. It's not much more work and it adds a good deal more flexibility in using the bean.

To set multivalue properties there are setter method signatures analogous to the getter method naming styles described earlier. The syntax for these methods is:

```
public void setProperty(int index, PropertyType value)
public void setProperty(PropertyType[] values)
```

Another type of method commonly implemented and recognized by bean containers is the `size()` method that can be used to determine the size of an indexed property. A typical implementation would be:

```
public int getPropertySize()
```

This is another method that is not required but increases the flexibility of the design to give page developers more options with which to work.

Example: a bean with indexed properties

In this example we will build a component that can perform statistical calculations on a series of numbers. The numbers themselves are stored in a single, indexed property. Other properties of the bean hold the value of statistical calculations like the average or the sum. This `StatBean`'s source code is shown in listing 8.3:

Listing 8.3 StatBean.java

```
package com.taglib.wdjsp.components;
import java.util.*;

public class StatBean {
  private double[] numbers;

  public StatBean() {
    numbers = new double[2];
    numbers[0] = 1;
    numbers[1] = 2;
  }

  public double getAverage() {
    double sum = 0;
    for (int i=0; i < numbers.length; i++)
      sum += numbers[i];
    return sum/numbers.length;
  }

  public double[] getNumbers() {
    return numbers;
  }

  public double getNumbers(int index) {
    return numbers[index];
  }

  public void setNumbers(double[] numbers) {
    this.numbers = numbers;
  }

  public void setNumbers(int index, double value) {
    numbers[index] = value;
```

```
    }
    public int getNumbersSize() {
      return numbers.length;
    }
}
```

Since the JSP bean tags deal exclusively with scalar properties, the only way to interact with indexed properties such as these is through JSP scriptlets and expressions. In this JSP page we'll use a JSP scriptlet in the body of the `<jsp:useBean>` tag to pass an array of integers to the bean's `numbers` property. We'll have to use a scriptlet to display back the numbers themselves, but we can use a `<jsp:getProperty>` tag to display the average. The page is shown in listing 8.4:

Listing 8.4 stats.jsp

```
<jsp:useBean id="stat" class="com.taglib.wdjsp.StatBean">
  <%
  double[] mynums = {100, 250, 150, 50, 450};
  stat.setNumbers(mynums);
  %>
</jsp:useBean>
<html>
<body>
The average of
<%
double[] numbers = stat.getNumbers();
for (int i=0; i < numbers.length; i++) {
  if (i != numbers.length)
    out.print(numbers[i] + ",");
  else
    out.println("" + numbers[i]);
}
%>
is equal to
<jsp:getProperty name="stat" property="average"/>
</body>
</html>
```

The use of custom tags, a technique that we will discuss in chapters 18 and 19, can greatly aid in working with indexed properties by eliminating the need for inline code by encapsulating common functionality into simple tag elements. With custom tags, we could eliminate the need for Java code in this example. We can also move this code inside the bean, which is what we'll do for now.

Accessing indexed values through JSP bean tags

We might also want to include a method that will enable us to pass in the array of numbers through a standard bean tag. Since bean tags deal exclusively with single values, we will have to perform the conversion ourselves in the property access methods. We'll create another pair of access methods that treat the array as a list of numbers stored in a comma delimited string. To differentiate between these two approaches, we will map the `String` versions of our new access methods to a new property we will call `numbersList`. Note that even though we are using a different property name, it is still modifying the same internal data, and will cause changes in the `average` and `numbers` properties. (Another example of this technique can be found in the Whois example of chapter 17.)

```
public void setNumbersList(String values) {
  Vector n = new Vector();
  StringTokenizer tok = new StringTokenizer(values, ",");
  while (tok.hasMoreTokens())
    n.addElement(tok.nextToken());
  numbers = new double[n.size()];
  for (int i=0; i < numbers.length; i++)
     numbers[i] = Double.parseDouble((String) n.elementAt(i));
}

public String getNumbersList() {
  String list = new String();
  for (int i=0; i < numbers.length; i++) {
    if (i != (numbers.length -1))
      list += numbers[i] + ",";
    else
      list += "" + numbers[i];
  }
  return list;
}
```

Now we can access this bean through JSP tags alone, as shown in listing 8.5.

Listing 8.5 stats2.jsp

```
<jsp:useBean id="stat" class="com.taglib.wdjsp.components.StatBean">
  <jsp:setProperty name="stat" property="numbersList" value="100,250,150,50,450" />
</jsp:useBean>
<html>
<body>
The average of <jsp:getProperty name="stat" property="numbersList" />
is equal to
<jsp:getProperty name="stat" property="average" />
</body>
</html>
```

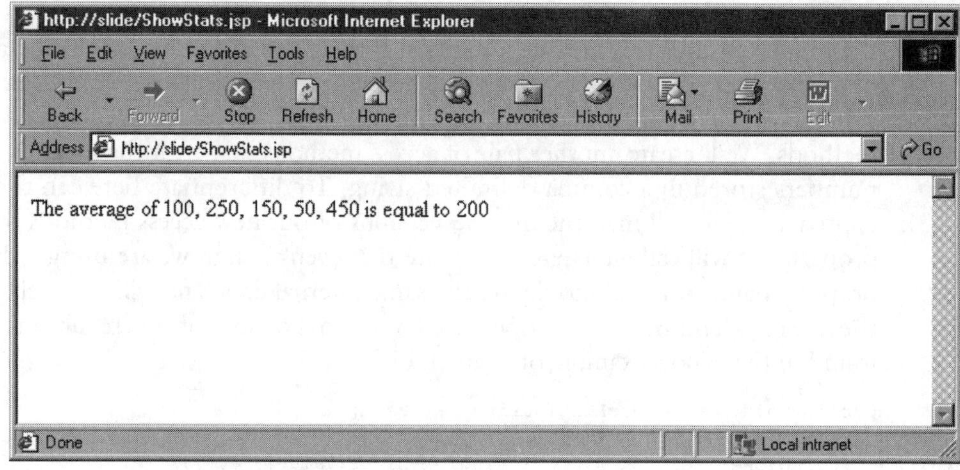

Figure 8.1 The ShowStat's page in action

The resulting display is shown in figure 8.1.

8.1.5 Implementing bean properties as cursors

Another technique for exposing the indexed properties of beans is creating a cursor. If you are familiar with JDBC's `ResultSet` class, or the `CachedRowSet` class of JDBC 2.0, then you can probably guess where we're headed. The idea here is to move the index inside the bean class as an instance variable, allowing us to access each indexed property though the `<jsp:getProperty>` tags by simply iterating the index. We provide a `next()` method which increments the index, returning `false` when the index counter has gone past the end of the list. This greatly reduces the amount of scriptlet code in the page, without introducing the complexity of custom tags. An example of a page using this technique is shown in listing 8.6. The `PlanetBean` referenced in the page is shown in listing 8.7 and the resulting display is shown in figure 8.2.

Listing 8.6 planets.jsp

```
<html>
<body bgcolor="white">
<jsp:useBean id="planet" class="wdjsp.PlanetBean"/>
<table border="1">
<tr><th>Planet</th> <th>Number of Moons</th></tr>
<% while (planet.next()) { %>
<tr><td><jsp:getProperty name="planet" property="name"/></td>
```

```
<td align="center"><jsp:getProperty name="planet" property="moons"/></td></tr>
<% } %>
</table>
</body>
</html>
```

Listing 8.7 PlanetBean.java

```
package wdjsp;

public class PlanetBean {
  private static final int numPlanets = 9;
  private static final String[] names = {
    "Mercury", "Venus", "Earth", "Mars", "Jupiter", "Saturn", "Uranus",
    "Neptune", "Pluto" };
  private static final int[] moons =
    { 0, 0, 1, 2, 16, 18, 20, 8, 1 };

  private int index;

  public PlanetBean() {
    index = -1;
  }

  public void first() {
    index = -1;
  }

  public boolean next() {
    index++;
    if (index >= numPlanets) {
      index--;
      return false;
    }
    else {
      return true;
    }
  }

  public String getName() {
    return names[index];
  }

  public int getMoons() {
    return moons[index];
  }
}
```

The `while` loop continues calling `next()`, incrementing the index, until it reaches the end of the list. Each time through, the index is pointing at a different planet's

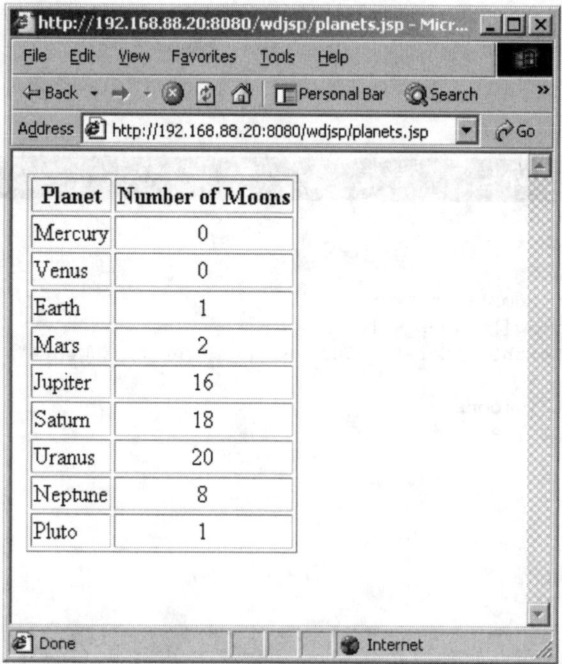

Figure 8.2 Output of planet.jsp

data. We can then use our JSP bean tags to retrieve the corresponding properties. Although we didn't use it in this example, we provided a `first()` method to rollback the index to just prior to first element. This lets us rewind if we need to display the list again. As this is a simple example, we've not implemented bounds checking on the properties.

8.1.6 Boolean properties

For boolean properties that hold only true or false values, you can elect to use another bean convention for getter methods. This convention is to prefix the property name with the word `is` and return a boolean result. For example, consider these method signatures:

```
public boolean isProperty();
public boolean isEnabled();
public boolean isAuthorized();
```

The container will automatically look for this form of method if it cannot find a property access method matching the getter syntax discussed earlier. Setting the value of a boolean property is no different then the setter methods for other properties.

```
public void setProperty(boolean b);
public void setEnabled(boolean b);
public void setAuthorized(boolean b);
```

8.1.7 *JSP type conversion*

A JSP component's properties are not limited to `String` values, but it is important to understand that all property values accessed through the `<jsp:getProperty>` tag will be converted into a `String`. A getter method need not return a `String` explicitly, however, as the JSP container will automatically convert the return value into a `String`. For the Java primitive types, conversion is handled by the methods shown in table 8.1

Table 8.1 Type conversions for `<jsp:getProperty>`

Property Type	Conversion to String
`boolean`	`java.lang.Boolean.toString(boolean)`
`byte`	`java.lang.Byte.toString(byte)`
`char`	`java.lang.Character.toString(char)`
`double`	`java.lang.Double.toString(double)`
`int`	`java.lang.Integer.toString(int)`
`float`	`java.lang.Float.toString(float)`
`long`	`java.lang.Long.toString(long)`
`object`	calls the Object's `toString()` method

Likewise, all property setter methods accessed with a `<jsp:setProperty>` tag will be automatically converted from a `String` to the appropriate native type by the JSP container. This is accomplished via methods of Java's wrapper classes as shown in table 8.2.

Table 8.2 Type conversions for `<jsp:setProperty>`

Property Type	Conversion from String
`boolean` or `Boolean`	`java.lang.Boolean.valueOf(String)`
`byte` or `Byte`	`java.lang.Byte.valueOf(String)`
`char` or `Character`	`java.lang.Character.valueOf(String)`
`double` or `Double`	`java.lang.Double.valueOf(String)`

Table 8.2 Type conversions for `<jsp:setProperty>` (continued)

Property Type	Conversion from String
`int` or `Integer`	`java.lang.Integer.valueOf(String)`
`float` or `Float`	`java.lang.Float.valueOf(String)`
`long` or `Long`	`java.lang.Long.valueOf(String)`
object	as if `new String(String)`

Properties are not restricted to primitive types. For objects, the JSP container will invoke the object's `toString()` method, which, unless you have overloaded it, will probably not be very representative of the data stored in the object. For properties holding objects rather than a String or native Java type you can set the property indirectly, for example allowing the user to set the hours and minutes separately through a pair of write-only properties and having a single read-only property called time.

Handling properties with null values

Property getter methods for Java's primitive types such as `int` and `double` cannot return a `null` value, which is only valid for methods that return objects. Sometimes however, a property really is undefined. For example, if a property represents a user's age, and a call to the database reveals that we don't know their age, what do we return? While not that critical in many applications, it may be important to some. In this case, we can simply establish a convention for this property, which says if the age is a negative number then we don't have any idea what the age is—it is undefined. It is up to the JSP developer in this case to understand the convention and react to such a situation accordingly.

Unfortunately, it's not always that easy. How would we handle a temperature reading, where negative numbers are perfectly valid? We could still pick an unreasonable number, like `-999`, as an indicator that this particular value is unknown. However, such an approach is not only messy—requiring too much in-depth understanding by the JSP designer—it is also dangerous. Who knows what will be a reasonable value for this application (or its decedents) ten years from now? A better approach to this problem is to add a boolean property which can verify the legitimacy of the property in question. In that case, it doesn't matter what the property is actually set to. For example we would define both a `getTempReading()` and `isValidTempReading()` methods.

8.1.8 Configuring beans

Many times a bean will require run-time configuration by the page initializing it before it can properly perform its tasks. Since we can't pass information into the bean's constructor we have to use the bean's properties to hold configuration information. We do this by setting the appropriate property values immediately after the container instantiates the bean in the body of the `<jsp:useBean>` tag or anywhere in the page before the bean's properties are accessed. It can be useful to set a flag in your class to indicate whether or not an instance is in a useful state, toggling the flag when all of the necessary properties have been set.

Even though the bean tags do not allow you to pass any arguments into a bean's constructor, you can still define constructors that take arguments. You will not however, be able to call them through bean tags. You can only instantiate an object requiring arguments in its constructor through a JSP scriptlet. For example:

```
<% Thermostat t = new Thermostat(78); %>
The thermostat was set at a temperature
of <%= t.getTemp() %> degrees.
```

One technique we have found useful is to provide a single method that handles all configuration steps. This method can be called by your constructors that take arguments, for use outside of bean tags, as well as by your property access methods once all the necessary properties have been configured. In this example we'll provide two constructors for this `Thermostat` class, as well as an `init()` method which would handle any necessary internal configuration. The zero argument constructor is provided for bean compatibility, calling the constructor which takes an initial temperature argument with a default value. Our `init()` method is then called through this alternate constructor.

```
public class Thermostat {
  private int temp;
  private int maxTemp;
  private int minTemp;
  private int fuelType;

  public Thermostat() {
    // no argument constructor for Bean use
    this(75);
  }

  public Thermostat(int temp) {
    this.temp = temp;
    init();
  }

  public void setTemp(int temp) {
    this.temp = temp;
```

```
    // initialize settings with this temp
    init();
  }
  public int getTemp() {
    return temp;
  }
  private void init() {
    maxTemp = this.temp + 10;
    minTemp = this.temp - 15;
    if (maxTemp > 150)
      fuelType = Fuels.DILITHIUM;
    else
      fuelType = Fuels.NATURALGAS;
  }
}
```

8.2 Some examples

In this section we will present a number of more detailed examples of creating JavaBeans for use in JSP. These examples are more in-depth than the ones we've been looking at so far, and they will help give you the feel for developing more complex components. For additional examples, see the beans we develop in chapters 9 and 11.

8.2.1 Example: a TimerBean

In the previous chapter we used a `TimerBean` to track the amount of time a user has been active in the current browsing session. In the bean's constructor we simply need to record the current time, which we will use as our starting time, into an instance variable:

```
private long start;

public TimerBean() {
  start = System.currentTimeMillis();
}
```

The `elapsedMillis` property should return the number of milliseconds that has elapsed since the session began. The first time we place a `TimerBean` into the session with a `<jsp:useBean>` tag, the JSP container will create a new instance of the bean, starting our timer. To calculate the elapsed time we simply compute the difference between the current time and our starting time:

```
public long getElapsedMillis() {
  long now = System.currentTimeMillis();
  return now - start;
}
```

The other property access methods are simply conversions applied to the elapsed milliseconds. We have chosen to have our `minutes` and `seconds` properties return whole numbers rather than floating points to simplify the display of properties within the JSP page and eliminate the issues of formatting and precision. If the application using our bean needs a finer degree of resolution, it can access the `milliseconds` property and perform the conversions themselves. You are often better off reducing component complexity by limiting the properties (and corresponding methods) you provide with the component. We have found it helpful to focus on the core functionality we are trying to provide, rather than attempt to address every possible use of the component.

```
public long getElapsedSeconds() {
  return (long)this.getElapsedMillis() / 1000;
}

public long getElapsedMinutes() {
  return (long)this.getElapsedMillis() / 60000;
}
```

For convenience we will add a method to restart the timer by setting our start to the current time. We'll then make this method accessible through the JSP bean tags by defining the necessary access methods for a `startTime` property and interpreting an illegal argument to `setStartTime()` as a request to reset the timer.

```
public void reset() {
  start = System.currentTimeMillis();
}

public long getStartTime() {
  return start;
}

public void setStartTime(long time) {
  if (time <= 0)
    reset();
  else
    start = time;
}
```

The complete source for the bean is shown in listing 8.8.

Listing 8.8 TimerBean

```
package com.taglib.wdjsp.components;
public class TimerBean {
  private long start;
  public TimerBean() {
    start = System.currentTimeMillis();
```

```
    }
    public long getElapsedMillis() {
      long now = System.currentTimeMillis();
      return now - start;
    }
    public long getElapsedSeconds() {
      return (long)this.getElapsedMillis() / 1000;
    }
    public long getElapsedMinutes() {
      return (long)this.getElapsedMillis() / 60000;
    }

    public void reset() {
      start = System.currentTimeMillis();
    }

    public long getStartTime() {
      return start;
    }

    public void setStartTime(long time) {
      if (time <= 0)
        reset();
      else
        start = time;
    }
}
```

Here's an example of a JSP page that pulls a `TimerBean` from the user's session (or instantiates a new Bean, if necessary) and resets the clock, using the approach described in listing 8.8:

```
<jsp:useBean id="timer" class="TimerBean" scope="session"/>
<jsp:setProperty name="timer" property="startTime" value="-1"/>
<html><body>
Your online timer has been restarted…
</body></html>
```

8.2.2 A bean that calculates interest

As a more complex example let's create a JSP component that knows how to calculate the future value of money that is accumulating interest. Such a bean would be useful for an application allowing the user to compare investments. The formula for calculating the future value of money collecting compounding interest is:

```
FV = principal(1 + rate/compounding periods)^(years * compounding periods)
```

This bean will require:

- The sum of money to be invested (the principal)
- The interest rate
- The number of years for the investment
- How often interest is compounded

This gives us the list of properties that the user must be able to modify. Once all of these properties have been initialized, the bean should be able to calculate the future value of our principal amount. In addition, we will need to have a property to reflect the future value of the money after the calculation has been performed. Table 8.3 defines the bean's properties.

Table 8.3 Properties of a bean that calculates interest

Property Name	Mode	Type
`principal`	read/write	`double`
`years`	read/write	`int`
`compounds`	read/write	`int`
`interestRate`	read/write	`double`
`futureValue`	read-only	`double`

Since users will probably want to display the input values in addition to configuring them, they have been given both read and write access. The `futureValue` property is designated read-only because it will reflect the results of the calculation. Retrieving the value of the `futureValue` property uses the other properties to calculate our results. (If you wanted to get fancy, you could write a bean that, given any four of the properties, could calculate the remaining property value.) We'll store our initialization properties in instance variables:

```
public class CompoundInterestBean {
  private double interestRate;
  private int years;
  private double principal;
  private int compounds;
```

It is a good practice to make your instance variables `private` since we plan to define access methods for them. This assures that all interaction with the class is restricted to the access methods allowing us to modify the implementation without affecting code that makes use of our class. Following the bean conventions, we must define a constructor that has no arguments. In our constructor we should set our initialization properties to some default values that will leave our bean property initialized. We cannot calculate the future value without our initialization properties being set to appropriate, legal values.

```
public CompoundInterestBean() {
  this.compounds = 12;
  this.interestRate = 8.0;
  this.years = 1;
  this.principal = 1000.0;
}
```

Since investments are generally compounded monthly (that is twelve times a year) it might be handy to provide a shortcut that allows the bean user to not specify the `compounds` property and instead use the default. It would also be nice if we could provide other clients of the bean with a more robust constructor that would allow them to do all their initialization through the constructor. This can be accomplished by creating a constructor that takes a full set of arguments and calling it from the zero-argument constructor with the default values we have selected for our bean's properties:

```
public CompoundInterestBean() {
  this(12, 8.0, 1, 1000.0);
}

public CompoundInterestBean(int compounds, double interestRate,
  int years, double principal) {
  this.compounds = compounds;
  this.interestRate = interestRate;
  this.years = years;
  this.principal = principal;
}
```

This is a good compromise in the design. The bean is now useful to both traditional Java developers as well as JSP authors. We must now define access methods for our initialization properties. For each one we will verify that they have been passed valid information. For example, money cannot be invested into the past, so the `year` property's value must be a positive number. Since the access methods are all similar, we'll just look at those for the `interestRate` property.

```
public void setInterestRate(double rate) {
  if (rate > 0)
    this.interestRate = rate;
  else
    this.interestRate = 0;
}
```

```
public double getInterestRate() {
  return this.interestRate;
}
```

When we catch illegal arguments, such as negative interest rates, we have to decide the appropriate way of handling it. We can pick a reasonable default value, as we did here for example, or take a stricter approach and throw an exception.

We chose to initialize our properties with a set of legitimate, but hard-coded values to keep our bean in a legal state. Of course, this approach might not be appropriate in every situation. Another technique for handling uninitialized data is setting up boolean flags for each property which has no legal value until it is initialized, and tripping them as each setter method is called. Another method could then be used to check the status of the flags to determine if the component had been initialized yet or not. For example, we could have defined our `futureValue` access method like this:

```
public double getFutureValue() {
  if (isInitialized())
    return principal * Math.pow(1 + interestRate/compounds,
      years * compounds);
  else
    throw new RuntimeException("Bean requires configuration!");
}

private boolean isInitialized() {
  return (compoundsSet && interestRateSet && yearsSet && principalSet);
}
```

In such a case, the bean is considered initialized if and only if the flags for each property are set to `true`. We would initialize each flag to `false` in our constructor and then define our setter methods as:

```
public void setYears(int years) {
  yearsSet = true;
  if (years >=1 )
    this.years = years;
  else
    this.years = 1;
}
```

The complete code is shown in listing 8.9:

Listing 8.9 CompoundInterestBean.java

```
package com.taglib.wdjsp.components;
public class CompoundInterestBean {
```

```
private double interestRate;
private int years;
private double principal;
private int compounds;

public CompoundInterestBean() {
  this(12);
}

public CompoundInterestBean(int compounds) {
  this.compounds = compounds;
  this.interestRate = -1;
  this.years = -1;
  this.principal = -1;
}

public double getFutureValue() {
  if ((compounds != -1) &&
    (interestRate != -1 ) &&
    (years != -1))
     return principal * Math.pow(1+interestRate/compounds, compounds*12);
  else
    throw new RuntimeException("Bean requires configuration!");
}

public void setInterestRate(double rate) {
  if (rate > 0)
    this.interestRate = rate;
  else
    this.interestRate = 0;
}

public double getInterestRate() {
  return this.interestRate;
}

public void setYears(int years) {
  if (years >=1 )
    this.years = years;
  else
    this.years = 1;
}

public int getYears() {
  return this.years;
}

public void setPrincipal(double principal) {
  this.principal = principal;
}

public double getPrincipal() {
  return this.principal;
```

```
    }

    public static void main(String[] args) {
      CompoundInterestBean bean = new CompoundInterestBean();
      bean.setInterestRate(0.06);
      bean.setYears(30);
      bean.setPrincipal(1200.00);
      System.out.println("FutureValue = " + bean.getFutureValue());
    }
  }
```

8.3 Bean interfaces

While not specifically required, there are a number of interfaces that you may choose to implement with your beans to extend their functionality. We'll cover them briefly in this section.

8.3.1 The BeanInfo interface

We learned about reflection earlier, but another way that a bean class can inform the bean container about its properties is by providing an implementation of the `BeanInfo` interface. The `BeanInfo` interface allows you to create a companion class for your bean that defines its properties and their corresponding levels of access. It can be used to adapt existing Java classes for bean use without changing their published interface. It can also be used to hide what would normally be accessible properties from your client, since sometimes Java's standard reflection mechanism can reveal more information than we would like.

To create a `BeanInfo` class use your bean's class name with the suffix `BeanInfo` and implement the `java.beans.BeanInfo` interface. This naming convention is how the bean container locates the appropriate `BeanInfo` class for your bean. This interface requires you to define methods that inform the container about your bean's properties. This explicit mapping eliminates the introspection step entirely.

There is also a `java.beans.SimpleBeanInfo` class that provides default, do-nothing implementations of all of the required `BeanInfo` methods. This often provides a good starting point when designing a `BeanInfo` class for a JSP bean, because many of the bean features designed for working with visual beans are irrelevant in the context of JSP, and are ignored by the JSP container.

One area where the `BeanInfo` approach is particularly useful is in visual, or WYSIWYG, JSP editors. JSP was designed to be machine-readable in order to support visual editors and development tools. By applying the `BeanInfo` interface to existing Java classes, developers can construct their own JSP components for use in such editors, even if the original component class does not follow the JavaBean conventions. Using `BeanInfo` classes you can designate which methods of an arbitrary class correspond to bean properties, for use with the `<jsp:setPropety>` and `<jsp:getProperty>` tags.

8.3.2 The Serializable interface

One of the JavaBean requirements that JSP does not mandate is that beans should implement the `Serializable` interface. This will allow an instance of the bean to be *serialized*, turning it into a flat stream of binary data that can be stored to disk for later reuse. When a bean is serialized to disk (or anywhere else for that matter), its state is preserved such that its property values remained untouched. There are several reasons why you might want to "freeze-dry" a bean for later use.

Some servers support indefinite, long-term session persistence by writing any session data (including beans) to disk between server shutdowns. When the server comes back up, the serialized data is restored. This same reasoning applies to servers that support clustering in heavy traffic environments. Many of them use serialization to replicate session data among a group of web servers. If your beans do not implement the `Serializable` interface, the server will be unable to properly store or transfer your beans (or other classes) in these situations.

Using a similar tactic, you might choose to store serialized copies of your beans to disk, an LDAP server, or a database for later use. You could, for example, implement a user's shopping cart as a bean, which you store in the database between visits.

If a bean requires particularly complicated configuration or setup it may be useful to fully configure the beans' properties as required, then serialize the configured bean to disk. This snapshot of a bean can then be used anywhere you would normally be required to create and configure the bean by hand, including the `<jsp:useBean>` tag via the `beanName` attribute.

The `beanName` attribute of the `<jsp:useBean>` tag is used to instantiate serialized beans rather than creating new instances from a class file. If the bean doesn't exist in the scope, then the `beanName` attribute is passed on to `java.beans.Bean.instantiate()`, which will instantiate the bean for the class loader. It first assumes that the name corresponds to a serialized bean file (identified by the .ser extension) in which case it will bring it to life, but if it can't find or invoke the serialized bean it will fall back to instantiating a new bean from its class.

8.3.3 The HttpSessionBindingListener interface

Implementing the Java Servlet API's `HttpSessionBindingListener` interface in your JavaBean's class will enable its instances to receive notification of session events. The interface is quite simple, defining only two methods.

```
public void valueBound(HttpSessionBindingEvent event)
public void valueUnbound(HttpSessionBindingEvent event)
```

The `valueBound()` method is called when the bean is first bound (stored into) the user's session. In the case of JSP, this will typically happen right after a bean is instantiated by a `<jsp:useBean>` tag that specifies a `session` scope, thus assigning the bean to the user's session.

The `valueUnbound()` method is called, as you would expect, when the object is being removed from the session. There are several situations that could cause your bean to be removed from the session. When the JSP container plans to expire a user's session due to inactivity, it is required to first remove each item from the session, triggering the `valueUnbound` notification. The JSP container will automatically recognize that the bean is implementing the `HttpSessionBindingListener` interface, hence there is no need to register the bean with the container as a listener. Alternatively, this event would be triggered if a servlet, scriptlet, or other Java code specifically removed the bean from the session for some reason.

Each of these events is associated with an `HttpSessionBindingEvent` object, which can be used to gain access to the session object. Implementing this interface will allow you to react to session events by, for example, closing connections that are no longer needed, logging transactions, or performing other maintenance activities. If you are implementing your own session persistence, such as saving a shopping cart, this would be where you would move your data off to disk or database.

8.3.4 Other features of the Bean API

In addition to the access methods and constructor conventions that we have examined here, the JavaBeans Specification defines several other features. When writing beans for use with JSP we do not generally need to concern ourselves with these remaining elements of the specification because they are more oriented toward visual beans, such as GUI components. While most of this extra functionality is not reflected into the bean tags, it can be useful working with beans through JSP scriptlets or as part of a larger system. For clarity and for the sake of completeness we will quickly point out these other features. For full details on these aspects of JavaBeans, see the JavaBeans Specification or Manning's *The Awesome Power of Java Beans.*

JavaBean event model

The JavaBeans API supports Java 1.1 style event handling, a feature intended primarily for visual components. Events allow visual beans to communicate with one another in a standard way, without each bean having to be too tightly coupled to other beans. However, JSP containers do not support the JavaBeans event model directly. Any bean-to-bean communication is the responsibility of the bean designer.

Bound properties

A bean can be designed to generate events any time changes are made to its properties. This allows users of the bean to be notified of the changes and react accordingly. If, for example, a bean contained information about the status of a radio button on a user interface which was modified by one of the bean's users, any other users of the bean would be notified and could update their displays accordingly.

Constrained properties

Constrained properties are properties whose values must fall within specific limits. For example a property representing a percentage value must be greater than or equal to zero, and less than or equal to one hundred. The only difference between the design patterns for setting a constrained versus an unconstrained property is that it must declare that it throws the `java.beans.PropertyVetoException`. Objects that want to support constrained properties must also implement methods that allow other objects to register with the bean so that they can play a part in the change approval process. Constrained property functionality is not directly implemented through the bean tags, although beans can still take advantage of this functionality internally. If a bean throws an exception in response to an illegal property value, the normal JSP error handling will take place.

8.4 Mixing scriptlets and bean tags

Since JSP bean tags, scriptlets, and expressions eventually are translated into the same single Java servlet class on the server, you can combine any of the elements. This allows you to take advantage of component-centric design while not being bound by the limits of the built-in tag commands. Using the `<jsp:useBean>` tag to create objects puts them into the scope of the page, making them available to both scriptlets and `<jsp:getProperty>` and `<jsp:setProperty>` tags.

8.4.1 Accessing beans through scriptlets

Since the `<jsp:useBean>` tag creates an object reference behind the scenes, you are free to access that object through scriptlets and expressions, using the bean's name as the object identifier. For example, it is perfectly valid to do either of these snippets, both of which produce the same results:

```
<jsp:useBean id="stocks" class="StockMarketBean" scope="page"/>
The Dow is at <jsp:getProperty name="stocks" property="dow"/> points
```

or

```
<jsp:useBean id="stocks" class="StockMarketBean" scope="page"/>
The Dow is at <%= stocks.getDow() %> points
```

Calling bean properties through an expression rather than the somewhat lengthy `<jsp:getProperty>` tag can be a handy shortcut if you aren't afraid of a little Java code in your page. A word of caution however! You can't always assume that a bean's property returns a String or maps directly to the method you expect. It may return a different type of data than you expect (which is all right if you are calling the method in an expression), or a `BeanInfo` class may be redirecting you to a completely different method—one for which you may not even know the name.

8.4.2 Accessing scriptlet created objects

The reverse of this operation is not true. Objects created through scriptlets are not guaranteed to be accessible through the bean tags, because there is no guarantee that these objects will become part of the page context. Consider the following JSP code for example, which is not valid in most JSP containers.

```
<html><body>
Auto-Shop 2000<br>
<% Car car = (Car)request.getAttribute("car"); %>
<% car.updateRecords(); %>
This car has <jsp:getProperty name="car" property="milage"/> miles on it…
</body></html>
```

In this example we have attempted to pull an object reference, `car`, out of the request and use it in the page. However, the `<jsp:getProperty>` tag will not have a reference to the object because it was not scoped into the page through a `<jsp:useBean>` tag. The corrected code is:

```
<html><body>
Auto-Shop 2000<br>
<jsp:useBean id="car" class="Car" scope="request"/>
<% car.updateRecords(); %>
This car has <jsp:getProperty name="car" property="milage"/> miles on it…
</body></html>
```

Notice that we can access the object through both scriptlets and JSP tags, allowing us to call the `updateRecords()` method directly. We can even change the object referenced by the named identifier specified by `<jsp:useBean>`—it is the identifier that's important, not the actual object reference.

Alternatively, you can scope the bean into the `pageContext` directly using the code:

```
pageContext.setAttribute("car", car);
```

Handling indexed properties

This technique is particularly useful in handling indexed properties, which JSP doesn't provide any easier way to deal with (other than custom tags, as we'll learn in chapters 18 and 19). We apply the same principles as before, creating objects with the `<jsp:useBean>` tag and referencing them through scriptlets and expressions. For example, to loop through an indexed property we write code similar to that which follows. The exact syntax will depend on your bean's properties and associated methods. In this example, `MusicCollectionBean` contains an array of `Album` objects, nested in its `albums` property. Each `Album` object in turn has a number of bean properties. Note however, that we must declare the `Album` object reference through a bean tag as a placeholder, or it will not be available to our page context and therefore inaccessible through the bean tags.

```
<jsp:useBean id="music" class="MusicCollectionBean"/>
<jsp:useBean id="album" class="Album"/>
<%
Album[] albums = music.getAlbums();
for (int j=0; j < albums.length; j++) {
  album = albums[j];
%>
Title: <jsp:getProperty name="album" property="title"/><BR>
Artist: <jsp:getProperty name="album" property="artist"/><BR>
Year: <jsp:getProperty name="album" property="year"/><BR>
<% } %>
```

This code will loop through each of the albums in the array returned by the `getAlbums()` method of `MusicCollectionBean`, assigning each to the variable `album` in turn. We can then treat `album` as a bean, accessing it through the `<jsp:getProperty>` tags. You can use this technique to create tables, lists, and other sequences of indexed properties.

Other bean methods

Since beans are just objects, they may also have methods that are accessible through JSP scripting elements. While it is desirable to create beans that can be used entirely through the tags, sometimes it is useful to create beans with two levels of complexity. These extra methods are not bean-related, but allow you to treat the bean as any other Java object for more benefits or advanced functionality.

Not all of your methods need to follow the bean conventions, although only those methods that can be found by introspection will be made available through the bean container. It is sometimes useful to provide basic functionality accessible through the bean container, such as JSP tags, and more advanced functionality only accessible through scriptlets or direct programmer intervention.

Removing a bean when done with it

At the end of a bean's life span, which is determined by its scope, all references to the bean will be removed and it will become eligible for garbage collection. Beans in the page or request scopes are automatically reclaimed at the end of the HTTP request, but session and application beans can live on. The life of a session bean is, as discussed, dependent on the JSP container while the application scope is tied to the life of the server. There are several situations where you might want to prematurely end the life of a bean. The first involves removing it from memory for performance reasons. When you have no more use for the bean, especially one in session or application scope, it's a good idea to get rid of it. Eliminating unused bean objects will improve the performance of your server-side applications by freeing as many of the JVM's resources as soon as possible.

Another reason you want to remove a bean is to eliminate it from the user's session for security reasons. A good example of this would be removing a user's login information from the session when the user has specifically advised that they are logging off. A typical approach to user authentication with JSP is to place the user's login credentials into the session following a successful login. The presence of these credentials in the session satisfies the login requirements for future visits to protected pages until the session expires. For security reasons however it is desirable to offer the visitor the ability to eliminate their login information from the session when they have completed their visit. We can accomplish this by simply removing their credentials from the session, returning them to their unauthenticated state. The methods available to you are summarized in table 8.4.

Table 8.4 Discarding a used bean from various scopes

Scope	Scriptlet	Servlet
session	`session.removeAttribute(name)`	`HttpSession.removeAttribute(name)`
request/page	`pageContext.remove-Attribute(name)`	`ServletRequest.remove-Attribute(name)`
application	`application.remove-Attribute(name)`	`ServletContext.remove-Attribute(name)`

The request bean

As discussed in previous chapters, JSP defines a number of implicit objects that reflect information about the environment. The request object encapsulates information about the request and has several properties that are accessible through the bean tags. Like other beans, we can access the properties of the request objects through `<jsp:getProperty>`. The `id` value assigned to the implicit request object is, as you probably guessed, `request`. For example, we can display the remote user name as follows:

```
<jsp:getProperty name="request" property="remoteUser"/>
```

Table 8.5 summarizes some of the more useful methods of the request object, which can be exposed as properties to the bean tags.

Table 8.5 Properties of the request bean

Name	Access	Use
`authType`	read	Gets the authentication scheme of this request or null if unknown. Same as the CGI variable `AUTH_TYPE`
`method`	read	Gets the HTTP method (for example, `GET`, `POST`, `PUT`) with which this request was made. Same as the CGI variable `REQUEST_METHOD`
`pathInfo`	read	Gets any optional extra path information following the servlet path of this request's URI, but immediately preceding its query string. Same as the CGI variable `PATH_INFO`
`pathTranslated`	read	Gets any optional extra path information following the servlet path of this request's URI, but immediately preceding its query string, and translates it to a real path. Same as the CGI variable `PATH_TRANSLATED`
`queryString`	read	Gets any query string that is part of the HTTP request URI Same as the CGI variable `QUERY_STRING`
`remoteUser`	read	Gets the name of the user making this request. The user name is set with HTTP authentication. Whether the user name will continue to be sent with each subsequent communication is browser-dependent. Same as the CGI variable `REMOTE_USER`
`requestURI`	read	Gets the URI corresponding to the original request
`characterEncoding`	read	Gets the character set encoding for the input of this request
`contentType`	read	Gets the Internet media type of the request entity data, or null if not known. Same as the CGI variable `CONTENT_TYPE`
`protocol`	read	Gets the protocol and version of the request as a string of the form <protocol>/<major version>.<minor version>. Same as the CGI variable `SERVER_PROTOCOL`

Table 8.5 Properties of the request bean (continued)

Name	Access	Use
`remoteAddr`	read	Gets the IP address of the agent that sent the request. Same as the CGI variable `REMOTE_ADDR`
`serverName`	read	Gets the host name of the server that received the request. Same as the CGI variable `SERVER_NAME`
`serverPort`	read	Gets the port number on which this request was received. Same as the CGI variable `SERVER_PORT`
`scheme`	read	Gets the scheme of the URL used in this request, for example "http," "https," or "ftp"
`remoteHost`	read	Gets the fully qualified host name of the agent that sent the request. Same as the CGI variable `REMOTE_HOST`

9 Working with databases

This chapter covers

- The link between Java's JDBC API and JSP
- Storing and retrieving JSP Beans with an RDBMS system
- Displaying database results with JSP
- Maintaining persistent connections

While long a bastion of large, well-funded enterprises, databases have found their way into a much wider range of web sites in recent years. Along with their traditional role as back office data sources, most large-scale web sites employ databases for at least some portion of the content. Ad management, users registration information, community services, and contact lists are just some of the features commonly managed through a database. JSPs and relational databases make a good combination. The relational database gives us the organizational capabilities and the performance necessary to manage large amounts of dynamic data, while JSP gives us a convenient way to present it. By combining the power of a relational database with the flexibility of JSP for content presentation and front-end design you can quickly develop rich, interactive web applications.

9.1 JSP and JDBC

Unlike other web scripting languages such as ColdFusion, Server Side JavaScript, and PHP, JSP does not define its own set of tags for database access. Rather than develop yet another mechanism for database access, the designers of JSP chose to leverage Java's powerful, popular, database API—JDBC.

When a JSP application needs to communicate with a database, it does so through a vendor-provided driver class written to the JDBC API. Accessing a database in JSP then is nothing new; it sticks to this tried and true workhorse from Sun. In practice, as we'll learn in chapter 10, we'll often isolate database access inside a servlet or a Bean, keeping the details hidden from the presentation aspects of the JSP page. Both of these approaches are illustrated in figure 9.1

Learning JDBC is beyond the scope of this book, and a wealth of valuable information already exists on the topic. If you aren't familiar with Java's JDBC API, a number of online tutorials can be found on Sun's JDBC web site, http://java.sun.com/products/jdbc. Check online or at your favorite bookstore if you need more information. In this chapter we'll focus instead on the relationship between JSP and JDBC.

NOTE The JDBC classes are part of the `java.sql` package, which must be imported into any Java class from which you wish to access JDBC, including your JSP pages. Additional, optional extensions for the 2.0 version of the JDBC API can be found in the `javax.sql` package, if it is installed on your system. If your JDBC driver is not in your JSP container's class path, you will have to either import it into your page or refer to it through its fully qualified class name.

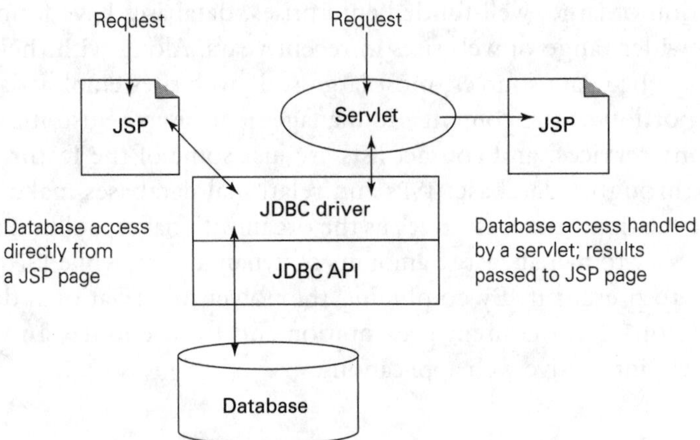

Figure 9.1 Database access options in JSP

9.1.1 JNDI and data sources

In ColdFusion and other template/scripting systems you access a database through a single identifier that corresponds to a preconfigured database connection (or connection pool) assigned by the system's administrator. This allows you to eliminate database connection information from your code, referring to your database sources by a logical name such as `EmployeeDB` or `SalesDatabase`. The details of connecting to the database are not exposed to your code. If a new driver class becomes available, the database server moves, or the login information changes, only the resource description needs to be reconfigured. Any components or code referencing this named resource will not have to be touched.

JSP does not define its own database resource management system; instead you can rely on JDBC 2.0's `Datasource` interface and Java Naming and Directory Interface (JNDI) technology for naming and location services. JNDI can be used to shield your application code from the database details such as the driver class, the username, password, and connection URI. To create a database connection with JNDI, specify a resource name which corresponds to an entry in a database or naming service, and receive the information necessary to establish a connection with your database. This shields your JSP code and supporting components from changes to the database's configuration. More information on using JNDI is available from Sun, at http://java.sun.com/products/jndi. Here's an example of creating a connection from a data source defined in the JNDI registry:

```
Context ctx = new InitialContext();
DataSource ds = (DataSource)ctx.lookup("jdbc/SalesDB");
Connection con = ds.getConnection("username", "password");
```

We can further improve upon this abstraction, and further simplify database access, through custom tags, which use JNDI to allow simple access to named database resources in a manner familiar to ColdFusion and other tag-style languages.

9.1.2 Prepared statements

Prepared statements allow us to develop a Structured Query Language (SQL) query template that we can reuse to handle similar requests with different values between each execution. Essentially we create the query, which can be any sort of SQL statement, leaving any variable values undefined. We can then specify values for our undefined elements before executing the query, and repeat as necessary. Prepared statements are created from a `Connection` object, just like regular `Statement` objects. In the SQL, replace any variable values with a question mark.

```
String query = "SELECT * FROM GAME_RECORDS WHERE SCORE > ? AND TEAM = ?";
PreparedStatement statement = connection.prepareStatement(query);
```

Before we can execute the statement we must specify a value for all of our missing parameters. The `PreparedStatement` object supports a number of methods, each tied to setting a value of a specific type—`int`, `long`, `String`, and so forth. Each method takes two arguments, an index value indicating which missing parameter you are specifying, and the value itself. The first parameter has an index value of 1 (not 0) so to specify a query that selects all high scores > 10,000 for the "Gold" team we use the following statements to set the values and execute the query:

```
statement.setInt(1, 10000);      // Score
statement.setString(2, "Gold"); // Team
ResultSet results = statement.executeQuery();
```

Once you have defined a prepared statement you can reuse it simply by changing parameters, as needed. There is no need to create a new prepared statement instance as long as the basic query is unchanged. So, we can execute several queries without having to create a statement object. We can even share a single prepared statement among an application's components or a servlet's users. When using prepared statements, the RDBMS engine has to parse the SQL statement only once, rather than again and again with each new request. This results in more efficient database operations.

Not only is this more efficient in terms of database access, object creation, and memory allocation but the resulting code is cleaner and more easily understood.

Consider this example again, but this time the queries are not hard coded, but come from a bean, `userBean`, which has been initialized from an input form.

```
statement.setInt(1, userBean.getScore());  // Score
statement.setString(2, userBean.getTeam()); // Team
ResultSet results = statement.execute();
```

The alternative is to build each SQL statement from strings, which can quickly get confusing, especially with complex queries. Consider the following example again, this time without the benefit of a prepared statement:

```
Statement statement = connection.getStatement();
String query = "SELECT * FROM GAME_RECORDS WHERE SCORE > " +
userBean.getScore() + " AND TEAM = '" +
userBean.getTeam() + "'";
ResultSet results = Statement.executeQuery(query);
```

Another, perhaps even more important, benefit of using prepared statements is evidenced here. When you insert a value into a prepared statement with one of its setter methods you do not have to worry about proper quoting of strings, escaping of special characters, and conversions of dates and other values into the proper format for your particular database. This is particularly important for JSPs that are likely to be collecting search terms input directly from users through form elements and are particularly vulnerable to special characters and unpredictable input. Since each database might have its own formatting peculiarities, especially for dates, using prepared statements can help further distance your code from dealing with any one particular database.

9.2 Database driven JSPs

There are a number of ways to develop database driven applications through JSP. In this chapter, we're concentrating on the database interaction itself, and less on program architecture. JSP application design will be covered in chapter 10 and again in chapter 11 which will feature a walk-through example of a database driven JSP project.

9.2.1 Creating JSP components from table data

You may have recognized a similarity between the tables of a relational database and simple JavaBean components. When building your applications think of tables as being analogous to JavaBeans. While JavaBeans have properties, data from a table has columns. A table's schema is like the class that defines a JavaBean—defining the names and types data that instances will hold. Like Java classes, tables are templates for storing a specific set of information like the data from a purchase order or details about inventory items and by themselves are not particularly useful.

It is only when we create instances of a JavaBean class or add rows to a table that we have something worthwhile. Each row is an instance of what the table represents, just as a bean is an instance of its class. Both classes and tables then serve as data models, a useful container for managing information about some real world object or event. Keep this relationship in mind as we learn about JSP database development. It will form the basis for many of our applications.

One of the most common areas for utilizing databases with JSP applications is to retrieve data stored in a table to create a bean for use within the page. The configuration of JSP components from information in the database is pretty straightforward if your table schema (or the results of a join between tables) closely corresponds to your bean's properties. We simply use the row access methods of the `ResultSet` class to configure the bean's properties with the values in the table's corresponding columns. If there is more than a single row in the result set we must create a collection of beans, one for each row of the results.

Database beans from scriptlets

You can use JSP scriptlets to configure a bean's properties when it is created. After establishing the connection, set its properties as appropriate through the data carried in the `ResultSet`. Don't forget to import the `java.sql` package into the page with the `<%@ page import="java.sql.*" %>` directive.

In this example we will use an `ItemBean` class used to represent a particular item from inventory, taking the item number from the request object.

```
<%@ page import="java.sql.*" %>
<jsp:useBean id="item" class="ItemBean">
<%
Connection connection = null;
Statement statement = null;
ResultSet results = null;
ItemBean item = new ItemBean();
try {
  Class.forName("oracle.jdbc.driver.OracleDriver");
  String url = "jdbc:oracle:oci8@dbserver";
  String id = request.getParameter(id);
  String query = "SELECT * FROM PRODUCTS_TABLE WHERE ITEM_ID = " + id;
  connection = DriverManager.getConnection(url, "scott", "tiger");
  statement = connection.createStatement();
  results = statement.executeQuery(query);
  if (results.next()) {
    item.setId(results.getInt("ITEM_ID"));
    item.setDesc(results.getString("DESCRIPTION"));
```

```
    item.setPrice(results.getDouble("PRICE"));
    item.setStock(results.getInt("QTY_AVAILABLE"));
  }
  connection.close();
}
catch (ClassNotFoundException e) {
  System.err.println("Could not load database driver!");
}
catch (SQLException e) {
  System.err.println("Could not connect to the database!");
}
finally {
  try { if (connection != null) connection.close(); }
  catch (SQLException e) { }
}
%>
</jsp:useBean>
<html>
<body>
<table>
<tr><td>Item Number</td><td>
<jsp:getProperty name="item" property="id"/></td></tr>
<tr><td>Description</td><td>
<jsp:getProperty name="item" property="desc"/></td></tr>
<tr><td>Price $</td><td>
<jsp:getProperty name="item" property="price"/></td></tr>
<tr><td>On hand</td><td>
<jsp:getProperty name="item" property="stock"/></td></tr>
</table>
</body>
</html>
```

When this code finishes we will have an `ItemBean` that is either empty (if the `SELECT` found no matches) or is populated with data from the `PRODUCTS_TABLE`. After creating our bean and using the database to populate it we then display its properties. In this approach we've ended up with a lot of Java code, supporting a small amount of HTML presentation. If we have several pages with similar needs, we'll end up rewriting (or using the cut and pasting operation, then maintaining) all of this code again. In chapter 10, we'll learn about architectures that help eliminate these problems. In the meantime, we could wrap the code into the bean, creating one that is self-populating.

Self-populating beans

You can use a similar technique to that used in the JSP page example earlier to create beans that populate themselves. In the bean's constructor, you can establish the database connection, perform the query, set your property values, close the connection, and be ready for business. You can also define some of your bean's properties as triggers that cause the bean to retrieve data from the database by including the database access code inside your property method. For example, changing the ID property of our `ItemBean` could cause it to fetch that row of data from the database and build up the other properties.

Outside influence

As we will learn in chapter 10, it is often desirable to keep the actual Java code in the JSP page to a minimum. Instead we can rely on servlets to package data from the database into the beans needed by the JSP page. The same approach that applies to database access still applies, but with a servlet we can share and reuse our database connection. We can move the management of database connections and the collection of data out of the page, and into a servlet.

9.2.2 JSPs and JDBC data types

Each database supports its own set of internal data types, which vary significantly among vendors. JDBC provides a layer of abstraction between Java's data types and those of the database. The JDBC layer frees a Java developer from having to worry about subtle type distinctions and proper formatting. JDBC deals with the difference in data types in two ways. It defines a set of SQL types that logically map back to native database types and it maps Java data types to the SQL types, and vice versa.

When dealing with the database directly, such as setting up a table's schema, you must deal with SQL types. However, when retrieving or storing data through JDBC, you work in Java's type system—the JDBC method calls you make determine how to convert the data into the appropriate SQL type. When building JSP components that interact with the database it is important to understand how such data is handled. The following information will give you a good feel for some of the more important SQL types and their handling by JDBC.

Integer data

JDBC defines four SQL types for handling integer data, but the major database vendors commonly support only two. The `SMALLINT` type represents 16-bit signed integers and is treated as a Java `short`. The `INTEGER` type is mapped to Java's `int` type and holds a 32-bit signed integer value. The remaining two types, `TINYINT` and `BIGINT`, represent 8-bit and 64-bit integers and are not commonly supported.

Floating-point numbers

There are two floating-point data types specified by JDBC, `DOUBLE` and `FLOAT`. For all practical purposes they are essentially the same, the latter being included for consistency with ODBC. Sun recommends that programmers generally stick with the DOUBLE type, which is analogous to Java's double type.

Textual data

JDBC defines two primary SQL types for handling text: CHAR and VARCHAR. Each is treated as a String object by JDBC. CHAR is widely supported by most databases, and holds text of a fixed length. VARCHAR, on the other hand, holds variable length text, up to a maximum specified width. Because CHAR is a fixed length data type, if the data placed into a CHAR column contains fewer characters than the specified width it will be padded with spaces by JDBC. While HTML browsers will ignore extra spaces in JSP output data, you can call String's trim() method before acting on the data to remove trailing spaces. A third text type defined by JDBC is LONG-VARCHAR, which holds especially large amounts of text. Because vendor support for LONGVARCHAR differs wildly, you probably won't use it much.

Dates and times

To handle date and time information JDBC defines three distinct types: DATE, TIME, and TIMESTAMP. DATE holds day, month, and year values only. TIME holds hours, minutes, and seconds. TIMESTAMP combines the information held in DATE and TIME, and adds a nanoseconds field. Unfortunately, none of these corresponds exactly to java.util.Date, which falls somewhere between each of these, due to its lack of a nanoseconds field.

All of these SQL types are handled in Java by one of three subclasses of java.util.Date: java.sql.Date, java.sql.Time, and java.sql.Timestamp. Since they are subclasses of java.util.Date, they can be used anywhere a java.util.Date type is expected. This allows you to treat them as you might normally treat date and time values, while retaining compatibility with the database. Understanding how each of these specialized subclasses differs from its common base class is important. For example, the java.sql.Date class zeros out the time values, while java.sql.Time zeros out the date values. Don't forget about these important distinctions when exchanging data between the database and your JSP components. If you need to convert a java.sql.Timestamp object into its closest approximate java.util.Date object, you can use the following code:

```
Timestamp t = results.getTimestamp("MODIFIED");
java.util.Date d;
d = new java.util.Date(t.getTime() + (t.getNanos()/1000000));
```

Some of the most common data type mappings you will encounter are listed in table 9.1, along with the recommended ResultSet access method for retrieving data of that type.

Table 9.1 Common Java-to-JDBC type mappings

Java type	JDBC type	Recommended JDBC access method
`short`	SMALLINT	`getShort()`
`int`	INTEGER	`getInt()`
`double`	DOUBLE	`getDouble()`
`java.lang.String`	CHAR	`getString()`
`java.lang.String`	VARCHAR	`getString()`
`java.util.Date`	DATE	`getDate()`
`java.sql.Time`	TIME	`getTime()`
`java.sql.Timestamp`	TIMESTAMP	`getTimestamp()`

Handling undefined column data

If a column in the database is not assigned a value it will be set to null. The problem is that there is no good way to represent an empty value with Java's primitive types like `int` and `double`, which are not objects and cannot be set to null. For example, a call to `getInt()` might return `0` or `-1` to indicate null, but those are both valid values. The problem exists for `String`s as well. Some drivers return an empty string (`""`), some return null, and still others return the string value `null`. The solution, which isn't particularly elegant but does work, is the `ResultSet`'s `wasNull()` method. This method returns true or false, depending on whether or not the last row access method called should have returned an actual null value.

We have this same problem when creating JSP components from JavaBeans. The interpretation of a null value by the `<jsp:getProperty>` tag is not consistent among vendors, so if we can't use a literal value to represent null we have to design an approach similar to that of JDBC. What we can do is define a boolean property that will indicate the validity of the property value in question. When we encounter a null value in the database, we set the property to some non-null value, then make certain the validity check will return false. In the following code we set the value of our quantity property using the `QTY_AVAILABLE` column of our `ResultSet`. We also set a flag to indicate whether or not the value was actually valid.

```
init() {
  . . .
  myQuantity = results.getInt("QTY_AVAILABLE");
  if (results.wasNull()) {
    myQuantity = 0;
    validQuantity = false;
  }
  else {
```

```
    validQuantity = true;
  }
  . . .
}

  isValidQuality() {
    return validQuantity;
}
```

Of course, that means that in our JSP code we will have to check the validity of the value before using it. We have to call our boolean check method:

```
Quantity Available:
<% if (item.isValidQuantity()) %>
<jsp:getProperty name="item" property="quantity"/> units
<% else %>
Unknown
```

An alternative, if the value were being used by the JSP only for display, would be to define a `String` property that would return an appropriate value, no matter the state of the property. While this approach would limit the flexibility of the bean, it might be worth it to gain simplicity in your JSP code.

```
getQuantityString() {
  if (validQuantity)
    return new Integer(quantity).toString();
  else
    return "Unknown";
  }
```

The most popular way to avoid this irritating problem is to not allow null values in the database. Most databases even allow you to enforce this at the schema level by flagging a column as not being allowed to have null values.

9.2.3 Maintaining persistent connections

Sometimes you may want to keep your database connection across several requests by the same client. You must be careful when you do this because the number of database connections that a single server can support is limited. While continuing the connection is all right for a few simultaneous users, if you have high traffic you will not want each request to have its own connection to the database. Unfortunately, establishing a connection to a database is probably one of the slowest parts of your application, so it is something to be avoided where possible.

There are a number of solutions to this. Connection pools—implemented either by the database driver or through connection pool classes—maintain a fixed number of live connections, and loan them as requested by your JSP pages or beans. A connection pool is a good compromise between having too many open connections and paying the penalty for frequent connections and disconnections.

Listing 9.1 creates a bean which encapsulates a database connection. Using this `ConnectionBean` allows us to easily shield our JSP page from database connection details, as well as enables us to keep our connection across several pages by storing it in the session. That way we needn't reconnect to the database each time. We've also included some convenience methods that call the corresponding methods on the wrapped connection object. (Note: To keep things simple here, we've hard coded our database access parameters. You would probably want to make these configurable.)

Listing 9.1 ConnectionBean.java

```
package com.taglib.wdjsp.databases;

import java.sql.*;
import javax.servlet.http.*;

public class ConnectionBean implements HttpSessionBindingListener {
  private Connection connection;
  private Statement statement;

  private static final String driver="postgresql.Driver";
  private static final String dbURL="jdbc:postgresql://slide/test";
  private static final String login="guest";
  private static final String password="guest";

  public ConnectionBean() {

    try {
      Class.forName(driver);
      connection=DriverManager.getConnection(dbURL,login,password);
      statement=connection.createStatement();
    }
    catch (ClassNotFoundException e) {
      System.err.println("ConnectionBean: driver unavailable");
      connection = null;
    }
    catch (SQLException e) {
      System.err.println("ConnectionBean: driver not loaded");
      connection = null;
    }
  }

  public Connection getConnection() {
    return connection;
  }

  public void commit() throws SQLException {
    connection.commit();
```

```
  }

  public void rollback() throws SQLException {
    connection.rollback();
  }

  public void setAutoCommit(boolean autoCommit)
    throws SQLException {
    connection.setAutoCommit(autoCommit );
  }

  public ResultSet executeQuery(String sql) throws SQLException {
    return statement.executeQuery(sql);
  }

  public int executeUpdate(String sql) throws SQLException {
    return statement.executeUpdate(sql);
  }

  public void valueBound(HttpSessionBindingEvent event) {
    System.err.println("ConnectionBean: in the valueBound method");
    try {
      if (connection == null || connection.isClosed()) {
        connection =
          DriverManager.getConnection(dbURL,login,password);
        statement = connection.createStatement();
      }
    }
    catch (SQLException e) { connection = null; }
  }

  public void valueUnbound(HttpSessionBindingEvent event) {
    try {
      connection.close();
    }
    catch (SQLException e) { }
    finally {
      connection = null;
    }
  }

  protected void finalize() {
    try {
      connection.close();
    }
    catch (SQLException e) { }
  }
}
```

This `ConnectionBean` class implements `HttpSessionBindingListener`, disconnecting itself from the database if the bean is removed from the session. This keeps the connection from living too long after we are done with it, and before it actually gets garbage collected.

This bean has been designed to shield our application from the database connection details, but we could also create a more generic bean which accepts the necessary configuration values (`url`, `username`, `password`, and `driver`) as properties that the JSP page would have to set to activate the connection.

9.2.4 Handling large sets of results

If your query to the database returns a large number of rows, you probably don't want to display all of them at once. A 15,000-row table is hard to read and the HTML resulting from your JSP can take a considerable amount of time to download and display. If your application design allows, enforce a limit on the amount of rows a query can return. Asking the user to restrict his or her search further can be the quickest way to eliminate this problem.

A better solution is to present results a page at a time. There are a number of approaches to solving this problem with JSPs. The `RowSet` interface was introduced in JDBC 2.0 to define a standard way to access cached data through a JavaBeans component, or across distributed systems.

Creating a persistent ResultSet

When you retrieve a `ResultSet` object from a query, not all of the results are stored in memory. The database actually maintains a connection to the database and doles out rows as needed. This result buffering behavior keeps traffic and memory requirements low, but means you will remain connected to the database longer—which might be an issue in high traffic environments where you want to recycle database connections quickly. The database driver will determine the optimum number of rows to fetch at a time, or, in JDBC 2.0, you can offer your own suggestion to the driver. Fetching a new set of rows occurs automatically as you advance through the `ResultSet`; you don't have to keep track of state yourself.

One strategy then is to page through the `ResultSet` a page at a time, say twenty rows per page. We simply loop through twenty rows, then stick the `ResultSet` into our session, and visit twenty more. The cursor position internal to the `ResultSet` won't change between requests; we'll pick up right where we left off when we pull it out of the user's session. You don't need to explicitly keep a reference to the original `Connection` object, the `ResultSet` itself does that. When your `ResultSet` goes out of scope and is garbage collected your `Connection` will be shut down. You might want to wrap your `ResultSet` in a bean and implement `HttpSessionBindingListener` to shut down your database connections as soon as they are no longer needed, or expose a cleanup method and call it at the bottom of your JSP page. One problem with this approach is you're keeping the database connection open for so long. We'll look at a couple of approaches that don't hold the connection open while the user browses from page to page.

Performing the query multiple times

In this technique we re-execute the search for each page of results we wish to show, storing our current window position in the user's session. At each step, we reissue the original query, then use the `ResultSet`'s `next()` method (or JDBC 2.0's `absolute()` method) to skip forward in order to start our listing at the appropriate position. We then display the next, say, twenty rows and stop. We skip ahead twenty rows the second time the JSP is loaded, forty rows on the third, and so on. If we wish to provide additional feedback as to where the user is in the `ResultSet`, simply note its size. Now that you know the number of rows, you can display the appropriate status information such as "page 1 of 5." One potential drawback to this technique is that each page represents a new look at the database. Should the data be modified between requests, the user's view could change from page to page.

Use a self-limiting query

This technique is less general then the others we've looked at, and can't be used in every situation. The strategy here is to show a page of data, then record the primary key of the last item you displayed. Then for each page you issue a new query, but fine-tune the search through your query's `WHERE` clause to limit the results of the search to those you have not shown the user.

This method works great in situations where your data is listed in sequence, say a series of product IDs. If the last product ID shown was 8375, store that number in the session, and modify your next query to use this number in the `WHERE` clause. For example:

```
SELECT * FROM PRODUCTS WHERE ID > 8375
```

The CachedRowSet Bean

An alternative way of handling more manageable query results—those that are bigger than a screen full, but not so big as to be a memory hog—is through `CachedRowSet`. Sun is working on an early implementation of the JDBC 2.0 `RowSet` interface, which encapsulates a database connection and associated query results into a JavaBean component, called the `CachedRowSet`. This bean provides a disconnected, scrollable container for accessing result set style data in your JSP page, or other JavaBean container. This is a very useful tool for working with database information from within JSP. Sun may eventually add this class to the JDBC 2.0 optional extensions; you can find out more at Sun's JDBC web page, http://java.sun.com/products/jdbc. Unlike `ResultSet`, `CachedRowSet` is an offline connection that caches all of the rows in your query into the object. No active connection is required because all of the data has been fetched from the database. While convenient, if the results of your database query are so large that memory usage is a problem, you will probably want to stick to a persistent result set.

`CachedRowSet` is very easy to use. Simply configure the appropriate properties—such as `username`, `password`, and the `URL` of your database—then set the command property to your SQL query. Doing so populates the `rowset` with results you can then browse through. You can also populate `CachedRowSet` using a `RowSet` object, created from another query.

Example: paging through results with a CachedRowSet

Let's build an example of paging through a series of results using Sun's `CachedRowSet` Bean and JSP. We'll pull in the data, then allow the user to browse through it five rows at a time, or jump back to the first row if desired. The same technique applies to using a persistent `ResultSet`, although we'd have to resort to JSP scriptlets or wrap our live `ResultSet` object into our own bean. In this example we'll page through a set of results five rows at a time. In figure 9.2 you can see a screen shot of our example in action.

And here in listing 9.2 is the source code:

Listing 9.2 CachedResults.jsp

```
<%@ page import="java.sql.*,javax.sql.*,sun.jdbc.rowset.*" %>
<jsp:useBean id="crs" class="CachedRowSet" scope="session">
  <%
  try { Class.forName("postgresql.Driver"); }
  catch (ClassNotFoundException e) {
    System.err.println("Error" + e);
  }
  %>
  <jsp:setProperty name="crs" property="url"
     value="jdbc:postgresql://slide/test" />
  <jsp:setProperty name="crs" property="username" value="guest" />
  <jsp:setProperty name="crs" property="password" value="apple" />
  <jsp:setProperty name="crs" property="command"
     value="select * from shuttles order by id" />
  <%
    try { crs.execute(); }
     catch (SQLException e) { out.println("SQL Error: " + e); }
  %>
```

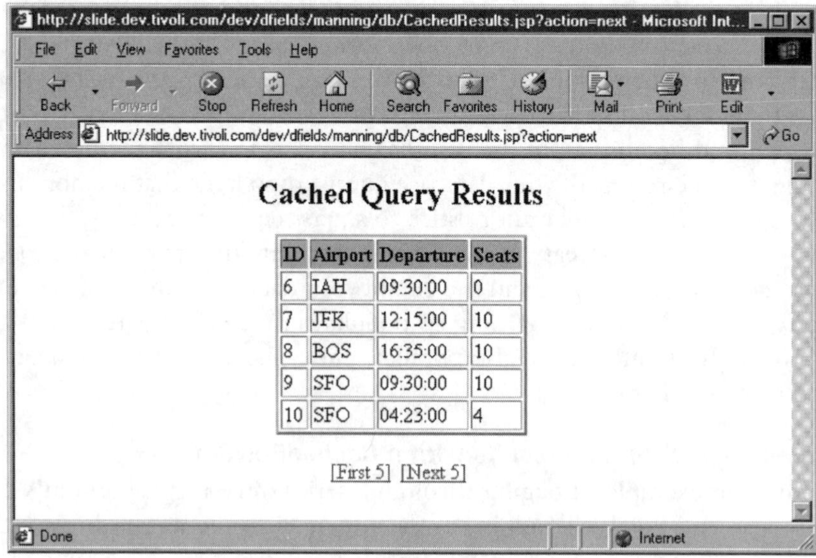

Figure 9.2 Browsing through data with a CachedRowSet

```
</jsp:useBean>

<html>
<body>
<center>
<h2>Cached Query Results</h2>
<P>
<table border="2">
<tr bgcolor="tan">
<th>id</th><th>Airport</th><th>Departure</th><th>Seats</th></tr>
<%
try {
  if ("first".equals(request.getParameter("action")))
    crs.beforeFirst();
  for (int i=0; (i < 5) && crs.next(); i++) {
%>
<tr>
<td><%= crs.getString("id") %></td>
<td><%= crs.getString("airport") %></td>
<td><%= crs.getString("time") %></td>
<td><%= crs.getString("seats") %></td>
</tr>
<% } %>
</table>
</p>
<%
```

```
if (crs.isAfterLast()) {
  crs.beforeFirst(); %>
<br>At the end of the result set<br>
<% } }
catch (SQLException e) { out.println("SQL Error" + e); }
%>

<a href="<%= HttpUtils.getRequestURL(request) %>?action=first">
[First 5]</a> 
<a href="<%= HttpUtils.getRequestURL(request) %>?action=next">
[Next 5]</a> 
</center>
</body>
</html>
```

NOTE The `HttpUtils` class has been deprecated as of Java Servlet API 2.3. These methods in that class were only useful with the default encoding and have been moved to the request interfaces. The call to the `HttpUtils.getRequestURL` method can be replaced by calling the `getRequestURL()` method of the request object directly.

In this example, we create a session scoped `CachedRowSet` in our `<jsp:useBean>` tag, and use the body of that tag to configure it and execute our query. It is important to note that we must call attention to the database driver *before* we set the `url` property of our bean. If we don't, the database `DriverManager` class will not recognize the URL as being associated with our driver, resulting in an error.

If the user clicks either link at the bottom of the page, a request parameter is set to indicate the desired action. So if the user clicks the "First 5" link, we move the cursor back to its starting position just before the first row of the `CashedRowSet`.

If the user selects the next five, the default, we don't have to do anything special. Since the `CashedRowSet` set is stored inside our session the cursor position will not change, and we'll simply pick up where we left off at the end of the previous viewing. We loop through the result with a `for` loop.

If more than five rows are left in the `CachedRowSet` the loop iterates through them. In each step we are advancing the cursor one position and making sure we don't go off the end of the results. The loop stops after five iterations or when `crs.next()` returns `false`—whichever occurs first. Inside the loop we simply display the data from the database. After the loop, we must move the cursor back to the beginning as if we had run out of data, essentially looping back through the data. Note the following code, near the end of the example:

```
<a href="<%= HttpUtils.getRequestURL(request) %>?action=next">
```

The `getRequestURL()` method of `HttpUtils` (part of `javax.servlet`, which is automatically imported by the JSP page) creates a link back to the current page, rather than hard coding our own URL. We include the `action` request necessary to indicate the user's selection by tacking it onto the end of the request in GET encoding syntax.

9.2.5 Transaction processing

Most of the JSP/database interactions we've been studying involve single step actions. That is, one SQL statement is executed and we are done. Oftentimes however, a single action is actually composed of a series of interrelated SQL statements that should succeed or fail together. For example, transferring money between two accounts is a two-step process. You have to debit one account and credit the other. By default, the database will process each statement immediately, an irrevocable action. In our funds transfer example, if the credit action went through but the debit one didn't, we would be left with accounts that don't balance.

Databases provide a mechanism known as *transactions* that help avoid such problems. A transaction is a block of related SQL statements treated as a single action, and subsequently recalled in the event that any one of the individual statements fails or encounters unexpected results. It is important to understand that to each statement in the transaction, the database will show any changes made by the previous statements in the same transaction. Anyone looking at the database outside the scope of the transaction will either not see the changes until the entire transaction has completed, or will be blocked from using the database until it is done. The behavior of the database during the transaction is configurable, but limited to the capabilities of the database with which you are working. This ability to block access to data you are working with lets you develop transactions composed of a complex series of steps without having to worry about leaving the database in an invalid state.

When you are satisfied with the results of your database statements, signal the database to accept the changes as final through the `commit()` method of your `Connection` object. Likewise, to revoke any changes made since the start of the transaction simply call your `Connection` object's `rollback()` method, which returns the database to the state it was after the last transaction was committed.

By default, JDBC assumes that you want to treat each SQL statement as its own transaction. This feature is known as *autocommit*, where each statement is committed automatically as soon as it is issued. To begin a block of statements under transaction control, you have to turn off the autocommit feature, as shown in the example which follows—a transaction where we'll swap funds between Bob's and Sue's accounts.

When we've completed all of the steps in our transaction, we'll re-enable the auto-commit feature.

```
connection.setAutoCommit(false);
try {
  Statement st = connection.createStatement();
  st.executeUpdate(
    "UPDATE ACCTS SET BALANCE=(BALANCE-100) WHERE OWNER = "Bob");
  st.executeUpdate(
    "UPDATE ACCTS SET BALANCE=(BALANCE + 100) WHERE OWNER = "Sue");
  connection.commit();
}
catch (SQLException e) { connection.rollback(); }
finally { connection.setAutoCommit(true); }
```

In the example we roll back the transaction if a problem occurs, and there are a number of reasons one could. Bob and Sue might not exist, or their account may not be accessible to our program, Bob's account may not have enough funds to cover the transaction, the database could explode between the first and second statements. Wrapping them into a transaction ensures that the entire process either completes, or the whole thing fails—not something in between.

9.3 Example: JSP conference booking tool

We'll wrap up this chapter with an example that ties together much of what we've learned about JSP database access: data retrieval, persistent connections, and multi-page transaction processing. Here we'll concentrate on the database code rather than the application architecture, which is covered in chapter 10.

9.3.1 Project overview

In this project we must build an application to support an upcoming JSP conference, which is being held in several major cities across the U.S. First, we must determine which conference (city) the user plans to attend and reserve a slot for him or her, as seating is very limited. Secondly, we must also reserve a seat for the user on one of the several shuttle buses which will transport participants from the airport to the conference. The tricky part is making sure that once the user has secured a ticket to the conference he or she doesn't lose it to other users while picking a shuttle option. This becomes a very real possibility when you consider thousands of users registering across the globe simultaneously.

9.3.2 *Our database*

Our database back end already exists and is populated with the relevant data in two tables, Conferences (table 9.2) and Shuttles (table 9.3). The tables are related through their respective Airport column, which holds the three-character identifier for each airport associated with each conference city. Once the user has selected a city, we can use the airport identifier to locate appropriate shuttle service.

Table 9.2 Schema for the Conferences table

Column	Type
ID	`int`
CITY	`varchar(80)`
AIRPORT	`char(3)`
SEATS	`int`

Table 9.3 Schema for the Shuttles table

Column	Type
ID	`int`
AIRPORT	`char(3)`
TIME	`time`
SEATS	`int`

9.3.3 *Design overview*

There are four basic steps in this process: picking a city, choosing a shuttle, reviewing selections, and confirming the transaction. A user will be presented a list of cities where the conference will be held and may select any one of them where space is available. Doing so should hold his or her seat in the database by starting a transaction. This will ensure that the user doesn't lose his or her seat while selecting the shuttle in the second step. The third and fourth steps in the process are to have the user review his or her selections and confirm them—committing the changes to the database—or abort the process, rolling back the selections to free them for other, less fickle attendees.

To maintain a transaction across several pages like this we'll need to use JSP's session management capabilities to store our connection to the database, which we'll wrap in the `ConnectionBean` we built earlier in this chapter. This will allow our transaction to span each page in the process. The pages, in order of application flow, are shown in figure 9.3. As you can see, we've also created a separate error page we can use to report any problem with the database or other element of the application.

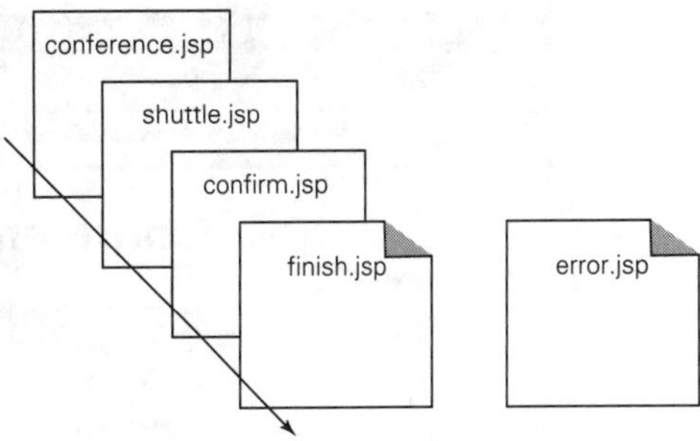

Figure 9.3 The JSP pages of our registration application

Step 1: conference.jsp

The responsibilities of the conference selection page (figure 9.4) are to present the user with a list of conference cities, pulled from the database, and allow him/her to select any of them which have openings. The source code is shown in listing 9.3.

Listing 9.3 conference.jsp

```
<%@ page import="java.sql.*,com.taglib.wdjsp.databases.*" errorPage="error.jsp" %>
<jsp:useBean id="connection" class="ConnectionBean" scope="session"/>
<html>
<body>
<center>
<font size="+2" face="arial"><b>Conference Registration</b></font>
<form action="shuttle.jsp" method="post">
<table border=1 bgcolor="tan" width="50%" align="center">
<tr><td>
<table border="0" bgcolor="white" cellspacing=0 width="100%">
<tr bgcolor="tan">
<th> </th><th>City</th><th>Tickets Remaining</th></tr>
<%
String sql = "SELECT * FROM CONFERENCES";
ResultSet results = connection.executeQuery(sql);
while (results.next()) {
  if (results.getInt("seats") > 0) {
%>
<td>
<input type="radio" name="show"
value="<%= results.getString("id") %>">
</td>
<% } else { %>
```

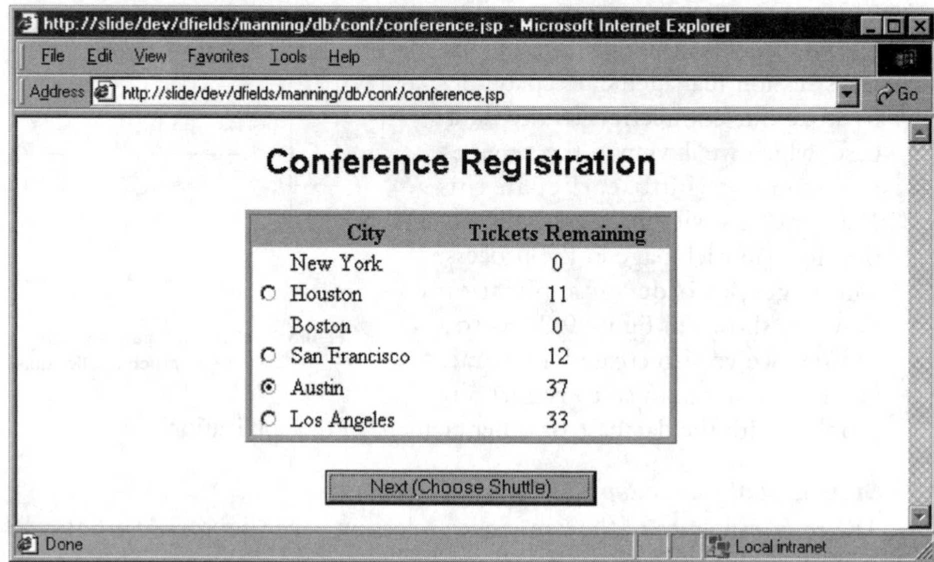

Figure 9.4 The conference selection page

```
<td> </td>
<% } %>
<td><%= results.getString("city") %></td>
<td align="center"><%= results.getString("seats") %></td>
</tr>
<% } %>
</table>
</td></tr></table>

<p>
<input type="submit" value="Next (Choose Shuttle)">
</form>
</center>

</body>
</html>
```

This is the entry point into our application, but because our simple `ConnectionBean` shields the database information from the page, we needn't do anything special to configure it. In fact, each page in our application starts with a block of code to import our database classes and reference the `ConnectionBean` from the session, or—in this case—create a `ConnectionBean` and place it into the session.

Once we have a connection to the database we can simply build our form using data from the Conference table by executing the appropriate query and looping

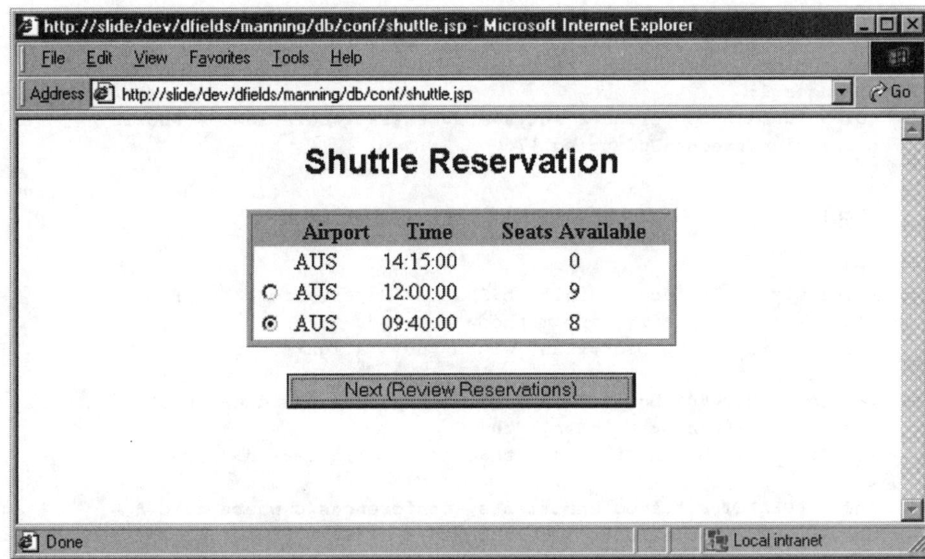

Figure 9.5 The shuttle selection page

through it with a `while` loop. For each row in the table, we verify that there are seats available before adding a radio button for this city, ensuring that we don't allow the user to pick a conference that is full. We use the ID of each conference as the value of the radio button, to which we have given the name `show`. We'll use that in the next page to hold their seat at the conference. The rest of the code is pretty straightforward HTML. Clicking Next directs the user to the next page of the application, shuttle.jsp (figure 9.5).

Step 2: shuttle.jsp

The shuttle selection page has a double duty. First it has to act on the information gathered on the conference selection page. We have to reserve the user a seat at the selected conference. Secondly, we have to allow the user to pick a conference shuttle selection based on which conference city he/she will be visiting. The source appears in listing 9.4.

Listing 9.4 shuttle.jsp

```
<%@ page import="java.sql.*,com.taglib.wdjsp.databases.*"
errorPage="error.jsp" %>
<jsp:useBean id="connection" class="ConnectionBean"
scope="session"/>
```

```
<%
String showID = request.getParameter("show");
connection.setAutoCommit(false);
String sql;
sql = "UPDATE conferences set seats=seats-1 where id=" + showID;
connection.executeUpdate(sql);
%>

<html>
<body>
<center>
<font size="+2" face="arial"><b>Shuttle Reservation</b></font>
<form action="confirm.jsp" method="post">
<table border=1 bgcolor="tan" width="50%" align="center">
<tr><td>
<table border="0" bgcolor="white" cellspacing=0 width="100%">
<tr bgcolor="tan"><th> </th>
<th>Airport</th><th>Time</th><th>Seats Available</th></tr>
<%
sql = "SELECT s.* from shuttles s, conferences c where c.id=" +
showID + " and s.airport = c.airport";
ResultSet results = connection.executeQuery(sql);
while (results.next()) {
  if (results.getInt("seats") > 0) {
%>
<td>
<input type="radio" name="shuttle"
value="<%= results.getString("id") %>">
</td>
<% } else { %>
<td> </td>
<% } %>
<td><%= results.getString("airport") %></td>
<td><%= results.getTime("time") %></td>
<td align="center"><%= results.getString("seats") %></td>
</tr>
<% } %>
</table>
</td></tr></table>
<p>
<input type="hidden" name="show" value="<%= showID %>">
<input type="submit" value="Next (Review Reservations)">
</form>
</center>

</body>
</html>
```

Now, after grabbing a reference to the `ConnectionBean` from the session, we grab the selected show ID from the request and stash it in a local variable. We'll need it to update the database, plus we'll pass it on to the pages that follow so we can summarize the user's selections on the last page.

```
String showID = request.getParameter("show");
```

We now actually reserve the user a seat at his or her selected conference, by reducing the open seat count by one. Before we do this however, we turn off the auto-commit feature of the database, thereby starting a transaction.

Generating our input form is no different than on the first page of the application, although the database query is more complicated.

```
"SELECT s.* from shuttles s, conferences c WHERE c.id=" +
showID + " and s.airport = c.airport"
```

That translates into a statement something like this:

```
SELECT s.* from shuttles s, conferences c
WHERE c.id=12 and s.airport = c.airport
```

Which, in English, means "perform a join on the table's shuttles and conferences, keeping only the shuttle table's columns, and select only those rows where the conference ID is 12 and the conference and shuttle are associated with the same airport." This gives us a subset of the available shuttles, showing only those available for our selected city. (Note that we can specify a table alias after each table's name (the `s` and `c` values) which keeps us from having to spell out the full table name each time we use it in the application.)

We then loop through the result set as before, again not allowing the user to select an entry that is already full. We'll still need the `showID` selected in the original page later in the application, so we'll carry that on through a hidden form field.

```
<INPUT TYPE="HIDDEN" NAME="show" VALUE="<%= showID %>">
```

We could have placed it into the session, but this is just as easy for now and involves fewer steps. Figure 9.6 shows how the user confirms his/her reservation.

Step 3: confirm.jsp

On this page we must reserve the user's seat on the selected shuttle, display a summary of his/her selections from the first two screens, and then ask the user to either commit or cancel the reservation. Listing 9.5 is the source code for the page:

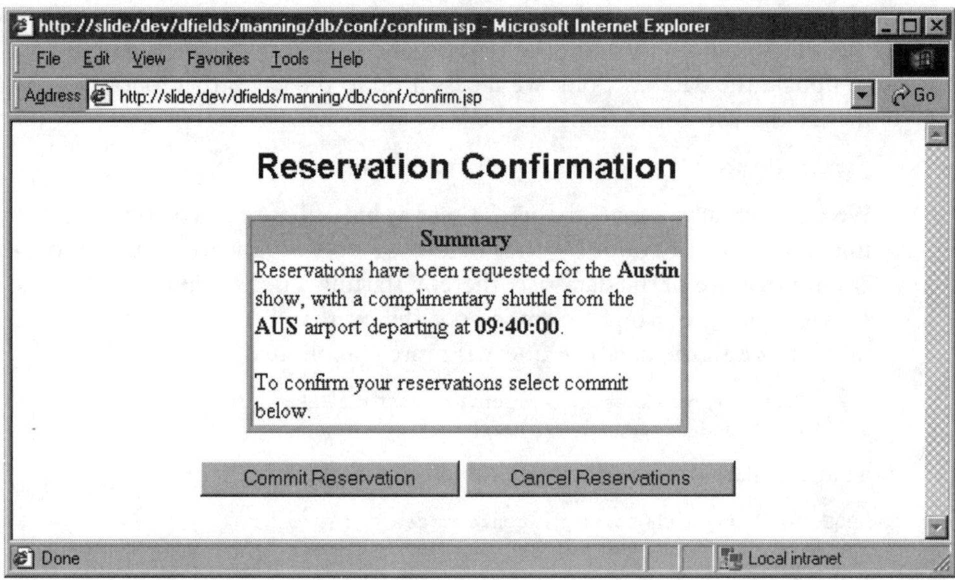

Figure 9.6 The confirmation request page

Listing 9.5 confirm.jsp

```
<%@ page import="java.sql.*,com.taglib.wdjsp.databases.*" errorPage="error.jsp" %>
<jsp:useBean id="connection" class="ConnectionBean" scope="session"/>
<%
String sql;
String shuttleID = request.getParameter("shuttle");
String showID = request.getParameter("show");
sql = "UPDATE shuttles set seats=seats-1 where id=" + shuttleID;
connection.executeUpdate(sql);
sql = "SELECT c.city, c.airport, s.time from conferences c, " +
  "shuttles s where c.id=" + showID + " and s.id=" + shuttleID;
ResultSet results = connection.executeQuery(sql);
results.next();
%>
<html>
<body>
<center>
<font size="+2" face="arial"><B>Reservation Confirmation</b></font>
<form action="finish.jsp" method=post>
<table border=1 bgcolor="tan" width="50%" align="center">
<tr><td>
<table border="0" bgcolor="white" cellspacing=0 width="100%">
<tr bgcolor="tan"><th>Summary</th></tr>
```

```
<tr><td>
Reservations have been requested for
the <b><%= results.getString("city") %></b>
show, with a complimentary shuttle from
the <b><%= results.getString("airport") %></b> airport
departing at <b><%= results.getTime("time") %></b>.
<p>
To confirm your reservations select commit below.
</td></tr>
</table>
</td></tr></table>

<p>
<input type="submit" name="commit" value="Commit Reservation">
<input type="submit" name="rollback" value="Cancel Reservations">
</body>
</html>
```

Again, there's not much new here. We decrement the appropriate shuttle seat count, just as we did earlier with the conference. We've now made all the changes we plan to make to the database, but remember we are still under transaction control since we turned off autocommit earlier. We have to disable autocommit only once, because it is a property of our connection, which we have stored in our session via the `ConnectionBean`.

```
sql = "UPDATE shuttles set seats = seats - 1 where id = " + shuttleID;
connection.executeUpdate(sql);
```

The query to get the summary information is a little complicated; we could have broken it into a couple of separate queries, extracting the appropriate data from each. However, it's not necessary.

```
sql = "SELECT c.city, c.airport, s.time from conferences c, shuttles s where
  c.id=" + showID + " and s.id=" + shuttleID;
```

This selects the columns we are interested in from the intersection of the `CONFERENCE` and `SHUTTLES` table where the corresponding ID values match the two selections the user already made. At that point, we are ready to move on to the final page (figure 9.7), which, depending on which button the user clicks, will commit the transaction or roll it back.

Step 4: finish.jsp

Listing 9.6 is the final segment of our application.

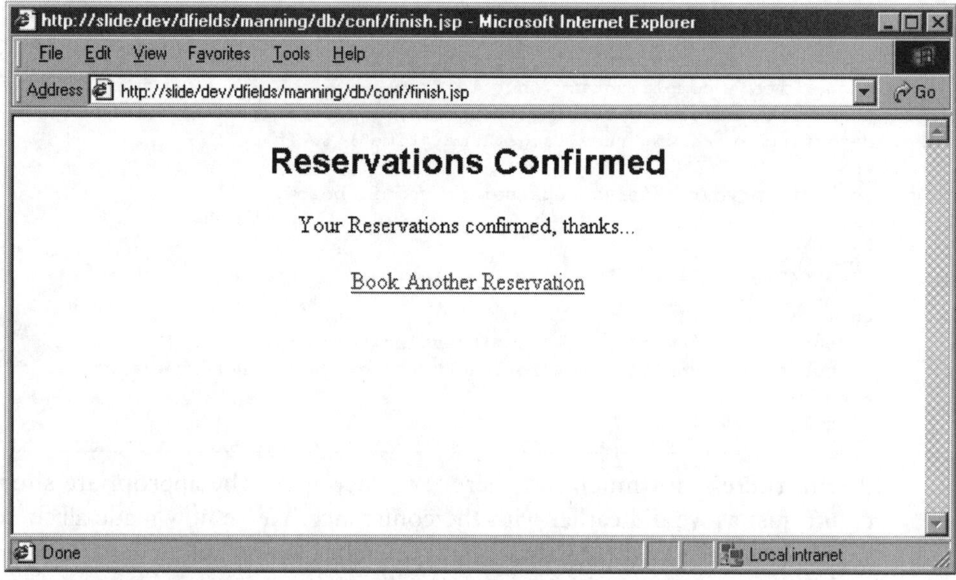

Figure 9.7 The final page

Listing 9.6 finish.jsp

```
<%@ page import="java.sql.*,com.taglib.wdjsp.databases.*"
errorPage="error.jsp" %>
<html>
<body>
<%
ConnectionBean connection =
(ConnectionBean)session.getValue("connection");
if (request.getParameter("commit") != null)
  connection.commit();
else
  connection.rollback();
session.removeAttribute("connection");
%>
<center>
<% if (request.getParameter("commit") != null) { %>
<font size="+2" face="arial"><b>Reservations Confirmed</b></font>
<p>
Your Reservations confirmed, thanks...
<% } else { %>
<font size="+2" face="arial"><b>Reservations Canceled</b></font>
<p>
Your reservations have been canceled.
```

```
<% } %>

<p>
<a href="conference.jsp">Book Another Reservation</a>

</body>
</html>
```

If the user selected Commit, it will show up as a request parameter. If we detect this we'll commit the transaction. Otherwise, we'll call rollback:

```
if (request.getParameter("commit") != null)
  connection.commit();
else
  connection.rollback();
```

After saving our changes, we must get rid of that `ConnectionBean` to free its resources, including the database we've been holding. So, we simply remove the connection object from the session.

```
session.removeAttribute("connection");
```

The last step is to give the user feedback, with an `if` block, based on his/her decision. All in all the flow through this example is straightforward and linear. To wrap this example up, let's look at the error page.

The error.jsp page

This page (listing 9.7) is referenced as an error handler for each page in the application. If any exception occurs in the course of communicating with the database, it will be forwarded to this page.

Listing 9.7 error.jsp

```
<%@ page import="java.sql.*,com.taglib.wdjsp.databases.*"
isErrorPage="true" %>
<html>
<body>
<%
if (exception instanceof SQLException) {
  try {
   ConnectionBean connection = (ConnectionBean)session.getAttribute("connection");
    connection.getConnection().rollback();
    session.removeAttribute("connection");
  }
  catch (SQLException e) { }
}
```

```
%>
<center>
<font size="+2" face="arial"><b>Application Error</b></font>
<p>
An error has occurred: <tt><%= exception %></tt>
<p>
<a href="conference.jsp">Book Another Reservation</a>
</center>
</body>
</html>
```

On this page we try to clean up some things and let the user know what has happened. In the code we abort our transactions and remove the connection object from our session when an error occurs. We'll see more detailed discussion on creating error pages in chapter 14.

10

Architecting JSP applications

This chapter covers

- Building applications with JSP alone
- Learning to combine servlets and JSP pages
- Understanding architectural tradeoffs

Now that we have covered the better portion of material on how to use JSP to build dynamic web pages, we will look at how we can construct complete web applications with this technology. In this chapter we will discuss several architectural models useful for developing JSP applications. We will examine architectural options available to us when we combine JSP pages with servlets, EJBs, HTML, and other software elements to create web-based applications.

10.1 Web applications

When designing a web application of any complexity, it helps to think of its high-level architecture in terms of three logical areas:

- The *presentation layer*, the front end which controls the look and feel and delivers results, also known as the view
- The *control layer*, which controls application flow, also known as the controller
- The *application logic* layer, which manages application data, performs calculations and communicates with back-end resources, also known as the model

The three layers (figure 10.1) aren't necessarily separate software elements or components (though as we shall see they can be), but rather they are useful constructs to help us understand our application's requirements. If you are familiar with design patterns, a collection of common strategies used in software development, you might recognize this three-part architecture as an implementation of the Model-View-Controller, or MVC, pattern. The MVC pattern is concerned with separating the information (the model) from its presentation (the view), which maps nicely into our strategy.

Each layer plays an important role in an application's architecture and will be discussed briefly in the sections which follow. It is often advantageous to treat each tier as an independent portion of your application. Isolating the logical portions of the application helps ensure that you've covered all the bases in the design, focuses attention on creating a robust architecture, and lays the groundwork for the implementation.

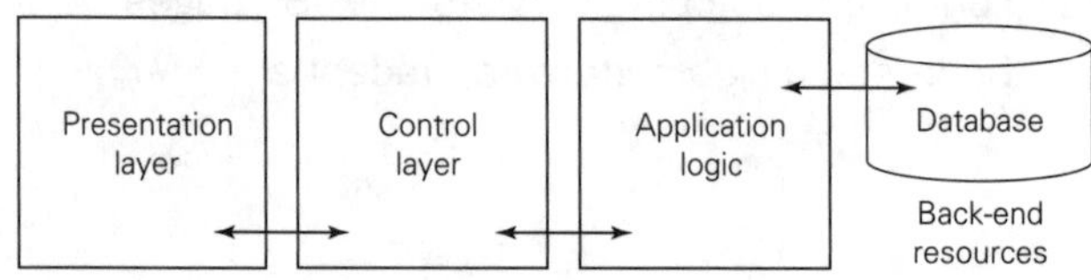

Figure 10.1 Web application layers

Do not confuse logical separation of responsibilities with actual separation of components. Each tier does not necessarily need to be implemented by separate components. Some or all of the tiers can be combined into single components to reduce application complexity, at the expense of modularity and high-level abstraction.

The presentation layer

This tier includes the client-side display elements, such as HTML, XML, or Java applets. The presentation layout tier can be thought of as the user interface for the application because it is used to get input from the end user and display the application's results. In the MVC paradigm, the presentation layout tier fills the role of the view. It is an application specific presentation of the information owned by the application logic, or model in MVC terms.

The presentation layout tier is not concerned with how the information was obtained, or from where. Its responsibilities lie only in displaying the information itself, while delegating any other activity up the chain to other tiers. For example, in an application which involves submitting a search query through a web form only the form itself and the corresponding results are the responsibility of the presentation layer. What happens in between, the processing of the request and the retrieval of the results, is not.

Application logic

The application logic layer is the heart of the application, responsible for actually doing whatever it is the application is supposed to do. It is responsible for performing queries against a database, calculating sales tax, or processing orders. This layer models the data and behavior behind the business process for which we are developing the application. It is an encapsulation of data and behavior that is independent of its presentation.

Unlike the presentation layer, this tier cares only about storing, manipulating, and generating data, not displaying it. For this reason, components designed to work as application logic can be relocated outside web-based applications, since the behavior they encapsulate isn't web-centric.

Control layer

The control layer determines the application's flow, serving as an intermediary between the presentation layer and the application logic. This tier serves as the logical connection between the user's interaction with the front-end and business services on the back end. In the MVC pattern this tier is acting as the controller. It delivers the model to the view and regulates communication between the two.

This tier is also responsible for making decisions among multiple presentations, when available. If a user's language, locale, or access level dictates a different presentation, this decision is made in the control layer. For example, an administrator might see all of the data from a database query, while an end user might see an alternate, more restrictive results page.

Each request enters the application through the control layer, which decides how the request should be handled and what information should be returned. Several things could happen at this point, depending on the circumstances of the request and the application.

For example, the control layer might determine that the requested URL is protected by access control, in which case it would forward the request to a logon page if the user has not yet been authenticated. This is an example of presentation logic controlling the application's flow from screen to screen. If any application work needs to be done, the application's presentation logic will collect data from the request, if necessary, and deliver it to the application logic tier for processing. When the application logic has completed its operation, the controller directs the request back to the user via the presentation layer.

10.1.1 Web application flow

Applications, no matter the platform, are designed with a particular flow in mind. Operations are expected to unfold in a series of steps, each with a specific purpose and each in an order anticipated by the application's designer. For example, to edit a user's profile you might prompt for a username whose profile you wish to edit, display that user's current profile information, ask for changes, process those changes, and then display or confirm the results of the operation. As programmers, we expect the user—indeed require the user—to proceed through each part of the application in a certain, predetermined order. We can't, for example, display user profile details without first selecting the username. The nature of the web however, can disrupt the rigid flow we've come to expect from applications.

Unlike traditional applications, web-based programs are forced to deal with strange interruptions that may occur in the expected flow of a program due to the inherent stateless request/response behavior of the HTTP protocol. The user can hit the Back button on the browser, hit reload, prematurely abort an in-process request, or open new browser windows at any time. In an application involving transactions, the application may require that certain activities happen under very specific circumstances or after certain prerequisites have been met. For example, you can't save a modified entry until you have first retrieved the original from the database; you can't delete an item until you have confirmed your selection; you can't submit an order twice, and so forth.

In a traditional, off-line application, the developer has full control over the program flow. Each step in the application's process logically flows through the program. A JSP application is a different story all together. Web applications are vulnerable to irregularities in the program flow. We're not talking malicious intent; it's a perfectly innocent action on the part of users, conditioned to browsing traditional web pages. They may bookmark the application halfway through the process, or may click the Back in an attempt to go back to a step in the application. Or, they may abort the request prematurely or attempt to reload the page. In any case, they break the program flow we might normally expect. It is the responsibility of the JSP application to ensure that proper program state and application flow is maintained.

10.1.2 Architectural approaches

Possibly the biggest choice you face in designing a JSP application is determining how to separate the responsibilities of presentation, control, and application logic. There are two basic approaches to take when architecting a JSP application: page-centric and servlet-centric.

In the first approach, control and application logic responsibilities are handled by the JSP pages themselves; in the second, an intermediate servlet (or servlets) are used. Cleanly separating a JSP application into presentation, control, and application logic subsystems makes it easier to develop, understand, and maintain.

10.2 Page-centric design

In the page-centric approach an application is composed solely of a series of interrelated JSP pages that handle all aspects—the presentation, control, and the application logic. In this approach client requests are handled directly by JSP pages that perform whatever tasks are necessary, including communicating with back-end data sources, performing operations, and generating dynamic content elements.

All of the application logic and control decisions about which page to visit next will be hard coded into the page itself or expressed through its beans, scriptlets, and expressions at run time. Commonly, the next page visited would be determined by a user clicking on a hyperlink anchor, for example `<A HREF="checkout.jsp">`, or through the action of submitting a form, `<FORM ACTION="processSearch.jsp">`.

10.2.1 Role-based pages

In the page-centric design model, each JSP page has a very specific role to play in the application. One page might display a menu of options, another might provide a form for selecting items from the catalog, and another would be needed to complete the shopping process. How a typical application might flow between these different pages is illustrated in figure 10.2.

We've combined the application logic and program flow layers of our applications at the page level. This doesn't mean that we lose our separation of presentation and content. We can still use the dynamic nature of JSP and its support for JavaBeans components to keep things squared away. We've just elected to use the JSP pages as containers for the application's control and logic, which ideally would still be encapsulated into discrete components wherever possible.

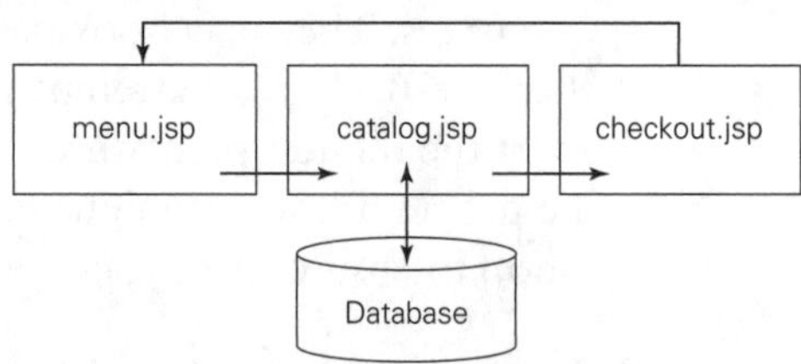

Figure 10.2 Page-centric program flow

A simple page-centric application

Here's a simple example of a trivial, two-page application using scriptlets for the application logic. In this application (and we are using the term very loosely) we are creating a system for rebel command to help sign up new recruits for Jedi training. Perhaps the most important part of the process is determining the Jedi name given to new recruits. This highly scientific calculation involves manipulating the letters of the user's first and last names with that of the hometown and mother's maiden name. This is a pretty typical two-step form application. The first page, `jediform.html`, contains an HTML form, which collects the information needed to perform processing, while the second screen, `jediname.jsp`, calculates and displays the recruit's new name (figure 10.3). The source codes for the operations are in listings 10.1 and 10.2.

Listing 10.1 jediform.html

```
<html>
<body>
<b>Jedi Registration Center</b>
<form action="jediname.jsp" method="post">
<input type="text" name="firstName"> First Name<BR>
<input type="text" name="lastName"> Last Name<BR>
<input type="text" name="mother"> Mother's Maiden Name<BR>
<input type="text" name="hometown"> Hometown<BR>
<p>
<input type="submit" value="Signup Now!">
</form>
</body>
</html>
```

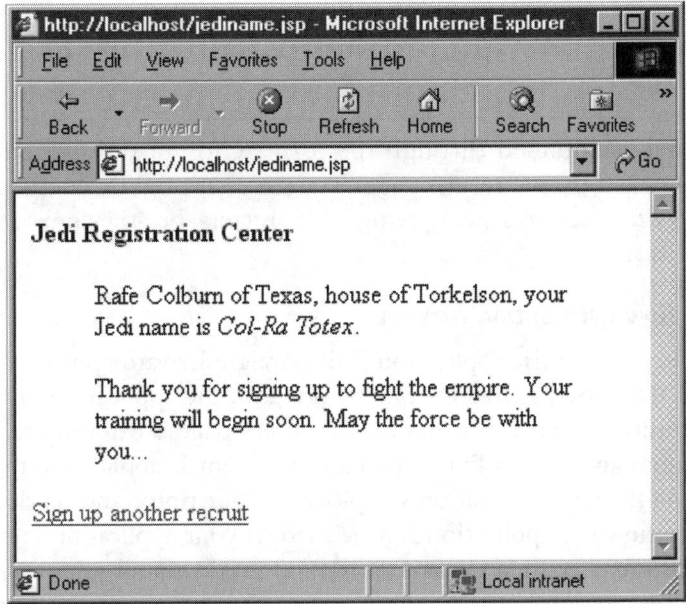

Figure 10.3 A page-centric application

Listing 10.2 jediname.jsp

```
<html>
<body>
<%
  String firstName = request.getParameter("firstName");
  String lastName = request.getParameter("lastName");
  String mother = request.getParameter("mother");
  String hometown = request.getParameter("hometown");

  String newFirst = lastName.substring(0,3) + "-" +
    firstName.substring(0,2);
  String newLast = mother.substring(0,2) +
    hometown.substring(0,3).toLowerCase();
  String jediname = newFirst + " " + newLast;
%>
<b>Jedi Registration Center</b>
<p>
<blockquote>
<%= firstName %> <%= lastName %> of <%= hometown %>,
house of <%= mother %>, your Jedi name is <i><%= jediname %></i>.
<p>
Thank you for signing up to fight the empire.
Your training will begin soon. May the force be with you...
```

```
</blockquote>
<a href="jediform.html">Sign up another recruit</a>
</body>
</html>
```

Application flow is maintained through the form action in the first page, and through the anchor tab on the results page. The pages are tightly coupled in this case. Not only do they need to sync up request parameters, but they must be aware of each other's URLs.

10.2.2 Managing page flow with action targets

One benefit of the page-centric application is the straightforward approach to page flow. It is immediately obvious to someone working on the application or web site what the intended flow is between pages because every page is explicitly referenced through form actions and anchor links. With a servlet-centric application the developer must examine the web application's deployment descriptor and servlet source code to determine how the application is processed. If your application logic is not hidden behind custom tags, then this approach tends to do a poor job of separating application and presentation logic. A compromise exists however, allowing you to keep an obvious and straightforward application flow while minimizing the mixing of application code and presentation. This approach, which we call action targets, isolates your application code into JSP pages whose only responsibility is processing a request and then forwarding the request on to another HTML or JSP page responsible for the presentation.

In this approach, which works particularlly well with form driven applications, the JSP page targeted by a form submission contains a JSP scriptlet which processes the request. This page is the action target. After processing, and possibly dependent on the outcome of the processing, the request is directed to the next page in the application.

The redict may be either a server-side redirect via a request dispatcher, or more commonly, a client-side redirect courtesy of `HttpServletResponse.sendRedirect()`. A client-side redirect actually sends a response header back to the client, redirecting it to another URL. No content is returned from the action target in either case. If you make use of the request dispatcher's `forward()` method, the original request is preserved and accessible by the presentation page. In the case of a client-side redirect, the request received by the presentation page is not the same request delivered to the action target. It does not contain request parameters, or attributes. It is possible to pass the request parameters to the presentation page by dynamically constructing the redirect URL to contain the appropriate parameters, in typically GET request fashion. You may also encode request parameters onto the URL to pass information from the action target. Take for example this action target for handling a bank account transfer. If the transfer succeeds, there is a single success page to visit. If it fails however, you want to include a brief error message. We could code this as shown in the following action target, taken from a banking application. In it, it receives information from an HTML form used to initiate a funds transfer.

```
<%
String src = request.getParameter("srcAccount");
String dest = request.getParameter("destAccount");
String amount = request.getParameter("amount");

int result = BankManager.instance().transfer(src, dest, amount);
if (result == 0) {
  response.sendRedirect("transferSuccessful.jsp?amount=" + amount);
}
else {
  String msg;
  if (result == 100)
    msg = "Insufficient Funds";
  else if (result == 200)
    msg = "Destination Account Invalid";
  else if (result == 300)
    msg = "Source Account Invalid";
  else
    msg = "Unknown Error: Transfer Failed";
  // encode the msg for for use as a request parameter
  response.sendRedirect("transferFailed.jsp?msg=" + msg);
}
%>
```

In the example, the hypothetical `BankManager` class actually attempts to perform the transfer, returning a result code to indicate the success or failure. In this case, a code of 0 indicates that everything went okay, while other codes are used to report error conditions. After processing, the client is redirected to either transferSuccessful.jsp or transferFailed.jsp for presentation, which would presumbably give the user appropriate feedback. We'd like to show the amount of the transfer on the success page, but with a client-side redirect the original request parameters are lost. Therefore, we pass the value of the amount parameter to the success page through a GET parameter. Moreover, the failure page is passsed a request parameter, `msg`, which contains the reason for the failure as determined by the result code returned from the `BankManager`'s `transfer` method.

WARNING Unlike the request dispatcher and the `<jsp:include>` tag, the path referenced in the `response.sendRedirect()` method is absolute to the document root of the server, not the servlet context. If you want to redirect the client to another document within your web application, you must prepend the servlet context to the path, as you must do with HTML references. For example:

```
<%
response.sendRedirect(request.getContextPath() + "
      /destination.jsp");
%>
```

Another fact that may influence the type of redirect to use (server or client) is how you want the browser to react. Using a request dispatcher preserves the original action URL in the browser, while a client redirect actually sends the browser to another URL.

The code in the action target could just as easily have been placed into a servlet (see the section of this chapter on developing servlet-centric applications), to create an additional layer of abstraction between the presentation and logic aspects. Whether this is a benefit or a hinderence to your project depends on a number of factors, including your comfort level with servlets and WAR files, as well as who will be working with the code most often and their familiarity with the application as a whole. One situation where the action target technique can be particularly helpful is during testing and debugging. If there is a problem with a particular form on the web site or application it is trivial for someone unfamiliar with the code to determine the source of the problem, even without access to the source code. If a form submission is going through a servlet reference specified in a web application, the tester may be unable to determine where the request started and where it is going without a good understanding of servlets, WAR files, and your application's architecture.

10.2.3 Building composite pages

The idea of creating composite pages expands on the single page approach illustrated earlier but doesn't change the fact that application presentation, logic, and control systems are confined to a series of JSP pages. However in this design style we combine a collection of small component pages, containing either HTML or JSP, to create each screen in the application. This is accomplished through the use of the `<jsp:include>` action and the `<%@ include>` directive.

Reducing complexity through decomposition

The composite page structure is a good approach when the pages that make up your application (or web site) are composed of a number of complex dynamic elements. For example, to display details of a catalog item we might break the page into several elements—a site standard header containing navigational elements and branding, the details of the item itself, and a footer to close the page. Each of these elements can be either static, such as a snippet of HTML code, or dynamic—another JSP file. We can take this strategy a step further by building our composite page of elements which are also composite pages themselves—iteratively breaking down each element into more manageable structures. Each portion of the page comes from a separate JSP or HTML file, as shown in figure 10.4.

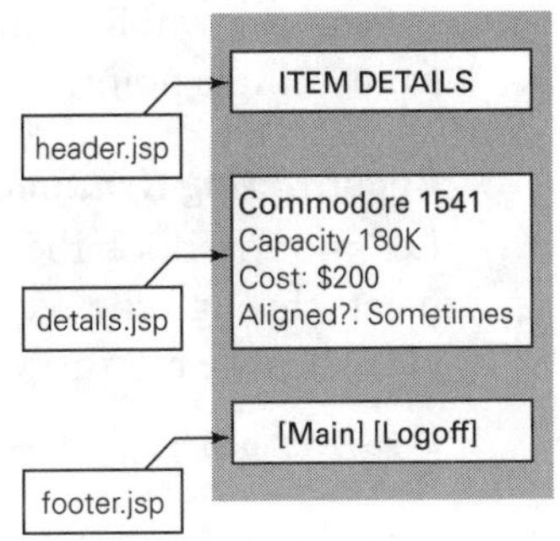

Figure 10.4 Component page

As illustrated, the header and footer files might be static HTML elements. We would then use the `<%@ include %>` directive to load the contents of the files in at run time. The item we wish to display however, might apply a boilerplate approach, by creating a JSP template, which we reuse throughout the site. This gives us the ability to isolate the presentation of an item's details (which might involve complex HTML code) from the higher-level layout of its containing page. The page designer could choose to include the item information anywhere on the page, and in any context desired.

At run time, the primary page and any of its dynamic elements will not have to be recompiled by the JSP engine unless they themselves have changed—static content is included dynamically and not through the compilation process. For example, a change to the header file will show up at run time, but will not compile a new version of its containing JSP page each time. An excerpt from such a compound catalog page code might look like this:

```
<html>
<body>
<jsp:include page="/headers/support_section.jsp" flush="true"/>
<center><h2>Catalog Item 7423</h2></center>
<jsp:include page="/catalog/item7423.jsp" flush="true"/>
<hr>
<jsp:include page="/footers/standard.html" flush="true"/>
</html>
</body>
```

We can concentrate on the design of each portion of the page independently of the system as a whole. This also gives us the ability to change the design at any time, from a single point.

Constructing dynamic page components

Let's not overlook the fact that you can pass information to your composite page elements through the request to provide page-specific or dynamic behaviors. For example, when we call the page we specify the title through a request parameter:

```
<jsp:include page="/headers/basic.jsp" flush="true">
  <jsp:param name="title" value="About Our Company"/>
  <jsp:param name="bgcolor" value="#FFFFFF"/>
</jsp:include>
```

And then in the /headers/basic.jsp file we retrieve the request parameters, and use JSP expressions to include their contents as part of the content we return through the include tag:

```
<html>
<head><title><%= request.getParameter("title") %></title></head>
<body bgcolor="<%= request.getParameter("bgcolor") %>">
<HR>
```

Or, revisiting our catalog item example, we might provide a more complex page component that allows you to pass in parameters to determine which catalog item to display.

```
<jsp:include page="/catalog/fetchItem.jsp" flush="true">
  <jsp:param name="item" value="7423"/>
</jsp:include>
```

We could of course configure the `item` parameter at run time, based on input parameters, giving us an even more useful dynamic page.

```
<jsp:param name="item" value="<%= request.getParameter("item") %>"/>
```

Any beans or other objects that have been loaded into request or application level scope will be available to pages included through the `<jsp:include>` action. Objects created in the default page level scope will not be available.

Component architecture, revisited

In many ways, the composite page view pattern mirrors the component architectural strategies we discussed in the chapter 7. We have broken out various content elements from our page design in order to improve the reusability and ease the process of presentation design and development. The approach we have used here, factoring out the dynamic portions of the page, is a good way to build up a composite page and reduce the complexity of any given JSP page.

The composite page approach provides excellent benefits among collections of pages that can share common elements. By factoring out reusable, redundant information and isolating it to its own files, we get two advantages. First, we reduce the number of files involved by reusing common code. Second, we improve our ability to manage site and application design by gaining the ability to delegate engineering and design resources to discrete subsections of the application—without the potential for stepping on each other's toes.

10.2.4 Limitations of the page-centric approach

A page-centric design is very simple from an architectural perspective. Because there are few moving parts, little abstraction, and a minimum of layers it can be a good approach for individuals and small teams of developers savvy in both HTML design and Java development to quickly create dynamic web pages and simple JSP applications. Because a page-centric approach requires less overall code it may also be a good choice for developing prototypes. However, for an application of any complexity, the page-centric approach suffers from a number of problems.

Maintainability

Because the JSP pages that compose the application contain both presentation and logic/control code, the application can be difficult to maintain. Significant mingling between HTML and JSP code blurs the distinction between web page designer and Java coder, often requiring a high degree of interaction between developers.

Flow contol

The inherent flow control issues of web applications can lead to a number of problems unless you take the proper steps, coding your JSP pages defensively to be prepared for receiving requests out of sequence. Since each segment of a page-centric JSP application is its own page represented by its own URL, there is really nothing to stop a user from executing the pages out of order. Each page of your application must check for valid request parameters, verify open connections, watch for changing conditions, and generally take an assume-nothing approach with regard to the order of operations of your pages. As you can imagine, this quickly becomes unmanageable for all but the simplest applications. A servlet-centric approach, which we discuss next, helps centralize flow control and reduce the complexity of the individual pages.

10.3 Servlet-centric design

Another, often more manageable approach to application design with JSPs is to use its pages only for presentation, with the control and application logic aspects of the application handled by a servlet, or group of servlets, on the back end. In this approach, requests are indirectly routed to the JSP front-end pages via a servlet, which performs whatever actions are needed by the application. A servlet can do any or all of three things for the application:

- Perform actions on behalf of the JSP, such as submitting an order
- Deliver data for display, such as a database record, to a JSP
- Control flow between related JSP pages in an application

After performing the task the servlet forwards the request on to the appropriate JSP, or, for that matter, a static HTML page. This approach is illustrated in figure 10.5.

If you are familiar with the mediator design pattern, this is the same approach only applied to the JSP pages and other components of our application rather than Java objects. In the mediator pattern we create a centralized component, in this case a servlet, whose job it is to control how the other components of the application interact with each other and the application's data resources. This approach loosens the coupling between the pages—allowing them to interact without having to be directly aware of each other, and improves the abstraction between presentation and application logic.

The goal in this approach to application design is to minimize the amount of work being done in the pages themselves, relying instead on application dedicated servlets to handle such aspects. This approach eliminates complexity from the front-end JSP code, reducing them to pure data display and input collection activities. Likewise, we eliminate the need for embedding presentation information inside the servlets. The servlets in this case should be concerned only with application flow and generating the data needed by the JSP pages for presentation to the user.

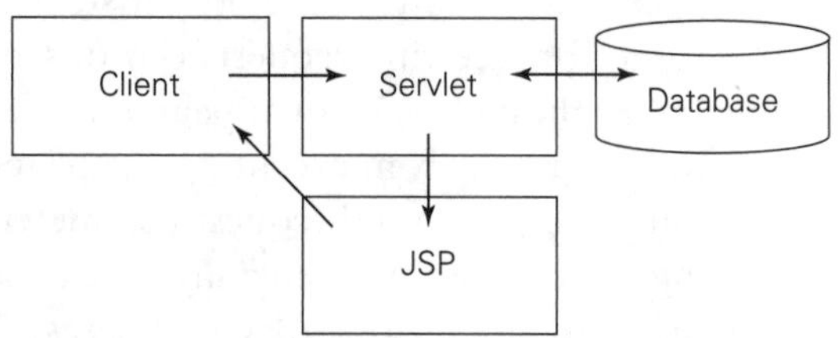

Figure 10.5 Program flow in a servlet-centric application

10.3.1 Hello, World—with servlets

Like any good programming book we started this one off with a couple of "Hello, World" examples—using JSPs with scriptlets and beans. We'll now add another one, using a servlet-centric approach. The request will actually come in to the servlet, which will in turn forward it on to this JSP page (helloFromservlet.jsp):

```
<% String msg = (String)request.getAttribute("message"); %>
<html>
<body>
<%= msg %>
</body
</html>
```

As you'll notice we aren't creating any beans here. The getAttribute() method of the request here is the key. It's similar to getParameter()—it pulls information from the request—but deals with any object rather than just simple Strings. Later in this chapter we'll learn more about how we can use getAttribute() (and its companion the setAttribute() method) to pass beans from servlets to JSP pages. For now though, just understand that it's looking for an object with an identifer of message and retrieving it from the request. How did it get there? The servlet put it there! Remember that this page is not designed to be called directly, but rather pass through our servlet first. The code for our servlet is:

```
package com.taglib.wdjsp.arch;

import java.io.*;
import javax.servlet.*;
import javax.servlet.http.*;

public class HelloWorldServlet extends HttpServlet {
  public void service(HttpServletRequest req,
           HttpServletResponse res)
    throws ServletException, IOException {
    String theMessage = "Hello, World";
    String target = "helloFromServlet.jsp";
    req.setAttribute("message", theMessage);
    RequestDispatcher rd;
    rd = getServletContext().getRequestDispatcher(target);
    rd.forward(req, res);
  }
}
```

When this servlet is called, it creates a "Hello, World" String object, places it into the request with the identifier of "message", creates a RequestDispatcher (a mechanism for finding servlets and JSP pages) for our JSP page, and forwards the request to it. Notice that the servlet hasn't done any presentation. There is not a single `out.println()` in there! The dynamic information is generated by the servlet, but it's the JSP page that is in charge of displaying it. We've taken all of the application logic from the JSP and moved it to the servlet. While you should be familiar with the basics of Java servlets for this section, don't worry if you aren't familiar with the new Servlet API features that JSP uses. We will cover those next.

10.3.2 JSP and the servlet API

There are a number of additions to the Servlet API with releases 2.1, 2.2, and 2.3 that enable the combination of JSPs and servlets. We'll quickly cover the relevant additions to the Java Servlet API and explain how they enable a servlet-centric approach to JSP application design. Visit Sun's site (http://java.sun.com/products/servlets) for more details.

Controlling flow: the RequestDispatcher

We've talked about passing control from the servlet to the JSP, but we haven't explained how to do this. Servlet API 2.1 introduced the `RequestDispatcher` interface that allows you to forward processing of a request to a JSP or another servlet, or call and include the output from a local document (a JSP, a servlet, an HTML page) into the existing output stream. A `RequestDispatcher` object is created by passing the URI of either the JSP page or the destination servlet to the `getRequestDispatcher()` method of either the incoming request object, or the servlet's `ServletContext`. The `ServletContext`'s method requires an absolute URI, while the request object's method allows you to use relative paths. The path is assumed relative to the servlet's request object. If the servlet that calls the methods in the following bit of code is mapped to the URI /store/fetchOrderServlet, then the following methods are equivalent.

```
req.getRequestDispatcher("showOrders.jsp")
getServletContext().getRequestDispatcher("/store/showOrders.jsp");
```

Why go through a `RequestDispatcher` if you already have the URI? Many things could affect the actual destination of the request—a web application, servlet mappings, and other server configuration settings. For example, the absolute path is rooted at the application level (which we will learn more about in chapter 14), which is not necessarily the same as your web server's document root. Once you have a `RequestDispatcher` object you can forward the request on, or include the output of the specified servlet JSP page in the output of the current servlet.

Once you have created a `RequestDispatcher` object corresponding to your JSP page (or another servlet for that matter) you have two choices. You can either hand control of processing the current request over to the page associated with the

`RequestDispatcher` with the `forward()` method, or you can include its contents in your servlet's response via the `include()` method. The `include()` method can be called at any time, but if you have done anything in your servlet to generate output, such as written to the output stream, trying to call `forward()` will generate an exception. Both methods need a reference to the current request and response object. The signatures of these two methods of the `RequestDispatcher` class are:

```
public void include(HttpServletRequest, HttpServletResponse)
public void forward(HttpServletRequest, HttpServletResponse)
```

As we will soon see, it is the `RequestDispatcher` that allows us to use servlets in the role of application controller. If the servlet code needs to perform any sort of output at all, it simply does its job, then forwards the request for handling by the JSP page. This is not a browser redirect—the browser's view of the URL will not change. The processing of the page is handled entirely by the server and the user will not experience a page reload or even see the URL of the JSP page. Note that a call to `RequestDispatcher.forward()` does not exit the `doGet` or `doPost` once the destination page has been executed. Any code that follows your forward statement will be processed once the request has been handled. Therefore it is important to include an empty `return` statement following your forward call to prevent the unwanted execution of additional call.

Passing data: request attributes

Request attributes are objects that are associated with a given request. Unlike String values, which can be expressed through request parameters, request attributes can be any Java object. They are placed into the request by the servlet container—usually to pass information between the servlet and another servlet or JSP page.

WARNING Attribute names beginning with `java.`, `javax.`, `sun.`, and `com.sun.` are reserved for internal usage by the servlet container and should not be used in your application. A good way to avoid attribute collisions between applications running on the same server is to use your package identifier as a prefix to your attribute name. The same approach applies for storing attributes in the session as well. If you need to maintain a consistent set of attribute names throughout a number of classes, consider defining them in a common interface that can be implemented by your servlets or other classes which need to refer to them.

Setting and getting request attributes is quite straightforward; simply use these two methods of the `ServletRequest` object, and remember that when retrieving an object stored as a request attribute, you'll have to cast it to the appropriate class.

```
public void setAttribute(String name, Object o)
public Object getAttribute(String name)
```

It is request attributes that enable servlets to handle application logic by providing a portable mechanism to exchange data between servlets and JSP pages. The data resulting from an operation, such as a database lookup, can be packaged into a bean or other object and placed directly into the request, where the JSP page can retrieve it for presentation. We'll discuss this concept in more detail later.

Effects of dispatching on the request

It is important to understand that when the `RequestDispatcher` transfers the request to a JSP page it modifies the path information in the request object to reflect the URL of the destination page. If you attempt to read the path information (such as with `HttpUtils.getRequestURL()` or `getServletPath()`) you will see only the JSP page URL, not the servlet URL as originally requested. There are a few exceptions to this rule. If you use the `include()` method rather than the `forward()` method, the servlet container will create the following request attributes to reflect the original path requested:

```
javax.servlet.include.request_uri
javax.servlet.include.context_path
javax.servlet.include.servlet_path
javax.servlet.include.path_info
javax.servlet.include.query_string
```

You can retrieve these request attributes if you need to determine the original request. For this reason, if your JSP pages need to connect back to the original servlet targeted request, and you want to determine the servlet's path at run time, you will have to use `RequestDispatcher.include()` in your servlet, rather than forwarding control on to the JSP directly.

There is another type of `RequestDispatcher` called the `NamedRequestDispatcher` that allows you to reference servlets by a logical name assigned to them at deployment time. A `NamedRequestDispatcher` can be obtained by calling the `getNamedRequestDispatcher()` method of the `ServletContext`. When using the `NamedRequestDispatcher` the request information is left intact, and is not modified to map to the new servlet. Servlets are named for these purposes as part of the Servlet API's web application packaging process—which we'll introduce in chapter 14.

10.3.3 Servlets for application control

One important role servlets in this architecture can play is to proxy transactions between the individual JSP pages that compose the front end of the application. By making certain that each HTTP request is first handled by a centralized controlling servlet, we can better tie the pages together by performing tasks that span the scope of any single page, such as authentication, and ensure that the application maintains proper state and expected flow between components.

Enforcing application level requirements

For example, we could use our controlling servlet to enforce proper authentication for accessing any portion of our application. Unauthenticated users would be detoured through a logon subsystem, which must be successfully completed, before arriving at their destination. Rather than try to build this complexity into each JSP page making up our application, we handle each request that comes in through the mediation servlet.

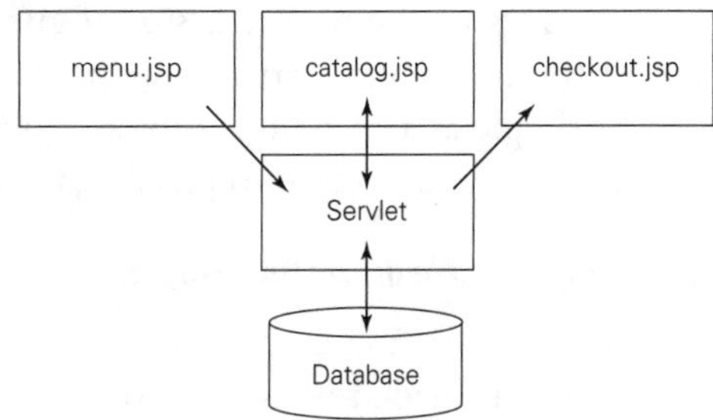

Figure 10.6 A servlet-centric catalog

In this architecture the servlet is managing flow through the application, rather than the flow being driven by HTML anchor links and forms hard coded into each JSP page. This eliminates some of the flow control problems inherent to HTTP-based communications as we find in a page-centric application. The page-centric application design we built earlier could be redesigned with a servlet-centric approach to JSP application development as shown in figur e10.6.

Directing application flow

Directing application requests through a servlet shields JSP presentation code from the complexities of application flow. We can use a servlet to provide a single URL that will serve as our application's entry point and encode the logical program flow into the servlet. After being called, the servlet determines the appropriate action to take, then uses a `RequestDispatcher` to route data to the appropriate JSP page. A `submitFeedback.jsp` page delivers its data to our controlling servlet, and doesn't have to know that the next step is to send the user back to the main web page. Compare this to one JSP page calling another. This approach not only leaves our pages free of application logic, but allows us to reuse them for several purposes, even across applications, because they have been reduced to their essence—as presentation devices.

One technique for managing this flow is by employing a *screen mapper*, a data structure that can associate a logical name with each of the screens that make up your application. Then, your servlet deals with application flow as a series of logical screen names, rather than actual file names. For example, a page featuring an input form asking for information for a new employee, might be logically mapped to the ID `NewEmployeeForm` and might refer to the URL /forms/employees/new.jsp. If you place your mappings into a property file, or even a database, you can make changes to the program's configuration without having to edit your servlet code. Although centralized storage permits sharing between applications, even something as simple as a hash table, initialized in your servlet's `init()` method, will help better manage your logical to physical file mapping.

10.3.4 Servlets for handling application logic

Servlets provide an excellent mechanism for creating reusable services for your JSP pages. Provided with the inputs (such as a purchase order number or customer ID) it can deliver your page the data it needs, via request attributes. You can create as many servlets for your application as needed: one that fetches purchase orders, one that grabs customer data, and so forth. Alternatively, you can wrap up all of your application's functionality into a single servlet, and use request parameters to direct the action to be taken.

Servlets provide services

In the case of an application displaying an item's detail information from the database, the servlet might get the item's ID from the request, perform the lookup, and package the item information into a bean. This bean could then be added to the request before forwarding control on to the JSP page containing the item presentation HTML. In the JSP page, we would be able to retrieve the bean from the request, and display its information accordingly. For example, we'll grab a `PurchaseOrderBean` and place it into the request object under the name `po`. In this example assume that `getPurchaseOrder()` uses the ID passed in from the JSP form to retrieve a record from the database. The `service()` method of our servlet would look like this:

```
String id = request.getParameter("id");
PurchaseOrderBean bean = getPurchaseOrder(id);
request.setAttribute("po", bean);
RequestDispatcher rd;
rd = getServletContext().getRequestDispatcher("/DisplayOrder.jsp");
rd.forward(req, res);
```

To get a reference to the `PurchaseOrderBean` we can either use the `<jsp:useBean>` tag, specifying `request` scope, or the `getAttribute()` method of the request object to reference the object in a scriptlet, casting it to the appropriate type.

```
<jsp:useBean name="po" class="PurchaseOrderBean" scope="request"/>
Purchase Order Number: <jsp:getProperty name="po" property="number"/>
```

or

```
<jsp:useBean name="po" class="PurchaseOrderBean"/>
<% po = (PurchaseOrderBean)request.getAttribute("po"); %>
Purchase Order Number: <jsp:getProperty name="po" property="number"/>
```

The servlet in this case is acting as a service for the JSP page.

10.3.5 Servlets as single entry points

If we send all of our requests through a single servlet we must encode action information into the request to declare our intentions—such as adding an item to the database or retrieving an existing one. We can do this through request parameters, using hidden form elements, URL encoding, or appending extra information after the base servlet path. For example, if the URI for the servlet controlling your application were /servlet/catalog, you could signal the desire to look up item 123 as follows by encoding request parameters:

```
/servlet/catalog?action=lookup&item=123
```

Another way to accomplish the same thing is by tacking additional information onto the end of the URI, which the servlet can pick up through the `getPathInfo()` method of its request object.

```
/servlet/catalog/lookup/123
```

The scheme by which you choose to communicate your progress is irrelevant, as long as you can easily retrieve the request information. Using request parameters makes it easy, since the servlet has built-in support for processing them. On the servlet side, we use these request parameters to determine where we are next headed in the application and to pass along any relevant information (such as the item code in the previous two examples). Once the desired action has been determined in the servlet, it can decide what needs to happen next.

Utilizing the command pattern

Many servlet-centric JSP applications involve command-oriented architecture. Requests from each JSP page include some sort of command identifier, which triggers behavior in the servlet or otherwise directs program flow. The command pattern, a design pattern (a commonly understood programming technique) familiar to GUI programmers, can help us better structure our servlet by reducing complexity and improving the separation between control and application logic.

Using this design pattern, we encapsulate each command our servlet can handle into its own class—allowing us to break their functionality out of the main servlet code. When a request comes in from the JSP page, the servlet dispatches the request to the particular object associated with performing that command. The knowledge of how that command corresponds to application logic is the domain of the command object only; the servlet merely mediates the request between the JSP and the command object. Consider this simple excerpt from a servlet's `service()` method which can dispatch a command request to our command class based on the command identified through the request.

```
String cmd = req.getParameter("cmd");
if (cmd.equals("save")) {
  SaveCommand saver = new SaveCommand();
  saver.save(); // do its thing
}
if (cmd.equals("edit")) {
  EditCommand editor = new EditCommand();
  editor.edit(); // do its thing
}
if (cmd.equals("remove")) {
  RemoveCommand remover = new RemoveCommand();
  remover.remove(); // do its thing
}
```

Without utilizing the command pattern, each `if` block of our servlet would have to contain all of the logic necessary to perform the command as requested. Instead, we now have a reusable, encapsulated set of behavior that makes our code clearer and more easily understood and has the added benefit of being able to be developed and tested independently of the web application itself. While the example code is an incremental improvement, what if our application has dozens of commands? We'll end up with a huge cascading group of `if/then/else` blocks.

We can improve on the example by eliminating the servlet's need to understand the exact relationship between a request command and the command object itself. If we create a common way to handle all command objects, the servlet can treat them all the same, in a single command-processing loop. Through an interface we can create a common way to perform each command, without having to understand its specifics. We treat the request command string as a unique identifier to obtain the particular type of command object we require. Once we get a reference to the appropriate command, we can call the methods defined in its interface to actually perform the command. Consider the following code excerpt, where `Command` is a common interface implemented by all command objects, and the `CommandFactory` class maps command identifiers to specific command objects, returning the appropriate object as type `Command`.

```
Command cmd = CommandFactory.getCommand(request.getParameter("command"));
cmd.execute();
```

This code is the heart of our servlet, and can handle any command with just those few lines. In the event that an unknown command comes through, we can have `CommandFactory` return a valid command object that doesn't actually do anything but throw an exception, or perform default behavior. There are a number of strategies for mapping command identifiers to `Command` classes. We can employ a simple `HashMap` for example. Another useful technique is utilizing the `Class.forName()` method to create a `Command` instance dynamically using the command identifier itself. Consider the following code snippet:

```
String cmdID = request.getParameter("command"));
Command cmd = Class.forName(cmdID + "Command").newInstance();
```

In the example we combine the command identifier in the request with the string `Command`, and attempt to locate the appropriate class. For example, if the command passed in were `GetUser` then we would try to create an instance of the `GetUserCommand` class. This technique requires you to establish a naming convention among your command handlers, and can get more complicated if you need to support several different types of constructors. The command pattern is an excellent way to simplify JSP/servlet interaction. In chapter 11 we will use the command pattern in a full length JSP application.

Ensuring transaction integrity

As we discussed earlier, web applications suffer somewhat from the stateless request/response nature of the HTTP protocol. Reloading a page or clicking Back can reissue requests or call them out of sequence—something we want to be sure to catch in a mission-critical application.

One way to solve this continuity problem is by recording a token in the user's session upon completion of activity prerequisites and requiring this token in the second step. When a request comes in to perform the second step of the transaction, the servlet can first verify that the prerequisite has been met by retrieving the token from the session. Once completed, the token is removed from the session. A token then gives the servlet the ability to perform an action, but only once. Secondary requests will find no matching token and can raise an exception. Depending on your application's requirements you can maintain either a list of tokens—which would simultaneously support multiple browser windows from the same user—or a single token, which is overwritten each time.

Let's say your transaction is purchasing an item from your store. The final steps of your checkout process are handled by `checkout.jsp`, a page that contains a form requesting the selections and asks for final confirmation. Clicking Confirm places an order for each item on the page, and then shows `thankyou.jsp` which thanks the visitor for the order. What happens if the user hits Reload at this point, or Back? Remember that as far as the browser is concerned it is submitting the contents of a form. It doesn't matter if a servlet or another JSP is receiving the action, the browser will remember the request parameter contained in the form and deliver it to its handler. Clicking Reload essentially repeats the process—resulting in the placement of a duplicate order.

To add our transaction token scheme to this example, we have to have both pages fall under the control of servlets (or the same servlet). When the user goes to check out, the servlet should first generate a single-use token and store it in the session before directing the request to `checkout.jsp` where we include the token as a hidden form element. When the form is submitted, the servlet verifies that the token in the form and the token on the server match. It then performs the action, and revokes the token before proceeding on to `thankyou.jsp`.

If the user were to click Reload on the thank-you page, the form action would be resubmitted, but this time there would be no corresponding token indicating to the servlet that it was all right to proceed with the transaction. The servlet could then decide to just ignore the duplicate request and reload `thankyou.jsp`. This process is illustrated in figure 10.7.

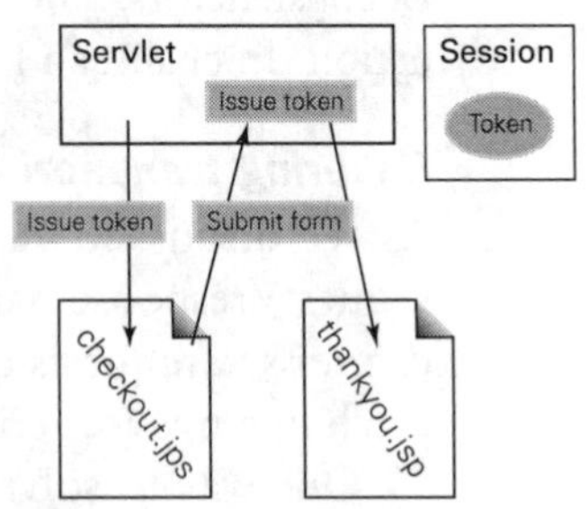

Figure 10.7 Transaction

One technique for generating a simple transaction token that is both unique to each session and nonrepeatable throughout the application is by computing a message digest from the user's unique session ID and the current system time. In chapter 11 we will apply this technique as part of our example application.

10.3.6 *Handling errors in the servlet*

If in the course of normal application events your servlet encounters an unexpected error, you have the option of passing the error on to a JSP error page. This keeps all of your exception handling and error processing consistent throughout the application, regardless of whether errors crop up in the JSP pages themselves or your

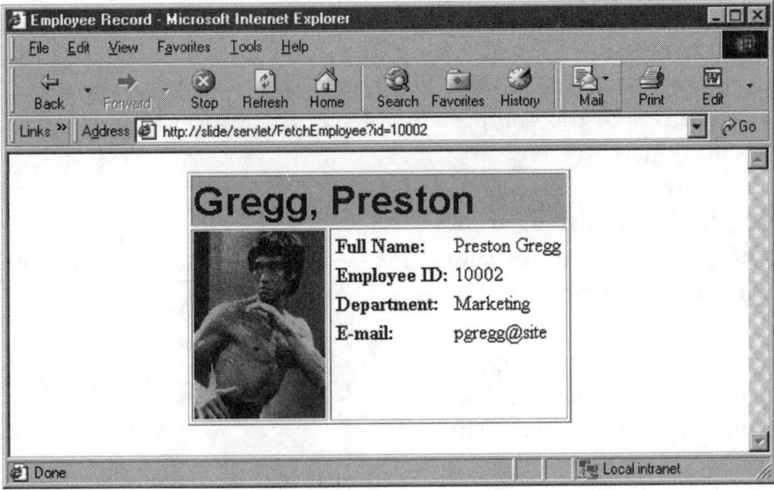

Figure 10.8 An employee's ID card

servlets. Simply catch the exception (which can be any subclass of `Throwable`) and put it into the request object under the name `javax.servlet.jsp.jspException`. Next use an instance of `RequestDispatcher` to forward your request on to your error handling page. For example:

```
String username = req.getParameter("user");
if (username == null)
  req.setAttribute("javax.servlet.jsp.jspException", new Exception("no user-
  name!"));
RequestDispatcher rd = getServletContext().getRequestDispatcher("/error.jsp");
rd.forward(req, res);
```

The `error.jsp` page in this example should be defined as a JSP error page as normal. When we stuff an exception object into the request with that attribute name (`javax.servlet.jsp.jspException`) the error page will automatically create the implicit exception object, and error handling can proceed. There is no difference between an exception created by our servlet in this example and one being generated by an error in another JSP page.

10.3.7 Example: servlet-centric employee browser

In this example we will develop an application that browses through personnel records of an existing database (figure 10.8). To keep things simple the user will not be allowed to modify or add records to the database, which will be treated as read-only. We'll build a more complex database application later in this book.

Design considerations

The employee database we are accessing may also be used by the payroll department, the logon security system, and who knows what—or who—else. It is a good idea therefore to design the components of this application to be as independent from the application as possible.

We'll need two main interfaces in this example, one to list all of the available employees, and another that can view the details about the employee selected from the list. The core component of our application will be a bean, `EmployeeBean`, which will encapsulate the information we are interested in. It will be the job of our central servlet to handle all of the database interaction. The application model can be seen in figure10.9.

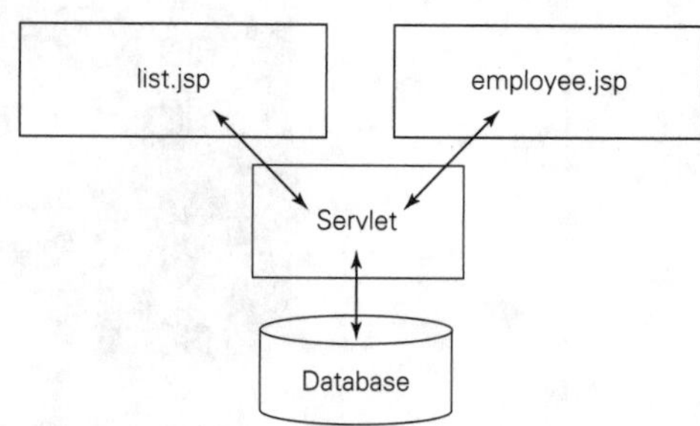

Figure 10.9 The employee database application

The database

We will be accessing an existing database that is accessible through JDBC. Thanks to the JDBC API, the Java code itself is database independent and should apply to whatever particular database you favor. The information we wish to access, employee records, is contained in a single table called `PEOPLE_TABLE`. While this was done for simplicity's sake in this example, spreading employee information across several tables would only complicate the discussion and the SQL query required to collect an individual's information, but not our Java code. The schema for `PEOPLE_TABLE` is shown in table 10.1:

Table 10.1 The PEOPLE_TABLE scheme

Column	Purpose	Type
ID	Unique Employee ID	`int`
FNAME	First Name	`varchar(80)`
LNAME	Last Name	`varchar(80)`
DEPARTMENT	Department	`varchar(80)`
EMAIL	Email Address	`varchar(80)`
IMAGE	URL of personal photo	`varchar(80)`

To access a particular employee's record, say employee #1000, we can use the following SQL query, which should return a single record since each ID number is unique to a single employee.

```
SELECT * FROM PEOPLE_TABLE WHERE ID = 1000
```

We can wrap the results of this query into an `EmployeeBean` that encapsulates all of the information we have about an employee. We can then use this Bean inside a JSP page to display the information, but we will also have a reusable component that we can apply to other applications that deal with employees and our database. Rather than including the code for accessing information from the database inside the functionality of our `EmployeeBean` or the JSP pages composing the front end, we have chosen to create a servlet that is responsible for dealing with the database and controlling the application.

10.3.8 EmployeeBean

The first thing we need to do is to define the JavaBean that will represent the employee data contained in each record of the table. To do this we simply map each column of the table to a bean property of the appropriate type. The property sheet for a bean designed to hold a record from our `PEOPLE_TABLE` is shown in table 10.2.

Table 10.2 An EmployeeBean

Name	Access	Java Type	Example
`id`	read-only	`int`	1000
`firstName`	read/write	`String`	Arlon
`lastName`	read/write	`String`	Fields
`department`	read/write	`String`	Engineering
`email`	read/write	`String`	afields@headquarters
`image`	read/write	`String`	http://server/1000.gif

The decision on what level of access to afford each property depends on how you expect the bean to be used in the application. The `id` property for example is unique to each record and will generally not be changed, even if we are editing an employee's details, so we will make it read-only to emphasize this fact. We still need to be able to specify the `id` value at some point however—as it needs to be reflected through the read-only property. To do so we will pass it in through the constructor.

The constructor will also set all of the instance variables, which are used to store property data, to empty strings.

```
public EmployeeBean(int id) {
  this.id = id;
  firstName = "";
  lastName = "";
  image = "";
  email = "";
  department = "";
}
```

Of course a JSP page will not be able to pass arguments to a constructor, and indeed won't be able to instantiate a bean without a zero argument constructor. We'll provide one that simply passes a dummy, impossible `id` value to the primary constructor. In this application however, we shouldn't need to create a bean in our JSP page anyway.

```
public EmployeeBean() {
  this(0);
}
```

This way we can create the bean and leave it in a state that tells us that we don't have a valid identifier for this bean yet, such as when we are creating a record. If we needed to construct a new database record from the data contained in the bean we will need to create a valid identifier, usually by asking the database for the next unique identifier. The `EmployeeBean` code (listing 10.3) is straightforward:

Listing 10.3 EmployeeBean

```
package com.taglib.wdjsp.arch;

public class EmployeeBean {
  private int id;
  private String firstName;
  private String lastName;
  private String image;
  private String email;
  private String department;

  public EmployeeBean(int id) {
    this.id = id;
    firstName = "";
    lastName = "";
    image = "";
    email = "";
    department = "";
  }
```

```
  public EmployeeBean() {
    this(0);
  }

  public int getId() {
    return this.id;
  }

  public void setFirstName(String firstName) {
    this.firstName = firstName;
  }

  public String getFirstName() {
    return this.firstName;
  }

  public void setLastName(String lastName) {
    this.lastName = lastName;
  }

  public String getLastName() {
    return this.lastName;
  }

  public void setImage(String image) {
    this.image = image;
  }

  public String getImage() {
    return this.image;
  }

  public void setEmail(String email) {
    this.email = email;
  }

  public String getEmail() {
    return this.email;
  }

  public void setDepartment(String department) {
    this.department = department;
  }

  public String getDepartment() {
    return this.department;
  }
}
```

10.3.9 FetchEmployeeServlet

`FetchEmployeeServlet` knows how to do only two things. It can, given an employee ID number, retrieve that employee's information from the database and forward it to the `employee.jsp` page for display, or return a `Vector` containing a Bean representing each employee in the database to the `list.jsp` page. The coding is in listing 10.4.

Listing 10.4 FetchEmployeeServlet.java

```
package com.taglib.wdjsp.arch;

import javax.servlet.*;
import javax.servlet.http.*;
import java.io.*;
import java.sql.*;
import java.util.*;

public class FetchEmployeeServlet extends HttpServlet {
  private final static String driver = "postgresql.Driver";
  private final static String url =
    "jdbc:postgresql://slide.dev/emp";
  private final static String user = "guest";
  private final static String password = "guest";
  private final static String sql =
    "select * from people_table where id = ?";
  private Connection connection = null;
  private PreparedStatement statement = null;
  private ServletContext context;

   public void init(ServletConfig config) throws ServletException {
    super.init(config);
    context = config.getServletContext();
    try {
      Class.forName(driver);
      connection = DriverManager.getConnection(url, user, password);
      statement = connection.prepareStatement(sql);
    }
    catch (ClassNotFoundException e) {
      System.err.println("Unable to load database driver");
      throw new ServletException("Unable to load database driver");
    }
    catch (SQLException e) {
      System.err.println("Unable to connect to database");
      throw new ServletException("Unable to connect to database");
    }
  }

  public void service(HttpServletRequest req,
          HttpServletResponse res)
```

```
    throws ServletException, IOException {
    String jsp;
    String cmd = req.getParameter("cmd");
    String idString = req.getParameter("id");
    int id;
    try { id = Integer.parseInt(idString); }
    catch(NumberFormatException e) { id=0; }

    if ("get".equals(cmd)) {
      EmployeeBean bean = fetchEmployee(id);
      req.setAttribute("employee", bean);
      jsp = "/employee.jsp";
    }
    else {
      Vector list = fetchAll();
      req.setAttribute("list", list);
      jsp = "/list.jsp";
    }
    RequestDispatcher dispatcher;
    dispatcher = context.getRequestDispatcher(jsp);
    dispatcher.forward(req, res);
  }

  public EmployeeBean makeBean(ResultSet results)
    throws SQLException {
    EmployeeBean bean = new EmployeeBean(results.getInt("id"));
    bean.setFirstName(results.getString("fname"));
    bean.setLastName(results.getString("lname"));
    bean.setEmail(results.getString("email"));
    bean.setDepartment(results.getString("department"));
    bean.setImage(results.getString("image"));
    return bean;
  }

  public EmployeeBean fetchEmployee(int id) {
    try {
      ResultSet results;
      synchronized (statement) {
        statement.clearParameters();
        statement.setInt(1, id);
        results = statement.executeQuery();
      }
      EmployeeBean bean = null;
      if (results.next()) {
        bean = makeBean(results);
      }
      if (results != null)
        results.close();
      return bean;
    }
    catch (SQLException se) { return null; }
```

```
  }

  public Vector fetchAll() {
    try {
      Vector list = new Vector();
      ResultSet results;
      Statement st = connection.createStatement();
      results = st.executeQuery("select * from people_table");
      while (results.next())
        list.add(makeBean(results));
      return list;
    }
    catch (SQLException se) { return null; }
  }

  public void destroy() {
    try {
      if (connection != null)
        connection.close();
    }
    catch (SQLException e) { }
  }
}
```

In the `init()` method of our servlet we establish a connection to the database that will remain throughout the life of the servlet. In the `destroy()` method, which will be called by the servlet container just prior to shutdown, we close this connection. Each time the servlet is requested, `service()` will be called. It is here that we encode our application's logic and flow control. We basically support two commands, `get` to fetch a specific employee, or anything else to create a `Vector` containing all possible employees.

```
String cmd = req.getParameter("cmd");
if ("get".equals(cmd)) {
  EmployeeBean bean = fetchEmployee(id);
  req.setAttribute("employee", bean);
  jsp = "employee.jsp";
}
else {
  Vector list = fetchAll();
  req.setAttribute("list", list);
  jsp = "list.jsp";
}
```

After processing, we've set the variable `jsp` to the URI of the JSP page which should be visited next by the application. We use a `RequestDispatcher` to transfer control to that page.

```
RequestDispatcher dispatcher = context.getRequestDispatcher(jsp);
dispatcher.forward(req, res);
```

Both `fetchEmployee()` and `fetchAll()` rely on the `makeBean()` method, which takes the current row of the `ResultSet` sent to it and extracts the appropriate columns to populate a newly created `EmployeeBean`.

```
public EmployeeBean makeBean(ResultSet results) throws SQLException {
  EmployeeBean bean = new EmployeeBean(results.getInt("id"));
  bean.setFirstName(results.getString("fname"));
  bean.setLastName(results.getString("lname"));
  bean.setEmail(results.getString("email"));
  bean.setDepartment(results.getString("department"));
  bean.setImage(results.getString("image"));
  return bean;
}
```

10.3.10 JSP employee list

This page receives the list of employees from the servlet in the form of a `Vector` filled with `EmployeeBean` objects. It simply uses scriptlets to extract each one, then builds a link back to the servlet to provide the user with a detail view of each entry. We pass each employee's ID number in through the link, which will allow our servlet to pick the proper one. The source code is in listing10.5.

Listing 10.5 list.jsp

```
<%@ page import="java.util.*,com.taglib.wdjsp.arch.EmployeeBean" %>
<jsp:useBean id="employee" class="com.taglib.wdjsp.arch.EmployeeBean"/>
<html>
<body>
<b>Current Employees</b>
<ul>
<%
  Vector v = (Vector)request.getAttribute("list");
  Iterator i= v.iterator();
  while (i.hasNext()) {
     employee = (EmployeeBean)i.next();
%>
<li>
<a href="/servlet/FetchEmployeeServlet?cmd=get&id=
<jsp:getProperty name="employee" property="id"/>">
<jsp:getProperty name="employee" property="lastName"/>,
<jsp:getProperty name="employee" property="firstName"/></a>
<% } %>
</ul>
</body>
</html>
```

10.3.11 JSP page viewer

The JSP code needed to view the information stored inside the bean is fairly straightforward. After we have a reference to the bean we simply display the values of the appropriate properties needed for our interface. To grab the bean, which has been placed into the request by our servlet, we specify a scope value of `request` and an ID with the same identifier value used by the servlet.

```
<jsp:useBean id="employee" class="com.taglib.wdjsp.arch.EmployeeBean"
  scope="request"/>
```

If the `id` value that we specify is not the same identifier used by the servlet when placing the bean into the request, or if the page is requested directly rather than through the servlet, the bean will not be found. If the bean is not found, the `<jsp:useBean>` tag will, of course, create an empty `EmployeeBean` and place it into the request. Once we have a reference to the bean we can use it to display the fields extracted from the database, as we do with any other bean.

```
<B>Department:</B> <jsp:getProperty name="employee" property="department"/>
```

We have in essence encapsulated a database record into a JSP accessible bean without muddying our page with database code. This solution also provides a high degree of abstraction for the page designer. As far as the JSP code is concerned it doesn't matter where the data came from—flat file, database, input form, or an LDAP server—the page still displays the record's fields. This not only allows the back-end implementation to change over time without affecting the front end, it allows this front-end code (listing 10.6) to be reused throughout the system.

Listing 10.6 employee.jsp

```
<:%@ page import="com.taglib.wdjsp.arch.EmployeeBean"%>
<jsp:useBean id="employee" class="com.taglib.wdjsp.arch.EmployeeBean"
  scope="request"/>
<html>
<head><title>employee record</title></head>
<body>
<table border="1" align="center">
<tr bgcolor="tan"><td colspan=2><font size=+3 face=arial><b>
<jsp:getProperty name="employee" property="lastname"/>,
<jsp:getProperty name="employee" property="firstname"/>
</b></font></td></tr>
<tr><td align=left valign=top>
<img height="150"
src="<jsp:getProperty name="employee" property="image"/>"></td>
<td align=left valign=top>
<table border=0>
```

```
<tr><td><b>full name:</b></td><td>
<jsp:getProperty name="employee" property="firstname"/>
<jsp:getProperty name="employee" property="lastname"/>
</td></tr>
<tr><td><b>employee id:</b></td><td>
<jsp:getProperty name="employee" property="id"/>
</td></tr>
<tr><td><b>department:</b></td><td>
<jsp:getProperty name="employee" property="department"/>
</td></tr>
<tr><td><b>e-mail:</b></td><td>
<jsp:getProperty name="employee" property="email"/>
</td></tr>
</table>
</td>
</tr>
</table>
</body>
</html>
```

10.4 Enterprise JavaBeans

The previous two JSP architectures we've discussed do not directly support complicated transaction management and distributed architectures. The introduction of the EJBs specification by Sun Microsystems and its adoption by major application server companies like Netscape and IBM promises to ease and speed the development of mission-critical applications. EJBs are positioned to play an increasingly important role in Java applications and pair up excellently with JSPs and servlets. However, teaching you the details of EJBs is beyond the scope of this book. We can only hope to introduce them to you, and leave you with an understanding of how they fit into JSP application design.

10.4.1 What are Enterprise JavaBeans?

EJBs are reusable business logic components for use in distributed, multitier application architectures. You can get up and running quickly by building applications around EJBs you have created or by leveraging the growing number of off-the-shelf components. The EJB framework provides functionality that traditionally has represented the biggest challenge to creating web-based applications.

For example, if you were developing a high-end e-commerce application, you might purchase one EJB component that performed real-time credit card approval, another that managed your customers, and another that calculated shipping costs. You would then tie these together within your application server by customizing the run-time properties of the EJBs, and there you would have it—an order processing system. The application server would automatically handle sticky issues such as balancing loads, maintaining security, monitoring transaction processes, sharing resources, ensuring data integrity, and so on.

10.4.2 JavaBeans vs. EJBs

How do EJBs and JavaBeans relate? They actually don't have much in common from a technical perspective, even if the philosophy behind them—enabling developers to take advantage of reusable components in their applications—is the same.

Like the beans we have been studying, EJBs are a Java-based software component. However these beans follow a completely different set of conventions and interfaces and are not accessible directly through bean containers or JSP tags (at least the standard tags). The purpose of EJBs is to encapsulate business logic (for example, the steps involved in depositing money into an account, calculating income tax, or selecting which warehouse to ship an order from) into reusable server-side components. In the EJB paradigm, an application is implemented as a set of business-logic-controlling components that have been configured in application-specific ways inside an EJB container such as an application server. Clients are then written to communicate with the EJB components and handle the results. The standardized interfaces exist to allow the EJB container to manage security and transactional aspects of the bean. We can use EJBs to create JavaBeans for use in our JSP page.

10.4.3 Application servers and EJB containers

Like JSPs, EJBs are designed to work in concert with a container, typically integrated into an application server such as Netscape Application Server (NAS) or IBM's WebSphere. An EJB container and a JSP container are different things, but many application servers offer support for both. EJB containers must support Sun's EJB specification, which details the interface between application server elements. EJBs can be used with any application server or other system providing an EJB container that implements these interfaces. EJB containers can also exist as part of other systems such as transaction monitors or database systems.

Application servers in particular are excellent environments to host EJB containers because they automate the more complex features of multitier computing. Application servers manage scarce resources on behalf of the components involved in the design. They also provide infrastructure services such as naming, directory services, and security. And they provide bean-based applications with the benefit of scalability—most application server environments will let you scale your application through the addition of new clusters of machines.

EJB containers transparently provide their EJBs with a number of important services. While you may not deal with these services directly since they're conveniently kept under the covers, EJBs couldn't function without them. These services are:

- **Life cycle management:** Enables initialization and shutdown of EJBs.
- **Load management:** Automatically distributes EJB objects across a cluster of servers.
- **Security management:** Enables EJBs to work with a variety of authentication schemes and approval processes.
- **Transaction support:** Manages such things as rolling back transactions that didn't fully complete and handling final commitment of transactions, plus transactions across multiple databases.
- **Persistence and state management:** Enables EJBs to keep information between sessions and individual requests, even if the container's server must be rebooted.

The EJB container also provides a communications channel to and from its beans, and it will handle all of its EJBs multithreading issues. In fact, the EJB specification explicitly forbids an EJB from creating its own threads. This ensures thread-safe operation and frees the developer from often-complicated thread management concerns.

10.4.4 Application design with EJBs

Now let's examine how we would build a JSP application employing EJBs. Because the role of an EJB is to handle only the core business logic of your application, you will still need JSPs to deal with presentation issues such as generating web pages to communicate results and servlets for control. While you can build your application from JSPs and EJBs alone, either through scriptlets or JSP JavaBeans, we don't generally recommend it. An application complex enough to benefit from EJBs would almost certainly employ a servlet-centric design. Similar to the use of the command pattern we described ealier, EJBs handle processing command requests or other application logic, freeing the servlet from direct responsibility over command execution.

For example, in a banking application a servlet might use the services of an EJB component to determine whether users are business or consumer customers and use a servlet to direct them to an appropriate JSP-controlled web page to show them their account balance. The application logic has been moved out of the servlet, in favor of the EJB, which might be better able to handle it (figure 10.10).

In such an approach, we'd want to shield the JSP pages themselves from the EJB's inner workings as much as possible. If the servlet's calls to the EJB server return particularly complex objects, we might be better off wrapping the results of the call into simpler data beans, which contain a view of the data relevant to the JSP page. For example, consider this excerpt from a servlet where we extract account information from an EJB and place it into a JavaBean before forwarding control on to our presentation page:

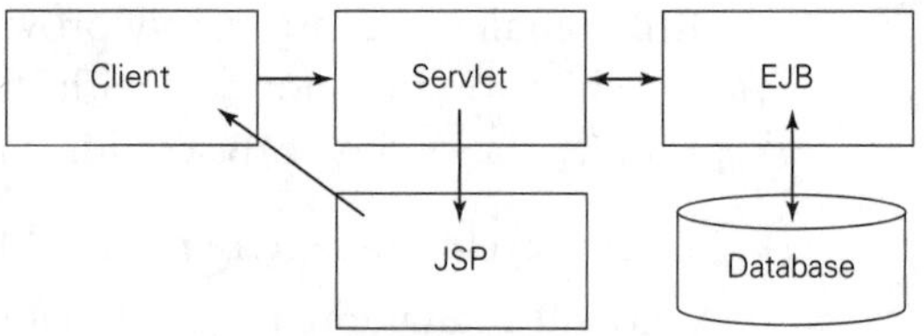

Figure 10.10 An EJB handling application logic

```
Context initial = new InitialContext();
Object objref = initial.lookup("AccountStatus");
AcctHome home;
home = (AcctHome)PortableRemoteObject.narrow(objref, AcctHome.class);
AccountStatus accountStatus = home.create();
AccountViewBean bean = new AccountViewBean();
bean.setBalance(accountStatus.getBalance());
bean.setLastUpdate(accountStatus.getLastModifiedTimeStamp());
request.setAttribute("accountview", bean);
RequestDispatcher rd;
rd = getServletContext().getRequestDispatcher("/AccountStatus.jsp");
rd.forward(req, res);
```

10.5 Choosing an appropriate architecture

So when is it appropriate to use each of these different architectures for your JSP application? Like most architectural decisions, it depends. It depends on a number of factors, including your own team's skills, experiences, personal preferences, and biases. Sophisticated, multitier architectures provide a larger degree of abstraction and modularity, but only at the cost of complexity and increased development time. In practice, large multifaceted JSP applications tend to make use of more than one single architectural model, using different models to fill different sets of requirements for each aspect of the application. When making your architectural selection there are several important aspects to consider, each with its own advantages, disadvantages, and tradeoffs.

10.5.1 Application environment

A JSP application's environment plays an important role in determining the best-fit architecture for a project. Every environment is different, but each places its own unique pressures on JSP application design and deployment.

Firewalls and the DMZ

Today's enterprise networks are pretty complicated places. Combined with the fact that many applications cross the firewall we must be aware of the different zones of accessibility in most enterprise situations. There are three basic access zones inside most enterprises: intranet (the networks inside the inner firewall); DMZ or no man's land (the area between the intranet firewall and the public web); and the public web or Internet (the network outside all firewalls).

Firewalls divide the corporate network into a series of distinct zones (figure 10.11), each of which is afforded a different level of accessibility. Of course in practice there are generally several different levels of accessibility within each zone, but for purposes of discussion these definitions will suffice.

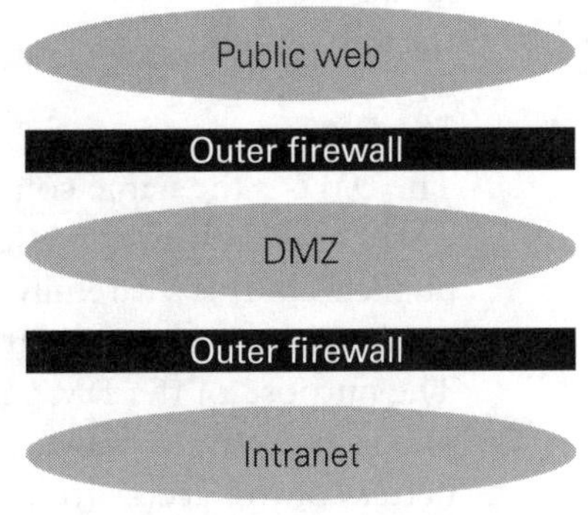

Figure 10.11 A typical enterprise network

The public web

Machines on the public web, with the exception of corporate public web servers, are generally restricted from any access to internal networks, including the DMZ. You can think of the public web as "the rest of the world," since it literally includes everyone on the Internet. This is the area that will host the web servers and JSP containers that the general public will connect to. While systems in this zone may include various levels of authentication designed to restrict access to information on the server, the important thing to remember is that the general public is given direct network connectivity to these systems, at least to some degree. Applications running in this segment of the network generally experience more traffic, and are more concerned with scalability and performance.

If a company runs an extranet for its business partners, it will generally be deployed from this network zone. While we often think of an extranet as being private, from a network connectivity point of view it still falls into the domain of public access, at least for the front end. On the other hand, *virtual private networks* (VPNs) created by corporations for their partners, employees, or field offices do not fall into this category. Although they carry information across the Internet they have been designed to map into the company's network in a transparent matter. For this reason, we treat VPNs as simply another segment of our intranet, or internal corporate network.

The intranet

The intranet is composed of internal networks and systems. Traditionally, systems on the intranet can access machines inside the DMZ and on the public web. JSP applications designed to run in the intranet can be entirely self-contained internal applications, relying totally on resources local to the intranet they run on. Or, JSP applications on the intranet may be acting on back-end data sources located in the DMZ or the public web. For example, a JSP application might let a content manager modify information ultimately displayed on the corporate web server, which lives in the public web.

The DMZ

The DMZ is the name commonly given to the area between public and private networks and is given some level of access to machines on both the intranet and the public web. It is a carefully restricted network zone. For this reason the DMZ can be used to host back-end databases and support services for front-end JSP services. The purpose of the DMZ is to provide the connectivity to communicate between public and private network zones, while establishing a buffer zone where you can better control access to information. Generally, the firewall is designed to let only web traffic into the DMZ.

Back-end resources

Back-end resources (also known as enterprise information systems) are databases, LDAP servers, legacy applications, and other sources of information that we will need to access through our JSP application. Projects for the enterprise generally require access to some sort of information system on the back end. Where are your databases located? What sort of access is granted between your JSP container and your information systems?

10.5.2 Enterprise software requirements

If you are building JSP applications for the enterprise, your choice of JSP application architecture is largely influenced by the requirements placed on it by the very nature and requirements of the enterprise itself. While every project is different, of course, any JSP application we might develop for use in the enterprise shares some common characteristics that are worth exploring.

10.5.3 Performance, scalability, and availability

Enterprise applications are particularly sensitive to performance and availability issues, especially in mission-critical situations and heavily loaded web servers. One strategy commonly employed to address scalability issues is web server clustering, using groups of machines to distribute the load across a single web site. If you will be deploying JSP applications into a clustered environment you must understand how your web servers, JSP containers, and application servers (if present) will handle requests. Distributed transactions, sessions, and object persistence will vary differently by vendor and program design. Some configurations will place restrictions on your JSP components, such as support for object serialization, while others may limit your use of persistence. If you are using JSP's session management services you must understand how your environment manages sessions across cluster nodes.

Maintenance and updates

Unlike retail software, which is developed around fixed schedules of release, applications designed for use within an enterprise are typically evolving constantly. If an application is critical to the success of the business it will certainly be the target of frequent bug fixes, improvements, and enhancements. In such a situation, modularity and design flexibility will be critical to the ongoing success of the project. One of JSP's big strengths is its ability to separate the presentation aspects of your application, allowing you to alter it independently of the application logic itself.

Understand risk factors

What task is your application performing? How much time should you spend ensuring transaction integrity and bulletproofing each step of the process? If you are building mission-critical applications, count on spending more time designing transaction-processing code and developing an architecture that reduces the risk of interruptions in the program flow, as this can often be the most complicated and time-consuming aspect of application design and testing.

10.5.4 Technical considerations

The technical nature of a JSP project will play a large role in determining the best architectural approach. The complexity and number of moving parts should, in a very real way, affect the project direction.

Complexity and scope

How complex and interrelated are the activities surrounding your application? If your application must deal with multiple data sources, resource pooling, or complex transaction management, a fairly sophisticated architecture will certainly be in order. It is very likely that you will want to employ servlets, and possibly EJBs to shield your JSP front-end from a complicated back end. On the other hand, if there are very few steps involved, placing all of your application logic directly into JSP pages in a page-centric approach eliminates complexity and will likely reduce the amount of development time required to complete the project

Potential for reuse

Could your application make use of components that already exist or would be useful in other applications? If the JSP application you are developing is part of a larger series of projects, the extra time involved in focusing on the development of components may pay off in the long run. If you can develop JavaBeans to model your domain objects you can reuse them throughout related applications—even if they are not JSP based.

Expected lifetime and propensity for change

How likely is it that requirements will change over the life of the application? A long life with an expectation for frequent change points to the need for a more modular architecture with a higher degree of flexibility. However, an application that you expect to use briefly and then discard would probably not benefit from the increased complexity of a loosely coupled component-based architecture.

10.5.5 Organizational considerations

Every organization's situation is different. What worked for you in your last job won't necessarily work in this one. The talents of your team and your organization's work style will play a big role in determining the most appropriate JSP architecture.

Team size and capabilities

How big is your team? Is it just you or are you lucky enough to have a large corporate development team at your command? Is your Java development team composed of beginners or seasoned veterans? Is there a high degree of variance in skill levels? Larger teams with a range of complementary skill sets tend to favor the more distributed models incorporating servlets and EJBs.

The ability to divide your application into discrete components promotes division of labor, developer specialization, and better manageability in the team. Less experienced developers can work on data beans and other less complicated aspects while your senior members can worry about the more complicated aspects of the architecture and application logic. If necessary you can even hire contractors to develop individual components beyond the area of expertise of your own developers, then integrate them into your project. Such a modular approach becomes less important if a single small team will handle the JSP project alone.

Removing the Java from the front-end code frees your design team to concentrate on the application interface rather than its implementation. On the other hand, if you are a lone wolf coding commando, then you will probably benefit from the simplicity of single source, JSP-only style applications. The makeup of your team will, in part play a role in determining the best architecture for your application.

Time and money

How much time and money has been allocated to your project? Increased levels of complexity generally mean more time and, in the case of EJBs, more money. Complexity and time are trade-offs, but you have to consider maintenance expenses as well. It doesn't do much good to create a rigid, hard to maintain design in an effort to save time and money up front if you are continually forced to devote development resources to maintaining the project in the future.

Control of assets and resources

How much control do you have over corporate resources that are important to your project? If your application will be accessing databases or other information sources that already exist or are beyond your control, you will probably want to select an architecture with the additional layers of abstraction necessary to shield your developers from a disparate and possibly variant interface.

11 An example JSP project

This chapter covers

- Building a servlet-centric application
- Component-based JSP development
- JSP/Database interaction
- Utilizing the command pattern
- Maintaining transaction integrity

Now we will apply the JSP programming techniques covered in previous chapters toward the design and development of a real-world enterprise application more complex than would be allowed as part of another chapter. We will develop a database driven system for creating, managing, and displaying a list of frequently asked questions (FAQs) and making them available through a web site. We hope it will help tie together all the concepts we have discussed so far.

11.1 An FAQ system

We selected an FAQ system as the example for this chapter for several reasons. It is a nontrivial application that illustrates many of the principals of JSP application design such as command handling, form element processing, database interaction, and transaction management. It was also important to present an application simple enough that it could be constrained to a readable number of pages.

Lastly, we wanted to end up with a web application that could be useful in its own right. While we will approach this project from an FAQ perspective, the project itself is applicable to maintaining and displaying any collection of information managed by a database through a browser with JSP. Just to show you where we are heading, a screen shot of the finished application in action is shown in figure 11.1.

11.1.1 Project motivations

A recent client of ours has been maintaining a list of FAQs to address common customer product issues. As the list has grown over the years it had became increasingly difficult to maintain and it had become necessary to maintain several different versions—a table of contents view, the whole list view, a list of new entries sorted by date, and so forth. Each version was maintained by hand from the master list. The web content team was responsible for updating the HTML based on the input of product management, technical support, the documentation team, and a host of others.

The combination of frequent updates and the need to maintain multiple views of the list was the driving force behind the desire to automate the FAQ administration process. This chapter-length example is based on this project, which we recently completed with the help of JSP technology.

11.1.2 Application requirements

The FAQ system we will build in this example is designed to allow the company's internal content owners (product managers, technical support, etc.) to add, update, and delete entries from the list without needing to enlist the help of the content team, and without having to edit individual HTML files. We'll use a simple

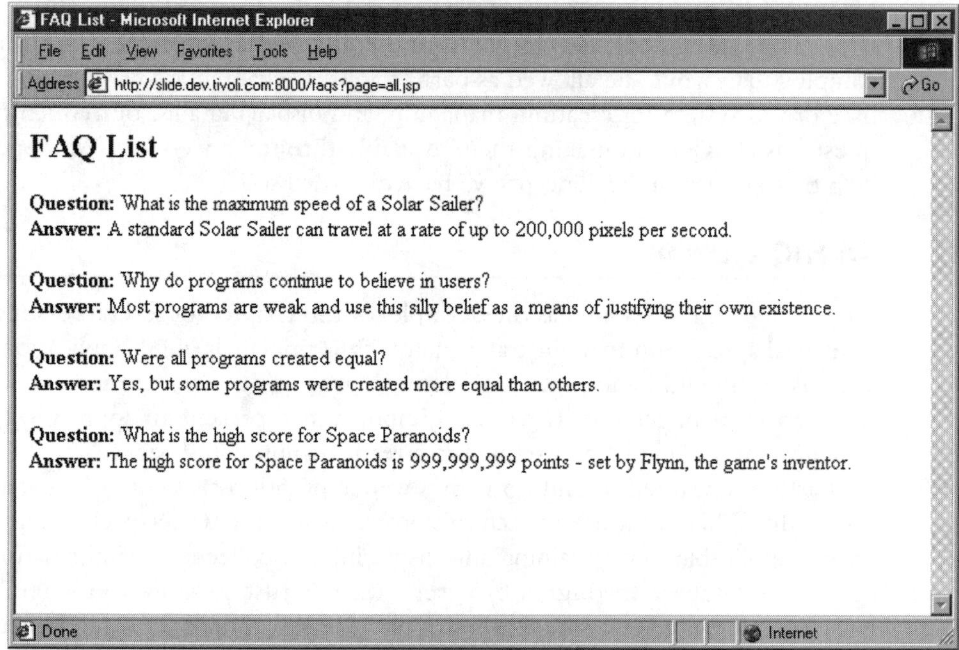

Figure 11.1 Viewing FAQs through our JSP application

web-based interface to allow them to manipulate the FAQ entries. FAQ information created by this process will be stored inside a database, and will be viewable in several forms and contexts through the company web site in place of the old, static pages.

After devising the concept and establishing our basic application goals, we must devise a list of specific features we expect the application to support. The goal here is not to dive into the details of the implementation behind each feature of the application, but rather to list activities and events that the application will be required to support:

- Each entry in the list will have a question, and an answer
- When an entry is modified we need to record the modification date
- FAQ entries should have a unique identifier that does not change, even if the wording of the question itself changes, so that it is possible to link a user to a particular FAQ
- FAQs must be visible in a variety of formats on the web—by title, by modification date, and so forth

- The FAQ lists on the web site should be generated dynamically, without the need for content engineers to perform production work
- Users need to view single FAQ or multiple FAQs as presentation dictates

Another important requirement was to fit into the client's network architecture. In this case, they had database servers in the DMZ accessible from both the public web servers and the intranet. We therefore decided that the most logical deployment scheme would be to let intranet users manage FAQs stored on the DMZ databases, and have the web servers access those same databases in order to display the FAQs.

11.1.3 Application modules

In order to start coding on this project we'll first separate the application into discrete modules which can then be built individually, without being burdened by the details of the implementation of the others. To accomplish this we looked for common areas of functionality that we could separate from the project as a whole. An important goal in this process was to create modules that were more or less independent of each other. After studying the different areas, functions, and requirements we had identified we defined three modules:

- Storage—stores and retrieves FAQs in the database
- Administration—lets administrators create and edit entries
- Web access—displays the FAQs on the public web site

Decomposing our FAQ system into three modules gave us a number of benefits—before, during, and after development. First, it allowed us to divide development tasks among our development team resources. As long as the requirements for interaction between modules were clear it was possible for each team to work more or less independently—at least until we were ready to integrate the modules.

This approach also tends to encourage abstraction and promotes looser coupling between modules and gives the ability to make changes to the implementation of one module without having to rewrite the supporting ones. In other words, future enhancements to one module can be made without involving the design teams of the others.

Storage module

The storage module manages access to the database where each FAQ entry is stored. We created it to shield the administration and web access modules from the complexities of dealing with the database, and provide a layer of abstraction in case we decided to make changes to the underlying storage mechanism as requirements changed. In this case we are using a relational database, but may in the future need to move to an object database or perhaps a simple flat file format.

Administration module

The administration module is the tool that product managers, support staff, and other internal users would use to create and maintain the database of FAQs. It includes a JSP-based user interface allowing them to add, delete, and update FAQs in the database. This module is designed to be used within the enterprise exclusively, and will not be exposed to the public web.

Web access module

This module is pretty much the reason we started this project. It allows us to retrieve FAQs from the database and display them on the web dynamically. The purpose of this module is to give our content team the JSP components and Java classes they need to easily include individual or whole collections of FAQs into web pages without having to constantly update them. It turns out that this module is pretty simple; building off of components created for use in the other modules, but is infinitely flexible in its capabilities. It essentially becomes a new service (fetching an FAQ from the database) available to the content designers.

11.1.4 Building an FAQ component

It is clear that each module will need to exchange data at some point. To do so, we'll create a class to represent each FAQ. This class will be the building block from each of our related modules, since, after all, it's the FAQs we are building this whole thing for in the first place. Since servlets and JSPs can both deal in terms of objects, a `FaqBean` object gives a common unit of exchange that will greatly simplify interaction between components. The `FaqBean` class defines a simple set of properties, as shown in table 11.1.

Table 11.1 FaqBean properties

Property	Java Type
`ID`	int
`question`	String
`answer`	String
`lastModified`	java.util.Date

Creating the bean is straightforward; we simply provide the getter and setter methods for each of the Bean's properties as shown in chapter 8. The source code is shown in listing 11.1.

Listing 11.1 FaqBean

```
package com.taglib.wdjsp.faqtool;

import java.util.Date;

public class FaqBean {
  private int id;
  private String question;
  private String answer;
  private Date lastModified;

  public FaqBean() {
    this.id = 0;
    this.question = "";
    this.answer = "";
    this.lastModified = new Date();
  }

  public void setQuestion(String question) {
    this.question = question;
    this.lastModified = new Date();
  }

  public String getQuestion() {
    return this.question;
  }

  public void setAnswer(String answer) {
    this.answer = answer;
    this.lastModified = new Date();
  }

  public String getAnswer() {
    return this.answer;
  }

  public void setID(int id) {
    this.id = id;
  }

  public int getID() {
    return this.id;
  }

  public Date getLastModified() {
    return this.lastModified;
  }
```

```
  public void setLastModified(Date modified) {
    this.lastModified = modified;
  }

  public String toString() {
    return "[" + id + "] " + "Q: " + question + "; A: " +
      answer + "\n";
  }
}
```

Modifying any property of the bean through a setter method triggers an update in the value of the `lastModified` property, which was initialized in the constructor to match its creation date. You may be wondering why we created setter properties for properties you might not expect the user to manipulate, such as `lastModified` and `ID`. Since we'll be constructing beans out of data from the database (and using them in our JSPs), we need to be able to manipulate all the properties of our bean in order to completely mirror their state in the database. The `ID` property for new beans is assigned by the storage module, rather than the bean itself, as we'll soon learn.

11.2 The storage module

The storage module must be accessible by several application components. We wanted to isolate all database activity into a single module—hiding database code behind a series of access methods that dependent components could use to add, remove, and update FAQ objects in the database.

The goal is to provide a single point of access into and out of the database. In fact, we decided that the other modules should not even need to know that there is a database; they simply request or deliver FAQs to the storage module, which magically handles the transaction. Likewise, we wanted the storage module to be application independent. It does not need to be concerned about how the information it manages is used by the other two modules, or any future modules for that matter.

The design we came up with was to create a Java class designed to handle any requests for access to FAQs stored in the database. This code is independent of the other modules in our database, but its interface would provide the necessary methods to manage FAQs. By isolating database specific code in this manner, we are able to pursue development of this module independently of the other two. It also restricts database or schema specific operations to a single module.

11.2.1 Database schema

For this application we created a single table, FAQS, with four columns. The table is used to store data for our FAQ objects. Each row of the table represents an FAQ (and its answer) and is identified by a unique ID value. The schema is summarized in table 11.2.

Table 11.2 The FAQ database schema

Column	SQL Type
id	int
question	varchar(255)
answer	varchar(4096)
modified	timestamp

Most of these mappings between database columns and `FaqBean` properties are fairly straightforward. The `modified` column is used to store the date the FAQ was last modified. The ID of each FAQ will be kept unique by maintaining a sequence on the database, which is incremented automatically with each new Bean we add to the table.

11.2.2 The FaqRepository class

The `FaqRepository` class is an example of the singleton pattern, a class which allows only one instance of itself to be created and provides clients with a means to access that instance. In this case, the singleton object provides a number of methods for manipulating FAQs stored in the database. All of the methods in this class deal with `FaqBean` objects, not strings or SQL data, improving the abstraction between this and its companion classes which will use it. We can build and debug this class independently of the other modules because, while the repository lets us manipulate Beans in the database, it does so with no direct ties to the main application. The `FaqRepository` class is shown in listing 11.2.

Listing 11.2 FaqRepository

```
package com.taglib.wdjsp.faqtool;

import java.util.*;
import java.sql.*;

public class FaqRepository {
  private static FaqRepository instance;
```

```
private static final String driver = "postgresql.Driver";
private static final String user= "guest";
private static final String pass = "guest";
private static final String dbURL =
  "jdbc:postgresql://slide/test";

private Connection connection;
private PreparedStatement getStmt;
private PreparedStatement putStmt;
private PreparedStatement remStmt;
private PreparedStatement getAllStmt;
private PreparedStatement updStmt;

public static FaqRepository getInstance()
  throws FaqRepositoryException {
  if (instance == null)
    instance = new FaqRepository();
  return instance;
}

private FaqRepository() throws FaqRepositoryException {
  String get="SELECT * FROM FAQS WHERE ID=?";
  String put=
    "INSERT INTO FAQS VALUES (NEXTVAL('faqid_seq'), ?, ?, ?)";
  String rem="DELETE FROM FAQS WHERE ID=?";
  String upd=
    "UPDATE FAQS SET QUESTION=?, ANSWER=?, MODIFIED=? WHERE ID=?";
  String all="SELECT * FROM FAQS ORDER BY ID";

  try {
    Class.forName(driver);
    connection = DriverManager.getConnection(dbURL, user, pass);
    getStmt = connection.prepareStatement(get);
    putStmt = connection.prepareStatement(put);
    remStmt = connection.prepareStatement(rem);
    getAllStmt = connection.prepareStatement(all);
    updStmt = connection.prepareStatement(upd);
  }
  catch (ClassNotFoundException e) {
    throw new FaqRepositoryException("No Driver Available!");
  }
  catch (SQLException se) {
    throw new FaqRepositoryException(se.getMessage());
  }
}

private FaqBean makeFaq(ResultSet results)
  throws FaqRepositoryException {
  try {
    FaqBean faq = new FaqBean();
    faq.setID(results.getInt("ID"));
    faq.setQuestion(results.getString("QUESTION"));
```

```
      faq.setAnswer(results.getString("ANSWER"));
      Timestamp t = results.getTimestamp("MODIFIED");
      java.util.Date d;
      d = new java.util.Date(t.getTime() + (t.getNanos()/1000000));
      faq.setLastModified(d);
      return faq;
    }
    catch (SQLException e) {
      throw new FaqRepositoryException(e.getMessage());
    }
  }

  public FaqBean getFaq(int id)
    throws UnknownFaqException, FaqRepositoryException {
    try {
      ResultSet results;
      synchronized (getStmt) {
        getStmt.clearParameters();
        getStmt.setInt(1, id);
        results = getStmt.executeQuery();
      }
      if (results.next())
       return makeFaq(results);
      else
       throw new UnknownFaqException("Could not find FAQ# " + id);
    }
    catch (SQLException e) {
      throw new FaqRepositoryException(e.getMessage());
    }
  }

  public FaqBean[] getFaqs()
    throws FaqRepositoryException {
    try {
      ResultSet results;
      Collection faqs = new ArrayList();
      synchronized(getAllStmt) {
        results = getAllStmt.executeQuery();
      }
      FaqBean faq;
      while (results.next()) {
        faqs.add(makeFaq(results));
      }
      return (FaqBean[])faqs.toArray(new FaqBean[0]);
    }
    catch (SQLException e) {
      throw new FaqRepositoryException(e.getMessage());
    }
  }
```

```
public void update(FaqBean faq)
  throws UnknownFaqException, FaqRepositoryException {
  try {
    synchronized(updStmt) {
      updStmt.clearParameters();
      updStmt.setString(1, faq.getQuestion());
      updStmt.setString(2, faq.getAnswer());
      Timestamp now;
      now = new Timestamp(faq.getLastModified().getTime());
      updStmt.setTimestamp(3, now);
      updStmt.setInt(4, faq.getID());
      int rowsChanged = updStmt.executeUpdate();
      if (rowsChanged < 1)
        throw new UnknownFaqException("Could not find FAQ# " +
      faq.getID());
    }
  }
  catch (SQLException e) {
    throw new FaqRepositoryException(e.getMessage());
  }
}

public void put(FaqBean faq) throws
  FaqRepositoryException {
  try {
    synchronized(putStmt) {
      putStmt.clearParameters();
      putStmt.setString(1, faq.getQuestion());
      putStmt.setString(2, faq.getAnswer());
      Timestamp now;
      now = new Timestamp(faq.getLastModified().getTime());
      putStmt.setTimestamp(3, now);
      putStmt.executeUpdate();
    }
  }
  catch (SQLException e) {
    throw new FaqRepositoryException(e.getMessage());
  }

}

public void removeFaq(int id)
  throws FaqRepositoryException {
  try {
    synchronized(remStmt) {
      remStmt.clearParameters();
      remStmt.setInt(1, id);
      int rowsChanged = remStmt.executeUpdate();
      if (rowsChanged < 1)
        throw new UnknownFaqException("Can't delete FAQ# "+ id);
```

```
      }
    }
    catch (SQLException e) {
      throw new FaqRepositoryException(e.getMessage());
    }
  }

  public void destroy() {
    if (connection != null) {
      try { connection.close(); }
      catch (Exception e) { }
    }
  }

}
```

The constructor

The constructor for a singleton class like this one is `private` to prevent outside classes from instantiating it. The only way to obtain an instance of the `FaqRepository` class then is through a `static` method of the `FaqRepository` itself. In the constructor we establish a connection to the database. For brevity, we've hard coded all of our database connection information, but in practice we would employ a `ResourceBundle`, a properties file, JNDI, or some other means of externally configuring this information. In the constructor we also create a number of prepared statements to support the various operations we require—adding FAQs, removing FAQs, and so forth.

Using prepared statements not only improves the performance, it keeps our database access particulars in one place. While we've hard coded the database connection and the SQL code for simplicity, we could pull database access and schema related statements out of the code, retrieving them from a properties file at run time, allowing us some more flexibility. Remember, we'll only have to go through this prepared statement setup process once, since the constructor will be called only once, when we create the sole instance of the class.

Referencing the instance

A `static` member of the class itself maintains a reference (`instance`) to a single instance of the class that will be passed to anyone calling the `getInstance()` method. The `getInstance()` method also takes care of creating the instance the first time it is called. Note that if there is a problem, we throw a `FaqRepositoryException` in the constructor and rethrow it here. This way we can alert the calling class that, for whatever reason, we are unable to create a `FaqRepository`.

To use the `FaqRepository` then, the calling class just calls `getInstance()` (within a `try` block of course), and then calls the appropriate `public` methods. For example, to get an FAQ from the database, we would use code such as this:

```
try {

  FaqRepository faqDatabase = FaqRepository.getInstance();
  FaqBean faq = faqDatabase.getFaq(10005);
  System.out.println("The Question Is: " + faq.getQuestion()");
}
catch (UnknownFaqException e1) {
  System.out.println("Could not find Faq 10005");
}
catch (FaqRepositoryException e2) {
  System.out.println("Could not get access to Faqs!");
}
```

We can use the code to write a test harness for this module and test each method of our `FaqRepository` class, even though the other modules may still be in development. Very handy.

Prepared statements

Note that our access methods all contain synchronized blocks around the prepared statements. This is necessary because we are reusing `PreparedStatement` objects. Because there is only a single instance of this class, there may be several threads executing these methods simultaneously. Without synchronization, one thread could be manipulating elements of the `PreparedStatement` object while another is attempting to use it. Not a good thing.

Each prepared statement handles a different type of operation and each works with the data stored inside the `FAQS` table of the database. As a typical example, notice the prepared statement we are using to add FAQs to the database:

```
String put="INSERT INTO FAQS VALUES (NEXTVAL('faqid_seq'), ?, ?, ?)";
```

This statement says that the first value (which maps to the ID of the FAQ) is determined by incrementing a sequence, `faqid_seq`, on the database. The operation `nextval()` is a built-in method of our database server. This keeps us from having to manage `id` allocation ourselves. Most, but not all, databases provide some sort of managed sequences. If necessary you can create your own table of sequence values and manage them yourself.

Access methods

Our FAQ access methods `getFaq()` and `getFaqs()` have a common operational requirement. Given a `ResultSet` as output from executing the appropriate prepared statement they need to turn each row into a `FaqBean` object. This is accomplished by creating an empty `FaqBean` object, and populating it with data from the appropriate columns of the current row of the result set. Take a look at the `getFaq()` method in the previous section. As you can see, we simplify things by delegating this common task off to a utility method, `makeFaq()`, which takes the `ResultSet` as its argument, and builds a bean mirroring the data in the `ResultSet`. Also note the conversion from the database `Timestamp` to the bean's `java.util.Date` type.

11.2.3 Storage module exceptions

In our methods that need to execute JDBC calls, we trap any `SQLExceptions` that arise and rewrap them into `FaqRepositoryExceptions`. We could have simply thrown them back, but since the decision was made to make the interface to `FaqRepository` independent of its implementation—meaning that calling classes shouldn't have to know that `FaqRepository` is accessing a database, and thus shouldn't have to deal with `SQLExceptions`. Besides, if they can't access the `FaqRepository`, there's not much the calling class can do about it, other than reporting it. Failure in this case is fatal. We do pass the message along in any case, to make things easier to debug.

We've created two simple exceptions classes to handle various error conditions that may arise inside the storage module. The first, `FaqRepositoryException`, is the base class. The second, `UnknownFaqException`, is a more specific exception that is thrown when a requested FAQ cannot be located. They are very simple classes. Their source code is shown in listings 11.3 and 11.4.

Listing 11.3 FaqRepositoryException

```
package com.taglib.wdjsp.faqtool;

public class FaqRepositoryException extends Exception {

  public FaqRepositoryException() {
    super();
  }

  public FaqRepositoryException(String msg) {
    super(msg);
  }
}
```

Listing 11.4 UnknownFaqException

```
package com.taglib.wdjsp.faqtool;

public class UnknownFaqException extends FaqRepositoryException {

  public UnknownFaqException() {
    super();
  }

  public UnknownFaqException(String msg) {
    super(msg);
  }
}
```

11.3 The administration module

The administration module is a tool allowing administrators to add, delete, and update FAQs in the system. It is composed of a series of interconnected screens that form the user interface to our application. The application's screens are a function of the various steps the user can take along the way. Transitioning between each step causes activity—such as adding an FAQ to the database or deleting an existing one—and results in different outcomes that lead us to new screens.

At each screen, we'll want to give the user a chance to go back to the main menu (aborting the current step), as well as perform the appropriate activity for that page. Therefore, from each screen in our application different choices take the user to different parts of the program. This is a typical tree-style application flow (figure 11.2). (For brevity and clarity in the diagram, we've left out the abort path which just takes the user back to the main menu from each screen.) Each path through the application adds another branch to the tree.

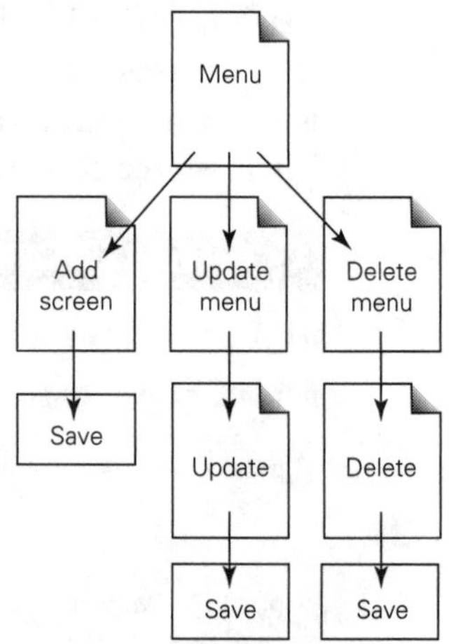

Figure 11.2 Flow through the administration application

In developing the administration portion of our FAQ management system we decided to create one central servlet, `FaqAdminServlet`, to handle the application logic and direct each request to the appropriate screen, depending on the state of the application and information specified in the request. The screens themselves are a series of JSP pages, which make use of data provided by the servlet. The servlet will be a mediator between the various pages that make up the user interface screens, and will direct requests to the appropriate application logic, which deals with the FAQ data itself.

11.3.1 The administration servlet

A servlet is at the heart of our application. We will direct each request to this servlet, and have it determine the actions to take and the next appropriate page to display. Our goal here is to use the JSPs for display and presentation purposes only, and have the servlet managing flow through the application and handling the application logic. We created an implementation of the command pattern approach discussed in chapter 10 to help better separate the application logic from the program control aspects of our servlet.

Utilizing the command pattern

In the command pattern, we associate application activities (such as adding an FAQ or editing an entry) with instances of classes that know how to perform the requested function. Each activity will be represented by a specific command. The implementation we elected to use for this project packages the application logic into a collection of independent command handler classes, all of which implement a common interface called `Command`. The `Command` interface specifies a single method, `execute()`:

```
package com.taglib.wdjsp.faqtool;
import javax.servlet.*;
import javax.servlet.http.*;

public interface Command {
  public String execute(HttpServletRequest req)
    throws CommandException;
}
```

The `execute()` method of each command handler takes an `HttpServletRequest`, allowing it to pull out from the request any parameters it needs to perform its operation. When complete, the command handler can then store its results as a request attribute before returning control to the servlet. The results of the operation can then be retrieved from the request by the JSP page ultimately handling the request. If anything goes wrong, an instance of `CommandException`, (listing 11.5), is thrown to alert the servlet to the problem. The big idea here is that we have created an interface which allows the servlet to delegate the handling of a command to a handler class, without having to know any details about the handler class itself, even its specific class name.

Listing 11.5 CommandException

```
package com.taglib.wdjsp.faqtool;

public class CommandException extends Exception {

  public CommandException() {
    super();
  }

  public CommandException(String msg) {
    super(msg);
  }
}
```

Mapping actions to commands

Each JSP screen will indicate the user's desired action to the servlet by passing in a value through the request parameter `cmd`. The value of `cmd` serves as a command identifier, telling us what to do next. So to delete an FAQ, the JSP page would simply pass in the appropriate identifier, say `delete`, signaling the servlet to hand the request off to the command handler for deletion. Each action we want to support in our application needs its own unique identifier that the JSP pages can use to request different actions to be performed.

However, processing a command is more than just calling the appropriate command handler's `execute()` method. We must also direct the request to the appropriate JSP page following successful completion of the action. We didn't want the pages themselves to have to be bound to specific pages or understand flow control issues. Therefore we've designed each of our command handlers to accept a `String` value in its constructor to specify the next page in the process. This `String` value is passed back to the controlling servlet from the `execute()` method as a return value, identifying the JSP page that should now receive the request.

In our servlet, we associate each command identifier with a separate instance of one of our command classes (each of which we'll discuss in a bit), which has been preconfigured with the file name of the destination screen we should visit next. We store each command class instance in a `HashMap`, using the command identifier used by our JSP pages as the key. We'll do this in the `init()` method of the servlet, which is run only the first time the servlet is started by the server. This operation is performed in the `initCommands()` utility method:

```
private void initCommands() {
  commands = new HashMap();
  commands.put("main-menu", new NullCommand("menu.jsp"));
  commands.put("abort", new AbortCommand("menu.jsp"));
```

```
    commands.put("add", new NullCommand("add.jsp"));
    commands.put("do-add", new AddCommand("menu.jsp"));
    commands.put("update-menu", new GetAllCommand("upd_menu.jsp"));
    commands.put("update", new GetCommand("update.jsp"));
    commands.put("do-update", new UpdateCommand("menu.jsp"));
    commands.put("delete-menu", new GetAllCommand("del_menu.jsp"));
    commands.put("delete", new GetCommand("delete.jsp"));
    commands.put("do-delete", new DeleteCommand("menu.jsp"));
  }
```

As you can see we've created ten different commands, each with its own unique identifier, which form the keys to our `HashMap`. Each command activity involves more than just mapping a command identifier to a command handler; it's a combination of command identifier, command handler class, and destination screen. Some command handlers can be used to handle several different command identifiers, by being configured with different destination pages. For example, both the update menu and delete menu JSP pages will need a list of the FAQs in the database to allow the user to make their selection. Collecting all of the FAQs for retrieval by the JSP page is the job of the `GetAllCommand` class. Creating two different instances of the `GetAllCommand` class with different destinations allows us to reuse the application logic isolated inside the command handler. We aren't required to create a unique class for each identifier, since only the destination screens are different in this case.

Processing commands

The implementation behind each command handler is, as we'll see, independent of the operations inside the servlet itself. We'll discuss each of these in turn. The `service()` method of our servlet is extremely simple in this design. We simply fetch the appropriate command handler from our list, call its `execute()` method, then redirect the request to the appropriate page. The `lookupCommand()` method simply pulls the appropriate object from the `HashMap` and provides sane defaults—sort of a factory method. The `CommandToken.set()` method creates a special token to help maintain transaction integrity, which will be explained soon.

```
public void service(HttpServletRequest req, HttpServletResponse res)
  throws ServletException, IOException {
  String next;
  try {
    Command cmd = lookupCommand(req.getParameter("cmd"));
    next = cmd.execute(req);
    CommandToken.set(req);
  }
  catch (CommandException e) {
    req.setAttribute("javax.servlet.jsp.jspException", e);
```

```
    next = error;
  }
  RequestDispatcher rd;
  rd = getServletContext().getRequestDispatcher(jspdir + next);
  rd.forward(req, res);
}
```

If executing the command throws an exception, we catch it and store it as a request attribute before forwarding the request on to our error-handling page. This allows us to handle both servlet originated exceptions and JSP exceptions in the same place. The complete source code for the servlet is shown in listing 11.6.

Listing 11.6 FaqAdministrationServlet

```
package com.taglib.wdjsp.faqtool;

import java.io.*;
import javax.servlet.*;
import javax.servlet.http.*;
import java.util.*;

public class FaqAdminServlet extends HttpServlet {
  private HashMap commands;
  private String error = "error.jsp";
  private String jspdir = "/jsp/";

  public void init(ServletConfig config) throws ServletException {
    super.init(config);
    initCommands();
  }

  public void service(HttpServletRequest req,
          HttpServletResponse res)
    throws ServletException, IOException {
    String next;
    try {
      Command cmd = lookupCommand(req.getParameter("cmd"));
      next = cmd.execute(req);
      CommandToken.set(req);
    }
    catch (CommandException e) {
      req.setAttribute("javax.servlet.jsp.jspException", e);
      next = error;
    }
    RequestDispatcher rd;
    rd = getServletContext().getRequestDispatcher(jspdir + next);
    rd.forward(req, res);
  }
```

```
  private Command lookupCommand(String cmd)
    throws CommandException {
    if (cmd == null)
      cmd = "main-menu";
    if (commands.containsKey(cmd.toLowerCase()))
      return (Command)commands.get(cmd.toLowerCase());
    else
      throw new CommandException("Invalid Command Identifier");
  }

  private void initCommands() {
    commands = new HashMap();
    commands.put("main-menu", new NullCommand("menu.jsp"));
    commands.put("abort", new AbortCommand("menu.jsp"));
    commands.put("add", new NullCommand("add.jsp"));
    commands.put("do-add", new AddCommand("menu.jsp"));
    commands.put("update-menu", new GetAllCommand("upd_menu.jsp"));
    commands.put("update", new GetCommand("update.jsp"));
    commands.put("do-update", new UpdateCommand("menu.jsp"));
    commands.put("delete-menu", new GetAllCommand("del_menu.jsp"));
    commands.put("delete", new GetCommand("delete.jsp"));
    commands.put("do-delete", new DeleteCommand("menu.jsp"));
  }
}
```

Transaction integrity

Now to explain the meaning of that `CommandToken.set()` call following a successful command execution. As explained in chapter 10, some actions in a JSP application are vulnerable to accidental re-execution due to the user reloading a page or clicking Back.

Take for example the steps involved in adding a new FAQ to the database. In the first step, we collect information for the new FAQ through a form. In the second step it takes the question and answer from the request, and instructs the `FaqRepository` to process it, adding it to the database. The FAQ is added and the user ends up back at the main menu. However, the URL that the browser has stored in memory for the current page request now includes the add request and the appropriate question and answer variables. If the user clicks Reload, the request is resubmitted, all the request parameters are resent, and another instance is added to the database. A similar problem can also happen with Delete and Update. We need to trap each of these cases and act accordingly. Something has to alert the servlet to the fact that we've already performed this operation once and that we should not do it a second or third time.

In our servlet we will apply the command token technique discussed in chapter 10 to assure that sensitive commands are performed only once. To issue and manage our tokens we'll use an application independent utility class we've designed called `CommandToken`, which has two public methods, both of which are static:

```
public static void set(HttpServletRequest req)
public static boolean isValid(HttpServletRequest req)
```

The first method, `set()`, creates a unique transaction token and stores it (as a string of hex characters) in the user's session and in the request as an attribute. The second method, `isValid()`, can be used to validate a request, and will search for the existence of a token in the request and the session and compare them for equality. If they are equal, it returns true—otherwise it returns false indicating that there is either a missing or mismatched token. The token itself is an MD5 message digest (a kind of checksum) generated from the combination of the user's session ID and the current system time. This assures that each token is unique to the user and will not be repeated. The code for the `CommandToken` class is in listing 11.7:

Listing 11.7 CommandToken

```
package com.taglib.wdjsp.faqtool;

import javax.servlet.http.*;
import java.security.*;

public class CommandToken {
  public static void set(HttpServletRequest req) {
    HttpSession session = req.getSession(true);
    long systime = System.currentTimeMillis();
    byte[] time  = new Long(systime).toString().getBytes();
    byte[] id = session.getId().getBytes();
    try {
      MessageDigest md5 = MessageDigest.getInstance("MD5");
      md5.update(id);
      md5.update(time);
      String token = toHex(md5.digest());
      req.setAttribute("token", token);
      session.setAttribute("token", token);
    }
    catch (Exception e) {
      System.err.println("Unable to calculate MD5 Digests");
    }
  }

  public static boolean isValid(HttpServletRequest req) {
    HttpSession session = req.getSession(true);
    String requestToken = req.getParameter("token");
```

```
    String sessionToken = (String)session.getAttribute("token");
    if (requestToken == null || sessionToken == null)
      return false;
    else
      return requestToken.equals(sessionToken);
  }

  private static String toHex(byte[] digest) {
    StringBuffer buf = new StringBuffer();
    for (int i=0; i < digest.length; i++)
      buf.append(Integer.toHexString((int)digest[i] & 0x00ff));
    return buf.toString();
  }
}
```

To make use of this class, we need to set a new token after the successful completion of each command. That's the reason for the call to `CommandToken.set()` in our servlet's `service()` method. We are essentially creating a single-use token each time to help regulate flow between pages. On pages that precede flow-critical commands we must include the token as a hidden element of our form data by retrieving it from the request. Then, we'll have each sensitive command pass the request object to the `isValid()` method to verify that this is a valid request before handling it. We'll see this in practice in the `AddCommand`, `UpdateCommand`, and `DeleteCommand` classes and their respective front-end JSP pages.

11.3.2 The main menu

This screen is the main interface for managing the FAQ list. Here the user can select to add, modify, or delete an entry. Selecting an action for an FAQ will lead to other screens. The user will be returned to this screen after completing any operations from the other screens, and should have a status message area that can be used to report the results of each operation.

You are taken to the main menu via the `main-menu` command. Visiting the main menu is also the default activity if no command identifier is specified. In either case, no action is required, and the command is handled by a very simple implementation of the `Command` interface called `NullCommand`.

The NullCommand class

The simplest of our commands, as you might expect, is the `NullCommand` class (listing 11.8). It simply returns its next URL value, performing no operation. This class is used for commands that are simply requests to visit a particular page, such as visiting the main menu and collecting the information necessary to add an FAQ to the database.

Listing 11.8 NullCommand

```
package com.taglib.wdjsp.faqtool;

import javax.servlet.*;
import javax.servlet.http.*;

public class NullCommand implements Command {
  private String next;

  public NullCommand(String next) {
    this.next = next;
  }

  public String execute(HttpServletRequest req)
    throws CommandException {
    return next;
  }
}
```

The AbortCommand class

We also created an `AbortCommand` class to handle the case where the user wants to abort the current operation and return to the main menu from any page. `AbortCommand` differs from `NullCommand` in only one way: it adds a message to the request in the form of a request attribute—creating a simple page-to-page communication system. This message is retrieved by the main menu JSP page, and used to update the status area of the main menu interface (figure 11.3.) This is a way to give feedback to the user about the status of the last operation. We'll use this technique in several other commands as well. The `AbortComand` code is shown in listing 11.9.

Listing 11.9 AbortCommand

```
package com.taglib.wdjsp.faqtool;

import javax.servlet.*;
import javax.servlet.http.*;

public class AbortCommand implements Command {
  private String next;

  public AbortCommand(String next) {
    this.next = next;
  }

  public String execute(HttpServletRequest req)
    throws CommandException {
    req.setAttribute("faqtool.msg", "Operation Aborted");
    return next;
  }
```

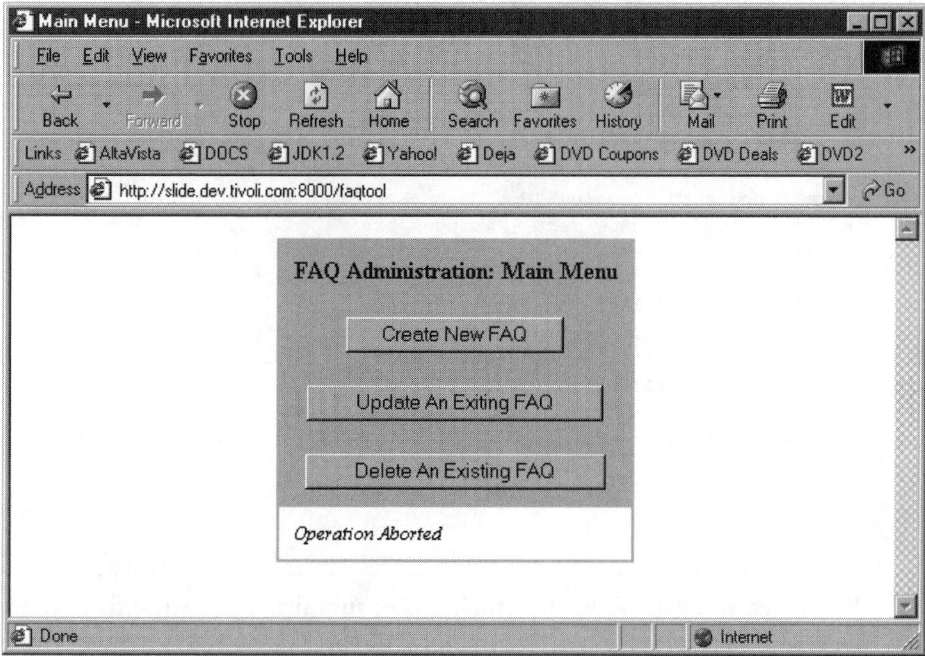

Figure 11.3 A status message on the main menu

The main menu JSP page

The operation of this page is straightforward. The main menu page allows the user to add, update, or delete an FAQ from the database. That is the page's only job. The source code for the main menu page, `menu.jsp` is shown in listing 11.10.

Listing 11.10 menu.jsp

```
<%@ page import="com.taglib.wdjsp.faqtool.*" errorPage="/jsp/error.jsp" %>
<html>
<head>
<title>Main Menu</title>
<script language="JavaScript">
function setCmd(value) {
  document.menu.cmd.value = value;
}
</script>
</head>
<body bgcolor="white">
<form name="menu" action="/faqtool" method="post">
```

```
<input type="hidden" name="cmd" value="">
<table bgcolor="tan" border="0" align="center" cellpadding="10">
<tr><th>FAQ Administration: Main Menu</th></tr>
<tr><td align="center">
<input type="submit" value="Create New FAQ"
onClick="setCmd('add')"></td></tr>
<tr><td align="center">
<input type="submit" value="Update An Existing FAQ"
onClick="setCmd('update-menu')"></td></tr>
<tr><td align="center">
<input type="submit" value="Delete An Existing FAQ"
onClick="setCmd('delete-menu')"></td></tr>
<tr><td bgcolor="white"><font size="-1">
<% if (request.getAttribute("faqtool.msg") != null) { %>
<i><%= request.getAttribute("faqtool.msg") %></i>
<% } %>
</font></td></tr>
</table>
</form>
</body>
</html>
```

We've created a simple form, which, upon submittal, posts the form data back to the URL /faqtool, which we've mapped to the `FaqAdminServlet` in our JSP container. The command action will be specified through the request parameter `cmd`, which must be set by our form. There are a number of ways to include this request parameter into our form submission. We could have three separate forms on the page each with its own appropriate values assigned to the hidden element called `cmd`, and the three selection buttons would be the submit buttons for each form. We could also have named our submit buttons `cmd`, and set the value of each to the appropriate command identifiers. We could have even used anchor tags with URLs such as the following, which encode the `cmd` identifier into the URL as a parameter:

```
<a href="/faqtool?cmd=add">Create New FAQ</a>
<a href="/faqtool?cmd=update-menu">Create New FAQ</a>
<a href="/faqtool?cmd=delete-menu">Create New FAQ</a>
```

The servlet and application logic classes don't care how the front-end code works, as long as it sets the appropriate request parameters. We chose to set the command identifier through a hidden element (`cmd`) by using JavaScript to change the value depending on the user's selection. Each button on the page is a submit button—all for the same, single form. However, each has its own JavaScript `onClick` event handler which sets the value of our `cmd` element to the appropriate value upon the user selecting the button. This approach gives us more flexibility in how we describe each button, and lets us stick to `POST` style form processing rather than mucking up our URLs by tacking on parameters as we did in the hypothetical example. If you change the form handler's method type to GET it will still work, and you will see that the resulting request looks exactly like those shown. We are just setting the same request parameters after all. The POST approach keeps our URLs nice and clean and avoids tempting the user to bookmark deep into the application.

At the bottom of our little interface we check for the presence of a status message, and display it if necessary. As we talked about in the discussion of the AbortCommand, feedback messages may be placed into the request by our other commands to update us as to the status of things.

11.3.3 Adding an FAQ

Adding an FAQ to the database involves two steps, but only one screen. The users first choose to create an FAQ from the main menu. We don't need to do anything database related at this point, so in our servlet we use the NullCommand (which does nothing, remember) to handle this activity, forwarding us to the add.jsp page, which collects the question and the answer information that make up an FAQ. From this form the user selects to either abort the action, which simply takes them back to the main menu courtesy of the AbortCommand class, or commit the new FAQ to the database via a do-add request, which calls the AddCommand class to add the FAQ to the database, ending back at the main menu once it has been added successfully.

The add page

We must remember our earlier discussion on transaction integrity for sensitive, flow-dependent commands which we do not want to inadvertently process multiple times. Adding an FAQ to the database definitely qualifies as a sensitive command, and it will be looking for a token in the request it receives which matches the one stored in the session. We therefore need to include the single use token, which was stored as a request attribute following the successful completion of the command that brought us to this page. This is simple enough to include in our form.

```
<input type="hidden" name="token"
value="<%= request.getAttribute("token") %>">
```

which turns into something like this at request processing time:

```
<input type="hidden" name="token" value="485a4b73c03ef8149e6a438b6aa749e3">
```

This value, along with input from the user detailing the new question and answer will be sent to FaqAdminServlet for processing by an instance of the AddCommand class, which we will discuss in a moment. The source code for add.jsp is shown in listing 11.11 and the page shown in figure 11.4

Listing 11.11 add.jsp

```
<%@ page import="com.taglib.wdjsp.faqtool.*" errorPage="/jsp/error.jsp" %>
<html>
<head><title>Add FAQ</title></head>
<body bgcolor="white">
<form name="menu" action="/faqtool" method="post">
<table bgcolor="tan" border="0" align="center" cellpadding="10">
<tr><th colspan="2">FAQ Administration: Add FAQ</th></tr>
<tr><td><b>Question:</b></td>
<td><input type="text" name="question" size="41" value="">
</td></tr>
<tr><td><b>Answer:</b></td>
<td>
<textarea name="answer" cols="35" rows="5">
</textarea>
</td></tr>
<tr><td colspan="2" align="center">
<input type="submit" value="Abort Addition">
<input type="submit" value="Add This FAQ"
  onClick="document.menu.cmd.value='do-add'">
</td></tr>
</table>
<input type="hidden" name="token"
value="<%= request.getAttribute("token") %>">
<input type="hidden" name="cmd" value="abort">
</form>
</body>
</html>
```

As with the main menu, we use JavaScript to manipulate the value of the hidden form field `cmd`, which directs our action within the controller servlet, which defaults to the `abort` directive, changing its value to `do-add` if the user indicates he or she wishes to add the FAQ to the database. If you refer to the `FaqAdminServlet`'s `initCommands()` method you will see that the `do-add` directive is handled by an instance of the `AddCommand` class.

The AddCommand class

The source for the `AddCommand` class is relatively straightforward, because most of the hard work is done inside the `FaqRepository` class we described earlier. We merely have to use the information placed into the request through the JSP form to build an `FaqBean` object to pass to the put method of `FaqRepository`, and carry out a few sanity checks. The code is shown in listing 11.12:

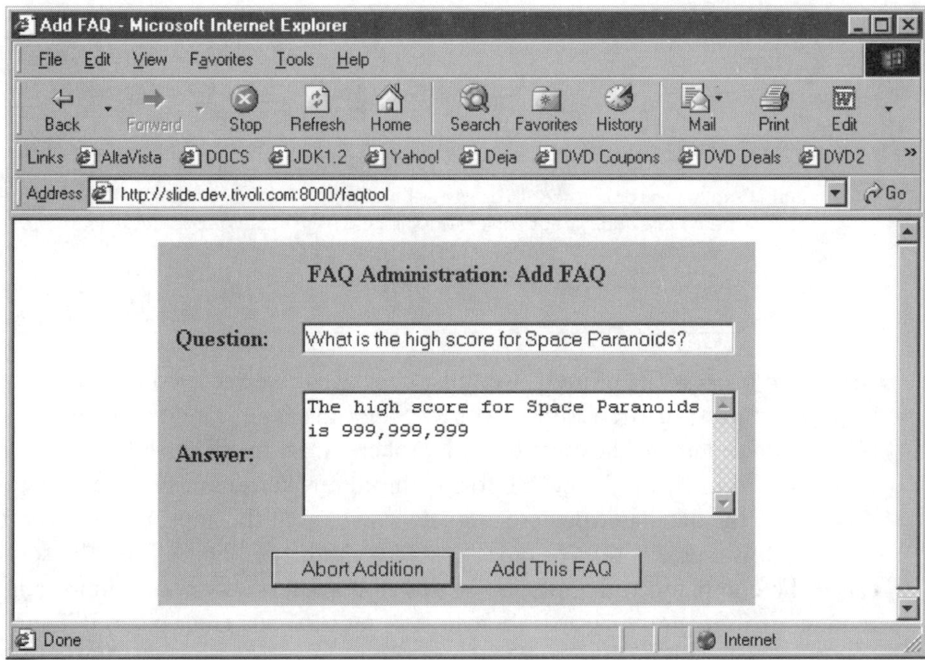

Figure 11.4 Adding an FAQ

Listing 11.12 AddCommand

```
package com.taglib.wdjsp.faqtool;

import javax.servlet.*;
import javax.servlet.http.*;

public class AddCommand implements Command {
  private String next;

  public AddCommand(String next) {
    this.next = next;
  }

  public String execute(HttpServletRequest req)
    throws CommandException {
    try {
      if (CommandToken.isValid(req)) {
        FaqRepository faqs = FaqRepository.getInstance();
        FaqBean faq = new FaqBean();
        faq.setQuestion(req.getParameter("question"));
        faq.setAnswer(req.getParameter("answer"));
        faqs.put(faq);
```

```
        req.setAttribute("faqtool.msg", "FAQ Added Successfully");
      }
      else {
        req.setAttribute("faqtool.msg", "Invalid Reload Attempted");
      }
      return next;
    }
    catch (FaqRepositoryException fe) {
      throw new CommandException("AddCommand: " + fe.getMessage());
    }
  }
}
```

Before we process the request, we must check that we received a valid token in the request by passing the request to the `CommandToken.isValid()` method. This command validator will expect to find a token in the user's session that matches the token passed in through the JSP form's hidden token field. If it does, we can add the FAQ to the database. If there is an error, we catch the appropriate exception and rethrow it as an exception of type `CommandException`. This allows the servlet that called the command to handle it—in this case `FaqAdminServlet` bundles it up as a request attribute and forwards the whole request to our error page. If it succeeds, it inserts an appropriate status message in the form of a request attribute to indicate what happened before returning the user to the main menu.

11.3.4 Deleting an FAQ

Deleting an FAQ takes three steps spread over two screens. After selecting delete from the main menu, the user is given a list of FAQs to select for removal. Before anything is deleted however, the FAQ's information is displayed and the user is asked for confirmation and given a final chance to abort the process and return to the main menu. Like adding an FAQ, deleting one is considered a sensitive operation, so we'll be checking that token again.

The GetAllCommand class

The first step in the deletion process, as you can see from the command mapping for the delete directive, is handled by the `GetAllCommand` class whose job is to retrieve the entire collection of FAQs from the database, wrap them into an array, and store them as a request attribute under the attribute name `faqs`. This allows the JSP page following this command to display a listing of all of the FAQs in the database. As before, most of the work is done inside the already covered `FaqRepository`. The source for this class is shown in listing 11.13.

Listing 11.13 GetAllCommand

```
package com.taglib.wdjsp.faqtool;

import javax.servlet.*;
import javax.servlet.http.*;

public class GetAllCommand implements Command {
  private String next;

  public GetAllCommand(String next) {
    this.next = next;
  }

  public String execute(HttpServletRequest req)
    throws CommandException {
    try {
      FaqRepository faqs = FaqRepository.getInstance();
      FaqBean[] faqList = faqs.getFaqs();
      req.setAttribute("faqs", faqList);
      return next;
    }
    catch (FaqRepositoryException fe) {
      throw new CommandException("GetCommand: " + fe.getMessage());
    }
  }
}
```

The deletion selection screen

The `del_menu.jsp` page is responsible for displaying the available FAQs and allowing the user to select one for deletion. It is delivered after `GetAllCommand` has retrieved the FAQs from the database and stored them as an array in `request`. We simply have to pull them out one by one, and build up our form. The end result is shown in figure 11.5, the source code is in listing 11.14. There are a few tricky parts, which we'll discuss.

Listing 11.14 del_menu.jsp

```
<%@ page import="com.taglib.wdjsp.faqtool.*"
 errorPage="/jsp/error.jsp" %>
<jsp:useBean id="faq" class="com.taglib.wdjsp.faqtool.FaqBean"/>
<%
  FaqBean[] faqs = (FaqBean[])request.getAttribute("faqs");
%>
<html>
<head><title>Delete Menu</title></head>
<form name="menu" action="/faqtool" method="post">
```

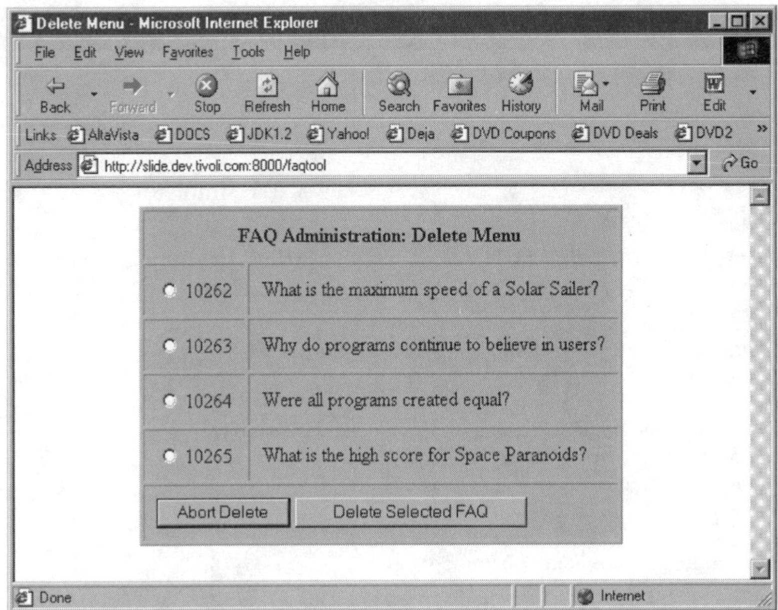

Figure 11.5 The deletion selection screen

```
<table bgcolor="tan" border="1" align="center" cellpadding="10">
<tr><th colspan="2">FAQ Administration: Delete Menu</th></tr>
<%
for (int i=0; i < faqs.length; i++) {
  faq = faqs[i];
%>
<tr>
<td><input type="radio" name="id"
value="<jsp:getProperty name="faq" property="ID"/>">
<jsp:getProperty name="faq" property="ID"/></td>
<td><jsp:getProperty name="faq" property="question"/></td>
</tr>
<% } %>
<tr><td colspan=2>
<input type="submit" value="Abort Delete">
<input type="submit" value="Delete Selected FAQ"
  onClick="document.menu.cmd.value='delete'">
<input type="hidden" name="cmd" value="abort">
</td></tr>
</table>
</form>
</html>
```

Looping through the array of `FaqBean` objects we pulled from the request seems straightforward, but there's a tricky part here. We wanted to use the Bean tags inside our loop, but remember that there are no standard tags for handling indexed properties or elements of an array like this. Therefore, we have to pull each item out of the array and create a reference to it accessible by the `PageContext` object, most importantly for the bean tag `<jsp:getProperty>`. We simply declare the reference, `faq`, at the top of the page via `<jsp:useBean>`, even though we actually assign a `FaqBean` object to the reference through a scriptlet. Leaving out the `<jsp:useBean>` tag would cause an error when the page tried to use `<jsp:getProperty>` on the `faq` variable.

The form itself is straightforward. We need to obtain the ID number of the FAQ that is to be deleted, as well as give the user the abort option. The submit buttons are handled as before, through JavaScript, and radio buttons give us an easy way to pick up the selected ID. If the user chooses to continue on to the second of the three steps, we set the `cmd` identifier to the delete action, which is handled by the `GetCommand` class to ask for confirmation.

The GetCommand class

The `GetCommand` class can retrieve a single FAQ from the database by its ID value. It looks in the request for the `id` parameter, then uses the `FaqRepository` class we created in our storage module to retrieve the matching FAQ from the database. We use the `id` value pulled from the request to call the `getFaq()` method of our `FaqRepository`. If we are successful fetching the FAQ from the database, we store it in the request under the attribute name `faq`. This allows the destination screen, in this case `delete.jsp`, to retrieve it from the request to make sure the user really wants to delete this FAQ. The only thing new here is that we have to catch several different exceptions and react accordingly. When we're done we return the next screen to the servlet. The source for the `GetCommand` class is shown in listing 11.15.

Listing 11.15 GetCommand

```
package com.taglib.wdjsp.faqtool;

import javax.servlet.*;
import javax.servlet.http.*;

public class GetCommand implements Command {
  private String next;

  public GetCommand(String next) {
    this.next = next;
  }
```

```
  public String execute(HttpServletRequest req)
    throws CommandException {
    try {
      FaqRepository faqs = FaqRepository.getInstance();
      int id = Integer.parseInt(req.getParameter("id"));
      FaqBean faq = faqs.getFaq(id);
      req.setAttribute("faq", faq);
      return next;
    }
    catch (NumberFormatException e) {
      throw new CommandException("GetCommand: invalid ID");
    }
    catch (UnknownFaqException uf) {
      throw new CommandException("GetCommand: " + uf.getMessage());
    }
    catch (FaqRepositoryException fe) {
      throw new CommandException("GetCommand: " + fe.getMessage());
    }
  }
}
```

The delete confirmation screen

This page allows the user to confirm the selection and triggers the deletion on the server. We simply need to retrieve the FAQ from the request, display its properties, and get the user's decision. Because the handler class for the `do-delete` action, `DeleteCommand`, is vulnerable we must include the current command token in our request, just as we did on the screen where we were creating an FAQ entry. The source for this page is shown in listing 11.16 and a screen is shown in figure 11.6

Listing 11.16 delete.jsp

```
<%@ page import="com.taglib.wdjsp.faqtool.*" errorPage="/jsp/error.jsp" %>
<jsp:useBean id="faq" class="com.taglib.wdjsp.faqtool.FaqBean" scope="request"/
  >
<html>
<head><title>Delete FAQ</title></head>
<form name="menu" action="/faqtool" method="post">
<table bgcolor="tan" border="0" align="center" cellpadding="10">
<tr><th colspan="2">FAQ Administration: Delete FAQ</th></tr>
<tr><td><b>ID:</b></td>
<td><jsp:getProperty name="faq" property="ID"/></td>
</tr>
<tr><td><b>Question:</b></td>
<td><jsp:getProperty name="faq" property="question"/></td>
</tr>
```

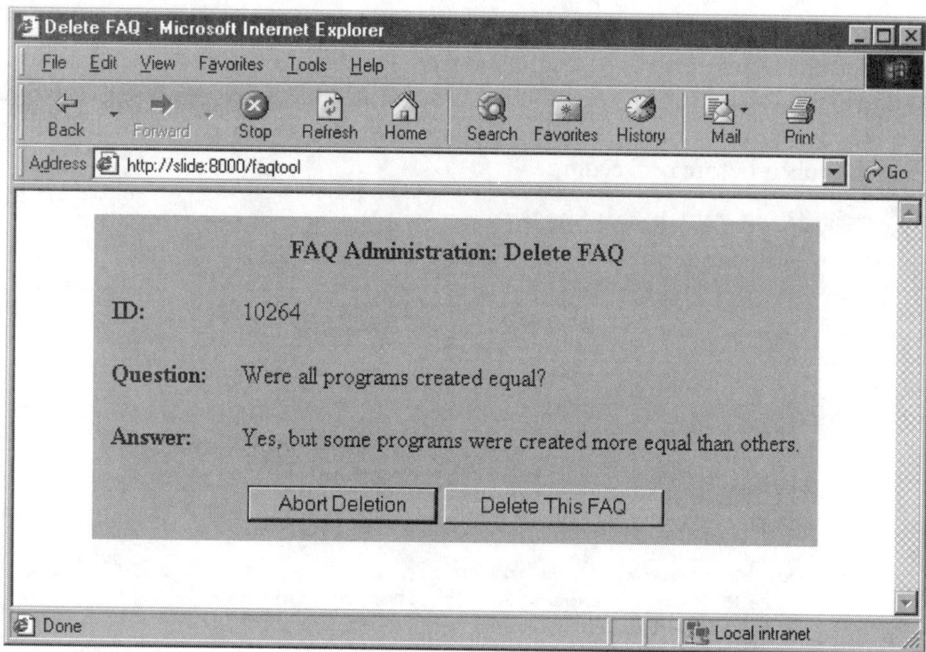

Figure 11.6 The deletion confirmation screen

```
<tr><td><b>Answer:</b></td>
<td><jsp:getProperty name="faq" property="answer"/></td>
</tr>
<tr>
<td colspan="2">
<input type="submit" value="Abort Deletion">
<input type="submit" value="Delete This FAQ"
onClick="document.menu.cmd.value='do-delete'">
</td></tr>
</table>
<input type="hidden" name="token"
value="<%= request.getAttribute("token") %>">
<input type="hidden" name="id"
value="<jsp:getProperty name="faq" property="id"/>">
<input type="hidden" name="cmd" value="abort">
</form>
</html>
```

The DeleteCommand class

Another straightforward command handler, `DeleteCommand`, requires an FAQ ID, which it obtains from the request. It calls the appropriate `FaqRepository` method, catching exceptions where appropriate. This is a sensitive command, so we check the token before proceeding.

```
package com.taglib.wdjsp.faqtool;

import javax.servlet.*;
import javax.servlet.http.*;

public class DeleteCommand implements Command {
  private String next;

  public DeleteCommand(String next) {
    this.next = next;
  }

  public String execute(HttpServletRequest req)
    throws CommandException {
    try {
      if (CommandToken.isValid(req)) {
        FaqRepository faqs = FaqRepository.getInstance();
        int id = Integer.parseInt(req.getParameter("id"));
        faqs.removeFaq(id);
        req.setAttribute("faqtool.msg", "FAQ Deleted Successfully");
      }
      else {
        req.setAttribute("faqtool.msg", "Invalid Reload Attempted");
      }
      return next;
    }
    catch (NumberFormatException e) {
      throw new CommandException("DeleteCommand: invalid ID");
    }
    catch (UnknownFaqException u) {
      throw new CommandException("DeleteCommand: "+u.getMessage());
    }
    catch (FaqRepositoryException fe) {
      throw new CommandException("DeleteCommand: "+fe.getMessage());
    }
  }
}
```

11.3.5 Updating an FAQ

Updating an FAQ—that is, editing its question and answer values—is a three-step process. In the first step, just as with deleting an FAQ, the user picks an FAQ from the list in the database. The next step is a screen which looks like the add screen we built earlier, but this time has default values equal to the current values for the selected FAQ in the database. Committing changes on this screen updates the database with the new values.

Update selection screen

This screen is nearly identical to the one we created for the Delete menu. Its source is shown in listing 11.17 and its screen shot in figure 11.7. Submitting the form on the page causes the servlet to execute the `GetCommand` on the selected servlet, in preparation for the update screen.

Listing 11.17 upd_menu.jsp

```
<%@ page import="com.taglib.wdjsp.faqtool.*" errorPage="/jsp/error.jsp" %>
<jsp:useBean id="faq" class="com.taglib.wdjsp.faqtool.FaqBean"/>
<%
  FaqBean[] faqs = (FaqBean[])request.getAttribute("faqs");
%>
<html>
<head><title>Update Menu</title></head>
<form name="menu" action="/faqtool" method="post">
<table bgcolor="tan" border="1" align="center" cellpadding="10">
<tr><th colspan="2">FAQ Administration: Update Menu</th></tr>
<%
for (int i=0; i < faqs.length; i++) {
  faq = faqs[i];
%>
<tr>
<td><input type="radio" name="id"
value="<jsp:getProperty name="faq" property="ID"/>">
<jsp:getProperty name="faq" property="ID"/></td>
<td><jsp:getProperty name="faq" property="question"/></td>
</tr>
<% } %>
<tr><td colspan=2>
<input type="submit" value="Abort Updating">
<input type="submit" value="Update Selected FAQ"
   onClick="document.menu.cmd.value='update'">
<input type="hidden" name="cmd" value="abort">
</td></tr>
</table>
</form>
</html>
```

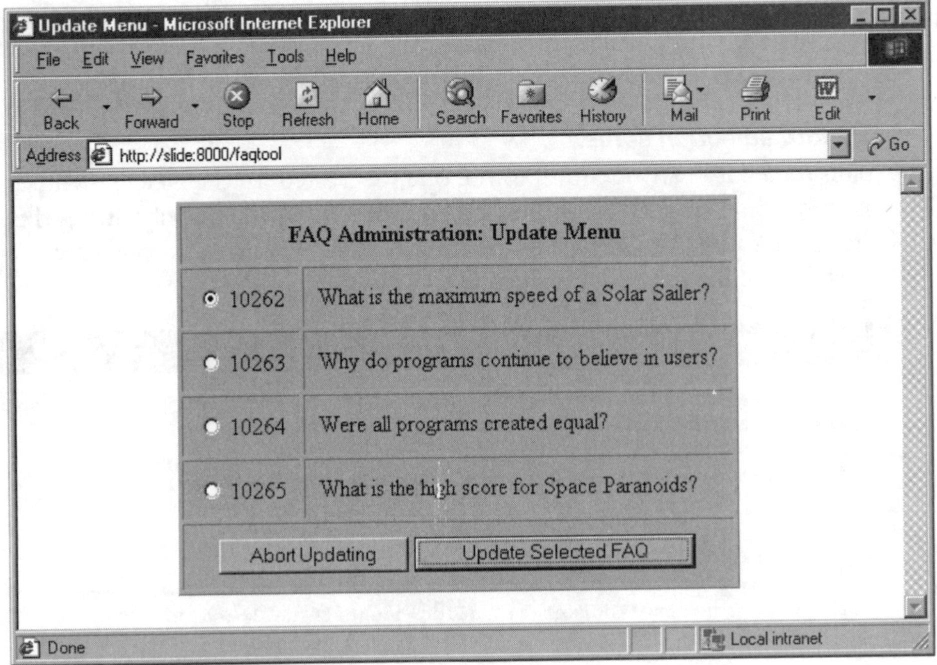

Figure 11.7 The Update menu

Update screen

This page operates nearly identically to the page for adding FAQs. The only difference (other than passing a different command identifier) is that we have to prepopulate the form fields with the current values for the selected FAQ. The `GetCommand` has placed a `FaqBean` corresponding with the selection into the request, so all we have to do is retrieve its values and place them into the form fields. More detailed information on populating forms—including radio buttons, select lists, and other elements—with JSP can be found in chapter 14. The listing for this page is shown in listing 11.18, and the screenshot in figure 11.8.

Listing 11.18 update.jsp

```
<%@ page import="com.taglib.wdjsp.faqtool.*" errorPage="/jsp/error.jsp" %>
<jsp:useBean id="faq" class="com.taglib.wdjsp.faqtool.FaqBean" scope="request"/
   >
<html>
<head><title>Update FAQ</title></head>
<body bgcolor="white">
```

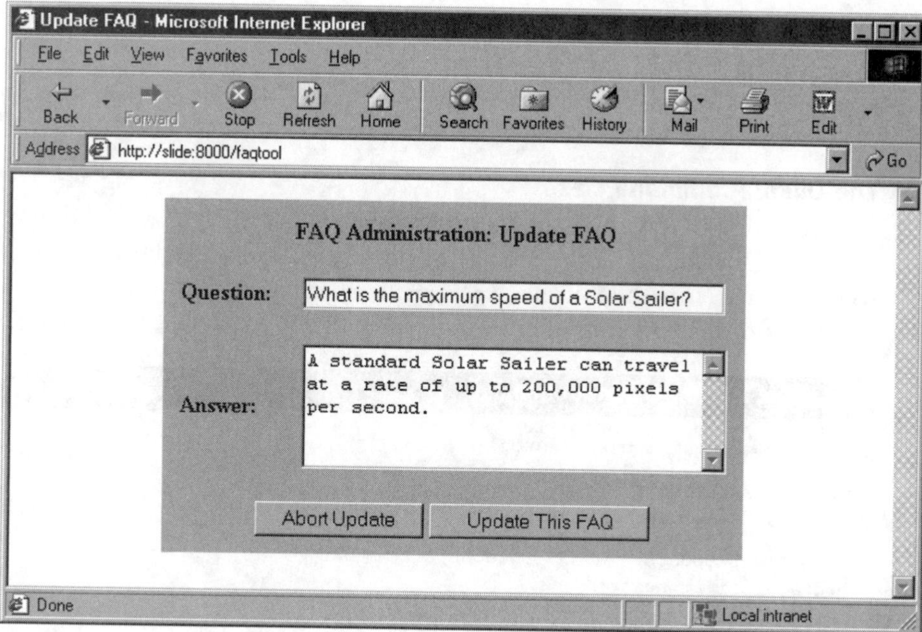

Figure 11.8 The update screen

```
<form name="menu" action="/faqtool" method="post">
<table bgcolor="tan" border="0" align="center" cellpadding="10">
<tr><th colspan="2">FAQ Administration: Update FAQ</th></tr>
<tr><td><b>Question:</b></td>
<td><input type="text" name="question" size="41"
value="<jsp:getProperty name="faq" property="question"/>">
</td></tr>
<tr><td><b>Answer:</b></td>
<td>
<textarea name="answer" cols="35" rows="5">
<jsp:getProperty name="faq" property="answer"/>
</textarea>
</td></tr>
<tr><td colspan="2" align="center">
<input type="submit" value="Abort Update">
<input type="submit" value="Update This FAQ"
onClick="document.menu.cmd.value='do-update'">
</td></tr>
</table>
<input type="hidden" name="cmd" value="abort">
<input type="hidden" name="token"
value="<%= request.getAttribute("token") %>">
<input type="hidden" name="id"
```

```
value="<jsp:getProperty name="faq" property="ID"/>">
</form>
</body>
</html>
```

The UpdateCommand class

The operation of this command is very similar to that of `AddCommand` discussed earlier. We take elements of the request to populate a `FaqBean` object which is passed to the `update()` method of the `FaqRepository` class. Again, we catch the appropriate exceptions. The source is shown in listing 11.19.

Listing 11.19 UpdateCommand

```
package com.taglib.wdjsp.faqtool;

import javax.servlet.*;
import javax.servlet.http.*;

public class UpdateCommand implements Command {
  private String next;

  public UpdateCommand(String next) {
    this.next = next;
  }

  public String execute(HttpServletRequest req)
    throws CommandException {
    try {
      if (CommandToken.isValid(req)) {
        FaqRepository faqs = FaqRepository.getInstance();
        FaqBean faq = new FaqBean();
        faq.setID(Integer.parseInt(req.getParameter("id")));
        faq.setQuestion(req.getParameter("question"));
        faq.setAnswer(req.getParameter("answer"));
        faqs.update(faq);
        req.setAttribute("faqtool.msg", "FAQ Updated Successfully");
      }
      else {
        req.setAttribute("faqtool.msg", "Invalid Reload Attempted");
      }
      return next;
    }
    catch (NumberFormatException e) {
      throw new CommandException("UpdateCommand: invalid ID");
    }
    catch (UnknownFaqException uf) {
      throw new CommandException("UpdateCommand: "+uf.getMessage());
    }
```

```
    catch (FaqRepositoryException fe) {
      throw new CommandException("UpdateCommand: "+fe.getMessage());
    }
  }
}
```

Error screen

This application has a single, very simple error screen, as shown in listing 11.20.

Listing 11.20 error.jsp

```
<%@ page isErrorPage="true" %>
<html>
<body>
The ERROR : <%= exception.getMessage() %>
<% exception.printStackTrace(); %>
</body>
</html>
```

11.4 The web access module

When we started thinking about how the FAQs would be represented on the web, we realized that with a JSP solution, it was less important to know how they would look (which would be determined by our content team), and more important to know what type of information they would need to convey. From talking with the content team we knew that they would need a way to access the information pertaining to a single FAQ in the database as well as a way to access the entire list of FAQs at once. With these capabilities, they could use JSP to design any number of displays. The decision then was to concentrate on providing them these necessary components (through JavaBeans), and leaving the details of the page design up to them. We also wanted to allow them to create pages in additional styles of formats without the development team having to modify any servlets.

An important consideration that went into the design of this module is that the exact requirements of how the FAQs will be displayed on the web will never be nailed down. We have some basic ideas, but in implementation it is limited only by the creativity of the design team and will certainly change over time and with each site redesign. The goal was to provide the content team with a collection of flexible JSP components that would allow them to fill just about whatever content needs might arise now, or in the future. We'll implement several possible FAQ presentations that work with the components we create.

11.4.1 The FaqServlet

For the web access module we created `FaqServlet` which can be used to retrieve either a single FAQ or all of the FAQs from the database. Its operation depends on the information passed into the servlet through request parameters. The servlet stores the FAQ (or FAQs) as a request attribute before forwarding it to the front-end JSP page, which, unlike our administration servlet, is also specified by the user through the request at run time. The source code for this servlet is shown in listing 11.21.

Listing 11.21 FaqServlet

```
package com.taglib.wdjsp.faqtool;

import java.io.*;
import javax.servlet.*;
import javax.servlet.http.*;
import java.util.*;

public class FaqServlet extends HttpServlet {
  private String jspdir = "/jsp/";
  private String error = "error.jsp";

  public void service(HttpServletRequest req, HttpServletResponse res)
    throws ServletException, IOException {
    String next;
    Command cmd;
    try {
      next = req.getParameter("page");
      if (next == null)
        throw new CommandException("Page not specified");
      if (req.getParameter("id") != null)
        cmd = new GetCommand(next);
      else
        cmd = new GetAllCommand(next);
      cmd.execute(req);
    }
    catch (CommandException e) {
      req.setAttribute("javax.servlet.jsp.jspException", e);
      next = error;
    }
    RequestDispatcher rd;
    rd = getServletContext().getRequestDispatcher(jspdir + next);
    rd.forward(req, res);
  }
}
```

We were able to reuse the GetCommand and GetAllCommand classes that were developed for the administration module in this servlet. However, since there are only a couple of possible actions in this servlet, we eliminated the command identifiers and instead base our actions on what parameters were present in the request. If a single FAQ is to be retrieved, its ID values should be passed in through the id request parameter. If this parameter doesn't exist, we'll default to fetching all of the FAQs. In either case, we need to know which JSP page will be ultimately handling the request, and this should be indicated through the page request parameter. If this parameter is missing we have no choice but to throw an exception and visit the error page. We mapped the servlet to /faqs/ on the external web server. So, for example, to retrieve FAQ number 1437 and display it in the JSP page showfaq.jsp we would use a URL such as this:

```
/faqs?page=showfaq.jsp&id=1437
```

This simple servlet is quite flexible; it is basically an FAQ lookup service for JSP pages. It allows the web team to develop many different pages that display FAQs in a variety of formats and styles without having to modify the application or control logic. They can have a hundred different versions if they want to. This simple core service can serve them all. Let's look at a couple of examples of how this service can be used to display FAQs.

11.4.2 Viewing a single FAQ

To view a single FAQ we simply pass in the page name, in this case single.jsp, and the ID number of the FAQ we want to display. We then retrieve the FAQ from the request and display its properties. The source for the page is shown in listing 11.22 and a screen shot in figure 11.9.

Listing 11.22 single.jsp

```
<%@ page import="com.taglib.wdjsp.faqtool.*" errorPage="/jsp/error.jsp" %>
<jsp:useBean id="faq" class="com.taglib.wdjsp.faqtool.FaqBean" scope="request"/
  >
<html>
<head>
<title>FAQ <jsp:getProperty name="faq" property="ID"/></title>
</head>
<body bgcolor="white">
<b>Question:</b> <jsp:getProperty name="faq" property="question"/>
<br>
<b>Answer:</b> <jsp:getProperty name="faq" property="answer"/>
<p>
```

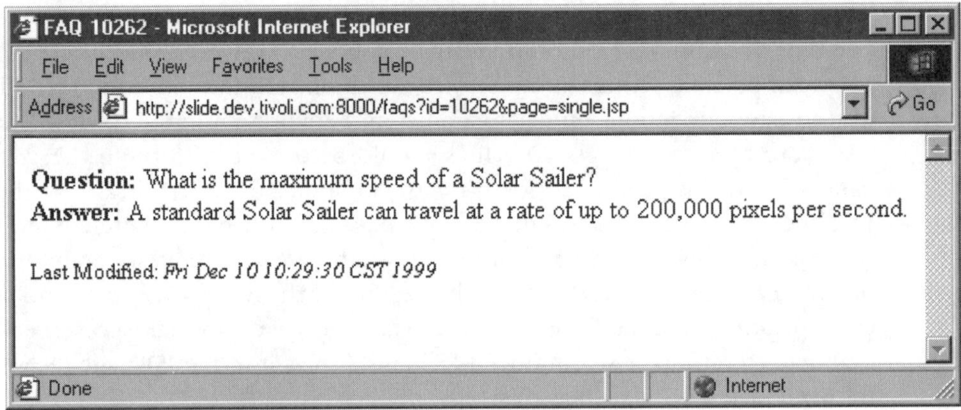

Figure 11.9 Viewing a single FAQ

```
<font size=-1>Last Modified:
<i><jsp:getProperty name="faq" property="lastModified"/></i>
</font>
</body>
</html>
```

11.4.3 Viewing all the FAQs

Showing the contents of all of the FAQs on a single page is not much different. We use the same looping constructs we developed for the delete and update menus in the Administration module to cycle through the FAQs. The source code is shown in listing 11.23, and a screen shot is shown in figure 11.10.

Listing 11.23 all.jsp

```
<%@ page import="com.taglib.wdjsp.faqtool.*"
 errorPage="/jsp/error.jsp" %>
<jsp:useBean id="faq" class=" FaqBean"/>
<% FaqBean[] faqs = (FaqBean[])request.getAttribute("faqs"); %>
<html>
<head><title>FAQ List</title></head>
<body bgcolor="white">
<h2>FAQ List</h2>
<%
for (int i=0; i < faqs.length; i++) {
  faq = faqs[i];
%>
<b>Question:</b> <jsp:getProperty name="faq" property="question"/>
<br>
```

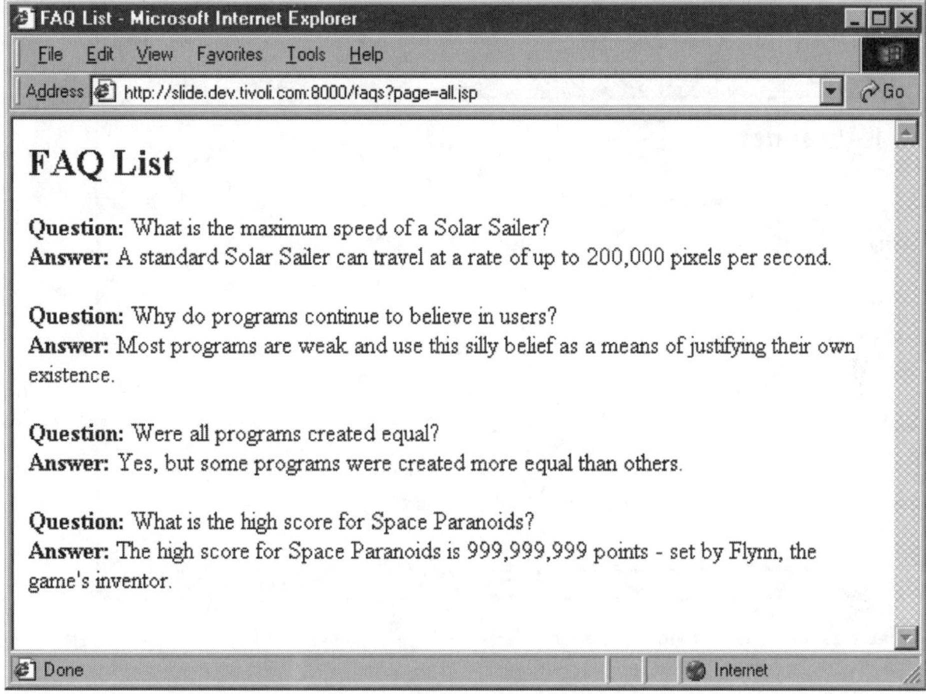

Figure 11.10 All the FAQs

```
<b>Answer:</b> <jsp:getProperty name="faq" property="answer"/>
<p>
<% } %>
</body>
</html>
```

11.4.4 A table of contents view

A more imaginative use of the FAQ lookup servlet is to create a table of contents view of the FAQs in the database. To do this we need to reference all of the FAQs, just as we did when we wanted to view all of them. This time, however, we only display the questions as a link to our single FAQ view. This dynamically generates links to each individual FAQ. The source for this page is shown in listing 11.24, and a screen shot in figure 11.11.

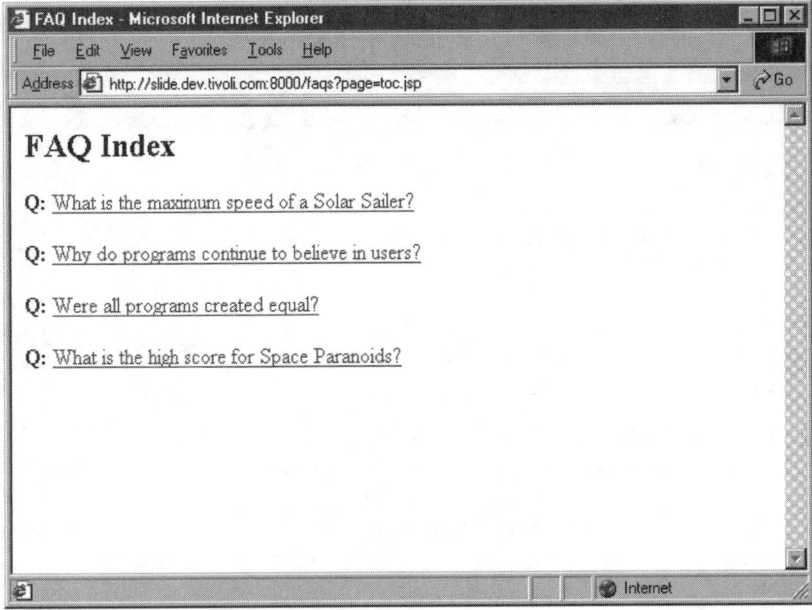

Figure 11.11 The FAQ index page

Listing 11.24 toc.jsp

```
<%@ page import="com.taglib.wdjsp.faqtool.*"
 errorPage="/jsp/error.jsp" %>
<jsp:useBean id="faq" class="com.taglib.wdjsp.faqtool.FaqBean"/>
<% FaqBean[] faqs = (FaqBean[])request.getAttribute("faqs"); %>
<html>
<head><title>FAQ Index</title></head>
<body bgcolor="white">
<h2>FAQ Index</h2>
<%
for (int i=0; i < faqs.length; i++) {
  faq = faqs[i];
%>
<b>Q:</b>
<a href="/faqs?page=single.jsp&id=
<jsp:getProperty name="faq" property="ID"/>">
<jsp:getProperty name="faq" property="question"/></a>
<p>
<% } %>
</body>
</html>
```

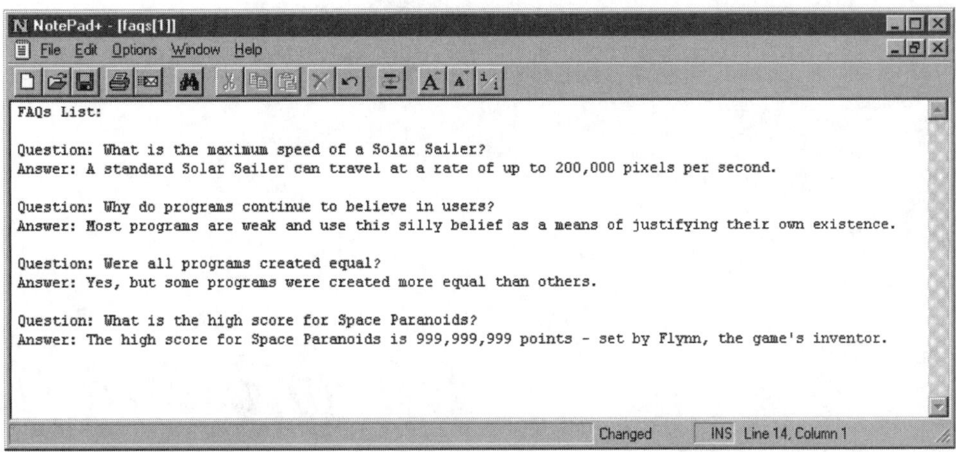

Figure 11.12 A plain text view

11.4.5 Plain text view

As an alternative view of the FAQs we create a plain text version of the list by simply changing the content type and omitting HTML code. This view is shown in listing 11.25 and can be seen in action (loaded into a text viewer) in figure 11.12.

Listing 11.25 plain.jsp

```
<%@ page import="com.taglib.wdjsp.faqtool.*" errorPage="/jsp/error.jsp" %>
<jsp:useBean id="faq" class=" FaqBean"/>
<% FaqBean[] faqs = (FaqBean[])request.getAttribute("faqs"); %>
FAQs List:
<%
for (int i=0; i < faqs.length; i++) {
  faq = faqs[i];
%>
Question: <jsp:getProperty name="faq" property="question"/>
Answer: <jsp:getProperty name="faq" property="answer"/>
<% } %>
```

12 Introducing filters and listeners

This chapter covers

- Life-cycle event listeners
- Filtering application resources
- Request and response wrappers

As described in previous chapters, JSP is an extension of Java servlets. The text of a JSP page is automatically translated into Java source code for a servlet that produces the content, both static and dynamic, designated by the original page. As such, each version of JSP is tied to an associated version of the Servlet specification. JSP 1.2, for example, is based on version 2.3 of the Servlet specification.

As a result, features added to the Servlet specification also become new features of the dependent JSP specification. In chapter 6, for example, we saw that JSP 1.2 supports both `true` and `false` values for the `flush` attribute of the `<jsp:include>` action, whereas JSP 1.1 requires this attribute to be `true` always. This enhanced functionality of JSP 1.2 is a result of improvements in Servlet 2.3.

Filters and life-cycle event listeners are two additional Servlet 2.3 features that can likewise be taken advantage of in JSP 1.2 applications. Filters allow developers to layer new functionality on top of existing web-based resources (e.g., servlets, JSP pages, and static content), by intercepting requests and responses and performing new operations on them, in addition to—or even instead of—those associated with the original resource. Listeners allow developers to hook into the operations of the container itself, running custom code in response to events associated with applications and HTTP sessions.

12.1 Life-cycle event listeners

Listeners allow web application developers to monitor certain types of operations performed by the container, and take appropriate application-specific actions in response to those operations. As of Servlet 2.3 and JSP 1.2, there are six such life-cycle event listeners, all taking the form of Java interfaces which define methods for receiving notifications of container activities. Four of these may be used to monitor session activity, and two are focused on application-level life-cycle events.

12.1.1 Session listeners

We have seen one example of a life-cycle event listener, the `javax.servlet.http.HttpSessionBindingListener` interface, described in chapter 8. By implementing this interface, objects that expect to be interacting with an end user's HTTP session can be notified whenever they are added to or removed from a session, via the methods summarized in table 12.1. An example of its use was presented in chapter 9, where the `HttpSessionBindingListener` interface is implemented by the `ConnectionBean` class.

Table 12.1 Methods of the `javax.servlet.http.HttpSessionBindingListener` interface

Method	Description
`valueBound(event)`	Notifies the listening object that it is being added to a session.
`valueUnbound(event)`	Notifies the listening object that it is being removed from a session.

This particular listener interface predates JSP 1.0. Five new listener interfaces have been added with Servlet 2.3, and are therefore only available with JSP containers supporting JSP 1.2 and higher.

The first, the `javax.servlet.http.HttpSessionActivationListener` interface, works very similarly to `HttpSessionBindingListener`. Objects that are added to the session whose classes implement the `HttpSessionActivationListener` interface will automatically be notified whenever the session is activated or passivated, using the methods listed in table 12.2. Activation and passivation are features of advanced application servers that supported distributed processing. Such servers implement load balancing by transferring sessions between different JVMs, running either on the same machine or on multiple machines across a network.

Table 12.2 Methods of the `javax.servlet.http.HttpSessionActivationListener` interface

Method	Description
`sessionDidActivate(event)`	Notifies the listening object that its session has been activated.
`sessionWillPassivate(event)`	Notifies the listening object that its session is about to be passivated.

When a session is being stored for transfer to another JVM, it is said to be *passivated*. Any objects currently stored as attributes of that session which happen to implement the `HttpSessionActivationListener` interface will be notified by calling their `sessionWillPassivate()` method. After the session has been migrated to the other JVM, it is said to be *activated*. When this happens, all session attributes implementing `HttpSessionActivationListener` will have their `sessionDidActivate()` methods called. In both cases, the method is passed an instance of the `javax.servlet.http.HttpSessionEvent`, from which the `HttpSession` object may be retrieved via the event's `getSession()` method.

NOTE Since `HttpSessionBindingListener` and `HttpSessionActivationListener` are interfaces, they are not subject to Java's restrictions regarding multiple inheritance of classes. Objects that expect to be placed in a session are therefore free to implement both `HttpSessionBindingListener` and `HttpSessionActivationListener`, allowing them to respond appropriately to both sets of events.

The other new life-cycle event handlers operate rather differently. The `HttpSessionBindingListener` and `HttpSessionActivationListener` interfaces must be implemented directly by the objects that are involved in session-related activity, and it is these objects that will receive, and must therefore respond to, the event notifications associated with the individual interactions with the session. Also, there is no need to register such listeners with the container; the association is automatic. If an object implementing `HttpSessionBindingListener` is added to a session, its `valueBound()` method is automatically called, just as its `valueUnbound()` method is automatically called when the object is removed from the session. For an object implementing `HttpSessionActivationListener`, its `sessionWillPassivate()` and `sessionDidActivate()` methods are automatically called when the session to which the object belongs is either passivated or activated.

In contrast to `HttpSessionBindingListener` and `HttpSessionActivationListener`, then, the other new listener interfaces are typically implemented via dedicated classes, rather than adding them to a class that is already performing some other application functionality. As a result, these listeners need to be explicitly registered with the application, since there is no way for the application to detect them automatically. This is accomplished via the application's deployment descriptor file, an XML document containing configuration information about the application. As an application is being loaded and initialized, it reads the configuration information in the deployment descriptor, including the set of listener classes registered there. The container then creates an instance of each such class, and begins sending it the appropriate events as they occur. Deployment descriptors are described in detail in chapter 14.

In addition, these other new interfaces are designed to receive all events associated with a particular category of container activity, rather than just those events affecting a single object. An object implementing `HttpSessionBindingListener` or `HttpSessionActivationListener` only receives events regarding its own interactions with the application. An object implementing one or more of the new life-cycle event listener interfaces receives all application events of the corresponding types, independent of the specific objects involved in the event. Of these remaining four listener interfaces, two are concerned with session-related activity and two are for monitoring activity of the applications.

Notification of events indicating the creation and destruction of sessions is provided by the `javax.servlet.http.HttpSessionListener` interface. As indicated in table 12.3, listeners implementing this interface are informed when new sessions are created by means of the interface's `sessionCreated()` method. When a session is destroyed, either because it has expired or because application code has called its `invalidate()` method, the container will notify the application's `HttpSessionListener` instances by calling their `sessionDestroyed()` methods. Both methods are passed an instance of the aforementioned `HttpSessionEvent` class as their sole parameter.

Table 12.3 Methods of the `javax.servlet.http.HttpSessionListener` interface

Method	Description
`sessionCreated(event)`	Notifies the listening object that the session has been loaded and initialized.
`sessionDestroyed(event)`	Notifies the listening object that the session has been unloaded.

Events related to session attributes are handled by the `javax.servlet.http.HttpSessionAttributeListener` interface. Its methods, summarized in table 12.4, allow the developer to monitor the creation, setting, and deletion of session attributes.

Table 12.4 Methods of the `javax.servlet.http.HttpSessionAttributeListener` interface

Method	Description
`attributeAdded(event)`	Notifies the listening object that a value has been assigned to a new session attribute.
`attributeReplaced(event)`	Notifies the listening object that a new value has been assigned to an existing session attribute.
`attributeRemoved(event)`	Notifies the listening object that an session attribute has been removed.

Whenever an attribute is added to a session—for example, by calling the session's `setAttribute()` method or via a `<jsp:useBean>` action with its `scope` attribute set to `"session"`—it will call the `attributeAdded()` method of all registered instances of the `HttpSessionAttributeListener` interface. A single parameter will be provided, in the form of an instance of the `javax.servlet.http.HttpSession-`

BindingEvent class. This event class is actually a subclass of the HttpSessionEvent class introduced previously, and supports two additional methods, getName() and getValue(), for recovering the name of the attribute being added and its initial value, respectively.

If a new value is subsequently assigned to such an attribute, the application will post a new event by calling these listeners' attributeReplaced() methods. The event will again be an instance of HttpSessionBindingEvent. In this case, however, the event instance's getValue() method will return the attribute's former value, not its new value. If the attribute is removed from the session, each HttpSessionAttributeListener will have its attributeRemoved() method called, again with an instance of HttpSessionBindingEvent as its sole argument. The event object's getName() method will return the name of the attribute that has been removed, while its getValue() method will return the last value assigned to that attribute before it was removed.

The HttpSessionAttributeListener thus provides very similar functionality to HttpSessionBindingListener. As already suggested, the primary difference is that HttpSessionBindingListener must be implemented directly by objects being added to the session, whereas classes implementing HttpSessionAttributeListener are not direct participants in session activity. The HttpSessionAttributeListener interface can thus be considered noninvasive, because it allows session activity to be monitored without needing to modify the objects involved in that session activity. Implementing HttpSessionBindingListener, however, requires access to the source code for the object whose session activity is to be monitored.

NOTE Direct access to the source code of a class to which you wish to add HttpSessionBindingListener support is not strictly required. You can always create a subclass of the original class that inherits the methods of the original and also implements the HttpSessionBindingListener interface. Alternatively, the delegation design pattern can be used to create a class implementing HttpSessionBindingListener, which incorporates an instance of the original class as one of its instance variables. The methods of HttpSessionBindingListener are implemented directly by this new class, while those of the original class are forwarded (i.e., delegated) to the object stored in this instance variable.

The choice of which listener to use is application-dependent. If a given object is generic and intended for use in a wide range of applications (i.e., not necessarily web-related) then `HttpSessionAttributeListener` may be more appropriate. By doing so, the session-related functionality can be isolated in a separate class that need only be included when the object is used in a web-based application. If the object is specifically geared toward deployment with servlets and JSP pages, then having its class also implement `HttpSessionBindingListener` may be preferred. This approach is particularly appropriate if the object needs to track session activation and passivation as well, since this will require it to also implement `HttpSessionActivationListener`.

12.1.2 Application listeners

The final pair of new life-cycle event listeners are concerned with the activity of the web application itself. As described in chapter 6, a set of interrelated servlets, JSP pages, and other resources are grouped as a web application. One feature of such an application is that all of its resources have URLs which share the same top-level directory name. The application's resources also share an associated instance of the `javax.servlet.ServletContext` class. This instance, which is made available to its JSP pages as the `application` implicit object, provides access to the application's global attributes and initialization parameters.

A given servlet or JSP container can be simultaneously running any number of web applications. Each such application is assumed to be self-contained, with no dependencies upon or detailed knowledge of the inner workings of any of the other applications running in the container. Based on this assumption, the container is allowed to load and unload individual applications as it sees fit. If, for example, a particular application's resources have not been accessed recently, the container is allowed to unload the application in order to free memory for the other applications it is running. As soon as it receives a new request for that resource, however, it must reload it in order to handle that request.

Because it is shared among all of its servlets and JSP pages, an application's `ServletContext` instance is often a convenient place to store long-lived global resources such as database connection pools or large in-memory data structures intended to be accessed by multiple users. When doing so, however, it is often necessary to take special action to manage these resources any time the application is loaded or unloaded. Keeping track of the loading and unloading of an application is the role of the `javax.servlet.ServletContextListener` interface, the methods of which are summarized in table 12.5.

Table 12.5 Methods of the `javax.servlet.ServletContextListener` interface

Method	Description
`contextInitialized(event)`	Notifies the listening object that the application has been loaded and initialized.
`contextDestroyed(event)`	Notifies the listening object that the application has been unloaded.

When a container loads an application that includes listeners implementing the `ServletContextListener` interface, all such listeners are sent a corresponding `javax.servlet.ServletContextEvent` instance via their `contextInitialized()` methods, indicating that the application is now ready to receive requests. The application's `ServletContext` instance can be retrieved from this event via its `getServletContext()` method. When the application is unloaded by the container, those listeners are then sent another `ServletContextEvent` event via their `contextDestroyed()` methods.

As indicated in chapter 6, an application's `ServletContext` instance—like its sessions—may also be used to store and retrieve attributes. A second listener has been provided in Servlet 2.3 for monitoring access to such application-level attributes. The methods of this interface, `javax.servlet.ServletContextAttributeListener`, are summarized in table 12.6.

Table 12.6 Methods of the `javax.servlet.ServletContextAttributeListener` interface

Method	Description
`attributeAdded(event)`	Notifies the listening object that a value has been assigned to a new application attribute.
`attributeReplaced(event)`	Notifies the listening object that a new value has been assigned to an existing application attribute.
`attributeRemoved(event)`	Notifies the listening object that an application attribute has been removed.

As indicated in table 12.6, `ServletContextAttributeListener`'s methods have the same names as those of the `HttpSessionAttributeListener` interface, and perform similar roles. The most significant difference between these methods and those of `HttpSessionAttributeListener` is the class of the event object serving as the methods' parameter. Where the `HttpSessionAttributeListener` methods are passed `HttpSessionBindingEvent` objects, the `ServletContextAttributeListener`'s methods are passed instances of the `ServletContextAttributeEvent` class.

`ServletContextAttributeEvent` is a subclass of `ServletContextEvent`, and therefore inherits its `getServletContext()` method. The `ServletContextAttributeEvent` class defines two additional methods, `getName()` and `getValue()`. `getName()` is used to retrieve the name of the attribute that was added, removed, or had its value replaced. For events associated with the `attributeAdded()` method, the `getValue()` method returns the value to be assigned to the new attribute. For those associated with the `attributeRemoved()` method, `getValue()` returns the last value assigned to the attribute prior to its removal. And for events associated with the `attributeReplaced()` method, the `getValue()` method will return the attribute's old value (i.e., the value that had been assigned to attribute just before it was set to its new, replacement value).

NOTE Listener classes to be added to a web application can implement any combination of one or more of these last four interfaces. An example listener to be presented in the next chapter implements both of the session life-cycle event listener interfaces, `HttpSessionListener` and `HttpSessionAttributeListener`.

12.2 Filters

For maximum modularity, servlets and JSP pages that are focused on delivering specific web-based content or resources are preferred. In a complex application, however, multiple layers of functionality may need to be added on top of the underlying content in order to satisfy overall system requirements. For example, access to resources may need to be restricted to properly authenticated users, or responses may need to be transformed before they are returned to the end user. Compression and encryption are common examples of response transformations, but more complex data manipulation, such as dithering of color images, is also possible. Or perhaps the application content takes the form of XML documents which must be translated (via a set of XSLT stylesheets, say) into platform-specific formats based on the origin of the request: requests from a browser are translated into HTML, while those from a WAP cell phone are translated into WML.

Prior to Servlet 2.3 and JSP 1.2, functionality such as this had to be built into any servlet or JSP page needing it, reducing the modularity of the resulting code. Early implementations of servlet technology (prior to the standardization efforts that led to Servlet 2.0) included a feature known as *servlet chaining* which allowed a sequence of servlets to be applied to a single request, each performing one step in the generation of a response. One servlet in the chain, for example, might supply the basic content, another performs user authentication, and a third performs data compression. Using this approach, multiple layers of application functionality could be implemented as individual servlets, and then combined in a modular fashion through servlet chaining.

Ultimately, the details of servlet chaining proved to be too idiosyncratic to be included in the formal servlet specification. Servlets intended to take part in servlet chaining needed to be implemented differently from servlets that were meant to be stand-alone. The resulting dual nature of servlets was not conducive to the technology standardization effort, so support for servlet chaining was dropped from the Servlet 2.0 specification.

12.2.1 How filters work

The functionality provided by servlet chaining is highly useful, however, and efforts to restore such capabilities to the servlet standard have materialized in Servlet 2.3 in the form of *filters*. Rather than the use of a sequence of servlets to layer functionality, a sequence of filters is used, each handing off control to the next as a request is being handled, until the resource that was originally requested is reached. This resource may be a servlet, a JSP page, an image file, or any other content to be delivered by the container. After the response representing this resource is constructed, control is handed back to the sequence of filters, this time in the reverse order, for further processing. At any point in the process, a filter can transfer control to another resource, by means of a `RequestDispatcher` or by calling the `sendRedirect()` or `sendError()` methods of the response object.

Filters are created as Java classes implementing the `javax.servlet.Filter` interface. In deference to their servlet-chaining heritage, when the container is building up the sequence of filters to be applied to a particular request, the resulting data structure is a container-specific Java object that implements the `javax.servlet.FilterChain` interface. Chain, however, may be a bit misleading in this case, because the relationship between the elements of the chain is more than just sequential. As indicated in figure 12.1, each filter is nested inside its predecessor, with the originally requested resource at the center of the nesting hierarchy, wrapped inside all of the filters comprising the chain.

A closer analogy would be Matryoshka dolls, the wooden dolls from Russia, in which each one fits inside the next. Like Matryoshka dolls, each filter in a chain is a shell around the next filter to be called. Inside the last filter is the resource being delivered, analogous to the true doll hidden inside all of the doll shells of a Matryoshka toy.

When a request is received, the container determines which resource the request is mapped to, as well as the set of applicable filters. This is akin to selecting a

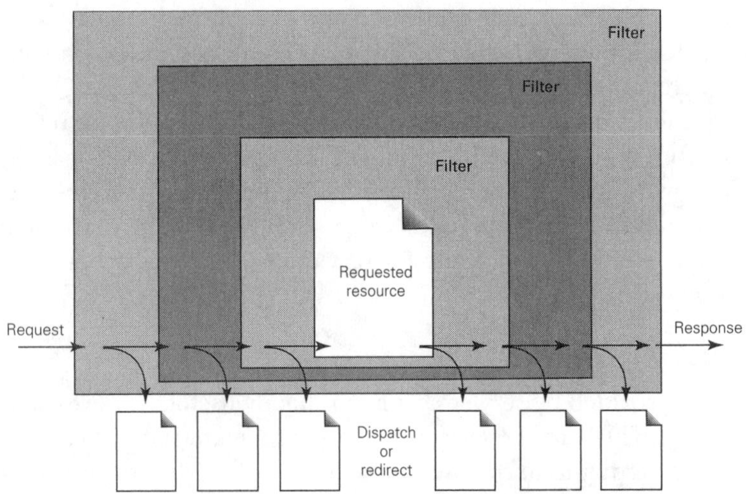

Figure 12.1 Nested processing of requests by a filter chain

particular set of Matryoshka dolls. The request is handled by first passing it to the outermost filter, which can allow processing to continue or can opt to dispatch or redirect the request to some other resource, or even return an error condition. If all of the filters allow processing to continue, the request will ultimately make its way to the resource (servlet, JSP page, static document, etc.) that was requested. Once that resource has generated its response, control passes back to the filters once more. Now that the response has been generated, each filter is given another opportunity to either continue or interrupt the handling of the request. The filter can dispatch to another resource via a `RequestDispatcher`, or transfer control back to the user's browser by calling the response's `sendRedirect()` or `sendError()` messages. Because the filters are called in a nested manner, control passes among the filters in the opposite order after the requested resource is processed as it was before. Control passes back to the innermost filter first, and then back up the filter chain to the outermost filter.

NOTE If a filter interrupts the handling of a request by creating a `RequestDispatcher` and calling its `forward()` or `include()` methods, the dispatched request will not be subject to filtering. Recall that when the `sendRedirect()` method of the `HttpServletResponse` class is called, it has the effect of causing the end user's browser to issue a new request for the resource indicated by the method's parameter. The bottom line, then, is that if you want to bypass further filtering, you should use a `RequestDispatcher`. If your filter wants to transfer control but requires the new request to also be filtered, then `sendRedirect()` is the right strategy to follow. Keep in mind, as well, that this choice also affects whether or not a new URL is displayed by the browser.

To continue the analogy, then, each doll is opened in turn, and given a chance to say whether or not the doll that was inside it should be opened. Ultimately, the innermost, solid doll—which represents the requested resource—is reached. Then the process of putting the dolls back together begins. The dolls must be assembled in the reverse order of their disassembly, just as the nested filters are processed in inverse order after the requested resource is reached. And as the dolls are put back together, each decides whether or not the reassembly should continue or halt.

Filters also have the opportunity to manipulate the request and/or the response being handled by the filter chain. By wrapping the request in an instance of the `javax.servlet.ServletRequestWrapper` or `javax.servlet.http.HttpServletRequestWrapper` class, request headers or other request data can be modified by a filter before passing control to the next item in the chain. Responses can likewise be wrapped via the `javax.servlet.ServletResponseWrapper` and `javax.servlet.http.HttpServletResponseWrapper` classes, allowing the filter to modify response header, content, and other data.

These wrapper classes implement the corresponding request and response interfaces, so no other elements in the chain—either another filter or the requested resource—can distinguish between the original request or response and a wrapped request or response. Each filter receives a request and a response, which it can optionally wrap and pass to the next item in the filter chain. It may in fact be the case, however, that the request and/or the response it received may already have been wrapped by a previous filter in the chain. As far as the filter is concerned, it is working with a standard request/response pair. There is no way, short of Java's `instanceof` operator, for the filter to determine whether or not it is working with a wrapped request or response.

To stretch the Matryoshka doll analogy nearly to its breaking point, request and response wrappers are like gloves that must be worn while taking the dolls apart and putting them back together. The wrapping of the request and/or response by a filter is analogous to a given doll requiring the owner to put on a pair of gloves before opening the next doll. In this case, the gloves must be kept on until the same doll is put back together again. Also, no doll is aware of any other doll's gloves. The toy's owner may already be wearing one or more pairs of gloves before the current doll adds another pair.

12.2.2 Filter classes

As indicated, filters classes must implement the `javax.servlet.Filter` interface. This interface defines three methods; any concrete filter class must provide implementations for all three. The first of these is the `init()` method which, as its name suggests, is used to run any initialization code required by the filter. This method takes a single parameter, an instance of the `javax.servlet.FilterConfig` interface, which may be used by the filter to access initialization parameters set in the application's deployment descriptor. A filter instance will not be called upon to process any requests until it has finished running its `init()` method.

The methods of the `FilterConfig` interface are presented in table 12.7.

Table 12.7 Methods of the `javax.servlet.FilterConfig` interface

Method	Description
`getFilterName()`	Returns the name of the filter, as specified in the deployment descriptor.
`getServletContext()`	Retrieves the servlet context for the application for which the filter is being created.
`getInitParameterNames()`	Constructs an enumeration of the names of the filter's initialization parameters.
`getInitParameter(name)`	Returns the value of the named initialization parameter.

The filter's `destroy()` method is called by the container to indicate that a filter instance is no longer needed (e.g., when the web application to which the filter belongs is being shut down, or the container needs to reclaim some memory).This method allows the developer to deallocate any long-term resources used by the filter while processing requests.

The actual handling of requests is the focus of the `Filter` interface's third and final method, whose signature is as follows:

```
void doFilter (ServletRequest request, ServletResponse response,
               FilterChain chain)
  throws ServletException, java.io.IOException
```

If this looks familiar, it is because it is very similar to the signatures of the `service()`, `doGet()`, and `doPut()` methods of the `Servlet` and `HttpServlet` classes, introduced in chapter 2. This method's only significant departure from its servlet counterparts is in its third parameter, which will be an instance of the `javax.servlet.FilterChain` interface.

The `FilterChain` instance represents the sequence of filters to be applied to the request. Surprisingly, it only exposes a single public method, also called `doFilter()`, with the following signature:

```
void doFilter (ServletRequest request, ServletResponse response)
  throws ServletException, java.io.IOException
```

This method, when applied to the chain passed to the filter's `doFilter()` method, causes the next item in the chain to be called upon to process the request and its response. In the course of running its own `doFilter()` method, then, the filter calls the chain's `doFilter()` method in order to hand off processing to the next filter or—if the end of the chain has been reached—the resource that was originally requested.

This call need not be the first or the final operation performed by the filter's `doFilter()` method. In order to allow for both pre- and post-processing of both requests and responses, the `doFilter()` method of a filter generally follows this structure:

```
void doFilter (ServletRequest request, ServletResponse response,
               FilterChain chain)
    throws ServletException, java.io.IOException {

  Pre-process request and/or response...
  Optionally wrap request and/or response...

  chain.doFilter(request or wrapped request, response or wrapped response);

  Post-process (optionally wrapped) request and/or response...

}
```

As this pseudocode indicates, if the filter introduces wrapped requests or responses, these are propagated down the chain by providing them, rather than the original request and/or response, as the arguments to the chain's `doFilter()` method. After the remaining elements of the chain have finished their processing, control returns back to the filter's `doFilter()` method, which can then postprocess the chain's results.

Note that, using this programming model, the filter has no information about where it is being called in the chain. It does not have access to any of the other filters in the chain, and in fact does not know whether the request and response objects passed as arguments to its `doFilter()` method are the genuine article, or just wrappers provided by some other filter that preceded it in the filter chain.

In fact, the only filter that is aware of the presence of request and response wrappers is the filter that created them and passed them down the chain via its `doFilter()` method. Any extraction of information or transformation of data to be performed via such wrappers must be performed by the filter that added them in the first place.

The programming model for filters thus requires them to be stand-alone, independent constructs that can be combined and reused in a modular fashion. Use of filters promotes separation of application functionality into small, targeted units that can be integrated with existing resources (servlets, JSP pages, image files, etc.) to add features as well as increase the maintainability of the overall application.

12.2.3 Wrapper classes

Four classes are provided in the Servlet 2.3 specification for wrapping requests and responses. For generic servlet applications, the `javax.servlet.ServletRequestWrapper` and `javax.servlet.ServletResponseWrapper` classes are provided. For applications based on the HTTP protocol, wrappers that support the additional functionality of HTTP requests and responses are also available, via the `javax.servlet.http.HttpServletRequestWrapper` and `javax.servlet.http.HttpServletResponseWrapper` classes.

The constructor for the `ServletRequestWrapper` class takes an instance of the `ServletRequest` interface as its sole argument, which may then be retrieved or replaced via the getter and setter methods listed in table 12.8. The `ServletRequestWrapper` class implements the `ServletRequest` interface, so it includes implementations of all of the methods associated with that interface. The default implementations of these interface methods simply forward the calls to the corresponding methods of the wrapped `ServletRequest` instance, so it is usually necessary to subclass the `ServletRequestWrapper` class in order to provide any required custom behavior. It is because `ServletRequestWrapper` implements the `ServletRequest` interface, of course, that it can stand in for a request in any method requiring one. This includes the `service()` method of a servlet, the `doFilter()` method of a filter or filter chain, and even the constructor and `setRequest()` methods of the `ServletRequestWrapper` class itself.

The `HttpServletRequestWrapper` class is a subclass of `ServletRequestWrapper`, and has the same relationship with the `HttpServletRequest` interface as `ServletRequestWrapper` has with the `ServletRequest` interface.

Table 12.8 Wrapper-specific methods of the `javax.servlet.ServletRequest` class

Method	Description
`getRequest()`	Retrieves the request being wrapped.
`setRequest(request)`	Sets the request being wrapped.

In a similar manner, the constructor the `ServletResponseWrapper` class takes an instance of the `ServletResponse` interface as its sole parameter, with corresponding getter and setter methods as listed in table 12.9. It also implements that interface, providing definitions for the interface's methods which delegate to this wrapped `ServletResponse` instance. Filters that employ response wrappers must therefore define their own subclasses of `ServletResponseWrapper` in order to implement filter-specific wrapper functionality. By implementing the `ServletResponse` interface, instances of the `ServletResponseWrapper` class are indistinguishable from actual response objects.

Like their request counterparts, the `HttpServletResponseWrapper` class is a subclass of `ServletResponseWrapper`, and has the same relationship with the `HttpServletResponse` interface as `ServletResponseWrapper` has with the `ServletResponse` interface.

Table 12.9 Wrapper-specific methods of the `javax.servlet.ServletResponse` class

Method	Description
`getResponse()`	Retrieves the response being wrapped.
`setResponse(response)`	Sets the response being wrapped.

12.3 Using filters and listeners

There are two primary steps in the application of filters and listeners. First, the Java classes that implement the required filter and/or listener behavior must be defined. In the case of filters, support for any associated initialization parameters must also be included in the class definition.

After these classes have been created, the second step is to incorporate the filters and listeners into the web application. For listeners, this is done by simply specifying the listeners classes which must be instantiated and registered with the application. Deployment of filters is slightly more complex. Like listeners, the filter classes to be instantiated must be specified, along with the values for their initialization parameters. In addition, the resources within the application to which each filter is to be applied must be specified. Filters can be mapped to individual resources (e.g., a servlet, a JSP page, or a static document such as an image or HTML file), or they can be applied to a collection of resources (such as those sharing the same directory or file extension). Filters can also be configured to cover all of an application's resources.

The implementation of filter and life-cycle event listener classes is demonstrated in chapter 13, in the context of an example web application to which both filter and listener classes will be added. The deployment of filters and listeners—as well as other web application resources—will be covered in chapter 14, with examples drawn from the sample application introduced in chapter 13.

13 Applying filters and listeners

This chapter covers

- An intranet example application
- Filters for access control
- A logging listener
- String replacement filter

Recall from chapter 12 that filters and life-cycle event listeners may be layered on top of existing applications in a modular fashion to provide enhanced functionality. To demonstrate this advantage, however, it is first necessary to have an application to which filters and listeners may be added. To that end, this chapter presents an example web application, a simple web-based intranet for the fictitious Encom Corporation, to which three filters and a listener will be applied to incrementally add new capabilities.

13.1 Application description

Before adding any filters and listeners, the original intranet application—as depicted in figure 13.1—consists of six JSP pages located in two directories. The top-level directory, named filters, contains a single page, representing the "front door" of the application. All of the content is stored in a subdirectory named departments, which has a welcome page for all users and three departmental home pages: one for management, one for the development team, and one for system administrators. The departments subdirectory also contains a fifth JSP page which contains navigational elements shared by all of the pages in this subdirectory. This header page is referenced by the other pages via the `<jsp:include>` action.

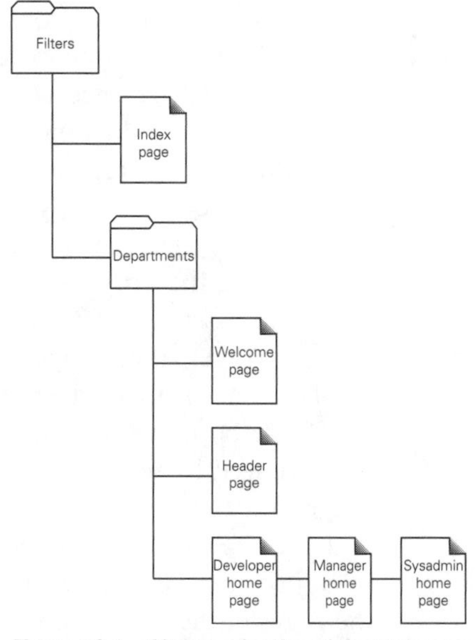

Figure 13.1 Site map for the original intranet application

The primary enhancement to be added to the intranet is user authentication. The company would like to personalize all content, as well as ensure that the information contained in these pages is accessed by authorized personnel only. All users will be required to log on to the intranet with a username and password. Individual access will be logged for auditing purposes. Furthermore, Encom management will restrict access to the various departmental pages to the employees of those departments.

To achieve maximum modularity, these requirements will be fulfilled using a combination of two filters and one listener. The first filter will be used to manage the login requirement, and enforce global access control. The second will provide local access control, implementing the departmental access restrictions using role-based security. The listener will implement the required logging functionality.

To support these new features, several modifications must be made to the contents of the site, as indicated in figure 13.2. First, the department's subdirectory has been renamed secure. This is strictly a cosmetic change, but it serves as a useful indication that all content in that subdirectory will be protected against unauthorized access.

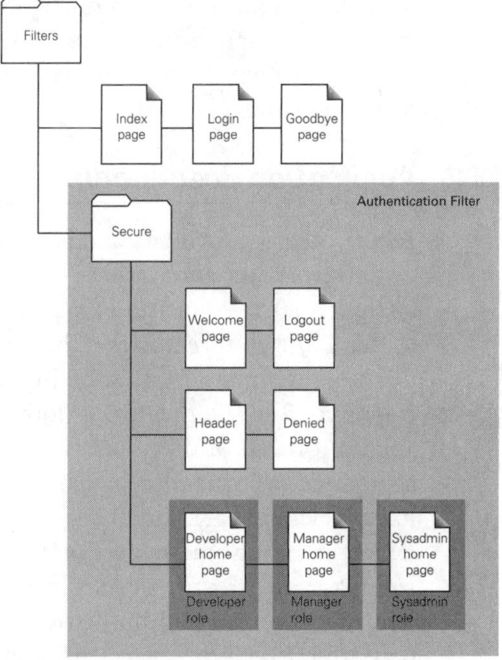

Figure 13.2 Site map for the revised intranet application, with filters

Next, two new documents have been added to the top-level filters directory. The first is a login page, which will contain the form used for entering the employee's username and password. The second is the good-bye page, which will be displayed after a user has logged out. Since both pages must be able to be viewed by users who are not logged in, they cannot be located in the secure subdirectory. (As indicated in figure 13.2, access to all of the pages in the secure subdirectory is controlled by the authentication filter.) The filter's directory, which is not subject to the authentication filter, provides a convenient location for insecure content such as this.

Two new pages have been added to the secure subdirectory. The logout page presents a form that enables users to log out. Since this action only makes sense for users who are already logged in, placing this page in the secure subdirectory ensures that it can only be viewed by users who have already been authenticated. The role-based security filter will be used to restrict access to the three departmental home pages. The other new page in this subdirectory, the denied page, contains content that will be displayed whenever a user attempts to access a departmental home page for which that user does not have the corresponding role.

Although it is not depicted in figure 13.2, we will also be adding two new servlets to the intranet application. These will be mapped to the /filters/login and /filters/logout application URLs and, as their names suggest, will be used to perform the actual login and logout operations for users visiting the site.

13.2 User authentication

Although our primary interest in this example application lies in its filters and listener, very little of the code that implements the underlying functionality is contained in the filter and listener classes themselves. As we will see later in the chapter, these particular classes are quite compact. Instead, most of the Java code is located in the auxiliary classes that implement the security mechanisms for user and role-based authentication.

13.2.1 User account representation

There are two key classes with respect to user authentication in this example application. The first is the `com.taglib.wdjsp.filters.UserBean` class, presented in listing 13.1. This JavaBean represents a user's login account information, including the username, first and last name, and assigned roles. Note that this bean is designed to be incorporated into a JSP page in order to personalize its content; for security reasons it does not include a property representing the user's password.

Listing 13.1 UserBean class

```
package com.taglib.wdjsp.filters;
import java.util.List;
import java.util.ArrayList;

public class UserBean {
  private String username, firstName, lastName;
  List roles;

  public UserBean () {
    this("", "", "");
  }
  public UserBean (String username, String firstName, String lastName) {
    this.username = username;
    this.firstName = firstName;
    this.lastName = lastName;
    this.roles = new ArrayList();
  }

  public String getUsername () { return username; }
  public String getFirstName () { return firstName; }
```

```
  public String getLastName () { return lastName; }

  public void setUsername (String username) { this.username = username; }
  public void setFirstName (String firstName) { this.firstName = firstName; }
  public void setLastName (String lastName) { this.lastName = lastName; }

  public void addRole (String role) {
    if (! roles.contains(role)) roles.add(role);
  }
  public void removeRole (String role) {
    int index = roles.indexOf(role);
    if (index >= 0) roles.remove(index);
  }
  public boolean hasRole (String role) {
      return roles.contains(role);
  }
}
```

Like other JavaBeans we have seen in previous chapters, `UserBean` includes a default constructor and getter and setter methods for its username, first name, and last name properties. It also includes a second constructor for setting those three properties during initialization, as well as a set of methods for managing and querying its roles, which are stored via an instance of the `java.util.ArrayList` class.

13.2.2 User management interface

The second key class is actually an interface, `com.taglib.wdjsp.filters.UserDataManager`. This interface, presented in listing 13.2, provides an abstraction layer intended to hide the details of the underlying authentication system. As the listing indicates, it defines only two methods, `validate()` and `lookupUserData()`. The `validate()` method returns a boolean value indicating whether or not the username and password provided as its parameters represent valid login credentials, while the `lookupUserData()` method is used to populate an instance of the `UserBean` class with the account information corresponding to the provided username.

Listing 13.2 UserDataManager interface

```
package com.taglib.wdjsp.filters;

public interface UserDataManager {
  public boolean validate (String username, String password);
  public UserBean lookupUserData (String username);
}
```

By using this interface, the other components of the application, such as the login servlet, do not need to be exposed to the mechanics of authenticating users. If the web components only interact with the authentication code via this interface, it becomes possible to plug in a variety of authentication schemes without having to alter those components in order to accommodate them. The same login servlet, for example, could be used with an authentication system based on a configuration file, an LDAP repository, or a complex database system, without modification.

NOTE Because this is example code, the `UserDataManager` interface, as presented here, is incomplete. At the very least, methods for modifying a user's password and other account information would be required in a production system. Methods for adding and removing accounts would likely also prove useful.

13.2.3 User management implementation

To keep things simple, our authentication system will rely on hard-coded usernames and passwords. This is not terribly practical, but hopefully possesses the virtue of being easy to understand and therefore not prone to distracting us from the topic at hand. With this in mind, the source code for the `com.taglib.wdjsp.filters.SimpleUserBase` class is presented in listing 13.3.

Listing 13.3 SimpleUserBase class

```
package com.taglib.wdjsp.filters;
import java.util.StringTokenizer;

public class SimpleUserBase {

  static public boolean validate (String username, String password) {
    int count = USER_DATA.length;
    for (int i = 0; i < count; ++i) {
      String[] entry = USER_DATA[i];
      if (username.equals(entry[0])) return password.equals(entry[1]);
    }
    return false;
  }
  static public void populate (UserBean bean, String username) {
    int count = USER_DATA.length;
    for (int i = 0; i < count; ++i) {
      String[] entry = USER_DATA[i];
      if (username.equals(entry[0])) populate(bean, entry);
    }
  }
  static private void populate (UserBean bean, String[] entry) {
    bean.setUsername(entry[0]);
```

```
      bean.setFirstName(entry[2]);
      bean.setLastName(entry[3]);
      StringTokenizer tokens = new StringTokenizer(entry[4], ":");
      while (tokens.hasMoreTokens()) {
        bean.addRole(tokens.nextToken());
      }
    }

  static private String[][] USER_DATA =
  {
    { "clu", "starman", "Kevin", "Flynn", "user:dev:admin" },
    { "tron", "scarecrow", "Alan", "Bradley", "user:dev" },
    { "yori", "galaxis", "Lora", "Morgan", "user:dev" },
    { "dumont", "doc", "Walter", "Gibbs", "user:mgr" },
    { "sark", "gorkon", "Ed", "Dillinger", "user:mgr:admin" },
  };
}
```

This class is simply a combination of static methods and a data structure, named `USER_DATA`, which stores the account information for a handful of employees. This data structure takes the form of a two-dimensional array of character strings, each row of which represents a single account. For each account, the username and password are listed, followed by the user's first name and last name. Finally, the roles assigned to the user are listed as a single text string in which multiple roles are delimited by colon characters.

The three static methods defined by this class perform authentication against the data in this array. The `validate()` method checks the array for the specified username/password combination, while the two `populate()` methods set the properties of a `UserBean` instance based on a provided username.

The methods of the `SimpleUserBase` class do not correspond to those required by the `UserDataManager` interface, so one more class is required to complete our user authentication system. The sole task of the `com.taglib.wdjsp.filters.SimpleUserDataManager` class is to provide a mapping between the `SimpleUserBase` class's methods and those of `UserDataManager`. Its source code is provided in listing 13.4. This class's `validate()` method simply calls the static `validate()` method of `SimpleUserBase`, while its `lookupUserData()` method creates a `UserBean` instance and then calls the `populate()` method of `SimpleUserBase` to set the new bean's properties.

Listing 13.4 SimpleUserDataManager class

```
package com.taglib.wdjsp.filters;

public class SimpleUserDataManager implements UserDataManager {
  public boolean validate (String username, String password) {
    return SimpleUserBase.validate(username, password);
  }
  public UserBean lookupUserData (String username) {
    UserBean data = new UserBean();
    SimpleUserBase.populate(data, username);
    return data;
  }
}
```

13.3 Web authentication

The objects described in the previous section for implementing user authentication, including the `UserBean` class, are not web-specific. These classes and interfaces could provide user authentication for other types of software requiring access control, such as desktop or client/server applications. From this point forward, however, our focus will be on applying this functionality to web-based settings in general, and our intranet example application in particular.

13.3.1 Session interactions

Since the only way to keep track of a user's ongoing interactions with a web site is via his or her session, this is an appropriate place to indicate whether or not the user has logged in. Since we will want to be able to customize content with a user's account information, a simple way to indicate login status is the presence or absence of a `UserBean` instance in the user's session. If the user has `UserBean` instance as the value of a designated session attribute, this is taken as an indication that the user has been authenticated. Furthermore, the properties of that `UserBean` can be assumed to reflect the session owner's account information.

To manage this interaction with the session, the `com.taglib.wdjsp.filters.UserSessionManager` class is introduced. This class has three static variables, one of which is used to implement the singleton pattern (introduced in chapter 11), as follows:

```
public class UserSessionManager {
  final static public String SESSION_USER_ATTRIBUTE = "user";
  final static public String SESSION_LOGINTARGET_ATTRIBUTE = "loginTarget";

  static private UserSessionManager INSTANCE = new UserSessionManager();
```

```
  private UserSessionManager () {}

  static public UserSessionManager getInstance () {
    return INSTANCE;
  }
  ...
}
```

The first two static variables are used to store attribute names for a pair of attributes to be stored in the session. The third static variable, `INSTANCE`, stores the singleton instance of this class, which may be retrieved via the `getInstance()` static method. Note that the constructor method is private, thereby preventing any other class from creating additional instances of `UserSessionManager`.

Instances of the `UserBean` class are stored in the session by means of the `setSessionUser()` method, defined as follows:

```
public void setSessionUser (HttpSession session, UserBean user) {
  session.setAttribute(SESSION_USER_ATTRIBUTE, user);
  if (user.hasRole("admin")) {
    session.setMaxInactiveInterval(60 * 60 * 8);
  } else {
    session.setMaxInactiveInterval(60 * 15);
  }
}
```

Given a session and a `UserBean`, this method stores the bean in the session using the attribute name specified in the class's `SESSION_USER_ATTRIBUTE` static variable. The `UserBean` instance is then checked to see whether or not the corresponding user has the `admin` role, in which case the session is set to expire after eight hours of inactivity, rather than the default fifteen minutes. The bean can subsequently be retrieved or removed from the session via the `getSessionUser()` and `removeSessionUser()` methods:

```
public UserBean getSessionUser (HttpSession session) {
  return (UserBean) session.getAttribute(SESSION_USER_ATTRIBUTE);
}
public void removeSessionUser (HttpSession session) {
  session.removeAttribute(SESSION_USER_ATTRIBUTE);
}
```

Like `setSessionUser()`, these methods take advantage of the `SESSION_USER_ATTRIBUTE` static variable to abstract the name of the session attribute.

In addition to managing the session attribute for storing the `UserBean` instance, this class is used to manage a second session attribute related to the user login process. The job of the authentication filter is to prevent access to content in the application's `secure` subdirectory by users who have not yet logged in. Once a user has successfully logged in, however, there is nothing preventing a user from creating a bookmark containing the URL for that secured content. If the user attempts to follow that bookmark at a later date without first logging in, the authentication filter will redirect them to the login page to be authenticated.

As a convenience, it is preferable to automatically take the user to the page they were originally trying to access, once the login has been authenticated (i.e., rather than sending them to a generic welcome page). In order to facilitate this behavior, store the URL for the page that was originally requested—referred to as the "login target"—in the user's session. This is accomplished by means of the `UserSessionManager` class's `setSessionLoginTarget()` method:

```
public void setSessionLoginTarget (HttpSession session, String loginTarget) {
  session.setAttribute(SESSION_LOGINTARGET_ATTRIBUTE, loginTarget);
}
```

The login target can subsequently be retrieved via the class's `getSessionLoginTarget()` method, which provides a second parameter for indicating whether or not the attribute should be removed from the session after it has been retrieved:

```
public String getSessionLoginTarget (HttpSession session, boolean clear) {
  String target = (String) session.getAttribute(SESSION_LOGINTARGET_ATTRIBUTE);
  if (clear) session.removeAttribute(SESSION_LOGINTARGET_ATTRIBUTE);
  return target;
}
```

Both methods make use of the `SESSION_LOGINTARGET_ATTRIBUTE` static variable for specifying the name of the attribute used to store the login target.

The final element of the `UserSessionManager` class is a static method named `doRedirect()`. As mentioned, the authentication filter will redirect unauthenticated users to the login page when they attempt to access restricted content. Redirection is also used to forward the user to the login target after they have been authenticated. The `doRedirect()` utility method allows the various steps required to perform this redirection to be defined once and reused throughout the application. It is defined as follows:

```
static public void doRedirect (HttpServletRequest request,
                               HttpServletResponse response, String url)
    throws IOException {
  String redirect = response.encodeRedirectURL(request.getContextPath() + url);
  response.sendRedirect(redirect);
}
```

The first step in this method is to call the request's `getContextPath()` method to retrieve the top-level directory name under which the application has been deployed (see chapter 14). This is prepended to the URL passed in as the method's third parameter, to result in an absolute URL as required by the response's `sendRedirect()` method. Before the `sendRedirect()` method can be called, however, the response's `encodeRedirectURL()` method must be called. This method will ensure that the user's session ID is encoded into the URL, should the user not have cookies enabled in the browser. Given the important role played by the session in our access control system, it is critical that the association between the user and their session not be lost. Finally, by defining this as a static method, it can easily be leveraged by the application's other classes.

The source code for the `UserSessionManager` class, in abbreviated form, appears in listing 13.5.

Listing 13.5 UserSessionManager class

```
package com.taglib.wdjsp.filters;
import javax.servlet.http.HttpSession;
import javax.servlet.http.HttpServletRequest;
import javax.servlet.http.HttpServletResponse;
import java.io.IOException;

public class UserSessionManager {
  final static public String SESSION_USER_ATTRIBUTE = "user";
  final static public String SESSION_LOGINTARGET_ATTRIBUTE = "loginTarget";

  static private UserSessionManager INSTANCE = new UserSessionManager();
  private UserSessionManager () {}

  static public UserSessionManager getInstance () { ... }

  public void setSessionUser (HttpSession session, UserBean user) { ... }
  public UserBean getSessionUser (HttpSession session) { ... }
  public void removeSessionUser (HttpSession session) { ... }

  public void setSessionLoginTarget (HttpSession session, String loginTarget) {
   ... }
  public String getSessionLoginTarget (HttpSession session, boolean clear) { ...
   }

  static public void doRedirect (HttpServletRequest request,
                                 HttpServletResponse response, String url)
    throws IOException { ... }
}
```

13.3.2 Login servlet

The process of logging in is implemented via the `com.taglib.wdjsp.filters.LoginServlet` class. This servlet validates login credentials and, when valid, adds a corresponding `UserBean` instance to the session. If the provided username and password are not valid, an error message is displayed and the user is given another opportunity to log in. If they are valid, the servlet will display the user's login target, if specified, or a generic welcome page, if it is not.

The `LoginServlet` class defines several instance variables, as well as a pair of static class variables:

```
public class LoginServlet extends HttpServlet {
  final private static String USERNAME_REQPARM = "username";
  final private static String PASSWORD_REQPARM = "password";

  private String loginPage;
  private String welcomePage;
  private UserDataManager userMgr;
  private UserSessionManager sessionMgr = UserSessionManager.getInstance();
  ...
}
```

The two class variables store the names of the request parameters that will be passed in by the form on the login page. The values of the `loginPage` and `welcomePage` instance variables will be passed in as initialization parameters, and will store URLs for the login form and for the default page to be displayed after a successful user authentication (i.e., in the absence of a login target). The `userMgr` instance variable stores an object implementing the `UserDataManager` interface, described earlier in the chapter, and is also set by means of an initialization parameter. The `sessionMgr` instance variable stores a pointer to the singleton `UserSessionManager` instance.

Initialization parameters are processed via the servlet's `init()` method, defined as follows:

```
public void init (ServletConfig config) throws ServletException {
  welcomePage = config.getInitParameter("welcomePage");
  if (welcomePage == null)
    throw new ServletException("The welcomePage init parameter"
                              + " must be specified.");
  loginPage = config.getInitParameter("loginPage");
  if (loginPage == null)
    throw new ServletException("The loginPage init parameter"
                               + " must be specified.");
  String userDataMgrClassname = config.getInitParameter("userDataManager");
  if (userDataMgrClassname == null)
    throw new ServletException("The userDataManager init parameter"
                              + " must be specified.");
  userMgr = (UserDataManager) makeInstance(userDataMgrClassname,
                                  UserDataManager.class, "user data manager");
}
```

The values of the `welcomePage` and `loginPage` initialization parameters are assigned directly to the instance variables of the same names, and an exception is raised if either of the two initialization parameters was not specified. An initialization parameter named `userDataManager` must also be specified, the value of which should be a fully qualified class name for a Java class that implements the `UserDataManager` interface. The specified class is instantiated by means of an auxiliary method named `makeInstance()`. This approach of specifying a class name, provided in the form of an initialization parameter, is a manifestation of the plug-in approach to user authentication enabled by our introduction of the `UserDataManager` interface.

The `makeInstance()` auxiliary method takes advantage of several methods defined by the `java.lang.Class` class to instantiate the class named by the `userDataManager` initialization parameter:

```
private Object makeInstance (String classname,
                             Class interfaceClass, String description)
  throws ServletException {
  try {
    Class klass = Class.forName(classname);
    if (! interfaceClass.isAssignableFrom(klass)) {
      throw new ServletException(classname + " does not implement required"
                                 + " interface" + interfaceClass.getName()
                                 + " for " + description + ".");
    }
    return klass.newInstance();
  }
  catch (ClassNotFoundException e) {
    throw new ServletException("Unable to instantiate" + description + ".", e);
  }
  catch (InstantiationException e) {
    throw new ServletException("Unable to instantiate" + description + ".", e);
  }
  catch (IllegalAccessException e) {
    throw new ServletException("Unable to instantiate" + description + ".", e);
  }
}
```

The `forName()` static method retrieves the `Class` object corresponding to a fully qualified class name. Once the class is retrieved, the `isAssignableFrom()` method (also defined by the `Class` class) is used to make sure that the named class implements the required interface. If so, the `Class` object's `newInstance()` method is called to create the required instance. Since the class of the instance cannot be known in advance, this method returns the result as an instance of the root `Object` class. The calling method (in this case, the servlet's `init()` method) must cast the result to the desired class (or, in this case, the desired interface).

Trying to construct an object from an arbitrary character string presumed to name a defined class is something of a risky proposition. The methods called upon to perform this task may throw a number of exceptions, which `makeInstance()` handles by rethrowing them as instances of the `ServletException` class.

For security reasons, it is recommended that request parameters corresponding to login passwords be submitted only via the HTTP POST method. Because the GET method passes request parameters as part of the URL, the values of those parameters are much more visible. On the client side, they will appear in the browser's history list of visited pages. They may also be stored in the activity logs of the web server hosting the login form. Based on this consideration, the `LoginServlet` class defines a `doPost()` method, but not a a `doGet()` method.

This `doPost()` method has three primary tasks: retrieve the request parameters for the username and password, validate them, and take appropriate action. The method is defined as follows:

```
public void doPost (HttpServletRequest request,
                    HttpServletResponse response)
  throws ServletException, IOException {
  String username = request.getParameter(USERNAME_REQPARM);
  if (username == null)
    throw new ServletException("No username specified.");
  String password = request.getParameter(PASSWORD_REQPARM);
  if (password == null)
    throw new ServletException("No password specified.");
  if (userMgr.validate(username, password)) {
    doLoginSuccess(request, response, username);
  } else {
    doLoginFailure(request, response, username);
  }
}
```

The request parameters are retrieved by calling the `getParameter()` method of the request object provided as the method's first argument. The static variables discussed earlier are used to reference the names of the two parameters, and an exception is raised if either is missing. Authentication of the username and password is accomplished by calling the `validate()` method of the `UserDataManager` object created in the servlet's `init()` method. Based on the results of this validation, one of two utility methods is called to indicate the success or failure of the login attempt.

If user authentication is successful, `doPost()` calls the servlet's `doLoginSuccess()` method:

```
private void doLoginSuccess (HttpServletRequest request,
                             HttpServletResponse response,
                             String username)
  throws IOException {
  UserBean user = userMgr.lookupUserData(username);
  HttpSession session = request.getSession(true);
  sessionMgr.setSessionUser(session, user);
  String targetPage = sessionMgr.getSessionLoginTarget(session, true);
  if (targetPage == null) {
    UserSessionManager.doRedirect(request, response, welcomePage);
  } else {
    targetPage = response.encodeRedirectURL(targetPage);
    response.sendRedirect(targetPage);
  }
}
```

This method's first step is to fetch a `UserBean` instance representing the user's account information from the servlet's `UserDataManager` object (stored in the `userMgr` instance variable). This bean is then stored in the user's session via the `setSessionUser()` method of the `UserSessionManager` singleton (referenced by the servlet's `sessionMgr` instance variable). The `UserSessionManager` object is then used to determine whether or not a login target has been stored in the user's session. If so, that class's `doRedirect()` static method is used to instruct the user's browser to issue a new request for the login target. If not, the `doRedirect()` method is used to send the user to the application's welcome page.

If the login validation fails, the servlet's `doPost()` method instead calls its `doLoginFailure()` method:

```
private void doLoginFailure (HttpServletRequest request,
                             HttpServletResponse response,
                             String username)
  throws IOException {
  String loginURL = loginPage + "?retry=true&username=" + username;
  UserSessionManager.doRedirect(request, response, loginURL);
}
```

This method also relies on the `doRedirect()` method of the `UserSessionManager` class, but instead sends the user back to the page with the login form. In addition, it appends two request parameters to the URL for the login page. The `retry` request parameter is a signal to the login page that a previous attempt at logging in failed, so that an appropriate error message may be displayed. The `username` request parameter is used to prefill the corresponding form field, presuming that the user is more likely to have mistyped the password (whose characters will have been masked during entry) than the username. (Also, the redirect operation will use the more vulnerable HTTP GET method, providing another good reason for not attempting to prefill the password field.)

This completes the methods of the LoginServlet class. The source code for the class is presented in abbreviated form in listing 13.6.

Listing 13.6 LoginServlet class

```
package com.taglib.wdjsp.filters;
import javax.servlet.ServletConfig;
import javax.servlet.http.HttpServlet;
import javax.servlet.http.HttpServletRequest;
import javax.servlet.http.HttpServletResponse;
import javax.servlet.http.HttpSession;

import javax.servlet.ServletException;
import java.io.IOException;

public class LoginServlet extends HttpServlet {
  final private static String USERNAME_REQPARM = "username";
  final private static String PASSWORD_REQPARM = "password";

  private String welcomePage;
  private String loginPage;
  private UserSessionManager sessionMgr = UserSessionManager.getInstance();
  private UserDataManager userMgr;

  public void init (ServletConfig config) throws ServletException { ... }
  private Object makeInstance (String classname,
                               Class interfaceClass, String description)
    throws ServletException {
    ...
  }
  public void doPost (HttpServletRequest request,
                      HttpServletResponse response)
    throws ServletException, IOException {
    ...
  }
  private void doLoginSuccess (HttpServletRequest request,
                               HttpServletResponse response,
                               String username)
    throws IOException {
    ...
  }
  private void doLoginFailure (HttpServletRequest request,
                               HttpServletResponse response,
                               String username)
    throws IOException {
    ...
  }
}
```

13.3.3 Login pages

Given this description of the operation of the login servlet, a look at the JSP pages supporting this servlet is in order. The first of these three pages is the `index.jsp` page for the filters directory, which displays a warning notice and provides a link to the login form. Its source code appears in listing 13.7. The only JSP element in this page is an expression which modifies the link to the login form by calling the `encodeURL()` method of the `response` implicit object. Like the `encodeRedirectURL()` method discussed previously, this method ensures that the user's session ID is encoded into the HTML link, for those users who have disabled cookies in their browser.

Listing 13.7 index.jsp

```
<html>
<head><title>Encom Intranet</title></head>
<body>
<h1>Encom Intranet</h1>
<p>
This is the Encom intranet. Unauthorized use is prohibited.
</p>
<p>
Click <a href='<%= response.encodeURL("login.jsp") %>'>here</a> to log in.
</p>
</body>
</html>
```

The source code for the login form, `login.jsp`, is presented in listing 13.8. The first JSP elements on this page are two scriptlets that conditionally include an error message in the presence of a request parameter named `retry`. As indicated in the previous section, this request parameter is set by the login servlet as an indicator that a previous login attempt has failed. The third scriptlet attempts to assign the value of a request parameter named `username` to a local variable of the same name, setting the local variable to an empty character string if the request parameter is not present.

Listing 13.8 login.jsp

```
<html>
<head><title>Please log in...</title></head>

<body>
<h1>Please log in...</h1>

<% if (request.getParameter("retry") != null) { %>
<p align=center><font color="red">
```

```
Invalid username/password combination.
</font></p>
<% } %>

<% String username = request.getParameter("username");
   if (username == null) username = ""; %>

<center>
<form action='<%= response.encodeURL(request.getContextPath()
                                     + "/filters/login") %>'
      method="POST">
<table>
<tr>
  <td align="right">Username:</td>
    <td align="left">
      <input type="text" name="username" size="16" value="<%= username %>">
    </td>
</tr>
<tr>
  <td align="right">Password:</td>
    <td align="left">
      <input type="password" name="password" size="20">
    </td>
</tr>
</table>

<input type="submit" value="Log In">
</form>
</center>

</body>
</html>
```

The remaining two JSP elements are expressions. The simpler is the second one, which inserts the value of the `username` local variable as the default value for the form field of the same name. The first expression is a bit more complex. Its task is to set the URL for the logon servlet as the `action` handler for the form. Once again, the `encodeURL()` method of the response object is employed to embed the session ID in the URL (if necessary). In addition, the `getContextPath()` method of the `request` implicit object is prepended to the URL for the logon servlet. This allows us to construct an absolute URL for the servlet, which includes the name of the top-level directory under which the application has been deployed. (For further discussion of application deployment issues, see chapter 14.) The page's static content implements the HTML layout of the form itself.

Figure 13.3 shows the logon form. Figure 13.4 shows the results of an unsuccessful logon attempt.

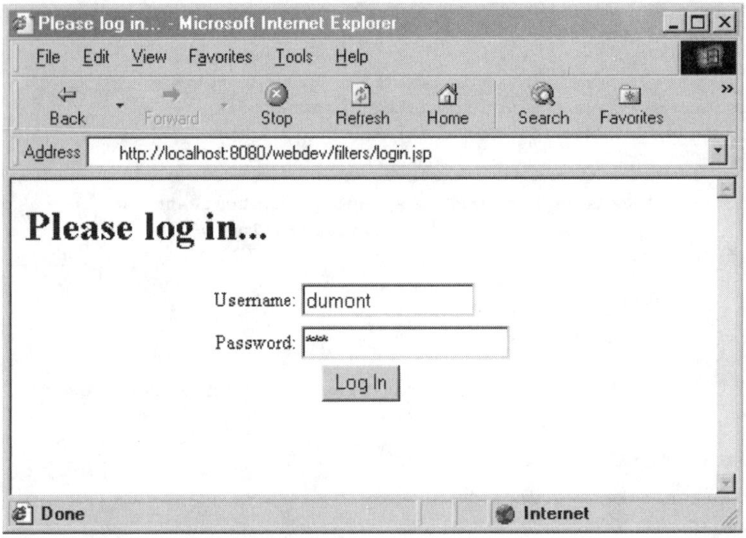

Figure 13.3 The logon form

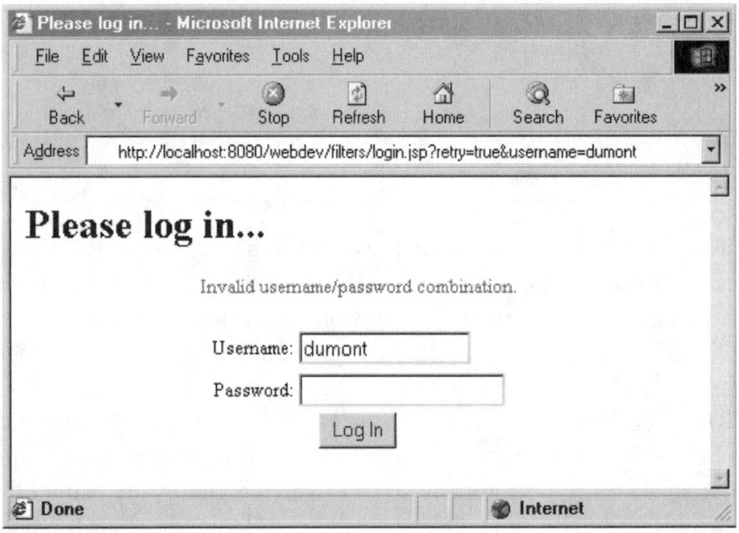

Figure 13.4 The logon form after an unsuccessful logon attempt

The third JSP page associated with the logon process is the welcome page, to which users whose session does not contain a logon target are directed after they log on. The welcome.jsp page is located in the secure subdirectory of the filters directory, and its source code is presented in listing 13.9.

Listing 13.9 welcome.jsp

```
<html>
<head><title>Welcome</title></head>

<body>
<jsp:include page="header.jsp" flush="false"/>

<h1>Welcome</h1>

<p>
...to the Encom intranet.
</p>

</body>
</html>
```

This JSP page has only one scripting element, used to include the navigational header for the content pages. (See listing 13.10.)

13.3.4 Content pages

The application has three content pages, corresponding to the three departmental home pages. Like the welcome page presented in the previous section, all are located in the secure subdirectory of the filters directory and use the <jsp:include> action to incorporate the content of the header page located in that subdirectory.

The source code for the header page appears in listing 13.10. As indicated in figure 13.2, all pages in the secure subdirectory will be subject to access control via the authentication filter. Anyone viewing these pages can therefore be presumed to be logged on. As indicated earlier in the chapter, this means that all users viewing content in the secure subdirectory will have an instance of the UserBean class in their session.

Listing 13.10 header.jsp

```
<center>

<jsp:useBean id="user" scope="session"
             class="com.taglib.wdjsp.filters.UserBean">
  <font color="red" size="+2">Illegal User Access!</font>
</jsp:useBean>

<font color="white">
<table bgcolor="grey">
```

```
<tr>
<td><b><jsp:getProperty name="user" property="username"/>@Encom:</b></td>
<td> </td>
<td><a href='<%= response.encodeURL("welcome.jsp") %>'>Home</a></td>
<td>|</td>
<td><a href='<%= response.encodeURL("development.jsp") %>'>Development</a></td>
<td>|</td>
<td><a href='<%= response.encodeURL("management.jsp") %>'>Management</a></td>
<td>|</td>
<td><a href='<%= response.encodeURL("admin.jsp") %>'>System
     Administration</a></td>
<td>|</td>
<td><a href='<%= response.encodeURL("logout.jsp") %>'>Log Out</a></td>
</tr>
</table>
</font>
</center>
```

The first JSP element in the header page, then, is a `<jsp:useBean>` action for making this bean available within the page. Note that, as a debugging aid, body content has been added to the action to print out a warning message if the `<jsp:useBean>` action does not find the bean already in the session and ends up instantiating a new one.

The remainder of the page implements an HTML table that provides a navigation banner for accessing each of the JSP pages in the secure subdirectory. As with previous links, the `response` object's `encodeURL()` method is called up to preserve the association between the user and the session if cookies have been disabled. In addition, the `<jsp:getProperty>` action is applied to display the username for the current user within the navigational banner. A screenshot of the welcome page described in the previous section, which incorporates the `header.jsp` page via the `<jsp:include>` action, is presented in figure 13.5.

The incorporation of the `UserBean` instance into the page by the included header can be taken advantage of by the other pages that use it. Each of the three departmental home pages, for example, displays one of the properties of this bean using the `<jsp:getProperty>` action. The development home page, presented in listing 13.11, uses this action to retrieve the user's first name, while the management home page, presented in listing 13.12, uses it to retrieve the user's last name. A screen shot of the management home page is depicted in figure 13.6.

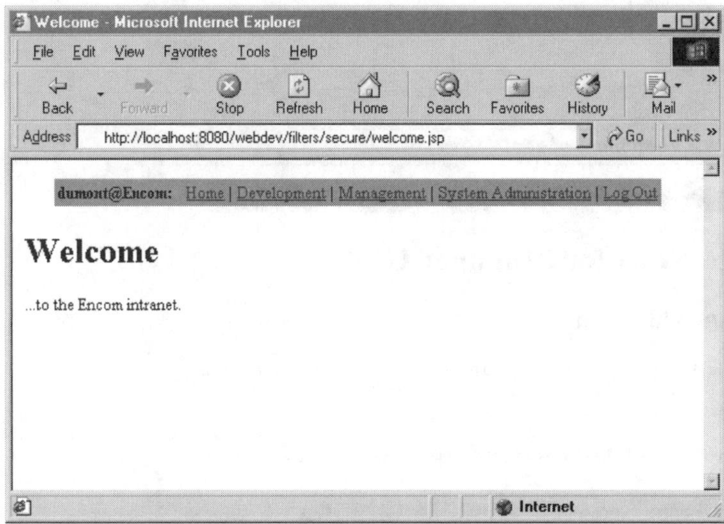

Figure 13.5 The welcome page, including the navigational header

Listing 13.11 development.jsp

```
<html>
<head><title>Development News</title></head>

<body>
<jsp:include page="header.jsp" flush="false"/>

<h1>Development News for
     <jsp:getProperty name="user" property="firstName"/></h1>

<ul>
<li>The development team meeting for Space Paranoids II will be next Tuesday
at 11 am.
<br>Bring your laptop.
<li>The Encom quarterly meeting will be next Friday at 9am.
<br>Bring your pillow.
</ul>

</body>
</html>
```

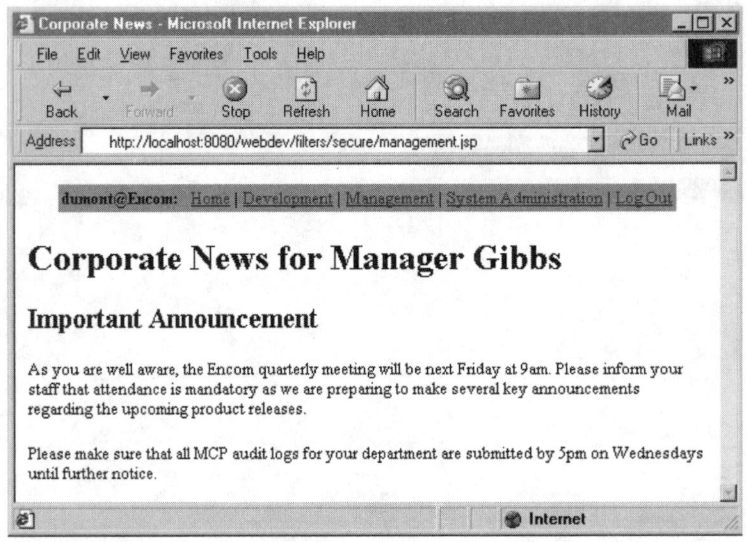

Figure 13.6 The management home page

Listing 13.12 management.jsp

```
<html>
<head><title>Corporate News</title></head>

<body>
<jsp:include page="header.jsp" flush="false"/>

<h1>Corporate News for Manager
     <jsp:getProperty name="user" property="lastName"/></h1>

<h2>Important Announcement</h2>

<p>
As you are well aware, the Encom quarterly meeting will be
next Friday at 9am. Please inform your staff that attendance is mandatory
as we are preparing to make several key announcements regarding the upcoming
product releases.
</p>

<p>
Please make sure that all MCP audit logs for your department are submitted by
5pm on Wednesdays until further notice.
</p>

</body>
</html>
```

The third and final departmental home page is presented in listing 13.13. Like the first two, it uses the `<jsp:getProperty>` action to retrieve a property from the `UserBean` stored in the user's session. An even more noteworthy characteristic of all three of these pages is what they do not include: nowhere within these pages do you see any code related to access control. The header page's `<jsp:useBean>` tag is an indirect dependence on the user authentication code, but there are no explicit checks in any of these JSP pages that the user is logged in or has been assigned the required role.

Instead, all of the code required to enforce the system's access control requirements will be provided by the filters to be introduced later in the chapter. No changes will need to be made to the pages themselves. As described in the previous chapter, this ability to add functionality to an application in a modular fashion, without having to modify existing resources, is one of the key advantages of both filters and listeners.

Listing 13.13 admin.jsp

```
<html>
<head><title>SysAdmin News</title></head>

<body>
<jsp:include page="header.jsp" flush="false"/>

<h1>SysAdmin News for user
     <jsp:getProperty name="user" property="username"/></h1>

<ul>
<li>Network status: The game grid is <b>up</b>.
</ul>

</body>
</html>
```

13.3.5 Logout servlet

The counterpart to the logon servlet is the logout servlet, which allows a user to cleanly exit the intranet application. It defines only two methods, an `init()` method and a `doPost()` method, as indicated in listing 13.14.

Listing 13.14 LogoutServlet class

```
package com.taglib.wdjsp.filters;
import javax.servlet.ServletConfig;
import javax.servlet.http.HttpServlet;
import javax.servlet.http.HttpServletRequest;
```

```
import javax.servlet.http.HttpServletResponse;
import javax.servlet.http.HttpSession;

import javax.servlet.ServletException;
import java.io.IOException;

public class LogoutServlet extends HttpServlet {

  private String goodbyePage;
  private UserSessionManager sessionMgr = UserSessionManager.getInstance();

  public void init (ServletConfig config) throws ServletException {
    goodbyePage = config.getInitParameter("goodbyePage");
    if (goodbyePage == null)
      throw new ServletException("The goodbyePage init parameter"
                                 + " must be specified.");
  }

  public void doPost (HttpServletRequest request,
                      HttpServletResponse response)
    throws ServletException, IOException {
    HttpSession session = request.getSession(true);
    sessionMgr.removeSessionUser(session);
    UserSessionManager.doRedirect(request, response, goodbyePage);
  }
}
```

The `com.taglib.wdjsp.filters.LogoutServlet` class also defines two instance variables. The first, `goodbyePage`, will hold the URL for the page to be displayed after a user has successfully logged out. Initializing this instance variable is the sole task of the servlet's `init()` method, which sets its value from an initialization parameter of the same name, throwing an exception if that initialization parameter is not found.

The servlet's second instance variable, `sessionMgr`, holds a reference to the `UserSessionManager` singleton, just like the `sessionMgr` instance variable of the `LoginServlet` class. This reference is used by the servlet's `doPost()` method to remove the `UserBean` instance from the user's session when logging them out. It then calls the `UserSessionManager` class's `doRedirect()` utility method to forward the user to the page specified by the servlet's `goodbyePage` instance variable.

13.3.6 Logout pages

There are two JSP pages in the application supporting the logout operation. The logout form is in a file named logout.jsp, which is in the secure subdirectory of the application's filters directory. After logging out, users are directed to goodbye.jsp, which resides in the filters directory itself.

The contents of the logout page are provided in listing 13.15. Like the content pages, it includes the header page containing navigational elements for the application, and it also uses the `<jsp:getProperty>` action to print the username of the account currently logged in. As was the case for the logon form, an expression using the `encodeURL()` method of the `response` object and the `getContextPath()` method of the `request` object is used to construct an absolute URL for the form handler (i.e., the logout servlet).

Listing 13.15 logout.jsp

```
<html>
<head><title>Log Out</title></head>

<body>
<jsp:include page="header.jsp" flush="false"/>

<h1>Logout</h1>

<p>
Select the button to log out account
<b><jsp:getProperty name="user" property="username"/></b>
from the Encom intranet.
</p>

<center>
<form action='<%= response.encodeURL(request.getContextPath()
                                + "/filters/logout") %>' method="POST">
<input type="submit" value="Log Out">
<form>
</center>

</body>
</html>
```

The good-bye page, presented in listing 13.16, is noteworthy in that it does not include any actual JSP elements. All of its content is static HTML. In particular, it does not use the `response` object's `encodeURL()` method to ensure that the user's session ID is preserved. This is because, having logged out, the user's connection to a particular session is no longer relevant.

Listing 13.16 goodbye.jsp

```
<html>
<head><title>Thank You</title></head>

<body>
<h1>Thank You</h1>
```

```
<p>
...for using the Encom intranet.<br>
Click <a href="login.jsp">here</a> to log back in.
</p>

</body>
</html>
```

Screen shots of the logout form and good-bye page appear in figures 13.7 and 13.8.

13.4 Access control filters

Now, with all the content and infrastructure in place, we are ready to return to the topics introduced in chapter 12. In this section, we will examine the two filters used to enforce the required access control policies on the intranet's JSP pages. The authentication filter restricts access to secure content to users who have successfully logged in. The role filter imposes an additional layer of access control, further restricting access to certain resources to users who have been assigned the corresponding role.

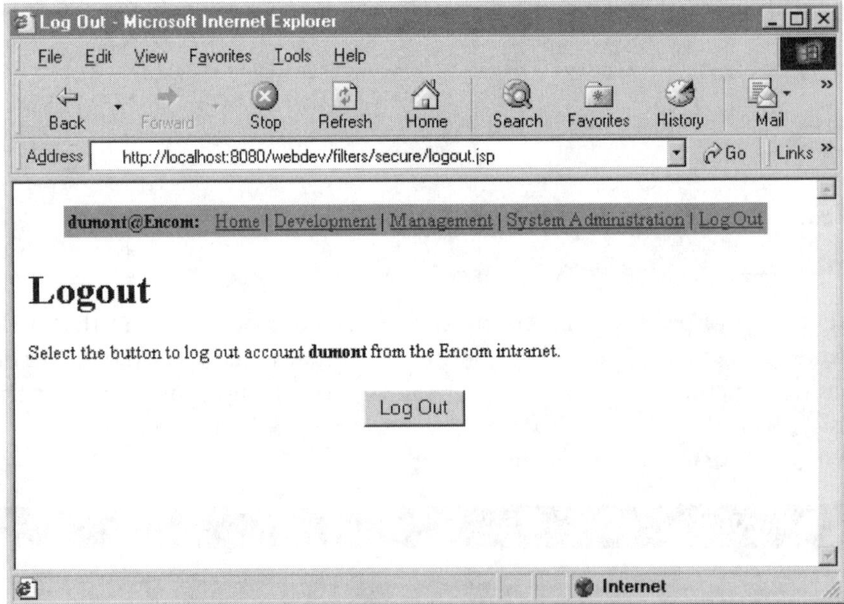

Figure 13.7 The logout form

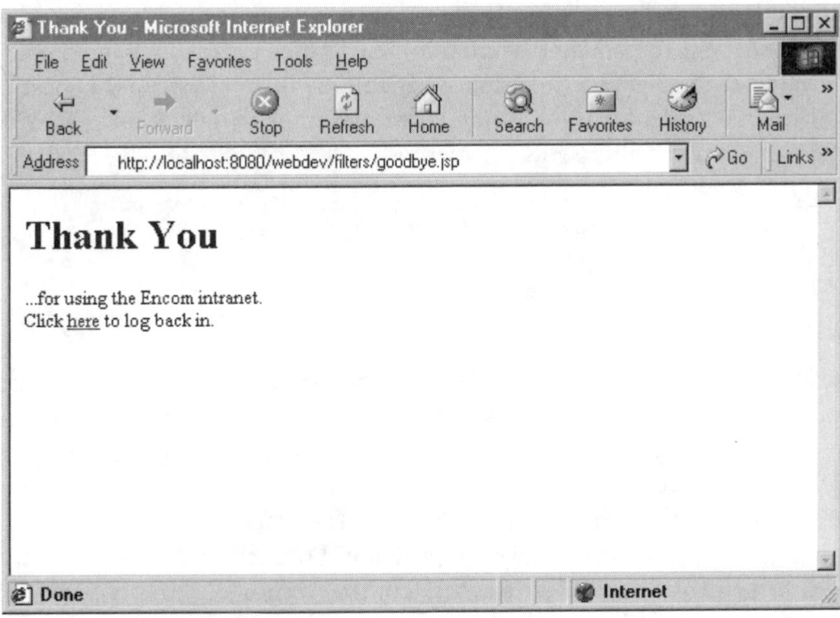

Figure 13.8 The goodbye page

13.4.1 Authentication filter

The authentication filter is implemented via the `com.taglib.wdjsp.filters.AuthenticationFilter` class. Its task is to ensure that a user is logged in before it will permit access to the resources to which it has been mapped. It does this by checking the user's session for the presence of a `UserBean` instance, which will only be present if the user has been authenticated via the login servlet. If the bean is present, access is permitted. If not, the user is redirected to the login form.

The `AuthenticationFilter` class defines two instance variables, one of which is set via a filter initialization parameter, and one of which is set by the class's constructor. The instance variables and constructors are defined as follows:

```
public class AuthenticationFilter implements Filter {
  private String loginPage;
  private UserSessionManager sessionMgr;

  public AuthenticationFilter () {
    sessionMgr = UserSessionManager.getInstance(); }
  ...
}
```

Like the logon and logout servlets, `AuthenticationFilter` also stores a reference to the `UserSessionManager` singleton in an instance variable named `sessionMgr`. The value of the `loginPage` instance variable—which will store the location of the application's logon form—is obtained from a filter initialization parameter of the same name, via the filter's `init()` method:

```
public void init (FilterConfig config) throws ServletException {
  loginPage = config.getInitParameter("loginPage");
  if (loginPage == null)
    throw new ServletException("The loginPage init parameter"
                               + " must be specified.");
}
```

Recall from the discussion in chapter 12 that filter initialization parameters are exposed to the filter via a corresponding `FilterConfig` object. The value of the `loginPage` parameter is obtained by calling this object's `getInitParameter()` method. If not found, an exception is raised. (Filter initialization parameter values are specified via the application deployment descriptor, an XML document for configuring the components of a web application. For further details, see chapter 14.)

Enforcement of the filter's access control responsibilities is provided by the `doFilter()` method. As indicated in the previous chapter, the signature of this method (as defined by the `Filter` interface) requires it to accept generic requests and responses. Because this filter must interact with the user's session, which is only applicable in the context of HTTP requests and responses, this method first ensures that its `request` and `response` parameters are actually instances of the `HttpServletRequest` and `HttpServletResponse` interfaces, respectively:

```
public void doFilter (ServletRequest request, ServletResponse response,
                      FilterChain chain)
  throws IOException, ServletException {
  if (request instanceof HttpServletRequest
      && response instanceof HttpServletResponse) {
    HttpServletRequest req = (HttpServletRequest) request;
    HttpSession session = req.getSession(true);
    UserBean user = sessionMgr.getSessionUser(session);
    if (user == null) {
      requireLogin(req, (HttpServletResponse) response, session);
    } else {
      chain.doFilter(request, response);
    }
  } else {
    throw new ServletException("Filter only applicable"
                               + " to HTTP and HTTPS requests.");
  }
}
```

If they are not, an exception is raised. If they are, then they are cast to the required interfaces, and the user's `HttpSession` object is retrieved from the request. The `getSessionUser()` method of the `UserSessionManager` singleton is then called upon to retrieve the user's corresponding `UserBean` instance for that session. If a `UserBean` object is present, then access to the requested resource is granted by calling the `FilterChain` parameter's `doFilter()` method, passing it the request and response objects originally passed to the filter itself. Control then passes to the next item in the chain, which will either be another filter or the resource that was originally requested.

If the required `UserBean` instance is not present in the user's session, the filter will instead call its `requireLogin()` method, defined as follows:

```
private void requireLogin (HttpServletRequest request,
                           HttpServletResponse response,
                           HttpSession session)
  throws IOException {
  StringBuffer buffer = request.getRequestURL();
  String query = request.getQueryString();
  if (query != null) {
    buffer.append('?');
    buffer.append(query);
  }
  sessionMgr.setSessionLoginTarget(session, buffer.toString());
  UserSessionManager.doRedirect(request, response, loginPage);
}
```

The `requireLogin()` method has three tasks. First, it reconstructs the URL which the user was trying to reach, including any query parameters (i.e., any request parameters passed in as part of the URL, via the HTTP GET method). This URL is then stored in the user's session as the logon target, via the `UserSessionManager` singleton's `setSessionLoginTarget()` method. That class's `doRedirect()` static method is then called upon to cause the user's browser to display the application's login form.

The full source code for the `AuthenticationFilter` class is presented in listing 13.17. As indicated there, the class also includes a definition of the `destroy()` method, as required by the `Filter` interface. Since this filter does not need to allocate any long-term resources, the body of its `destroy()` method is empty.

Listing 13.17 AuthenticationFilter class

```
package com.taglib.wdjsp.filters;
import javax.servlet. Filter;
import javax.servlet.FilterChain;
import javax.servlet.FilterConfig;
```

```
import javax.servlet.ServletRequest;
import javax.servlet.ServletResponse;
import javax.servlet.http.HttpServletRequest;
import javax.servlet.http.HttpServletResponse;
import javax.servlet.http.HttpSession;

import javax.servlet.ServletException;
import java.io.IOException;

public class AuthenticationFilter implements Filter {
  private String loginPage;
  private UserSessionManager sessionMgr;

  public AuthenticationFilter () { ... }
  public void init (FilterConfig config) throws ServletException { ... }
  public void doFilter (ServletRequest request, ServletResponse response,
                        FilterChain chain)
    throws IOException, ServletException {
    ...
  }
  private void requireLogin (HttpServletRequest request,
                             HttpServletResponse response,
                             HttpSession session)
    throws IOException {
    ...
  }
  public void destroy () {}
}
```

Just as the content pages have no direct knowledge of the filter that will be applied to them in order to implement access control, the filter itself has no direct knowledge of the resources to which it will be applied. The only JSP page it knows anything about is the login page, and even then the location of this page is provided via an initialization parameter to provide maximum flexibility. The ability to keep the functionality of the filter completely separate from the functionality of the application's other resources improves the reusability of both, and leads to greater maintainability and more flexible deployment of applications that leverage this approach.

13.4.2 Role filter

The implementation of the role filter is very similar to that of the authentication filter. One minor difference is that its class, `com.taglib.wdjsp.filters.RoleFilter`, has three instance variables rather than just two:

```
public class RoleFilter implements Filter {
  private String role, denyPage;
  private UserSessionManager sessionMgr;
```

```
  public RoleFilter () { sessionMgr = UserSessionManager.getInstance(); }
  ...
}
```

As was the case for the `AuthenticationFilter` class, this class's `sessionMgr` instance variable holds a reference to the `UserSessionManager` singleton and is initialized in the filter's constructor. The other two instance variables, `role` and `denyPage`, get their values from like-named initialization parameters, via the class's `init()` method:

```
public void init (FilterConfig config) throws ServletException {
  role = config.getInitParameter("role");
  if (role == null)
    throw new ServletException("The role init parameter"
                               + " must be specified.");
  denyPage = config.getInitParameter("denyPage");
  if (denyPage == null)
    throw new ServletException("The denyPage init parameter"
                               + " must be specified.");
}
```

The `role` instance variable stores the name of the role which the filter is to restrict access to, while the `denyPage` instance variable stores the location of the resource to be displayed to users who attempt to access a resource protected by this filter but do not have the required role. An exception is thrown if either of the corresponding initialization parameters is not specified.

Enforcement of role-based security is performed by the filter's `doFilter()` method, defined as follows:

```
public void doFilter (ServletRequest request, ServletResponse response,
                      FilterChain chain)
  throws IOException, ServletException {
  if (request instanceof HttpServletRequest
      && response instanceof HttpServletResponse) {
    HttpServletRequest req = (HttpServletRequest) request;
    HttpSession session = req.getSession(true);
    UserBean user = sessionMgr.getSessionUser(session);
    if ((user != null) && user.hasRole(role)) {
      chain.doFilter(request, response);
    } else {
      HttpServletResponse resp = (HttpServletResponse) response;
      UserSessionManager.doRedirect(req, resp, denyPage);
    }
  } else {
    throw new ServletException("Filter only applicable"
                               + " to HTTP and HTTPS requests.");
  }
}
```

Like its counterpart in the `AuthenticationFilter` class, this method's interaction with the user's session requires that the filter only be applied to HTTP requests and responses. This method's first step, then, is to make sure that the request and response instances passed in as its first two parameters are of the appropriate types. If not, an exception is raised.

If the request and response objects are of the required types, the cast operator is applied to allow the user's session to be retrieved from the request. The `getSessionUser()` method of the `UserSessionManager` singleton is then called to retrieve the `UserBean` instance for the user. If a `UserBean` object is present, its `hasRole()` method is called to determine whether or not the user has been assigned the role named in the filter's `role` instance variable. If so, the `doFilter()` method of the `FilterChain` object provided as the method's third parameter is called in order to continue processing the request. If not, the user is redirected to the location specified by the filter's `denyPage` instance variable, using the `doRedirect()` method of the `UserSessionManager` class.

The filter class's remaining method is `destroy()`. It is required to implement this method by the `Filter` interface, but because it allocates no long-term resources, this method performs no operations. This method, as well as abbreviated versions of the `RoleFilter` class's other methods, is presented in listing 13.18.

Listing 13.18 RoleFilter class

```
package com.taglib.wdjsp.filters;
import javax.servlet.Filter;
import javax.servlet.FilterChain;
import javax.servlet.FilterConfig;
import javax.servlet.ServletRequest;
import javax.servlet.ServletResponse;
import javax.servlet.http.HttpServletRequest;
import javax.servlet.http.HttpServletResponse;
import javax.servlet.http.HttpSession;

import javax.servlet.ServletException;
import java.io.IOException;

public class RoleFilter implements Filter {
  private String role, denyPage;
  private UserSessionManager sessionMgr;

  public RoleFilter () { ... }
  public void init (FilterConfig config) throws ServletException { ... }
  public void doFilter (ServletRequest request, ServletResponse response,
                        FilterChain chain)
    throws IOException, ServletException {
    ...
```

```
    }
    public void destroy () {}
}
```

Note that, since there are three different resources (i.e., the departmental home pages) to be restricted to three different roles, the application will have to create three different instances of the `RoleFilter` class. This allows each instance to have a different value for its `role` instance variable, and to be mapped to a different resource. (The mapping of filters to application resources is covered in the next chapter.) In contrast, only a single instance of the `AuthenticationFilter` class is required, since only one setting is needed for its `loginPage` instance variable.

The final element in the implementation of the role-based security requirement is the application's access denial page, the `denied.jsp` page located in the secure subdirectory of the filters directory. This is the resource that will be displayed when a user who has not been assigned the required role attempts to access a resource protected by the role filter. The source code for this JSP page, which leverages the navigational header page introduced earlier in the chapter, is presented in listing 13.19, and a representative screen shot appears in figure 13.9. Although each of the required `RoleFilter` instances has its own value for the `role` instance variable, each can share this single access denial page as the value for each of their `denyPage` instance variables.

Listing 13.19 denied.jsp

```
<html>
<head><title>Access Denied</title></head>

<body>
<jsp:include page="header.jsp" flush="false"/>

<h1>Access Denied</h1>

<font color="red">
<p>
The <b><jsp:getProperty name="user" property="username"/></b> account
is not authorized to access the requested resource.<br>
Please make another selection.
</p>

</body>
</html>
```

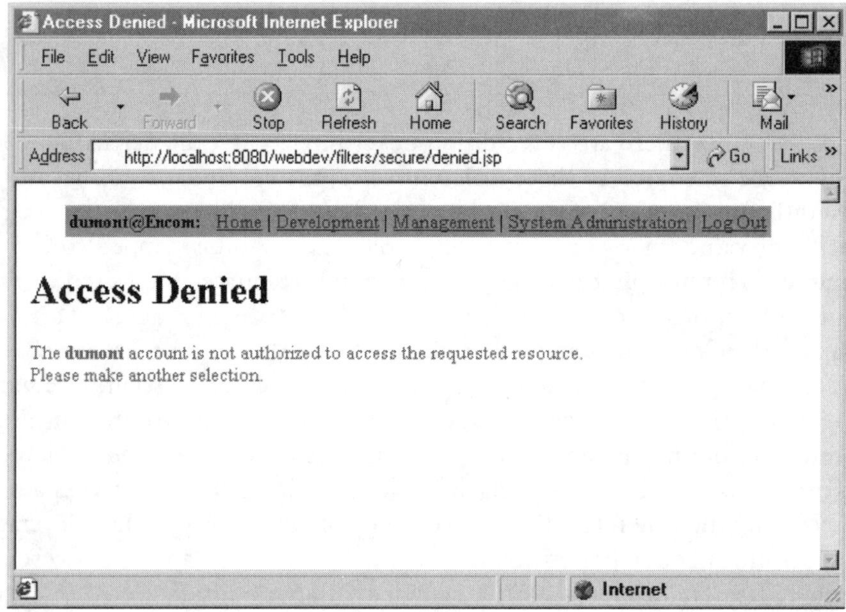

Figure 13.9 The access denial page

13.5 Logging listener

The authentication and role filters, when applied to the application's resources as illustrated in 13.2, implement all of the access control requirements described earlier in the chapter. The last of the desired enhancements to the original application is the addition of logging features. As was the case for the implementation of access control via the two filter classes, this will be accomplished without making any changes to the existing code, including that of the two filters.

The logging functionality will be implemented by means of a life-cycle event listener named `com.taglib.wdjsp.filters.LoginSessionListener`. Given that a user's logon status is represented by the presence or absence of a session attribute named `user` holding an instance of the `UserBean` class, monitoring that status is most easily accomplished by implementing the `HttpSessionAttributeListener` interface. (This monitoring could also be accomplished using the `HttpSessionBinding-Listener` interface, but that would necessitate modifications to the `UserBean` class, which we would prefer to avoid. The `HttpSessionAttributeListener` interface allows us to accomplish our goals without adding web-specific code to that class.) As a debugging aid, we will also have our new listener class implement the `HttpSessionListener` interface, so that we can monitor session creation and destruction.

13.5.1 *HttpSessionListener methods*

For this `HttpSessionListener` interface, two methods must be defined: The first, `sessionCreated()`, is defined as follows:

```
public void sessionCreated (HttpSessionEvent event) {
  HttpSession session = event.getSession();
  System.out.println(new Date().toString() + ": session created"
                     + " (" + session.getId() + ")");
}
```

This method retrieves the newly created session from the event passed in as the method's sole parameter, and then prints a log message containing a timestamp and the ID of the new session. (To keep things simple for this example, all logging messages are printed to the `System.out` output stream. In practice, a dedicated log file for all messages related to access control would be preferable.)

The other method required by this interface, `sessionDestroyed()`, is defined similarly:

```
public void sessionDestroyed (HttpSessionEvent event) {
  HttpSession session = event.getSession();
  System.out.println(new Date().toString() + ": session destroyed"
                     + " (" + session.getId() + ")");
}
```

This method's only significant difference from the `sessionCreated()` method is the wording of its log message.

13.5.2 *HttpSessionAttributeListener methods*

Three methods must be defined in order to implement the `HttpSessionAttributeListener`: interface: `attributeAdded()`, `attributeReplaced()`, and `attributeRemoved()`. The first of these is defined as follows:

```
public void attributeAdded (HttpSessionBindingEvent event) {
  if (event.getName().equals(UserSessionManager.SESSION_USER_ATTRIBUTE)) {
    UserBean user = (UserBean) event.getValue();
    HttpSession session = event.getSession();
    System.out.println(new Date().toString()
                       + ": session login for " + user.getUsername()
                       + " (" + session.getId() + ")");
  }
}
```

First, the name of the newly added attribute is extracted from the event via its `getName()` method. If the attribute's name matches that used by the `UserSessionManager` singleton for storing the `UserBean` instance, then that instance is retrieved from the session and used to print a logon message that includes a timestamp, the username associated with that `UserBean`, and the session ID. Since this specific attribute is only added to the session by the logon servlet, the logging message will only be produced while the user is in the process of logging on. Of course, this is exactly when we want the message to be produced.

An individual user's `UserBean` object is never replaced within a session (the user only logs in once), so no method body is required for the `LoginSessionListener` class's `attributeReplaced()` method (see listing 13.20).

The listener's `attributeRemoved()` method is very similar in structure to its `attributeAdded()` method:

```
public void attributeRemoved (HttpSessionBindingEvent event) {
  if (event.getName().equals(UserSessionManager.SESSION_USER_ATTRIBUTE)) {
    UserBean user = (UserBean) event.getValue();
    HttpSession session = event.getSession();
    System.out.println(new Date().toString()
                       + ": session "
                       + (isTimedOut(session) ? "timeout" : "logout")
                       + " for " + user.getUsername()
                       + " (" + session.getId() + ")");
  }
}
```

Again, the name of the removed attribute is retrieved from the event, and checked against the attribute name used to store the `UserBean` object in the user's session. If they match, an appropriate log message is generated.

In this case, however, two different circumstances may be responsible for the attribute removal event. If the user logs out of the application via the logout form, the logout servlet will call the `removeSessionUser()` method of the `UserSessionManager` singleton, thereby explicitly removing the attribute holding the `UserBean` instance. If the user neglects to log out, eventually the session will expire. As part of the session expiration process, the container will automatically remove all of the attributes stored in the session.

In order to distinguish between these two possible causes, the `attributeRemoved()` method calls a utility method named `isTimedOut()`. This method's task is to determine whether the session has expired (i.e., timed out) or the user logged out, and is defined as follows:

```
private boolean isTimedOut (HttpSession session) {
  try {
```

```
    long idle = new Date().getTime() - session.getLastAccessedTime();
    return idle > (session.getMaxInactiveInterval() * 1000);
  }
  catch (IllegalStateException e) { return true; }
}
```

First, this method determines how long the session provided as its sole parameter has been idle, by subtracting the time it was last accessed from the current time. This value, in milliseconds, is compared against the session's expiration period, as retrieved via its `getMaxInactiveInterval()` method, which must be multiplied by 1,000 in order to convert from seconds to milliseconds. If the idle period is greater than the expiration period, then the session must have timed out. If not, the user must have explicitly logged out.

Upon expiring a session, however, the container may refuse to allow methods such as `getLastAccessedTime()` and `getMaxInactiveInterval()` to be called. If so, attempts to call those methods will result in an `IllegalStateException`. For this reason, the `isTimedOut()` method includes a `try/catch` block for intercepting these exceptions. If such an exception is caught, the session can be presumed to have timed out, and the method will therefore return a value of `true`.

Listing 13.20 LoginSessionListener class

```
package com.taglib.wdjsp.filters;
import javax.servlet.http.HttpSession;
import javax.servlet.http.HttpSessionEvent;
import javax.servlet.http.HttpSessionListener;
import javax.servlet.http.HttpSessionBindingEvent;
import javax.servlet.http.HttpSessionAttributeListener;
import java.util.Date;

public class LoginSessionListener
  implements HttpSessionListener, HttpSessionAttributeListener {

  public void sessionCreated (HttpSessionEvent event) { ... }
  public void sessionDestroyed (HttpSessionEvent event) { ... }

  public void attributeAdded (HttpSessionBindingEvent event) { ... }
  public void attributeReplaced (HttpSessionBindingEvent event) {}
  public void attributeRemoved (HttpSessionBindingEvent event) { ... }

  private boolean isTimedOut (HttpSession session) { ... }
}
```

The resulting source code of the `LoginSessionListener` class (in abbreviated form) is presented in listing 13.20. A transcript of representative output from the listener appears in listing 13.21.

Listing 13.21 LoginSessionListener output

```
package com.taglib.wdjsp.filters;
Mon Jul 02 23:45:37 CDT 2001: session created (9910339382D7D242C44545C0357)
Mon Jul 02 23:45:53 CDT 2001: session login for sark
   (9910339382D7D242C44545C0357)
Mon Jul 02 23:46:16 CDT 2001: session logout for sark
   (9910339382D7D242C44545C0357)
Mon Jul 02 23:46:22 CDT 2001: session created (39D1C293B7D5D2D751F5D417826)
Mon Jul 02 23:46:38 CDT 2001: session login for dumont
   (39D1C293B7D5D2D751F5D417826)
Mon Jul 02 23:48:55 CDT 2001: session created (A4611187A5F480C4B121C477F14)
Mon Jul 02 23:49:07 CDT 2001: session login for yori
   (A4611187A5F480C4B121C477F14)
Mon Jul 02 23:49:16 CDT 2001: session logout for yori
   (A4611187A5F480C4B121C477F14)
Tue Jul 03 00:01:41 CDT 2001: session destroyed (9910339382D7D242C44545C0357)
Tue Jul 03 00:01:41 CDT 2001: session timeout for dumont
   (39D1C293B7D5D2D751F5D417826)
Tue Jul 03 00:01:41 CDT 2001: session destroyed (39D1C293B7D5D2D751F5D417826)
Tue Jul 03 00:04:41 CDT 2001: session destroyed (A4611187A5F480C4B121C477F14)
```

13.6 Content filter

The two filters presented earlier in this chapter are focused on access control. Access to specific resources is filtered according to the credentials (or lack thereof) associated with the user submitting the request.

As indicated in chapter 12, however, filters can also be used to manipulate the content provided by a resource. This is typically accomplished by means of request and/or response wrappers, for which the examples presented thus far have not had any need. In order to demonstrate this second type of filter, as well as the use of wrapper classes, we will close the chapter with the presentation of one final filter, embodied in the `com.taglib.wdjsp.filters.StringReplaceFilter` class.

As its name suggests, this filter may be used to replace one string with another in the content associated with a response. Without making any changes to the original documents of the application, occurrences of a specified string within the body of a response will be translated into occurrences of the specified replacement text. If, for example, the Encom Corporation were to change its name, the string replacement filter could be used to immediately replace all occurrences of the original name with the new corporate moniker. Such an effect could readily be achieved by mapping an instance of the `StringReplaceFilter` class to all of the resources comprising the application, as indicated in figure 13.10.

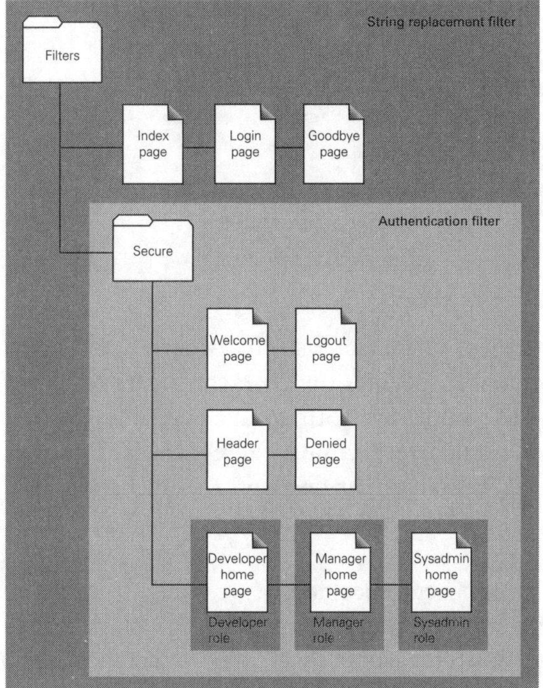

Figure 13.10 Final site map, including the string replacement filter

The string replacement filter operates by placing a wrapper around the response it passes down the filter chain. This wrapper introduces a second, temporary output stream to which the remaining items in the chain, including the resource originally requested, will write their content. When control returns to the filter after the response has been written, the contents of this temporary output stream are copied in the output stream of the response originally passed to the result, substituting all occurrences of a given string with the specified replacement string. The response wrapper and its temporary output stream are implemented via a pair of inner classes named `StringReplaceResponse` and `TmpServletOutputStream`, respectively.

13.6.1 Filter methods

Two instance variables are defined for the `StringReplaceFilter` class, both of whose values are set in the class's `init()` method.

```
public class StringReplaceFilter implements Filter {
  private String from, to;
```

```
  public void init (FilterConfig config) throws ServletException {
    from = config.getInitParameter("from");
    if (from == null)
      throw new ServletException("The from init parameter"
                                 + " must be specified.");
    to = config.getInitParameter("to");
    if (to == null)
      throw new ServletException("The to init parameter"
                                 + " must be specified.");
  }
  ...
}
```

The `from` instance variable specifies the character string, occurrences of which are to be replaced. The `to` instance variable specifies the character string to be substituted in place of those occurrences. The values for both instance variables are provided by filter initialization parameters with corresponding names. Initialization parameter values are set in the application's deployment descriptor (see chapter 14), and are made available to the filter via the `FilterConfig` instance passed as the sole parameter to its `init()` method. A new `ServletException` is raised if a value for either of the initialization parameters has not been specified.

The filtering of response content is performed by the class's `doFilter()` method. As already described, this filter works by creating a wrapped response that diverts the output of the remaining items in the filter to a temporary output stream. The output is then copied to the output stream associated with the real response, performing the specified string replacement in the process.

For compatability with the other filters defined for this application, however, the filter must be careful to wrap HTTP responses via the `HttpResponseWrapper` class, rather than the more generic `ResponseWrapper` class. Rather than trying to handle both cases, this filter—like its predecessors—will restrict itself to working with only HTTP requests and responses. The first step in the `doFilter()` method, then, is to check the types of the request and response objects passed in as the method's first two parameters:

```
public void doFilter (ServletRequest request, ServletResponse response,
                      FilterChain chain)
  throws IOException, ServletException {
  if (request instanceof HttpServletRequest
      && response instanceof HttpServletResponse) {
    HttpServletResponse resp = (HttpServletResponse) response;
    StringReplaceResponse wrappedResponse = new StringReplaceResponse(resp);
    chain.doFilter(request, wrappedResponse);
    transferData(wrappedResponse, resp);
  } else {
```

```
      throw new ServletException("Filter only applicable"
                                 + " to HTTP and HTTPS requests.");
    }
  }
```

An exception is raised if the request and response are not of the required types. Otherwise, the response is cast to the required class and then provided as the sole parameter for the wrapped response's constructor.

The original request and the wrapped response are then passed to the filter chain's `doFilter()` method, to allow the remaining items in the chain to handle the request. After these items have finished processing the request/response pair, control will be returned to the string replacement filter's `doFilter()` method, which then calls its `transferData()` private method to copy the output stored by the wrapped response to the output stream of the original response.

NOTE As pointed out in chapter 12, the original response passed in as the second parameter to the filter's `doFilter()` method may itself have been wrapped by another filter that preceded it in the chain. A response wrapper can wrap another response wrapper, just as easily as it can wrap a true response.

The inner workings of the `transferData()` method are dependent upon the two inner classes used to implement the wrapped response and its output stream. For this reason, we will first examine the details of those inner classes before reviewing the remaining methods of the `StringReplaceFilter` class.

13.6.2 Response wrapper inner class

The response wrapper used by the `StringReplaceFilter` class is implemented as an inner class named `StringReplaceResponse` as follows:

```
private class StringReplaceResponse extends HttpServletResponseWrapper {
  TmpServletOutputStream surrogate = new TmpServletOutputStream();

  private StringReplaceResponse (HttpServletResponse response) {
    super(response);
  }
  public ServletOutputStream getOutputStream ()
    throws java.io.IOException {
    return surrogate;
  }
  public PrintWriter getWriter ()
    throws java.io.IOException {
    return new PrintWriter(new OutputStreamWriter(surrogate));
  }
}
```

The wrapper class extends the `HttpServletResponseWrapper` base class present in chapter 12, and defines one instance variable and three methods.

The `surrogate` instance variable holds an instance of the filter's other inner class, `TmpServletOutputStream`. The response wrapper overrides the `getOutputStream()` and `getWriter()` methods of the `javax.servlet.ServletResponse` class to return this surrogate output stream (wrapped in a `java.io.PrintWriter` instance in the case of the latter method) to all items that follow the `StringReplaceFilter` in the filter chain. By overriding these two methods, all response output generated by those items will be written to this surrogate stream, rather than the output stream associated with the response object originally passed to the filter.

The other method defined by this class is its constructor, which takes that original response object as its parameter and passes it to the constructor of its `HttpServletResponseWrapper` superclass. As a result, all `HttpServletResponse` methods except for `getOutputStream()` and `getWriter()` will automatically be delegated to the original response.

13.6.3 Output stream inner class

The `TmpServletOutputStream` inner class implements the temporary stream to which subsequent filters and resources in the filter chain will write their output. For compatibility with the `ServletResponse` class's `getOutputStream()` method, this class is a subclass of the `javax.servlet.ServletOutputStream` class, and is defined as follows:

```
private class TmpServletOutputStream extends ServletOutputStream {
  private ByteArrayOutputStream baos = new ByteArrayOutputStream(1024);

  public void write (int b) { baos.write(b); }
  public void write (byte[] b, int off, int len) {
    baos.write(b, off, len);
  }

  private ByteArrayInputStream getInputStream () {
    return new ByteArrayInputStream(baos.toByteArray());
  }
}
```

Implementing an output stream is basically a matter of providing definitions for the two `write()` methods indicated in the definition of the `TmpServletOutputStream` class. The default implementations for all of the other output methods defined by the `java.io.OutputStream` base class ultimately call one of these two methods, so a subclass that defines both—and provides some place for the output to go—will have sufficient functionality to act as a Java output stream.

In the case of `TmpServletOutputStream`, an instance of the `java.io.ByteArrayOutputStream` class serves as the destination for all output, and the inner class's two `write()` methods delegate to this `ByteArrayOutputStream` instance. This instance provides an in-memory byte array (set in its constructor to an initial size of 1 KB) for storing all data written to the `TmpServletOutputStream` object.

Such data can be subsequently read from that byte array via the `java.io.ByteArrayInputStream` instance returned by the inner class's `getInputStream()` method. This method first retrieves the output written to the `ByteArrayOutputStream` by calling the output stream's `toByteArray()` method, and then creates an input stream for reading the data directly from the resulting byte array.

13.6.4 More filter methods

We are now ready to return to the methods of the top-level filter class, `StringReplaceFilter`. As indicated in the discussion of the filter's `doFilter()` method, `transferData()` is a private method defined by the filter that copies the data stored in a wrapped response to the output stream of another response:

```
private void transferData (StringReplaceResponse fromResponse,
                           HttpServletResponse toResponse)
  throws IOException {
  ByteArrayInputStream bais = fromResponse.surrogate.getInputStream();
  BufferedReader reader =
    new BufferedReader(new InputStreamReader(bais));
  ServletOutputStream original = toResponse.getOutputStream();
  PrintWriter writer =
    new PrintWriter(new OutputStreamWriter(original));
  String line;
  while ((line = reader.readLine()) != null) {
    writer.println(doReplacement(line));
  }
  writer.close();
  reader.close();
}
```

Since the call to `transferData()` occurs after the filter chain's `doFilter()` method is called, the output generated by the requested resource and any intervening filters will have already been written to the temporary output stream associated with the response wrapper. The first action taken by the `transferData()` method, then, is to call the `getInputStream()` method of the wrapper's surrogate output stream so that the data that has been written to it can be read. In order to read this data one line at a time, the `ByteArrayInputStream` returned by the `getInputStream()` method is wrapped in an instance of the `java.io.BufferedReader` class. (This is accomplished by means of an intermediate `java.io.InputStreamReader` class to bridge the gap between Java's byte-oriented input stream classes and its character-oriented reader classes.) For similar reasons, the `ServletOutputStream` instance associated with the original request object is wrapped in an instance of the `java.io.PrintWriter` class.

The method then reads from the `BufferedReader`, one line at a time, until all of the data is consumed (i.e., until the reader's `readLine()` method returns null). Each line is then written to the `PrintWriter` representing the original request object's output stream, after being processed by the filter's `doReplacement()` utility method. The reader and writer are then closed.

The job of the `doReplacement()` utility method is to perform text substituion for the filter on a single `String` object, passed in as a parameter to the method. Within that `String` instance, all occurrences of the character string stored in the filter's `from` instance variable are replaced by the character string stored in the filter's `to` instance variable. The method is defined as follows:

```
private String doReplacement (String s) {
    int start = s.indexOf(from);
    if (start < 0) {
      return s;
    } else {
      return s.substring(0, start) + to
        + doReplacement(s.substring(start + from.length()));
    }
  }
```

The method operates by locating the first occurrence of `from` in the string passed in as the method's parameter. If none is found, the string parameter is returned unmodified. If an occurrence of `from` is found, a new string in constructed to serve as the return value of the `doReplacement()` method. This return value is created by appending the replacement text in the `to` instance variable to the portion of the string that precedes the occurrence of `from`. Finally, the result of applying the `doReplacement()` method to the remainder of the string is also appended to the return value. This recursive call to `doReplacement()` ensures that any additional occurrences of `from` are also replaced.

In addition to the four methods already presented, the filter class defines a default constructor and a `destroy()` method, as indicated in listing 13.22. Because this filter allocates no long-term resources, however, both of these methods do nothing.

Listing 13.22 StringReplaceFilter class

```
package com.taglib.wdjsp.filters;
import javax.servlet.Filter;
import javax.servlet.FilterChain;
import javax.servlet.FilterConfig;
import javax.servlet.ServletRequest;
import javax.servlet.ServletResponse;
import javax.servlet.http.HttpServletRequest;
import javax.servlet.http.HttpServletResponse;
import javax.servlet.http.HttpServletResponseWrapper;
import javax.servlet.ServletOutputStream;

import java.io.OutputStream;
import java.io.ByteArrayOutputStream;
import java.io.ByteArrayInputStream;
import java.io.InputStreamReader;
import java.io.BufferedReader;
import java.io.OutputStreamWriter;
import java.io.PrintWriter;

import javax.servlet.ServletException;
import java.io.IOException;

public class StringReplaceFilter implements Filter {
  private String from, to;

  public StringReplaceFilter () {}
  public void init (FilterConfig config) throws ServletException { ... }
  public void doFilter (ServletRequest request, ServletResponse response,
                        FilterChain chain)
    throws IOException, ServletException {
    ...
  }
  public void destroy () {}
  private void transferData (StringReplaceResponse fromResponse,
                             HttpServletResponse toResponse)
    throws IOException {
    ...
  }
  private String doReplacement (String s) { ... }

  private class StringReplaceResponse extends
    HttpServletResponseWrapper {
    ...
  }

  private class TmpServletOutputStream extends ServletOutputStream { ... }
}
```

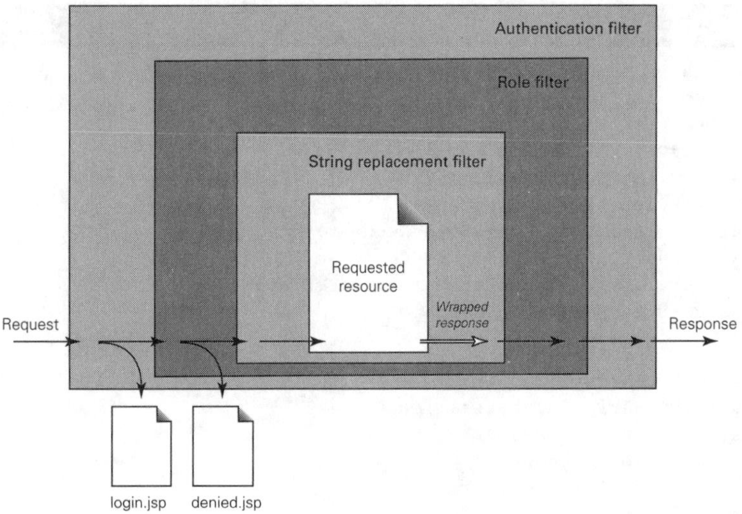

Figure 13.11 Default page for the filters directory, after string replacement

13.6.5 Filter results

Upon adding this filter to the other two being used by the intranet application, the overall flow of requests and responses for resources to which all three filters have been mapped is as depicted in figure 13.11. First, requests are passed to the authentication filter to check whether or not the user has logged on. Users who have not been authenticated are redirected to the logon page, `login.jsp`.

If the user is logged on, the request is then passed to the role filter. This filter examines the roles that have been assigned to the user, attempting to find a match for the filter's own role. Note that roles can only be checked after the user has logged on and thus been identified. It is therefore criticial that the role filter follow the authentication filter in the filter chain. If the current user has been assigned the required role, the request is passed to the next item in the filter chain. If not, the user is redirected to the access denial page, `denied.jsp`.

Since additional resources (in the form of a `ByteArrayOutputStream`) must be allocated in order to run the string replacement filter, it is best to place this filter last in the filter chain. In this way, the overhead associated with allocating the `ByteArrayOutputStream` can be avoided until it is clear that those resources will be required. When run, this filter passes a wrapped response to the next item in the filter chain which, in this case, will be the resource that was originally requested. This

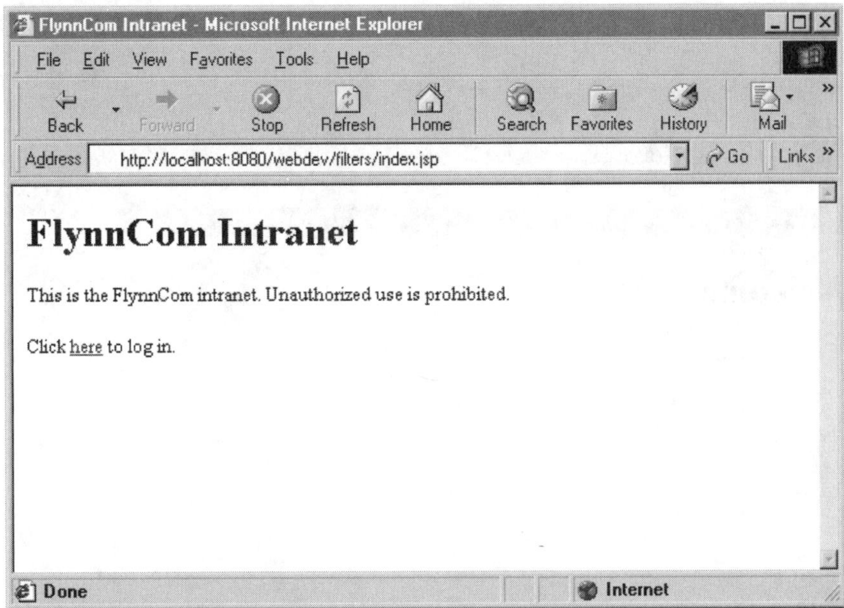

Figure 13.12 Default page for the filters directory, after string replacement

resource writes its content to the wrapped response, and control is passed back to the string replacement filter.

The filter then unwraps the response, performing the string substitution in the process. The other two filters need take no special action during this phase of the processing, so the unwrapped response is ultimately returned to the user.

Representative results of applying this filter to the intranet sample application, replacing all occurrences of the name Encom with the alternative name Flynncom, are depicted in figures 13.12–13.14. As indicated in figures 13.13 and 13.14, note that the contents of the header page, incorporated via the `<jsp:include>` action, are also subject to string replacement.

13.6.6 Other content filters

The same basic approach used to implement `StringReplaceFilter` can also be applied to other filters for manipulating content. The actions taken by this class's `doFilter()` method can be summarized as follows:

1. Creates a response wrapper which provides temporary storage for all output intended for the original response.

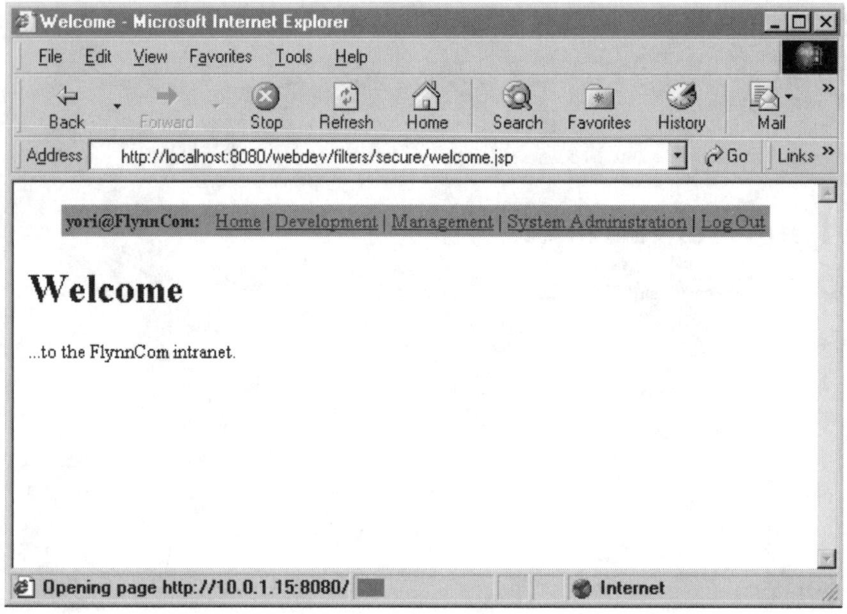

Figure 13.13 The welcome page, after string replacement

2. Passes the wrapped response to the filter chain for further processing.
3. When control returns to the filter, extracts the chain's output from temporary storage, transforms it, and writes the transformed output to the output stream associated with the original response.

The only aspect which will vary from one filter to the next is the type of transformation to be applied. For `StringReplaceFilter`, this transformation is content substitution.

A wide range of other transformations can be imagined. For example, a filter could be used to transform dynamically generated XML (such as a Simple Object Access Protocol [SOAP] or XML-RPC [remote procedure call] response) into a more user-friendly presentation format. For example, the filter could examine the `User-Agent:` or `Accept:` header of a request in order to select an appropriate XSLT style sheet for displaying the dynamic content. If the header indicates a web browser, a style sheet for rendering HTML might be selected. If the header indicates a Wireless Application Protocol (WAP) browser, a style sheet for rendering WML would be chosen instead. The filter would apply the selected XSLT stylesheet to the

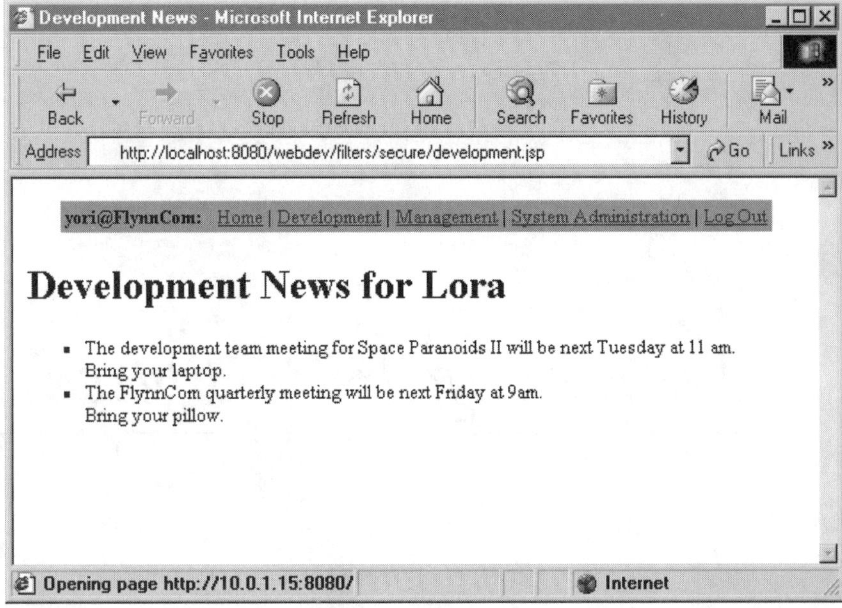

Figure 13.14 The development home page, after string replacement

generated XML stored by the response wrapper, and write the results to the output stream associated with the original response.

Similarly, consider the case of a PNG image generated dynamically by a servlet (for example, a bar chart depicting the current load on the server). As browser support for the PNG image format is relatively new, a filter could be wrapped around this servlet to determine which image formats (GIF, JPEG, etc.) are supported by the browser making the request, by examining the `Accept:` header supplied with that request. For browsers that don't support the PNG format, the filter could translate the image into an alternate, supported format on the fly. In this case, binary streams would be required rather than the character-oriented streams more common in JSP applications (i.e., the `java.io.Reader` and `java.io.Writer` subclasses, such as used in the `transferData()` method), but the underlying approach is the same.

14 Deploying JSP applications

This chapter covers

- Web application archives
- Components of WAR files
- Application deployment descriptors
- Developing for deployment

Regardless of the components or architecture you have selected for your JSP development, a web-based application can't be used until it has been successfully deployed on a web server. Whereas desktop applications are often packaged with customized installation programs that walk the user through the required configuration and deployment steps, the installation of applications targeted toward the server environment has historically been somewhat less user-friendly.

In an effort to remedy this situation, at least for Java-based web applications, the Servlet and JSP specifications support the bundling of an application's files into a single *web archive*, which can be deployed as is to a Java-enabled web server. All of the resources required for a given web application—JSP files and servlets, as well as associated content such as HTML documents, images, applets, and JavaBeans—are deposited in a web archive, along with an XML-based configuration file. This archive can then be placed into a designated directory on the web server and, after customizing the included configuration file as necessary, the associated application is run straight from the archive file. When requests are received for URLs corresponding to the contents of the archive, the JSP container extracts those resources as needed. Processing then resumes as if the extracted resources were part of the server's normal document hierarchy.

14.1 This means WAR

Web archives take the form of JAR files, the standard file archive format for the Java platform. Each web archive also contains a special descriptor file describing how the files in the archive are used to implement a web-based application. So that tools can easily distinguish between web archives and other JAR files, web archives are assigned the extension .war, and for this reason are commonly referred to as WAR files.

As mentioned in chapters 5 and 6, a Java web application is mapped to a directory hierarchy, rooted in a single top-level directory. The URLs for all of the elements of the application will therefore all begin with the same initial directory, the name of which also serves as the name of the application. In an application named clu, for example, its resources are all accessed in or below a top-level directory named clu, using URLs such as http://server/clu/index.jsp, http://server/clu/servlet/dashboard, and http://server/clu/images/reticle.gif.

As also described in chapter 6, all Java-based resources in an application (i.e., servlets and JSPs) share the same `javax.servlet.ServletContext` instance, which is made available to the application's JSP pages via the `application` implicit object. This object, by means of the standard attribute methods outlined in table 6.2, provides a simple data-sharing mechanism for use within an application, which serves as the foundation for storing objects (e.g., beans) with `application` scope.

WAR files are designed to store the contents of a single application. The hypothetical clu application introduced previously would therefore be stored in a web archive named clu.war. By registering the WAR file with the JSP container, all of the resources stored in that file become available for use by the container and, by extension, end users accessing the associated HTTP server.

NOTE The process by which WAR files are registered is currently container-specific. Some containers provide graphical tools for dragging and dropping new web applications, while others have designated directories into which WAR files must be copied in order to be automatically deployed. Still others rely on the editing of a container-specific configuration file, and many support a combination of these approaches.

14.1.1 WAR is XML

In addition to its web application content, a WAR file also contains a deployment descriptor file—formally referred to as the Web Application Descriptor file—that specifies how that content is used to provide the corresponding application functionality. For example, the descriptor file itemizes the servlets contained in an application, providing any associated initialization parameters or URL mappings. A web application can also contain JSP pages that have already been compiled into servlets, and the descriptor file is where the JSP container looks to find the original URLs for such pages.

TIP By deploying JSP pages as precompiled servlets, you can avoid the run-time overhead of compiling a page the first time it is requested by an end user. It also eliminates the need to include a Java compiler on the production web server, thereby reducing the memory footprint for the server's JVM. Techniques for JSP precompilation are described later in this chapter.

The descriptor file is named web.xml, and resides in a special top-level directory of the WAR file named WEB-INF. This subdirectory is an analog of the META-INF subdirectory found in all JAR files, containing *metainformation* about the archive itself. An archive serves as a repository of information; the data it stores about itself is therefore considered metainformation, in the sense that it is information about information. In a similar vein, the WEB-INF subdirectory contains information about how the contents of the repository are deployed via the Web, with the web.xml file serving as the central configuration file for the archive.

As its file extension suggests, the markup language for the data in the web.xml file is XML. For example, the contents of a basic deployment descriptor file for the intranet example presented in the previous chapter would take the following form:

```
<?xml version="1.0" encoding="ISO-8859-1" ?>
<!DOCTYPE web-app PUBLIC
          "-//Sun Microsystems, Inc.//DTD Web Application 2.3//EN"
          "http://java.sun.com/j2ee/dtds/web-app_2.3.dtd">
<web-app>
  <display-name>Encom Intranet</display-name>
  <filter>
    <filter-name>authentication</filter-name>
    <filter-class>
      com.taglib.wdjsp.filters.AuthenticationFilter</filter-class>
    <init-param>
      <param-name>loginPage</param-name>
      <param-value>/filters/login.jsp</param-value>
    </init-param>
  </filter>
  <filter>
    <filter-name>devRole</filter-name>
    <filter-class>com.taglib.wdjsp.filters.RoleFilter</filter-class>
    <init-param>
      <param-name>role</param-name>
      <param-value>dev</param-value>
    </init-param>
    <init-param>
      <param-name>denyPage</param-name>
      <param-value>/filters/secure/denied.jsp</param-value>
    </init-param>
  </filter>
  <filter>
    <filter-name>mgrRole</filter-name>
    <filter-class>com.taglib.wdjsp.filters.RoleFilter</filter-class>
    <init-param>
      <param-name>role</param-name>
      <param-value>mgr</param-value>
    </init-param>
    <init-param>
      <param-name>denyPage</param-name>
      <param-value>/filters/secure/denied.jsp</param-value>
    </init-param>
  </filter>
  <filter>
    <filter-name>adminRole</filter-name>
    <filter-class>com.taglib.wdjsp.filters.RoleFilter</filter-class>
```

```
    <init-param>
      <param-name>role</param-name>
      <param-value>admin</param-value>
    </init-param>
    <init-param>
      <param-name>denyPage</param-name>
      <param-value>/filters/secure/denied.jsp</param-value>
    </init-param>
  </filter>
  <filter-mapping>
    <filter-name>authentication</filter-name>
    <url-pattern>/filters/secure/*</url-pattern>
  </filter-mapping>
  <filter-mapping>
    <filter-name>devRole</filter-name>
    <url-pattern>/filters/secure/development.jsp</url-pattern>
  </filter-mapping>
  <filter-mapping>
    <filter-name>mgrRole</filter-name>
    <url-pattern>/filters/secure/management.jsp</url-pattern>
  </filter-mapping>
  <filter-mapping>
    <filter-name>adminRole</filter-name>
    <url-pattern>/filters/secure/admin.jsp</url-pattern>
  </filter-mapping>
  <listener>
  <listener-class>com.taglib.wdjsp.filters.LoginSessionListener</listener-class>
  </listener>
  <servlet>
    <servlet-name>login</servlet-name>
    <servlet-class>com.taglib.wdjsp.filters.LoginServlet</servlet-class>
    <init-param>
      <param-name>userDataManager</param-name>
      <param-value>
        com.taglib.wdjsp.filters.SimpleUserDataManager
      <param-value>
    </init-param>
    <init-param>
      <param-name>loginPage</param-name>
      <param-value>/filters/login.jsp</param-value>
    </init-param>
    <init-param>
      <param-name>welcomePage</param-name>
      <param-value>/filters/secure/welcome.jsp</param-value>
    </init-param>
  </servlet>
  <servlet>
    <servlet-name>logout</servlet-name>
    <servlet-class>com.taglib.wdjsp.filters.LogoutServlet</servlet-class>
    <init-param>
```

```
      <param-name>goodbyePage</param-name>
      <param-value>/filters/goodbye.jsp</param-value>
    </init-param>
  </servlet>
  <servlet-mapping>
    <servlet-name>login</servlet-name>
    <url-pattern>/filters/login</url-pattern>
  </servlet-mapping>
  <servlet-mapping>
    <servlet-name>logout</servlet-name>
    <url-pattern>/filters/logout</url-pattern>
  </servlet-mapping>
</web-app>
```

The details of the entries in a web.xml file will be presented later in the chapter. This particular example indicates that the intranet web application contains four filters and two servlets, all of which are mapped to corresponding URL patterns, and one listener.

Note that this deployment descriptor says nothing about the JSP pages used by this application. One might infer that the application does not make use of JSP, but as we saw in chapter 13, this is definitely not the case. Instead, because JSP servlets are generated as needed and are automatically mapped to URLs based on their original file names, there is no need to specify configuration information for them in the web.xml file. As a result, the JSP container is able to gather all of the information it typically requires about an application's JSP pages by simply scanning the contents of its WAR file.

14.1.2 Waging WAR

Like most configuration files, even though it uses a human-readable format, the web.xml file is a bit awkward to work with. For this reason, most of the commercial application servers that include graphical tools for installing web applications usually include user-friendly tools for creating and maintaining them as well. In addition to allowing developers to graphically select class files and web content (JSP pages, HTML documents, image files, etc.) for inclusion in the application, such tools typically provide forms for specifying URL mappings and other configuration settings in order to construct the corresponding web.xml file automatically.

If your budget doesn't support investing in feature-rich application servers, however, you may find your platform of choice does not include any bundled "wizards" for constructing and deploying web applications. If this is the case, you will likely find it necessary to package your web application by hand, including the manual construction and editing of deployment descriptors. And even if you are using a JSP container that does have all the bells and whistles, you may choose not to use them. Integrating a graphical web application deployment tool into your existing source code control and build processes, for example, may prove not to be the right approach for your development organization.For these and other reasons, then, understanding the contents of a web.xml file and knowing how to construct WAR files manually are useful skills to have. To that end, the next section of this chapter focuses on the structure of WAR files and the entries which comprise an archive's `web.xml` deployment descriptor.

14.2 The art of WAR

Deploying a Java-based application, then, has two phases. First, all of the files used by an application are bundled, along with a web.xml deployment descriptor, into a WAR file. The packaging of an application is the responsibility of the development team. The second phase is the installation of the packaged application on the web server.

Because installation is a server-specific operation, our focus here will be on constructing the web archive. WAR files are meant to be portable between JSP containers. As such, their contents and those of the deployment descriptor are well-defined by the servlet and JSP specifications. In the sections to follow we will provide an overview of the WAR file format, and then describe the web.xml entries required to specify an application's servlets and JSP pages.

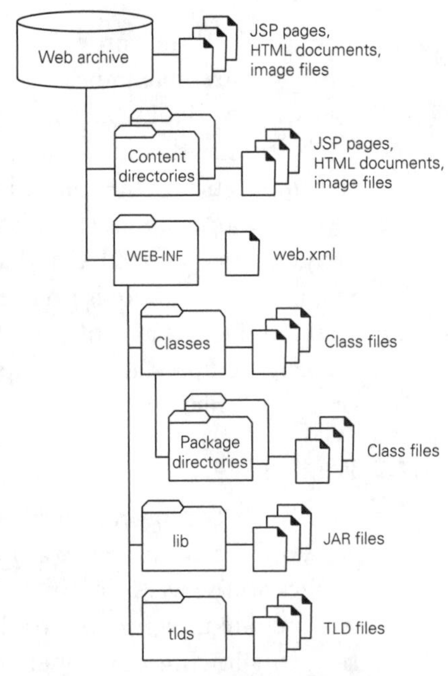

Figure 14.1 Contents of a WAR file for web application deployment

14.2.1 WAR materiel

As already described, a WAR (figure 14.1) file is essentially a JAR file that contains extra information allowing its contents to be deployed in a servlet or JSP container. This extra information is stored in the WAR file's top-level WEB-INF directory, which contains the archive's web.xml deployment descriptor, as well as two special subdirectories for storing Java classes.

The web-based content for an application can appear at the top-level of a web archive, or in arbitrary content directories and subdirectories. As indicated in figure 14.1, this content typically consists of JSP pages, HTML documents, and image files, but any file type that may be delivered over the web—including sound files, animations, portable documents, and Java applets—can be placed in a WAR file. That file will then be accessible from the web server to which the WAR file is deployed. Listing 14.1 is the source code for contents of an example WAR file.

Listing 14.1 Contents of an example WAR file, webdev.war

```
index.jsp
commontasks/error.jsp
filters/goodbye.jsp
filters/login.jsp
filters/index.jsp
filters/secure/admin.jsp
filters/secure/denied.jsp
filters/secure/development.jsp
filters/secure/header.jsp
filters/secure/logout.jsp
filters/secure/management.jsp
filters/secure/welcome.jsp
filters/secure/admin.jsp
images/logo.gif
images/icons/security.gif
images/icons/role.gif
images/edillinger.jsp
WEB-INF/web.xml
WEB-INF/classes/com/taglib/wdjsp/filters/AuthenticationFilter.class
WEB-INF/classes/com/taglib/wdjsp/filters/LoginServlet.class
WEB-INF/classes/com/taglib/wdjsp/filters/LoginSessionListener.class
WEB-INF/classes/com/taglib/wdjsp/filters/LogoutServlet.class
WEB-INF/classes/com/taglib/wdjsp/filters/RoleFilter.class
WEB-INF/classes/com/taglib/wdjsp/filters/SimpleUserBase.class
WEB-INF/classes/com/taglib/wdjsp/filters/SimpleUserDataManager.class
WEB-INF/classes/com/taglib/wdjsp/filters/UserBean.class
WEB-INF/classes/com/taglib/wdjsp/filters/UserDataManager.class
WEB-INF/classes/com/taglib/wdjsp/filters/UserSessionManager.class
WEB-INF/lib/mail.jar
WEB-INF/lib/activation.jar
WEB-INF/lib/mut.jar
WEB-INF/tlds/mut.tld
```

Content in a Java-based web application is accessed via a URL that begins with the name of the application. Consider, for example, an application named webdev that is packaged in a web archive named webdev.war with the contents in listing 14.1.

An end user accessing this application's index.jsp file would use a URL of the form http://server/webdev/index.jsp, in which the name of the application, webdev, provides the top-level directory for all URLs that reference the application's content. Directories and subdirectories are treated similarly. The URL for retrieving the image named security.gif, for instance, would be http://server/webdev/images/icons/security.gif.

On the front

Note from listing 14.1 that the WAR file itself contains no references to a top-level directory named webdev. This directory name is automatically recognized by the JSP container once the application has been registered with the container. Application names are arbitrary, and are assigned at the time of installation. The name of an application is completely independent of the name of the corresponding WAR file. It is common, but not mandatory for them to be the same. If the local server administrator wished to install the webdev.war file as an application named intranet, the JSP container will be happy to translate URLs such as http://server/intranet/filters/login.jsp into the corresponding content from the webdev.war archive.

This top-level URL directory, then, is completely under the control of the container. The directory name is mapped to an application, and is removed from the URL behind the scenes when translating it into a file name for retrieving content from the WAR file. Given that the application name is not built into the application, you may be wondering how the pages within an application can refer to one another via URLs. Relative URLs function as expected, but if the first directory in an absolute URL cannot be known until the application is installed, it would appear that absolute URLs must be avoided within an application's documents.

To address this deficiency, JSP containers are required to automatically account for this top-level directory when processing elements that use absolute URLs. Specifically, when a JSP page that is part of an application calls the `include` directive, the `<jsp:include>` action, or the `<jsp:forward>` action with an absolute URL, the container is required to map that URL into the page's application. In effect, the application name is transparently added to the beginning of such absolute URLs so that references within the application are properly maintained. For example, the login.jsp file for the sample application in listing 14.1 might wish to forward control to the welcome.jsp file in the `secure` directory, using an absolute URL as follows:

```
<jsp:forward page="/filters/secure/welcome.jsp" />
```

If the application has been named webdev, then when the JSP container processes this action it will automatically map the page reference to /webdev/filters/secure/

welcome.jsp. If intranet was chosen as the application name, it would instead map this absolute URL to /intranet/filters/secure/welcome.jsp.

References to URLs from standard HTML tags, however, are not automatically mapped. A relative URL appearing in the `SRC` attribute of an `<IMG>` tag or the HREF attribute of an `<A>` tag would be resolved correctly, but when an absolute URL is more convenient, an alternate approach is warranted. The most direct approach to using absolute URLs is to mandate a specific name under which the application must be installed on the server.

A more flexible approach is to take advantage of HTML's `<BASE>` tag. When this tag is specified in the `<HEAD>` section of an HTML document, all relative URLs in the document are resolved relative to the value specified for this tag's `HREF` attribute. In a JSP page, then, the following construct can be used to set this base URL to that of the application, as in the following page fragment:

```
<HTML>
<HEAD>
<BASE HREF="<%= request.getScheme() %>://<%= request.getServerName()%>:<%=
  request.getServerPort() %><%= request.getContextPath() %>/">
...
<HEAD>
<BODY>
...
<A HREF="filters/index.jsp"><IMG SRC="images/logo.gif"></A>
...
</BODY>
</HTML>
```

The `getContextPath()` method of the `javax.servlet.http.HttpServlet-Request` class is used to retrieve the top-level directory of the URL associated with the request, which will correspond to the name assigned to the application on the server. Note that the result returned by this method will start with an initial forward slash character, but will not end with one. The closing directory delimiter is therefore added explicitly by specifying it as static text in the `<BASE>` tag (i.e., immediately following the final JSP expression).

If the application has been assigned the name webdev, the result of calling the `getContextPath()` method will be `"/webdev"`. When the JSP page is processed, the resulting `<BASE>` tag sent back to the end user's browser will therefore be something like the following:

```
<BASE HREF="http://www.example.com:80/webdev/">
```

In the example page, the two relative URLs will be resolved by the browser relative to this base URL, resulting in an effective URL of /webdev/filters/index.jsp for the link and /webdev/images/logo.gif for the image. In this way, it becomes possible to reference other resources within the application using URLs that behave very similarly to absolute URLs, without having to know in advance the name (and therefore the top-level URL directory) of the installed application.

The fog of WAR

The translation by the JSP container of URLs into WAR file contents applies to all files and directories in the archive except those appearing within the WEB-INF directory. More specifically, the contents of the directory and its subdirectories cannot be accessed via URLs at all. Instead, these files are reserved for use by the JSP container, and fall into four major categories.

NOTE The `ServletContext` object associated with an application, accessible from its JSP pages via the application implicit object, is able to programmatically access the contents of the WAR file's WEB-INF directory, using its `getResource()` and `getResourceAsStream()` methods. In this way, developers can use the WEB-INF directory for storing additional application-specific data that can be accessed via Java code, but is not directly exposed to end users via URLs.

The first type of file found in the WEB-INF directory, the web.xml deployment descriptor, has already been mentioned. This file provides configuration information for the JSP container to use when running the application contained in the archive, the details of which are provided later in this chapter.

The second type are compiled Java class files. As illustrated in figure 14.1, Java class files appear in the classes subdirectory of the WEB-INF directory. Classes which are part of the default Java package should be placed directly in the classes directory, while those with explicitly named packages should be placed in subdirectories whose names correspond to the various elements of the package's name. For example, the `LoginServlet` and `UserBean` classes were defined in the previous chapter as being part of the `com.taglib.wdjsp.filters` package. Their class files thus appear in listing 14.1 within the `com/taglib/wdjsp/filters` subdirectory of the `classes` directory.

The classes appearing in the WAR file in the WEB-INF/classes directory and its subdirectories are automatically added to the class path used by the JSP container's JVM whenever it is accessing the application associated with the archive. As such, it is intended to provide a convenient location for storing the Java classes used by the application's servlets and JSP pages. The classes implementing the servlets themselves can appear here, as well as any auxiliary classes used by those servlets. JavaBeans, filters, listeners, and other Java classes referenced by the application's JSP pages can also be stored here.

The third type are JAR files, stored in the lib subdirectory of the WEB-INF directory. Like the individual class files found in the WEB-INF/classes directory, all of the classes found in the JAR files located here are automatically added to the JVM's class path whenever the JSP container is accessing the corresponding application. For the web archive presented in listing 14.1, classes stored in mail.jar would automatically be available when responding to requests for the webdev application's servlets and JSP pages.

The fourth type of file often found in the WEB-INF directory are Tag Library Descriptor (TLD) files for custom tag libraries. By convention, these are placed in a subdirectory named tlds. The deployment of custom tag libraries and TLDs will be discussed later in this chapter, but for the complete details see chapters 18–20.

In the absence of custom deployment tools, a common means for creating WAR files is Java's standard application for creating archive files, the `jar` command-line tool. The `jar` command can be used to create archives and to extract their contents. It can also be used to list the contents of an existing JAR file. When creating an archive, `jar` takes a list of files to be archived, as well as a file name for the archive. To create a WAR file, simply provide the `jar` command with a list of all of the files to be placed in the archive—web content files as well as those appearing in the WEB-INF directory—and specify a file name with a .war extension as the destination for the new archive.

NOTE When creating an archive, the `jar` command automatically inserts a top-level directory named META-INF, to which is added a file named MANIFEST.MF. This manifest file contains a listing of the contents of the archive, and may optionally be augmented with additional information about the archive's files. When the `jar` command is used to create a WAR file, the resulting web archive will also contain a META-INF/MANIFEST.MF file. Like the contents of the archive's WEB-INF directory, the JSP container will not make a manifest file accessible over the web via a URL.

For further details on the use of `jar`, including descriptions of the command line options that control its behavior, consult the documentation that accompanies the Java Development Kit (JDK), available from Sun Microsystems.

14.2.2 Drafting deployment descriptors

We next set our sights on a single file within the archive, the web.xml deployment descriptor. As discussed previously, this file contains entries describing the configuration of the application's Java-based assets. In the sections to follow, we will outline the format of this file and describe the XML directives used in the deployment descriptor to manage an application's servlets and, where appropriate, its JSP pages.

A prelude to WAR

As an XML document, the deployment descriptor must begin with the standard XML header material. Typically, a tag declaring the XML version number and the document's character encoding appear first, followed by a specification of the DTD for the document. As its name implies, it describes the valid tags for a given document type, and may thus be used to validate the syntax of an XML document.

For a Web Application Descriptor file, the DTD is provided by Sun Microsystems, at a published URL associated with the J2EE specification. A typical header for a web.xml file targeting a JSP 1.1 container would therefore be as follows:

```
<?xml version="1.0" encoding="ISO-8859-1" ?>
<!DOCTYPE web-app PUBLIC
        "-//Sun Microsystems, Inc.//DTD Web Application 2.2//EN"
        "http://java.sun.com/j2ee/dtds/web-app_2.2">
```

For applications that take advantage of JSP 1.2 and/or Servlet 2.3 features, the following header is required:

```
<?xml version="1.0" encoding="ISO-8859-1" ?>
<!DOCTYPE web-app PUBLIC
        "-//Sun Microsystems, Inc.//DTD Web Application 2.3//EN"
        "http://java.sun.com/j2ee/dtds/web-app_2.3.dtd">
```

The root element for deployment descriptors in either case is the `<web-app>` tag. All of the elements of a web.xml file, except for the header items just described, must appear within the body content of a single `<web-app>` tag, as in the intranet example presented earlier in this chapter.

Several subelements of the `<web-app>` tag are available for specifying properties of the application itself, as illustrated in the following `web.xml` fragment:

```
<web-app>
  <icon>
    <large-icon>/icons/encom32x32.gif</large-icon>
    <small-icon>/icons/encom16x16.gif</small-icon>
  </icon>
  <display-name>Encom Intranet</display-name>
  <description>
```

```
    Provides departmental information to authorized users.
  </description>
  <distributable/>
  ...
  <welcome-file-list>
    <welcome-file>default.html</welcome-file>
    <welcome-file>index.jsp</welcome-file>
  </welcome-file-list>
  ...
</web-app>
```

All of these subelements are optional, and should appear at most once within the parent `<web-app>` element. The `<description>` tag is used to document the application, while the `<icon>` tag and its subelements, `<large-icon>` and `<small-icon>`, are provided for use with graphical configuration tools, as is the `<display-name>` tag.

The `<welcome-file-list>` element is used to specify which file within an application directory should be displayed to the end user when a URL is requested that contains only a directory. Each such file name is specified via the `<welcome-file>` tag, and order is significant. When a directory URL is requested, the JSP container will search the corresponding directory in the application for the files in this list, in the order in which they appear in the deployment descriptor. The first one found generates the response to that request. If none is found, the response will contain an appropriate error message.

The remaining element in this example is the `<distributable>` tag. Unlike the others, this tag has no body content, but simply signals whether or not the application is distributable by its presence or absence. If this tag is included in the deployment descriptor, it serves as an indicator that the application has been written in such a way as to support distributing the application across multiple JSP containers. If the tag is not present, it must be assumed that distributed processing is not supported.

DEFINITION A distributed web application runs in multiple JSP containers simultaneously, typically on multiple web servers, while sharing some common resources and/or functionality. As discussed in chapter 4, the capacity for a web-based application to be distributed is an important consideration for scalability.

Targeting servlets

A web application's servlets are specified in the deployment descriptor via the `<servlet>` tag and its subelements, as in the following example:

```
<web-app>
  ...
  <servlet>
    <icon>
      <small-icon>/images/icons/security.gif</small-icon>
    </icon>
    <servlet-name>logout</servlet-name>
    <display-name>Logout Handler</display-name>
    <description>
      Logs a user out of the application.
    </description>
    <servlet-class>
      com.taglib.wdjsp.filters.LogoutServlet
    </servlet-class>

    <init-param>
      <param-name>goodbyePage</param-name>
      <param-value>/filters/goodbye.jsp</param-value>
      <description>
        The page to which users are sent after a successful logout.
      </description>
    </init-param>
    <load-on-startup>3</load-on-startup>
  </servlet>
  ...
</web-app>
```

Within the body of the `<servlet>` tag, the `<description>`, `<display-name>`, and `<icon>` tags play an analogous role to those they play when appearing at the top level in the body of the `<web-app>` tag. The functionality of the other tags is specific to servlets. Only the `<servlet-name>` and `<servlet-class>` tags are mandatory.

The `<servlet-name>` tag, as you might expect, provides a name for the servlet. The value provided in the body of this tag can be used to request the servlet via a URL composed of the application name, a subdirectory named `servlet`, and the specified servlet name. For example, if the servlet specified here were part of an application named webdev, the URL for accessing this servlet would be http://server/webdev/servlet/login. Note, therefore, that servlet names must be unique. No two servlet specifications within a single application deployment descriptor can have the same values for their `<servlet-name>` elements

The `<servlet-class>` tag specifies the Java class that implements the servlet. The JSP container instantiates this class in order to respond to requests handled by the servlet.

After instantiating the servlet class, but before servicing any requests, the container will call the class's `init()` method. Initialization parameters, which are passed to the servlet's `init()` method via an instance of `javax.servlet.ServletConfig`, are specified via the `<init-param>` tag. This tag has three subelements, `<param-name>`, `<param-value>`, and `<description>`, the last of which is optional. There should be one `<init-param>` tag for each initialization parameter to be passed to the `init()` method.

As their names suggest, the body of the `<param-name>` tag corresponds to the parameter name, while the body of the `<param-value>` tag supplies its value. In the example above, an initialization parameter named `goodbyePage` has been assigned a value of `/filters/goodbyePage`. Note that parameter names and values are both passed to the servlet as `String` objects. If the parameter value is intended to represent some other type of data (e.g., a numeric value), it is up to the servlet's `init()` method to parse the value appropriately. As has been the case elsewhere, the `<description>` tag is provided for documentation purposes.

The remaining `<servlet>` subelement is the `<load-on-startup>` tag. The presence of this tag indicates to the JSP container that this servlet should be loaded into the container's JVM (and initialized via its `init()` method) during the JSP container's startup process. If this tag is not present, the container is free to wait until a request is received for the servlet before loading it.

The `<load-on-startup>` tag can be specified either as an empty tag (i.e., `<load-on-startup/>`), or with body content specifying an integer value. This tag's body content is used to indicate when the servlet should be loaded, relative to others which are also designated as being loaded on startup. If the tag is empty, the JSP container is free to load the servlet whenever it wishes during startup. If the body content specifies an integer value, that value is used to order the loading of all servlets that specify integer values for this tag. Lower values are loaded first, followed by servlets specifying higher values. If more than one servlet specifies the same value for `<load-on-startup>`, the ordering of the servlets within that group is arbitrary. The effect is that all servlets which specify a value of `1` for this tag will be loaded first (in an unspecified order), followed by all servlets which specified a value of `2`, then all servlets specifying a value of `3`, and so on.

Typically, the servlets within one application are not dependent upon those in another. As long as you specify unique values for the `<load-on-startup>` tags within a single application, you can be assured that the servlets within that application will be loaded in the specified order. Servlets from other applications may also be loaded within that sequence, but you can at least be certain that any order dependencies within an individual application will be maintained.

Mapping the terrain

It is often desirable to specify an alternate URL for a servlet. It is good programming practice to hide the implementation details of a given set of functionality, and URLs that contain the word "servlet" are pretty much a dead giveaway that the underlying implementation of an application is based on servlets. This is not to suggest that you shouldn't be proud of selecting servlets as your implementation technology—indeed, the authors would wholeheartedly endorse that decision—but studies have shown that memorable URLs improve the usability of a web site and, frankly, end users don't care about what makes it work.

Given that the default URL for an application's servlets, as described in the previous section, includes a subdirectory component named servlet, those wishing to follow this advice need a mechanism for specifying alternate URLs. This is accomplished in the web.xml file via use of the `<servlet-mapping>` tag, as in the following example:

```
<web-app>
  ...
  <servlet-mapping>
    <servlet-name>logout</servlet-name>
    <url-pattern>/filters/logout</url-pattern>
  </servlet-mapping>
  ...
</web-app>
```

Here, the `<servlet-name>` tag identifies the servlet for which the alternate URL is being specified, and should correspond to a servlet defined elsewhere in the deployment descriptor via the `<servlet>` tag. The body of the `<url-pattern>` tag specifies a URL pattern, such that requests whose URLs match the specified pattern will be handled by the indicated servlet. Both subelements are required.

Like all URLs associated with an application, any URL specified in this manner must be preceded by the name of the application when it is requested by an end user. For the example shown here then, the alternate URL for the `logout` servlet, again assuming webdev is the name assigned to the application, will be http://server/webdev/filters/logout.

Although the URL pattern in the example shown here is an alphabetic string specifying a directory and a file name, more complex patterns are also supported. The number of directory levels is completely arbitrary. There can be none, as in `<url-pattern>/control</url-pattern>`, or there can be many. If even the file name portion is left out, as in `<url-pattern>/</url-pattern>`, then the servlet becomes the default resource for the web application. If a request is received that specifies no directory or file name components beyond that of the application, this default servlet will handle the request. (In fact, it will even override the functionality specified via the `<welcome-file-list>` element, if present.)

In addition, an asterisk can take the place of the final element in such mappings—for example, `/filters/access/group7/*`— indicating that all URLs that start with the specified directory pattern (plus the application name, of course), should be mapped to the corresponding servlet. As a special case, a URL pattern of /* indicates that all requests associated with the application should be mapped to the associated servlet. In either case, the additional directory and file name components of the actual URL used to access such a servlet will be available via the `getPathInfo()` method of `javax.servlet.http.HttpServletRequest`.

This tag can also be used to map requests for specific file types—based on their file name extensions—to a servlet. In this case the body of the `<url-pattern>` tag should take the form of an asterisk followed by a period and the extension to be mapped. For example, a URL pattern of `*.user` would map all requests within an application that have an extension of .user to the corresponding servlet.

NOTE In fact, this is how JSP itself works: all requests for files ending with the .jsp extension are mapped to a special servlet—historically referred to as the page compiler servlet—that maps requests for JSP pages into calls to the compiled servlets implementing those pages. This servlet will also take care of compiling the JSP page into a servlet if this is the first time it has been requested, or if its contents have changed since the last time it was compiled.

While a given servlet may be mapped to multiple URL patterns, the reverse is not true. A given URL pattern can be mapped to only one servlet, otherwise the servlet container would not be able to determine which servlet should be applied to requests that match the overloaded pattern.

There is still the potential for ambiguity, however, since even though two URL patterns are not identical, it is possible to imagine requests that match both patterns. Imagine, for example, three servlets mapped to three different URL patterns, `/*`, `/filters/*`, and `*.jsp`. A request for the URL http://server/filters/index.jsp would match all three of these patterns, so which servlet should the container actually call upon to handle the request?

To resolve situations such as this, a set of precedence rules have been specified. First, if a URL pattern is an exact match for the path in the request, the servlet associated with that pattern is to be called. If there is no exact match, then the directory-style patterns—those specifying one or more directory names followed by an asterisk—are next compared against the request path. Following these, servlets corresponding to URL patterns based on file name extensions (i.e., `*.jsp` and the like) are matched. If the path in the request does not match any of the URL patterns following these forms, then the servlet mapped to the default path, `/*`, is called. If there is no such default servlet, then an HTTP status code of 404, indicating the requested resource was not found, is returned.

WAR and JSPs

Since this is a JSP book, why has so much space been devoted here to the configuration of servlets. The first reason, as indicated in chapter 10, is that servlets and JSPs are natural companions in the construction of complex web applications. If you will be deploying an application that uses JSP pages, there's a strong chance the application also includes servlets.

In addition, recall that JSP pages are implemented as servlets. As a result, the deployment descriptor elements provided for configuring an application's servlets are also, in most cases, applicable to the configuration of its JSP pages. As already mentioned in this chapter, it is usually not necessary to mention an application's JSP pages in the web.xml file. When it is necessary, however, the servlet-related tags again come into play.

In the discussion of the `<servlet>` tag earlier in this chapter, it was pointed out that the only required subelements are the `<servlet-name>` and `<servlet-class>` tags. This is not completely true. When referencing JSP pages, the `<servlet-class>` tag is replaced by, appropriately enough, the `<jsp-file>` tag. In the interest of full disclosure then, the only required subelement of the `<servlet>` tag is the `<servlet-name>` tag. In addition, either the `<servlet-class>` tag or the `<jsp-file>` tag must be present.

In this way, the initialization parameters and startup behavior of the servlet corresponding to a JSP file can be configured using the same techniques described earlier for configuring servlets. The body of the `<jsp-file>` tag is used to specify the full path to the JSP page within the application, as in the following example:

```
<web-app>
  ...
  <servlet>
    <servlet-name>developmentHome</servlet-name>
    <jsp-file>/filters/secure/development.jsp</jsp-file>
    <description>Home page of the development group.</description>
    <init-param>
      <param-name>conferenceRoom</param-name>
      <param-value>Klaatu</param-value>
      <description>
        Current location for the weekly development meeting.
```

```
      </description>
    </init-param>
    <load-on-startup>4</load-on-startup>
  </servlet>
  ...
</web-app>
```

As with other application-specific paths, the body of the `<jsp-file>` tag does not include the top-level directory named after the application. Note also that when the `<load-on-startup>` tag is specified in the `<servlet>` tag for a JSP page, it is an indication to the JSP container that the page should be compiled as well as loaded during container startup.

Instead of precompiling the JSP servlet during container startup, however, it might be desirable under certain circumstances to deploy the fully compiled servlet rather than the original JSP page. This can also be accomplished via the web.xml deployment descriptor. After writing the JSP file and deploying it in a JSP container, a copy can be made of the compiled JSP servlet constructed by the container. Suppose, for example, that the `/filters/secure/development.jsp` page from our example intranet application has been compiled into a servlet class named `_jsp_filters_secure_development_JspImpl`. A copy of the generated class file, _jsp_filters_secure_development_JspImpl.class, can be added to the application's WAR file, in place of the original /filters/secure/development.jsp file. Appropriate `<servlet>` and `<servlet-mapping>` tags must then be added to the deployment descriptor to mimic the original JSP behavior, as in the following web.xml fragment:

```
<web-app>
  ...
  <servlet>
    <servlet-name>developmentHome</servlet-name>
    <servlet-class>_jsp_filters_secure_development_JspImpl</servlet-class>
  </servlet>
  <servlet-mapping>
    <servlet-name>developmentHome</servlet-name>
    <servlet-mapping>/filters/secure/development.jsp</servlet-mapping>
  </servlet-mapping>
  ...
</web-app>
```

As a result of this mapping, the URL associated with the original JSP page is explicitly mapped to the corresponding servlet, rather than relying on the aforementioned page compiler servlet to make this association automatically. In fact, when responding to requests for a JSP page mapped in this fashion, the page compiler servlet is bypassed altogether, and requests are routed directly to the precompiled page servlet.

WARNING Recall from chapter 5 that the requirement imposed by the JSP specification on servlets generated from JSP pages is that they implement the `javax.servlet.jsp.JspPage` interface. The concrete superclass for generated JSP pages is therefore implementation-specific. Keep in mind, then, that if you use the technique described here for deploying JSP pages as precompiled servlets, the resulting WAR file will not be portable. By virtue of its reliance on an implementation-specific servlet class, the WAR file will be compatible only with the JSP container originally used to generate the precompiled servlet.

In addition to the `<load-on-startup>` element, JSP provides a second mechanism for triggering the precompilation of deployed pages, by means of a special request parameter. When a request that includes a `jsp_precompile` is sent to a JSP page, this will be interpreted by the JSP container as a signal to compile that page without executing it. The request parameter should have a value of `true`, or no value, as in the following examples:

```
http://server/filters/secure/development.jsp?jsp_precompile
http://server/filters/secure/admin.jsp?jsp_precompile=true
```

A value of `false` is also acceptable, but this will result in the normal behavior when a request is sent to a JSP page: it is compiled if necessary, and then the request is delivered to the corresponding servlet for processing. Other values for this request parameter are invalid.

A successful precompilation request will cause the JSP container to compile the page into a servlet and send back a container-specific response, which is typically either a simple "compilation successful" message or a list of compilation errors. This simple precompilation protocol makes it easy to test the syntax of your JSP pages without an elaborate setup, and also has the advantage of being vendor-neutral. It is fairly easy, for example, to put together a small program or shell script which visits each page of your application immediately after deployment to trigger precompilation. Keep in mind that this is just a compilation test, however. Like any Java code, just because it compiles, that doesn't mean it works. This test won't detect potential run-time errors.

NOTE Some JSP containers also support other, nonstandard mechanisms for precompiling pages. The Tomcat reference implementation, for example, includes a command-line utility named `jspc` that can be run to precompile JSP pages without requiring them to first be deployed to a server.

Mobilizing custom tag libraries

In previous chapters, custom tag libraries have been described as a powerful feature for adding functionality to JSP pages. As indicated in chapter 5, tag libraries are loaded into a JSP page by means of the `taglib` directive, which locates a tag library based on a URL. Until now, however, we haven't been in a position to discuss where this URL comes from.

A custom tag library has two basic components: a set of Java classes implementing the custom actions provided by the tag library and a TLD file which provides a mapping between the library's tags and those implementation classes.

A tag library's classes are typically bundled into a JAR file, for storage in an application's WEB-INF/lib directory. Alternatively, the individual class files may be placed in the appropriate package-specific subdirectories of the application's WEB-INF/classes directory. As already mentioned, TLD files are typically stored in the WEB-INF/tlds directory.

The `taglib` directive loads a custom tag library by referencing the library's TLD file in its `uri` attribute. Because the contents of the WEB-INF directory are not normally accessible via URLs, it is usually necessary to provide a mapping for the TLD file in the application's deployment descriptor. This is accomplished via the `<taglib>` tag, as in the following web.xml fragment:

```
<web-app>
  ...
  <taglib>
    <taglib-uri>/mutlib</taglib-uri>
    <taglib-location>/WEB-INF/tlds/mut.tld</taglib-location>
  </taglib>
  ...
</web-app>
```

As illustrated in this example, the `<taglib>` tag has two subelements, `<taglib-uri>` and `<taglib-location>`, both of which are required. The `<taglib-uri>` tag is used to specify the URI by which `taglib` directives in the application's JSP pages can access the TLD. The `<taglib-location>` tag specifies the actual location of that TLD within the application's file hierarchy. Multiple `<taglib>` elements may appear in a single web.xml file, one for each custom tag library used by the application.

NOTE When referencing the URI of a TLD in a `taglib` directive, the top-level directory corresponding to the application name should not be specified. To access the TLD in the example presented here, then, the appropriate directive would be of the form `<%@ taglib uri="/mutlib" prefix="mut" %>`.

Note that in JSP 1.2, the tag library itself can specify the URI of its TLD, obviating the need for deployment descriptor `<taglib>` elements under some circumstances. For further details, see chapter 20.

Infiltrating the supply lines

For containers supporting Servlet 2.3 and JSP 1.2, filters are specified using the `<filter>` and `<filter-mapping>` tags. The `<filter>` tag supports six subelements, as in this example:

```
<filter>
  <icon>
    <small-icon>/images/icons/replace16x16.gif</small-icon>
    <small-icon>/images/icons/replace32x32.gif</small-icon>
  </icon>
  <filter-name>stringReplace</filter-name>
  <display-name>String Replacement Filter</display-name>
  <description>
    Replaces all occurrences of the &quot;from&quot; string
    with the contents of the &quot;to&quot; string.
  </description>
  <filter-class>
    com.taglib.wdjsp.filters.StringReplaceFilter
  </filter-class>
  <init-param>
    <param-name>from</param-name>
    <param-value>Encom</param-value>
  </init-param>
  <init-param>
    <param-name>to</param-name>
    <param-value>FlynnCom</param-value>
  </init-param>
</filter>
```

By now, the `<icon>`, `<display-name>`, and `<description>` subelements should be quite familiar. The `<description>` tag is used to specify a documentation string for the filter, while the other two are used to support graphical tools.

The `<init-param>` subelement is also familiar, and plays the same role for filters as it does for servlets: specifying the names and values of its initialization parameters. As you will recall from chapter 12, all filters are required to implement an init() method which takes an instance of the javax.servlet.FilterConfig class as its sole argument. This FilterConfig instance in turn provides methods that enable the filter to access the initialization parameters specified in the deployment descriptor via the <init-param> tag and its <param-name> and <param-value> subelements.

The final two elements, however, are unique to filters, and are the only two <filter> subelements which are not optional. The first is the <filter-name> tag, which is used to provide a unique name for the filter within the application. The second is the <filter-class> tag, which specifies the Java class to be instantiated when constructing the filter. These elements are thus analogous to the <servlet> tag's <servlet-name> and <servlet-class> elements.

The similarities between filter specification and servlet specification don't end there. Just as the URLs to which servlets are mapped are specified via the <servlet-mapping> tag, the <filter-mapping> tag is used to specify the resources to which filters are to be applied. The <filter-mapping> element takes two forms. First, a filter can be mapped to a specific servlet, by specifying them both by name:

```
<filter-mapping>
  <filter-name>stringReplace</filter-name>
  <servlet-name>login</url-pattern>
</filter-mapping>
```

The filter to be mapped is indicated via the <filter-name> tag, the body of which must match a filter name that is also specified via the <filter-name> element of a corresponding <filter> tag. The servlet to which the filter is to be applied is specified via the <servlet-name> tag, which must similarly match a servlet name specified via the <servlet-name> element of a corresponding <servlet> tag.

Alternatively, a filter can be mapped to a set of resources matching a given URL pattern, as in this example:

```
<filter-mapping>
  <filter-name>stringReplace</filter-name>
  <url-pattern>/filters/*</url-pattern>
 </filter-mapping>
```

Here, the <filter-name> tag once again identifies which filter is being mapped, and must match the name of a filter specified elsewhere in the deployment descriptor via the <filter> element. The <url-pattern> element indicates to which requests the filter should be applied. The named filter will be applied to all requests whose path matches the specified pattern. All of the different forms of URL patterns supported by the <url-pattern> subelement of the <servlet-mapping> tag may also be used within the <url-pattern> subelement of the <filter-mapping> tag.

As with servlets, a given filter may be mapped to multiple URL patterns or servlet names. Unlike servlets, however, you are also permitted to map more than one filter to the same URL pattern or servlet name. This is because, as described in chapter 12, all of the filters applicable to a given request will be chained together, each handing off the request to the next filter in the chain for further processing, receiving the resulting response as it is passed back up the chain.

For filters, then, there is no need for rules to determine which filter to apply when a request path matches multiple servlet names and/or URL patterns: all of the matching filters are applied. Instead, the issue is in what order those matching filters should be applied.

Consider, for example, the three example filters presented in the previous chapter. It does not make sense to check the user's role until after they have logged in and you know who they are. Requests should therefore be validated by the `AuthenticationFilter` before being passed on to the `RoleFilter`. For efficiency reasons, it would also be preferable to avoid the overhead of instantiating the `java.io.ByteArrayOutputStream` object associated with the `StringReplaceFilter` until you're certain you're going to be using it. Since the login and role validation filters can cause a request to be redirected, it would be preferable to place the string replacement filter at the end of the chain. That way, if the original request is redirected by either of the other two filters, the `doFilterMethod()` of `StringReplaceFilter` will never be called, and the overhead of wrapping its response and creating the `ByteArrayOutputStream` will never be incurred.

The ability to control the order in which filters are applied to requests is thus very important. To that end, Servlet 2.3 containers are required to follow two basic rules for determining the order in which filters are to be applied, both of which are based on the order in which `<filter-mapping>` elements appear within an application's deployment descriptor. For a given request, first all of the matching filters which have been mapped via URL patterns are applied. These filters must be applied in the order in which the corresponding `<filter-mapping>` elements occur within the web.xml file. Next all of the matching filters which have been mapped via explicit servlet names are applied, again in the order in which their `<filter-mapping>` elements appear.

For this reason, it is generally a good rule of thumb to keep the `<filter-mapping>` elements separated within the deployment descriptors. First specify all of the `<filter-mapping>` tags which include `<url-pattern>` subelements, and then specify all of the `<filter-mapping>` tags which include `<servlet-name>` subelements. By following this practice, the ordering that will be imposed on the application's filters by the container will exactly match the ordering within the `web.xml` file. A quick visual examination of that file will then suffice to remind you how the container will be handling any given request: simply examine each of the `<filter-mapping>` elements in order, and each filter which is mapped to the resource specified in that request will become part of the `FilterChain` created for handling that request, in exactly the same order as they are encountered in the file.

The proper sequence of `<filter-mapping>` elements for the filters introduced in the previous chapter, then, is as follows:

```
<filter-mapping>
  <filter-name>authentication</filter-name>
  <url-pattern>/filters/secure/*</url-pattern>
</filter-mapping>
<filter-mapping>
  <filter-name>devRole</filter-name>
  <url-pattern>/filters/secure/development.jsp</url-pattern>
</filter-mapping>
<filter-mapping>
  <filter-name>mgrRole</filter-name>
  <url-pattern>/filters/secure/management.jsp</url-pattern>
</filter-mapping>
<filter-mapping>
  <filter-name>adminRole</filter-name>
  <url-pattern>/filters/secure/admin.jsp</url-pattern>
</filter-mapping>
<filter-mapping>
  <filter-name>stringReplace</filter-name>
  <url-pattern>/filters/*</url-pattern>
</filter-mapping>
```

where the filter names are as specified in the example `<filter>` tags presented previously in this chapter. This sequence ensures that the login authentication filter is applied first, and the string replacement filter is applied last, with the role authentication filters running in between. Note that the login authentication and string replacement filters use directory-style URL patterns, while the role authentication filters are only applied to specific URLs (in this case, three different individual JSP pages).

Developing listening posts

Like filters, listeners are a new feature introduced by the Servlet 2.3 specification, and are therefore available in JSP 1.2. Listeners are added to a web application via the intuitively named `<listener>` element, which has a single, required subelement. For the `LoginSessionListener` introduced in chapter 13, the corresponding `<listener>` element for incorporating that listener into a web application is as follows:

```
<listener>
  <listener-class>
```

```
    com.taglib.wdjsp.filters.LoginSessionListener
  </listener-class>
</listener>
```

For each such `<listener>` element appearing in the deployment descriptor, the container will create one instance of the Java class specified in the body of its `<listener-class>` subelement. The instance will then be registered with the container according to which of the five life-cycle event handler interfaces it implements, and will automatically begin receiving the events specified by those interfaces as they occur. The class specified via the `<listener-class>` tag must implement at least one of these five interfaces:

- `javax.servlet.ServletContextListener`
- `javax.servlet.ServletContextAttributeListener`
- `javax.servlet.http.HttpSessionListener`
- `javax.servlet.http.HttpSessionAttributeListener`
- `javax.servlet.http.HttpSessionActivationListener`

The `LoginSessionListener`, defined in chapter 13, implements both `HttpSessionListener` and `HttpSessionAttributeListener`.

Special forces

In addition to standard web file types, such as HTML and JSP documents and GIF and JPEG images, it is often desirable to provide access to other types of information via a web server. For this reason, whenever the server sends a document to a web browser, it includes a specification of the type of document it is sending, referred to as the document's MIME type. MIME was originally developed for identifying documents sent as electronic mail attachments. It is now used for many applications, including the identification of document types on the Web.

Most web servers are configured to associate MIME types with specific file name extensions. For instance, file names ending with .html are typically associated with the `text/html` MIME type, while those whose extension is .doc might be assigned the `application/msword` MIME type, identifying them as Word documents. By examining the MIME type returned by the server for a given request, the browser can determine how to handle the data contained in the response. If the MIME type of the response is text/html, the browser will render that data as an HTML document. If the MIME type is application/msword, the browser might instead attempt to open Word in order to view the document contents.

TIP The official registry of Internet MIME types is managed by the IANA, and is available from its website at http://www.iana.org.

For web applications running in a JSP container, the web server will forward all URLs associated with the application (i.e., all URLs whose top-level directory corresponds to the name of the application) to the application itself for processing. The application is therefore responsible for assigning a MIME type to the generated response. Most JSP containers will automatically recognize the standard extensions for HTML, GIF, and JPEG files, and return the correct MIME type. The default MIME type for responses generated by servlets and JSP files is text/html, but this can be overridden. In a servlet, the `setContentType()` method of `javax.servlet.ServletResponse` may be used to set the MIME type of the response. The `contentType` attribute of the page directive provides the same functionality in a JSP page.

If you are deploying a web application that includes other document types, you must configure the application to recognize the extensions used by those documents and assign the appropriate MIME type. The `<mime-mapping>` tag is provided for this purpose, as demonstrated in this web.xml fragment:

```
<web-app>
  ...
  <mime-mapping>
    <extension>pdf</extension>
    <mime-type>application/pdf</mime-type>
  </mime-mapping>
  ...
</web-app>
```

The `<mime-mapping>` tag has two subelements, `<extension>` and `<mime-type>`. The `<extension>` element is used to specify the file name extension to be mapped to a particular MIME type, while the `<mime-type>` element identifies the MIME type to which it should be mapped. In our example, the pdf extension is mapped to the application/pdf MIME type, indicating that file names ending with .pdf are to be identified as being in Adobe's Portable Document Format.

A web.xml file can contain an arbitrary number of `<mime-mapping>` elements. While each individual extension should be mapped to only a single MIME type, the reverse is not necessarily the case: multiple extensions can be mapped to the same MIME type. For example, web servers commonly map both the .jpg and .jpeg file extensions to the same image/jpeg MIME type.

Controlling the theater of operations

In addition to its capabilities for configuring servlets and JSP pages, the deployment descriptor provides applications with the ability to control certain aspects of the JSP container in which it is running. For example, security restrictions may be specified for controlling access to an application's resources. If the JSP container also happens to be an EJB container, the web.xml file can be used to specify means for referencing EJBs.

While we will not cover topics such as these in-depth, there are three more deployment descriptor tags we will discuss. First, we will see how the `<session-config>` tag may be used to control the behavior of sessions created by an application. Second is the use of the `<context-param>` tag to specify initialization parameters for the application as a whole. Finally, it is the `<error-page>` tag, which can be used to indicate specific URLs to which control should be transferred when various types of errors occur.

The `<session-config>` tag is used to specify a default time-out value for sessions created by the application's servlets and JSP pages, via its single required subelement, the `<session-timeout>` tag. The body of `<session-timeout>` should be an integral value indicating how many minutes of inactivity are required before a session is considered to have expired, as in the following example:

```
<web-app>
   ...
   <session-config>
      <session-timeout>30</session-timeout>
   </session-config>
   ...
</web-app>
```

In this case, the application's sessions are set to expire, by default, after half an hour of inactivity. This default value can be explicitly overridden for individual sessions by means of the `setMaxInactiveInterval()` method of the `javax.servlet.http.HttpSession` interface. At most one `<session-config>` element may appear in a web.xml application descriptor. Note that a value of zero or less in the body of the `<session-timeout>` tag indicates to the JSP container that, by default, sessions should never time-out. In such a case, the `setMaxInactiveInterval()` method should be used to set the expiration period programmatically, or the application should itself take care of keeping track of and invalidating sessions. Otherwise, the container will keep accumulating sessions that never expire until it runs out of memory.

NOTE As the language here suggests, sessions are application-specific. A session object created by one application running in a JSP container cannot be accessed from another application running in that same container. As a result, objects stored in the session as attributes by one application cannot be retrieved from the session by code running in another. The `<session-timeout>` tag, therefore, only controls the expiration of sessions associated with the application defined in the web.xml file in which that tag appears.

As described earlier, the `<init-param>` tag specifies values for a servlet's or filter's initialization parameters. In a similar manner, the `<context-param>` tag specifies initialization parameter values for an entire application or, more specifically, the `ServletContext` object associated with an application. The `<context-param>` tag supports the same three subelements as the `<init-param>` tag, serving analogous roles, as in this web.xml fragment:

```
<web-app>
   ...
   <context-param>
      <param-name>dbUsername</param-name>
      <param-value>sark</param-value>
      <description>Username for the employee database.</description>
   </context-param>
   <context-param>
      <param-name>dbPassword</param-name>
      <param-value>gorgon</param-value>
      <description>Password for the employee database.</description>
   </context-param>
   ...
</web-app>
```

Here, two application initialization parameters, `dbUsername` and `dbPassword`, are specified. Their values are automatically set when the container first loads the application, and can be retrieved from the `ServletContext` object associated with the application by means of its `getInitParameter()` method. Within the JSP pages of the application, this `ServletContext` object is available via the `application` implicit object. Because this object is accessible from all of an application's servlets and JSP pages, it provides a convenient mechanism for specifying configuration data that is applicable across multiple resources within the same application.

The `<error-page>` element is used to configure the behavior of the container when exceptional circumstances occur, and takes two different forms. The first is used to specify the behavior of the container when it detects an HTTP status code indicating an error, as in this example:

```
<error-page>
  <error-code>404</error-code>
  <location>/errors/fileNotFound.jsp</location>
</error-page>
```

If a servlet or JSP page chooses to return an HTTP status code to indicate an error (via the `setStatus()` method of the `javax.servlet.http.HttpServletResponse` class, for example), the container will typically send this response back to the browser and allow it to display an appropriate error message. Using the `<error-page>` element, however, it is possible to provide a custom error message. This example tells the container to display one of the application's JSP pages, located at /errors/fileNotFound.jsp, whenever a response whose status code is 404 is encountered. The `<error-code>` subelement specifies the value of the status code, while the `<location>` subelement indicates the URL within the application whose contents are to be returned in responses having that status code value.

The second form of the `<error-page>` element allows the application deployer to specify content to be returned whenever an uncaught exception of a particular class is encountered. In this example, the container is instructed to forward to the /errors/brokenDB.jsp page whenever an uncaught `SQLException` is raised:

```
<error-page>
  <exception-type>java.sql.SQLException</exception-type>
  <location>/errors/brokenDB.jsp</location>
</error-page>
```

In this case, the `<exception-type>` element specifies the fully qualified class name of the exception with which the error response is to be associated. Once again, the `<location>` element indicates the application-specific URL whose contents are to be presented when the error condition occurs.

A deployment descriptor can include as many `<error-page>` elements as desired. Each `<error-page>` element must include exactly one `<location>` subelement, as well as either an `<error-code>` or an `<exception-type>` element.

Marching orders

As an XML file, the application deployment descriptor must conform to the DTD specified in its XML header (described earlier in this chapter). DTDs tend to be rather strict about the order in which elements appear in the XML file, a consideration we have so far ignored in the interest of presenting the `web.xml` elements in logical groupings. If you are interested in constructing deployment descriptors by hand, or need to debug a web.xml file generated by a deployment tool, knowing the order in which the various elements must appear is crucial. Containers will reject deployment descriptors that do not conform to the official DTD. The required ordering for the subelements of the <web-app> root element is presented in listing 14.2.

Listing 14.2 Required ordering of <web-app> subelements in the application deployment descriptor

```
<web-app>
  <icon>...</icon>
  <display-name>...</display-name>
  <description>...</description>
  <distributable/>
  <context-param>...</context-param> entries
  <filter>...</filter> entries
  <filter-mapping>...</filter-mapping> entries
  <listener>...</listener> entries
  <servlet>...</servlet> entries
  <servlet-mapping>...</servlet-mapping> entries
  <session-config>...</session-config>
  <mime-mapping>...</mime-mapping> entries
  <welcome-file-list>...</welcome-file-list>
  <error-page>...</error-page> entries
  <taglib>...</taglib> entries
  ...
</web-app>
```

With respect to the ordering of elements within the bodies of the various <web-app> subelements, the examples shown in this chapter are accurate. For example, the subelements of the example <filter> tag for the StringReplaceFilter, presented earlier in this chapter, conform to the ordering requirements of the web application deployment descriptor DTD.

14.3 Maintaining a WAR footing

WAR files, then, establish directory conventions for organizing the components of a web application, as well as a standard configuration file for managing its resources. In return, they simplify the deployment of web applications from development to production web servers, and do so in a portable manner. Web applications packaged as WAR files are compatible with all JSP containers that comply with version 1.1 and higher of the JSP specification.

One aspect of WAR files that has not been discussed thus far, is the ability of many JSP containers to work with web applications that have been expanded from their WAR files—that is, web archives whose contents have been extracted into the corresponding individual files. Such applications employ the same file hierarchy as WAR files, including the WEB-INF directory, but use actual directories and files instead of consolidating resources into a single archive file. By way of example, the file hierarchy for an expanded application based on the WAR file presented in listing 14.1 is depicted in listing 14.3. Once again, webdev has been selected as the application name.

Listing 14.3 File hierarchy for the expanded webdev application

```
/webdev/index.jsp
/webdev/commontasks/error.jsp
/webdev/filters/goodbye.jsp
/webdev/filters/login.jsp
/webdev/filters/index.jsp
/webdev/filters/secure/admin.jsp
/webdev/filters/secure/denied.jsp
/webdev/filters/secure/development.jsp
/webdev/filters/secure/header.jsp
/webdev/filters/secure/logout.jsp
/webdev/filters/secure/management.jsp
/webdev/filters/secure/welcome.jsp
/webdev/filters/secure/admin.jsp
/webdev/images/logo.gif
/webdev/images/icons/security.gif
/webdev/images/icons/role.gif
/webdev/images/edillinger.jsp
/webdev/WEB-INF/web.xml
/webdev/WEB-INF/classes/com/taglib/wdjsp/filters/AuthenticationFilter.class
/webdev/WEB-INF/classes/com/taglib/wdjsp/filters/LoginServlet.class
/webdev/WEB-INF/classes/com/taglib/wdjsp/filters/LoginSessionListener.class
/webdev/WEB-INF/classes/com/taglib/wdjsp/filters/LogoutServlet.class
/webdev/WEB-INF/classes/com/taglib/wdjsp/filters/RoleFilter.class
/webdev/WEB-INF/classes/com/taglib/wdjsp/filters/SimpleUserBase.class
/webdev/WEB-INF/classes/com/taglib/wdjsp/filters/SimpleUserDataManager.class
/webdev/WEB-INF/classes/com/taglib/wdjsp/filters/UserBean.class
/webdev/WEB-INF/classes/com/taglib/wdjsp/filters/UserDataManager.class
/webdev/WEB-INF/classes/com/taglib/wdjsp/filters/UserSessionManager.class
/webdev/WEB-INF/lib/mail.jar
/webdev/WEB-INF/lib/activation.jar\
/webdev/WEB-INF/lib/mut.jar
/webdev/WEB-INF/tlds/mut.tld
```

The advantage of this approach is that modifying the application is simpler. To change a JSP page, you edit the file and save the new version in place of the old. To change the value of an initialization parameter, edit and save the web.xml file (and, typically, restart the JSP container). For applications stored in WAR files, modifications such as these first require you to extract the file to be changed, make the changes, then update the archive to include the modified file. Clearly, expanded applications are much easier to work with when many changes must be made to their contents, while WAR files are preferable when it comes time to deploy them.

For this reason, it is good practice to use expanded applications for development, and WAR files for deployment. This allows for rapid turnaround of changes while developing an application, and convenient packaging when deploying it. Because both application forms share the same directory structure, it is a simple task to transform the expanded application used for development into a web archive: simply create a JAR file rooted in the top-level directory of the expanded application, containing the latest versions of all of the development application's files. Assign this JAR file an extension of .war, and it's ready to be deployed. *Vive la guerre!*

15 Performing common JSP tasks

This chapter covers

- Storing and retrieving cookies
- JSP error pages
- Managing and validating forms
- Building a shopping cart

In this chapter we will illustrate common tasks associated with web-based applications, and how they may be performed using JSP. For example, the primary means for interacting with end users over the web is via forms. To that end, we include here multiple sections on managing and validating forms. Data associated with end users is often stored in cookies, so JSP techniques for storing and retrieving cookies, among other topics, are also discussed. All of the examples presented here take the form of building blocks that can serve as basic ingredients in the construction of full-fledged web applications.

15.1 Handling cookies

Cookies are the standard mechanism provided by the HTTP protocol for a web server (or a group of web servers sharing the same Internet domain) to store small amounts of persistent data in a user's web browser for later retrieval. By default, cookies expire as soon as the user exits the browser application. Alternatively, they may be configured to persist across browser sessions until a specified expiration date.

The data stored in a cookie is set by the web server, and therefore can contain only information known to the server. For security reasons, a cookie may be retrieved only by the server that supplied it. Optionally, a cookie can be made accessible to other servers in the same domain as the originating server. A cookie can also be restricted to a specific URL directory hierarchy on the server or servers from which it is accessible. In addition to the data it stores, a cookie is assigned a name; a server can then set multiple cookies and distinguish between them via their names.

15.1.1 Managing cookies

Cookies are set by a web server via HTTP response headers. When a browser requests a URL whose server and directory match those of one or more of its stored cookies, the corresponding cookies are sent back to the server in the form of request headers. If that URL is for a JSP page, the page can access those cookies via the `getCookies()` method of the `request` implicit object (an instance of the `javax.servlet.http.HttpServletRequest` class). In a similar manner, cookies are set by a JSP page via the `addCookie()` method of the `response` implicit object (which is an instance of the `javax.servlet.http.HttpServletResponse` class). These methods are summarized in table 15.1.

For both methods, HTTP cookies are represented as instances of the `javax.servlet.http.Cookie` class. The `getCookies()` method of the `request` object returns an array of `Cookie` instances, while the `addCookie()` method of the `response` object takes an instance of this class as its sole argument.

Table 15.1 Methods of the JSP implicit objects for managing cookies

Implicit Object	Method	Description
`request`	`getCookies()`	Returns an array of the cookies accessible from the page.
`response`	`addCookie(cookie)`	Sends a cookie to the browser for storage/modification.

15.1.2 The Cookie class

Interacting with cookies in a JSP page, therefore, is accomplished by manipulating instances of the `javax.servlet.http.Cookie` class. A single constructor is provided for creating instances, which takes two `String` arguments representing the name of the cookie and the corresponding value, as in the following example statement:

```
Cookie cookie = new Cookie("Favorite", "chocolate chip");
```

Here, the first argument represents the name of the cookie (i.e., `"Favorite"`) and the second its value (i.e., `"chocolate chip"`).

As summarized in table 15.2, accessors are provided for storing and retrieving the properties of a cookie. Note that the text data stored in a cookie value can be modified after its construction using the `setValue()` method, but a cookie's name can only be set using the constructor.

Table 15.2 Common methods of the `javax.servlet.http.Cookie` class

Method	Description
`getName()`	Returns the name of the cookie.
`getValue()`	Returns the value stored in the cookie.
`getDomain()`	Returns the server or domain from which the cookie may be accessed.
`getPath()`	Returns the URL path from which the cookie may be accessed.
`getMaxAge()`	Returns the time remaining (in seconds) before the cookie expires.
`getSecure()`	Indicates whether the cookie is restricted to HTTPS requests.
`setValue()`	Assigns a new value for the cookie.
`setDomain()`	Sets the server or domain from which the cookie may be accessed.
`setPath(uri)`	Sets the URL path from which the cookie may be accessed.
`setMaxAge(sec)`	Sets the time remaining (in seconds) before the cookie expires.
`setSecure(flag)`	Indicates whether the cookie should be restricted to HTTPS requests.

When using this class, remember that instances of `javax.servlet.http.Cookie` reside in the JSP container. After constructing a new instance, or modifying one retrieved via `getCookies()`, you must use the `addCookie()` method of the `response` object in order to update the cookie data stored in the browser.

TIP Although it may seem counterintuitive, this approach is also required to delete a cookie. First, call `setMaxAge()` of the cookie instance with a value of zero (indicating that the cookie is to be deleted). Then—and here's the unintuitive part—call `addCookie()` to inform the browser that the cookie is to be deleted (i.e., by replacing it with a cookie that has been set to expire immediately).

Cookie data is communicated from the server to the browser via response headers. Recall from earlier chapters that all headers must be set before any body content is sent to the browser. As such, in order for the `addCookie()` method to succeed in a JSP page, it must be called before the page's output buffer is flushed. This can occur when the buffer becomes full (depending upon the setting of the `autoflush` attribute of the `page` directive). The output buffer is also flushed any time the `<jsp:include>` action is encountered. The status of output buffering is obviously an important consideration when constructing JSP pages that set cookies.

15.1.3 Example 1: setting a cookie

The first step, then, in using a cookie within a JSP page is to set it. This is accomplished by creating an instance of the `javax.servlet.http.Cookie` class and calling `addCookie()` of the `response` implicit object. Listing 15.1 presents a JSP page, /webdev/red-cookie.jsp, which accomplishes these tasks via a scriptlet:

Listing 15.1 A JSP page called /webdev/red-cookie.jsp

```
<html>
<head>
<title>The Red Cookie Page</title>
</head>
<%@ page import="java.util.Date" %>
<%@ page import="java.net.*" %>
<% String cookieName = "RedCookie";
   Date now = new Date();
   String timestamp = now.toString();
   Cookie cookie = new Cookie(cookieName,
                              URLEncoder.encode(timestamp));
   cookie.setDomain(".taglib.com");
```

```
    cookie.setPath("/webdev");
    cookie.setMaxAge(7 * 24 * 60 * 60);  // One week
    cookie.setVersion(0);
    cookie.setSecure(false);
    cookie.setComment("Timestamp for red cookie.");
    response.addCookie(cookie);
%>
<body>
<font color="red">
<h1>The Red Cookie Page</h1>
<p>
This is the <i>red</i> cookie page.<br>
The blue cookie page is <a href="blue-cookie.jsp">here</a>.
</p>
</font>
</body>
</html>
```

In this case, the cookie is identified by the string `"RedCookie"`, and is assigned a value containing a string representation of the time at which the request was received by the JSP page. The HTTP protocol imposes certain restrictions on the types of characters that may appear in a cookie's value, so it is generally good practice, as is done here, to URL-encode cookie values via the `java.net.URLEncoder.encode()` static method.

In addition, the domain and path (i.e., base URL directory) are set for the cookie to ensure that it is accessible from related pages on other servers in the host domain. It is set to expire within one week. For maximum browser compatibility, it is set to adhere to version 0 of the cookie specification. Secure cookies can only be sent using the HTTPS protocol, which encrypts requests and responses. Here, the argument to the new cookie's `setSecure()` method is `false`, indicating the cookie should be transferred via the standard unencrypted HTTP protocol. After supplying a comment for the cookie, it is marked for transmission back to the browser via the `addCookie()` method.

The response sent to the browser from this JSP page is depicted in figure 15.1. For this page, there is no dynamic content in the rendered output. Instead, all of the dynamic content is in the headers, where the request-specific cookie value is supplied.

15.1.4 Example 2: retrieving a cookie

The effect of the JSP page presented in the previous example is to update a time stamp whenever the user visits the page. This time stamp is stored in a cookie, and may be retrieved by other JSP pages which share the domain and path originally assigned to the cookie.

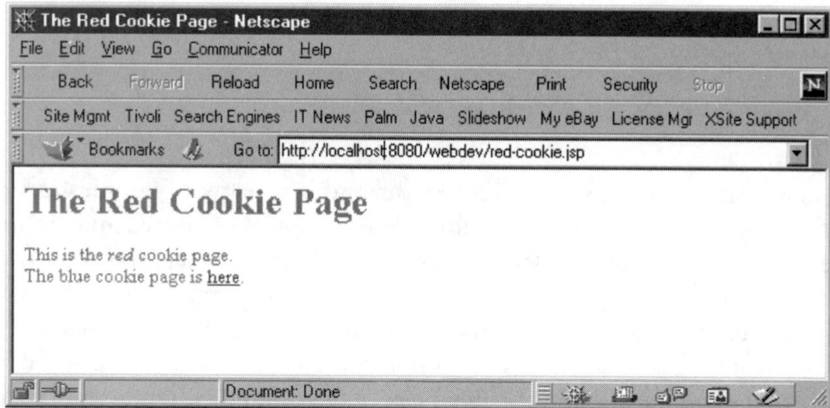

Figure 15.1 Output of JSP page that sets a cookie

Cookies are retrieved via the `getCookies()` method of the `request` implicit object. Here is a sample JSP page, /webdev/blue-cookie.jsp, which attempts to retrieve the cookie set by the page in the previous example:

```
<html>
<head>
<title>The Blue Cookie Page</title>
</head>
<%@ page import="java.net.*" %>
<% String cookieName = "RedCookie";
   Cookie cookies[] = request.getCookies();
   Cookie redCookie = null;
   if (cookies != null) {
     for (int i = 0; i < cookies.length; ++i) {
       if (cookies[i].getName().equals(cookieName)) {
         redCookie = cookies[i];
         break;
       }
     }
   }
%>
<body>
<font color="blue">
<h1>The Blue Cookie Page</h1>
<p>
This is the <i>blue</i> cookie page.<br>
You last visited the <a href="red-cookie.jsp">red cookie page</a>
<% if (redCookie == null) { %>
    over a week ago.
<% } else { %>
```

```
    on <%= URLDecoder.decode(redCookie.getValue()) %>.
<% } %>
</p>
</font>
</body>
</html>
```

The first scriptlet on this page iterates through the array of cookies returned by `getCookies()` until it finds one named `"RedCookie"`. The dynamic content displayed by this page is then based on whether or not this cookie was found.

If no such cookie were found, then the conditional scriptlet near the end of the page will cause the page to display the text indicated in figure 15.2. The presumption here is that if the cookie is not found, it must have expired. Another possibility is that the cookie has not been set in the first place, which would be the case if the user had never visited the page which sets the cookie. The important point here is it is not possible to tell the difference between the expiration of a cookie and its absence.

If, on the other hand, the cookie is present, the iterative search through the array returned by the `getCookies()` method will succeed and the `redCookie` variable will not be `null`. In this case, the second clause of the conditional scriptlet will be exercised, resulting in the output depicted in figure 15.3. Here, the `java.net.URLDecoder.decode()` static method is used to decode the value stored in the cookie so that it may be displayed in its original form.

WARNING The `java.net.URLDecoder` class was added in Java 2. Earlier versions of the Java specification do not include this class. The `java.net.URLEncoder` class, however, is present in the 1.0 and 1.1 releases.

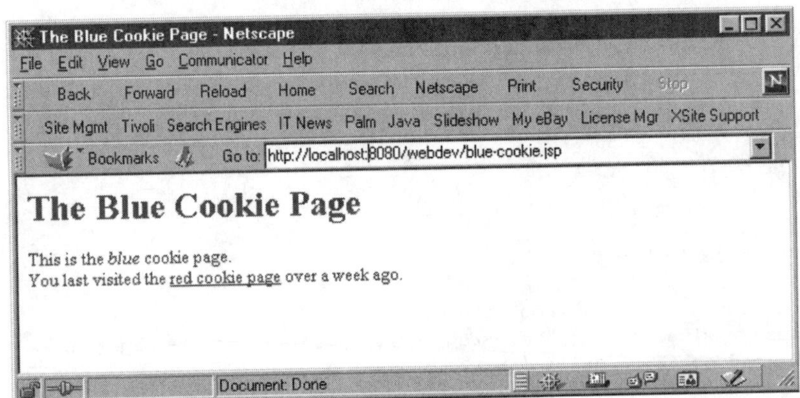

Figure 15.2 Output of JSP page that retrieves a cookie when it has not been set

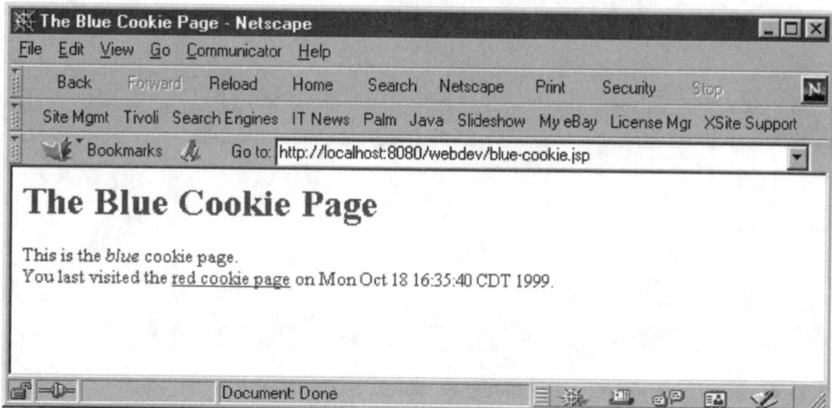

Figure 15.3 Output of JSP page that retrieves a cookie which has been set

When taking advantage of HTTP cookies, a number of restrictions on their use should be kept in mind. First, the data stored in a cookie (i.e., its name and value) can occupy at most 4 KB of storage. Also, while it is possible for a given server or domain to set multiple cookies, the browser is only required to store up to twenty cookies per domain setting. At the same time, the browser need only store up to 300 cookies. If either limit is exhausted, the browser is expected to delete cookies, beginning with those which have been used least recently.

The domain assigned to a cookie must have at least two periods in its name. This will automatically be the case if a fully qualified server name is used, such as www.example.com. If the domain is used instead, it should take the form .example.com in order to satisfy the two-period requirement. This rule is in place to prevent the specification of cookies which can be read across an entire top-level domain (i.e., .com, .org, .net, etc.). Note that if no domain is specified for a cookie, it may only be read by the host which originally set it.

15.2 Creating error pages

As mentioned in chapter 6, the typical behavior when an error occurs while processing a JSP page is to display an error message—possibly including a stack trace—within or in place of the output from that page. Figure 15.4 displays the results generated by one JSP container when processing a page that attempts to divide a number by zero. The result is not particularly user-friendly, nor does it provide much information that the development team could use to track down the problem.

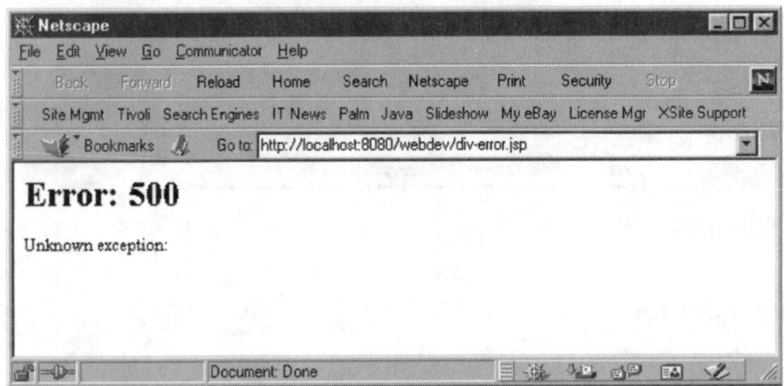

Figure 15.4 Output from a JSP page that generates a run-time error

Fortunately, JSP provides a means for addressing both of these issues via the `errorPage` attribute of the `page` directive, introduced in chapter 5. This feature allows you to designate an alternate JSP page to which control will be forwarded whenever the processing of a page causes an error. Furthermore, the exception that is thrown when the error occurs will be accessible from the selected error page via the `exception` implicit object. By taking advantage of this capability, you can ensure the user is clearly informed that a problem has occurred, and reassured that it will be fixed. At the same time, the full circumstances surrounding the error can be captured for use by the developers in resolving it.

JSP error pages can also be used for handling servlet errors. As mentioned in chapter 10, a JSP error page expects to find the `Throwable` object representing the error in an attribute of the `request` implicit object associated with the name `"javax.servlet.jsp.jspException"`. Servlet code that has the potential of throwing an exception can use a `try/catch` block to catch the exception, store it as a request attribute, then forward it to a JSP error page. The error page is then responsible for displaying an error message to the user and recording the circumstances under which the error occurred.

In this section, an error page will be presented that displays a brief summary and apology to the end user, while constructing a detailed error message behind the scenes which is then sent to the webmaster via email. Sun's JavaMail API is used to deliver the electronic mail message.

15.2.1 An erroneous page

In order to test this error page, we first need a page that will generate errors. Here, for example, is a small JSP page, /webdev/div-error.jsp, which is guaranteed to throw an exception every time it is requested because it attempts to divide a number by zero:

```
<html>
<head>
<%@ page errorPage="error.jsp" session="false" %>
<title>Arithmetic Error</title>
</head>
<body bgcolor="white">
<h1>Arithmetic Error</h1>
<% int x = 5; %>
<P>
In Java, dividing by zero raises an exception:
<tt>25/0 = <%= 25/(5-x) %></tt>
</P>
</body>
</html>
```

Note that, because the compiler recognizes that an explicit divide-by-zero expression is invalid, the local variable x is introduced to make page compilation succeed. When a request is received for this page, however, the arithmetic expression will generate a run-time error when the division by zero is detected.

In the absence of the JSP page directive near the beginning of this file, a request for this page will generate results such as those depicted in figure 15.4. By incorporating this directive, however, more graceful and more thorough handling of the error is possible.

15.2.2 Data collection methods

Before examining the error page itself, we will first consider a set of utility methods it will use to collect information about the error. Note that control will be transferred to the error page as if the <jsp:forward> action had been used, meaning that the error page will have access to the request implicit object corresponding to the original page request, as well as an exception implicit object representing the error that occurred there.

The first of these utility methods is makeErrorReport(), which takes values corresponding to both of these implicit objects as its arguments:

```
public String makeErrorReport (HttpServletRequest req, Throwable e) {
  StringBuffer buffer = new StringBuffer();
  reportException(buffer, e);
  reportRequest(buffer, req);
  reportParameters(buffer, req);
  reportHeaders(buffer, req);
  reportCookies(buffer, req);
  return buffer.toString();
}
```

This method serves as the control routine for collecting information about the request and the resulting error. An instance of `java.lang.StringBuffer` is constructed for storing this information, which is then passed to a series of other methods that store various categories of data into this `StringBuffer`. Once all of the data has been collected, the contents of the buffer are used to generate a full-fledged `String` object.

The first of these methods that add data to the `StringBuffer` is `reportException()`, which collects information about the error itself:

```
public void reportException (StringBuffer buffer, Throwable e) {
  StringWriter writer = new StringWriter();
  e.printStackTrace(new PrintWriter(writer));
  buffer.append(writer.getBuffer());
  buffer.append('\n');
}
```

More specifically, this method wraps a `java.io.PrintWriter` around a `java.io.StringWriter`, into which the exception's stack trace is written. The contents of the `StringWriter` are then added to the `StringBuffer` passed in as an argument to this method.

The stack trace contains all of the information available about the error that occurred, including its type, a brief explanatory message, and the stack of method calls that were in effect when the exception was thrown. As a result, the remaining data collection methods are focused not on the error, but on the context in which the error occurred, as embodied in the request.

Basic information about the request is collected via the `reportRequest()` method. This method reconstructs the URL used to request the original page, as well as information about the user's session (if applicable), and is defined as follows:

```
public void reportRequest (StringBuffer buffer, HttpServletRequest req) {
  buffer.append("Request: ");
  buffer.append(req.getMethod());
  buffer.append(' ');
  buffer.append(HttpUtils.getRequestURL(req));
  String queryString = req.getQueryString();
  if (queryString != null) {
    buffer.append('?');
    buffer.append(queryString);
  }
  buffer.append("\nSession ID: ");
  String sessionId = req.getRequestedSessionId();
  if (sessionId == null) {
    buffer.append("none");
  } else if (req.isRequestedSessionIdValid()) {
    buffer.append(sessionId);
```

```
    buffer.append(" (from ");
    if (req.isRequestedSessionIdFromCookie())
      buffer.append("cookie)\n");
    else if (req.isRequestedSessionIdFromURL())
      buffer.append("url)\n");
    else
      buffer.append("unknown)\n");
  } else {
    buffer.append("invalid\n");
  }
}
```

To reconstruct the URL, the HTTP method (e.g., `GET`, `POST`, etc.) and query string are retrieved from the `javax.servlet.http.HttpServletRequest` object passed in via the `req` argument. The protocol, host name, and port number are not directly accessible from this object, however; instead one of the utility methods provided by the `javax.servlet.http.HttpUtils` class, `getRequestURL()`, is used to recreate the base URL.

The methods of the `javax.servlet.http.HttpUtils` class are summarized in table 15.3. This class has been deprecated in version 2.3 of the Servlet specification, upon which JSP 1.2 is based. Instead, an analogous `getRequestURL()` method has been added to the `HttpServletRequest` class itself.

Table 15.3 Methods of the javax.servlet.http.HttpUtils class

Method	Description
`getRequestURL(request)`	Recreates the URL used by the browser to make the request.
`parsePostData(length, stream)`	Parses HTML form data submitted via a POST request.
`parseQueryString(string)`	Parses the query string of a requested URL into a hash table of parameters and values.

The session information reported by this method is likewise retrieved from the request. If session information is present and valid, this information will include the user-specific session identification code, and an indication of how the session information is being transferred between the server and the browser (i.e., via either cookies or URL rewriting). This is accomplished via standard methods provided by the `javax.servlet.http.HttpServletRequest` class, first described in chapter 4.

The next data collection method, `reportParameters()`, lists the request parameters that accompanied the original page request. Note that the `HttpServletRequest` class does not distinguish between parameters supplied in the URL via a query string and those provided in the body of an HTTP `POST` request. In fact, both may be present in the same request, and will be combined into one overall set of parameters. If values for the same parameter are provided multiple times, all of the values are stored. In such a case, the first value supplied for a parameter takes precedence, and parameter values set in the URL take precedence over those set in the body of the request. The code for this method is as follows:

```
public void reportParameters (StringBuffer buffer, HttpServletRequest req) {
  Enumeration names = req.getParameterNames();
  if (names.hasMoreElements()) {
    buffer.append("Parameters:\n");
    while (names.hasMoreElements()) {
      String name = (String) names.nextElement();
      String[] values = req.getParameterValues(name);
      for (int i = 0; i < values.length; ++i) {
        buffer.append("    ");
        buffer.append(name);
        buffer.append(" = ");
        buffer.append(values[i]);
        buffer.append('\n');
      }
    }
  }
}
```

Here, the `getParameterNames()` method is called to obtain an enumeration of all of the parameters known to the request. If there is at least one parameter present, the next step is to print the name of each parameter, and its values. Since one parameter may have multiple values, a nested iteration loop is required to iterate over all of the values returned by the `getParameterValues()` method.

After listing the request parameters, the next step is to list the request headers, using the following `reportHeaders()` method:

```
public void reportHeaders (StringBuffer buffer, HttpServletRequest req) {
  Enumeration names = req.getHeaderNames();
  if (names.hasMoreElements()) {
    buffer.append("Headers:\n");
    while (names.hasMoreElements()) {
      String name = (String) names.nextElement();
      String value = (String) req.getHeader(name);
      buffer.append("    ");
      buffer.append(name);
      buffer.append(": ");
      buffer.append(value);
      buffer.append('\n');
    }
  }
}
```

Headers contain information about the browser that made the request, as well as any cookies the browser is submitting with the request. The code for this method is similar to that of `reportParameters()`. Here, the `getHeaderNames()` method of the `HttpServletRequest` instance is called to generate an enumeration of the names of the headers present in the request. We then iterate through this result, adding the name of the header and its corresponding value—retrieved via the `getHeader()` method of `HttpServletRequest`—to the `StringBuffer` object being used to accumulate our error report.

Unfortunately, even though the HTTP protocol allows requests to specify multiple headers with the same name, the `HttpServletRequest` class only provides methods for fetching one header of a given name. In practice, most headers are only ever specified once, but there are a few which regularly appear multiple times in a single request. In particular, when a request includes multiple cookies, each cookie is generally specified by its own header. For a request containing multiple cookies, only one of the cookie headers will be listed by the `reportHeaders()` method described previously.

For this reason, the `reportCookies()` method is provided to ensure that all of the cookies that are relevant to the request are included in the error report. The code for this method is as follows:

```
public void reportCookies (StringBuffer buffer, HttpServletRequest req) {
  Cookie[] cookies = req.getCookies();
  int l = cookies.length;
  if (l > 0) {
    buffer.append("Cookies:\n");
    for (int i = 0; i < l; ++i) {
      Cookie cookie = cookies[i];
      buffer.append("    ");
      buffer.append(cookie.getName());
      buffer.append(" = ");
      buffer.append(cookie.getValue());
      buffer.append('\n');
    }
  }
}
```

This function relies on several of the cookie-related methods discussed earlier in this chapter in order to iterate through the request's cookies and list their names and values.

15.2.3 Sending electronic mail

Given all of these methods for constructing a description of an error and the request that generated it, we next need a mechanism for delivering this text to someone who can fix the underlying problem. For this example, that mechanism will be an electronic mail message. The methods described previously will be used to generate the body of this mail message, which is then sent to one or more recipients by means of the JavaMail API. This specification defines a set of Java classes for interacting with mail servers in order to send and receive electronic mail messages.

While a complete description of the JavaMail API is beyond the scope of this book, we will discuss a small subset of this specification in the context of a simple utility method, `sendEmail()`, which encapsulates all of the JavaMail calls needed to connect to an SMTP server and send a simple text-based mail message. (The full functionality provided by the JavaMail API extends well beyond the straightforward task presented here. For example, JavaMail includes support for retrieving messages from both POP and IMAP servers, as well as for sending messages incorporating styled text and/or attachments.)

For use in a JSP error page, however, sending a plain text message is sufficient. To this end, the `sendEmail()` method is defined as follows:

```
public void sendEmail (String mailServer, String subject,
                       String to[], String from, String messageText)
  throws AddressException, MessagingException {
  // Create session
  Properties mailProps = new Properties();
  mailProps.put("mail.smtp.host", mailServer);
  Session mailSession = Session.getDefaultInstance(mailProps, null);
  // Construct addresses
  int toCount = to.length;
  InternetAddress[] toAddrs = new InternetAddress[toCount];
  for (int i = 0; i < toCount; ++i) {
    toAddrs[i] = new InternetAddress(to[i]);
  }
  InternetAddress fromAddr = new InternetAddress(from);
  // Create and initialize message
  Message message = new MimeMessage(mailSession);
  message.setFrom(fromAddr);
  message.setRecipients(Message.RecipientType.TO, toAddrs);
  message.setSubject(subject);
  message.setContent(messageText.toString(), "text/plain");
  // Send message
  Transport.send(message);
}
```

All of the arguments to this method are instances of the Java `String` class, with the exception of the `to` argument, representing the intended recipients, which is an array of strings. The `mailServer` parameter is the name of a network host running an SMTP server that will handle the actual sending of the message. The `subject` argument represents the subject line for the message. The `from` parameter identifies the email address from which the message is being sent. The validity of this return address may or may not be confirmed, depending upon how the SMTP server has been configured. The final argument, `messageText`, should be a string containing the text to be sent as the body of the email message.

A central concept of the JavaMail API is that of a *mail session*, representing a set of interactions with a mail server. Mail sessions are represented by an instance of the `javax.mail.Session` class, which is initialized from an instance of the `java.util.Properties` class. For our purposes here, the only information that needs to be in the property list for this mail session is the identity of the SMTP host, as indicated by a property named `mail.smtp.host`. The next step is to convert the email addresses passed in as `String` values via the `to` and `from` arguments into instances of the `javax.mail.internet.InternetAddress` class. Next, an instance of the `javax.mail.Message` class is constructed. This is an abstract class, however, so the actual object created is an instance of the `javax.mail.internet.MimeMessage` class, whose constructor takes a `MailSession` instance as its sole argument. The properties of this message are then set to identify the sender, subject, recipients, and body. Note that in the call to `setContent()` the MIME type of the message body is set to `"text/plain"`, indicating that the text of the message is standard ASCII text. Finally, the static `send()` method of the `javax.mail.Transport` class is called to actually deliver the message.

Within the body of this method, several of the JavaMail method calls have the potential to throw exceptions. As we will see in the next section, for the current application within a JSP error page it is more convenient to pass these exceptions to callers of the `sendEmail()` method, rather than attempt to handle them locally. For this reason, `sendEmail()` is declared as throwing two exception classes, `javax.mail.internet.AddressException` and `javax.mail.MessagingException`.

15.2.4 The error page

These utility methods for collecting data and sending electronic mail can be combined in a JSP error page that serves both end users and developers. Here is the content of such a page, /webdev/error.jsp, where the method bodies have been removed for brevity's sake:

```
<html>
<head>
<%@ page isErrorPage="true" %>
<%@ page import="java.util.*, java.io.*" %>
<%@ page import="javax.mail.*, javax.mail.internet.*" %>
<title>Oops!</title>
</head>
<body bgcolor="white">
<p>
Sorry, an error has occurred:<br>
<center> <b><%= exception %></b> </center>
</p>
<% try {
   String mailServer = "mail.taglib.com";
   String subject = "JSP Error Notification";
   String [] to = { "webmaster@taglib.com" };
   String from = "JSP Container <webmaster@taglib.com>";
   sendEmail(mailServer, subject, to, from,
             makeErrorReport(request, exception)); %>
<p>Not to worry, though! The guilty parties have been notified.</p>
<% }
   catch (AddressException e) { %>
<p>Invalid e-mail address(es) for error notification.</p>
<% }
   catch (MessagingException e) { %>
<p>Unable to send e-mail for error notification.</p>
<% } %>
</body>
</html>
<%!
  public String makeErrorReport (HttpServletRequest req, Throwable e) {
    ...
  }
  public void reportException (StringBuffer buffer, Throwable e) {
    ...
  }
  public void reportRequest (StringBuffer buffer, HttpServletRequest req) {
    ...
  }
  public void reportParameters (StringBuffer buffer,
                                HttpServletRequest req) {
    ...
  }
  public void reportHeaders (StringBuffer buffer, HttpServletRequest req) {
    ...
  }
  public void reportCookies (StringBuffer buffer, HttpServletRequest req) {
    ...
  }
  public void sendEmail (String mailServer, String subject,
```

```
                    String to[], String from, String messageText)
    throws AddressException, MessagingException {
    ...
  }
%>
```

The first JSP element on this page is the page directive, which uses isErrorPage to indicate that this page serves as an error page for one or more other JSP pages. As a result, the exception implicit object will be available for use by other JSP elements on the page.

The two additional page directives which follow are used to import classes from multiple Java packages. These classes are used in the utility methods which appear in a JSP declaration at the end of the page. By using the import attribute of the page directive in this manner, it is unnecessary to prefix the class names with their corresponding package names when they are referred to in the method bodies.

The page directives are followed by a combination of HTML and JSP elements that present the error message to the user, as depicted in Figure 15.5. A JSP expression is used to print a brief description of the error, by taking advantage of the toString() method provided by the java.lang.Throwable class. The final line in the browser output is determined by the success (or lack thereof) of the code that submits the error report to the development team.

This last step is accomplished by means of a set of JSP scriptlets implementing a try/catch block. Within the try clause, the first step is to configure the site-specific mail parameters. These parameters are then supplied as arguments to the sendEmail() method, along with body text generated via the makeErrorReport()

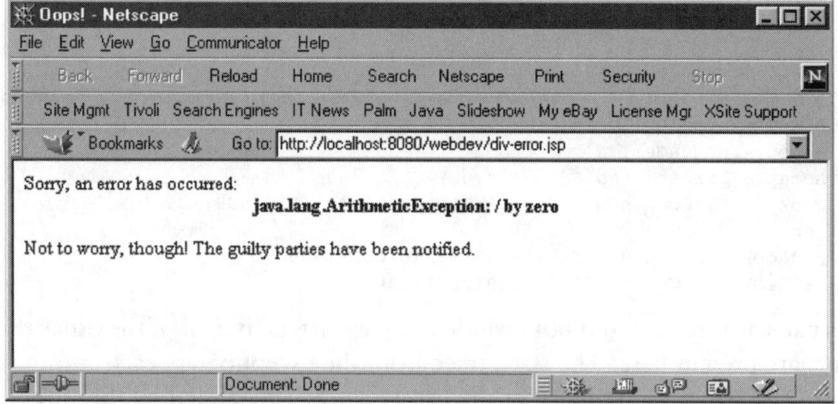

Figure 15.5 Output sent to the browser by the example error page

method. If any exceptions are thrown by the underlying JavaMail code, an indication to this effect will appear in the JSP output.

When the configuration parameters are set properly and the mail server is accessible, execution of these methods should succeed and no exceptions will be thrown within the error page itself. Under these circumstances, the "guilty parties" message will appear in the JSP output and a report such as the following will be sent to the designated recipients:

```
From: JSP Container <webmaster@taglib.com>
To: webmaster@taglib.com
Subject: JSP Error Notification

java.lang.ArithmeticException: / by zero
    at home.server.user.web-
       dev.div_error_jsp_1._jspService(div_error_jsp_1.java:72)
    at com.sun.jsp.runtime.HttpJspBase.service(HttpJspBase.java:87)
    at javax.servlet.http.HttpServlet.service(HttpServlet.java:840)
    at com.sun.jsp.runtime.JspServlet$JspServletWrapper.service(JspServ-
       let.java:88)
    at com.sun.jsp.runtime.JspServlet.serviceJspFile(JspServlet.java:218)
    at com.sun.jsp.runtime.JspServlet.service(JspServlet.java:294)
    at javax.servlet.http.HttpServlet.service(HttpServlet.java:840)
    at com.sun.web.core.ServletWrapper.handleRequest(ServletWrapper.java:155)
    at com.sun.web.core.Context.handleRequest(Context.java:414)
    at com.sun.web.server.ConnectionHandler.run(ConnectionHandler.java:139)

Request: GET http://localhost:8080/webdev/div-error.jsp
Session ID: To1010mC8608781812051488At (from cookie)
Headers:
    Connection: Keep-Alive
    User-Agent: Mozilla/4.5 [en] (WinNT; U)
    Pragma: no-cache
    Host: localhost:8080
    Accept: image/gif, image/x-xbitmap, image/jpeg, image/pjpeg, image/png, */*
    Accept-Encoding: gzip
    Accept-Language: en
    Accept-Charset: iso-8859-1,*,utf-8
    Cookie: RedCookie=Mon+Oct+18+16%3A35%3A40+CDT+1999;SESSIONID=To1010m…
Cookies:
    RedCookie = Mon+Oct+18+16%3A35%3A40+CDT+1999
    SESSIONID = To1010mC8608781812051488At
```

This particular request did not include any parameters, but all of the other report elements are present here. The stack trace from the exception appears, and the description of the request indicates that the exception was generated by the /webdev/div-error.jsp page. The session ID code appears, with an indication that it is being stored in a cookie. This is followed by listings of nine request headers and two cookies.

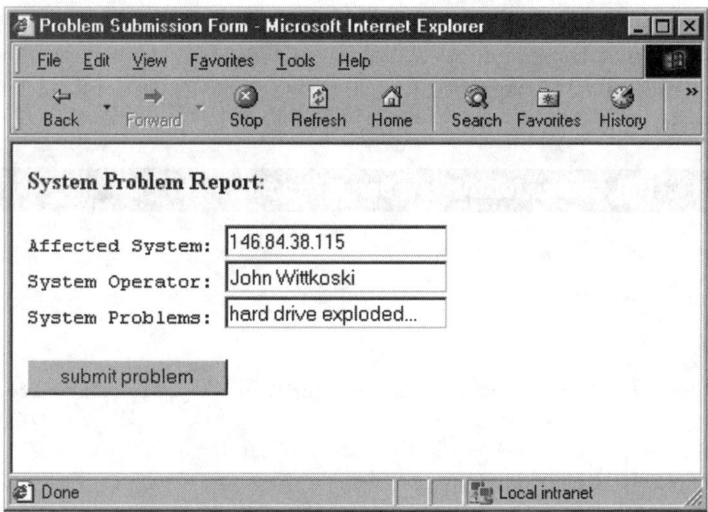

Figure 15.6 Problem submission form

These headers indicate, among other things, that the request originated from version 4.5 of Netscape's browser (nicknamed Mozilla), running on the Windows platform. The cookies correspond to the session ID code and the time stamp cookie associated with the JSP cookie example presented earlier in this chapter. Note that, as mentioned in the earlier discussion of the `reportHeaders()` method, only one of the two cookie headers appears among the header listings.

15.3 Mixing JSP and JavaScript

JSP can work in conjunction with JavaScript (and other client-side technologies) to add server-side processing to operations typically limited to client-side activities. As an example, we'll build a simple form for reporting system problems. As an additional requirement, we've decided that we want to verify the validity of the host name specified by the user before allowing it to submit the problem. We also require that the problem host be identified by its IP address, rather than its host name. The resulting form is shown in figure 15.6.

When the user inputs a host name into the Affected System field of our form, it is changed into the corresponding IP address when they tab over to the next field. (If an actual IP address is supplied, it is not changed.) Furthermore, if the user inputs an invalid host name, an alert window will notify him or her of this fact and he or she will not be allowed to submit the form until the problem is corrected. All of this happens on the client before submitting the form, and without the user having to manually reload the page. As a matter of fact, the form page, shown in listing 15.2, is not even a JSP page, it's just standard HTML, with a little JavaScript thrown in. How, then, do we perform this little trick? We cheat.

Listing 15.2 HTML source for the JavaScript example form

```
<html>
<head>
<script language="javascript">
resolved=false;

function resolve(element) {
  top.resolver.document.location = "resolver.jsp?host=" + element.value;
}

function isResolved() {
  alert(resolved);
  return resolved;
}
</script>
</head>
<body>
<b>System Problem Report:</b>
<P>
<form name="info" action="/servlet/problem" onSubmit='return isResolved()'>
<TT>
Affected System: <input type="text" name="host" onChange='resolve(this)'> <BR>
System Operator: <input type="text" name="user"> <BR>
System Problems: <input type="text" name="problem"> <BR>
</TT>
<P>
<input type="submit" value="submit problem">
</form>
</body>
</html>
```

If you closely examine the HTML in the listing, you will notice that we are making references to another frame called `resolver`, which we direct to load the page `resolver.jsp`. It is this second page—which *is* a JSP page—that performs the host name resolution for us. It appears at the bottom of the page in a hidden frame, using the frameset code shown in listing 15.3.

Listing 15.3 HTML source for the JavaScript example frameset

```
<html>
<head><title>Problem Submission Form</title></head>
<frameset rows="100%, 0%" border=0 frameborder="no">
<frame src="form.html" name="theform">
<frame name="resolver">
</frameset>
</html>
```

When the user makes a change to the Affected System field, the `onChange()` handler in the field's `<input>` tag calls the `resolve()` function—a client-side JavaScript function—to load our JSP into the hidden frame. This function also appends the value of the field to the request, giving our JSP page the host name it needs to verify. In the JSP page, we attempt to resolve the host name. If we are successful we have two tasks to do. We have to change the value of the Affected System field to the verified IP address, and we have to alert the document that a valid host name has been entered. We do this with cross-frame JavaScript:

```
<script>
top.theform.document.info.host.value="<%= ip %>";
top.theform.resolved=true;
</script>
```

If the host name turns out to be invalid, we alert the user to its evil ways, flip the `resolved` flag to false, and clear the offending value from the form field:

```
<script>
alert("Invalid Hostname: <%= host %>");
top.theform.document.info.host.value="";
top.theform.resolved=false;
top.theform.document.info.host.focus();
</script>
```

Note that we can embed JSP commands into the midst of our JavaScript code here. This may seem strange at first, but keep in mind how a JSP page is processed. After all the JSP code is handled, what you are left with is the HTML, JavaScript, or other data containing your JSP elements. In this case, we are conditionally inserting blocks of JavaScript into our output. The full source to the resolver.jsp page is presented in listing 15.4.

Listing 15.4 The resolver.jsp page

```
<%@ page import="java.net.*" %>
<html>
<body>
<%
String host = request.getParameter("host");
String ip = host;
if (host != null) {
   try {
     ip = java.net.InetAddress.getByName(host).getHostAddress();
%>
<script>
top.theform.document.info.host.value="<%= ip %>";
top.theform.resolved=true;
</script>
<%
   }
   catch (UnknownHostException e) {
%>
<script>
alert("Invalid Hostname: <%= host %>");
top.theform.document.info.host.value="";
top.theform.resolved=false;
top.theform.document.info.host.focus();
</script>
<% }
}
%>
</body>
</html>
```

Note that the `getHostAddress()` method throws an `UnknownHostException` if it is unable to resolve the name correctly. Therefore, we execute it in a `try/catch` block, which has the side effect of determining which block of JavaScript we end up calling.

Autocompleting form fields

This same technique can be used for other client/server cooperative activities. One good example of this is simulating fields with automatic completion through the use of an `onKeyPress()` handler. This JavaScript handler is triggered with each key press, not just when tabbing out of a field or hitting return. With each press, you pass the current value of the field to your hidden JSP, which searches the database for a match, based on what the user has typed so far. So in our example above, as soon as the user typed `"John W"` into the System Operator field, our JSP could search the user database and automatically fill in the rest of the name.

15.4 Building interactive interfaces

Using JSP we can create web-based applications which look and feel more like traditional desktop programs. Even though we must cope with the transient nature of web requests, it is possible to build interfaces whose elements have a more interactive feel, preserving their state between actions. While dynamic HTML and JavaScript have begun to allow such behavior for client-side operations, we can also achieve similar results with applications based on server-side operations. To do this, we combine the data collection form and its handler into a single JSP page whose form elements provide an application interface that retains its state across multiple requests.

15.4.1 Sticky widgets

Java developers creating applications or applets with Swing or AWT build their interface around input elements such as text fields, check boxes, and buttons. These elements allow the developer to collect information and direction from the user. When a user clicks a button, the developer uses information from the input elements to perform the corresponding function. When we develop an application using JSP we use HTML form elements in this same role. One important difference, however, is that the stateless nature of HTTP forces us to do more work ourselves in order to maintain the state of the user interface.

When an HTML page containing a form is loaded into the browser the state of its elements is encoded into the HTML. If you fill out a form once and then revisit it, the state and contents of all of the elements on the page are lost and the form reverts to its original condition as specified in the HTML. HTTP requests, unless cookies (which have limited storage capacity) are being used, have no memory. The only way that form elements on a page can appear to maintain state between requests is by dynamically generating the HTML that controls the layout and contents of the form to represent the state you wish to present.

The approach we will follow is to create a JSP page that collects information from its form elements and then targets itself as its own form handler. This HTML interface should emulate the behavior of traditional applications. When the JSP lays out its form on subsequent requests it should reflect the form's most recent state and content. If a user selected a check box or radio button before submitting the form, it should be selected again when the form is redisplayed. If a text field had text in it then it should again contain that same text.

While it is easy to combine the form and the results into a single page, creating this interactive interface requires us to understand how each form element can be configured through JSP's dynamic HTML generation capabilities. Each input element's state is preserved through the data in the form submission. For each element of our interface we have a value that represents its state just prior to clicking Submit. The values of the form elements are then submitted as request parameters, from which they may be extracted when the next form request—initiated by the form submission itself—is processed.

15.4.2 Utility methods

To aid in extracting parameter values from requests, we first introduce a set of utility methods that will be used throughout this form-handling example. The first, `getParam()`, is defined as:

```
public String getParam (HttpServletRequest request, String param) {
  if (request.getParameter(param) == null)
    return "";
  else
    return request.getParameter(param);
}
```

This method retrieves the value of the named parameter from the indicated request. As a convenience, if the parameter is not present in the request, an empty `String` is returned. (For the `request` object's own `getParameter()` method, a `null` value is returned for parameters that have not been specified.)

For those parameters which may have multiple values assigned to them, a `getParamValues()` method is provided. Here is the code for this method:

```
public String getParamValues (HttpServletRequest request, String param) {
  String values[] = request.getParameterValues(param);
  if (values == null) return "";
  int count = values.length;
  switch (count) {
    case 1:
        return values[0];
    default:
        StringBuffer result = new StringBuffer(values[0]);
        int stop = count - 1;
        if (stop > 1) result.append(", ");
        for (int i = 1; i < stop; ++i) {
          result.append(values[i]);
          result.append(", ");
        }
        result.append(" and ");
        result.append(values[stop]);
        return result.toString();
  }
}
```

Like getParam(), this method returns an empty String when the parameter has not been specified. When one or more values are specified, however, getParamValues() will combine them into one String, adding comma separators and the word "and" where appropriate.

This next method, requestContains(), is used to determine whether or not a specific value has been specified for a request parameter, and is defined as follows:

```
public boolean requestContains (HttpServletRequest request,
                                String param, String testValue) {
  String rp[] = request.getParameterValues(param);
  if (rp == null)
    return false;
  for (int i=0; i < rp.length; i++)
    if (rp[i].equals(testValue))
      return true;
  return false;
}
```

In this method, all of the values specified for a parameter are compared to the specified testValue. This method only returns true if there is a match.

The last two utility methods extend the functionality of the requestContains() method to return specific String values when a matching value is detected. Here are the definitions for isChecked() and isSelected():

```
public String isChecked (HttpServletRequest request,
                         String param, String testValue) {
  return (requestContains(request, param, testValue)) ? "checked" : "";
}
public String isSelected (HttpServletRequest request,
                          String param, String testValue) {
  return (requestContains(request, param, testValue)) ? "selected" : "";
}
```

As we will see, these last two methods will be particularly useful in the initialization of radio buttons, check boxes, and select boxes.

15.4.3 The example form

The form we will use to motivate this example is depicted in figures 15.7 and 15.8. As illustrated in figure 15.7, various form elements are used to collect input data from the user:

- A text field, for entering a name
- A select box, for choosing a device
- A set of check boxes, for selecting one or more colors

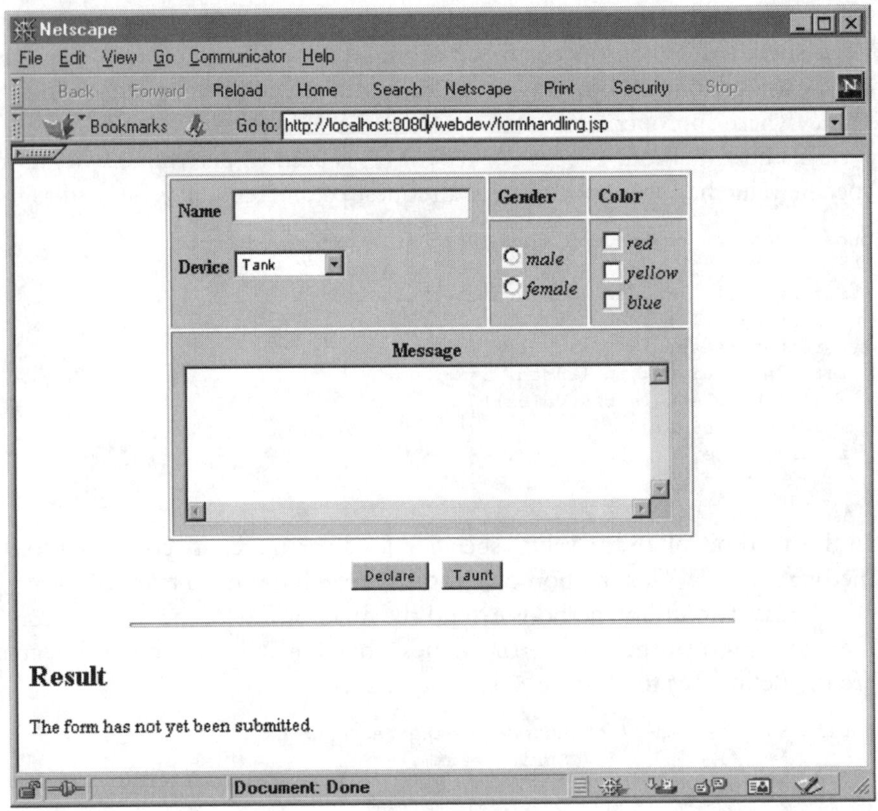

Figure 15.7 The example form, prior to submission

- Radio buttons, for selecting a gender
- A text area, for entering a multiline message
- Two form submission buttons

When either of the form submission buttons is clicked, the form calls itself to process the form data and redisplay the form. The result of processing the form—in this case, a sentence constructed from the values selected for the form elements—is displayed at the bottom of the page (figure 15.8). The form widgets are *sticky*: each time the form is displayed, the default values for all of the input fields are based on the final input values from the last time the form was submitted.

Based on this description of the form, then, let's examine how this behavior is implemented as a JSP page.

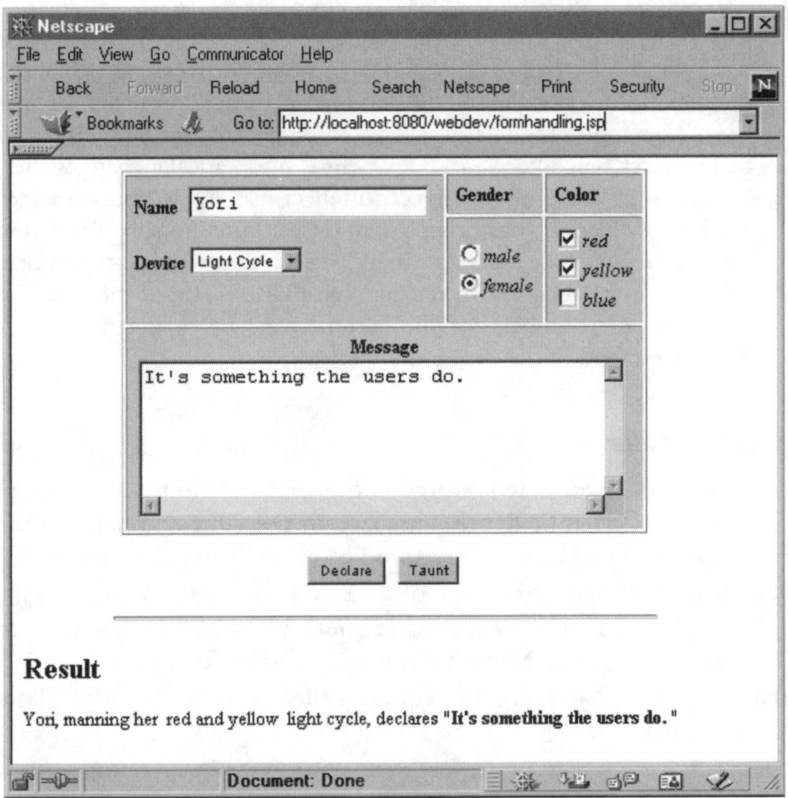

Figure 15.8 The example form, after submission

15.4.4 Setting up the form

We can use the following JSP expression to create a form that targets itself no matter what URL it was called from. This will allow us to move our application to any location without having to modify any code.

```
<FORM action="<%= HttpUtils.getRequestURL(request) %>" method="POST">
```

This JSP expression will insert the full URL to the form as its `action` target. Submitting the form, then, will call back to the same URL to handle the form as was used to bring up the form in the first place.

WARNING This technique of querying the request to determine the URL necessary to reach the current page will work only in situations where the JSP was accessed directly. If, for example, the JSP was loaded through a servlet using the `forward()` method of the `RequestDispatcher` class, the path information may be incorrect, since `RequestDispatcher` automatically changes the path information in the `request` object to reflect its new destination address. This can be a problem if your original request was intentionally directed to a servlet, since subsequent requests will likely need to go back through that servlet. In this case, it is possible to obtain a local URL (without the host name, protocol, or port number) for the current page by calling the `getServletPath()` method of the `request` object.

15.4.5 Text and hidden fields

The initial content of a text field is stored in the `value` attribute of the `<input>` tag defining that field. Hidden fields are initialized in the same manner, but their contents are not displayed and therefore cannot be edited by the end user. To make one of these element types reflect the state of a request parameter, we use a JSP expression containing a call to the `getParam()` method inside the `value` attribute's quotes. In our interface the Name field is specified using a text field. When the form is recreated after processing the request it should retain the original query. We do this as shown here:

```
<input type="text" name="character"
       value="<%= getParam(request, "character") %>">
```

The identifier for the Name input field is specified as `"character"`, using the `name` attribute of the `<input>` tag. If, then, the value submitted for this field was the character string `"Lora"`, when the JSP page is processed as a result of the form submission, it will generate the following output for this tag:

```
<input type="text" name="character" value="Lora">
```

As a result, the default value for this input field—specified via the value attribute—will be `"Lora"`. We have thus rewritten the input tag to contain a default value equal to the last value entered into the form. This is how we maintain the form's state between each request.

WARNING You must escape any quotes in the string you are using to populate the `value` attribute of a text field. If you don't, then any quotes in the value will cause a premature end to the `value` attribute, resulting in invalid HTML.

15.4.6 Text areas

In our example form, we provide a text area for entering the message to be included in our output result. Setting the initial contents of the text area from the request data is even more straightforward than initializing a text field: a pair of starting and ending `<textarea>` tags defines a text area, and the body enclosed by these tags defines its initial contents. The Message field and its initial value can therefore be specified as follows:

```
<textarea cols="40" rows="5" name="message">
<%= getParam(request, "message") %>
</textarea>
```

Again, the `getParam()` method is used to obtain the value of the request parameter, which in this case is named `message`. (As with all form elements, the name of the request parameter corresponds to the identifier specified for the form element via the `name` attribute.)

The text area itself can contain any text whatsoever. HTML tags will not be afforded special treatment—they will come through as plain text. Any HTML entities, such as `"` or `&`, will be converted into their character equivalents, the double quote and the ampersand. The only exception to this rule is the text area's closing tag. If the contents of your text area might contain a literal `</textarea>` tag, you will want to protect the form field from this value by converting its angle braces into their HTML entity equivalents, `<` and `>`.

15.4.7 Radio buttons

Unlike text fields and text areas whose values are determined by the user, radio buttons have a fixed set of possible values. A user's interaction with these elements does not affect these values, it only determines which of the provided options has been selected. Typically you will have a group of multiple radio buttons with the same name, forming a group. To specify that one of these form elements should be enabled when the page loads, you must include the keyword `checked` inside its `<input>` tag. Only one input element in the button group should be marked as checked. In our example form we are using radio buttons to allow the user to select the corresponding gender-specific pronoun for the value supplied in the Name field. When we load the page after servicing a request we want to ensure that the user's choice is reflected in our interface by enabling the radio button that corresponds to the current selection. This involves comparing the value attribute of each radio button with the user's selection, via the `isChecked()` method:

```
<input type="radio" name="gender" value="his"
       <%= isChecked(request, "gender", "his") %>><i>male</i><BR>
<input type="radio" name="gender" value="her"
       <%= isChecked(request, "gender", "her") %>><i>female</i><BR>
```

We use this utility method to compare the value assigned to each radio button with that stored in the request parameter. If there is a match, then this was the selected radio button and we insert the `checked` keyword into the input tag. Otherwise, we insert an empty `String`, which has no effect on the form element.

TIP Note that the values for these radio button form elements—the pronoun strings `"his"` and `"her"`—are different from the labels that appear on the form itself. HTML does not require that the values and labels match. JSP elements, however, only have access to the values of request parameters, and have no knowledge of the labels displayed for the form elements. The third argument to the `isChecked()` method, therefore, must indicate the value to be checked, not the label.

15.4.8 Select boxes

While certainly visually different, select boxes are quite similar in many respects to a group of radio buttons. They allow the user to make a selection from a set of choices. The initial selection for the group is indicated by the keyword `selected` inside the `<option>` tag defining the selection. We can therefore apply a similar technique to that used for radio buttons:

```
<select name="device">
<option value="tank" <%= isSelected(request, "device", "tank") %>>Tank
<option value="disk" <%= isSelected(request, "device", "disk") %>>Disk
<option value="light cycle"
  <%= isSelected(request, "device", "light cycle") %>>Light Cycle
</select>
```

With respect to the JSP elements, the only difference from the radio button example is the replacement of the request parameter names and values, and the use of the `isSelected()` utility method in place of `isChecked()`. The change in methods merely reflects the change in keywords between radio buttons and select boxes.

15.4.9 Check boxes

Check boxes can be used to select multiple choices from a set of possible values for a request parameter. Whether or not a check box should be enabled is determined by the presence of the `checked` keyword, as was the case for radio buttons. In the case of check boxes, however, it is not a problem if more than one check box is marked as enabled. In the example form, check boxes are used to select one or more colors, and are specified as follows:

```
<input type="checkbox" name="colors" value="red"
       <%= isChecked(request, "colors", "red") %>><i>red</i><BR>
<input type="checkbox" name="colors" value="yellow"
       <%= isChecked(request, "colors", "yellow") %>><i>yellow</i><BR>
<input type="checkbox" name="colors" value="blue"
       <%= isChecked(request, "colors", "blue") %>><i>blue</i><BR>
```

Note that the same identifier, `colors`, is specified for all three check boxes via the `name` attribute of the `<input>` tag. As a result, any and all values selected will be assigned as multiple values to the corresponding request parameter (also named colors).

15.4.10 Form source

The form depicted in figures 15.7 and 15.8 is constructed by combining these form elements into a JSP page. An HTML table is used to control the layout of the form, and a JSP declaration element is used to define the utility methods introduced earlier. The complete contents of the JSP file are presented in listing 15.5 (the method definitions have been abbreviated to conserve space).

For the form itself, two Submit buttons have been provided. The JSP code at the bottom of the page, which implements the form handler, can distinguish between these buttons by checking the value of a request parameter named `submittedVia`, which corresponds to the identifier assigned to these two Submit buttons via the `name` attribute of the corresponding `<input>` tags. Furthermore, the form handling code can deduce from the absence of this request parameter that the form has yet to be submitted, as indicated by the scriptlet which checks the result of the `getParam()` call for this parameter to see if it is empty.

Listing 15.5 JSP source code for the example form

```
<html>
<body>
<%!
public String getParam (HttpServletRequest request, String param) { ... }
public String getParamValues (HttpServletRequest request, String param) { ... }
public boolean requestContains (HttpServletRequest request,
                                String param, String testValue) { ... }
public String isChecked (HttpServletRequest request,
                         String param, String testValue) { ... }
public String isSelected (HttpServletRequest request,
                          String param, String testValue) { ... }
%>
```

```
<form action="<%= HttpUtils.getRequestURL(request) %>" method="post">
<table bgcolor="lightgrey" align="center" border="1" cellpadding="5">
<tr align="left" valign="top">
<td valign="top" rowspan="2">
<b>Name</b> 
<input type="text" name="character"
       value="<%= getParam(request, "character") %>">
<P>
<b>Select Box</b>
<select name="device">
<option value="tank" <%= isSelected(request, "device", "tank") %>>Tank
<option value="disk" <%= isSelected(request, "device", "disk") %>>Disk
<option value="light cycle"
        <%= isSelected(request, "device", "light cycle") %>>Light Cycle
</select>
</td>
<td><b>Gender</b></td>
<td><b>Color</b></td></tr>
<tr>
<td>
<input type="radio" name="gender" value="his"
       <%= isChecked(request, "gender", "his") %>><i>male</i><BR>
<input type="radio" name="gender" value="her"
       <%= isChecked(request, "gender", "her") %>><i>female</i><BR>
</td>
<td>
<input type="checkbox" name="colors" value="red"
       <%= isChecked(request, "colors", "red") %>><i>red</i><BR>
<input type="checkbox" name="colors" value="yellow"
       <%= isChecked(request, "colors", "yellow") %>><i>yellow</i><BR>
<input type="checkbox" name="colors" value="blue"
       <%= isChecked(request, "colors", "blue") %>><i>blue</i><BR>
</td>
</tr>
<tr>
<td colspan="3" align="center" valign="center">
<b>Message</b><br>
<textarea cols="40" rows="5" name="message">
<%= getParam(request, "message") %>
</textarea>
</td>
</tr>
</table>
<P>
<center>
<input type="submit" name="submittedVia" value="Declare">
 
<input type="submit" name="submittedVia" value="Taunt">
</center>
</P>
```

```
<hr width="75%">
<%-- FORM HANDLING CODE --%>
<h2>Result</h2>
<% String submission = getParam(request, "submittedVia");
   if (submission.equals("")) { %>
       The form has not yet been submitted.
<% } else {
      String verb = (submission.equals("Taunt")) ? "taunts" : "declares";
%>
  <%= getParam(request, "character") %>, manning
  <%= getParam(request, "gender") %>
  <%= getParamValues(request, "colors") %>
  <%= getParam(request, "device") %>,
  <%= verb %> "<b><%= getParam(request, "message") %></b>"
<% } %>
</form>
</body>
</html>
```

Thus, if the form has not yet been submitted, a message to that effect is displayed at the bottom of the page. If it has, the values of the request parameters are combined via a set of JSP scriptlets and expressions to generate a sentence based on the user's selections.

15.5 Validating form data

When we are collecting information for processing on the server through an HTML input form we often need to validate the data we get from the client browser to make sure it is in the format we expect before passing it off to a JSP or servlet. If we ask for a year, we might want to verify that the user typed in a four-digit year rather than a two-digit one. Indeed we'd want to make sure he/she entered *numbers* in the year field and not letters! Or, we may require that certain fields not be left blank. In any case, there are two choices for how we perform our validation—on the client or the server.

15.5.1 Client- and server-side validation

Client-side input field validation is performed with JavaScript. The general approach is to add an `onSubmit` handler to our form and use JavaScript methods to check each form field for whatever constraints we wish to enforce on the data. The user is prevented from submitting the form until the data in the input fields meets our requirements. Of course, since it is client-controlled there is nothing to enforce this but the browser—and who said the user is running a browser? The truth is users can submit anything they want by building their own form, creating their own client software, or connecting to the HTTP server directly. If your JSP or servlet isn't prepared to handle illegal or unexpected data you could have a problem. Bottom line: never trust the client to perform important tasks on its own.

Server-side validation on the other hand is completely under your control as the application developer. Server-side validation can be performed in the servlet or JSP which receives the form action and is responsible for processing the information. The server is able to validate the form data only after it has been submitted by the client. At that point it must verify that the data is within limits and either accept it, display an error message, or return the user to the form and give some indication of what needs to be done to correct the problem. This cycle is repeated until the user enters valid data, or gives up and goes home. This is also a good time to massage the data into your preferred form; for example, you want something in all lower case or want to strip out dashes and spaces. Once valid data is received, the form handler servlet or JSP can proceed with populating the database, sending email, or whatever it is we had set out to do. This process is illustrated in figure 15.9.

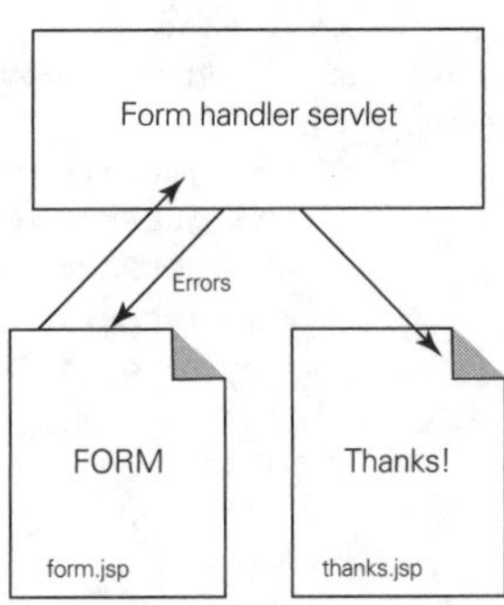

Figure 15.9 Server-side form validation

When you send the user back to the form following an error, we don't want him/her to have to fill in all of the fields again; we want to preserve the form data. This is where JSP comes in. If we make our input forms JSP-based, then the servlet can pass the current form field values back to the JSP, which can update the form's values. We used a similar technique earlier in this chapter to build interactive interfaces, but the approach works equally well with plain old forms.

Server-side validation has the downside of the user having to resubmit requests for validation each time. The delay between updates on the client side and the extra load on your server may be unacceptable in some situations. A good compromise is to do both types of validation on the form. Build in client-side validation to catch what you can, but double-check it once the data is submitted to the server. This gives you the performance you would like while preserving the security of server-validated data.

15.5.2 Example: server-side validation

In this example we will collect information from a JSP form and validate it through the servlet serving as our form handler. We've got three simple fields in our form:

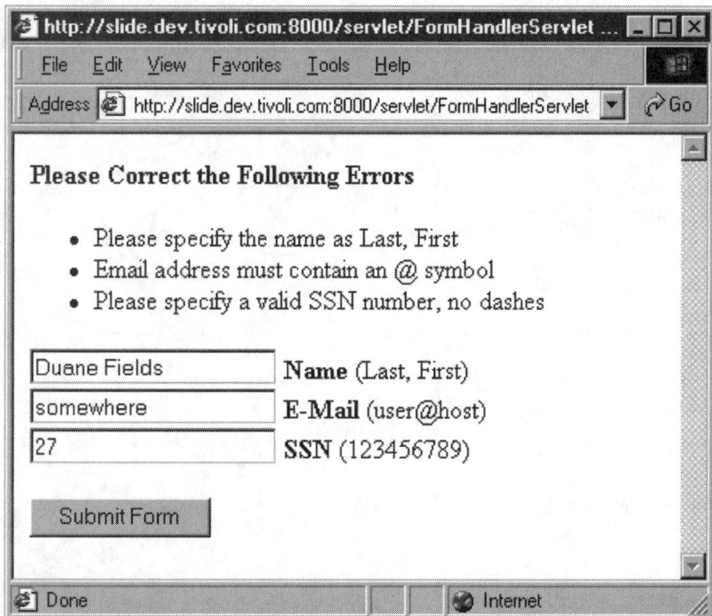

Figure 15.10 Form validation in progress

Name, Email, and Social Security number (a unique nine-digit number assigned to U.S. citizens). Since this is only an example, we'll perform extremely simple validation on the data. We want to make sure that the user enters his/her name in the format "Last, First," that the email address appears to really be an email address, and that he/she has entered enough digits for the Social Security number. If an error occurs, we'll send them back to the form to try again, as illustrated in figure 15.10.

We'll build the servlet—which for this example doesn't do anything other than validate the data, the form page, and the results page—where we'll acknowledge our acceptance of the data and redisplay it to show the user what we accepted.

The FormBean

Encapsulating our form data into a JavaBean makes it easy to repopulate the form fields with the user's data following an invalid submission. As you'll see shortly, we can populate the bean directly from the request parameters and use the bean tags to update each form field (listing 15.6).

Listing 15.6 FormBean.java

```
package com.taglib.wdjsp.commontasks;

public class FormBean {

  private String name;
  private String email;
  private String ssn;

  public FormBean() {
    name = "";
    email = "";
    ssn = "";
  }

  public void setName(String name) {
    this.name = name;
  }

  public String getName() {
    return name;
  }

  public void setEmail(String email) {
    this.email = email;
  }

  public String getEmail() {
    return email;
  }

  public void setSsn(String ssn) {
    this.ssn = ssn;
  }

  public String getSsn() {

    return ssn;
  }
}
```

The JSP form

The JSP form we use in this example has several jobs. First, it must populate a `FormBean` object using any data present in the request. If there is a problem validating the data following submission, the request will be redirected back to this page, populating the bean with the data. Each time the page is accessed directly a new `FormBean` will be created, with its default empty values. Empty bean or not, we use the `<jsp:getProperty>` tags to populate the default values of our form fields, giving us sticky form fields. If any errors were detected from a previous submittal attempt, the page must display them above the form data. We'll talk about each of these tasks in detail shortly. The source is shown in listing 15.7.

Listing 15.7 form.jsp

```
<jsp:useBean id="form" class="com.taglib.wdjsp.commontasks.FormBean">
  <jsp:setProperty name="form" property="*"/>
</jsp:useBean>
<html>
<body bgcolor="white">
<%
  String[] errors = (String[])request.getAttribute("errors");
  if (errors != null && errors.length > 0) {
%>
<b>Please Correct the Following Errors</b>
<ul>
<% for (int i=0; i < errors.length; i++) { %>
<li> <%= errors[i] %>
<% } %>
</ul>
<% } %>

<form action="/servlet/FormHandlerServlet" method="post">
<input type="text" name="name"
value="<jsp:getProperty name="form" property="name"/>">
<b>Name</b> (Last, First)<br>

<input type="text" name="email"
value="<jsp:getProperty name="form" property="email"/>">
<b>E-Mail</b> (user@host)<br>

<input type="text" name="ssn"
value="<jsp:getProperty name="form" property="ssn"/>">
<b>SSN</b> (123456789)<br>
<p>
<input type="submit" value="Submit Form">
</form>
</body>
</html>
```

The form handler

Before we can talk about the aspects of the code in the JSP form we must understand how it relates to our servlet. The servlet is responsible in this case for validating the code, performing whatever operation is required by the application, and directing the user to the next page in the process. Take a look at the source in listing 15.8, and then we'll explain the process in detail.

Listing 15.8 FormHandlerServlet.java

```
import java.io.*;
import javax.servlet.*;
import javax.servlet.http.*;
import java.util.*;

public class FormHandlerServlet extends HttpServlet {

  public void service(HttpServletRequest req,
           HttpServletResponse res)
    throws ServletException, IOException {
    Vector errors = new Vector();

    String name = req.getParameter("name");
    String ssn = req.getParameter("ssn");
    String email = req.getParameter("email");

    if (! isValidName(name))
      errors.add("Please specify the name as Last, First");
    if (! isValidEmail(email))
      errors.add("Email address must contain an @ symbol");
    if (! isValidSSN(ssn))
      errors.add("Please specify a valid SSN number, no dashes");

    String next;
    if (errors.size() == 0) {
      // data is OK, do whatever
      // dispatch to wherever
      next = "thanks.jsp";
    }
    else {
      // data has errors, try again
      String[] errorArray = (String[])errors.toArray(new String[0]);
      req.setAttribute("errors", errorArray);
      next = "form.jsp";
    }

    String base = "/validate/";
    RequestDispatcher rd;
    rd = getServletContext().getRequestDispatcher(base + next);
    rd.forward(req, res);
  }

  private boolean isValidSSN(String ssn) {
    // check for 9 characters, no dashes
    return (ssn.length() == 9 && ssn.indexOf("-") == -1);
  }

  private boolean isValidEmail(String email) {
    // check an "@" somewhere after the 1st character
    return (email.indexOf("@") > 0);
  }
```

```
  private boolean isValidName(String name) {
    // should be Last, First - check for the comma
    return (name.indexOf(",") != -1);
  }
}
```

Handling validation errors

Regardless of what type of data the user enters into the form fields of `form.jsp`, the data will be sent to the server, as we are not doing any client-side validation in this case. Also keep in mind that the bean we created on that page disappears as soon as the page is finished displaying. The form submission is a straight HTTP request, and cannot deliver anything other than name/value pairs to the servlet.

When the request comes in to the servlet, it extracts from the request the three parameters in which we are interested and validates them using three very simplistic checks. For each one of these validations that fails, the servlet adds a new message to the `errors` array, a list of all errors detected during validation. If no errors were found, the servlet dispatches the request to the thank you page, thanks.jsp.

When errors are encountered, they are packaged as a request attribute before dispatching back to `form.jsp`, from whence it came. When this request is processed by the JSP, both the original request parameters and the list of error messages are present. The `<jsp:useBean>` tag creates an instance of `FormBean` and uses a wild card to populate it from this new request with the original form data. Just prior to displaying the form, we must check for the presence of the error list, looping through and displaying each one as a bullet in an unordered list:

```
<%
  String[] errors = (String[])request.getAttribute("errors");
  if (errors != null && errors.length > 0) {
%>
<b>Please Correct the Following Errors</b>
<ul>
<% for (int i=0; i < errors.length; i++) { %>
<li> <%= errors[i] %>
<% } %>
</ul>
<% } %>
```

The thank you page

When the form is successfully submitted, we again populate a fresh bean with data from the successful request. This allows us to display the data to the user, with a message that the form was accurately processed (listing 15.9 and figure 15.11).

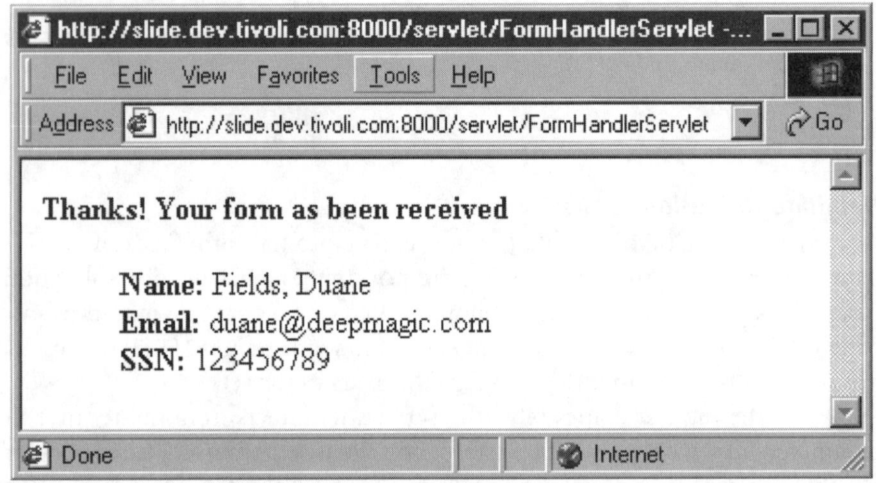

Figure 15.11 Form successfully processed

Listing 15.9 thanks.jsp

```
<jsp:useBean id="form" class="validate.FormBean">
  <jsp:setProperty name="form" property="*"/>
</jsp:useBean>
<html>
<body bgcolor="white">
<b>Thanks! Your form as been received.</b>
<ul>
<b>Name:</b> <jsp:getProperty name="form" property="name"/><br>
<b>Email:</b> <jsp:getProperty name="form" property="email"/><br>
<b>SSN:</b> <jsp:getProperty name="form" property="ssn"/><br>
</ul>
</body>
</html>
```

15.6 Building a shopping cart

One of the questions we were most frequently asked after the first edition of this book is "How do I build a shopping cart?" Every e-commerce site on the net makes use of such a component, allowing shoppers to browse the site accumulating items for eventual purchase. This example shows one way to build a simple, session-based shopping cart. It is not meant to be a commercial-ready software component, but should put you well on your way to building your own component that meets the unique needs of your site.

Figure 15.12 The shopping cart in action

15.6.1 Overview

The basic operation of a shopping cart is centered around a JavaBean placed into the user's session when they first visit the site. This bean, `ShoppingCart`, must be able to store a collection of items, each with its own description, part number, price and other properties. Each time the user selects an item to add to the cart, the `ShoppingCartBean` is called up and the item added to it. Each time the user adds an item, or when the user is ready to check out, we'll want to give the option of looking at the items in the cart to view the total and modify the selections. There are dozens of different shopping cart interfaces, but ours will give the option of removing items one at a time. We'll also want to keep subtotals as well as a grand total for the contents of the cart. The resulting full shopping cart is shown in figure 15.12.

The JSP file which displays the contents of the cart will only need to lay out the table and invoke the bean from the session. The subtotals and currency formatting will all come from the bean itself. I'm sure you can probably make a nicer looking cart then we did. We'll get to the actual implementation shortly, but let's look at the catalog page.

15.6.2 The catalog page

The catalog page shows a list of items for sale and allows the users to add one of them to their cart. Each item could, of course, be on a separate page. Since descriptions change and would be unwieldy, we'll key item selections off of a unique part number. Almost all e-commerce applications operate on such a concept, such as the UPC code you find on items in the grocery store. The shopping cart page will be responsible for not only displaying the cart's contents, but adding and removing items as well. So, we'll make each item link to the shopping cart and pass in its part number as a request parameter. We need to be able to remove items as well, so we'll have two different request parameters:

```
shoppingcart.jsp?addItem=partnumber
shoppingcart.jsp?removeItem=partnumber
```

How the shopping cart responds to these parameters we'll soon see. The finished catalog page is shown in figure 15.13 and the code shown in listing 15.10. Notice that the catalog page in this example is straight HTML. In real life however, you would probably generate your product listing dynamically, so we went ahead and made it a JSP.

Listing 15.10 catalog.jsp

```
<html>
<body bgcolor="white">
<h2>Catalog Items</h2>
<p>Select an item to add to your shopping cart:
<ul>
<li> <a href="shoppingcart.jsp?addItem=T7535">Light Cycle
<li> <a href="shoppingcart.jsp?addItem=T9515">Grid Bug Repellent
<li> <a href="shoppingcart.jsp?addItem=T8875">Digital Tank Grease
<li> <a href="shoppingcart.jsp?addItem=T6684">Input/Output Hat
</ul>
</p>
<p>
<a href="shoppingcart.jsp">View Shopping Cart</a>
</p>
</body>
</html>
```

15.6.3 ShoppingCartItem and InventoryManager

Since each item in our cart will have multiple properties, we'll need a supporting bean to represent each item. For our shopping cart we've elected to also store a

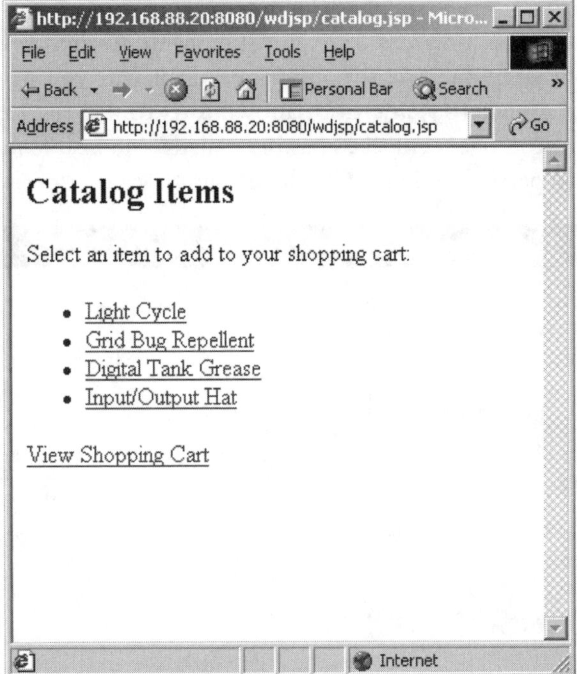

Figure 15.13 The Catalog Page

quantity for each item, making it easier to deal with multiple items of the same type. We've also added methods for calculating and displaying the price of the item, and the extended price (the subtotal for items of that type, the price x the quantity). The pricing and other information comes from a class called `InventoryManager`. In our example, `InventoryManager` contains a hard-coded list of parts and their prices. In a real application, this is where you would pull the item information from the database. If different types of items had different business rules (like quantity discounts) you might want to make `ShoppingCartItem` an interface or base class, extending the functionality as necessary to support unique business requirements.

One tricky aspect of shopping carts that we don't address in this example is how to deal with price changes and availability of goods. If I place an item in my shopping cart when it is priced at $5, then the price is raised to $10, what am I billed at checkout? Am I grandfathered in at the old price? Are items removed from inventory when they go into the cart, or is availability verified at checkout? There are a lot of business issues that must be determined when building your own.

The code for ShoppingCartItem and InventoryManager is shown in listings 15.11 and 15.12. Note that for some accessors, we just delegate to the Inventory-Manager, but this approach simplifies the shopping cart display as you'll see later. We've also implemented the equals() method, allowing us to use the items in a HashTable or other Collection class. The class has been made serializable in case we want the server to be able to persist the items (as part of our ShoppingCart).

Listing 15.11 ShoppingCartItem.java

```
package wdjsp;

import java.text.*;
import java.io.*;

public class ShoppingCartItem implements Serializable {
  private String itemNumber;
  private int count;
  private NumberFormat currencyFormat;

  public ShoppingCartItem(String itemNumber) {
    this.itemNumber = itemNumber;
    this.count = 1;
    currencyFormat = NumberFormat.getCurrencyInstance();
  }

  public int getCount() {
    return count;
  }

  public String getItemNumber() {
    return itemNumber;
  }

  public String getDescription() {
    return InventoryManager.instance().getDescription(itemNumber);
  }

  public String getUnitPriceString() {
    double price = getUnitPrice();
    return currencyFormat.format(price);
  }

  public double getUnitPrice() {
    double price = InventoryManager.instance().getPrice(itemNumber);
    return price;
  }

  public String getExtendedPriceString() {
    double price = getExtendedPrice();
    return currencyFormat.format(price);
  }
```

```
  public double getExtendedPrice() {
    double price = InventoryManager.instance().getPrice(itemNumber);
    return price * count;
  }

  public void incrementCount(int delta) {
    count = count + delta;
  }

  public boolean equals(Object o) {
    if (! (o instanceof ShoppingCartItem)) {
      return false;
    }
    else {
      ShoppingCartItem item = (ShoppingCartItem)o;
      return item.getItemNumber().equals(this.itemNumber);
    }
  }

  public int hashCode {
    return item.hashCode();
  }
}
```

Listing 15.12 InventoryManager.java

```
package wdjsp;

import java.util.*;

public class InventoryManager {
  private static InventoryManager instance;
  private Map descriptions;
  private Map prices;

  public static InventoryManager instance() {
    if (instance == null) {
      instance = new InventoryManager();
    }
    return instance;
  }

  private InventoryManager() {
    // load up some hard coded descriptions
    descriptions = new HashMap();
    descriptions.put("T7535", "Light Cycle");
    descriptions.put("T9515", "Grid Bug Repellent");
    descriptions.put("T8875", "Digital Tank Grease");
    descriptions.put("T6684", "Input/Output Hat");
    // and some prices
    prices  = new HashMap();
    prices.put("T7535", new Double(1003.10));
```

```
    prices.put("T9515", new Double(20.12));
    prices.put("T8875", new Double(10.50));
    prices.put("T6684", new Double(19.95));
  }

  public double getPrice(String sku) {
    if (prices.containsKey(sku)) {
      return ((Double)prices.get(sku)).doubleValue();
    }
    else {
      return 0D;
    }
  }

  public String getDescription(String sku) {
    if (descriptions.containsKey(sku)) {
      return (String) descriptions.get(sku);
    }
    else {
      return "No Description Available";
    }
  }
}
```

15.6.4 The ShoppingCart bean

Finally, we are ready to discuss the `ShoppingCart` bean itself. The `ShoppingCart` bean is built around an item list (an `ArrayList`, which is like a `Vector`) which will hold the `ShoppingCartItems` we built earlier, as each is added to the cart. Since items have a quanity property (count) we only need to store one copy of each one, incrementing that copy's count if we already have one in our cart. To add and remove items from the cart we've implemented the private `changeItemCount` method which accepts an increment (positive or negative). This allows us some flexibility and keeps the list management logic in a single place. A convenience method was added to total all the items in the cart as well, and the class has been made serializable to support container persistence (listing 15.13).

Listing 15.13 ShoppingCart.java

```
package wdjsp;

import java.util.*;
import java.text.*;
import java.io.*;

public class ShoppingCart implements Serializable {
  private List items;
```

```
  private NumberFormat currencyFormat;

  public ShoppingCart() {
    items = new ArrayList();
    currencyFormat = NumberFormat.getCurrencyInstance();
  }

  public void setAddItem(String itemNumber) {
    changeItemCount(itemNumber, 1);
  }

  public void setRemoveItem(String itemNumber) {
    changeItemCount(itemNumber, -1);
  }

  public ShoppingCartItem getItem(int i) {
    return (ShoppingCartItem)items.get(i);
  }

  public int getItemSize() {
    return items.size();
  }

  public String getTotalPrice() {
    Iterator i = items.iterator();
    double price = 0.00;
    while (i.hasNext()) {
      ShoppingCartItem item = (ShoppingCartItem)i.next();
      price += item.getExtendedPrice();
    }
    return currencyFormat.format(price);
  }

  private void changeItemCount(String itemNumber, int delta) {
    ShoppingCartItem item = new ShoppingCartItem(itemNumber);
    if (items.contains(item)) {
      // change the count for this item
      ShoppingCartItem existingItem;
      existingItem = (ShoppingCartItem)items.get(items.indexOf(item));
      existingItem.incrementCount(delta);
      if (existingItem.getCount() <= 0) {
        items.remove(existingItem);
      }
    }
    else {
      // new item, store it if positive change
      if (delta > 0) {
        items.add(item);
      }
    }
  }
}
```

15.6.5 Displaying the shopping cart

This page has three functions. First and foremost, it displays the contents of the user's shopping cart. It also handles additions and removals from the cart. Don't worry, we've done the hard parts already. Actually displaying the contents of the shopping cart, and hooking up the ability to add and remove items is pretty easy. We've cheated a bit, and used a custom tag from chapter 18 to loop through the items in the cart. For now, just understand that the `<mut:forProperty>…</mut:forProperty>` creates a loop similar to the scriptlet:

```
<%
for (int i=0; i < cart.getItemSize(); i++) {
  ShoppingCartItem item = cart.getItem(i);
%>
// jsp code here
<% } %>
```

Aren't the custom tags prettier? Just thought we would tweak your interest in things to come a bit. Inside the loop we just access the item's properties to display the price, description, and so forth. We use each item's part number to build the removal links as we loop through the cart. The interesting lines are at the top:

```
<jsp:useBean id="cart" class="wdjsp.ShoppingCart" scope="session"/>
<jsp:setProperty name="cart" property="addItem" param="addItem"/>
<jsp:setProperty name="cart" property="removeItem" param="removeItem"/>
```

The `<jsp:useBean>` tag pulls the cart from the user's session (or creates one if it doesn't exist) while the `<jsp:setProperty>` tags take care of adding and removing items. While this doesn't exactly follow the typical `setPropertyName` naming scheme, it works the same. Behind the scenes the `setRemoveItem` method gets called, with the item number as the argument. Maybe a better property name might be `itemForRemoval` with the method `setItemForRemoval`. Regardless of which you prefer they work the same. If either of the request parameters is not set (and in our case only one of them should be in each case) the `<jsp:setProperty>` tag is ignored. Notice that we don't try to instantiate `ShoppingCartItem` objects and pass them into the `ShoppingCart`; all we need is the part number. The `ShoppingCart` will create the item if necessary. The listing is shown in listing 15.14.

Listing 15.14 shoppingcart.jsp

```
<html>
<body bgcolor="white">
<%@ taglib uri="/mutlib" prefix="mut" %>
<jsp:useBean id="cart" class="wdjsp.ShoppingCart" scope="session"/>
```

```
<jsp:setProperty name="cart" property="addItem" param="addItem"/>
<jsp:setProperty name="cart" property="removeItem" param="removeItem"/>

<h2>Your Shopping Cart</h2>
<table border="1">
<tr><th>Item #</th><th>Description</th><th>Qty.</th>
<th>Unit Price</th><th>Extended Price</th><th> </th></tr>
<mut:forProperty name="cart" property="item" id="item"
className="wdjsp.ShoppingCartItem">
<tr>
<td><jsp:getProperty name="item" property="itemNumber"/></td>
<td><jsp:getProperty name="item" property="description"/></td>
<td><jsp:getProperty name="item" property="count"/></td>
<td><jsp:getProperty name="item" property="unitPriceString"/></td>
<td><jsp:getProperty name="item" property="extendedPriceString"/></td>
<td><a href="shoppingcart.jsp?removeItem=<jsp:getProperty name="item"
property="itemNumber"/>">remove</a></td>
</tr>
</mut:forProperty>
<tr>
<td align="right" colspan="4"><b>Total:</b></td>
<td><jsp:getProperty name="cart" property="totalPrice"/></td>
<td> </td>
</tr>
</table>

<p>
<a href="catalog.jsp">Return To Catalog</a>
</body>
</html>
```

15.7 Miscellaneous tasks

We conclude this chapter with a set of short examples that demonstrate three additional common tasks. Rather than demonstrate broad principles, however, these examples are focused on implementing very specific functionality. As such, only brief discussions are provided to clarify the accompanying code.

15.7.1 Determining the last modification date

Having a JSP page display its last modification date turns out to be trickier than you might think. We first have to map the page's path to a physical file on disk. We can use the `getServletPath()` method of the `request` implicit object to determine its path relative to the application, then use the `application` implicit object (an instance of `ServletContext`) to determine the real path to the underlying JSP file. This in turn allows us to create a `Date` object, based on the last modification time of the JSP file itself:

```
<%@ page import="java.io.*,java.util.*" %>
<% File f =
     new File(application.getRealPath(request.getServletPath()));
%>
<% Date modified = new Date(f.LastModified()); %>
<HTML>
<BODY>
This page last modified on: <%= modified %>
</BODY>
</HTML>
```

Based on the brevity of this code and its general utility, one might consider packaging this functionality so that it may be easily reused. One mechanism for doing this is to create a small JSP page that can be incorporated into other JSP pages via the `include` directive. (Note that the `<jsp:include>` tag is not an option here, as it would end up computing the last modification date of the included file.) Alternatively, a custom tag could be created which uses similar code to compute and insert the last modification date.

15.7.2 Executing system commands

Just like other Java programs, you can use JSPs to execute external commands. You can even use the Java Native Interface to execute native code stored inside libraries or DLLs. (Remember, of course, that we are talking about code native to the platform of the server, not the client, since JSP pages are executed on the server.) If you are converting your CGI scripts to JSPs and servlets, or building front ends to system administration tasks, the following code example shows how you can display the results of executing a command on the server. This example displays the current uptime and load average for a UNIX server, as reported by the server's `/usr/bin/uptime` command.

```
<%@ page import="java.io.*" %>
<%!
public String runCmd(String cmd) {
  try {
    Runtime rt = Runtime.getRuntime();
    Process p = rt.exec(cmd);
    InputStreamReader in = new InputStreamReader(p.getInputStream());
    BufferedReader reader = new BufferedReader(in);
    StringBuffer buf = new StringBuffer();
    String line;
    String newline = "\n";
    while ((line = reader.readLine()) != null) {
      buf.append(line);
      buf.append(newline);
    }
```

```
        reader.close();
        p.getInputStream().close();
        p.getOutputStream().close();
        p.getErrorStream().close();
        p.waitFor();
        return buf.toString();
    }
    catch (Exception e) {
        return (e.getMessage());
    }
}
%>
<html>
<body>
The system uptime is currently: <%= runCmd("/usr/bin/uptime") %>
</body>
</html>
```

Note that we are using an instance of `java.io.BufferedReader` in this example, reading output one line at a time. This is the most efficient method—especially for large amounts of data (unlike our example). Additionally, recall that, by default, JSP pages have an 8 KB buffer. As a result, we won't see the results of long-running commands immediately, but rather in 8 KB bursts. If your application demands that buffering be turned off, you will need to modify the loop of the `runCmd()` method to grab each character from the input stream, rather than buffered lines, and you'll also need to disable buffering on the page. In this case, replace the initial lines of the previous example with:

```
<%@ page buffer="none" import="java.io.*" %>
<%!
public String runCmd(String cmd) {
    try {
        Runtime rt = Runtime.getRuntime();
        Process p = rt.exec(cmd);…
          InputStreamReader in = new InputStreamReader(p.getInputStream());
          int c;
          StringBuffer buf = new StringBuffer();
          while ((c = in.read()) != -1) {
              buf.append((char)c);
          }
        ...
```

16 Generating non-HTML content

This chapter covers

- How JSP generates different content formats
- The relationship between the browser and a document's MIME type
- How to create text, XML, and even spreadsheets with JSP

16.1 Working with non-HTML content

The most popular use of JSP is to generate dynamic HTML in support of web applications. Because of this, one of the misconceptions many developers have about JSP is that it is exclusively geared toward generating dynamic HTML. In fact, JSP can generate just about any type of textual data required. On the web this capability can be used to display a single piece of information in a variety of formats, supporting a variety of clients or end user applications. For example, JSPs can be used to display database records as XML, HTML, WML, or even an Excel spreadsheet.

To generate other forms of content with JSP it is important to understand that JSP is simply a dynamic content creation language and not an HTML generator. The JSP language doesn't contain any HTML specific tags—it only generates what you tell it to. There isn't a JSP tag that results in bold text or an HTML table. All of this is specified by the page designer, forming a template into which JSP generates dynamic data.

In this chapter you will see some of the often-overlooked flexibility that JSP provides for generating different types of dynamic content, for the browser or otherwise. Once you grasp the simple elegance of the JSP architecture, realizing that it's about content not format, the sky's the limit.

16.1.1 The importance of MIME

The key to generating different types of dynamic content is understanding the relationship between web content, the browser, and MIME types. When a web server returns data to the browser it must identify the type of information it is delivering by setting the document's content type. This content type identifier is expressed as a text code known as the MIME type, a value contained in the HTTP response header behind the scenes. The MIME system itself was originally created for expressing the nature of email attachments (hence M.I.M.E—the Multipurpose Internet Mail Extensions) but has now expanded to identify content for everything from helper applications to browser plug-ins.

The MIME type of a document is used by the browser to determine exactly how the information should be interpreted and displayed. For example, image files have a content type of image/gif or image/jpg, while HTML is identified through the type text/html. When the server returns a static file, it typically uses the file's extension to determine the appropriate content type for the data. This mapping between file extension and MIME type is specified in the server's configuration, or for J2EE web applications in the web.xml deployment descriptor.

16.1.2 Controlling the content type

For JSP pages you can specify the content type of any page through the `contentType` attribute of the page directive. This attribute sets the MIME type and if unspecified, defaults to the familiar text/html response code. Most of the time this is appropriate, but as we'll see it is sometimes necessary to specify an alternate content type in order to generate non-HTML data. Here's an example of setting the MIME type to force a plain text display:

```
<%@ page contentType="text/plain" %>
```

The page directive's `contentType` attribute can also be used to specify an alternate character set for the JSP page, enabling the display of localized content using the language encoding most appropriate for the text. The character set is specified after the MIME type, as part of the `contentType` attribute. For example, the following directive specifies an HTML response using the ISO-8859-1 character set, which is as it turns out the default:

```
<%@ page contentType="text/html; charset=ISO-8859-1" %>
```

Of course setting the MIME type only tells the browser what to expect, and has no effect on the actual data being sent. It is up to the page designer to create content which corresponds to the desired content type and then it is up to the browser to interpret that data appropriately. The browser bases its decision on not only the content type, but in some cases the extension of the requested file as well. This is another important point, as we will see later.

16.1.3 Detecting your client

To determine what type of content to return, the first step is analyzing the client browser to determine the most appropriate format for it. For example, a Netscape browser might best be sent HTML, while you may wish to send a plain text version of your document for text only browsers such as Lynx, or a WML optimized page for cell phone users.

Keying off of the user-agent

The most obvious way to determine the type of browser you are dealing with is by reading the User-Agent header. Every HTTP request includes this header to identify the browser. For example, Internet Explorer sets the header's value to: Mozilla/4.0 (compatible; MSIE 4.01; Windows NT). (If you are wondering about the Mozilla business, that's IE trying to look like Netscape—an artifact of the browsers wars.) The User-Agent generally identifies the browser's developer, version, and platform. Unfortunately there's no set format for the structure of the User-Agent string, making them difficult to parse. For just Netscape and IE alone there are over a hundred variations between all of the versions and platforms. A number of commercial products, such as BrowserHawk from cyScape, specialize in detecting the browser type and translating it to a list of capabilities. Generally, this is good for getting a general idea that you are talking to a PC-based web browser. The header is easy to get to, just use the `getHeader` method of the request object. For example:

```
<% if ((request.getHeader("User-Agent").indexOf("MSIE") != -1) { %>
Welcome Internet Explorer User!
<% } else { %>
Welcome patriot!
<% } %>
```

This method of detecting your client can be a good way to fine-tune your content to meet the quirks of the browsers' makers varying support for standards. It is also a good way to address support for very narrow sets of clients. Say for example your field sales force uses a web-enabled phone to access the corporate intranet. By detecting the phone's unique User-Agent string, you can tailor your content appropriately. For a more generic approach, there's another way.

Keying off of the accept header

Many modern web clients, especially those with particularly restrictive vocabularies set the Accept header to indicate the formats of content that they understand. This can be a great way to negotiate with the browser to determine the appropriate type of content to return. Not only does it specify the types of content it is willing to accept, but it ranks them in terms of preference, and for some formats quality level. This header's content can change from request to request, depending on the context in which the browser is operating. When the browser requests an image for example (in response to an `<IMG>` tag) it informs the server that it will only accept image data in return. Cell phones looking for WAP content would generally include the following in the Accept header: text/vnd.wap.wml. Such content of the Accept header is usually a sure sign of support, and generally the best way to separate one type of client from another.

16.1.4 Designing multiformat applications

The modern web, if you can call it that, is a complex place. Not only are there dozens of browser versions and software platforms, but now we have Palm Pilots, Windows CE devices, cell phones, voice browsers, robots and who knows what else. Often these devices support significantly different types of content. For instance cell phones make use of WML, while the Palm Pilot uses its own special HTML extensions for its wireless web clipping applications. Supporting multiple types of content can provide its own set of challenges. If your application will be accessible from a variety of clients you have several options on how to organize your content effectively.

There are a number of strategies for actually organizing your content and routing it appropriately. The best choice for your application depends on a number of factors, including your own personal tastes. Like any architectural decision there are tradeoffs at every corner.

The most straightforward approach would be to maintain separate hierarchies of content, one for each type of client you plan to support. For example, your WML version of the site could live under /wml, and more traditional content gets stored under /html. Either have your clients direct themselves to the appropriate path, or use one of the client detection techniques we discussed earlier to enact the routing automatically.

Another useful technique can be to ask the user which type of content they prefer. This eliminates the need for browser detection, at the expense of requiring user input. After selection is made, you can set a cookie to make their choice stick.

16.1.5 Controlling the file extension

Often the MIME type indicates a content type that can't be displayed directly in the browser. When this happens the browser passes the file off to a helper application or a plug-in. This is often the case with media files, spreadsheets, and the like. Once the document is passed to one of these helper applications, it uses the file extension to determine the type of data it is loading. If the document was generated through JSP and downloaded from the web, it typically ends in .jsp, an extension that means nothing to the helper application. What we want to do is create a JSP file that appears (at least to the browser and helper application) to have an extension appropriate for the content type in question. Of course changing the name of our file directly doesn't work because our web server needs the .jsp extension to recognize the file as a JSP source file that should be rendered before delivery. Since we can't change the file name, we have to create an alias to it with the desired extension. This can be done through the web.xml file, the deployment descriptor used when deploying J2EE applications.

Using the `<servlet>` container tag we name a new servlet, using the JSP file that generates our document data, as shown in the following excerpt. Note that as far as the deployment descriptor is concerned JSPs are just servlets. The name we choose is arbitrary, but must be unique to the application, as it is used as a label for identifying the servlet throughout the deployment descriptor. In this case, we'll call it `myPage`.

```
<servlet>
  <servlet-name>myPage</servlet-name>
  <jsp-file>/myPage.jsp</jsp-file>
</servlet>
```

Now that we have named the servlet (masquerading behind our JSP file) we can assign that servlet to any URL we'd like through the `<servlet-mapping>` container tag, again in our web.xml deployment descriptor. In this example, we'll map the file to a .txt extension, indicating a plain text file.

```
<servlet-mapping>
  <servlet-name>myPage</servlet-name>
  <url-pattern>/myPage.txt</url-pattern>
</servlet-mapping>
```

Changing the file name and/or extension can also be useful if you want to hide the fact that you are using JSP or want to create URLs that are the same for both static and dynamic content. See chapter 14 for more information on the deployment descriptor.

16.2 Text content formats

While it has special meaning to an Internet browser, HTML is in essence plain text. By extension, JSPs can be used to create a variety of other text-based formats, from plain ASCII text to complicated XML formats.

16.2.1 Plain text output

Now that we understand how to control the content type specification of a page, let's learn how to control the page content itself. Let's start with something simple, straight ASCII text. Listings 16.1 and 16.2 show two examples of a classic Hello, World style JSP program, one that generates formatted HTML as output and another resulting in plain text.

Listing 16.1 HelloWorldHTML.jsp

```
<%@ page contentType="text/html" %>
<html>
<body>
<h1>Hello World</h1>
Greetings world, the date is <%= new java.util.Date() %>.
</body>
</html>
```

Listing 16.2 HelloWorldASCII.jsp

```
<%@ page contentType="text/plain" %>
Hello World
Greetings world, the date is <%= new java.util.Date() %>.
```

Both programs produce similar output, but if you try them out you'll see that the first example has full HTML layout while the second is shown as plain text, including fixed width font and hard formatting, similar to output you might see using HTML's `<pre>` tag. Unfortunately, browsers don't always interpret the content as you might expect. Internet Explorer for example tends to ignore the text/plain content type for any content that contains valid HTML tags, interpreting and displaying the content as HTML instead. One can only guess that Microsoft is trying to be helpful in displaying pages with what it assumes must be an incorrectly set MIME type. So much for standards.

16.2.2 WYGIWYG output (what you generate is what you get)

One thing to watch for when using JSP to create non-HTML content is the handling of white space. When JSP pages are parsed by the servlet engine white space (tabs, spaces, carriage returns, and new lines) is handled according to XML conventions; it is considered insignificant but is nonetheless preserved. Translation—if you don't want white space in your output you can't include it in the JSP source page. When dealing with HTML it's usually acceptable to have extraneous white space hanging around because the browser crunches it all together, wrapping the text as necessary. Not so for plain text. What you generate is what you get. For example look at the following text. It displays as a single line when interpreted as HTML by the browser, but as three distinct lines of text when viewed as plain text.

```
This is line 1.
This is line 2.
This is line 3.
```

While HTML is certainly more forgiving about extra line feeds and white space, there are circumstances where it becomes important to be aware of what's happening, namely when specifying attribute values. Take for example the following excerpt of JSP code that creates an `<img>` tag from a file name stored as a `String` property of a JavaBean:

```
<img src="
<jsp:getProperty name="branding" property="logoURL"/>
">
```

The resulting page shows a broken image placeholder where our logo should have been, even though we verified that the bean contains the property URL. What could be happening? We can use the browser's ability to view the HTML source to find out. After parsing by the servlet engine, the following HTML code is returned to the browser:

```
<img src="
/images/logo.gif
">
```

Aha! The extra line feed was retained, creating a bogus file name reference. This is not a bug, it's doing exactly as it is supposed to, preserving white space. To correct the problem we have to modify the JSP code to make sure that no extra white space ends up in the value of the image tag's `src` attribute.

```
<img src="<jsp:getProperty name="branding" property="logoURL"/>">
```

There's no rule that requires everything to be on a single line, but we must avoid introducing spaces where things will cause problems. Remember that HTML and XML ignore white space between attributes and tags, making this a good place to break the line. Alternatively therefore we could write:

```
<img
src="<jsp:getProperty name="branding" property="logoURL"/>"
>
```

16.3 XML documents

Generating XML data from a JSP page is not very different from generating HTML or plain text. Instead of our page containing HTML tags however, we are creating an XML template and using JSP to insert the data. Generating dynamic XML is easier to maintain through JSP files over using servlets directly. If something changes, you can simply apply the edits to the JSP page, rather than recompiling. Typically, you will generate XML in conjunction with a servlet or EJB, which delivers the actual content to the JSP page via a JavaBean stored in a request attribute. Here's a simple example that follows this pattern and displays an employee record, presumably pulled from a backend database:

Listing 16.3 EmployeeXML.jsp

```
<%@ page contentType="text/xml" %><?xml version="1.0"?>
<jsp:useBean id="employee" class="Employee" scope="request"/>
<employee>
  <name>
    <jsp:getProperty name="employee" property="name"/>
  </name>
  <salary>
    <jsp:getProperty name="employee" property="salary"/>
  </salary>
</employee>
```

There is an important WYGIWYG gotcha to watch out for when generating XML like this. While generally forgiving, XML is particularly picky about extraneous spaces in one specific circumstance, the opening `<?xml>` tag. It requires no leading spaces; therefore we must place it flush against our opening page directive to assure it is the first line of the resulting XML content. Other than that, we are free to indent and space the elements of the code however we feel is the most readable and maintainable, but remember that the space will be included in the final output. Once rendered, the output produced by the above example would look something like this:

```
<?xml version="1.0">
<employee>
  <name>
    Duane Fields
  </name>
  <salary>
    350K
  </salary>
</employee>
```

There's really not much difference between XML and HTML generation, the audience is just different. Humans and browsers typically prefer HTML, while machines and servlets better understand data represented as XML. Often we'll need to use both types of content in the course of an application. For instance the code above might be used by an internal process to generate paychecks, while an HTML representation might be needed for a manager reviewing his employee's pay levels. We can reuse existing backend code, and display the same data with the following HTML JSP:

Listing 16.4 EmployeeHTML.jsp

```
<%@ page contentType="text/html" %>
<jsp:useBean id="employee" class="Employee" scope="request"/>
<html>
<body>
<h1>Employee Record</h1>
<b>Name:</b> <jsp:getProperty name="employee" property="name"/>
<b>Salary:</b> <jsp:getProperty name="employee" property="salary"/>
</body>
</html>
```

16.3.1 Creating voice XML documents

More and more new types of data are being managed through XML. One particularly interesting new format is voice XML, or VXML. VXML is an XML document format for building interactive voice response systems featuring text-to-speech and voice recognition. Systems such as telephone banking use interactive voice response (IVR) to provide automated account access. With VXML, it is easy to build phone systems that interact with existing enterprise data systems using your existing web services. A VXML application is composed of VXML documents that specify menus ("Press 1 for your current balance") and forms ("Please enter your account number"). The specification allows the documents to submit the form values back to an address on the server, much like HTML documents. VXML therefore is an excellent candidate for generation with dynamic content generation systems such as JSP.

Without going into the details of the VXML command set, it is enough to understand that it is simply an XML document that follows the VXML DTD. VXML can direct systems to prompt users for input (using speech recognition or touch tones), play audio messages for feedback, and direct the caller to additional information. Given that, we treat VXML just like the XML documents we looked at earlier with the one exception. Most VXML phone systems expect a content type of `text/vxml` or `application/x-vxml` to identify that it is indeed a VXML document and not just any old XML document. Listing 16.5 is an example of a simple VXML application that validates a user's logon. The first document, login.vxml, collects the user's account number and PIN (personal identification number) and submits that data to the second page, validateLogin.jsp (listing 16.6). The account is validated (or invalidated) and an appropriate response is generated.

Listing 16.5 login.vxml

```
<?xml version="1.0"?>
<vxml version="1.0">

  <!-- keep track of login attempts -->
  <var name="attempts" expr="1"/>

  <!-- the login form -->
  <form id="login">
    <field name="account" type="digits">
      <prompt>
         <audio src="">
         Welcome to MegaBank. Please say or enter your account number.
         </audio>
      </prompt>
    </field>
```

```
    <field name="pin" type="digits">
      <prompt>
        <audio src="">
        Please say or enter your PIN.
        </audio>
      </prompt>
    </field>

    <block>
      <audio src="">
      Please wait while we access your account.
      </audio>
    </block>

    <subdialog src="validateLogin.jsp" namelist="account pin" caching="safe">
      <catch event="event.login.success">
        <goto next="welcome.vxml"/>
      </catch>
      <catch event="event.login.failure">
        <assign name="attempts" expr="attempts + 1"/>
        <if cond="attempts > 3">
          <goto next="#tooManyAttempts"/>
        </if>
        <audio src="">
        Invalid login. Please try again.
        </audio>
        <goto next="#login"/>
      </catch>
    </subdialog>
  </form>

  <!-- too many invalid login attempts -->
  <form id="tooManyAttempts">
    <block>
      <audio src="">
      Too many invalid login attempts. Goodbye.
      </audio>
      <goto next="#goodbye"/>
    </block>
  </form>

  <!-- hangup -->
  <form id="goodbye">
    <block>
      <exit/>
    </block>
  </form>
</vxml>
```

Listing 16.6 validateLogin.jsp

```
<?xml version="1.0"?>

<%@ page contentType="text/vxml" %>

<%
String account = request.getParameter("account");
String pin = request.getParameter("pin");
String event = null;

ValidatePhoneUserCommand validator =
  new ValidatePhoneUserCommand(account, pin);
SystemEngine.instance().executeCommand(validator);
if (validator.isValidAndActive()) {
  ObjectID userId = validator.getUserId();
  StartSessionCommand sessionCmd = new StartSessionCommand(userId);
  SystemEngine.instance().executeCommand(sessionCmd);
  String sessionId = sessionCmd.getSessionID().toString();
  Cookie cookie = new Cookie("session", sessionId);
  cookie.setPath("/phone");
  cookie.setMaxAge(-1);
  response.addCookie(cookie);
  event = "event.login.success";
}
else {
  event = "event.login.failure";
}
%>

<vxml version="1.0">
  <form>
    <block>
      <return event="<%= event %>"/>
    </block>
  </form>
</vxml>
```

As you can see the validateLogin.jsp page delivers a valid VXML document which returns an event that the main page reacts to. When we call the page through the `<subdialog>` tag, note that we are careful to use the `caching="safe"` attribute to assure that the VXML browser (the phone) doesn't cache the results of our validation by mistake. Safe caching tells the phone browser to always go back to the server to ensure that it has the latest content. Another way to use JSP with VXML is to simply generate the forms themselves. However, by keeping the main application as VXML files you can achieve a more flexible deployment.

16.4 External content

We learned earlier how JSP can include JSP or HTML content at request time through the `<jsp:include>` action and the `<%@ include %>` directive. Beyond this, HTML itself allows for several forms of embedded content that cause data included by the browser at request time. Images, style sheets, JavaScript libraries, applet code, media files are all considered forms of external content that is referenced through the requested document and not actually contained within it. An `<img>` tag for example, has a `src` attribute which specifies a remote image document to be included in the context of the page.

External content is imported into the document by the browser, not the server, and thus happens subsequent to the original request. What happens is this: the initial request is made, either to a JSP page, a servlet, or a static HTML document. The source is scanned for references to external content (such as the `<img>` tag) which are then retrieved (usually two or three at a time in parallel) and made available to the original content. You can think of this process as a "client-side include" mechanism, even if it's not necessarily a literal cut-and-paste like server-side includes.

These subsequent requests for content are unique requests against the server generated by the browser itself and do not share the properties of the original request, such as request parameters. Likewise, these subsequent requests do not share the request scope of the original request and therefore cannot access request attributes such as JavaBeans available to the original request. However, because these requests originate from the same browser session as the original request, they share the same session and contain cookies, authentication headers, user agent information, and the like. This means that they can take advantage of user specific information stored in the session or application contexts. Additionally, these requests will include a reference to their referrer, the URL of the page that originally requested them.

TIP If you need to pass request parameters to the external content requests, you can do so by dynamically appending the request parameters to the remote document via URL rewriting.

The most common example of this is the HTML `<img>` tag, which allows the browser to issue follow-on requests for image data. While JSP is probably not appropriate for generating dynamic images (although a servlet certainly is), there are two other forms of embedded content that can be quite easily controlled through JSP: style sheets and JavaScript. One advantage is that because this is a client-side technique, it allows static HTML pages to include some form of dynamic content, even if the local server does not support a technology such as JSP.

WARNING One downside is that older browsers don't support external style sheets or JavaScript source, however the 4.0 and 5.0 browsers do, as do some of the 3.0 browsers. If you plan to rely on these features in your site, make certain that your audience can take advantage of them.

16.4.1 JSP style sheets

The most common use for style sheets in web publishing is to provide a standardized look and feel for all of the pages on the site, without having to stylize the colors, fonts, and layout of each page separately. To this end browsers can make use of the `<link>` tag to embed references to external style sheet documents into their HTML. Typically, the link tag looks like this:

```
<link rel="stylesheet" type="text/css" href="style.css">
```

It is important to understand that the `href` attribute that defines the external style sheet is pointing to the URL of a document somewhere out on the network. The document doesn't have to be local to the current server, and it doesn't even have to have a .css extension. After loading the initial page, the browser will spawn an additional request to download the style sheet. Regardless of the location or file extension, the browser will expect what comes back from the server to be only a list of CSS style directives. No HTML is allowed. A typical style sheet then might contain something like the following:

```
P { color: red; font-size=14pt;  margin-left: 2em; }
P.hilite { background-color: yellow; }
```

Since this style information is just text, we are free to create our own style sheet through JSP, allowing us to customize the style on a per-request, or per-session basis. We're not going to go into the details of how style sheets work. If you aren't familiar with them all you need to know is that they tell the browser how different content elements (such as tables, paragraphs, etc.) should look and be laid out. In this simple example (listing 16.7) we'll create a style sheet that creates a random color scheme by selecting a new combination of background, text, and anchor colors for each page request.

Listing 16.7 random-css.jsp

```
<%@ page contentType="text/css" %>
<%!
String[] colors = { "red", "green", "blue", "yellow", "black", "white" };

private String getRandomColor() {
  return colors[(int)(Math.random() * colors.length)];
}
%>

BODY { background-color: <%= getRandomColor() %> }
P { color: <%= getRandomColor() %> }
A:link { color: <%= getRandomColor() %> }
A:active { color: <%= getRandomColor() %> }
A:visited { color: <%= getRandomColor() %> }
```

You can load this page into your browser directly to see the results. Notice how it changes with each reload. (If it doesn't, you'll probably need to modify your browsers caching behavior to assure it reloads the style sheet from the network each time, or see the caching section in this chapter for information on how to have the page direct the browser's caching behavior itself). Here's a typical result:

```
BODY { background-color: green }
P { color: black }
A:link { color: yellow }
A:active { color: red }
A:visited { color: blue }
```

To reference this style sheet in our documents (table 16.8), we make use of the link tag, substituting the URL of the dynamic style sheet we just created:

Listing 16.8 random.html

```
<html>
<head>
<link rel="stylesheet" type="text/css" href="random-css.jsp">
</head>

<body>
<p>
Welcome to a page with a random style.
</p>
</body>
</html>
```

This style sheet can be referenced by any HTML document, including static HTML and JSP files. It is now accessible from other servers as well. Dynamic style sheets are a useful way to modify the look and feel of your existing pages without having to convert the entire site's web pages to JSP. There are layout effects that can't be done without style sheets, like carefully controlling the font size, margins, and borders of the content. We could take advantage of this technique to allow the user to control the style of the page recording their choices in their session, and by retrieving this information to construct our dynamic style sheet. Another useful technique is adapting the style sheet based on the platform or the vendor of the client's browser. For example, we might need to bump up the default font size for UNIX browsers, or modify a table style to achieve parity between Netscape and Internet Explorer.

16.4.2 JavaScript

Like style sheets, JavaScript can be either included directly in the HTML page, or imported by the browser at request time. The `src` attribute of the `<script>` tag can be used to specify an external file that contains JavaScript functions, variables, or commands that should be made available to the page. Typically, this capability is used to create libraries of JavaScript functions that are available to multiple pages on the site. A typical reference looks like this:

```
<script src="loans.js">
</script>
```

And the file loans.js (which could be anywhere on the network) would contain functions to calculate loan payments, interest rates, and so forth. As with style sheets this file could be a JSP that modified the commands or functions based on the current users, their browsers, and so on. For example, the functions for calculating loans might take the user's local interest or tax rates into account. This provides a way of centralizing application logic in a single-client side module, by introducing server-side dependencies.

A more interesting technique is using dynamic imported JavaScript to pass information between the client and the server. In this example we'll pretend that we run an online bookstore and we are looking for a way to provide a "book of the month" that our associates and partners can promote through their own web sites. It's simple enough to select a book each month, but we want a way that the partners can promote it without having to manually change the book's information each month and would like to display the current number available for purchase. We also can't assume that every affiliate site is running a JSP capable server or has access to servlets. What we can do is provide a dynamic JavaScript library on our server that can be referenced by HTML on the associate's server to display information about the currently selected book. That gives our associates a 100 percent client-side solution, backed up by our JSP generated JavaScript library. Listing 16.9 is a simplified example of the JSP that will form this JavaScript library.

Listing 16.9 bookOfTheMonth-js.jsp

```
<%
//
// In real-life this information would come from a backend database
// and stored in a bean, rather than through a scriptlet as shown here
String isbn = "1884777996";
String title = "Web Development With JavaServer Pages";
String price = "$44.95";
// We'll fake an every changing inventory
int inventory = (int) (Math.random() * 200);
%>
<!-- JavaScript Variables -->
var isbn = "<%= isbn %>";
var title = "<%= title %>";
var inventory = "<%= inventory %>";
var price = "<%= price %>";
```

When a request comes in, the information about the current book of the month is looked up (or in this case made up) and reflected into a series of JavaScript variables. If you were to request and view this page directly it would look something like figure 16.1:

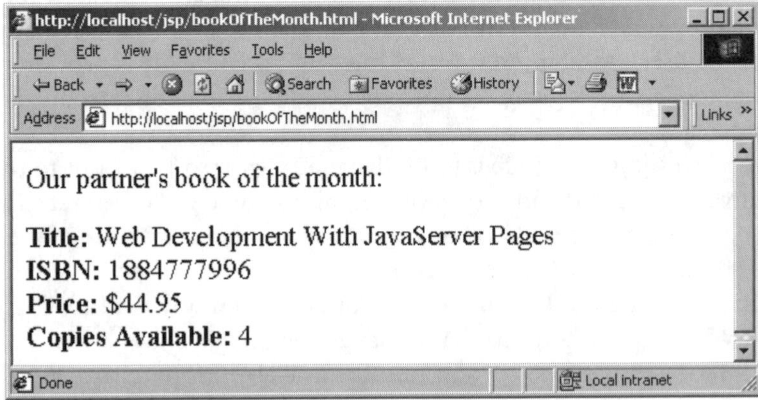

Figure 16.1 The fully rendered Book Of The Month selection

```
var isbn = "1884777996";
var title = "Web Development With JavaServer Pages";
var inventory = "34";
var price = "$44.95";
```

When an HTML document requests external JavaScript it interprets all of the returned data as JavaScript. It shouldn't be wrapped in `<script>` or other HTML tags. In this case, we aren't defining functions but are declaring global variables that will be available throughout the page. The associate would reference this external JavaScript with a page such as listing 16.10, which then uses document.write methods to display the values stored in the variables.

Listing 16.10 bookOfTheMonth.html

```
<html>

<head>
<script src="http://partner.example.com/jsp/bookOfTheMonth-js.jsp">
</script>
</head>

<body>
Our partner's book of the month:<p>

<b>Title:</b>
<script>document.write(title);</script>
<br>

<b>ISBN:</b>
<script>document.write(isbn);</script>
<br>

<b>Price:</b>
<script>document.write(price);</script>
<br>

<b>Copies Available:</b>
<script>document.write(inventory);</script>
<br>

</body>
</html>
```

16.5 Advanced content formats

Leaving the world of plain text behind, let us now explore something a little different. While not as straightforward, JSP can also be quite helpful in creating more interesting types of content that you might not expect it capable of at first.

16.5.1 Excel spreadsheets

In the previous two examples we've generated content not targeted at any particular application; we've simply specified the content type and let nature take its course. In this example (listing 16.11) we'll create a page that opens directly into Microsoft Excel. To accomplish this we'll have to control not only the content type, but the file extension as well. Remember that despite all of our best efforts, the server can't force the client to do something it doesn't want to do. If the client's file associations are different than expected, or for that matter doesn't have Excel installed, you're out of luck. However, if you control the client at least we know it can be set up to do what we require.

The content type we'll want to use in this case is application/x-msexcel, an application specific association recognized by Excel. Setting this content type will cause the page to be passed on to Excel, which will rely on the file extension to determine how to best handle the file. To generate our spreadsheet data, we'll create a simple page that displays Java's system properties as a table of comma separated values.

Listing 16.11 SystemProperties.jsp

```
<%@ page contentType="application/x-msexcel" import="java.util.*" %>
"Property Name","Property Value"
<%
Properties sysprops = System.getProperties();
Enumeration keys = sysprops.propertyNames();
while (keys.hasMoreElements()) {
  String name = (String)keys.nextElement();
  String value = sysprops.getProperty(name);
%><%= name %>,<%= value %>
<% } %>
```

If you were to view this page you'd see that it displays the system properties inside an Excel spreadsheet, assuming your system is configured to handle the application/x-msexcel content type. But we're not done yet. When loading this page into Excel, it displays both the property name and value fields together in the first column. Why hasn't it correctly parsed our data into two columns? The answer lies in the file extension.

Excel, like other applications, uses the file extension to determine the type of data it is loading. In our case the document loaded from the web ends in .jsp, an extension that means nothing to Excel. What we want to do is create a page with the extension .csv, which tells Excel that these are comma-separated values, a common way of importing data into a spreadsheet. As explained earlier, this can be accomplished by setting up our own servlet-mapping in the deployment descriptor.

```
<servlet>
  <servlet-name>SysProps</servlet-name>
  <jsp-file>/SystemProperties.jsp</jsp-file>
</servlet>

<servlet-mapping>
  <servlet-name>SysProps</servlet-name>
  <url-pattern>/SystemProperties.csv</url-pattern>
</servlet-mapping>
```

Now we can direct the browser to /SystemProperties.csv (relative to the application context, if it's not the default application on the server) and get exactly the same data as before, but this time with a file extension that Excel knows how to handle properly.

16.5.2 Code generation

Not all dynamic content is intended for publication. JSP can also be used to generate configuration files, database schema, and even source code for internal usage. A novel use of JSP is as an easy code generator. Less typing is always better, and code generators provide a short cut to producing Java code. In this example (listing 16.12) we build a simple tool to generate JavaBean class files from a list of properties and their types. Its benefit is obvious from the screenshots in figure 16.2. This tool can save hours of monotonous typing while reducing errors and encouraging consistent style and formatting. While simple, it illustrates a powerful concept that you can certainly take further and apply to new situations.

How it works is simple. A simple HTML form provides class details and a list of property name/type pairs. The form is submitted to the beanMaker.jsp file shown in listing 16.12. This file produces plain text as discussed earlier, substituting the appropriate names to complete the source code. Notice again the WYGIWYG principle which causes us to pay close attention to formatting, especially line feeds. For example, to place our package statement on the first line of our output file we have to jut it up against our content type declaration. Once complete, you can use your browser's Save feature to write your generated source file to disk.

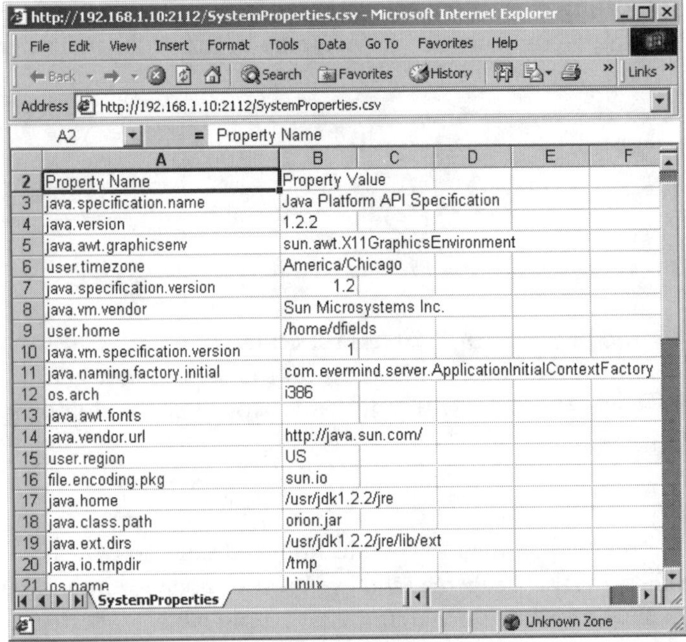

	A	B
2	Property Name	Property Value
3	java.specification.name	Java Platform API Specification
4	java.version	1.2.2
5	java.awt.graphicsenv	sun.awt.X11GraphicsEnvironment
6	user.timezone	America/Chicago
7	java.specification.version	1.2
8	java.vm.vendor	Sun Microsystems Inc.
9	user.home	/home/dfields
10	java.vm.specification.version	1
11	java.naming.factory.initial	com.evermind.server.ApplicationInitialContextFactory
12	os.arch	i386
13	java.awt.fonts	
14	java.vendor.url	http://java.sun.com/
15	user.region	US
16	file.encoding.pkg	sun.io
17	java.home	/usr/jdk1.2.2/jre
18	java.class.path	orion.jar
19	java.ext.dirs	/usr/jdk1.2.2/jre/lib/ext
20	java.io.tmpdir	/tmp
21	os.name	Linux

Figure 16.2 A dynamic spreadsheet, courtesy of JSP

Listing 16.12 A JavaBean Generator

```
<%@ page contentType="text/plain" %>package <%= request.getParameter("pkg") %>;

/**
 * Generated code for the <%= request.getParameter("class") %> class.
 *
 * @author BeanMaker
 */
public class <%= request.getParameter("class") %> {
<% for (int i=1; i < 5; i++) {
  if (! "".equals(request.getParameter("type" + i))) {
    String propertyName = request.getParameter("property" + i);
    String propertyType = request.getParameter("type" + i);
%>  private <%= propertyType %> <%= propertyName %>;
<% } } %>
  public <%= request.getParameter("class") %>() {
    // add constructor code here
  }
<% for (int i=1; i < 5; i++) {
  if (! "".equals(request.getParameter("type" + i))) {
```

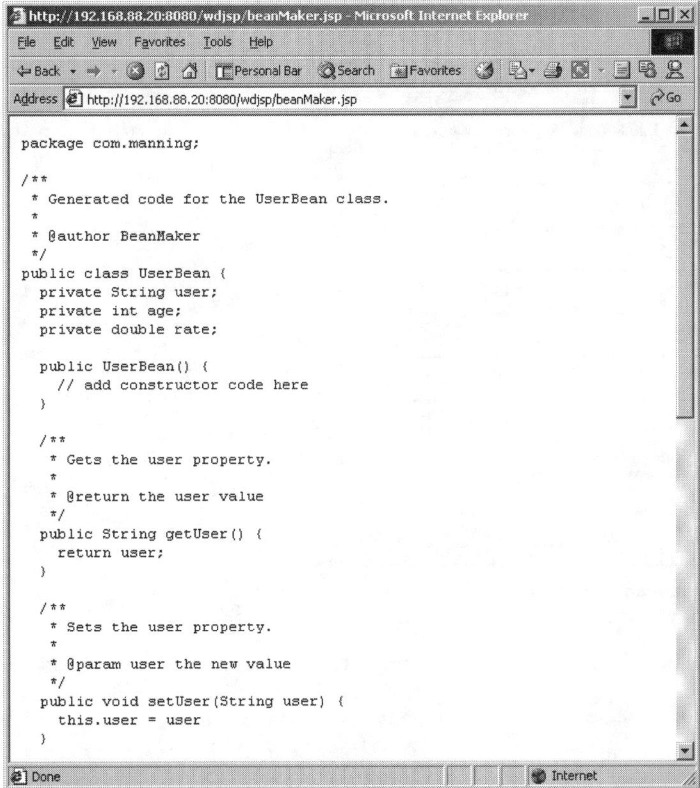

Figure 16.3 Java source code, courtesy of JSP

```
    String propertyName = request.getParameter("property" + i);
    String propertyType = request.getParameter("type" + i);%>
  /**
   * Gets the <%= propertyName %> property.
   *
   * @return the <%= propertyName %> value
   */
  public <%= propertyType %> get<%= fixcase(propertyName) %>() {
    return <%= propertyName %>;
  }

  /**
   * Sets the <%= propertyName %> property.
   *
   * @param <%= propertyName %> the new value
   */
```

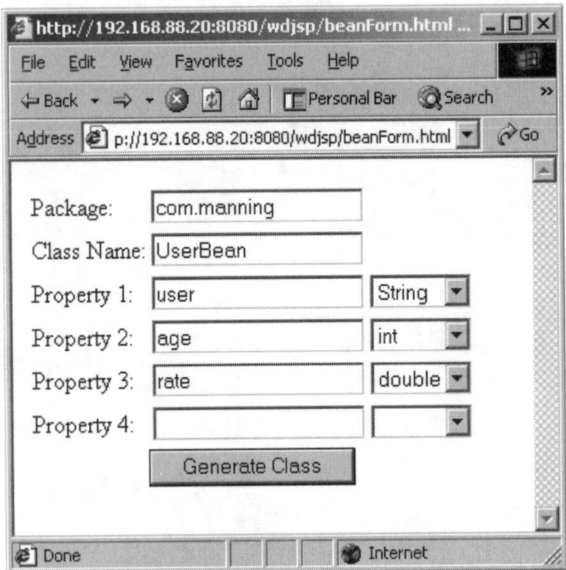

Figure 16.4 The JavaBean generator

```
  public void set<%= fixcase(propertyName) %>(<%= propertyType %> <%= proper-
   tyName %>) {
    this.<%= propertyName %> = <%= propertyName %>
  }
<% } } %>
}

<%!
private String fixcase(String s) {
  return s.toUpperCase().substring(0,1) + s.substring(1);
}
%>
```

In this chapter we've looked at several HTML alternatives that can benefit from JSP's dynamic content generation capabilities. These are just a few of the formats we can produce with JSP. If, for example, you need to dynamically generate richer, more print-ready documents, try dynamic RTF or PostScript documents. Leaving the realm of documents, you can also use JSP to generate complicated configuration files, data files, or Perl code. Once you grasp the simple elegance of the JSP content generation capabilities, the sky's the limit.

17 JSP by example

This chapter covers

- Rotating an ad banner
- Generating a random quote
- Mailing a link to the current page
- Accessing the Whois database
- Generating an index file
- Viewing raw JSP code

In this chapter we will present additional examples of JSP programming. While we will highlight important or confusing segments of the code, our main purpose is to add context and real world examples to the programming syntax and theory covered earlier in the book. For those of you who learn best by example, this chapter will help tie together the concepts we've been discussing.

17.1 A rotating banner ad

Banner ads are now a common fixture on web pages. Typically, these ads are comprised of graphical images conforming to a fixed size requirement, to be displayed across the top of a page or some other standard location. A site will often be presenting multiple banner ads on its pages at the same time, alternating which banner is displayed as the user moves from page to page. For this reason, an automated mechanism for selecting a banner from those available and displaying it on a page is highly desirable.

This example, because it will be used from multiple pages, utilizes JSP's JavaBeans tags to promote reusability. The first requirement, then, is a working bean that provides the required functionality.

17.1.1 The BannerBean

For the purposes of this example, it is assumed that the banners take the form of image files accessible via URLs. The primary role of this bean, then, is to select one entry from a set of such URLs to serve as the value for the `src` attribute of an HTML `img` tag in order to display the banner.

This is accomplished by means of a `bannerURL` property, provided by the bean's `getBannerURL()` method. In addition, the bean must keep track of all of the available banner images, and rotate among them each time the `bannerURL` property is retrieved. The complete source code for this bean is shown in listing 17.1:

Listing 17.1 BannerBean

```
package com.taglib.wdjsp.byexample;
import java.util.Random;

public class BannerBean {
  private int index, count;
  static private String[] BANNER_URLS = {
    "/webdev/images/PlainBanner.gif",
    "/webdev/images/StripedBanner.gif",
    "/webdev/images/SpottedBanner.gif" };
  public BannerBean () {
    count = BANNER_URLS.length;
```

```
        Random r = new Random();
        index = r.nextInt(count);
    }
    public String getBannerURL () {
        return BANNER_URLS[nextIndex()];
    }
    private int nextIndex () {
        if (++index == count) index = 0;
        return index;
    }
}
```

As you may recall from the discussion in chapter 8, the aspects of this class definition that qualify it as a bean are its constructor, which takes no arguments, and the `getBannerURL()` method, which provides an abstract interface for accessing the bean's sole property, `bannerURL`.

For simplicity's sake, the URLs of the available banners are stored in a `String` array, which is referenced by the static variable `BANNER_URLS`. Similarly, although a variety of schemes might be imagined for determining the selection and/or order in which the banners should be displayed—for example, based on which pages have already been viewed, or on demographic information tied to a specific user—a simple iterative approach is taken here. An integer instance variable, `index`, indicates which of the banners to display. A random value is used to initialize this variable, which is incremented each time the `bannerURL` property is accessed via the `getBannerURL()` method. Incrementing is performed via the `nextIndex()` method, which resets the counter to zero if the number of available URLs is exceeded.

17.1.2 Using the bean

By storing an instance of this bean in the user's session, the user is guaranteed to see a new banner on each page which uses it. This is because each request for the `bannerURL` property increments the instance's `index` variable. When the bean is stored in the session, it will not be necessary to create a bean each time a page which uses the bean is encountered. Instead, the bean will be retrieved from the session and reused. Here is the source code for a sample JSP page, /webdev/banner.jsp, that implements this approach:

```
<%@page import="com.taglib.wdjsp.byexample.*"%>
<html>
<head>
<title>Banner Page</title>
</head>
<body>
```

```
<center>
<jsp:useBean id="banner" scope="session" class="com.taglib.wdjsp.byexample.Ban-
  nerBean"/>
<img src="<jsp:getProperty name="banner" property="bannerURL"/>">
</center>
<P>Click <a href="banner.jsp">here</a> to see the next banner.</P>
</body>
</html>
```

Note that only two JSP elements are needed to access the banner rotation functionality, a `<jsp:useBean>` tag and a `<jsp:getProperty>` tag. To enhance the reusability of this code even further, the two lines containing these JSP elements could be placed in a separate JSP file for inclusion by multiple pages using either the `include` directive or the `<jsp:include>` action. Alternatively, the `BannerBean` could provide the basis for a custom tag.

The output for this JSP page is depicted in figure 17.1. Here, the URL selected for the banner was the third value in the `BANNER_URLS` array, `/webdev/images/SpottedBanner.gif`. If the page's link were followed, the browser would redisplay the same page, since the link points back to /webdev/banner.jsp. Because this would correspond to a new request for that page, however, the JSP container would be required to process the page again. In doing so, `<jsp:useBean>` tag would cause the original `BannerBean` instance to be retrieved from the session, after which the `<jsp:getProperty>` tag would result in a new call to the bean's `getBannerURL()` method. This would cause the next image in the rotation to be displayed. In this case, since the `BANNER_URLS` array only has three elements, the `index` variable would loop to the beginning, so that the next image to be displayed would be `/webdev/images/PlainBanner.gif`.

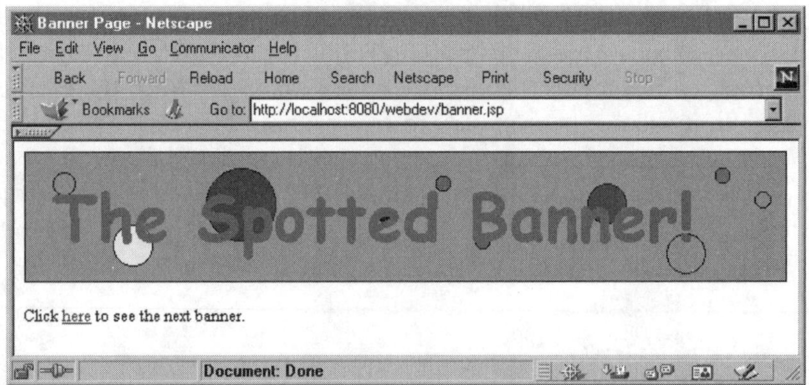

Figure 17.1 Output sent to the browser by the banner page

17.2 A random quote generator

In this example, which builds on the preceding banner rotation example, we select a random quote for the user from a list read from disk at run time. Here we'll see how to bring in our quotes from a file and select a random element for inclusion. The resulting bean provides a great way to add dynamic hints and tips or fortune cookie quotes to your pages.

17.2.1 The QuoteBean

The `QuoteBean` class will store all of our quotes, which are loaded from disk using a file name supplied through the `quoteFile` property. Changing the `quoteFile` property will cause the bean to reload its quote selections from disk. This means that we will want the bean to stick around since it's a relatively expensive operation to go to disk each time. The solution here is to put the bean in the application scope and reuse it for all users visiting our site.

The source for `QuoteBean`: is shown in listing 17.2:

Listing 17.2 QuoteBean

```
import java.io.*;
import java.util.*;

public class QuoteBean {
  private String[] quotes = {"No quotes today!"};
  private Random rand;

  public QuoteBean() {
    rand = new Random();
  }

  public void setQuoteFile(String path) {
    try {
      File file = new File(path);
      ArrayList quoteList = new ArrayList();
      String quote;
      FileReader stream = new FileReader(file);
      BufferedReader reader = new BufferedReader(stream);
      while ((quote = reader.readLine()) != null)
        quoteList.add(quote);
      if (quoteList.size() > 0)
        quotes = (String[])quoteList.toArray(quotes);
    }
    catch (IOException e) {
        System.err.println("Error: " + e.getMessage());};
  }
```

```
  public String getQuote() {
    return quotes[rand.nextInt(quotes.length)];
  }
}
```

In our constructor we need to create an instance of the `java.util.Random` class, which provides a set of easy-to-use pseudorandom number generation methods, and stores it in an instance variable. All of the quotes will be stored in a simple `String` array called `quotes`. Notice that we make sure that the array always has something in it by initializing it to a default value, and not modifying it directly until we've read in our file completely. We could also elect to load in a default file of quotes in the constructor, but we chose to keep the implementation simple for this example.

We use a `BufferedReader` to read each quote, one quote per line, from the file specified through the argument to the `quoteFile` property. Note that this file's path is not assumed to be relative to your web server's document root directory—it can be anywhere on your system. The initial working directory location will be determined by the process that starts your JVM, but in practice this can be difficult to determine and you will likely find it easiest to stick to absolute paths.

Each time you access the `quote` property of this Bean, a new quote is selected by choosing a random array index value, and returning the corresponding `String`. Because we process the entire file in the `setQuoteFile()` method, we don't have to go back to the disk for a new quote each time—only when we change the quote file from which we are selecting.

17.2.2 Using the bean

As we mentioned, this bean was designed to be reused between requests, and would typically be placed into application scope, as shown here. We use the body of the `<jsp:useBean>` tag to initialize the bean by setting the path to our quote file.

```
<jsp:useBean id="quotes" class="com.taglib.wdjsp.byexample.QuoteBean"
  scope="application">
<jsp:setProperty name="quotes" property="quoteFile"
 value="/games/fortunes.txt"/>
</jsp:useBean>
<html>
<body>
Tip of the day: <jsp:getProperty name="quotes" property="quote"/>
</body>
</html>
```

Another way you could use this bean is at the session scope level, with the selection of quote file based on other parameters such as the user's native language, status, or other dynamic attributes which you can determine at run time. Here's an example of selecting the quote file dynamically on a per-user basis, based on the authenticated username—we'll assume that we've created a quote file based on each user's name, in the /quotes/ directory. So for example, user `cwalton` would correspond to `/quotes/cwalton.txt`.

```
<jsp:useBean id="quotes" class="com.taglib.wdjsp.byexample.QuoteBean"
   scope="session">
<jsp:setProperty name="quotes" property="quoteFile"
  value="<%= "/quotes/" + request.getRemoteUser() + ".txt" %>"/>
</jsp:useBean>
<html>
<body>
Greetings <%= request.getRemoteUser() %>, our advice to you is:
<jsp:getProperty name="quotes" property="quote"/>
</body>
</html>
```

17.3 The Tell a Friend! sticker

In this example we'll build a JSP component that will provide the capability of mailing the current page to a friend or colleague. This feature is found on many of the popular news sites because it is an easy way to get your users to promote your site and attract new users. We'll create a Tell a Friend! module that can easily be added to any page on the site to provide this new capability. The module adds a sticker (so called because it's a reusable element that we can stick onto any page) to the page from which it is called (figure 17.2). Clicking the sticker activates the module, asking the user for the friend's email address before sending the mail and returning the user to the original page.

There are several parts to this example. There's the sticker itself, a page that gets the information required to send the email, and the page or servlet that actually sends the email. The flow between them is illustrated in figure 17.3. The sticker may be included on any page. Clicking the sticker activates this process, directing the user to a page that asks for the information required to send the mail, such as the intended recipient's email address. This form then submits its information to another page (or a servlet) to send the mail, and the user is redirected back to the original page. It's all simpler than it looks.

You could apply this same principal in other ways, skipping the second step if you didn't need any additional information from the user before sending the mail.

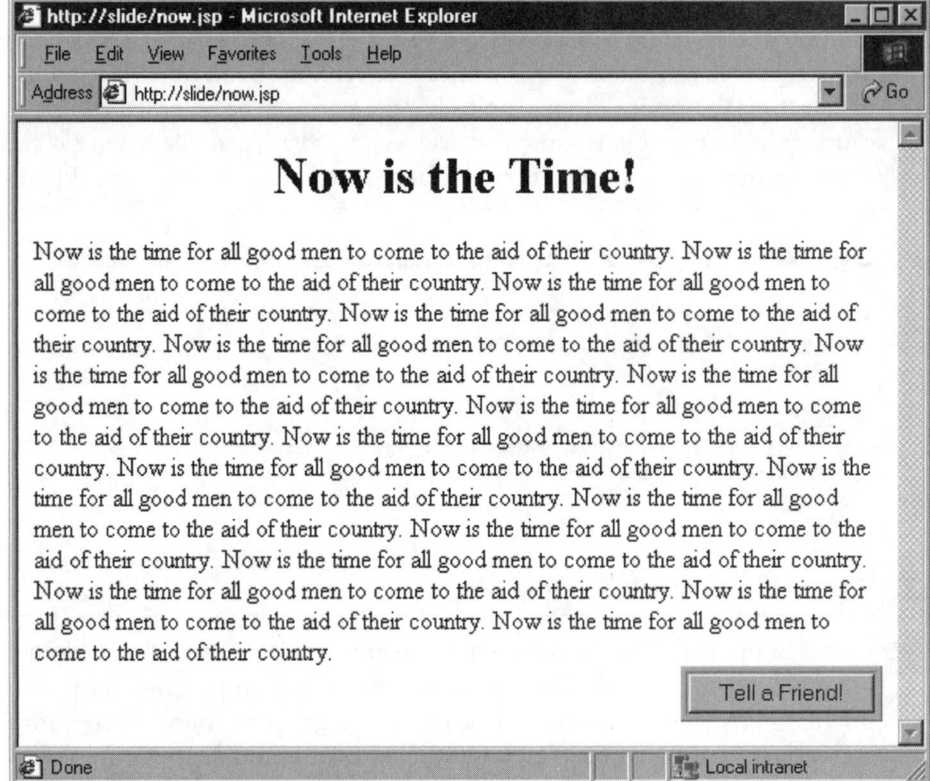

Figure 17.2 The Tell a Friend! sticker in action

17.3.1 The sticker

The sticker is the little icon, table, form, or link that we want to appear on pages throughout our site. Clicking it is what initiates the mailing process. We'll use a little form button in this example, but an image link would work just as well. The beauty of this approach is that the design of the sticker itself is independent of its usage and its HTML source code is isolated to its own file. Because the sticker will be added to each page at run time, you are free to alter its look at any time and it will be instantly updated throughout the site.

Creating the sticker

The Tell a Friend! sticker itself isn't necessarily a JSP. Its specific contents are unimportant. Its only job is to create a link from the current page to our MailForm page so we can get the information we need to send the email message. The real work is done once we get to the MailForm page. Here's a simple example sticker which creates a small tan table with a Submit button to create the linkage we need:

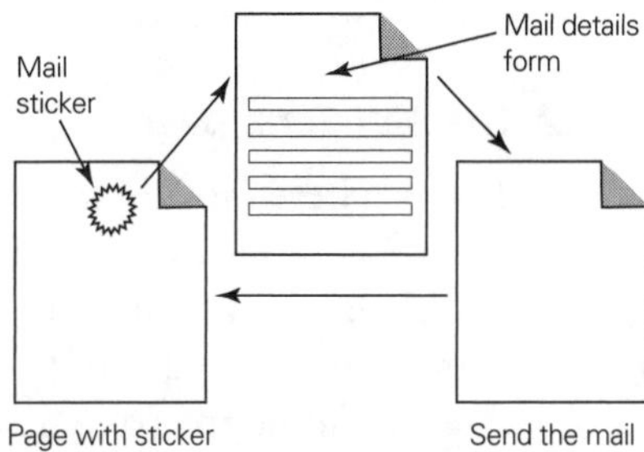

Figure 17.3 Page interactions for implementing the mail this page sticker

```
<table bgcolor="tan" border="1">
<form action="MailForm.jsp" method="post">
<tr><td align="Center">
<input type="Submit" value="Tell a Friend!">
</td></tr>
</form>
</table>
```

Since the mail sticker page will be included in another page, we don't need this to be a complete HTML document (in fact it should not be). Therefore we don't need `<HTML>` or `<BODY>` tags here. Here's another example sticker that uses an image and an anchor to create the link. Note that it's not necessary to have a form on this page.

```
<a href="MailForm.jsp">
<img src="/images/mailsticker.gif">
</a>
```

Again, the reason we have a separate page is to componentize our sticker, so that its look and feel can be managed separately from that of the pages on which it will appear. You could even create several different stickers for different areas of the site.

Using the sticker

Using the sticker is very easy; simply include it in the page with the `include` action:

```
<html>
<body>
Now is the time!
<div align="right">
<jsp:include page="MailSticker.jsp" />
</div>
</body>
</html>
```

The contents will be added to the page at run time, and will automatically pick up any changes to the MailSticker.jsp page.

17.3.2 The MailForm page

This is where most of the action takes place, but as you'll see it's still easy to understand. What we have to do here is to grab the contents of the REFERER header, a hidden bit of information enclosed in the HTTP request from the user's browser that tells us the URL of the page from which the request originated, which in our case should be the page the sticker was on (figure 17.4).

Note that it is not the URL of the sticker itself: recall that we included its contents directly into our page. This is the URL that we mail to the address specified by the user, and is the URL that we will send the user back to when we are finished with the whole process. We need to pass the referrer information, along with some mail-related details, to our servlet or JSP page that will handle the actual sending of the mail. The contents of the MailForm.jsp page are shown in listing 17.3.

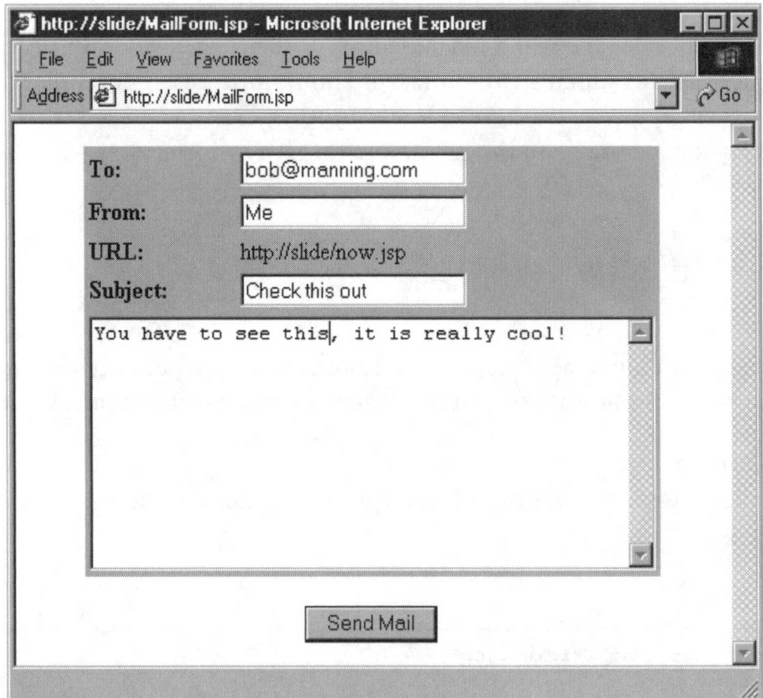

Figure 17.4 Passing along the referrer information via email

Listing 17.3 MailForm.jsp page

```
<html>
<body>
<form action="SendMail.jsp" method="post">
<table border="0" align="center" bgcolor="tan">
<tr><td><b>To:</b></td><td>
<input type="TEXT" name="to"></td></tr>
<tr><td><b>From:</b></td><td>
<input type="TEXT" name="from"></td></tr>
<tr><td><b>URL:</b></td><td>
<%= request.getHeader("REFERER") %></td></tr>
<tr><td><b>Subject:</b></td><td>
<input type="TEXT" name="subject" value="Check this out"></td></tr>
<tr><td colspan="2"><textarea name="body" rows=10 cols=45>
Check out this site, it is really cool!
</textarea>
</td></tr>
</table>
<p>
<input type="HIDDEN" name="destination"
value="<%= request.getHeader("referer") %>">
<center><input type="SUBMIT" value="Send Mail"></center>
</form>
</body>
</html>
```

There is only one JSP element on this page, which we use to grab the value of the referrer and store it in a hidden form element called `destination`. The form handler will use this information, and the `to` and `from` fields, to know what to send and where to send it.

17.3.3 Sending the mail

The form handler `SendMail.jsp` is responsible for taking the input data from the form, sending the corresponding email message, and returning the user to the original page. The code for our example is shown in listing 17.4, but there are, of course, a number of ways to process the request. We've omitted the JavaMail code that sends the email, as it's the same as discussed in chapter 14.

Listing 17.4 Sending email and returning user to the page

```
<html>
<%@ page import="javax.mail.*, javax.mail.internet.*" %>
<%
  try {
    String mailServer = "devmail.dev.tivoli.com";
    String subject = request.getParameter("subject");
    String[] to = { request.getParameter("to" };
    String from = request.getParameter("from");
    String body = request.getParameter("destination") +
      "\n\n" + request.getParameter("body");
    sendEmail(mailServer, subject, to, from, body);
 %>
<body>
<P> Mail has been sent! </P>
<% }
  catch (AddressException e) { %>
<P>Invalid e-mail address(es) for forwarding</P>
<% }
  catch (MessagingException e) { %>
<P>Unable to send e-mail notification</P>
<% } %>
Return to
<a href="<%= request.getParameter("destination") %>">
Original Page</a>
</body>
</html>
```

This JSP page uses a scriptlet and a pair of method declarations to implement the form handler. The `getParameter()` method of the request object is used to retrieve the form inputs, which are then used with the `sendEmail()` method, introduced in chapter 11, to deliver the electronic mail message.

Instead of mailing the interesting URL to the user we could have directed the request to a servlet which would read in the contents of the URL (perhaps even converting it to plain text) and then send the whole thing off to the indicated user as an email attachment.

Also, rather than redirecting the user to the original page, we could have the sticker create a separate pop-up window, which would ask for the mail details. This would keep the user's main browser on the same page the entire time. When complete, we could simply close the pop-up window.

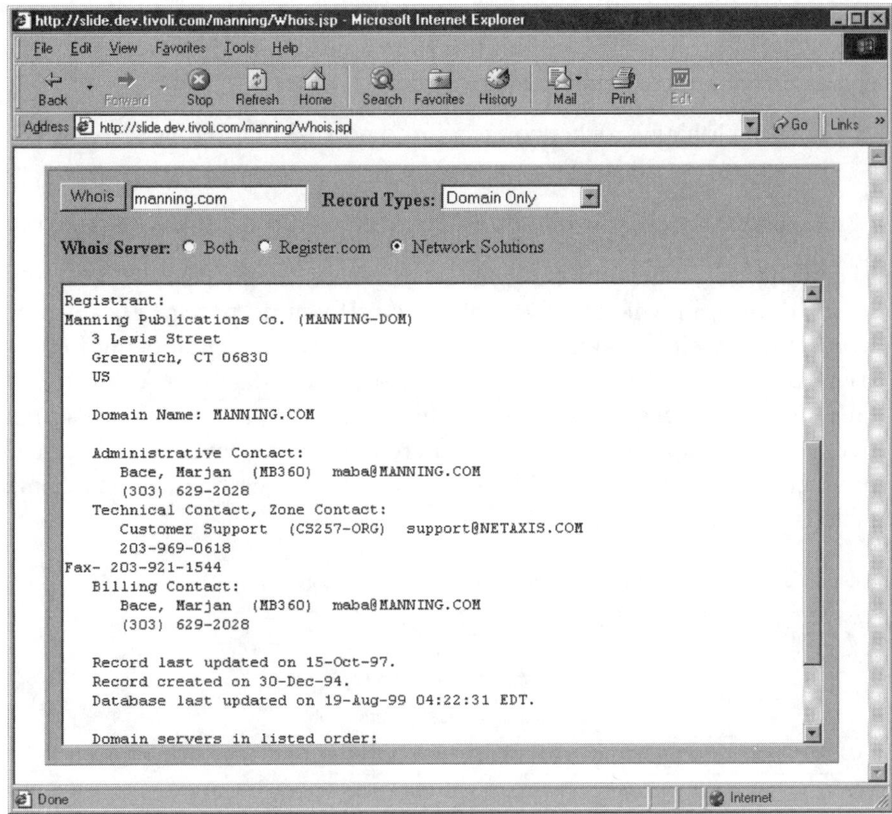

Figure 17.5 User interface for the JSP-based Whois client

17.4 A JSP Whois client

The *Whois* database is an Internet directory service that stores contact information for Internet domains and the administrators responsible for running them. A Whois client can search the contents of this database to find out the owner of a particular domain name, the contact information, and when the name was registered. In this example we will use JSP to design a Whois client with a web interface (figure 17.5).

17.4.1 The Whois protocol

In order to build this application we must understand a little bit about the Whois protocol, which is defined by RFC954, and decide what features we will support. The Whois protocol is a simple query/response service that is hosted by the companies authorized by the Internet Corporation for Assigned Names and Numbers (ICANN) to handle Internet domain name registration. Searching the Whois database with a client application involves:

1. Establishing a socket connection to port 43 of a Whois server
2. Sending a search query terminated with a line feed
3. Retrieving results from the Whois server, which will then close the connection

The format of a Whois search query is fairly basic: simply pass the name of the person or domain in which you are interested. If you do not specify any search keywords, the default action is to conduct a very broad search, looking for matches to your query in any field of any type of record in the database. You can prefix your query with a special set of keywords, which can be used to restrict the search to particular record types or fields. While there are many keywords and search control parameters supported by the Whois service, the most useful ones are summarized in table 17.1.

Table 17.1 Common search keywords for the Whois protocol

Keyword	Function
DO	Restrict searches to domain records only
HO	Restrict searches to host records only
GA	Restrict searches to gateway records only
Full	Gives a long display for each record
SUM	Return only summaries

Prior to the explosive growth of the Internet, a single company was responsible for registering top-level Internet domain names. This meant that by searching a single Whois server you could retrieve information about any .com, .net, or .org site on the Internet. In October 1998, the U.S. government developed a shared registration System that permits multiple registrars to provide registration services for the Internet, and appointed ICANN to oversee this system. Several new registrars have been approved, and more are planned. This makes searching for registration information a somewhat more challenging task because records for new domain name registrations are now spread across a growing number of individual Whois databases. It is uncertain whether or not anyone plans to consolidate information from each of the registrars into a single database.

NOTE Information on the implementation of NSI's Shared Registration System is available at http://www.nsiregistry.com, while information about ICANN's registrar accreditation process is available at http://www.icann.org.

17.4.2 Requirements and design considerations

What we are building is a Whois client that can be accessed through a web browser, making it accessible to anyone on our network, no matter what type of computer he/she has. While the primary interface will be designed in HTML, this project involves remote network connections, so some server-side code will be required.

Unlike the Whois clients that are built into UNIX or bundled with most networking packages, our client will need to be able to search multiple Whois databases simultaneously, so that we can locate records regardless of which registrar's database they happen to be on. We should also expect that new registrars will be approved in the future, and be prepared to handle these new servers as they become available.

Our client should also include options that allow the user to restrict searches to certain sets of records or fields. While we could simply require the user to encode the query with the appropriate keywords and modifiers, it is preferable to assume that not all of our users are quite so familiar with the Whois protocol.

From an architectural perspective it makes sense to divide our development tasks into two parts: a front-end user interface and a back-end network service. The capability to look up records in a Whois server will be encapsulated into a JavaBean running on the server. We can develop this component independently from our front-end interface, which might change over time.

17.4.3 The WhoisBean

All of the code required to perform searches against a Whois database will be encapsulated into our server-side component for this application, the `WhoisBean`. The `WhoisBean` can provide Whois lookup services to any application capable of accessing its properties. In this case we are building an HTML interface through JSP, but a servlet, applet, or Java application could just as easily use the bean's services. By packaging our service into a JavaBean like this, we don't have to worry about how or when it will be used, and we won't need to rewrite it for every project or new user interface that comes up.

To perform the lookup, we first create a socket connection to port 43 of the server. Once connected, we issue our query to the socket's `OutputStream` and read the results from its `InputStream`. The following code will establish a connection to the Whois server at Networks Solutions, Inc. (whois.internic.net), which will search for the domain manning.com and print the response to the screen.

```
Socket connection = new Socket("whois.internic.net", 43);
out = new PrintStream(connection.getOutputStream());
in = new BufferedReader(new InputStreamReader(connection.getInputStream()));
out.println("DO manning.com");
while ((line = reader.readLine()) != null)
  System.out.println(line + "\n");
```

Code like this will form the core of our `WhoisBean` class, as it performs the primary service we are interested in delivering. The rest of the code for this class will be concerned with supporting our bean's properties, which will form the interface required to access the bean through JSP.

Bean properties

The first step in designing our bean is to determine what properties it will support. We know that at minimum the front-end interface will need to set a query and view the results of the search, so there are two properties right there: `query` and `results`. How should we handle the search keywords and options? One choice would be to implement properties and corresponding access methods for each search option supported by the Whois protocol. While this might seem to be the most exacting approach, it would create a needlessly complex interface that could be eliminated by simply accepting all search modifiers through a single property, `options`. We'll make the `query` and `options` properties read/write, since the front-end code might need to view their state as well as modify it. The `results` property however, will be read-only because instead of reflecting the state of an instance variable it will actually be used to return the response from the Whois server. Since the value of the `results` property will be computed dynamically each time it is requested, it requires only a getter method, not a setter.

It would also be a good idea to allow the front-end code to specify which Whois servers we wish to search. Because the growth of the Internet is creating the need for additional registrars and Whois databases, we can expect that we will need to update our code to include support for additional Whois server addresses in the future. That being said, we should try to isolate that portion of the code to the front-end, which is easier to revise. It also gives us a more flexible solution. The front-end code can decide what servers are searched and give the user as many or as few options as desired. Otherwise, we would be restricted to a rigid, bean-enforced selection of servers each time, or end up with an overly complex interface between the Bean and the front-end code. We've therefore added an indexed property, `servers`, which holds the names of the Whois servers we wish to search. We've also included a convenience property that allows the JSP page to treat the `servers` property as a single `String` value by separating each server name with a comma. In the absence of custom JSP tags for handling indexed properties, this will make the front-end JSP code much cleaner.

The property sheet for this bean is presented in table 17.2.

Table 17.2 Property sheet for `com.taglib.wdjsp.byexample.WhoisBean`

Name	Access	Java Type	Use
`query`	read/write	`java.lang.String`	Specifies the query data
`options`	read/write	`java.lang.String`	Searches keywords and modifiers
`results`	read only	`java.lang.String`	Results from whois
`servers`	read/write	`java.lang.String[]`	Whois servers to search through
`serverList`	read/write	`java.lang.String`	Convenience property for setting servers, accepts a comma separated list of servers

Instance variables and constructor

In order to maintain its state, our `WhoisBean` class will need instance variables for the query, the search options, and the list of servers.

```
public class WhoisBean {
  private String query;
  private String options;
  private String[] servers;
}
```

In the constructor we will initialize our state variables with empty data.

```
public WhoisBean() {
  query = "";
  options = "";
  servers = new String[0];
}
```

Access methods

The access methods for our `query` and `options` properties are relatively straightforward. Each can map directly to an instance variable, with getters and setters that access these instance variables to manage the bean's state.

```
public String getQuery() {
  return query;
}
public void setQuery(String query) {
  this.query = query;
```

```
}
public String getOptions() {
  return options;
}
public void setOptions(String options) {
  this.options = options;
}
```

Designing the access methods for the `servers` and `serverList` properties is a little more complex. Internally, we can store our list of Whois servers as an array of `String` objects. This will let us easily loop through the list of servers to perform our searches. In order to better support JSP access to this bean, we decided that our list of servers could be modified by the user through two different properties, `servers` and `serverList`. This means that we need to create methods to read and write the array through both properties. `Servers` is an indexed property that deals with arrays directly, and its access methods are fairly straightforward. Don't forget however, that while not entirely necessary, it's a good idea to go ahead and add additional access methods that can be used to access the entire contents of the list at once as an array:

```
public String getServers(int index) {
  return servers[index];
}
public void setServers(String server, int index) {
  servers[index] = server;
}
public String[] getServers() {
  return servers;
}
public void setServers(String[] servers) {
  this.servers = servers;
}
```

Writing the `serverList` property access methods requires us to do more work. We must convert the `servers` array to and from a comma-delimited list. It is important to preserve the ordering of the list of servers so that the front-end code will get consistent results back from the property. We have used the `java.util.Vector` class to assure that we preserve the order of the elements in the list.

```
public void setServerList(String values) {
  Vector v = new Vector();
  StringTokenizer tok = new StringTokenizer(values, ", ");
  while (tok.hasMoreTokens())
    v.addElement(tok.nextToken());
  servers = new String[v.size()];
  for (int i=0; i < servers.length; i++)
```

```
    servers[i] = (String)v.elementAt(i);
}

public String getServerList() {
  String values = "";
  for (int i=0; i < servers.length; i++) {
    values += servers[i];
    if (i < (servers.length - 1))
      values += ", ";
  }
  return values;
}
```

The `results` property access method will be read-only, so we only need to create the method `getResults()`. As indicated, this getter method will perform the specified query. The first step is to create the query string that we will send to each Whois server. Recall from our discussion of the Whois protocol, we build our query string by prepending our search options to the string for which we wish to search. We'll also need to test for the possibility that there aren't any options, in which case we will use the query property as the search string, as follows:

```
String queryString;
if (options.length() > 0)
  queryString = options + " " + query;
else
  queryString = query;
```

We'll use the networking code we looked at earlier as the core of this method. To simplify the implementation, we'll collect the search results from all of the servers we're interested in by looping through the array of servers, conducting a search against each one, and appending the results of each search to a `String` variable that will by returned by the `getResults()` method.

```
String output = "";
for (int i=0; (i < servers.length) && (query.length() > 0); i++) {
  try {
    String line = "";
    Socket connection = new Socket(servers[i], 43);
    InputStream sock = connection.getInputStream();
    PrintStream out = new PrintStream(connection.getOutputStream());
    BufferedReader in = new BufferedReader(
     new InputStreamReader(sock));
    output += "Results from " + servers[i] + " for \"" +
     query + "\"\n\n";
    out.println(query);
    while ((line = in.readLine()) != null)
      output += line + "\n";
  }
```

```
    catch(Exception e) {
      output += "Could not contact Whois server on "+servers[i]+ "\n";
    }
    output += "\n\n\n";
  }
  return output;
```

As far as handling error conditions, we've decided here to keep things simple. Attempting to access the `results` property without properly setting the query or servers properties is an error condition, but rather then throw an exception we will simply return an empty string from `getResults()`. This approach will keep the front-end code simple and will allow it to display the `results` property, which evaluates to an empty `String` in such cases, without having to test for error states or valid properties. Likewise, if we encounter an error contacting or reading data from the Whois server we will simply include the error message in our results. If one particular server did not respond, we would still like to receive results from the others in the list. This seems reasonable for this particular bean: if you haven't set the `query` or `servers` properties, the `results` property will be empty. Other beans might require more sophisticated error-handling capabilities.

The complete source for the `WhoisBean` class is provided in listing 17.5.

Listing 17.5 com.taglib.wdjsp.byexample.WhoisBean class

```
package com.taglib.wdjsp.byexample;

import java.io.*;
import java.net.*;
import java.util.*;

public class WhoisBean {
  private String query;
  private String options;
  private String[] servers;
  private String serverList;

  public WhoisBean() {
    this.query = "";
    this.options = "";
    this.servers = new String[0];
  }

  public void setOptions(String options) {
    this.options = options;
  }

  public String getOptions() {
    return this.options;
  }
```

```
public String getQuery() {
  return query;
}

public void setQuery(String query) {
  this.query = query;
}

public String getServers(int index) {
  return servers[index];
}

public String[] getServers() {
  return servers;
}

public void setServers(String server, int index) {
  servers[index] = server;
}

public void setServers(String[] servers) {
  this.servers = servers;
}

public void setServerList(String values) {
  Vector v = new Vector();
  StringTokenizer tok = new StringTokenizer(values, ",");
  while (tok.hasMoreTokens())
    v.addElement(tok.nextToken());
  servers = new String[v.size()];
  for (int i=0; i < servers.length; i++)
    servers[i] = (String)v.elementAt(i);
}

public String getServerList() {
  String values = "";
  for (int i=0; i < servers.length; i++) {
    values += servers[i];
    if (i < (servers.length - 1))
      values += ",";
  }
  return values;
}

public String getResults() {
  String queryString;
  if (options.length() > 0)
    queryString = options + " " + query;
  else
    queryString = query;
  String output = "";
  for (int i=0; (i< servers.length) && (query.length()>0); i++) {
    try {
```

```
        String line = "";
        Socket connection = new Socket(servers[i], 43);
        InputStream sock = connection.getInputStream();
        PrintStream out =
          new PrintStream(connection.getOutputStream());
        BufferedReader in =
          new BufferedReader(new InputStreamReader(sock));
        output += "Results from " + servers[i] +
          " for \"" + queryString + "\"\n\n";
        out.println(queryString);
        while ((line = in.readLine()) != null)
          output += line + "\n";
      }
      catch(Exception e) {
        output += "Could not contact Whois server at " +
          servers[i] + "\n";
      }
      output += "\n\n\n";
    }
    return output;
  }

  public static void main(String[] args) {
    WhoisBean bean = new WhoisBean();
    bean.setServerList("whois.internic.net");
    bean.setQuery("manning.com");
    System.out.println(bean.getResults());
    bean.setQuery("metafirm.com");
    System.out.println(bean.getResults());
  }
}
```

Improving the design of the bean

If instances of this bean were handling lots of requests or performing a critical service, we might want to make a few minor improvements to its design. We could, for example, only perform a new Whois lookup when one of the input parameters—the contents of the query and options properties—has changed. To do this we would create an internal boolean cache variable that would be flipped to `true` in the `getResults()` method, and back to `false` in any of the setter methods for our properties. Of course when we use this bean in conjunction with JSP, such a change would provide no benefits unless the bean instances were reused across multiple requests. To do so, the JSP developer would need to place user-specific instances of the `WhoisBean` into the session scope.

Another minor improvement we could introduce would be better handling of the error conditions that might arise. We could, for example, remove Whois servers that aren't responding from our server list, throw more meaningful exceptions, and/or validate property values in our setter methods.

17.4.4 Building the front end

Now that we have completed the `WhoisBean` implementation, we need to design the JSP page that will form the user interface of our application. Various approaches are possible for implementing the front end. The traditional approach to web applications such as this is to implement a form in HTML, which then calls a CGI program to perform the specified query. In light of the form-handling example presented in chapter 11, however, a form that incorporates sticky widgets via JSP elements would seem to provide a more user-friendly interface. When coupled with the functionality available in the `WhoisBean`, however, the JSP approach is a natural fit, the results of which are presented in figure 17.5.

Coupling the use of a bean with the sticky widgets approach provides two additional benefits. First, initialization of the bean properties is greatly simplified by supplying identifiers for the form elements that map directly to those properties. This allows us to use the wild card setting for the `property` attribute (i.e., `property="*"`) of the `<jsp:setProperty>` tag. As a result, we can create and initialize our bean with just two tags:

```
<% @page import="com.taglib.wdjsp.byexample" %>
<jsp:useBean id="whois" class="com.taglib.wdjsp.byexample.WhoisBean"
  scope="request"/>
<jsp:setProperty name="whois" property="*"/>
```

Recall that the input values from the form elements are translated into request parameters when the form is submitted. The effect of the wild card value in the `<jsp:setProperty>` tag is to create a mapping from request parameters to bean properties, meaning that we can now access all of the data from the form inputs via the bean instance.

NOTE In the JSP code for this form, as presented in listing 17.6, we use four tags to create and initialize the `WhoisBean` instance. Two additional tags are required to add a body to the `<useBean>` tag in which we provide a default value for the bean's `serverList` property.

This in turn means that, rather than embedding scripting elements into our page for interacting with request parameters, we can use JSP's built-in JavaBeans tags to manipulate these request parameters via the corresponding bean properties. For example, the text field corresponding to the Whois query can be initialized via the

<jsp:getProperty> tag, rather than via a JSP expression as in the earlier example, as follows:

```
<INPUT type="text" name="query" SIZE="20"
 value="<jsp:getProperty name="whois" property="query"/>">
```

Note that the identifier specified for the <input> tag, query, has the same name as the bean property. This ability to replace scripting elements with bean tags is the second added benefit implementing form-handling with JavaBeans: eliminating Java code from the JSP page in order to promote greater separation of presentation and implementation.

Rather than relying extensively on scripting elements containing raw Java code to initialize form fields and handle requests, the Whois client has little Java code in the page itself. What Java code remains in the page is focused entirely on the presentation: setting the action attribute for the <form> tag, and determining which of the select box options and radio buttons should be enabled. All of the application-specific code (i.e., contacting the Whois servers and collecting the results) resides in the implementation of the WhoisBean class.

Another noteworthy aspect of this example is the use of a text area for displaying the results of the Whois lookup. In this case, the text area form element is used for output rather than input. This was done primarily for stylistic reasons, so that the form as a whole resembles a self-contained window from a conventional desktop application. By presenting the query results in a text area with a fixed size and its own scroll bar, the form itself maintains a fixed size that is more consistent with the behavior of desktop application windows (listing 17.6).

Listing 17.6 The JSP Whois form

```
<%@page import="com.taglib.wdjsp.byexample.*" %>
<jsp:useBean id="whois" class="com.taglib.wdjsp.byexample.WhoisBean"
   scope="session">
  <jsp:setProperty name="whois" property="serverList"
    value="whois.internic.net,whois.register.com"/>
</jsp:useBean>
<jsp:setProperty name="whois" property="*"/>
<HTML>
<HEAD><TITLE>Whois Client</TITLE></HEAD>
<BODY BGCOLOR="white">
<TABLE bgcolor="tan" align="center" border="1" cellpadding="10">
<FORM action="<%= HttpUtils.getRequestURL(request) %>" method="GET">
<TR><TD>
<INPUT type="submit" value="Whois">
<INPUT type="text" name="query" SIZE="20"
 value="<jsp:getProperty name="whois" property="query"/>">
```

```
 
<B>Record Types:</B>
<SELECT name="options" SIZE="1">
<OPTION <%= whois.getOptions().equals("")?"selected":"" %>
  VALUE="">All
<OPTION <%= whois.getOptions().equals("Do")?"selected":"" %>
VALUE="Do">Domain Only
<OPTION <%= whois.getOptions().equals("Person")?"selected":"" %>
VALUE="Person">People Only
<OPTION <%= whois.getOptions().equals("Organization")?"selected":"" %>
 VALUE="Organization">Organizations Only
</SELECT>
<P></P>
<B>Whois Server:</B>
<INPUT TYPE="RADIO" NAME="serverList"
<%= whois.getServerList().equals("whois.internic.net,whois.register.com")
    ?"checked":"" %> VALUE="whois.internic.net,whois.register.com">
Both  
<INPUT TYPE="RADIO" NAME="serverList"
<%= whois.getServerList().equals("whois.register.com")
    ?"checked":"" %>
VALUE="whois.register.com">
Register.com  
<INPUT TYPE="RADIO" NAME="serverList"
<%= whois.getServerList().equals("whois.internic.net")?"checked":"" %>
VALUE="whois.internic.net">
Network Solutions
<P></P>
<TEXTAREA rows="24" cols="80">
<jsp:getProperty name="whois" property="results"/>
</TEXTAREA>
</TD></TR>
</TABLE>
</FORM>
</BODY>
</HTML>
```

17.5 An index generator

In this example we'll build a JSP page which generates an index of the files in its directory. It is typical for a web server to look for a welcome file, a default file name to display if a browser requests a directory, rather than a specific file. Typically this file is called index.html, but JSP web servers can be configured to look for the presence of an index.jsp file, and load that instead. Most web servers have some built-in mechanism to generate a file listing for directories that do not have an appropriate welcome file. Typically, these look like a raw directory listing, with anchors to each file, allowing you to browse the file tree without having to create your own index pages.

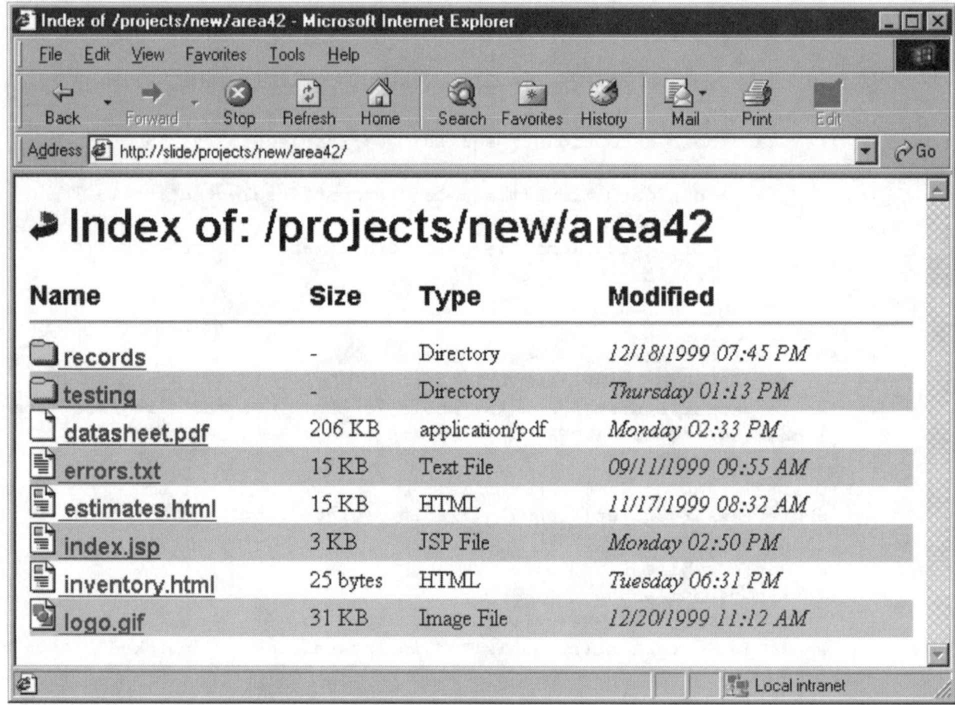

Figure 17.6 Our new and improved index in action

In this example, we'll create our own index.jsp page which can be used as a replacement to your web server's built-in directory listing mechanism. We'll add a number of new features over the average web server, including icons that are sensitive to the type of items in the directory, and alphabetical sorting. Now even if you're happy with the directory listings created by your web server, there are a number of advantages to rolling your own. First, you have complete control of the look and feel of your page—you can make it look as fancy as you'd like. You can also add your own security, filtering, or other options to your index page. An example of the page we created is shown in figure 17.6.

17.5.1 A basic implementation

First, let's create a very basic index which provides an equivalent bare-bones implementation like that provided by most web servers by default. This will help us understand the concepts without being overburdened by the decorative details for now.

Directory independence

One of the initially tricky things about this example is achieving directory independence. We didn't want to have to hard code the directory path, the document root, or other directory location dependent information into the page, modifying them for each directory we wanted to enable with our index generator. Ideally, we can have one copy of the index page, shared by all of our directories.

To use our autoindexing JSP page, we'll configure the web server to look for index.jsp (or whatever we would like to call this welcome page). We'll store the index page in a shared directory as /utils/index.jsp. We will then create a link or copy of the page called index.jsp pointing to this index file from every directory we want to use it. Some web servers will let you specify an absolute path to your welcome file, allowing you to use the same file for all directories, eliminating the need for the link.

We therefore have to make the page itself determine both the logical path that the user sees, as well as the physical path to the directory in order to access details about its files. The first thing then, is to determine the logical path to the current directory. This can be done by examining the request:

```
String cd = new File(request.getRequestURI()).getParent();
```

The request will return something like `/projects/stuff/index.jsp`. We'll temporarily convert this string into a `File` object, so we can utilize its `getParent()` method, which chops off the last bit of the path to yield `/projects/stuff`. (The `File` object's constructor doesn't care if the file exists, it can still manipulate the file names in a platform-independent manner). We then use the `getRealPath()` method of the `application` object to locate the physical directory beneath the server's document root.

```
File realPath = new File(application.getRealPath(cd));
```

Now we're home free. We use the `listFiles()` method of the `File` object (a method new to Java 2) to retrieve an array of `File` objects corresponding to each file in that directory. We can then loop through this list, and interrogate each file for its information, displaying them in a table.

```
File[] files = realPath.listFiles();
for (int i=0; i < files.length; i++) {
  // display file info
}
```

The complete source code for this simple indexer is shown in listing 17.7 and a screen shot in figure 17.7.

Listing 17.7 simpleindex.jsp

```
<%@ page import="java.io.*,java.util.*" %>
<%
  String cd = new File(request.getRequestURI()).getParent();
  File realPath = new File(application.getRealPath(cd));
%>
<html>
<body>
Index of: <%= cd %><p>
<table border="0" cellpadding="0" cellspacing="0" width="100%">
<tr><td>Name</td><td>Size</td><td>Modified</td></tr>
<tr><td colspan="3"><hr></td></tr>
<%
  File[] files = realPath.listFiles();
  for (int i=0; i < files.length; i++) {
%>
<tr>
<td><a href="<%= files[i].getName() %>">
<%= files[i].getName() %></a></td>
<td><%= files[i].length() %></td>
<td><i><%= new Date(files[i].lastModified()) %></i></td>
</tr>
<% } %>
</table>
</body>
</html>
```

As you can see, implementing the basic functionality was easy. Now we'll get fancy and add improvements over most built-in indexes.

17.5.2 An improved version

The source code for the final page is shown in listing 17.8; the screen shot in figure 17.6 was generated from this source, which is greatly enhanced over the simple example in listing 17.7. Other than basic HTML formatting, most of the work to make our index more useful comes from better interpreting information about each file. The raw dates, file sizes, and ordering returned from the underlying operating system are not necessarily the most convenient way to display that data. Therefore, as you can see, we've created a number of utility methods.

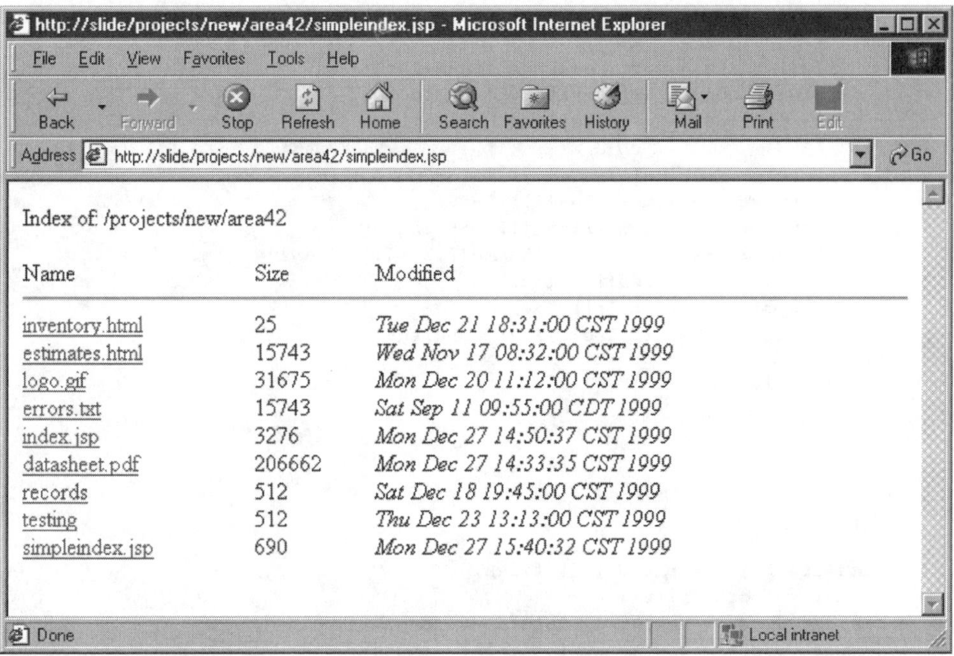

Figure 17.7 A simple index

Listing 17.8 autoindex.jsp

```
<%@ page import="java.io.*,java.util.*,java.text.*" %>
<%
  String cd = new File(request.getRequestURI()).getParent();
  File realPath = new File(application.getRealPath(cd));
%>
<html>
<head><title>Index of <%= cd %></title></head>
<body bgcolor="White">
<% if (! cd.equals("/")) { %>
<a href=".."><img src="/icons/back.gif" border="0"></a> 
<% } %>
<font face="arial" size="+3"><b>Index of: <%= cd %></b></font><p>

<table border="0" cellpadding="0" cellspacing="0" width="100%">
<tr>
<td><font size="+1" face="arial"><b>Name</b></font></td>
<td><font size="+1" face="arial"><b>Size</b></font></td>
<td><font size="+1" face="arial"><b>Type</b></font></td>
<td><font size="+1" face="arial"><b>Modified</b></font></td>
</tr>
```

```
<tr><td colspan="4"><hr></td></tr>
<%
  File[] files = sort(realPath.listFiles());
  String[] colors = { "white", "#cccccc" };
  for (int i=0; i < files.length; i++) {
%>
<tr bgcolor="<%= colors[i % 2] %>"><td>
<a href="<%= getName(files[i]) %>">
<img src="<%= getIcon(files[i]) %>" border="0">
<font face="arial"><b><%= getName(files[i]) %></b></font></a></td>
<td><%= getSize(files[i]) %></td>
<td><%= getType(files[i]) %></td>
<td><i><%= getDate(files[i]) %></i></td>
</tr>
<% } %>
</table>

</body>
</html>

<%!

private File[] sort(File[] files) {
  Arrays.sort(files);
  List dirs  = new ArrayList(files.length);
  List other = new ArrayList(files.length);
  for (int i=0; i < files.length; i++) {
    if (files[i].isDirectory())
      dirs.add(files[i]);
    else
      other.add(files[i]);
  }
  dirs.addAll(other);
  return (File[])dirs.toArray(files);
}

private String getName(File file) {
  return file.getName();
}

private String getIcon(File file) {
  if (file.isDirectory()) return "/icons/folder.gif";
  if (file.toString().endsWith(".jsp")) return "/icons/html.gif";
  String type = getServletContext().getMimeType(file.toString());
  if (type == null) return "/icons/unknown.gif";
  if (type.equals("text/html")) return "/icons/html.gif";
  if (type.startsWith("text/")) return "/icons/text.gif";
  if (type.startsWith("image/")) return "/icons/image2.gif";
  return "/icons/generic.gif";
}

private String getType(File file) {
```

```
    if (file.isDirectory()) return "Directory";
    if (file.toString().endsWith(".jsp")) return "JSP File";
    String type = getServletContext().getMimeType(file.toString());
    if (type == null) return "Unknown";
    if (type.equals("text/html")) return "HTML";
    if (type.startsWith("text/")) return "Text File";
    if (type.startsWith("image/")) return "Image File";
    return type;
  }

  private String getSize(File file) {
    if (file.isDirectory()) return ("-");
    long size = file.length();
    if (size > 1024)
      return ((size / 1024) + " KB");
    return size + " bytes";
  }

  private String getDate(File file) {
    String pattern = "";
    Calendar now = Calendar.getInstance();
    now.roll(Calendar.DATE, true);
    now.add(Calendar.DATE, -7);
    Date fileDate = new Date(file.lastModified());
    if (fileDate.before(now.getTime()))
       pattern = "MM/dd/yyyy hh:mm a";
    else
       pattern = "EEEE hh:mm a";
    SimpleDateFormat formatter;
    formatter = new SimpleDateFormat(pattern);
    return formatter.format(fileDate);
  }
%>
```

Creating color bars

We made each row easier to see by alternating the background color of our table rows with each time through the loop. This is a useful technique that can be applied to any iterative situation. We do this by selecting one color for the odd rows, and another for the even rows. We first create a two-element array, the first color will be used on even-numbered rows (those divisible by 2) and the second will be used by odd-numbered rows. Since we'll be using these values inside HTML, any valid HTML color value can be used, for example, to get white and gray bars we would use this:

```
String[] colors = { "white", "#cccccc" };
```

To display a color, we simply take the remainder (using the modulo operator) of the index counter divided by 2. Even numbered rows will have a remainder of 0, corresponding to the first element of our `colors` array while the odd numbered ones will have a remainder of 1.

```
<tr bgcolor="<%= colors[i % 2] %>"><td>
```

Sorting the files

One annoying aspect about our first implementation of this application is that all of the directories and files are displayed in a jumbled order. We'll fix that by sorting the files by name, with directories listed first. This operation is performed in the `sort()` method. We simply sort the entire array of files first, then extract directories and files to separate arrays. This gives us a sorted set of files, and a sorted set of directories; we simply put the two arrays together, directories first.

Determining the file type and selecting an icon

We can use the `application.getMimeType()` method to determine the type of file with which we are dealing. This method relies on the file's extension and the server's configuration to assign a MIME type. In the `getType()` method, we determine the MIME type directly, and in the `getIcon()` method we choose an appropriate icon. If we wanted to get fancy, we could easily group like files together in the listing by sorting on their respective types.

WARNING From scriptlets in the page we can use the `application` implicit object to gain reference to the current servlet context. However, inside a page's declared methods (such as our `getType()` method in this example) the implicit objects are not defined, and we can only use the methods provided by the Servlet and JSP APIs. The current `PageContext` instance, obtainable through the `getPageContext()` method, can be used to access any of the implicit objects available to the page.

A more flexible modification date

To make our dates a little more relevant, we decided that any date younger than a week would be shown simply as being modified on the day of the week, rather than the full date. Therefore, something modified on Monday of this week at 4 P.M. says "Mon 4:00pm" instead of "Monday, January 10, 2000 4:00:00 pm."

Cleaning up file size

We also wanted to convert file size information from a confusing byte format, to terms of kilobytes and megabytes. We simply divide by the appropriate numbers to convert bytes to the appropriate format. This is done in the `getSize()` method.

17.5.3 Going further

There are a number of ways to expand on this example. Instead of creating a generic index, you could create a more topical one, using the JSP to automatically generate a table of contents for a particular directory to save you the hassle of updating it, for example. You could also add more features to the listing, such as the ability to view, delete, or edit the files in the listing. You could use native methods to retrieve ownership information (if supported by your OS) and other details.

17.6 A button to view JSP source

One thing about JSP development that can be a bit confusing at first is that if you attempt to use the browser's view source feature to look at the HTML behind the JSP page you are visiting you will see the rendered HTML, rather than the JSP code you might first expect. This, of course, is because the JSP code is processed by the server into HTML—the browser never sees the original JSP code. In this example, we'll build a button and a bookmark that allow you to view the original JSP source that lies behind the current HTML page. This restores our ability to look at source code on the fly, without having to have direct access to the web server. Figure 17.8 shows our source code viewer in action.

17.6.1 Displaying the source

This isn't, as it turns out, very complicated—but unfortunately it's more complicated than it should be. All we have to do in theory is calculate the URL of the page we are looking at, and then use the `application.getRealPath()` method to determine the path to the actual file on the server. Knowing the location of the original JSP page, we simply load the contents of the file, set the `contentType` attribute of the page to a value of `text/plain` (so that the page doesn't render HTML tags), and display the contents of the file to the screen. However, some browsers blatantly ignore the server-specified content type of the page, instead attempting to guess the format. The presence of any HTML tags in the contents of the page will cause such browsers to go ahead and render it as HTML, regardless of the server's insistence that it should be shown as text.

So we have to eliminate the HTML tags from the file, but, of course, deleting them would defeat the purpose of this project, so that won't work. What we do then is bend to the browser and display everything in HTML, but convert the angle brackets of HTML tags (and the ampersands of existing entity tags) into their HTML entity forms: `<`, `>`, and `&`. Wrapping the file contents between `<pre>` tags and converting the angle brackets like this gives us the source code.

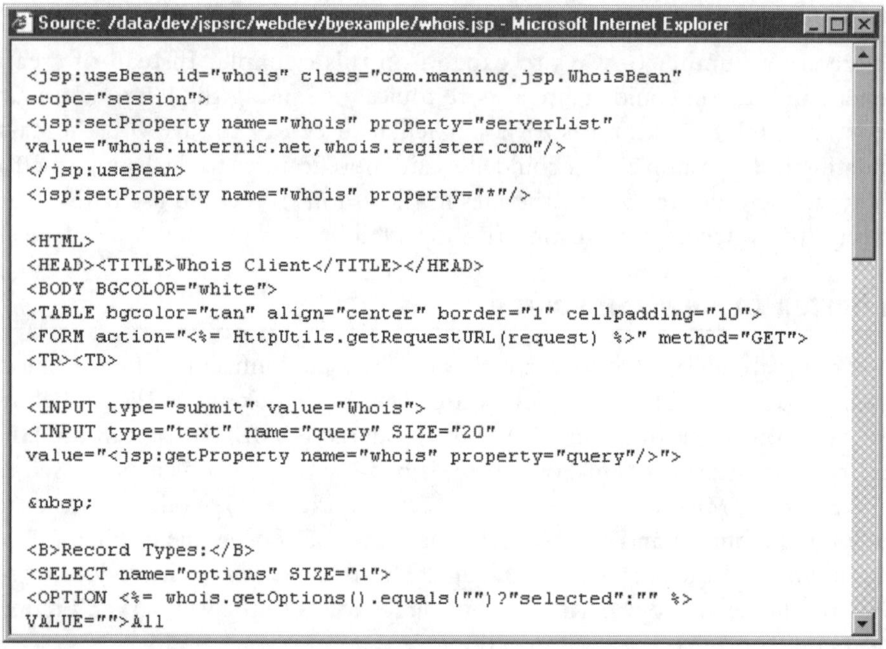

Source: /data/dev/jspsrc/webdev/byexample/whois.jsp - Microsoft Internet Explorer

```
<jsp:useBean id="whois" class="com.manning.jsp.WhoisBean"
scope="session">
<jsp:setProperty name="whois" property="serverList"
value="whois.internic.net,whois.register.com"/>
</jsp:useBean>
<jsp:setProperty name="whois" property="*"/>

<HTML>
<HEAD><TITLE>Whois Client</TITLE></HEAD>
<BODY BGCOLOR="white">
<TABLE bgcolor="tan" align="center" border="1" cellpadding="10">
<FORM action="<%= HttpUtils.getRequestURL(request) %>" method="GET">
<TR><TD>

<INPUT type="submit" value="Whois">
<INPUT type="text" name="query" SIZE="20"
value="<jsp:getProperty name="whois" property="query"/>">

 

<B>Record Types:</B>
<SELECT name="options" SIZE="1">
<OPTION <%= whois.getOptions().equals("")?"selected":"" %>
VALUE="">All
```

Figure 17.8 Viewing JSP source from a browser

We'll create a page which takes a URL as a request argument, locates the file, converts its contents into HTML friendly text, and displays the results (listing 17.9).

Listing 17.9 viewsource.jsp

```
<%@ page import="java.io.*" %>
<%
String url = request.getParameter("url");
if (url.indexOf("..") > -1)
  throw new java.io.IOException("Relative paths are not allowed");
File realPath = new File(application.getRealPath(url));
%>
<html><head><title>Source: <%= url %></title></head><body><pre>
<%
FileInputStream fis = null;
try {
  fis = new FileInputStream(realPath);
  BufferedReader reader;
  reader = new BufferedReader(new InputStreamReader(fis));
  String line;
  while ((line = reader.readLine()) != null) {
    line = replace(line, "&", "&amp;");
```

```
      line = replace(line, "<", "&lt;");
      line = replace(line, ">", "&gt;");
      out.println(line);
    }
  }
  catch (IOException e) {
    out.println("IOException: " + e.getMessage());
  }
  finally { if (fis != null) fis.close(); }
  %>
  </pre></body></html>
  <%!
  public String replace(String s, String old, String replacement) {
     int i = s.indexOf(old);
     StringBuffer r = new StringBuffer();
     if (i == -1) return s;
     r.append(s.substring(0,i) + replacement);
     if (i + old.length() < s.length())
       r.append(replace(s.substring(i + old.length(), s.length()),
        old, replacement));
     return r.toString();
  }
  %>
```

17.6.2 Limitations of the view source program

There are limitations to this approach however. Since we are relying on the application object's ability to determine the actual path to our JSP file, the application will only be able to handle JSP pages on the same server as itself. In fact, it will only be able to handle JSPs in the same application as itself. If you are using multiple servers or your server has multiple JSP applications installed, you will have to have multiple copies of the JSP page.

17.6.3 Adding a view source button to a page

As you can see, this code must be passed to the URL of the page for which we are interested in seeing the source, through the `url` request parameter. To make it as easy as possible, we'll create another JSP page, vsbutton.jsp, which contains the necessary form elements and JSP code to add an HTML form button to the page (listing 17.10).

Listing 17.10 vsbutton.jsp

```
<%@ page import="java.io.*,java.util.*,java.text.*" %>
<% String me = request.getRequestURI(); %>
<script language="JavaScript">
function show(url) {
  opts="height=400,width=600,scrollbars=yes,resizable=yes"
  window.open("viewsource.jsp?url=" + escape(url), "src", opts);
}
</script>
<form><div align="right">
<input type="button" value="View Source"
onClick="show('<%= me %>')"></div>
</form>
```

We can then include this page into any other page to which we wish to add the button. It will appear wherever we like on the page, and clicking it will display the source code for the page in its own little window, thanks to JavaScript.

```
<jsp:include page="vsbutton.jsp" flush="true"/>
```

This is cool, but it requires us to add a line of code to each and every page for which we would like to view source. That's not real handy, and we can do better.

17.6.4 Viewing source through a bookmark

To avoid adding code to each page, we can encapsulate our request into a JavaScript URL which we can add to our browser's bookmark list. Clicking the bookmark will pop up a window displaying the source code of the current page, just as our button did. This works because a JavaScript URL in a bookmark is executed in the context of the current document, meaning it can determine the document location, which it passes to the original viewsource.jsp page through the `url` parameter (listing 17.11).

Listing 17.11 jsvvs.html

```
<html>
<body>Right Click and add to Boomarks/Favorites:
<a href="javascript:void
window.open('/utils/viewsource.jsp?url='+escape(location.pathname),
'src','height=400,width=600,scrollbars=yes,resizable=yes');">
View JSP Source</a>
</body>
</html>
```

18 Creating custom tags

This chapter covers

- How custom tags work
- Constructing tag libraries and tag library descriptors
- Java classes for implementing custom tags
- Custom tag examples for content substitution and content translation

Custom tags are the standard extension mechanism for JSP, and are among its newest features. While the `taglib` directive was introduced in version 1.0 of the JSP specification, the Java classes that could be used to implement custom tags in a portable fashion were not added until version 1.1. Furthermore, many of the new features introduced in JSP 1.2 are related to custom tags. In this chapter, we discuss both the use and implementation of custom tags for JSP. We start by examining their role and capabilities, and provide an overview of how they work. We next take a look at the set of Java classes and interfaces provided by JSP for developing custom tags, and then demonstrate their features by applying them to the implementation of basic custom tags. These, in combination with the advanced custom tags to be presented in chapter 19 and the custom tag validators to be covered in chapter 20, will form the basis of a small library for demonstrating their use in a series of example pages.

18.1 Role of custom tags

As discussed in chapter 3, a key advantage of JSP over many of the other commonly used dynamic content systems is its ability to separate presentation from implementation through the use of HTML-like tags. By avoiding the use of JSP elements that embed scripting language code in the page, maintenance of JSP pages is greatly simplified, and the opportunity to reuse the Java code that provides the underlying functionality is preserved.

Unfortunately, JSP provides only three built-in actions for interacting with JavaBeans objects: `<jsp:useBean>`, `<jsp:getProperty>`, and `<jsp:setProperty>`. With the exception of these three bean tags, the only standard means provided by JSP for accessing arbitrary Java code are the scripting elements (i.e., scriptlets and expressions). If the needs of your application cannot be met via the standard bean tags, it would appear that the need to embed Java code in the page is unavoidable.

Fortunately, JSP provides custom tags as an extension mechanism for adding new action tags. As such, custom tag libraries can be written to provide added functionality for a JSP application without having to resort to the use of Java code within your JSP pages.

Similarly, as pointed out in chapter 3, it is undesirable to implement dynamic HTML generation via JavaBeans properties, because beans are intended to be standalone components that are independent of the type of application within which they are used. Dynamic HTML generation is a fairly uncommon requirement outside of the context of JSP, suggesting that beans which generate HTML may be too closely tied to a specific application.

On the other hand, custom tags are explicitly designed to add functionality to JSP pages, including the dynamic generation of page content such as HTML. If you need to generate HTML content programmatically via Java, custom tags are an ideal implementation technique. Custom tags can be used to insert text into the page, and also to implement flow of control. Attributes can be specified for custom tags, as parameters that influence their behavior. Custom tags can be empty or have bodies, which contain either nested JSP elements (including other custom tags) or tag-specific content to be processed by the tag itself. Custom tags can also interact with each other, either by requesting information through the hierarchy of nested tags, or by introducing new scripting variables which may be accessed by subsequent custom tags, as well as by the standard JSP scripting elements.

As with all other JSP features, custom tags are implemented via Java objects. Developers who are creating their own custom tags do so by creating Java classes that produce the desired functionality. As such, custom tags can access the full range of Java APIs. For example, custom tags can employ the JDBC classes to make database calls, or use the JavaMail API to send or receive electronic mail.

Of course, embedding too much functionality into custom tags has its disadvantages. In particular, since custom tags are only meant to be accessed from JSP pages, any operations built into the implementation of these tags can be used only from JSP. To promote reusability, it is preferable to implement the underlying functionality via JavaBeans, EJBs, or generic Java classes, and use custom tags for controlling presentation and translating between bean properties and class methods and the page markup language.

The implication, then, is that there are no limits on the types of behavior that can be implemented via custom tags. If you have need for a specific computational task to be accomplished on a JSP page, an implementation based on a combination of custom tags and other Java code can be developed which maintains a strong separation between presentation and implementation.

18.2 How tag libraries work

As described in chapter 5, a JSP page that uses custom tags must first load the libraries containing those custom tags by means of the `taglib` directive. Two attributes must be specified with this directive, a URL indicating the location of the TLD file for the library, described next, and a string specifying a page-specific XML namespace for the library's tags.

When the JSP container is compiling a page that uses a custom tag library, its first response to the `taglib` directive is to determine whether or not it needs to load

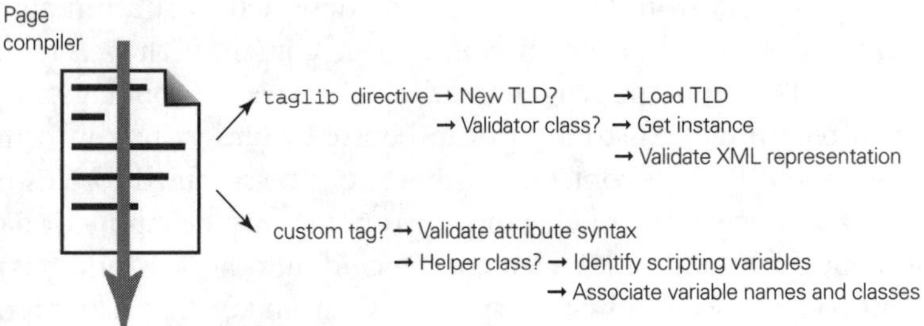

Figure 18.1 Page compilation steps for custom tags

the corresponding TLD (figure 18.1). If this is the first time the specified library has been requested by a page, the JSP container will read the TLD from the indicated URI. If, however, the specified library has been encountered before, such as during compilation of another page that uses the same library, the TLD will not be loaded a second time.

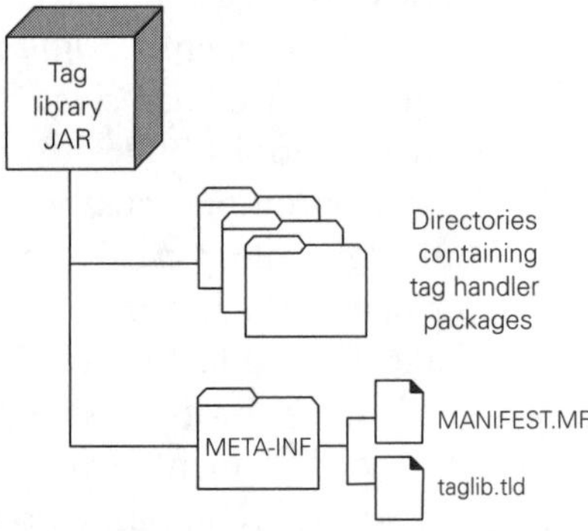

Figure 18.2 JAR file structure for custom tag libraries

A tag library is typically packaged as a JAR file, which in turn contains the class files that implement the library's tags. If you are familiar with the JAR format, then you know that, in addition to Java class files, a JAR file includes a top-level directory named META-INF that stores information about the archive itself. For example, standard JAR files include a file named MANIFEST.MF in this META-INF directory that contains a listing of all of the files in the archive, along with authentication data that may be used to verify the archive's integrity. JAR files representing JSP tag libraries must also include a file named taglib.tld in this directory, which holds a copy of the library's TLD (figure 18.2). The TLD is an XML document that identifies and describes the custom tags provided by the library.

You may recall from chapter 14 that a copy of the TLD also typically resides in the WEB- INF/tlds directory associated with the application making use of the tag library. The name used for this copy is arbitrary. The application's web.xml deployment descriptor is used to designate a URI for this copy of the TLD, and it is this URI that is referenced in the `uri` attribute of the `taglib` directive within the application's JSP pages.

NOTE When naming the TLD stored in the WEB-INF/tlds subdirectory, the convention is to use the name of the library, the current version number, and the same .tld extension as the copy in the library's JAR file. For version 1.7 of a library named EncomTags, for example, this TLD would typically be named EncomTags_1_7.tld.

While compiling a page, the JSP container need only examine the TLD in order to validate most of the page's custom tags. This is because the TLD fully specifies each tag's attributes, including which are required and which are optional, as well as whether or not the tag supports body content (and what the body may contain). Each custom tag encountered while the page is being compiled can be compared against the corresponding specification in the TLD to make sure that the syntax of the tag call is correct. Thus, there is no need to unpack and load the implementation class for the tag just to check its syntax.

If a custom tag is used to introduce new scripting variables, however, some additional work must be done. In this case, the TLD specifies a helper class that can be loaded by the JSP container to identify the names and types of the scripting variables introduced by a specific occurrence of the custom tag. This helper class can also be used to perform additional validation of the custom tag, beyond the simple syntax checks described earlier. For example, if the attributes of a custom tag have mutual dependencies between them, the helper class can be used to check the values specified for those attributes to ensure those dependencies are satisfied.

These helper classes, because they have limited functionality, are often much smaller than the tag implementation classes with which they are associated. In fact, their small size—and the resulting efficiency in their use—is their primary reason for existence. Since the page compilation servlet can get much of the information it needs about a page's custom tags from a combination of the TLD and the helper classes identified by the TLD, it can compile a page much more efficiently than if it had to load the classes which actually implement the custom tags.

Neither the TLD nor the helper classes provide any capabilities for validating the global properties of a JSP page. For example, relationships between tags such as ordering or nesting requirements cannot be enforced via either helper classes or the TLD. To address this deficiency, JSP 1.2 has introduced a third validation mechanism, the tag library validator class. If a library specifies such a validator class in its TLD, this class will be instantiated and given the opportunity to examine the entire contents of the page before it is compiled. This step actually takes place between the two steps described previously: first the page's custom tags are compared against

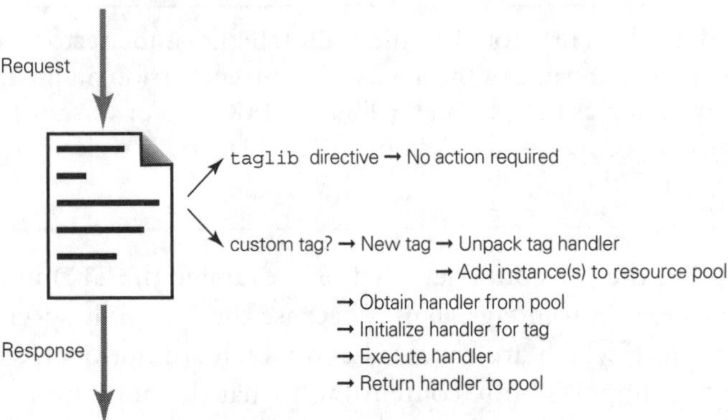

Figure 18.3 Request-time processing of custom tags

the syntax information in the TLD, then any validator classes for the page's tag libraries are applied, and finally the helper classes are consulted.

Thus, by using the result of the TLD syntax validation, along with the information provided by any validator or helper classes associated with a page's custom tags, the JSP container is able to compile the page into a servlet. As with other JSP pages, this servlet is then run whenever a request is received for the corresponding JSP page. It is when the servlet is run, as depicted in figure 18.3, that the tag implementation classes—commonly referred to as *tag handlers*—are unpacked from their library's JAR file, loaded into the container's JVM, and executed.

As another concession to run-time efficiency, custom tag handlers are stored in a shared resource pool. As a result, instances of the tag handler classes are reused by the JSP container as it processes pages, rather than creating an instance each time the corresponding tag is encountered on a page. Because object instantiation is one of the most expensive operations performed by the JVM, the reuse of tag handlers afforded by using such a resource pool can result in significant run-time efficiency when processing pages that make heavy use of custom tags.

Implementing a custom JSP tag, then, requires two major components: the class that implements its handler, and a corresponding entry for the TLD of the library that includes the tag. In the case of tags that define new scripting variables, or which need additional validation beyond the standard syntax checking, validator and/or helper classes must also be defined. The classes, along with the completed TLD, are then packaged into a JAR file for deployment to JSP containers.

18.3 Tag library descriptors

The TLD is an XML document, and, as such, it must include the standard XML header information, including specification of its DTD. The appropriate header for a JSP 1.2 tag library descriptor is as follows:

```
<?xml version="1.0" encoding="ISO-8859-1" ?>
<!DOCTYPE taglib PUBLIC
 "-//Sun Microsystems, Inc.//DTD JSP Tag Library 1.2//EN"
 "http://java.sun.com/j2ee/dtds/web-jsptaglibrary_1_2.dtd">
```

As you can see from its URL, the standard DTD for TLD files is maintained by Sun Microsystems and stored with the other J2EE DTDs on the java.sun.com webserver. If compatibility with JSP 1.1 is desired, the following header should be used:

```
<?xml version="1.0" encoding="ISO-8859-1" ?>
<!DOCTYPE taglib PUBLIC
 "-//Sun Microsystems, Inc.//DTD JSP Tag Library 1.1//EN"
 "http://java.sun.com/j2ee/dtds/web-jsptaglibrary_1_1.dtd">
```

When using this TLD header, the tag library itself should not rely on any JSP 1.2 features.

The root element for a TLD is the `<taglib>` element, which supports several subelements. Three of these, the `<validator-class>` element, the `<listener>` element, and the `<tag>` element, support their own subelements and are used to specify the library's validators, listeners, and tags, respectively. The other subelements specify properties of the library itself.

18.3.1 Library elements

Eight `<taglib>` subelements are provided for describing the library, as in the following TLD fragment:

```
<taglib>
    <tlib-version>1.0</tlib-version>
    <jsp-version>1.2</jsp-version>
    <short-name>mut</short-name>
    <uri>/mut</uri>
    <display-name>Manning Utility Tags</display-name>
    <small-icon>/WEB-INF/icons/mut_small.gif</small-icon>
    <large-icon>/WEB-INF/icons/mut_large.gif</large-icon>
    <description>Utility tags for JSP.</description>
     ...
</taglib>
```

None of these elements has attributes. Their values are specified only through the element bodies. Of these eight, only the `<tlib-version>` and `<short-name>` elements are required.

NOTE The `<display-name>`, `<small-icon>`, and `<large-icon>` elements were introduced in JSP 1.2. In addition, the `<tlib-version>`, `<jsp-version>`, `<short-name>`, and `<description>` elements instead went by the names `<tlibversion>`, `<jspversion>`, `<shortname>` and `<info>`, respectively, in JSP 1.1. The motivation for these JSP 1.2 changes is greater consistency with the XML-based descriptor files utilized by other J2EE technologies (such as the Web Application Descriptor presented in chapter 14).

The `<tlib-version>` element is used to provide a version number for the tag library. As new versions of a tag library are released, the version number should be increased so that pages and tools which interact with the tag library can be aware of version information and any related compatibility issues. The full format for version numbers is *N.N.N.N*, where each *N* is a single-digit integer. In the case where *N*=0 and all subsequent *N*s are zero, they may be omitted, but under no circumstances may the major version number (i.e., the *N* preceding the first period) be omitted.

The `<jsp-version>` element indicates the version of the JSP specification with which the tag library is compatible. The default value is `1.1`, the first version of the specification that fully supports custom tag libraries.

The `<short-name>` tag is used to specify an abbreviated name for the tag library. Because it will be made available to the JSP container and JSP development tools for the creation of variable names, it is required to begin with an alphabetic character and contain no white space characters. It may also serve as the default namespace prefix for the tag library when used by JSP development tools in the authoring of pages.

The optional `<uri>` element, as of JSP 1.2, allows tag library developers to provide a default value for the URI by which the TLD is accessed from pages using its custom tags (i.e., the value specified for the `uri` attribute of the `taglib` directive). For a demonstration of this functionality, see the discussion on packaging custom tag libraries at the end of chapter 20. This element had a somewhat vaguer meaning in JSP 1.1, which has been superseded by this new role.

The `<display-name>`, `<small-icon>`, and `<large-icon>` elements are provided to support graphical configuration tools. The `<display-name>` element is used to provide a short name for display by tools, while the icon elements are for specifying icons to graphically represent the tag library. Each should specify a relative path within the tag library to a GIF or JPEG image. The small icon should be 16×16 pixels in size, while the large icon should be 32×32.

The <description> element is used to supply a documentation string for the custom tag library. The default value is the empty string.

18.3.2 Validator elements

Tag library validator classes are specified via the <validator> element, which has two subelements, <validator-class> and <init-param>, as in the following TLD fragment:

```
<taglib>
    ...
  <validator>
    <validator-class>com.taglib.wdjsp.mut.NestingTLV</validator-class>
    <init-param>
          <param-name>inner</param-name>
          <param-value>index</param-value>
          <description>Name of the inner tag.</description>
    </init-param>
    <init-param>
          <param-name>outer</param-name>
          <param-value>forProperty</param-value>
          <description>Name of the outer tag.</description>
    </init-param>
    <description>Validates nesting of inner and outer tags.</description>
  </validator>
    ...
</taglib>
```

The <validator-class> subelement is required and can only occur once, while the optional <init-param> subelement can appear multiple times. The <validator> tag and its subelements are JSP 1.2 features.

The body of the <validator-class> subelement indicates the name of the Java class implementing the library's validator, which must be a subclass of javax.servlet.jsp.tagext.TagLibraryValidator.

The <init-param> subelement is used to specify one or more initialization parameters, whose values are to be passed to the validator instance before validating a page that uses the tag library. This tag supports three subelements of its own, of which the <param-name> and <param-value> subelements are required. The <param-name> subelement names an initialization parameter, while the <param-value> tag provides its corresponding value. The optional <description> tag is used to document the initialization parameter.

The <description> tag may also be provided as a subelement of the <validator> tag to support documentation of the validator itself.

For further details on the use, definition, and initialization of tag library validators, see chapter 20.

18.3.3 Listener elements

As discussed in chapters 12 and 13, Servlet 2.3 and JSP 1.2 web applications can define event listeners which respond to various life-cycle events within the application. In much the same way, custom tag libraries can also specify event listeners that will be applied to any web application that uses the tag library. This is accomplished by means of the optional TLD `<listener>` element.

Multiple `<listener>` elements may appear within a TLD. Each requires a single `<listener-class>` subelement, as in the following example:

```
<taglib>
    ...
  <listener>
    <listener-class>com.taglib.wdjsp.mut.AccountListener</listener-class>
  </listener>
    ...
</taglib>
```

The `<listener-class>` tag specifies the class of the listener, an instance of which is to be registered with the web application. Listener classes must implement one of the four interfaces provided by the Servlet 2.3 API for handling web application life-cycle events:

- `javax.servlet.ServletContextListener`
- `javax.servlet.ServletContextAttributeListener`
- `javax.servlet.http.HttpSessionListener`
- `javax.servlet.http.HttpSessionAttributeListener`

18.3.4 Tag elements

The `<taglib>` element of a TLD is also required to specify one or more `<tag>` subelements. There will be one `<tag>` specification for each custom tag defined in the library. The `<tag>` element itself supports eight subelements for specifying the properties of the tag, as well as two additional subelements for specifying the tag's scripting variables and attributes, if any. The tag property subelements are demonstrated in the following TLD fragment:

```
<tag>
    <name>forProperty</name>
    <tag-class>com.taglib.wdjsp.mut.ForPropertyTag</tag-class>
    <tei-class>com.taglib.wdjsp.mut.ForPropertyTEI</tei-class>
```

```
    <body-content>JSP</body-content>
    <display-name>Indexed Property Iteration Tag</display-name>
    <small-icon>/WEB-INF/icons/for_property_small.gif</small-icon>
    <large-icon>/WEB-INF/icons/for_property_large.gif</large-icon>
    <description>Loop through an indexed property.</description>
    ...
</tag>
```

Of these eight subelements, only the <name> and <tagclass> elements are required.

NOTE The <display-name>, <small-icon>, and <large-icon> elements were introduced in JSP 1.2. In addition, the <tag-class>, <tei-class>, <body-content>, and <description> tags were instead called <tag-class>, <teiclass>, <bodycontent>, and <info> in JSP 1.1. The motivation for these JSP 1.2 changes is greater consistency with the XML-based descriptor files utilized by other J2EE technologies (such as the Web Application Descriptor presented in chapter 14).

The <name> element is used to specify an identifier for the tag, which will be used in combination with the library's namespace prefix to name the tag when it is used on a JSP page. For the example shown here, then, a JSP page using this tag's library with a prefix of mut would call this tag using the name <mut:forProperty>.

The <tag-class> element is used to specify the class that implements the handler for this tag, fully qualified with its package name. The <tei-class> element is used to specify the helper class for this tag, if any. The name of this element is derived from the javax.servlet.jsp.tagext.TagExtraInfo class, which is the base class that all tag handler helper classes must extend.

The next <tag> subelement, <body-content>, is used to indicate the type of body content that may appear between opening and closing tags of the current type. The three valid values for this element are empty, JSP, and tagdependent. The empty value indicates that no body content is supported by the tag, while the JSP value indicates that additional JSP elements (including other custom tags) may appear within the body of the tag. In both cases, the JSP container will perform syntax validation on the body of the tag when it is encountered during normal page compilation.

If the value of the <body-content> element is tagdependent, the body of the tag is expected to be interpreted by the tag itself. For example, a custom tag for executing database queries might specify the query as its body content, as follows:

```
<db:query connection="conn">
   SELECT ID, SALARY FROM EMPLOYEES WHERE SALARY > 50000
</db:query>
```

As formulated here, the body of this tag is an SQL statement. Since the query is to be interpreted by the tag (presumably by means of JDBC), the TLD specification for this tag should specify a value of `tagdependent` for its `<body-content>` element.

The `<display-name>`, `<small-icon>`, and `<large-icon>` elements are provided to support graphical configuration tools, and play a similar role for individual tags as they do for the tag library itself when appearing as subelements of the `<taglib>` element. The final element, `<description>`, may be used to specify a documentation string for the custom tag. Its default value is the empty string.

18.3.5 Variable elements

The `<variable>` subelement (added in JSP 1.2) is only for custom tags that may be used to introduce scripting variables, and takes two different forms, depending upon how the scripting variable is to be named. If a fixed name is to be used, the `<variable>` tag takes the following form:

```
<tag>
     ...
    <variable>
      <name-given>account</name-given>
      <variable-class>com.taglib.wdjsp.filters.UserBean</variable-class>
      <declare>true</declare>
      <scope>AT_END</scope>
      <description>
        Exposes the user's account bean as a scripting variable.
      </description>
    </variable>
     ...
</tag>
```

Of the four subelements, only `<name-given>` is required.

The `<name-given>` tag is used to specify the name for the scripting variable, while the optional `<variable-class>` tag is used to specify the type of the scripting variable, in the form of a Java class. The default value for the `<variable-class>` element is `java.lang.String`. The example presented here indicates that the Java object implementing the associated custom tag will cause a scripting variable named `account` to be assigned an instance of the `com.taglib.wdjsp.filters.UserBean` class.

The `<declare>` element is used to indicate whether or not the scripting variable introduced by the custom tag needs to be declared, and defaults to `true`. The `<scope>` element indicates over what extent of the JSP page's content the scripting variable should be considered valid. The permitted values are `NESTED`, `AT_BEGIN`, and `AT_END`, of which `NESTED` is the default. Further details on declaring and scoping custom tag scripting variables is presented in the discussion of helper classes later in this chapter.

The <description> element, a JSP 1.2 addition, is provided to enable documentation of the scripting variable.

The <variable> tag can also be used to specify scripting variables whose names are to be obtained from the value of one of a custom tag's attributes. In this case, a second form is used:

```
<tag>
   ...
   <variable>
     <name-from-attribute>accountVar</name-from-attribute>
     <variable-class>com.taglib.wdjsp.filters.UserBean</variable-class>
     <declare>true</declare>
     <scope>AT_END</scope>
     <description>
       Exposes the user's account bean as a scripting variable.
     </description>
   </variable>
   ...
</tag>
```

When this form is used, only the <name-from-attribute> subelement is required.

The body of the <name-from-attribute> tag must be the name of one of the custom tag's attributes. The value assigned to this attribute when the tag appears on a JSP page will be used as the name for the scripting variable introduced by that specific occurence of the tag. The other three subelements have the same semantics as in the first case. For this second <variable> example, then, each appearance of the associated custom tag in a JSP must specify a variable name via its accountVar attribute. A scripting variable using this name will then be made available on the page and assigned an instance of the com.taglib.wdjsp.filters.UserBean class by the associated tag handler.

18.3.6 Attribute elements

If a custom tag takes attributes, these are specified using the <attribute> element, which is the tenth subelement supported by the <tag> element. The <attribute> element itself has four subelements, as in the following TLD fragment:

```
<tag>
   ...
   <attribute>
     <name>id</name>
     <required>true</required>
     <rtexprvalue>false</rtexprvalue>
     <type>int</type>
     <description>Names the scripting variable.</description>
   </attribute>
```

```
    ...
</tag>
```

There will be one `<attribute>` element for each of the tag's attributes. Only the `<name>` subelement is required; the other three are optional.

The `<name>` element, used to identify the attribute, represents the string that will be used to name the attribute when it appears in a tag. For the example shown here, if it were associated with the example tag presented in the previous section, the attribute and its value would be specified as:

```
<mut:forProperty id="loopVar">
```

Because it will be used in this manner, the attribute name should begin with an alphabetic character, and should not contain any white space characters.

The `<required>` element indicates whether the attribute is required or optional. Required attributes must be explicitly specified whenever the associated tag appears. The permitted values for this element are `true` and `false`. The default value is `false`, indicating that the attribute is optional.

The `<rtexprvalue>` element indicates whether or not a request-time attribute value may be used to specify the attribute's value when it appears in the tag. As with the `<required>` element, the permitted values for this element are `true` and `false`. When this element is set to `false` (the default), only fixed, static values may be specified for the attribute, as for the `id` attribute in the previous example. When this element is set to `true`, a JSP expression may be used to specify the value to be assigned to the attribute, as in the following example tag:

```
<mut:item text="<%= cookies[i].getName() %>"/>
```

As indicated in chapters 6 and 7, several of JSP's built-in actions support request-time attribute values, including the `value` attribute of the `<jsp:setProperty>` and `<jsp:param>` actions and the `page` attribute of the `<jsp:forward>` and `<jsp:include>` actions. In all of these cases save one, the value of the expression providing the request-time attribute value is required to be a character string. The exception to this requirement is the `value` attribute of `<jsp:setProperty>`. For this specific attribute, an expression whose value is the same type as the corresponding bean property is also permitted. For example, the `FaqBean` introduced in chapter 11 has a property named `lastModified` whose value is an instance of the `java.util.Date` class. For an instance of this bean class named `faq`, the value of this property could be set within a JSP page using the following action:

```
<jsp:setProperty name="faq" property="lastModified"
                  value="<%= new java.util.Date() %>"/>
```

When used in this fashion, there is no need to coerce the result of the expression into a character string, and then parse the string to construct a value of the required type. These two steps are bypassed altogether, and the original value of the expression is passed directly to the bean's corresponding setter method.

As of JSP 1.2, custom actions are also able to take advantage of this behavior. This is accomplished via the `<attribute>` subelement, `<type>`, a JSP 1.2 addition to the TLD specification. The `<type>` tag is used by the custom tag developer to declare to the JSP container the Java type of an attribute value, so that the container can recognize when an expression of the appropriate type has been provided for the attribute, in the form of a request-time attribute value. When such an expression is encountered, conversion to and from a character string can be skipped; instead, the corresponding setter method of the underlying tag handler is called directly. The `<type>` element is optional, and need only be specified when the value of the `<rtexprvalue>` element is `true`. The default value for the `<type>` element is `java.lang.String`.

The final subelement, `<description>`, allows the developer to provide an optional documentation string for the attribute. This element is also a a JSP 1.2 addition.

18.3.7 Example element

As of JSP 1.2, the `<tag>` element also supports a new subelement named `<example>`. This subelement can be used to provide additional documentation of the tag's use including, as its name suggests, one or more examples of the tag's application. Its use is demonstrated in the following TLD fragment:

```
<tag>
    ...
    <example><![CDATA[
      To iterate over the indexed property "program" of a Bean named
      "flynn", use this tag as follows:
          <forProperty name="flynn" property="program"
                       id="prog" class="com.encom.Program">
              body content
          </forProperty>
       Within the body of the tag, a scripting variable named "prog"
       will be bound to various instances of the com.encom.Program class,
       representing the successive elements of the "program" indexed
       property. The specified class must be compatible with the type
       of the indexed property.
    ]]></example>
    ...
</tag>
```

Because custom tags follow XML syntax conventions, the appearance of example uses in the body content of this element has the potential to violate the well-formedness of the TLD as an XML document. If the TLD is not well-formed, then the JSP container is likely to throw an exception when it tries to read it.

As a result, it is typically necessary to wrap the body content of the `<example>` element in an XML CDATA (character data) element, as illustrated. This marks the body content as literal text, not meant to be interpreted as XML.

18.4 API overview

All of the classes and interfaces provided by JSP for implementing tag handlers and helper classes are in the `javax.servlet.jsp.tagext` package. This package also has four auxiliary classes used by the JSP container in interpreting the contents of a TLD.

18.4.1 Tag handlers

Tag handlers are the Java objects that perform the action associated with a custom tag. When a request is received by the JSP container for a page containing custom tags, each time a custom tag is encountered, an instance of the corresponding tag handler is obtained. The tag handler is initialized according to any attribute values explicitly set by the tag on the page, then methods of the tag handler are called to perform the corresponding action. Once the action has been performed, the tag handler is returned to a resource pool for reuse.

The methods that the tag handler must support in order to perform the custom action are prescribed by the `javax.servlet.jsp.tagext` package's `Tag`, `IterationTag`, and `BodyTag` interfaces. By specifying tag handlers in terms of interfaces, JSP allows developers to turn existing classes, which may already have a well-defined inheritance hierarchy, into tag handlers. If you will be developing tag handlers from scratch, however, your task will be simplified by using one of the two tag handler base classes also available in the `javax.servlet.jsp.tagext` package, named `TagSupport` and `BodyTagSupport`. These classes provide default implementations for all of the methods in the corresponding interfaces, so that you will only have to redefine those methods that require custom behavior in order to implement the desired action.

You may be wondering why there are three tag handler interfaces. In practice, tags which manipulate their body content tend to be more complicated than tags which are either empty or just pass the contents of the tag body straight through to the page. In recognition of this, the `BodyTag` interface and the corresponding `BodyTagSupport` class are geared toward the implementation of tags that need to

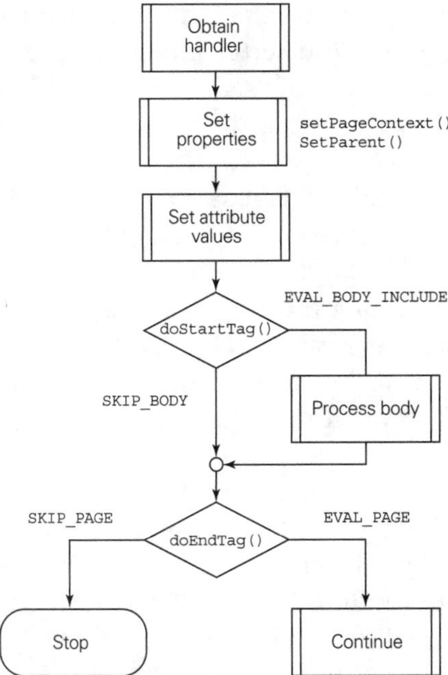

Figure 18.4 Flow of control for handlers implementing the Tag interface

process their body content in some manner, while the `Tag` and `IterationTag` interfaces and the `TagSupport` class are geared toward the simpler case. Fewer methods are required by the `Tag` and `IterationTag` interfaces. Of course, both types of tag handlers must provide the same base functionality. As a result of this underlying commonality, `BodyTag` is implemented as an extension of the `IterationTag` interface, which is itself an extension of the `Tag` interface. The `BodyTagSupport` class is likewise a subclass of `TagSupport`.

The application of a tag handler implementing the `Tag` interface is depicted in figure 18.4. The first step is to obtain an instance of the appropriate class, either from the tag handler resource pool or, if no instances are currently available, by creating one. Next, tag handler properties are set. First, the handler's `setPageContext()` method is called by the JSP container to assign it the appropriate `PageContext` object (see chapter 6 for a description of the `PageContext` class). Next, the handler's `setParent()` method is called. This provides access to the tag handler instance, if any, within whose body the current handler appears.

After these properties have been set, the attribute values specified by the tag, if any, are set. Tag attributes are handled like JavaBeans properties, via accessor methods defined by the tag handler class. A custom tag attribute named `id`, for instance, should have corresponding getter and setter methods: `getId()` and `setId()`, or equivalents specified via an associated `BeanInfo` class. These setter methods are called by the JSP container to assign the attribute values specified in the tag to the corresponding tag handler instance.

The JSP container next calls the tag handler's `doStartTag()` method. At this point, all of the contextual information needed to execute the tag handler will have been provided by the JSP container (i.e., the tag handler properties and attribute values), so `doStartTag()` can begin performing the action associated with its custom tag. This should return one of two integer values indicating how processing is to proceed. `Tag.SKIP_BODY` indicates that any body content of the tag should be ignored. `Tag.EVAL_BODY_INCLUDE` indicates that the body content should be processed normally.

In either case, the next step is to call the handler's `doEndTag()` method. As with `doStartTag()`, the actions performed are tag-specific. The method is expected to return one of two integer values indicating how processing is to proceed. A return value of `Tag.SKIP_PAGE` from `doEndTag()` indicates to the JSP container that processing of the page should be halted immediately. Any further content on the page should be ignored and any output generated thus far should be returned to the user's browser. A return value of `Tag.EVAL_PAGE` indicates that page processing should continue normally.

Regardless of the result returned by `doEndTag()`, the tag handler instance is made available for reuse. If there are other calls to the same custom tag on the page, the JSP container may, under certain circumstances, reuse the handler within the same page. If the handler can't be reused on the current page, it will ultimately be returned to the resource pool for reuse during subsequent JSP page requests.

The `IterationTag` interface, as its name suggests, adds provisions for processing the custom tag's body iteratively. As indicated in figure 18.5, the flow of control for tag handlers implementing the `IterationTag` interface incorporates a simple extension to the flow of control supported by the `Tag` interface to enable repeated application of the custom tag's body content. As before, the first step is to obtain an instance of the tag handler. Properties and attributes are then set, followed by a call to `doStartTag()`. If this returns `Tag.SKIP_BODY`, then the body content is ignored and control passes to the `doEndTag()` method. If `doStartTag()` returns `Tag.EVAL_BODY_INCLUDE`, the body content is processed and control passes to the `doAfterBody()` method. This method can also return one of two possible values: `Tag.SKIP_BODY` or `IterationTag.EVAL_BODY_AGAIN`. A return value of `Tag.SKIP_BODY` will transfer control to `doEndTag()`. A return value of `Iteration-`

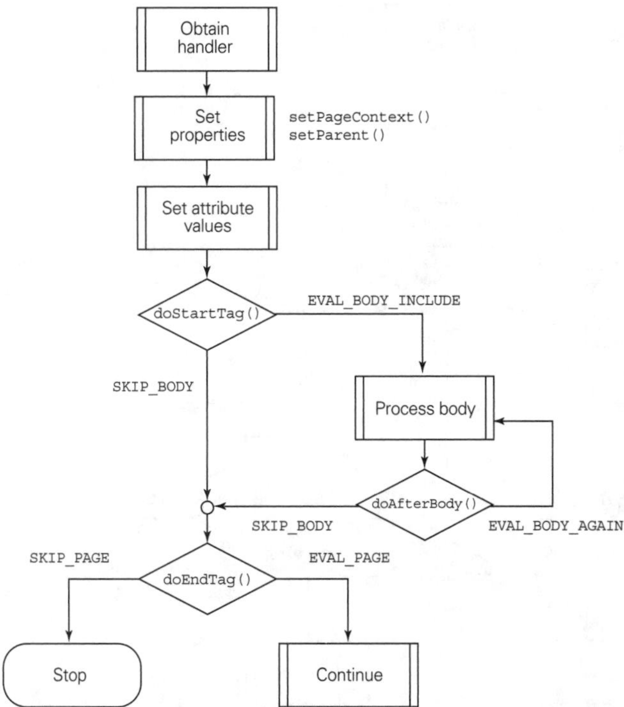

Figure 18.5 Flow of control for handlers implementing the IterationTag interface

Tag.EVAL_BODY_AGAIN will cause the body content to be processed once again, followed by another call to doAfterBody(). This subsequent call to doAfterBody() can once again return either Tag.SKIP_BODY or IterationTag.EVAL_BODY_AGAIN, either terminating the iteration or initiating yet another application of the tag's body content. The primary role of doAfterBody() then, is to control this looping over the body content.

Once control is passed to doEndTag(), it is that method's role to determine whether or not processing of the page itself should continue. If doEndTag() returns Tag.SKIP_PAGE, further processing of the JSP page will be aborted. If doEndTag() returns Tag.EVAL_PAGE, processing of the JSP page will continue normally. In either case, the custom tag handler then becomes available for reuse.

The BodyTag interface generalizes the tag handler flow of control even further. As indicated in figure 18.6, this interface supports a third return value for the doStartTag() method that allows the tag handler to access and manipulate the results of processing its body content. If the call to doStartTag() returns either

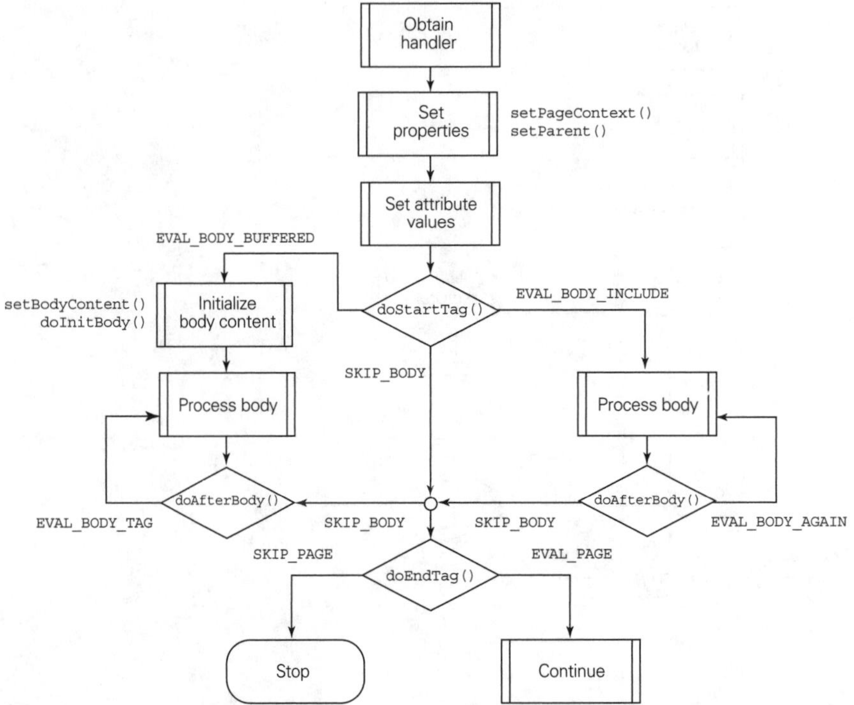

Figure 18.6 Flow of control for handlers implementing the `BodyTag` interface

`Tag.SKIP_BODY` or `Tag.EVAL_BODY_INCLUDE`, the behavior is identical to that of the `IterationTag` interface. A return value of `BodyTag.EVAL_BODY_BUFFERED`, however, indicates to the JSP container that, not only should the tag's body content be processed, but that the results of that processing must be stored for manipulation by the tag handler itself.

The results of processing the body content are stored by means of the `BodyContent` class. `BodyContent` is a subclass of `JspWriter`, an instance of which is used to represent the output stream for the content generated by a JSP page (chapter 6). Rather than buffer its output for eventual submission to the user's browser, as is the case with `JspWriter`, the `BodyContent` class stores its output for use by the tag handler. It is then up to the tag handler to decide whether that output should be discarded or sent to the browser in either its current or some modified form.

In order to process the body content, then, the first step is to create (or obtain from a resource pool) an instance of the `BodyContent` class. This is assigned to the tag handler by means of its `setBodyContent()` method. The JSP container then calls the tag handler's doInitBody(), in order to give the tag handler an opportunity to perform additional initialization steps after the BodyContent instance has been assigned. The body is then processed, with all of its output going to the BodyContent instance.

WARNING While processing the body content of a custom tag which implements the BodyTag interface, the out implicit object, accessible as a scripting variable via the JSP scripting elements, will reference the tag handler's BodyContent instance. After processing of the custom tag is completed, the out implicit object will reference its previous value.

After processing of the body content, the JSP container calls the tag handler's doAfterBody() method. The action performed by this method is typically tag-dependent, and often includes interactions with the tag's BodyContent instance. As was the case for the IterationTag interface, this method is expected to return either Tag.SKIP_BODY or IterationTag.EVAL_BODY_AGAIN. If the latter value is returned, then the tag's body content will be processed a second time, after which *doAfterBody()* will be called once again. Repeated processing of the body content will continue until the doAfterBody() method returns Tag.SKIP_BODY. This path can thus also be used to implement custom tags which process their body content iteratively.

Once processing of the body content has been skipped (either by doStartTag() or doAfterBody()), control is passed to the tag handler's doEndTag() method. From this point, processing is identical to that of a tag handlers implementing either the Tag or the IterationTag interface.

NOTE In addition to the introduction of the IterationTag interface, modifications were also made to the invocation protocol for the BodyTag interface as part of the JSP 1.2 specification. In particular, the static variables representing the values to be returned by two of the interface's invocation methods were changed. As described, JSP 1.2 expects the doStartTag() method of the BodyTag interface to return BodyTag.EVAL_BODY_BUFFERED to indicate that the tag's body content should be processed and stored, and a return value of IterationTag.EVAL_BODY_AGAIN from the doAfterBody() method to indicate that processing of the body content should be repeated. In JSP 1.1, a return value of BodyTag.EVAL_BODY_TAG fulfilled both roles.

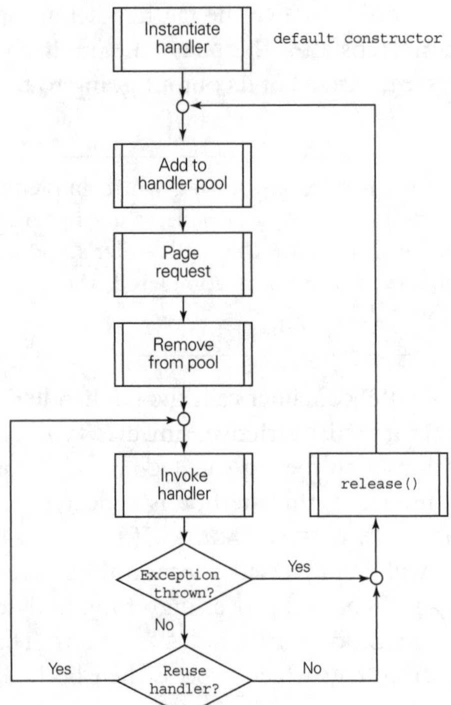

Figure 18.7 Default life cycle of a custom tag handler

18.4.2 Tag handler life-cycle

As indicated in the previous section, after a tag handler is instantiated, the JSP container is permitted to reuse it over and over again, both within a single page request and across multiple page requests by multiple users. We now turn our attention to the specifics of tag handler reuse, in the context of understanding how the overall life cycle of a tag handler instance affects its class design.

Like any other Java class, tag handlers are instantiated via the `new` operator, which has the side effect of calling one of its constructors. Tag handlers are automatically instantiated by the JSP container, and since no constructor arguments are provided by the container, the class's default constructor will be used. After the constructor is called, the tag handler is added to a resource pool managed by the JSP container.

As indicated in figure 18.7, the tag handler instance remains in the resource pool until it is needed by the container to handle a request for a JSP page that calls the corresponding custom tag. It is then removed from the resource pool, to keep other request threads from using it at the same time.

The tag handler instance is then invoked by the container to implement a specific custom tag occurrence within the page. The tag handler methods called within that single invocation are as described in the previous section, and thus are dependent upon which tag handler interface it implements. Regardless of its interface, however, there is a chance that the invocation will fail. In particular, the signatures for all of the tag handler methods that are typically written by the custom tag implementer—`doStartTag()`, `doEndTag()`, `doInitBody()`, and `doAfterBody()`—provide for throwing an instance of `javax.servlet.jsp.JspException`.

If no exceptions are raised during the invocation, the container is permitted to reuse the handler within the current page request. The circumstances under which a handler is reused within a page are somewhat restrictive, however: a tag handler instance can only be used multiple times during a given page request when subsequent custom tags specify the same set of attributes as the custom tag to which the handler was originally applied.

Consider a custom tag named `ifProperty`, which has required attributes named `name` and `property` and one optional attribute named `action`. Consider also a JSP page fragment in which this tag appears three times:

```
<mut:ifProperty name="timeOfDay" property="morning" action="include">
    <p>Good Morning!</p>
</mut:ifProperty>
<mut:ifProperty name="timeOfDay" property="afternoon">
    <p>Good Afternoon!</p>
</mut:ifProperty>
<mut:ifProperty name="timeOfDay" property="daytime" action="exclude">
    <p>Good Night!</p>
</mut:ifProperty>
```

In this fragment, the second use of the `ifProperty` tag sets only the required attributes, while the first and third also set the optional `action` attribute. As a result, at least two instances of the `ifProperty` tag handler will be required whenever the page containing this fragment is requested, one for the first and third occurrences of the tag, and another for the second. The tag handler used for the first `ifProperty` tag can be reused for the third, but because the second `ifProperty` tag employs a different set of attributes from the other two, it requires its own instance of the `ifProperty` tag handler.

This restriction on reuse is a result of the way custom tag attributes are modeled as JavaBeans properties of the corresponding tag handler objects. When a tag handler is applied to a specific occurrence of a custom tag, the tag handler setter methods corresponding to the attributes appearing in the custom tag are called. There are no "unsetter" methods, however, that might be called for attributes that are not specified by the custom tag. If a tag handler that has been applied to a custom tag that does include a specific attribute (such as the `action` attribute in our example) were to be applied to a custom tag that does not include a value for that attribute, then the tag handler would still have the value for that attribute that was set by the original custom tag. Because the setter would not be called when the second tag is encountered, the tag handler property corresponding to that attribute would still have the value set by the first custom tag. This would make the results of a custom tag dependent upon the attribute settings of previous occurrences of custom tags within the page. Such nonintuitive behavior would make custom tags much more difficult for page designers to use; hence, the restrictions on how custom tags may be reused within a single page request.

As one final twist on the reuse of tag handlers within a single JSP page, consider the following page fragment:

```
<mut:ifProperty name="timeOfDay" property="morning" action="include">
    <p>Good Morning!</p>
</mut:ifProperty>
<mut:ifProperty name="timeOfDay" property="afternoon" action="include">
    <p>Good Afternoon!</p>
</mut:ifProperty>
<mut:ifProperty name="timeOfDay" property="daytime" action="exclude">
    <p>Good Night!</p>
</mut:ifProperty>
```

The only difference between this fragment and the previous one is the specification of the `action` attribute in the second `ifProperty` tag. One effect of this change is that only a single tag handler instance is required to handle all three occurrences of the custom tag, since all three specify values for the same attribute set.

Notice, however, that the values of the `action` attributes are the same for the first two tags, and that the values of the `name` attributes are the same for all three. As a concession to efficiency, the JSP container is permitted to forego calling the setter method for the attribute property when reusing a tag handler and setting the attribute to the same value to which it was most recently set.

For the example above, then, in which the same handler instance can be applied to all three occurrences of the `ifProperty` tag, the sequence of setter operations is as follows:

- For the first occurrence, the `setName()`, `setProperty()`, and `setAction()` methods are called to set the values of each of the three specified attributes. (This assumes this is the first occurrence of the `ifProperty` tag on the page.)

- For the second occurrence, only the tag handler's `setProperty()` method is called, since the values of the other two attributes are unchanged.
- For the third occurrence, the `setProperty()` and `setAction()` methods are called.

An important implication of this behavior is that attribute property setter methods should be free from side effects. As the example shows, there is no guarantee that the setter methods will be called for each application of the tag handler; hence, any associated side effects might not be performed for each application. Typically, such side effects should be performed in the handler's `doStartTag()` method (which the JSP container is not permitted to skip), since all of the attribute values will have been set (or preserved from the previous invocation) before it is called.

Once the page request is completed, and all opportunities for tag handler reuse within the page have been exhausted, the `release()` method of each tag handler is called, and the tag handler instance is returned to the container's resource pool. The intent of the `release()` method is to free any resources allocated by the tag handler during the page request. If, say, the tag handler opened a database or network connection, the `release()` method provides an assured means for closing that connection, since it is guaranteed that the method will be called before the tag handler is returned to the resource pool. The `release()` method should also set the values of any tag handler instance variables—particularly those representing tag attribute values—back to their initial, default values. In this way, it plays an analogous role within the context of tag handler reuse that Java's `finalize()` method does in the context of garbage collection.

In the case where an exception is raised by a tag handler method, or a result of processing the corresponding body content, the standard JSP error-handling mechanism is invoked: uncaught exceptions cause control to be forwarded to an error page, and processing of the current page request is aborted. In that case, the `release()` method for all of the tag handlers in use by the page are called, including that of the tag handler which caused the exception. These tag handler instances are then returned to the JSP container's resource pool.

The default life cycle for tag handler instances thus provides for limited reuse of tag handlers at both a local (page-specific) and global (container-wide) scale. In addition, global reuse of tag handlers is robust to exceptions raised at the local level. The default life cycle, however, does not support local handling of exceptions. More specifically, tag handlers cannot intercept exceptions raised while processing their body content. In addition, while the `release()` method provides a mechanism for freeing resources at the page request level, there is no corresponding mechanism for freeing resources at the level of an individual custom tag invocation.

In response to these two deficiencies, a new interface class, `javax.servlet.jsp.tagext.TryCatchFinally`, has been introduced in JSP 1.2. This interface is intended to be implemented by any custom tag handler that needs additional control over its life cycle, as a supplement to the standard `Tag`, `IterationTag`, and `BodyTag` interfaces.

Table 18.1 Methods of the `TryCatchFinally` interface.

Method	Description
`doCatch(throwable)`	Handles an exception raised in the body content or invocation methods of a tag handler.
`doFinally()`	Called after all invocation methods or in the event of an exception.

The `TryCatchFinally` interface (table 18.1) has two methods. For tag handlers that implement this interface, if an exception is raised while processing the corresponding tag's body content, or by its `doStartTag()`, `doEndTag()`, `doAfterBody()`, or `doInitBody()` method, the instance's `doCatch()` method will be called, with the exception itself as its sole parameter. The `doCatch()` method can then attempt to handle the exception, as if control had been passed to a standard Java `catch` clause. As in a standard catch clause, `doCatch()` also has the option of rethrowing the exception, or of throwing a new one.

In the case of nested custom tags, if both have tag handlers that implement `TryCatchFinally` and the inner tag's `doCatch()` method chooses to throw (or rethrow) an exception, then control will be transferred to the `doCatch()` method of the tag handler for the outer tag. Exceptions that propagate all the way up the chain of eligible `doCatch()` methods cause control to be forwarded to an error page. If any of the eligible `doCatch()` methods intercepts the exception and opts not to throw its own exception, processing of the page will resume with the page content following the end tag of the corresponding custom tag.

After the tag handler's `doCatch()` method is called, `doFinally()` is called, regardless of whether `doCatch()` elects to throw an exception itself. Note that if `doCatch()` throws an exception, then `doFinally()` will be called before any outer tag's `doCatch()` method is called.

Even if no exceptions are raised by the body content or the invocation methods, the `doFinally()` method of a tag handler implementing `TryCatchFinally` will always be called. In the case where no exceptions are raised (and, therefore, `doCatch()` is not called), the `doFinally()` method will be called immediately after the tag handler's `doEndTag()` method is called. The `doFinally()` method, then, can be relied upon to perform any cleanup code required after each application of

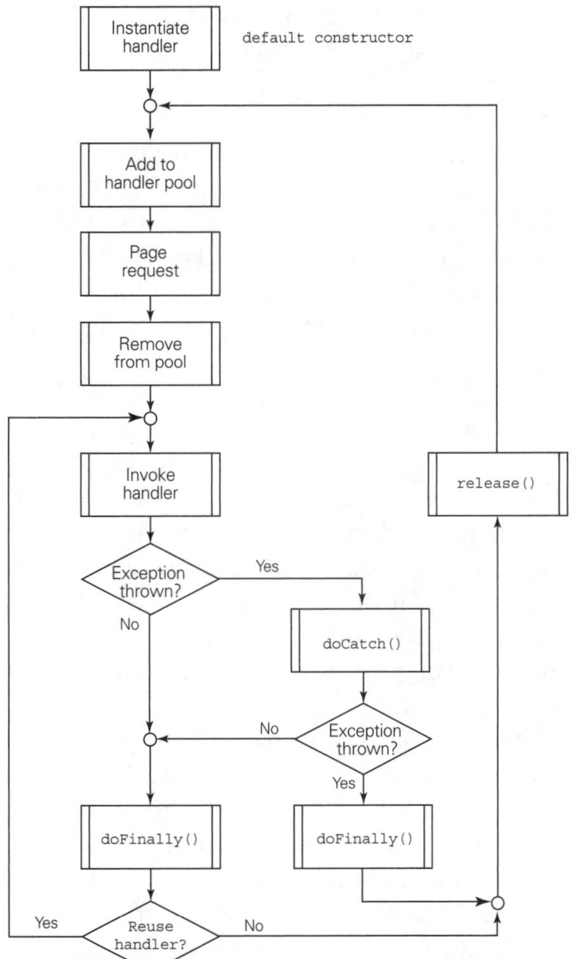

Figure 18.8 Life cycle of a custom tag handler implementing the `TryCatchFinally` interface

the tag handler. Note that this method should not try to reset the handler's attributes, given the container's ability, as previously described, to reuse attribute state by not calling attribute setters when values are not changed.

The net effect of these life-cycle methods is that only two methods are guaranteed to be called when a tag handler is invoked: `doStartTag()` and `release()`. The `doStartTag()` method will be called when the tag is first applied to an occurrence of the corresponding custom tag within the JSP page, and `release()` will be called when the tag handler is returned to the container's resource pool. For all of the other methods presented here, an exception thrown during the invocation of the handler or while processing its body content can abort further processing and prevent the method from being called.

For tag handlers that implement the `TryCatchFinally` interface, the `doFinally()` method is also guaranteed to be called. For this reason, programmers who are implementing custom tags are advised to restrict tag handler resource management to these three methods. The `doStartTag()` method is well-suited to performing request-time attribute validation, side effects based on attribute values, and resource allocation. In contrast, `doFinally()` is ideal for deallocation of per-invocation resources, while `release()` is intended for resetting attribute state and deallocating per-request resources.

18.4.3 Helper classes

As mentioned earlier, all tag handler helper classes are subclasses of the `javax.servlet.jsp.tagext.TagExtraInfo` class. When the JSP container is compiling a page that includes a custom tag whose TLD specification includes a `<tei-class>` entry, the container will create (or obtain from a resource pool) an instance of the indicated helper class. The role of this helper class is twofold: to provide information about any scripting variables introduced by the tag and/or to perform tag-level validation beyond the automatic syntax validation and any library-level validation performed by the page compiler.

To accomplish this, the `TagExtraInfo` base class specifies two methods that subclasses are expected to override as necessary. The `getVariableInfo()` method is called to obtain information about scripting variables, while the `isValid()` method is called to allow the subclass to perform tag-specific validation.

Both of these methods take a single argument, which is an instance of the `TagData` class. This instance will contain a representation of all of the attribute/value pairs specified in the custom tag being examined. Consider, for example, the following custom tag:

```
<mut:timeOfDay id="tod" timezone="EST"/>
```

When calling the helper class associated with this tag (assuming one exists), the `TagData` object would have entries for both of the specified attributes. The methods defined by the `TagData` class allow the developer to obtain the value associated with a given attribute name. In the particular case of an attribute whose value is specified via a request-time attribute value, these methods will return `TagData.REQUEST_TIME_VALUE` to indicate that no static value is available for use during page compilation. In this way, `getVariableInfo()` and `isValid()` can obtain information about tag attributes in order to perform their required tasks.

The contract of `isValid()` is quite straightforward. Given access to the data stored in the supplied `TagData` object, if the custom tag is considered valid, the method should return `true`. Otherwise, the method should return `false`. The default implementation of this method in the `TagExtraInfo` base class simply returns `true`.

This method allows the developer to perform additional checks on the attributes and their values beyond those performed by the page compiler based on the information in the TLD. For example, the TLD can only indicate whether an individual attribute is optional or required. Your tag might have an attribute that is normally optional, but must always appear whenever some other attribute is specified. The TLD does not provide a mechanism for specifying relationships between attributes, so dependencies such as this can only be verified by means of the `isValid()` method, or by using a tag library validator as described in chapter 20.

The `getVariableInfo()` method is a bit more involved. Its task is to return an array of `VariableInfo` instances that specify the scripting variables to be introduced by the corresponding tag. There should be one element in this array for each scripting variable. The default implementation of `getVariableInfo()` returns an empty array, indicating that no scripting variables are being introduced.

Four pieces of information are required for each scripting variable, all of which must be specified as arguments to the `VariableInfo` constructor. First, the name of the scripting variable must be specified, as well as the object class for the variable's value. This information is used by the page compiler to resolve variable references appearing later on the page. The variable name is also used by the JSP container when processing requests to find the value of the scripting variable at run time. Values of scripting variables are expected to be stored as attributes of the `PageContext` object associated with the page. The tag handler should set this attribute, from which the JSP container will extract the value of the scripting variable. The container can then make the appropriate assignment and continue processing the request, resolving references to the variable name with the retrieved value.

The next argument to the `VariableInfo` constructor is a boolean flag—referred to as the *declare flag*—that indicates whether the tag is introducing a new variable, or simply assigning a new value to an existing variable. (This is used to determine whether or not the scripting language needs to specify a declaration for the variable.) The fourth and final argument specifies the scope of the scripting variable. In the context of custom tag scripting variables, scope—also referred to as *visibility*—indicates the range of page content over which the variable remains valid, and is specified relative to the locations of the custom tag's start and end tags within the page. Three static variables are provided for specifying scripting variable scope, as follows:

- `VariableInfo.AT_BEGIN`—Indicates that the scripting variable is in scope immediately after the start tag.
- `VariableInfo.AT_END`—Indicates that the scripting variable is not in scope until after the end tag.
- `VariableInfo.NESTED`—Indicates that the scripting variable is in scope only between the start and end tags (i.e., within the body of the tag).

For the `<mut:timeOfDay>` example tag presented previously, then, the corresponding call to the `VariableInfo` constructor for the indicated attribute values might take the following form:

```
new VariableInfo("tod", "com.taglib.wdjsp.mut.TimeOfDayBean",
                 true, VariableInfo.AT_BEGIN);
```

The resulting `VariableInfo` instance thus specifies a scripting variable named `tod`, whose value will be an instance of the `com.taglib.wdjsp.advtags.TimeOfDay-Bean` class. The declare flag is set to `true`, indicating that this will be a new variable. Finally, its scope is set to `VariableInfo.AT_BEGIN`, indicating that the `tod` scripting variable will be available immediately following the associated `<mut:timeOfDay/>` tag, and will remain in scope until the end of the page.

As indicated earlier in the chapter, JSP 1.2 has added the capability to specify information about scripting variables in the TLD itself, obviating the need for `TagExtraInfo` classes in many circumstances. The subelements of the TLD's `<variable>` tag, in fact, correspond directly to the parameters of the described `VariableInfo` constructor. The `<name-given>` and `<name-from-attribute>` tags correspond to the constructor's first argument, while the `<variable-class>` and `<declare>` tags correspond to its second and third, respectively. The `<scope>` tag maps to its fourth parameter, and the values supported by this tag take their names from the corresponding static variables of the `TagExtraInfo` class, and have the same meanings.

For our `<mut:timeOfDay>` example tag, then, the developer could avoid having to create a `TagExtraInfo` helper class for the tag handler by adding the following `<variable>` subelement to its TLD entry:

```
<variable>
    <name-from-attribute>id</name-from-attribute>
    <variable-class>com.taglib.wdjsp.mut.TimeOfDayBean</variable-class>
    <declare>true</declare>
    <scope>AT_BEGIN</scope>
</variable>
```

As in the VariableInfo constructor call presented previously, this <variable> entry indicates that the scripting variable will be an instance of the com.taglib.wdjsp.advtags.TimeOfDayBean class, that it must be declared, and that it will be in scope from the location of the tag through the end of the page. Unlike the constructor call, however, which must explicitly specify the name of the scripting variable, the <variable> tag can take advantage of the <name-from-attribute> subelement to indicate that the name of the scripting variable will be obtained from the value of the tag's id attribute.

18.4.4 Auxiliary classes

There are four auxiliary classes provided by the javax.servlet.jsp.tagext package for use by the JSP container to represent the contents of a TLD file. These are TagLibraryInfo, TagInfo, TagAttributeInfo, and TagVariableInfo. Because these classes are intended for use by the JSP container, their use by web developers and library implementers is rare.

The TagLibraryInfo class stores information on the library as a whole, and provides accessors for retrieving its properties. Among them is a listing of the tags provided by the library, which are represented by instances of the TagInfo class. These instances in turn store the set of attributes and scripting variables associated with each tag, which are represented by instances of the TagAttributeInfo and TagVariableInfo classes, respectively. For further details, see appendix F.

18.5 Example tag library

To take this discussion of custom tags from the abstract to the concrete, the remainder of this chapter will focus on examples, as will chapter 19. We will examine in detail the implementation of several custom tags, and demonstrate their use within corresponding JSP pages. As discussed earlier in this chapter, use of custom tags within a JSP page first requires the construction of a tag library containing the tag handler classes and the associated TLD. To this end, we will also be packaging up our example tags into a custom tag library at the end of chapter 20.

A well-designed custom tag library will typically contain a focused set of interrelated tags that provide common or integrated functionality. For example, one library might contain a set of debugging tags for use during page development, while another might provide extensions to the standard JSP bean tags for improved flow control. Alternatively, a set of application-specific tags—for example, custom tags for interacting with the FAQ tool presented in chapter 11—would be a good candidate for a stand-alone tag library.

In order to give the reader exposure to a variety of custom tag examples, the library we will be constructing here will not be quite so unified in purpose. While this library will focus on general-purpose rather than application-specific tags, its tags cover a broad range of functionality, such as debugging, flow control, and extended HTML support. Any one of these areas would be an appropriate domain for a tag library of its own. Combining a few tags from each category into a single library is less than ideal, but hopefully acceptable in a pedagogical context such as this. In recognition of the rather mongrel nature of the tag library presented here, it will be referred to as the Manning Utility Tags library, fittingly abbreviated by the namespace prefix `mut`.

The TLD for this library is outlined in listing 18.1. The TLD entries for the tags will follow and must be inserted into the TLD in the indicated location in order to provide a complete specification of the tag library.

Listing 18.1 Skeleton TLD for the custom tag library

```
<?xml version="1.0" encoding="ISO-8859-1" ?>
<!DOCTYPE taglib PUBLIC
"-//Sun Microsystems, Inc.//DTD JSP Tag Library 1.2//EN"
"http://java.sun.com/j2ee/dtds/web-jsptaglib_1_2.dtd">
<taglib>
    <tlib-version>1.0</tlib-version>
    <jsp-version>1.2</jsp-version>
    <short-name>mut</short-name>
    <uri>/mutlib</uri>
    <info>
      Manning Utility Tags from
      Web Development with JavaServer Pages.
    </info>

    <validator></validator> entries
    <listener></listener> entries
    <tag></tag> entries

</taglib>
```

18.6 Content substitution

The most basic type of custom JSP action simply substitutes some text—often dynamically generated—in place of the custom tag. The first example tag for our library is of this sort, and is a debugging tag for displaying the status of a page's output buffer. This tag will be named `debugBuffer`, and will take no attributes, so its TLD entry is fairly straightforward:

```
<tag>
    <name>debugBuffer</name>
    <tag-class>com.taglib.wdjsp.mut.DebugBufferTag</tag-class>
```

```
    <body-content>empty</body-content>
    <description>
          Report the current status of output buffering.
    </description>
</tag>
```

As indicated in this TLD fragment, the class name for `debugBuffer`'s tag handler is `com.taglib.wdjsp.mut.DebugBufferTag`. A documentation string is provided via the `<description>` element, which will be available for use by JSP page development tools that wish to use this library. In addition, this tag's `<body-content>` entry indicates that there is no body content associated with this tag. If the page compiler encounters usage of this custom tag with associated body content, a compilation error will occur.

NOTE It is standard practice to name the tag handler class after the tag, with an added `Tag` suffix. This class, as with all of the tag handler classes in the `mut` library, is defined in the `com.taglib.wdjsp.mut` package.

Because there is no body content associated with this tag, it needs only to implement the `Tag` interface, rather than the more complicated `BodyTag` interface. Furthermore, since we will be developing this custom tag from scratch, we can take advantage of the `TagSupport` class to simplify the implementation. As a result, the only method that needs to be implemented by the `DebugBufferTag` class is `doStartTag()`. The full source code for the tag handler appears in listing 18.2.

Listing 18.2 DebugBufferTag tag handler

```
package com.taglib.wdjsp.mut;

import java.io.IOException;
import java.io.PrintStream;
import java.text.NumberFormat;
import javax.servlet.jsp.JspWriter;
import javax.servlet.jsp.PageContext;
import javax.servlet.jsp.tagext.Tag;
import javax.servlet.jsp.tagext.TagSupport;
import javax.servlet.jsp.JspException;
import javax.servlet.jsp.JspTagException;

public class DebugBufferTag extends TagSupport {
     public int doStartTag () throws JspException {
       JspWriter out = pageContext.getOut();
       int total = out.getBufferSize();
       int available = out.getRemaining();
       int used = total - available;
```

```
      try {
        out.print("Buffer Status: ");
        out.print(Integer.toString(used));
        out.print('/');
        out.print(Integer.toString(total));
        out.print(" = ");
        NumberFormat percentFmt = NumberFormat.getInstance();
        percentFmt.setMinimumFractionDigits(1);
        percentFmt.setMaximumFractionDigits(3);
        out.print(percentFmt.format((100D * used)/total));
        out.println("%");
      }
      catch(IOException e) {
        throw new JspTagException("I/O exception "
                                  + e.getMessage());
      }
      return SKIP_BODY;
    }
}
```

The first tag handler property set by the JSP container when applying a tag handler is its `PageContext` object. As indicated in chapter 6, the methods of the `PageContext` class provide programmatic access to all of the implicit objects available to the JSP scripting elements (table 6.16), as well as to all of the standard attribute scopes (table 6.19). Because tag handlers are passed a reference to the local `PageContext` instance during their initialization, they in turn will have access to all of these objects and attributes through that instance. Indeed, the `PageContext` object is the tag handler's primary window into the workings of the JSP container.

For tag handler classes that extend either `TagSupport` or `BodyTagSupport`, the local `PageContext` instance will be available through an instance variable named `pageContext`. This instance variable is set when the JSP container calls the handler's `setPageContext()` method which, as indicated in figures 18.4, 18.5, and 18.6, is one of the first steps in invoking a tag handler. The `DebugBufferTag` class takes advantage of this instance variable in the very first line of its `doStartTag()` method, in order to retrieve the page's `JspWriter` instance. It then calls methods defined by the `JspWriter` class to determine the current status of the output buffer, which are then displayed on the page by calling the same object's output methods, with help from the `java.text.NumberFormat` class to control the display of the numerical results.

Recall that, with respect to error handling, all of the tag handler life-cycle methods are specified as potentially throwing instances of the `JspException` class. By convention, however, when an error is thrown by a tag handler method it takes the form of a `JspTagException` instance, to signal that the error originated in a tag handler rather than some other JSP entity. All of the tag handler methods presented here and in chapter 19 follow this practice. As you might expect, `JspTagException` is a subclass of `JspException`, so the fact that the `throws` clause in the method signature only mentions `JspException` is not an issue.

Finally, the default behavior of the `doEndTag()` method, inherited by the `DebugBufferTag` class from `TagSupport`, is simply to return `Tag.EVAL_PAGE`, indicating that normal processing of the remainder of the page should continue.

An example page which uses this tag, as well as the resulting output, are presented in the next section.

18.7 Tag attributes

Now we take a closer look at how tag handlers manage the attributes of a custom tag. For this example, we will consider a second debugging tag that allows the developer to display the cookies available on the current page. The TLD entry for this tag is:

```
<tag>
   <name>debugCookies</name>
   <tag-class>com.taglib.wdjsp.mut.DebugCookiesTag</tag-class>
   <body-content>empty</body-content>
   <description>
     List the cookies accessible from this page.
   </description>
   <attribute><name>style</name></attribute>
</tag>
```

This tag is named `debugCookies`, and is implemented via the `DebugCookiesTag` class. As with the `debugBuffer` tag, it has no body content, but unlike the `debugBuffer` tag, this one supports a single attribute named `style`.

Note that the `<attribute>` entry does not specify either the `<required>` or the `<rtexprvalue>` subelement. As a result, the default values for those subelements apply, implying that this is an optional attribute that may not be specified via a request-time attribute value.

The `style` attribute will be used to control how the cookie information reported by the tag is to be displayed. Since the tag needs to be able to display multiple cookies, the tag can present either a plain text version (as was the case with the `debugBuffer` tag), or an HTML list. As such, the style attribute will accept two different string values, either `text` or `HTML`, depending upon how the results are to be displayed.

As mentioned earlier in the chapter, tag attributes are represented in the tag handler class as JavaBeans properties. For the `style` attribute, then, the `DebugCookiesTag` class must define the appropriate instance variables and methods, as in the following:

```
public class DebugCookiesTag extends TagSupport {
    private String style = "text";

    public void setStyle (String style) {
       this.style = style;
    }
    public String getStyle () {
       return style;
    }
     ...
}
```

When the JSP container is processing a page request and encounters the `debugCookies` tag, the value specified for the `style` attribute will be passed to the corresponding `DebugCookiesTag` instance via its `setStyle()` method. The default value for this optional tag attribute is `text`.

For the `DebugCookiesTag` class, two of the standard tag handler invocation methods must be implemented: `doStartTag()` and `release()`. The default implementation of the `doEndTag()` method can be used as is. The code for this class's `doStartTag()` method is as follows:

```
public int doStartTag () throws JspException {
       JspWriter out = pageContext.getOut();
       javax.servlet.ServletRequest req = pageContext.getRequest();
       if (req instanceof HttpServletRequest) {
          HttpServletRequest httpReq = (HttpServletRequest)req;
          Cookie[] cookies = httpReq.getCookies();
          int l = cookies.length;
          try {
             boolean doHTML = style.equalsIgnoreCase("HTML");
             if (doHTML) out.println("<ul>");
             for (int i = 0; i < l; i++) {
                Cookie cookie = cookies[i];
                if (doHTML) out.println("<li><b>");
                out.println(cookie.getName());
                if (doHTML) out.println("</b>");
                out.println(" = ");
                out.println(cookie.getValue());
                out.println('\n');
             }
             if (doHTML) out.println("</ul>");
          }
```

```
            catch(IOException e) {
               throw new JspTagException("I/O exception "
                  + e.getMessage());
            }
        }
        return SKIP_BODY;
}
```

Here, the pageContext instance variable is used to fetch both the output stream and the request object for the page on which the tag appears. The request object must first be cast to the appropriate HTTP-specific class in order to retrieve its array of Cookie instances, after which the cookie's names and values are written to the output stream in accordance with the selected style. If the value of the style instance variable is HTML, then the HTML markup for displaying an unordered list is produced, along with some gratuitous boldfacing. Otherwise, the cookie data is output as multiple lines of text, one per cookie.

This class must also provide its own implementation of the release() method. Recall that the purpose of this method is to restore the tag handler instance to its original state before returning it to the shared resource pool, so that it may be reused during subsequent JSP requests. For this particular tag, then, it is necessary to reset the value of its style instance variable to text, as follows:

```
public void release () {
    super.release();
    style = "text";
}
```

This is done so that the tag handler will use its proper default value for the corresponding style attribute if the next tag this handler is applied to does not explicitly specify a value for that attribute. If this instance variable is not reset, any tag which does not explicitly set that attribute will simply reuse the style value from the tag to which the handler was last applied, which may or may not be the correct default value.

TIP Note the call to super.release() as the first operation in the tag handler's own release() method. When resource management is a concern, it is essential to make certain that all of the classes in the inheritance hierarchy are accounted for.

Note that resetting the attribute property to its default value is not an issue for reuse within the same JSP page. As previously described, the tag handler can only be reused within a page when a later tag provides values for the same set of attributes as the original. If a `DebugCookiesTag` instance is first applied within a given page to a tag that explicitly sets the `style` attribute, it can only be reapplied within that page request to another `debugCookies` tag that also explicitly sets the `style` attribute.

The final source code for this tag handler is presented in abbreviated form in listing 18.3.

Listing 18.3 DebugCookiesTag tag handler

```
package com.taglib.wdjsp.mut;

import java.io.IOException;
import javax.servlet.http.Cookie;
import javax.servlet.http.HttpServletRequest;
import javax.servlet.jsp.JspWriter;
import javax.servlet.jsp.tagext.TagSupport;

public class DebugCookiesTag extends TagSupport {
    private String style = "text";

    public void setStyle (String style) {
      this.style = style;
    }
    public String getStyle () {
       return style;
    }
    public int doStartTag () { ... }
    public void release () { ... }
}
```

To see this tag handler in action, along with `DebugBufferTag`, the following example JSP page is presented:

```
<%@ taglib uri="/mutlib" prefix="mut" %>
<html>
<head>
<title>Debugging Tags</title>
</head>
<body>
<h1>Debugging Tags</h1>

<h2>Cookies</h2>
<mut:debugCookies style="html"/>

<h2>Output Buffering</h2>
<mut:debugBuffer/>

</body>
</html>
```

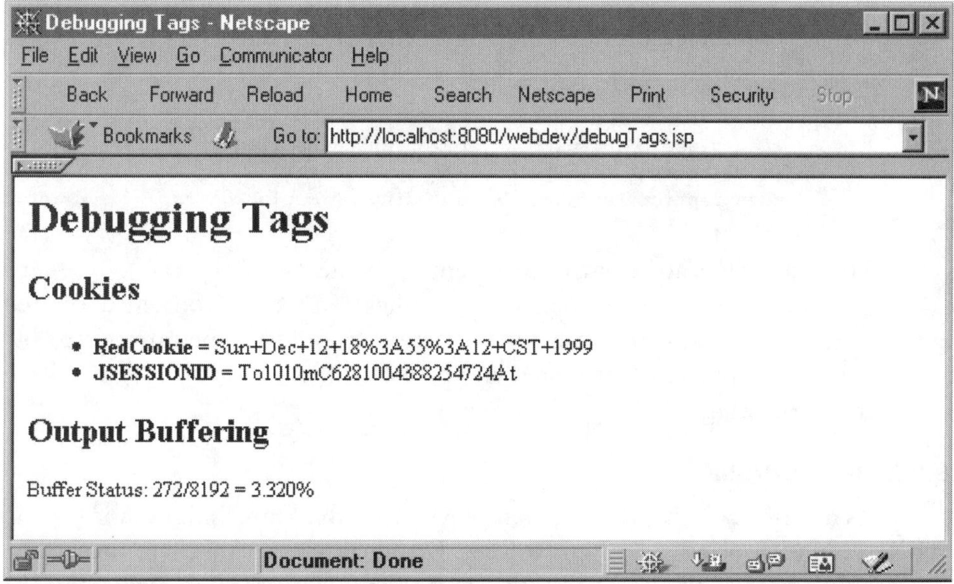

Figure 18.9 Output generated by the example debugging tags

This page simply loads the tag library via the `taglib` directive and calls the two custom tags just as it might call any other JSP tags. The resulting output is presented in figure 18.9.

18.8 Content translation

As we continue to add complexity to our tag handler implementation classes, the next step is to demonstrate tags that interact with their body content. To that end, we introduce tags named `url` and `encodeHTML`, which perform request-time translation on the body content enclosed by their start and end tags. The `url` tag performs automatic URL rewriting in support of the session management features in the servlet and JSP APIs. The `encodeHTML` tag is a more general-purpose variant of HTML's built-in `<pre>` tag: it translates any characters in its body which are special to HTML into their equivalent entities, in order to display that content literally, rather than having it be interpreted by the browser.

The TLD entries for these two tags are as follows:

```
<tag>
    <name>url</name>
    <tag-class>com.taglib.wdjsp.mut.UrlTag</tag-class>
```

```
    <body-content>tagdependent</body-content>
    <description>Perform URL rewriting if required.</description>
</tag>
<tag>
    <name>encodeHTML</name>
    <tag-class>com.taglib.wdjsp.mut.EncodeHtmlTag</tag-class>
    <body-content>tagdependent</body-content>
    <description>Perform HTML encoding of enclosed text.</description>
</tag>
```

The only new feature in these two entries is the use of the `tagdependent` value in the `<body-content>` elements. This indicates that the content delimited by the start and end tags for these custom actions should not be interpreted by the JSP container, but should be stored and passed to their respective tag handlers for further processing.

18.8.1 URL rewriting

As described in chapter 4, JSP employs two different techniques for managing user sessions: cookies and URL rewriting. Using cookies means that no changes need to be made to your site's pages in order to support session management, since the HTTP protocol supports cookies transparently and the JSP API handles session management cookies behind the scenes. Unfortunately, many users disable cookie support in their browsers due to privacy concerns. If you cannot mandate that your users enable cookie support, then URL rewriting is your only alternative for foolproof session management. Unfortunately, URL rewriting has a major drawback: every URL on every page must be rewritten dynamically in order to embed the user's session ID in every request.

Using only the tags built into JSP, URL rewriting can only be accomplished via scripting. To alleviate this burden, the `url` tag described here can be used to cause any URL delimited by this tag to be rewritten each time the page it appears on is requested, as in the following JSP page fragment:

```
<ul>
<li> <a href="<mut:url>bin/programs.jsp</mut:url>">Programs</a>
<li> <a href="<mut:url>employees/users.jsp</mut:url>">Users</a>
<li> <a href="<mut:url>sbin/mcp.jsp</mut:url>">Master Control</a>
</ul>
```

The presence of the custom `url` tags here ensures that each of the URLs associated with these three links will be rewritten. Furthermore, the rewriting is applied intelligently: URLs are only rewritten if the user has disabled cookie support. If cookies are enabled, the underlying code will recognize this and refrain from adding the session ID to the URL. And while this markup code may appear a bit crowded, it is arguably much cleaner than using three JSP expressions containing scripting code to perform the URL rewriting (as was the case, for example in listing 13.10).

Because the action implemented by this tag requires access to its body content, this tag must implement the `BodyTag` interface, rather than the simpler `Tag` interface. For this tag, however, all of the work takes place in its `doAfterBody()` method. By extending the `BodyTagSupport` class and taking advantage of its default method implementations, this tag handler can be implemented with just a single method definition, as indicated in listing 18.4.

Listing 18.4 UrlTag tag handler

```
package com.taglib.wdjsp.mut;

import javax.servlet.http.HttpServletResponse;
import javax.servlet.jsp.tagext.*;
import javax.servlet.jsp.*;
import java.io.IOException;

public class UrlTag extends BodyTagSupport {
  public int doAfterBody () throws JspException {
        BodyContent body = getBodyContent();
        String baseURL = body.getString();
        body.clearBody();
        try {
          HttpServletResponse response =
             (HttpServletResponse) pageContext.getResponse();
          String encodedURL = response.encodeURL(baseURL);
          getPreviousOut().print(encodedURL);
        }
        catch (IOException e) {
          throw new JspTagException("I/O exception "
             + e.getMessage());
        }
        return SKIP_BODY;
  }
}
```

The first step in this handler's `doAfterBody()` method is to obtain the `BodyContent` instance associated with processing the tag's body content. Since this is the `doAfterBody()` method, the body content will already have been processed by the time it is called, so the next step is to retrieve the body content as a `String` instance—to be stored in a local variable named `baseURL`–via the `getString()` method of the `BodyContent` class. Because the `<bodycontent>` element of the TLD entry for this tag was specified as `tagdependent`, this String will contain the original, unmodified contents of the tag's body. The `clearBody()` method is then called to clear out the contents of the BodyContent instance, allowing it to be safely reused by the JSP container after this method returns.

The next step is to encode the URL extracted from the tag's body content. This is most easily accomplished by taking advantage of the encodeURL() method defined by the HttpServletResponse class. The response object is obtained from the tag handler's pageContext instance variable and cast to the appropriate class. The encodeURL() method, which implements all of the logic required to determine whether or not a session ID is required and whether the user's session is being managed via cookies or URL rewriting, is then called to actually encode the URL as necessary.

The next step is to obtain an output stream for printing the transformed URL. This is accomplished by calling the getPreviousOut() method, provided by the BodyTagSupport base class. This method returns the JspWriter instance for the content immediately surrounding the custom tag being processed, which is then used to print the encoded URL. The doAfterBody() method concludes by returning Tag.SKIP_BODY, since no iterative processing of the body content is required.

TIP At this point, you may be wondering why getPreviousOut() is being called to obtain the JspWriter instance, rather than fetching it from the pageContext instance variable, or from the response object. This is done to account for custom tags which are nested inside one another. When custom tags are nested, the output from the inner custom tag may require further processing by the outer tag. If this is the case, we need to make sure that the output from the inner tag is written to the BodyContent object associated with the outer tag, rather than to the outermost JspWriter associated with the page. (Recall that BodyContent is a subclass of JspWriter.) The getPreviousOut() method returns the next BodyContent or JspWriter instance currently associated with the processing of the page's output, and is thus the recommended method for obtaining an output stream for tag handlers which implement the BodyTag interface.

The use of this tag is demonstrated in the following example page, which uses the url tag to rewrite the URL of a linked page. In addition, the page also prints out the user's session ID.

```
<%@ page session="true" %>
<%@ taglib uri="/mutlib" prefix="mut" %>
<html>
<head>
<title>URL Tag</title>
```

```
</head>
<body>
<h1>URL Tag</h1>
<p>
<a href="<mut:url>urlDest.jsp</mut:url>">Here</a> is a link to another page.
</p>
<p>
Your session ID is <%= session.getId() %>.
</p>
</body>
</html>
```

If this page is the first page requested from the server, output such as that depicted in figure 18.10 will result. Note that the link destination displayed at the bottom of the browser includes a request parameter specifying the session ID. If cookie support is enabled in the browser, subsequent requests for the page will generate output such as that in figure 18.11, in which the session ID no longer appears in the link destination display. If cookie support is not enabled, all requests for the page will produce the results displayed in figure 18.10.

Finally, note that since this tag handler doesn't set any attribute properties or allocate any additional resources, no handler-specific `release()` method is required. Instead, it can rely on the default implementation provided by the `BodyTagSupport` base class.

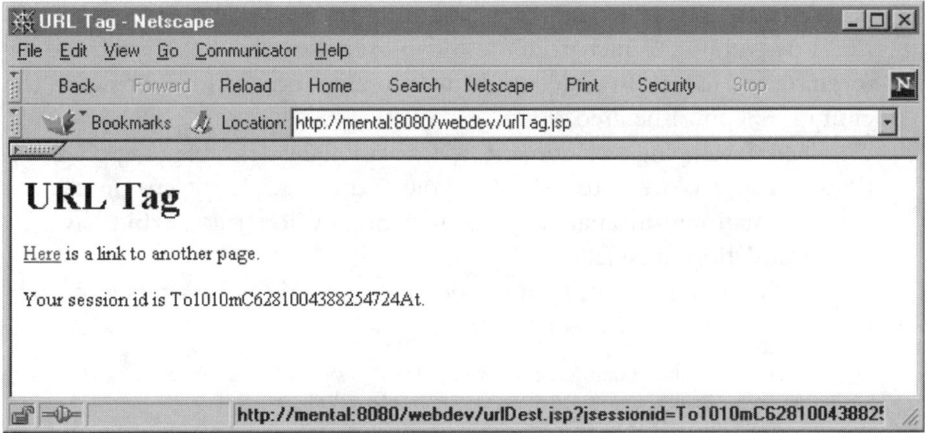

Figure 18.10 Output of URL rewriting tag for the first request, and all requests when cookie support is disabled

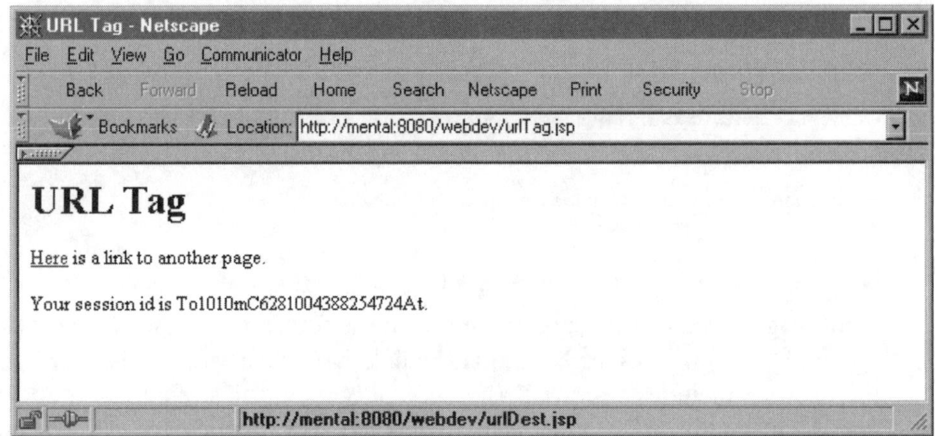

Figure 18.11 Output of URL rewriting tag for subsequent requests when cookie support is enabled

18.8.2 HTML encoding

Browsers interpret HTML content by applying special interpretations to certain characters, such as the < and > characters which delimit HTML tags. In order to cause these special characters to appear in the browsers, it is necessary to replace them with other special HTML constructs, referred to as *entities*. For example, the HTML entity for the < character is < and the HTML entity for the > character is >. As you might infer from these two examples, the & character also has special meaning in HTML. In order to display an ampersand in the browser, the HTML entity & must be used.

When developing web content, it is occasionally desirable to apply these translations to a large block of text. It is the role of the encodeHTML custom tag to perform such translations automatically, so that the developer can avoid having to apply these translations manually.

The first requirement, then, is code for translating characters into their equivalent HTML entities, such as the following:

```
static private Hashtable translations = makeTranslationTable();
static private Hashtable makeTranslationTable () {
    Hashtable table = new Hashtable();
    table.put(new Character('<'), "&lt;");
    table.put(new Character('>'), "&gt;");
    table.put(new Character('&'), "&amp;");
    table.put(new Character('"'), "&quot;");
    table.put(new Character('\n'), "<BR>");
    table.put(new Character('\t'), "  ");
```

```
        return table;
    }
    static public String getTranslation (char c) {
        return (String) translations.get(new Character(c));
    }
```

Here, a `Hashtable` is used to store the characters to be translated and their corresponding HTML entities. (Only a representative sampling of the available HTML entities is presented here.) Also, because the translation table need only be constructed once and can be shared by all tag handler instances, static variables and methods are used to implement the translation routine.

As was the case with `UrlTag`, the tag handler class for the `encodeHTML` tag, by taking advantage of the `BodyTagSupport` base class, needs only to override the definition of `doAfterBody()` in order to implement the desired functionality. The definition of this method for the `com.taglib.wdjsp.mut.EncodeHtmlTag` tag handler class follows:

```
public int doAfterBody () throws JspException {
     BodyContent body = getBodyContent();
     String orig = body.getString();
     body.clearBody();
     int length = orig.length();
     StringBuffer result =
         new StringBuffer(Math.round(length * 1.1f));
     for (int i = 0; i < length; ++i) {
         char c = orig.charAt(i);
         String translation = getTranslation(c);
         if (translation == null) {
          result.append(c);
         } else {
          result.append(translation);
         }
     }
     try {
         getPreviousOut().print(result.toString());
     }
     catch (IOException e) {
         throw new JspTagException("unexpected IO error");
     }
     return SKIP_BODY;
}
```

This method follows the same general outline as the `doAfterBody()` method of the `UrlTag` class, obtaining the tag's body contents in the form of a `String`, performing a translation operation on that `String`, and then printing the translation results. In this case, however, the translation is carried out on a character-by-character basis

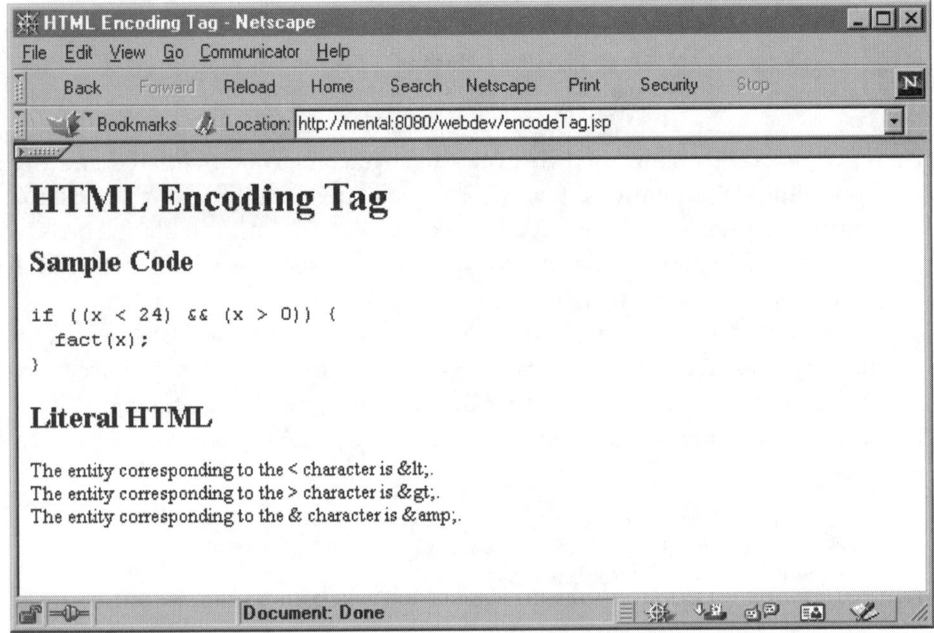

Figure 18.12 Output of the HTML encoding tag

using the static `getTranslation()` method. For efficiency reasons, the translation results are accumulated into an instance of `StringBuffer`, which is later transformed into a `String` for output.

The full source code for the `EncodeHtmlTag` class is presented in abbreviated form in listing 18.5. An example JSP page that makes use of the `encodeHTML` tag appears in listing 18.6. Note that, in order to prevent excessive translation of carriage return characters into `<BR>` tags, the `<mut:encodeHTML>` tags in this sample page appear on the same line as the content being encoded. The results of processing this example page are depicted in figure 18.12.

Listing 18.5 UrlTag tag handler

```
package com.taglib.wdjsp.mut;

import javax.servlet.jsp.PageContext;
import javax.servlet.jsp.tagext.*;
import javax.servlet.jsp.*;
import java.io.IOException;
import java.util.Hashtable;
```

```
public class EncodeHtmlTag extends BodyTagSupport {
    public int doAfterBody () throws JspException { ... }
    static private Hashtable translations = makeTranslationTable();
    static private Hashtable makeTranslationTable () { ... }
    static public String getTranslation (char c) { ... }
}
```

Listing 18.6 EncodeHTML custom tag

```
<%@ taglib uri="/mutlib" prefix="mut" %>
<html>
<head>
<title>HTML Encoding Tag</title>
</head>
<body>
<h1>HTML Encoding Tag</h1>

<h2>Sample Code</h2>
<tt><mut:encodeHTML>if ((x < 24) && (x > 0)) {
    fact(x);
}</mut:encodeHTML></tt>

<h2>Literal HTML</h2>
<mut:encodeHTML>The entity corresponding to the < character is &lt;.
The entity corresponding to the > character is &gt;.
The entity corresponding to the & character is &amp;.
</mut:encodeHTML>

</body>
</html>
```

18.9 Exception handling

The final custom tag for this chapter will take advantage of the `BodyTag` and `TryCatchFinally` interfaces to provide an alternative to JSP's standard exception-handling mechanism. Instead of forwarding control to an error page when an uncaught exception is raised, this custom tag allows the page designer to designate sections of the page within which errors are, effectively, to be ignored.

The syntax for this `failsafe` tag is as follows:

```
<mut:failsafe alt="fallback text">
    ...
</mut:failsafe>
```

Here, the body of the tag designates the content over which errors are to be ignored, and the optional `alt` attribute specifies alternative text, if any, to be substituted in place of the body content should an exception be raised. The corresponding TLD entry takes this form:

```
<tag>
    <name>failsafe</name>
    <tag-class>com.taglib.wdjsp.mut.FailsafeTag</tag-class>
    <body-content>JSP</body-content>
    <description>
      Ignore content and optionally print out alternative text
      in the event of an uncaught exception.
    </description>
    <attribute>
      <name>alt</name>
      <required>false</required>
      <rtexprvalue>true</rtexprvalue>
    </attribute>
</tag >
```

The `FailsafeTag` class which implements the tag handler has two instance variables, one for storing the value of the tag's `alt` attribute, and a second, `caught`, which acts as a flag indicating whether or not an exception was raised while the tag's body content was being processed:

```
public class FailsafeTag
    extends BodyTagSupport implements TryCatchFinally {

    private String alt = null;
    private boolean caught = false;
    ...
}
```

The `alt` instance variable requires appropriate getter, setter, and `release()` methods, as has previously been the case for instance variables representing custom tag attributes:

```
public class FailsafeTag
    extends BodyTagSupport implements TryCatchFinally {
    ...
    public String getAlt () { return alt; }
    public void setAlt (String alt) { this.alt = alt; }

    public void release () {
      super.release();
      this.alt = null;
    }
    ...
}
```

In order to make sure the `caught` instance variable is properly initialized even if it is reused within the same page request, the tag handler provides its own definition of `doStartTag()`, as follows:

```
public int doStartTag () {
     caught = false;
     return BodyTag.EVAL_BODY_BUFFERED;
}
```

This method ensures that `caught` is set to `false`, then returns `BodyTag.EVAL_BODY_BUFFERED` to indicate that the results of processing the body content should be buffered for later processing.

If no exceptions are raised while processing this body content, control will be transferred to the handler's `doAfterBody()` method, which takes the following form:

```
public int doAfterBody throws JspException () {
     BodyContent body = getBodyContent();
     String content = body.getString();
     body.clearBody();
     try {
        getPreviousOut().print(content);
     }
     catch (IOException e) {
        throw new JspTagException("I/O exception " + e.getMessage());
     }
     return Tag.SKIP_BODY;
}
```

All this method does is retrieve the body content in the form of a `String`, and then print it to the output stream, using the same methods as the previous two `doAfterBody()` methods. It then returns `Tag.SKIP_BODY` to indicate that the body content should only be processed once.

This may seem a bit pointless, since this is basically what the JSP container would have done with that body content on its own. The key factor, however, is what the JSP container would also have done if an exception were thrown by the body content. By taking over the original duties of the JSP container with respect to the body content, we can override the default exception handling behavior and replace it with our own.

The final elements of this tag handler that make this possible are the two `TryCatchFinally` methods, `doCatch()` and `doFinally()`. The `doCatch()` method, which is called only in the event that an exception is actually raised, is quite simple. It just sets the `caught` flag and ignores the thrown exception:

```
public void doCatch (Throwable t) {
     caught = true;
}
```

The `doFinally()` method is a bit more involved:

```
public void doFinally () {
     if (caught && (alt != null)) {
        try {
           getPreviousOut().print(alt);
        }
        catch (IOException e) {}
     }
}
```

Since `doFinally()` will be called whether or not an exception was raised, its first task is to check the `caught` flag. If no exception was raised, there is nothing for the method to do. Similarly, it must also check whether or not any alternate content has been specified. If so, then the final task of this method is to print that content to the current output stream, retrieved via the tag handler's `getPreviousOut()` method. Note that `doFinally()` is not permitted to throw its own exceptions. As a result, if this output operation throws any exceptions, they are silently ignored.

The finished source code for this tag handler is presented in abbreviated form in listing 18.7.

Listing 18.7 FailsafeTag tag handler

```
package com.taglib.wdjsp.mut;

import javax.servlet.jsp.tagext.Tag;
import javax.servlet.jsp.tagext.BodyTag;
import javax.servlet.jsp.tagext.BodyTagSupport;
import javax.servlet.jsp.tagext.BodyContent;
import javax.servlet.jsp.tagext.TryCatchFinally;

import java.io.IOException;
import javax.servlet.jsp.JspException;
import javax.servlet.jsp.JspTagException;

public class FailsafeTag
        extends BodyTagSupport implements TryCatchFinally {
     private String alt = null;
     private boolean caught = false;

     public String getAlt () { ... }
     public void setAlt (String alt) { ... }

     public int doStartTag () { ... }
     public int doAfterBody () throws JspException { ... }
     public void release () { ... }
```

```
    public void doCatch (Throwable t) { ... }
    public void doFinally () { ... }
}
```

An example page utilizing this custom tag handler is depicted in listing 18.8. Scriptlets in the body content of the page's `failsafe` tag are employed to throw an exception in the event that a value of zero is supplied for the (optional) `divisor` request parameter. If a non-zero integral value is provided for the `divisor` parameter, no exception is raised and the page output resembles that of figure 18.13.

If, however, a URL of the form http://server/webdev/customtags/failsafe.jsp?divisor =0 is used to request this page and pass in a value of zero for the request parameter, then an `ArithmeticException` will be raised as a result of the attempt to divide an integer by zero. This will cause the tag handler's `doCatch()` method to be called, which will set the value of the tag handler's `caught` instance variable to `true`. Because an exception was thrown, the tag handler's `doAfterBody()` method will not be called. As a result, none of the tag's body content will be displayed. Instead, when the tag handler's `doFinally()` method sees that `caught` is set to `true`, it will write out the tag's `alt` text, as depicted in figure 18.14.

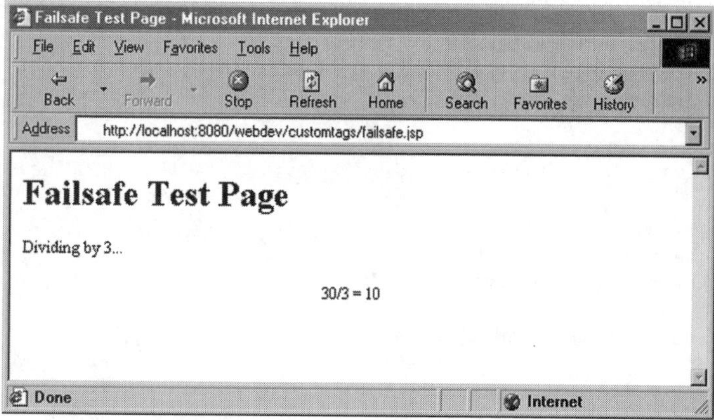

Figure 18.13 Output of the failsafe tag when no exception is raised by the body content

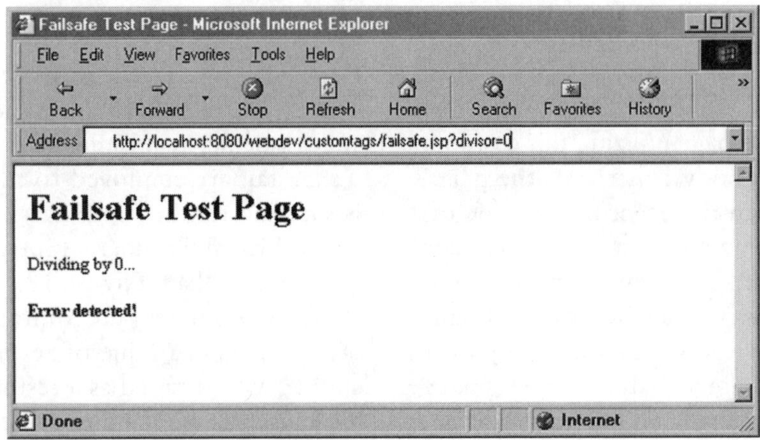

Figure 18.14 Output of the failsafe tag when an exception is raised by the body content

Listing 18.8 Sample page employing the failsafe custom tag

```
<%@ taglib prefix="mut" uri="/mut" %>
<%   int x = 30;
     int divisor = 3;
     String parm = request.getParameter("divisor");
     try { if (parm != null) divisor = Integer.parseInt(parm); }
     catch (NumberFormatException e) {} %>

<html>
<head><title>Failsafe Page</title></head>
<body>
<h1>Failsafe Page</h1>
<p>Dividing by <%= divisor %>...<p>
<mut:failsafe alt="<b>Error detected!</b>">
     <p align="center">
     <%= x>/<%= divisor %> = <%= x/divisor %>
     </p>
</mut:failsafe>
</body>
</html>
```

18.10 To be continued

In this chapter, we have looked at how custom tags are compiled and executed by a JSP container, and how their operation is reflected in the underlying `javax.servlet.jsp.tagext` class hierarchy. We have also described the use of TLD files and the packaging of tag libraries into JAR files, and examined a number of example tags.

The examples presented thus far have focused on key custom tag functionality such as content generation and translation. In the next chapter, we will consider tags that take advantage of more advanced features of JSP and Java, in order to implement paired tags that interact with one another within a single JSP page, as well as tags that set scripting variables and interact with JavaBeans components. In chapter 20, we will look at tag library validation and briefly revisit the topic of packaging tag libraries, to complete our presentation of the `mut` tag library.

19 Implementing advanced custom tags

This chapter covers

- Tags that introduce scripting variables
- Custom tags for flow of control
- Using introspection and reflection to access JavaBeans properties
- Creating families of interacting tags

In chapter 18, we introduced the classes used to create JSP custom tags, and described how those classes interact with the JSP container to perform custom actions within a page. Example tags and their implementations were presented, as was the use of JAR files and TLDs to package tags into a library. Now it is time to build upon that foundation to develop additional tags that leverage advanced JSP and Java APIs to provide enhanced capabilities.

First, we will describe how tags can be used to introduce scripting variables on a page. We will then create a pair of custom actions that provide tag-based flow of control for JSP pages. These tags will also take advantage of Java's introspection and reflection facilities to access JavaBeans properties, in much the same manner as the built-in `<jsp:getProperty>` and `<jsp:setProperty>` tags. We will then describe how data can be transferred between the tags on a page in order to spread functionality across two or more interacting custom actions, to be demonstrated via a fourth JSP custom tag.

19.1 Tag scripting variables

JSP provides two mechanisms for specifying custom actions that introduce scripting variables: the TLD `<variable>` element and `TagExtraInfo` helper classes. This first example will utilize the former approach; a second tag that requires the use of an associated `TagExtraInfo` class will be presented later in the chapter.

Regardless of how the scripting variable is specified, the same process is used to add it to a JSP page: it is assigned to an attribute with page-level scope, using the `setAttribute()` method of the tag's `pageContext` instance variable. The name of the scripting variable serves as the name of the attribute. When invoking a custom tag, the JSP container knows from its TLD entry whether or not it introduces any scripting variables (either via its `<variable>` elements or by means of the helper class specified in its `<tei-class>` entry). If it is expecting a scripting variable to be set, the JSP container will automatically examine the page's `PageContext` instance for the values to which those scripting variables are to be set. The actual mechanics of creating the scripting variable and assigning the value are handled by the container itself; the developer needs only to create the attribute and set its value, and leave the heavy lifting to the container.

19.1.1 Example tag

To demonstrate this functionality, we will implement a custom tag named `timeOf-Day`, which is used to create a scripting variable whose value will be an instance of a

JavaBean named `TimeOfDayBean`. This tag can thus be thought of as a special case of the built-in `<jsp:useBean>` action. The syntax for the `timeOfDay` tag is as follows:

```
<mut:timeOfDay id="bean" timezone="timezone"/>
```

Here, the `id` attribute is used to provide a name for the scripting variable, while the optional `timezone` attribute allows the user to provide a specific time zone in which the current time of day is sought.

As already indicated, the TLD entry for this tag uses the `<variable>` tag to specify that it introduces a scripting variable:

```
<tag>
  <name>timeOfDay</name>
  <tag-class>com.taglib.wdjsp.mut.TimeOfDayTag</tag-class>
  <body-content>empty</body-content>
  <description>
    Sets a scripting variable to the current time of day.
  </description>
  <variable>
    <name-from-attribute>id</name-from-attribute>
        <variable-class>com.taglib.wdjsp.mut.TimeOfDayBean</variable-class>
        <declare>true</declare>
        <scope>AT_BEGIN</scope>
  </variable>
  <attribute>
    <name>id</name><required>true</required>
  </attribute>
  <attribute>
    <name>timezone</name>
    <required>false</required>
    <rtexprvalue>true</rtexprvalue>
  </attribute>
</tag>
```

Furthermore, the scripting variable is defined as being an instance of `com.taglib.wdjsp.mut.TimeOfDayBean` and as taking its name from the value of the tag's `id` attribute. This TLD entry also specifies the tag's two attributes, indicating that the `timezone` attribute is optional and that its value may be specified via a request-time expression.

The tag handler class itself is presented in listing 19.1. There are instance variables for storing the values of the two attributes, as well as corresponding getter and setter methods. A `release()` method is also provided for resetting those instance variables to their default values when returning the tag handler to the JSP container's resource pool.

Listing 19.1 TimeOfDayTag tag handler

```
package com.taglib.wdjsp.mut;

import javax.servlet.jsp.tagext.Tag;
import javax.servlet.jsp.tagext.TagSupport;

public class TimeOfDayTag extends TagSupport {
     private String id, timezone;

     public void setId (String id) { this.id = id; }
     public String getId () { return id; }
     public void setTimezone (String timezone) { this.timezone = timezone; }
     public String getTimezone () { return timezone; }

     public int doStartTag () {
        TimeOfDayBean tod = (timezone == null) ?
           new TimeOfDayBean() : new TimeOfDayBean(timezone);
        pageContext.setAttribute(id, tod);
        return Tag.SKIP_BODY;
     }
     public void release () {
        super.release();
        this.id = null; this.timezone = null;
     }
}
```

As with many of the custom tags already presented, the essence of this tag handler's implementation is concentrated in its `doStartTag()` method; the rest is just bookkeeping. This method has two main tasks: instantiate the bean, and perform the attribute assignment. The `TimeOfDayBean` instance is created by calling one of its two constructors, dependent upon whether or not the tag's optional `timezone` attribute has been set. The method's second task, assigning the resulting bean instance to an attribute, is accomplished by calling the `setAttribute()` method of the handler's `pageContext` instance variable, using the value of the tag handler's `id` property as the name of the attribute. Note that since no explicit value for the attribute scope has been provided as a third argument to the `setAttribute()` method, the default value of `PageContext.PAGE_SCOPE` is assumed. Finally, since there is no body content associated with this tag, `doStartTag()` returns `Tag.SKIP_BODY`.

19.1.2 Scripting variable JavaBean

The final ingredient in the implementation of this custom tag is the specification of its associated JavaBean. To this end, the source code for the `com.taglib.wdjsp.mut.TimeOfDayBean` class is presented in listing 19.2. As you can see, this bean implements getters for three boolean properties named `morning`, `afternoon`, and `daytime`. The `morning` property is `true` between 6 A.M. and noon, while the `afternoon` property is `true` from noon to 6 P.M. The `daytime` property is `true` whenever either of the other two properties is `true`. An accessor for an integer property named `hour` is also available for accessing the current time of day directly.

The bean itself is just a wrapper around an underlying instance of the `java.util.Calendar` class, created by the bean's constructors, which it uses to access the current time. Note also the reliance on the `java.util.TimeZone` class in the second constructor to represent the desired time zone. Its static `getTimeZone()` method is used to parse the value of the supplied zone constructor argument, which must match one of the time zone names recognized by the underlying class. (The complete list of recognized names can be obtained by calling the `TimeZone.getAvailableIDs()` static method.)

Listing 19.2 TimeOfDayBean class

```
package com.taglib.wdjsp.mut;
import java.util.Calendar;
import java.util.TimeZone;

public class TimeOfDayBean {
     Calendar now;

     public TimeOfDayBean () { now = Calendar.getInstance(); }
     public TimeOfDayBean (String zone) {
        now = Calendar.getInstance(TimeZone.getTimeZone(zone));
     }
  public int getHour () { return now.get(Calendar.HOUR_OF_DAY); }

  public boolean isMorning () {
    int hour = getHour();
    return (hour >= 6) && (hour < 12);
  }
  public boolean isAfternoon () {
    int hour = getHour();
    return (hour >= 12) && (hour < 18);
  }
  public boolean isDaytime () {
    return isMorning() || isAfternoon();
  }
}
```

An example page which uses the `timeOfDay` custom tag (as well as the `TimeOfDayBean` class, of course) will be presented in the context of demonstrating the `ifProperty` tag presented later in the chapter.

19.2 Flow of control

As discussed in chapter 5, the only mechanism provided by JSP for implementing conditional or iterative presentation logic is the scriptlet. If you wish to reduce the use of scripting language code in your JSP pages, but still need to apply such constructs, custom tags are your only alternative.

To that end, we present here a pair of custom tags for implementing flow of control. These tags are modeled after JSP's built-in bean tags, keying off of bean properties to control conditional content and iteration. The TLD entries for these two tags, `ifProperty` and `forProperty`, appear in listing 19.3.

Listing 19.3 Tag library descriptor entries for the flow of control custom tags

```
<tag>
  <name>ifProperty</name>
  <tag-class>com.taglib.wdjsp.mut.IfPropertyTag</tag-class>
  <body-content>JSP</body-content>
  <description>
    Conditionally include or exclude page content
    based on a bean property.
  </description>
  <attribute>
    <name>name</name><required>true</required>
  </attribute>
  <attribute>
    <name>property</name><required>true</required>
  </attribute>
  <attribute><name>action</name></attribute>
</tag>
<tag>
  <name>forProperty</name>
  <tag-class>com.taglib.wdjsp.mut.ForPropertyTag</tag-class>
  <tei-class>com.taglib.wdjsp.mut.ForPropertyTEI</tei-class>
  <body-content>JSP</body-content>
  <description>
    Loop through an indexed property.
  </description>
  <attribute>
    <name>name</name><required>true</required>
  </attribute>
  <attribute>
    <name>property</name><required>true</required>
  </attribute>
  <attribute>
    <name>id</name><required>true</required>
  </attribute>
  <attribute>
```

```
    <name>class</name><required>true</required>
  </attribute>
</tag>
```

The only feature in these TLD entries that is not present in earlier examples in this book is the specification of a `<tei-class>` entry for the `forProperty` tag. This is required because the `forProperty` tag introduces a scripting variable to represent the current iteration element of an indexed property, the class of which is not known in advance. (Recall that the TLD `<variable>` tag requires an explicit specification of the type of the scripting variable, via its `<variable-class>` subelement.) As such, a helper class is necessary to transmit information about the scripting variable to the JSP container during page compilation.

19.2.1 Conditionalization

As indicated in the TLD, the `ifProperty` tag supports three attributes, two of which are required. The basic syntax for the `ifProperty` tag is:

```
<mut:ifProperty name="bean" property="property" action="action">
    bodyContent
</mut:ifProperty>
```

The `name` and `property` attributes have the same meaning as in the standard `<jsp:getProperty>` and `<jsp:setProperty>` tags: the `name` attribute identifies a JavaBean introduced earlier via `<jsp:useBean>`, and the `property` attribute names one of that bean's properties. In this case, however, it is expected that the bean property thus specified has a boolean value.

The `action` attribute specifies what to do with the tag's body content when the value of that boolean property is `true`. If the `action` attribute is set to `"include"`, the body content will become part of the displayed page. If the `action` attribute is set to `"exclude"`, the body content will be ignored. Furthermore, if the value of the specified bean property is `false`, the opposite action will be taken. As indicated in the TLD entry for this tag, the `name` and `property` attributes are required, while the `action` attribute is optional. The default value for `action` is `"include"`.

The `ifProperty` tag is implemented via a tag handler class named `IfPropertyTag`. The tag's attributes, as was the case for the previous `DebugCookiesTag` and `TimeOfDayTag` classes, are implemented as bean properties, the code for which is in listing 19.4. Each attribute is represented by an instance variable of class `String`, with a corresponding getter and setter method.

Although this tag has an effect on its body content, it does not need to interact with it directly, as was the case with the content translation tags. Because it is simply controlling whether or not the body content is processed, this tag can be implemented using only the `Tag` interface, rather than `BodyTag`. More specifically, by extending the `TagSupport` base class, the only tag handler invocation methods that need to be overridden are `doStartTag()` and `release()`, the first of which is defined as:

```
public int doStartTag () throws JspException {
    try {
        boolean propertyValue = evalPropertyValue();
        boolean exclude = action.equalsIgnoreCase("exclude");
        if (exclude) propertyValue = (! propertyValue);
        return propertyValue ? EVAL_BODY_INCLUDE : SKIP_BODY;
    }
    catch (IntrospectionException e) {
        throw new JspTagException(e.getMessage());
    }
}
```

The first thing this method does is retrieve the value of the bean property specified by the tag's `name` and `property` attributes, via a call to the auxiliary method `evalPropertyValue()`. If the tag's `action` attribute is set to `"exclude"`, then the sense of this boolean value is reversed (content exclusion is the opposite effect to content inclusion). Finally, based on the resulting value for the retrieved property, the method returns either `Tag.EVAL_BODY_INCLUDE` or `Tag.SKIP_BODY`, in order to control whether or not the tag's body content is processed.

Up to this point, the implementation is fairly straightforward. It's clear, though, that most of the real work is hidden in the `evalPropertyValue()` method, since it is responsible for turning a pair of strings describing a bean property into the value represented by those strings.

There are three major steps by means of which this magical transformation takes place, as outlined in the source code of the method itself:

```
private boolean evalPropertyValue ()
  throws IntrospectionException {
    Object bean = pageContext.getAttribute(name);
    if (bean != null) {
        Method reader = getPropertyReader(bean);
        return readProperty(bean, reader);
    }
    throw new IntrospectionException(
        "Bean \"" + name +"\" not found for <ifProperty> tag.");
}
```

The first step, then, is obtaining the bean instance from its name, and this is performed via the `pageContext` object. All beans introduced via the `<jsp:useBean>`

tag, in the course of being made available for use in scripting elements, are stored as attributes of the page. As a result, they can be retrieved by means of the `pageContext` object's `getAttribute()` method.

After retrieving the bean, the next step is to obtain a reference to the getter method for accessing the desired property. This computation is encapsulated in the call to the `getPropertyReader()` method, which takes advantage of Java's *introspection* API. The final step, represented by the call to the `readProperty()` method, is to call the getter method in order to obtain the actual property value. This process is accomplished via the Java *reflection* API.

Introspection

In the `getPropertyReader()` method, the `java.beans.Introspector` class obtains information about the class of the bean being accessed by the tag. In particular, the `Introspector` class provides access to the `BeanInfo` object that describes the bean class and its properties. For classes that conform with the standard bean naming conventions, the corresponding `BeanInfo` object can be constructed automatically. Remember that bean developers can also provide their own implementations of the `BeanInfo` interface for classes that do not strictly adhere to the bean conventions.

In either case, the `Introspector` class provides a static method named `getBeanInfo()` for obtaining the `BeanInfo` instance corresponding to a given class. Calling this method is one of the first steps performed by the `getPropertyReader()` method:

```
private Method getPropertyReader (Object bean)
    throws IntrospectionException {
    Class beanClass = bean.getClass();
    BeanInfo beanInfo = Introspector.getBeanInfo(beanClass);
    PropertyDescriptor[] descriptors =
        beanInfo.getPropertyDescriptors();
    int stop = descriptors.length;
    for (int i = 0; i < stop; ++i) {
        PropertyDescriptor descriptor = descriptors[i];
        if (descriptor.getName().equals(property)
            && (descriptor.getPropertyType() == boolean.class)) {
            return descriptor.getReadMethod();
        }
    }
    throw new IntrospectionException(
        "Bean \"" + name + "\" has no boolean property named \""
        + property + "\" for <ifProperty> tag.");
}
```

Once the appropriate `BeanInfo` instance has been obtained, the next step is to query its properties. This is accomplished by calling its `getPropertyDescriptors()` method, which returns an array of instances of the class `java.beans.PropertyDescriptor`. Each `PropertyDescriptor` instance contains information about the name and type of the corresponding bean property, and provides accessors for retrieving the property's getter and setter methods. The `getPropertyReader()` method iterates through this array of `PropertyDescriptor` instances looking for a property whose value is a boolean and whose name matches the string value supplied for the tag's property attribute. If an appropriate descriptor is found, its `getReadMethod()` method is called to retrieve the corresponding getter method. Otherwise, an error is signaled.

Reflection

Assuming the desired method is found, it is the role of the tag handler's `readProperty()` method to call this method in order to obtain the bean property's current value. This is accomplished via the Java reflection API, the classes of which are found in the `java.lang.reflect` package. In this case, we are interested in the `java.lang.reflect.Method` class, an instance of which should have been returned by the tag handler's `getPropertyReader()` method. The method represented by this `Method` instance is called by the instance's `invoke()` method:

```
private boolean readProperty (Object bean, Method reader)
    throws IntrospectionException {
    try {
        Object result = reader.invoke(bean, null);
        return ((Boolean) result).booleanValue();
    }
    catch (InvocationTargetException e) {
        throw new IntrospectionException(
          "Unable to access property \"" + property
          + "\" of bean \"" + name
          + "\" for <ifProperty> tag.");
    }
    catch (IllegalAccessException e) {
        throw new IntrospectionException(
          "Unable to access  property \"" + property
          + "\" of bean \"" + name
          + "\" for <ifProperty> tag.");
    }
}
```

The `invoke()` method takes two arguments: the instance for which the `Method` instance's method should be invoked, and an array of objects representing the arguments with which that method should be invoked. Since the method to be invoked is the property's getter method, the object for which it should be invoked is the bean. Since the getter method takes no arguments, the `null` value is provided as the second argument to `invoke()`.

JARGON If this is your first exposure to introspection and reflection, you have probably come to the conclusion that they are very powerful features, but an explanation of their use makes for very convoluted sentences. Bear with us: we're almost out of the woods, at least as far as the `ifProperty` tag is concerned.

In order to support the most general case, the result returned by `invoke()` takes the form of an instance of Java's `Object` class. Because the property's getter method returns a boolean value, it will be packaged by `invoke()` as an instance of the `java.lang.Boolean` class. The `Object` returned by `invoke()` must therefore first be cast to a `Boolean`, after which its `booleanValue()` method can be called to retrieve the actual value.

Of course, calling `invoke()` can be a fairly dangerous operation, since there's no guarantee that the method being invoked, the instance on which it is being invoked, and the arguments supplied for invoking it are mutually compatible. Numerous exceptions can be raised if such incompatibilities arise, as indicated by the `catch` clauses in the `readProperty()` method. For convenience, if any of these exceptions are thrown, they are transformed into instances of the `java.beans.IntrospectionException` class, which is caught by our original `doStartTag()` method.

Cleanup

The final step is the implementation of its `release()` method, which is defined as:

```
public void release () {
  super.release();
  name = null; property = null;
  action="include";
}
```

As with the `release()` methods presented earlier in this book, the first step is to call the `release()` method of the superclass. The next step is to reset all of the instance variables to their original values. As before, this allows the values used while processing the current tag to be garbage collected, and ensures that the appropriate default values are in place for the next tag.

The full source code for the tag handler is presented in abbreviated form in listing 19.4.

Listing 19.4 IfPropertyTag tag handler

```
package com.taglib.wdjsp.mut;

import javax.servlet.jsp.PageContext;
import javax.servlet.jsp.tagext.TagSupport;
import javax.servlet.jsp.JspException;
import javax.servlet.jsp.JspTagException;
import java.lang.reflect.*;
import java.beans.*;

public class IfPropertyTag extends TagSupport {
    private String name, property;
    private String action="include";

    public void setName (String name) {
        this.name = name;
    }
    public String getName () {
        return name;
    }
    public void setProperty (String property) {
        this.property = property;
    }
    public String getProperty () {
        return property;
    }
    public void setAction (String action) {
        this.action = action;
    }
    public String getAction () {
        return action;
    }
    public int doStartTag () throws JspException { … }
    private boolean evalPropertyValue ()
        throws IntrospectionException { … }
    private Method getPropertyReader (Object bean)
        throws IntrospectionException { … }
    private boolean readProperty (Object bean, Method reader)
        throws IntrospectionException { … }
    public void release () { … }
}
```

Application

In order to see the ifProperty tag in action, we first need a JavaBean with one or more boolean properties, to which the tag can be applied. Fortunately, we have already seen a bean with not just one, but three boolean properties: the com.taglib.wdjsp.mut.TimeOfDayBean introduced in conjunction with the timeOfDay custom tag. Taking advantage of this bean and its associated custom tag, we can readily construct a JSP page that combines them with our forProperty tag. Here is the source code for such a page:

```
<%@ taglib uri="/mutlib" prefix="mut" %>
<mut:timeOfDay id="tod" timezone="EST"/>
<html>
<head>
<title>Conditional Tag</title>
</head>
<body>
<h1>Conditional Tag</h1>

<p>The hour is now
<jsp:getProperty name="tod" property="hour"/>.</p>

<mut:ifProperty name="tod" property="morning">
<p>Good Morning!</p>
</mut:ifProperty>

<mut:ifProperty name="tod" property="afternoon">
<p>Good Afternoon!</p>
</mut:ifProperty>

<mut:ifProperty name="tod"
                property="daytime" action="exclude">
<p>Good Night!</p>
</mut:ifProperty>

</body>
</html>
```

Using the <mut:timeOfDay> tag, this page first creates an instance of the TimeOfDayBean named tod, and then displays the value of its hour property via the <jsp:getProperty> tag. The remainder of the page contains three uses of the ifProperty tag, conditionalizing the content to be displayed based on the bean's three boolean properties. The first two ifProperty tags rely on the default setting of the action attribute to include their body content whenever the corresponding property is true, while the third explicitly sets its action attribute to "exclude". As a result, the body content of the third ifProperty tag is only displayed when the value of the corresponding bean property is false.

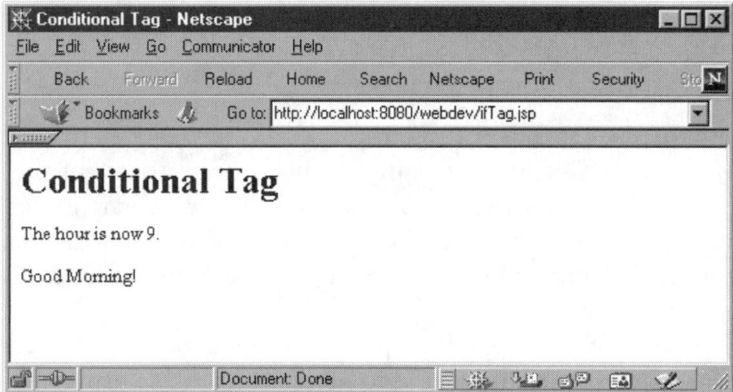

Figure 19.1 Output of the conditional tag

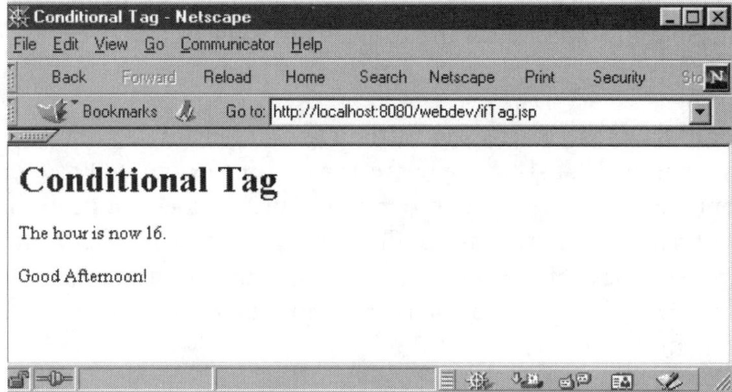

Figure 19.2 Later that same day

The results of requesting this page at different times of the day are displayed in figures 19.1 and 19.2.

19.2.2 Iteration

The `forProperty` tag performs iteration over the elements of a JavaBean's indexed property. In retrieving the values of that indexed property, our implementation of this custom action will again utilize the introspection and reflection APIs. In addition, because this tag makes the current element available as a scripting variable whose type is determined during page compilation, it will require a helper class.

Here is the syntax for the `forProperty` tag:

```
<mut:forProperty name="bean" property="property"
                 id="id" class="class">
    bodyContent
</mut:forProperty>
```

As was the case for the `ifProperty` tag, the `name` and `property` attributes of the `forProperty` tag have the same meaning as their counterparts in the built-in `<jsp:getProperty>` and `<jsp:setProperty>` tags. These two attributes identify the bean being accessed, and the specific property over whose elements the tag will iterate. The property identified by the `property` attribute should, of course, be an indexed one.

The body content of this tag will be processed once for each element of that indexed property. The `id` attribute is used to specify the variable name by which the element may be referenced within the body content. Finally, because the custom tag API does not provide enough information for inferring the class of an indexed property's elements during page compilation, the `class` attribute is provided for specifying it explicitly. All four attributes of the `forProperty` tag are required.

Tag handler

As you will recall from the discussion of the tag handler invocation diagrams in chapter 18 (i.e., figures 18.4–18.6) only the `IterationTag` and `BodyTag` interfaces are capable of processing body content iteratively. Since it does not need to interact with its body content directly, the tag handler for the `forProperty` custom action is implemented as a subclass of `TagSupport`, implementing the `IterationTag` interface. Four instance variables are provided for storing the tag's attribute values, with corresponding getters and setters:

```
public class ForPropertyTag
       extends BodyTagSupport implements IterationTag {
  private String name, property, id;
  private Class elementClass;

  public void setName (String name) {
    this.name = name;
  }
  public String getName () {
    return name;
  }
  public void setProperty (String property) {
    this.property = property;
  }
  public String getProperty () {
    return property;
  }
  public void setId (String id) {
```

```
    this.id = id;
  }
  public String getId () {
    return id;
  }
  public void setElementClass (String className)
    throws ClassNotFoundException {
    elementClass = Class.forName(className);
  }
  public String getElementClass () {
    return elementClass.getName();
  }
  ...
}
```

In a slight departure from previous tag handler implementations, note that the setter for the tag's `class` attribute, `setElementClass()`, automatically performs the translation of the `String` value specified for the attribute into an actual Java class object. This is accomplished via the `Class.forName()` static method, the result of which is then stored in the handler's `elementClass` instance variable. Note also that the getter and setter methods are named `getElementClass()` and `setElementClass()`, rather than `getClass()` and `setClass()`.

This is because the handler already has a `getClass()` method, inherited from `java.lang.Object`. As with all Java object classes, tag handlers are subclasses of Java's root `Object` class, which defines `getClass()` as a method for obtaining an object's class. Furthermore, this method is marked as `final`, which prohibits subclasses from overriding it. `ForPropertyTag` therefore cannot define its own `getClass()` method, no matter how much we might want it to. Hence, alternative method names are required; here, they are named as if the corresponding bean property was called `elementClass`. On the other hand, we are not prohibited from using `class` as an attribute name, and can thereby support a syntax for the `forProperty` tag which incorporates familiar elements from the built-in `<jsp:useBean>` and `<jsp:getProperty>` tags.

In order to map the `class` attribute name to the alternate method names, however, a custom `BeanInfo` class must be created. Like its `TagExtraInfo` helper class, the tag handler's `BeanInfo` class will be presented later in the chapter. Returning to the tag handler itself, there is additional data that it must keep track of, which (like its attribute values) will also be stored via instance variables. As a result of this tag's iterative nature, run-time performance can be improved by maintaining references to the bean, the method used for accessing the indexed property's elements, the size of the indexed property, and the current status of the iteration. These references take the form of the following four instance variables:

```
public class ForPropertyTag extends BodyTagSupport {
    ...
    private Object bean;
    private Method elementMethod;
    private int size, index;

    public int getIndex () { return index; }
    ...
}
```

Note also the presence of a public getter method for the index instance variable. While this method is not strictly required to implement the handler for the `forProperty` custom tag, it will prove to be critical to the implementation of another tag handler, presented later in the chapter.

It is the job of the tag handler's `doStartTag()` method to initialize these instance variables, and to prepare for the first iteration of the tag's body content. Here is the implementation of that method:

```
public int doStartTag () throws JspException {
     bean = pageContext.getAttribute(name);
     if (bean != null) {
         Class beanClass = bean.getClass();
         initSize(beanClass);
         if (size > 0) {
          initElementMethod(beanClass);
          index = 0;
          assignElement();
          return EVAL_BODY_TAG_INCLUDE;
         } else {
          return Tag.SKIP_BODY;
         }
     } else {
         throw new JspTagException("No bean \"" + name
          + "\" available for <forProperty> tag.");
     }
}
```

The first step is to initialize the `bean` instance variable. As was the case for the `evalPropertyValue()` method of `IfPropertyTag`, this is accomplished by means of the `getAttribute()` method associated with the `pageContext` object for the current page. If the specified bean is present, the `doStartTag()` method then proceeds to retrieve its `Class` object. If not, an error is signaled.

If bean initialization succeeds, `doStartTag()` next calls the tag handler's `initSize()` method to initialize the `size` instance variable. This method is defined as follows:

```
private void initSize (Class beanClass) throws JspException {
     Method method =
        getReader(beanClass, property + "Size", int.class);
     Object sizeWrapper = invokeMethod(method, "size");
     size = ((Integer) sizeWrapper).intValue();
}
```

The first step here is to retrieve the getter method for the indexed property's size. By convention, the size of an indexed property is itself exposed as an integer-valued bean property with the same name as the indexed property, plus the suffix `Size`. To obtain the size of the indexed property, then, we must first obtain the getter method for this `size` property. This is accomplished by means of a utility introspection method named `getReader()`, to be presented later in this chapter, which either returns the requested getter or throws a `JspException`.

Once the method is found, it is invoked in order to obtain the property value (i.e., the `size` property). Another utility method, `invokeMethod()`, is called upon to perform this reflection operation (or throw a `JspException` if it can't). The `invokeMethod()` method will be described later in the chapter. The final step of the `initSize()` method is to unwrap the `java.lang.Integer` object returned by `invokeMethod()` which contains the actual integer value representing the size of the indexed property.

Returning to the `doStartTag()` method, processing then depends upon whether or not the indexed property actually has any elements. If the indexed property's size is zero, then the tag's body can be skipped. This is accomplished by returning `Tag.SKIP_BODY`.

If one or more elements are present, however, the next step for `doStartTag()` is to call `initElementMethod()` to initialize the tag handler's `elementMethod` instance variable. This method is defined as follows:

```
private void initElementMethod (Class beanClass)
     throws JspException {
     elementMethod =
        getIndexedReader(beanClass, property, elementClass);
}
```

Like the first line of `initSize()`, this method simply relies on a utility introspection method for retrieving the getter method for the indexed property. As before, this utility method will be presented later in the chapter.

The remaining steps in the `doStartTag()` method when elements are present is to initialize the `index` instance variable to zero and then call `assignElement()` to initialize the tag's scripting variable prior to the first iteration. The method then returns `Tag.EVAL_BODY_INCLUDE` to indicate that processing of the custom action should continue with its body content.

The `assignElement()` method is also a key element of the tag handler's `doAfterBody()` method, which is defined as:

```
public int doAfterBody () throws JspException {
    if (++index < size) {
        assignElement();
        return IterationTag.EVAL_BODY_AGAIN;
    } else {
        return Tag.SKIP_BODY;
    }
}
```

Unlike the `doAfterBody()` methods for `UrlTag` and `HtmlEncodeTag` (chapter 18), this method does not need to concern itself with writing the results of processing the body content. This is taken care of automatically for tags that implement `IterationTag`, and is one of that interface's chief advantages over the `BodyTag` interface. The primary responsibility of `ForPropertyTag`'s `doAfterBody()` method, then, is to decide whether or not the iteration should continue.

To that end, its first step is to increment the `index` instance variable and compare its new value to the stored size of the indexed property. If there are no elements left, then the method returns `Tag.SKIP_BODY` to indicate to the JSP container that no further iterations are required. Otherwise, `assignElement()` is called to set the value of the scripting variable for the next iteration, and `IterationTag.EVAL_BODY_AGAIN` is returned to indicate that the body content should be processed again.

The code for the `assignElement()` method is itself fairly straightforward:

```
private void assignElement () throws JspException {
     Object element =
        invokeMethod(elementMethod, index, "element");
     pageContext.setAttribute(id, element);
}
```

Once again, a utility method, `invokeMethod()`, is called to perform the reflection operations required to retrieve the next element of the indexed property. Its role is to call the getter method for the indexed property, passing it the current value of the `index` instance variable as its sole argument. Then, just as the original bean was retrieved from the `pageContext` object via its `getAttribute()` method, assignment of the scripting variable for the element is accomplished by calling the `pageContext` object's `setAttribute()` method. This action, in combination with information provided to the JSP container via this handler's helper class, is the only step required for a custom tag to assign a value to a scripting variable. The JSP container handles all of the behind-the-scenes details required to subsequently access this value using the associated page's scripting language.

The final element is the `release()` method, defined as follows:

```
public void release () {
  super.release();
  name = null; property = null; id = null; elementClass = null;
  bean = null; index = 0; size = 0; elementMethod = null;
}
```

Like the `release()` methods presented for previous tag handlers, the primary task of this method is to reset the object's instance variables, so that the tag handler instance may be reused by the JSP container.

The complete source for the `ForPropertyTag` class is presented in abbreviated form in listing 19.5. The definitions of the introspection and reflection utility methods will be presented in the next two sections.

Listing 19.5 ForPropertyTag tag handler

```
package com.taglib.wdjsp.mut;

import javax.servlet.jsp.PageContext;
import javax.servlet.jsp.tagext.*;
import javax.servlet.jsp.*;
import java.lang.reflect.*;
import java.beans.*;
import java.io.IOException;

public class ForPropertyTag extends BodyTagSupport {
    private String name, property, id;
    private Class elementClass;

    public void setName (String name) { ... }
    public String getName () { ... }
    public void setProperty (String property) { ... }
    public String getProperty () { ... }
    public void setId (String id) { ... }
    public String getId () { ... }
    public void setElementClass (String className)
      throws ClassNotFoundException { ... }
    public String getElementClass () { ... }

    private Object bean;
    private Method elementMethod;
    private int size, index;

    private void assignElement () throws JspException { ... }
    private void initSize (Class beanClass)
```

```
      throws JspException { ... }
    private void initElementMethod (Class beanClass)
      throws JspException { ... }
    public int doStartTag () throws JspException { ... }
    public int doAfterBody () throws JspException { ... }
    public void release () { ... }

    private Method getReader (Class beanClass,
                              String property, Class returnType)
       throws JspException { ... }
    private Method getIndexedReader (Class beanClass,
                                     String property,
                                     Class returnType)
      throws JspException { ... }

    private Object invokeMethod (Method method, String label)
      throws JspException { ... }
    private Object invokeMethod (Method method, int arg,
                                 String label)
      throws JspException { ... }
    private Object invokeMethod (Method method, Object[] args,
                                 String label)
      throws JspException { ... }
}
```

Introspection methods

The `ForPropertyTag` class defines two utility methods for retrieving bean property accessors via Java's introspection API: `getReader()` fetches the getter method for a standard JavaBean property; `getIndexedReader()` retrieves the getter method for an indexed JavaBean property.

In the implementation of `ForPropertyTag`, `getReader()` is used to obtain the getter method for the property corresponding to the size of the indexed property (i.e., the number of elements over which the iteration is to occur). The `getIndexedReader()` method is used to obtain the getter method for accessing the actual elements of the indexed property.

Because each method is used only once, it may seem overkill to provide utility methods for performing these operations. Noting that we have already performed similar introspection operations while implementing the `IfPropertyTag` class, being able to abstract these operations into a set of utility methods that could potentially be reused by multiple tag handler classes is an attractive idea. These utility methods represent a first step in that direction.

Here is the code for implementing `getReader()`:

```
private Method getReader (Class beanClass,
                          String property, Class returnType)
  throws JspException {
  try {
    BeanInfo beanInfo = Introspector.getBeanInfo(beanClass);
    PropertyDescriptor[] descriptors =
      beanInfo.getPropertyDescriptors();
    int stop = descriptors.length;
    for (int i = 0; i < stop; ++i) {
      PropertyDescriptor descriptor = descriptors[i];
      if (descriptor.getName().equals(property)
          && (descriptor.getPropertyType() == returnType)) {
        return descriptor.getReadMethod();
      }
    }
    throw new
      JspTagException("Bean \"" + name +
                      "\" has no property named \"" + property +
                      "\" of type " + returnType.getName() +
                      " for <ifProperty> tag.");
  }
  catch (IntrospectionException e) {
    throw new JspTagException(e.getMessage());
  }
}
```

As might be expected, this method has much in common with the `getPropertyReader()` method of `IfPropertyTag`. The primary difference is that this method has no dependencies on the class's instance variables. Instead, the method's parameters are its primary source of data.

Like `getPropertyReader()`, this method starts out by retrieving the `BeanInfo` object for the JavaBean class whose properties are being examined (the method's first argument), and then uses this object to retrieve an array of property descriptors. This array is searched for a property whose name and value match those passed in as `getReader()`'s second and third parameters. Once found, the descriptor's `getReadMethod()` is called to obtain and return the `Method` object corresponding to the getter method for the property. If the search fails to turn up an appropriate property descriptor, a `JspTagException` is thrown. For convenience— given this utility method's intended role in implementing custom tags—if an `IntrospectionException` is thrown, it is caught and used to initialize a new `JspTagException` for notifying the caller of any introspection errors.

The implementation of `getIndexedReader()` is quite similar:

```
private Method getIndexedReader (Class beanClass,
                                 String property,
                                 Class returnType)
```

```
  throws JspException {
  try {
    BeanInfo beanInfo = Introspector.getBeanInfo(beanClass);
    PropertyDescriptor[] descriptors =
      beanInfo.getPropertyDescriptors();
    int stop = descriptors.length;
    for (int i = 0; i < stop; ++i) {
      PropertyDescriptor descriptor = descriptors[i];
      if (descriptor instanceof IndexedPropertyDescriptor
          && descriptor.getName().equals(property)) {
        IndexedPropertyDescriptor ipd =
          (IndexedPropertyDescriptor) descriptor;
        if (ipd.getIndexedPropertyType() == returnType) {
          return ipd.getIndexedReadMethod();
        }
      }
    }
    throw new
      JspTagException("Bean \"" + name +
                      "\" has no indexed property named \"" +
                      property +
                      "\" of type " + returnType.getName() +
                      " for <ifProperty> tag.");
  }
  catch (IntrospectionException e) {
    throw new JspTagException(e.getMessage());
  }
}
```

The primary difference between `getIndexedReader()` and `getReader()` is in the code for checking property descriptors. The introspection API provides a special subclass of `PropertyDescriptor`, named `IndexedPropertyDescriptor`, for representing indexed properties. For this reason, the `getIndexedReader()` method only examines property descriptors that are instances of this subclass. Note also that the `IndexedPropertyDescriptor` subclass renames the methods for retrieving the property type and getter method. These methods are called `getIndexedPropertyType()` and `getIndexedReadMethod()` respectively.

Reflection methods

Three utility methods are implemented by the `ForPropertyTag` class for supporting reflection. All three are variants of `invokeMethod()`, the principal version of which is defined as follows:

```
private Object invokeMethod (Method method, Object[] args,
                             String label)
  throws JspException {
  try {
```

```
    return method.invoke(bean, args);
  }
  catch (IllegalAccessException e) {
    throw new JspTagException("Unable to invoke " + label
                              + " method corresponding to property \""
                              + property + "\" of bean \"" + name
                              + "\" for <forProperty> tag.");
  }
  catch (InvocationTargetException e) {
    throw new JspTagException("Unable to invoke " + label
                              + " method corresponding to property \""
                              + property + "\" of bean \"" + name
                              + "\" for <forProperty> tag.");
  }
}
```

Obviously this method is basically a wrapper around the `invoke()` method of class `Method`, which catches any exceptions thrown during method invocation and then throws corresponding instances of the `JspTagException` class. To simplify the argument list, this method uses some of `ForPropertyTag`'s instance variables (specifically, `bean` and `property`), but it would not be too difficult to eliminate this dependency.

To simplify the invocation of methods that take no arguments, the following variant of `invokeMethod()` is provided:

```
private Object invokeMethod (Method method, String label)
  throws JspException {
  return invokeMethod(method, new Object[0], label);
}
```

This form simply provides a default, empty value for the second argument of the original version of `invokeMethod()`. `ForPropertyTag` calls this version of `invokeMethod()` in its `initSize()` method.

A third form of `invokeMethod()` is provided for calling methods which take a single, integer argument:

```
private Object invokeMethod (Method method, int arg, String label)
  throws JspException {
  Integer[] args = { new Integer(arg) };
  return invokeMethod(method, args, label);
}
```

Here, the integer argument is wrapped in an instance of the `java.lang.Integer` class. This `Integer` object is itself packaged in an array, which again serves as the value for the second argument when calling the original version of `invokeMethod()`.

BeanInfo class

As indicated previously, the default behavior of the `Introspector` class is to rely on method name conventions to identify bean properties. For cases when those conventions cannot be adhered to, the developer can provide an associated `BeanInfo` class to provide custom control over those properties and methods.

Providing such custom control is necessary here because the `forProperty` tag handler wishes to override the default read-only `class` property implicitly provided by the `getClass()` method of Java's root base class, `java.lang.Object`. The `BeanInfo` class that implements this custom tag, which must be named `ForPropertyTagBeanInfo` in order for it to be found by the `Introspector` class, is presented in listing 19.6.

Listing 19.6 ForPropertyTagBeanInfo class

```
package com.taglib.wdjsp.mut;
import java.util.beans.*;
import java.lang.reflect.*;
public class ForPropertyTagBeanInfo extends SimpleBeanInfo {
  public PropertyDescriptor[] getPropertyDescriptors () {
        try {
          PropertyDescriptor[] result = new PropertyDescriptor[4];
          result[0] = new PropertyDescriptor("name", ForPropertyTag.class);
          result[1] = new PropertyDescriptor("property",
                                             ForPropertyTag.class);
          result[2] = new PropertyDescriptor("id", ForPropertyTag.class);
          result[3] = new PropertyDescriptor("class",
                                              getClassGetter(),
                                              getClassSetter());
          return result;
        }
        catch (NoSuchMethodException e) {
          System.err.println(e.toString());
        }
        catch (IntrospectionException e) {
          System.err.println(e.toString());
        }
        return null;
    }
    private Method getClassGetter()
        throws NoSuchMethodException, SecurityException {
        Class klass = ForPropertyTag.class;
        return klass.getMethod("getElementClass", new Class[0]);
    }
    private Method getClassSetter()
        throws NoSuchMethodException, SecurityException {
```

```
        Class klass = ForPropertyTag.class;
        return klass.getMethod("setElementClass", new Class[]{String.class});
    }
}
```

The first thing to note about the `ForPropertyTagBeanInfo` class is that it is a subclass of the `java.beans.SimpleBeanInfo` class. This base class provides default implementations of all the methods required by the `BeanInfo` interface, simplifying the developer's task considerably. In this particular case, only the `getPropertyDescriptors()` method needs to be overridden by `ForPropertyTagBeanInfo`.

As we know from its use in the tag handler itself, the `getPropertyDescriptors()` method is used to fetch an array of `PropertyDescriptor` objects that map a bean's properties to its getter and setter methods. Here, that array must be constructed explicitly, rather than rely on the default mapping provided by the JavaBeans naming conventions. This is done by first allocating an array of length four, and then populating that array by making four calls to the `PropertyDescriptor` class's constructors. The first three constructor calls pass in only the name of the property and the bean's class (i.e., the tag handler). This constructor will automatically look up the getter and setter methods based on the standard naming conventions. Since each of these first three properties have getters and setters that follow those conventions, the simplified constructor will suffice.

For the `class` property, however, its getter and setter methods are required to use alternative names, due to a conflict with `Object`'s `getClass()` method. In this case, the getter and setter methods themselves must also be provided as arguments to the `PropertyDescriptor` constructor. A pair of auxiliary methods, `getClassGetter()` and `getClassSetter()`, are thus introduced to retrieve these methods.

The same approach is taken to retrieve both the getter and setter methods. First, a reference to the tag handler class is obtained. Next, the `getMethod()` method provided by `java.lang.Class` is called to perform the actual method lookup. This method takes a method name as its first argument, and an array of `Class` objects as its second. This second argument represents the parameter types for the method being retrieved. The getter method has no parameters, so an array of length zero is supplied. The setter method takes one argument, a string, so an array of length one, containing only a reference to the `String` class, is provided. The selected names of the `class` property's getter and setter methods, `getElementClass` and `setElementClass`, respectively, are provided as the first arguments to the corresponding `getMethod()` calls.

Helper class

As indicated earlier in the chapter, because the behavior of the `forProperty` tag includes setting a scripting variable whose class cannot be specified in the TLD, a helper class is required. This helper class will be instantiated (or fetched from a resource pool) whenever a page using the tag is compiled, in order to enable the JSP container to determine the variable's name and type. In this way, references to the scripting variable within the tag's body content can be resolved and statically checked during page compilation. The name of the helper class, as specified by the TLD entry for the `forPropertyTag` provided in listing 19.3, is `ForPropertyTEI`.

NOTE It is standard practice to name the tag helper class after the tag, with an added `TEI` suffix. As you recall, TEI is an acronym for `TagExtraInfo`, the base class that all JSP custom tag helper classes must extend.

The source code for `ForPropertyTEI` is provided in listing 19.7. As required for tag handler helper classes, `ForPropertyTEI` is a subclass of `javax.servlet.jsp.tag-ext.TagExtraInfo`, and provides implementations for its two primary methods, `getVariableInfo()` and `isValid()`.

Listing 19.7 ForPropertyTEI helper class

```
package com.taglib.wdjsp.mut;

import javax.servlet.jsp.tagext.*;

public class ForPropertyTEI extends TagExtraInfo {

  public VariableInfo[] getVariableInfo (TagData data) {
    String varName = data.getId();
    String className = data.getAttributeString("class");
    VariableInfo info =
      new VariableInfo(varName, className,
                       true, VariableInfo.NESTED);
    VariableInfo[] result = { info };
    return result;
  }
  public boolean isValid (TagData data) {
    return true;
  }
}
```

As discussed in chapter 18, `getVariableInfo()` is used to pass information about scripting variables to the JSP container. For the `forProperty` tag, the name of the scripting variable is provided by the `id` attribute, and its type is provided by the `class` attribute. The values for these two attributes are obtained from the `TagData` object passed in as the argument to this method via its `getId()` and `getAttributeString()` methods, respectively.

These two attribute values are used as the first two constructor arguments in creating an instance of the `VariableInfo` class. The third argument is `true`, indicating that this is a new scripting variable, for which a corresponding declaration may be required (depending upon the page's scripting language). The value for the fourth argument is `VariableInfo.NESTED`, indicating that the scripting variable is only in scope within the body of the `forProperty` tag.

NOTE The `getId()` method of the `TagData` class is shorthand for calling the `getAttributeString()` method with an argument of `"id"`. It is provided in support of the JSP convention that the `id` attribute is used to bind new scripting variables, whereas the `name` attribute is used to reference them. This convention is exemplified by the standard JavaBeans tags: `<jsp:useBean>` has an attribute named `id` for adding a bean to a page, while `<jsp:getProperty>` and `<jsp:setProperty>` have `name` attributes for accessing an existing bean's properties. The `getId()` convenience method is only useful in helper classes for custom tags that follow this convention.

Since this tag creates only a single scripting variable, a `VariableInfo` array of length one is then created. The `VariableInfo` instance that was just constructed serves as its sole element. This `array` is the return value of the `getVariableInfo()` method.

No special checks are performed by the `isValid()` method of `ForPropertyTEI`, so it simply returns `true`, indicating that the tag described by its `TagData` argument is valid. Recall that the JSP container automatically performs certain compile-time checks based on the tag's TLD entry, in addition to calling the `isValid()` method of the tag's helper class (if any).

Unfortunately, the `TagData` object passed in as the argument to both `getVariableInfo()` and `isValid()` provides access only to information about the custom tag currently being compiled by the JSP container. In particular, there is no way for these methods to obtain information about the context in which the custom tag appears.

The methods of `ForPropertyTEI`, for example, could certainly benefit from knowing about the beans present on the page. During the course of compiling the page, the JSP container will determine the class of the bean specified by the `forProperty` tag's `name` attribute. If this information were made available to the `isValid()` method, it would be possible for that method to validate the value specified for the tag's `class` attribute, using introspection. Alternatively, if this information were available from the `getVariableInfo()` method, use of the `class` attribute could be avoided. The introspection API could be used to infer the appropriate class of the scripting variable, and supply it to the `VariableInfo` constructor automatically. Tag library validators, described in chapter 20, expose some global information about a page, but a complete solution to the problem of identifying the Java objects accessible at any given point in a JSP page is not currently provided in the specification.

Example bean

Before we can demonstrate the use of this tag, we will need a bean with an indexed property that can be used in an example page. Actually, we will need two beans, since the elements of the indexed property should themselves be instances of a bean class. The two beans are presented in listings 19.8 and 19.9.

The first class, `PlotBean`, represents a set of *(x, y)* coordinates by means of two bean properties, `data` and `dataSize`. The first, `data`, is an indexed property that stores the plot's coordinates as an array of instances of our second example class, `DataBean`. The `dataSize` property merely reflects the size of this array. In something of a departure from other indexed properties we have seen, however, the setter for the `dataSize` property (i.e., `setDataSize()`) has an important side effect. By calling the bean class's `makeDataPoints()` method, the `dataSize` setter will generate an array of data points, using the zero-argument constructor provided by the `DataBean` class.

Listing 19.8 PlotBean class

```
package com.taglib.wdjsp.advtags;

public class PlotBean {
  private DataBean[] dataPoints;

  public PlotBean () {
    makeDataPoints(0);
  }
  public int getDataSize () {
    return dataPoints.length;
  }
  public void setDataSize (int size) {
    makeDataPoints(size);
  }
  public DataBean getData (int index) {
    return dataPoints[index];
  }
```

```
  public void setData (int index, DataBean data) {
    dataPoints[index] = data;
  }

  private void makeDataPoints (int count) {
    dataPoints = new DataBean[count];
    for (int i = 0; i < count; ++i) {
      dataPoints[i] = new DataBean();
    }
  }
}
```

As indicated in listing 19.9, this zero-argument `DataBean` constructor generates a new bean that has random values for its `x` and `y` properties. This is accomplished by means of `randomCoordinate()`, a static method defined by the `DataBean` class which generates random values between 0 and 100. This method in turn relies on a statically stored instance of the `java.util.Random` class, whose `nextDouble()` method is used to generate random, double-precision floating-point values between 0 and 1.

The `DataBean` class also provides a two-argument constructor for specifying its coordinates explicitly, as well as the standard getter and setter methods for the properties corresponding to those coordinates.

Listing 19.9 DataBean class

```
package com.taglib.wdjsp.advtags;
import java.util.Random;
public class DataBean {
  private double x, y;

  public DataBean () {
    this(randomCoordinate(), randomCoordinate());
  }
  public DataBean (double x, double y) {
    this.x = x;
    this.y = y;
  }
  public double getX () {
    return x;
  }
  public void setX (double x) {
    this.x = x;
  }
  public double getY () {
    return y;
  }
```

```
  public void setY (double y) {
    this.y = y;
  }
  static private Random rnd = new Random();
  static private double randomCoordinate () {
    return 100d * rnd.nextDouble();
  }
}
```

Sample page

A sample page demonstrating the application of the `forProperty` tag to an instance of the `PlotBean` class is provided in listing 19.10. Note the use of the `<jsp:setProperty>` tag in the body of the `<jsp:useBean>` tag to set the number of data points to `12`. Recall that this action has the side effect of replacing the contents of the bean's `data` indexed property with a dozen new, random data points.

The `forProperty` tag appears toward the end of the page, where it is used to iterate through the elements of this `data` property. In the body of the `forProperty` tag, table rows are generated for displaying the coordinates of the data points. The resulting output is depicted in figure 19.3.

Listing 19.10 The forProperty tag example page

```
<%@ taglib uri="/mutlib" prefix="mut" %>
<jsp:useBean id="plot"
             class="com.taglib.wdjsp.advtags.PlotBean"/>
  <jsp:setProperty name="plot" property="dataSize" value="12"/>
</jsp:useBean>
<html>
<head>
<title>Iteration Tag</title>
</head>
<body>
<h1>Iteration Tag</h1>
<center><table border=1>
<tr><th>X</th><th>Y</th></tr>
<mut:forProperty name="plot" property="data"
                 id="point" class="com.taglib.wdjsp.advtags.DataBean">
  <tr><td><jsp:getProperty name="point" property="x"/></td>
      <td><jsp:getProperty name="point" property="y"/></td></tr>
</mut:forProperty>
</table></center>
</body>
</html>
```

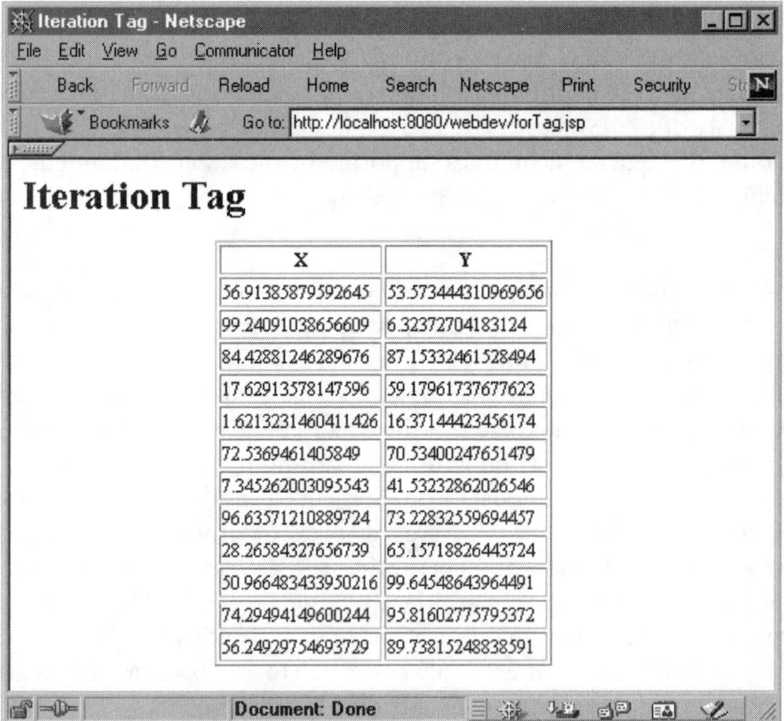

Figure 19.3 Output of the iteration tag

19.3 *Interacting tags*

HTML contains a number of tags whose behavior is dependent upon the context in which they appear. For example, the `<LI>` tag for designating the items in a list produces bulleted content when enclosed in a `<UL>` tag, and numbered content when it appears within the `<OL>` tag. The `<TD>` tag is only meaningful within the body of a `<TR>` tag, which itself must appear within the body of a `<TABLE>` tag.

The built-in JSP tags also include such interdependencies, for example, the relationship among the `<jsp:getProperty>`, `<jsp:setProperty>`, and `<jsp:useBean>` tags. The `page` directive, with its ability to set global properties such as imported packages, the scripting language, and participation in session management, has the potential to influence almost every JSP element that appears in a page.

19.3.1 Interaction mechanisms

As you can see, the ability for tags to interact can add powerful capabilities to a markup language. In recognition of their potency, support for interacting tags is an important part of the JSP custom tag API. JSP provides two different mechanisms, in addition to the general techniques supported by the Java programming language, for enabling data transfer between tag handlers.

Attributes

The simplest mechanism for tags to interact is the use of object attributes. Through their access to the local `PageContext` instance, as described in chapter 18, a tag handler can gain access to all four of the standard implicit objects which are capable of storing attributes: the application object, the session object, the request object, and the `PageContext` instance itself. If the data to be stored in an attribute by a custom tag has the scope associated with the corresponding implicit object, this is a reasonable way of transmitting data from one tag to another. It is somewhat unreliable, however, because there is no way to prevent others from using the same attribute name and inadvertently corrupting the data stored there. Since a given page may include any number of arbitrary scriptlets, `<jsp:useBean>` tags, and custom tags from other libraries—all of which can get and set any of the attributes accessible from that page—there is always the chance, however slim, that another developer has chosen to use the same attribute name as you.

If the visibility of the shared data does not match that of any of the standard scopes, an alternate approach should be taken. This will be true, for example, if the data to be shared should only be accessible within the body of an enclosing tag. In cases such as this, a more direct transfer of data between tag handlers is required. In fact, unless the data has application or session scope (which can only be stored by means of attributes), the approach we describe next is preferable to setting attributes with page or request scope because it does not introduce the possibility of namespace collisions.

The custom tag hierarchy

From the discussion of how tag handlers work in the previous chapter (figures 18.4, 18.5, and 18.6), recall that one of the first methods called when a tag handler is invoked is `setParent()`. The JSP container uses this method to keep track of the context in which a tag appears by means of a parent/child hierarchy. If one custom tag is called within the body of another, the outer tag is designated as the parent of the inner. After the JSP container has assigned a tag's parent—in the form of a tag handler instance—via `setParent()`, that handler can later be retrieved by its child using the corresponding `getParent()` method.

NOTE While any tag handler can access its parent handler by means of the `getParent()` method, the custom tag API provides no methods for determining a tag handler's children. As a result, the parent/child hierarchy can only be traversed in a bottom-up manner.

By calling its `getParent()` method, then, a tag can obtain a reference to its parent tag, and thereby retrieve data by calling its parent's methods. Because nesting of tags is arbitrary, though, you should never make assumptions about the parenthood of a given tag. Even if your tag library defines two tag handlers named `myParentTag` and `myChildTag`, with an implied relationship between the two, there is no way to guarantee that every instance of `myChildTag` will have an instance of `myParentTag` as its immediate parent. Perhaps the page author is also using the `mut` library, and has wrapped a call to the `<mut:encodeHTML>` tag between your two tags in order to encode the output of your `myChildTag` handler. While the `myChildTag` instance may still be descended from an instance of your `myParentTag` handler within the page's parent/child hierarchy, the result of calling `getParent()` from your `myChildTag` handler will yield an instance of `EncodeHtmlTag`, rather than an instance of `myParentTag`.

Coping with this inevitability is the role of `findAncestorWithClass()`, a static method defined by the `TagSupport` class. As its name suggests, this method is used to search up the parent/child hierarchy for the first ancestor of a tag that is an instance of a particular class. The signature for this method is:

```
static Tag TagSupport.findAncestorWithClass(Tag from, Class class)
```

The first argument, *from*, identifies the child tag from which the search is initiated. The second argument, *class*, specifies the tag handler class (or interface) for which an instance is sought. Starting from the handler identified by *from*, then, its parent handler is checked to see if it is an instance of *class*. If so, the parent handler is returned. If not, the parent's parent is checked. This process continues recursively until an instance of *class* is found, or a tag handler with no parent is reached, in which case the method returns `null`. In this way, a handler searching for an enclosing tag of a certain type can locate it by means of its class.

NOTE The base requirement for custom tag handlers is that they implement the `Tag` interface. The `findAncestorWithClass()` method is provided by the `TagSupport` class so that a full implementation can be provided, since interfaces can only specify abstract methods. Because it is a static method, however, it can readily be called by tag handlers based on the `Tag`, `IterationTag`, or `BodyTag` interfaces, as well as those extending the `TagSupport` and `BodyTagSupport` classes.

19.3.2 Index tag

To demonstrate the use of `findAncestorWithClass()`, we will implement an `index` tag for use with the `forProperty` tag introduced previously. This tag can be used to print the value of the index counter for the current iteration. The retrieval of this value from the parent `forProperty` tag handler by the child `index` tag handler is accomplished via `findAncestorWithClass()`.

The syntax for the index tag is as follows:

```
<mut:forProperty ...>
     ...
     <mut:index start="offset"/>
     ...
</mut:forProperty>
```

The tag has no body content and supports only a single, optional attribute named `start`. This attribute allows the user to specify an offset which is to be added to the index value before it is displayed. This option is provided because Java, like many programming languages, starts its count from zero when iterating through a set of indexed values. Natural languages, as well as HTML, treat such counts as starting from one. If the optional `start` attribute is omitted, the Java convention is followed. A value of one for this attribute mimics the natural language convention.

Given this description of its syntax, the corresponding TLD entry for the index tag takes this form:

```
<tag>
     <name>index</name>
     <tag-class>com.taglib.wdjsp.mut.IndexTag</tag-class>
     <body-content>empty</body-content>
     <description>
       Prints the index value for the current iteration.
     </description>
     <attribute>
       <name>start</name>
       <required>false</required>
       <rtexprvalue>true</rtexprvalue>
     </attribute>
</tag>
```

Thus, the index tag is implemented by means of an `IndexTag` tag handler class and has no body content. Its only attribute, which is optional, is named `start`.

Tag handler

The `IndexTag` handler class is presented in listing 19.11. Once again, the `doStartTag()` method is the primary workhorse in implementing the functionality of the custom tag, with support from one instance variable, its corresponding getter and setter methods, and a `release()` method for resetting its value prior to returning the tag handler to its resource pool.

Listing 19.11 IndexTag tag handler

```
package com.taglib.wdjsp.mut;

import javax.servlet.jsp.tagext.Tag;
import javax.servlet.jsp.tagext.TagSupport;
import javax.servlet.jsp.JspWriter;

import java.lang.IOException;
import javax.servlet.jsp.JspException;
import javax.servlet.jsp.JspTagException;

public class IndexTag extends TagSupport {
    private int start = 0;

    public void setStart (int start) { this. start = start; }
    public int getStart () { return start; }

    public int doStartTag throws JspException () {
      ForPropertyTag outer = (ForPropertyTag)
        TagSupport.findAncestorWithClass(this, ForPropertyTag.class);
      if (outer == null)
        throw new JspTagException("No enclosing ForPropertyTag instance.");
      JspWriter out = pageContext.getOut();
      try {
        out.print(start + outer.getIndex());
        return Tag.SKIP_BODY;
      }
      catch (IOException e) {
        throw new JspTagException("I/O exception " + e.getMessage());
      }
    }
    public void release () {
      super.release();
      this.start = 0;
    }
}
```

The first action taken by the handler's `doStartTag()` method is to call the `TagSupport.findAncestorWithClass()` method to locate the tag handler for the enclosing `forProperty` tag, if any, and assign it to a local variable named `outer`. Since this is a static method, the calling tag handler is passed in as the first argument, in the form of the this variable. The `ForPropertyTag` handler class acts as the second argument, indicating the type of enclosing handler that is sought. The `index` tag is only valid when nested inside a `forProperty` tag; if no enclosing instance of `ForPropertyTag` is found, a `JspTagException` is raised to report the error.

If the enclosing handler is found, the `JspWriter` representing the current output stream is retrieved from the handler's `pageContext`. The handler then writes out the index value, incremented by the value of the `start` instance variable, to this stream. The index value is itself retrieved by calling the `getIndex()` method of the enclosing `ForPropertyTag` instance, now referenced by the `outer` local variable. This method, introduced earlier in the chapter, is of no direct utility to its defining class; it is essential, however, to the operation of the `IndexTag` handler. The `doStartTag()` method then concludes by returning `Tag.SKIP_BODY`, consistent with the absence of body content for this custom tag.

Sample page

A final sample page demonstrating the interaction of the `index` and `forProperty` tags is presented in listing 19.12. This page is, of course, based on the original sample page for the `forProperty` tag, and only minor modifications were made to incorporate the second tag. Specifically, a new column was added to the table for displaying the index value of each row. The content of this column is provided by the `index` tag in the first line of the `forProperty` tag's body. A value of one has been specified for the `index` tag's `start` attribute, so that the row count starts at one instead of zero. In addition, a corresponding column heading was added to the table, and the page's title was changed. The resulting JSP page is depicted in figure 19.4.

Listing 19.12 The index tag example page

```
<%@ taglib uri="/mutlib" prefix="mut" %>
<jsp:useBean id="plot"
             class="com.taglib.wdjsp.advtags.PlotBean"/>
  <jsp:setProperty name="plot" property="dataSize" value="12"/>
</jsp:useBean>
<html>
<head>
<title>Index Tag</title>
</head>
<body>
<h1>Index Tag</h1>
<center><table border=1>
<tr><th>i</th><th>X</th><th>Y</th></tr>
```

```
<mut:forProperty name="plot" property="data"
                 id="point" class="com.taglib.wdjsp.advtags.DataBean">
  <tr><td><mut:index start="1"/></td>
      <td><jsp:getProperty name="point" property="x"/></td>
      <td><jsp:getProperty name="point" property="y"/></td></tr>
</mut:forProperty>
</table></center>
</body>
</html>
```

19.4 The final ingredient

The `index` tag completes the set of JSP custom actions to be included in the `mut` tag library. There is one more element to be added to the library before it is complete, however.

As indicated, the index tag can only be used within the body of a `forProperty` tag. Attempting to apply it outside the body of a `forProperty` tag results in a runtime error. In a traditional programming language, though, nesting requirements such as these are often enforced syntactically, allowing them to be detected during

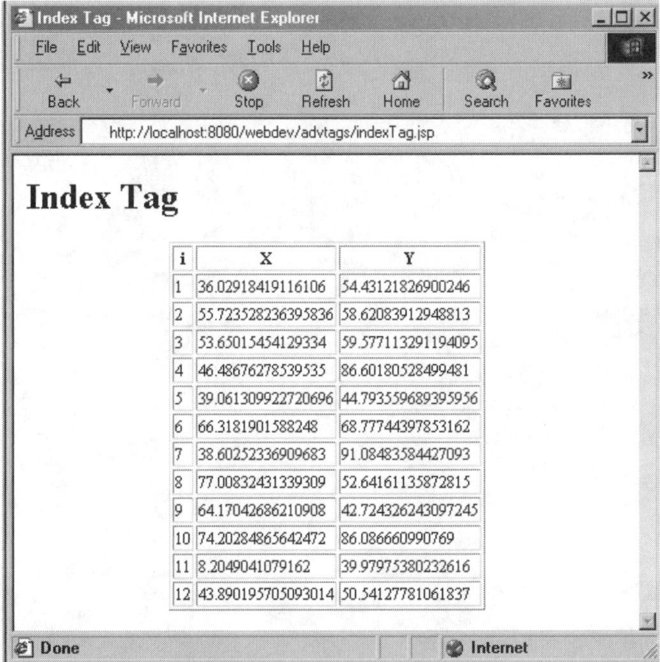

Figure 19.4 Output of the iteration index tag

compilation. Since compile-time errors tend to be detected earlier in the development process than run-time errors—particularly if you take advantage of JSP's precompilation protocol (chapter 14)—providing a compile-time mechanism for enforcing this relationship should prove advantageous.

Fortunately, this is exactly the sort of functionality provided by tag library validators. This feature, introduced in JSP 1.2, is the topic of our final chapter, and a validator for enforcing the nesting of `forProperty` and `index` tags which will be the final ingredient in our example tag library.

20 Validating custom tag libraries

This chapter covers

- XML representation of JSP pages
- How tag library validators work
- Implementation of tag library validators
- Packaging the example tag library

In the previous two chapters, we examined the design and operation of tag handlers for implementing JSP custom actions. We saw how information in the TLD is used by the JSP container to validate the syntax of custom tags and their attributes. We also discussed how the `isValidMethod()` of the `TagExtraInfo` class may be used to further validate individual applications of a specific custom tag. The two approaches are limited, however, in that they are applied to each individual occurrence of a custom tag within a JSP page.

Validating the complete set of custom tags present within a page—for example, to enforce uniqueness constraints or verify that dependencies among interacting tags are met—requires a different approach. This is the role of JSP 1.2's tag library validators, the primary topic of this final chapter. We will start by examining how JSP pages may be represented as XML documents, and then discuss how tag library validators interact with this XML representation to validate a page's custom tags. Several examples will be presented, including one for use with the example library presented in chapters 18 and 19. This validator will then be combined with the tag handlers from those chapters to constuct a JAR file for the completed `mut` custom tag library.

20.1 Two representations of JSP

As indicated in chapters 4 and 5, JSP supports two different representations of its pages. The standard representation, in which JSP markup tags are embedded in template text for dynamic content generation, has been used throughout the examples presented thus far. The format of this template text is arbitrary. It can take the form of HTML, WML, or any other text-based content, such as a table of comma-separated values to be displayed as a spread sheet.

The template text can also be an XML document, with the JSP markup tags used to supply content for that document dynamically. Application of JSP to XML in this way was demonstrated in the VXML example presented in chapter 16. When taking this approach, the underlying JSP page, containing the template text and JSP markup, is not a valid XML document. This is because the JSP markup tags are not part of the governing DTD for the document being generated. While standard actions and custom tags employ an XML-based syntax, they are in namespaces that are unrelated to the content being delivered. The remaining JSP markup tags, which use `<%` and `%>` as their delimiters, are completely invalid as XML elements.

It is only after the page has processed by the JSP container in response to a request that a valid XML document will result. All of the JSP markup will have been

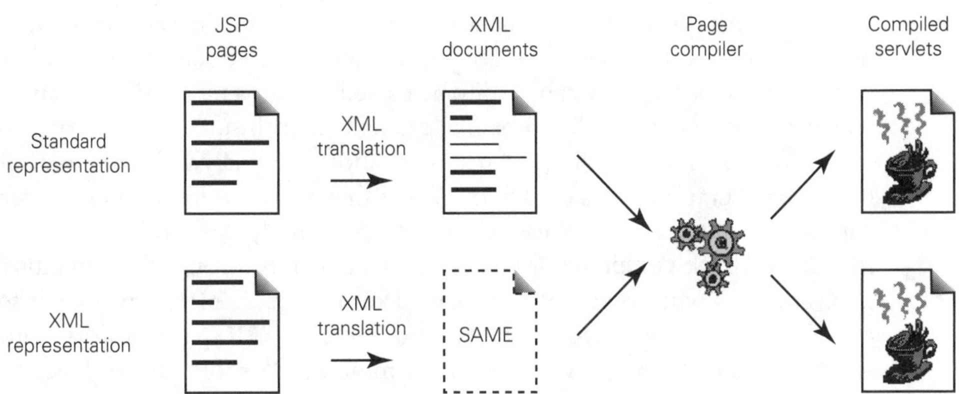

Figure 20.1 Compilation of JSP pages as XML documents

replaced by the generated content, which (presumably) fills in the template text to create well-formed XML.

As of JSP 1.2, however, an alternative is available. Although the XML variants of the various JSP markup tags were introduced in version 1.1 of the JSP specification, it was not until version 1.2 that a complete representation for JSP pages as well-formed XML documents was provided. Whereas the standard representation calls for template text interspersed with JSP markup tags, the XML representation of a JSP page conforms to a JSP-specific DTD, with dedicated elements for the markup tags as well as the template text.

For every JSP page written using the standard representation, then, there is an equivalent XML document that may be written using the XML representation. This equivalent XML document, when deployed in a JSP container, will produce exactly the same result in response to a request as the original JSP page (assuming, of course, that the context—request parameters, session attributes, etc.—for the two requests is identical). In fact, given that such an equivalent XML document exists for every possible JSP page using the standard representation, the JSP 1.2 specification mandates its use by the page compiler. As indicated in figure 20.1, fully compliant JSP containers are expected to create this equivalent XML page whenever a request is received for a JSP page that uses the standard representation and has not already been compiled into a servlet. Once it has been translated into the XML representation, it is this XML version of the page that is used to generate the servlet source code for the page which is then compiled and loaded into the JSP container. Pages originally written using the XML representation, of course, do not require this extra translation step. As depicted in figure 20.1, such pages are compiled directly.

The primary advantage of the XML representation is its regularity. Because JSP pages using this representation are well-formed XML documents, conforming to published standards, they can readily be parsed by software needing to analyze their contents. JSP containers would be one example of such software, but tools for creating, editing, and maintaining JSP pages are another equally valid example. The standard representation relies on arbitrary text files with JSP markup tags interspersed within the template text. While this approach is highly flexible and easy for authors to work with, this underlying flexibility makes the resulting files difficult for programs to work with, because they are difficult to parse. XML is, in comparison, very easy to parse, as evidenced by the large number of XML parsers, both commercial and free, available to the development community. A tool that produces JSP pages using the XML representation can readily read that file back in for modification at a later date, simply by parsing the page as an XML document. In contrast, when working with the standard representation, it is fairly easy to create JSP pages, but because there is no structure to the resulting document, reading it back in again is considerably more complex.

Finally, the ability of the XML representation to be easily parsed also greatly simplifies the task of validating JSP pages, as we shall soon see.

20.2 JSP pages as XML documents

In chapter 5, the XML equivalents of the various JSP markup tags were presented. For example, the `page` and `include` directives have corresponding XML elements named `<jsp:directive.page>` and `<jsp:directive.include>`, respectively. When constructing a JSP page using the XML representation, however, simply replacing the original markup tags with the appropriate XML forms is insufficient. XML documents have additional requirements, such as a top-level root element, that must be met in order for the document to be considered well-formed. XML is also strict about the characters that may appear within the body content of a tag. Some of the characters that commonly occur in Java code, including quotation marks and mathematical symbols such as < and >, require special treatment when they appear in the body of an XML tag. XML also does not allow one tag to be embedded within another, as is the case for JSP request-time attribute values. Additional modifications are required, then, to satisfy such requirements. If they are not satisfied, the document will be rejected when it is parsed by the page compiler.

20.2.1 The root element

The root element for all JSP pages using the XML representation is `<jsp:root>`. All elements on the page are thus delimited by matching `<jsp:root>` and `</jsp:root>` tags. This root element accepts multiple `xmlns` attributes identifying the XML namespaces used by the tags in the document. There will always be at least one `xmlns` attribute corresponding to the `jsp` namespace used by the standard JSP markup tags (e.g,. `<jsp:directive.include>`, `<jsp:expression>`, `<jsp:setProperty>`, etc.). A `version` attribute, indicating the version of the JSP specification to which the document adheres, is also required. The basic syntax for the root element, then, is:

```
<jsp:root version="1.2" xmlns:prefix1="uri1" xmlns:prefix2="uri2" ... >
  page content
</jsp:root>
```

where each `xmlns` attribute includes the namespace prefix as part of the attribute's name, and specifies the URI of the TLD for that namespace as its value.

For JSP pages that only use the built-in JSP tags, the root element takes this form:

```
<jsp:root version="1.2" xmlns:jsp="http://java.sun.com/JSP/Page">
  page content
</jsp:root>
```

Since only the standard markup tags are being used, only the specification of the `jsp` namespace is required. The URI for the namespace of the standard tags is http://java.sun.com/JSP/Page.

As mentioned in chapter 5, there is no direct XML equivalent for the JSP `taglib` directive. Instead, custom tags are referenced as additional namespaces for the root element. For a page using our `mut` tag library with `mut` as the chosen prefix for those tags, the root element would be

```
<jsp:root version="1.2" xmlns:jsp="http://java.sun.com/JSP/Page"
  xmlns:mut="urn:jsptld:/mutlib">
  page content
</jsp:root>
```

Instead of an explicit element specifying the tag library being used, an `xmlns` attribute for that tag library is added to the root element. The namespace prefix for the custom tag library appears in the name of the `xmlns` attribute, while the URI pointing to its TLD—in this case, /mutlib—serves as the attribute's value. These correspond to the values of the `prefix` and `uri` attributes, respectively, of the standard `taglib` directive. Using the standard representation, there is one `taglib` directive for each custom tag library used by a page. In the XML representation, there is one `xmlns` attribute for each custom tag library, plus an additional `xmlns` attribute for the standard tags (i.e., the `jsp` namespace).

Note in the previous example that the local URI for the custom tag library's TLD is specified as urn:jsptld:/mutlib, whereas the URI for the standard tags is a conventional http URL. This is because the TLD resides on the local server, using a mapped URI dictated by the web application to which the JSP page belongs (see chapter 14). Since the full URL is deployment-specific, this alternative URI syntax lets the JSP container know that it should use its own internal mechanisms to locate the TLD.

20.2.2 Template text

Template text within a JSP page is modeled in the XML representation as the body content of one or more `<jsp:text>` elements. In addition, to ensure that the body content of this element complies with XML data requirements, it is typically wrapped inside an XML CDATA element, indicating that it contains character data that is to be treated as literal text, rather than interpreted as XML tags.

Consider, for example, the following fragment of text to be included in a JSP page:

```
A world inside the computer where man has never been.
```

Since none of the characters in this text have any special meaning as XML, they can be wrapped directly in a `<jsp:text>` element without any negative side effects:

```
<jsp:text>A world inside the computer where man has never been.</jsp:text>
```

Consider, though, this second fragment, which includes HTML markup:

```
Never before <i>now</i>.
```

In this case, the delimiters for the HTML italics tags in this fragment do have meaning as XML. When parsing this fragment as XML, the parser would attempt to interpret the `<i>` and `</i>` tags as XML elements, most likely causing an error in the process. To ensure that template text such as this is treated literally, it is embedded in a CDATA element, like this:

```
<jsp:text> <![CDATA[Never before <i>now</i>.]]></jsp:text>
```

Wrapping the template text inside the CDATA element protects it from being interpreted as XML when the document is parsed.

20.2.3 Scripting elements

As indicated in chapter 5, JSP provides the `<jsp:declaration>`, `<jsp:scriptlet>`, and `<jsp:expression>` tags for specifying the three forms of JSP scripting elements in XML. As is the case for template text, however, the Java (or other scripting language) code that appears in such elements may not always comply with XML data requirements. For that reason, scripting code in the body of these three XML tags is also commonly wrapped inside an XML CDATA element, to avoid potential errors when the XML document containing these elements is parsed.

For example, consider the following method declaration using the standard representation:

```
<%! public long fact (long x) {
      if (x < 2) return 1;
      else return x * fact(x -1);
    } %>
```

Due to the presence of the < character in the second line of this declaration, the method definition cannot simply be placed between a set of `<jsp:declaration>` tags. If it were, an XML parser would attempt to interpret this character as the opening delimiter of a nested tag, which it obviously is not. By wrapping the Java code inside a CDATA element, however, parsing of the method body as XML is preempted. The equivalent XML representation for this declaration, then, is as follows:

```
<jsp:declaration><![CDATA[
 public long fact (long x) {
      if (x < 2) return 1;
      else return x * fact(x -1);
    }]]>
</jsp:declaration>
```

For the purposes of XML parsing, the Java code is thus treated as literal text.

Scriptlets and top-level expressions are treated similarly when using the XML representation.

20.2.4 Request-time attribute values

When expressions are used to provide request-time attribute values for JSP actions, the standard representation calls for them to be embedded within the action tag containing the attribute whose value they are setting. This is not permitted in well-formed XML, however. While it is legal for one or more XML tags to appear in the body content of another XML tag, XML does not permit such nesting within the tags themselves.

In order to accommodate request-time attribute values in the XML representation, then, JSP takes a slightly different approach. Rather than represent the request-time attribute value as an XML element, special character-based delimiters are used to signify the presence of scripting code representing a request-time attribute value. More specifically, the beginning of an expression providing a request-time attribute value is indicated by the characters `%=`, while the end of the expression is delimited by a `%`.

Consider the following action, which includes a request-time attribute value, using the standard representation:

```
<jsp:setProperty name="pizzaBean" slices="<%= fact(4) %>"/>
```

The equivalent action, using the XML representation, is:

```
<jsp:setProperty name="pizzaBean" slices="%= fact(4) %"/>
```

As you can see, the only difference between these two actions is the absence of the < and > delimiters on the request-time attribute value in the XML representation.

Note, however, that if the scripting code in such expressions uses any characters that have special meaning in XML, they must be properly escaped. For Java code, the character most likely to cause such difficulties is the quotation mark, since the XML parser would attempt to interpret it as the closing delimiter for the attribute value. There are three approaches to avoiding this problem.

The first takes advantage of the fact that both the standard representation and the XML representation support the use of the apostrophe (or single quote) character as a delimiter for attribute values. When there are quotation marks present in the expression, simply use this alternative delimiter to avoid conflicts, as in the following example, which uses the standard representation:

```
<jsp:setProperty name="user" nickname='<%= user.getLastName() + "ster" %>'/>
```

Unfortunately, if the expression contains both quotation marks and apostrophes, this approach is inadequate.

The second option is based on Java's built-in support for Unicode escape sequences. The escape sequence for quotation marks is \u0022, and can appear anywhere in the expression to stand in for a quotation mark. Here is the same tag using the XML representation and Unicode escape sequences:

```
<jsp:setProperty name="user" nickname="%= user.getLastName() +
  \u0022ster\u0022 %"/>
```

When the text of this expression is passed to the Java compiler, the escape sequences will automatically be recognized as representing a pair of quotation marks.

A third alternative is to use XML entities, as in this example:

```
<jsp:setProperty name="user" nickname="%= user.getLastName() +
   &quot;ster&quot; %"/>
```

In this case, it is the XML parser that is performing the character translation, recognizing the `"` entities as representing quotation marks intended to be part of the attribute value, rather than delimiters.

20.2.5 Directives and actions

The XML representation for the `taglib` directive has already been described: custom tag libraries are specified via the `xmlns` attribute of the `<jsp:root>` element. The other two JSP directives, `page` and `include`, have explicit XML equivalents, as described in chapter 5. All JSP actions, including those provided by a custom tag library, already employ a syntax that is compatible with XML.

When authoring a JSP page using the XML representation, then, `page` and `include` directives are specified using the equivalent XML syntax, rather than their standard form. Actions (both standard and custom) take the same form as in the standard representation.

When the JSP container translates a JSP page from the standard representation into the equivalent XML document, `page` and `include` directives are mapped into their XML equivalents. Action tags do not themselves require any mapping, unless they have attributes whose values are provided via request-time attribute values. In this case, the JSP expressions representing those request-time attribute values are transformed as described in the previous section. Finally, if there is any body content associated with the action, it too must be translated.

20.2.6 Sample page

A sample JSP page, expressed using both the standard and XML representations, is presented in listings 20.1 and 20.2. Note that the `taglib` directive in the standard representation is replaced by an `xmlns` attribute of the root element in the XML representation. Also note the two approaches to handling the quotation marks in the request-time attribute value for the `timezone` attribute of the `<mut:timeOfDay>` custom action, and the usage of `<jsp:text>` and associated CDATA elements in the XML representation to preserve the line spacing of the version using the standard representation.

Listing 20.1 Sample JSP page using the standard representation

```
<%@ page session="false" %>
<%@ taglib prefix="mut" uri="/mutlib" %>

<% String zone = request.getParameter("timezone"); %>
<mut:timeOfDay id="timeOfDay" timezone='<%= (zone == null) ? "EST" : zone %>"/>

<html>
<head>
<title>Standard and XML Representations</title>
</head>
<body>
<mut:ifProperty name="timeOfDay" property="daytime" action="include">
<p align="center">Good Day!</p>
</mut:ifProperty>
<mut:ifProperty name="timeOfDay" property="daytime" action="exclude">
<p align="center">Good Night!</p>
</mut:ifProperty>

</body>
</html>
```

Listing 20.2 Sample JSP page using the XML representation

```
<jsp:root version="1.2" xmlns:jsp="http://java.sun.com/JSP/Page"
          xmlns:mut="/mutlib">
<jsp:directive.page session="false"/>
<jsp:text><![CDATA[

]]>
</jsp:text>
<jsp:text><![CDATA[

]]>
</jsp:text>
<jsp:scriptlet><![CDATA[
 String zone = request.getParameter("timezone");
   if (zone == null) zone="EST"; ]]>
</jsp:scriptlet>
<jsp:text><![CDATA[

]]>
</jsp:text>
<mut:timeOfDay id="timeOfDay"
   timezone="%= (zone == null) ? &quot;EST&quot; : zone %"></mut:timeOfDay>
<jsp:text><![CDATA[

<html>
<head>
<title>Standard and XML Representations</title>
```

```
</head>
<body>

]]>
</jsp:text>
<mut:ifProperty name="timeOfDay" property="daytime" action="include">
<jsp:text><![CDATA[

<p align="center">Good Day!</p>
]]>
</jsp:text>
</mut:ifProperty>
<jsp:text><![CDATA[

]]>
</jsp:text>
<mut:ifProperty name="timeOfDay" property="daytime" action="exclude">
<jsp:text><![CDATA[

<p align="center">Good Night!</p>
]]>
</jsp:text>
</mut:ifProperty>
<jsp:text><![CDATA[

</body>
</html>
]]>
</jsp:text>
</jsp:root>
```

20.3 Tag library validation

As listing 20.2 suggests, the XML representation of a JSP page is considerably more verbose than the standard representation. At first glance, the XML representation also appears to be more complex, at least from the standpoint of readability. Assuming, of course, you are a human being.

If you happen to be a computer, however, the XML representation is much more readable. This is because XML documents are highly structured and therefore much easier to parse. For this reason, it is the XML representation of a JSP page that is exposed to tag library developers for the purpose of validating their libraries' custom tags.

Each custom tag library is permitted to specify a single tag library validator for validating pages that employ its custom tags. As described in chapter 18, when the JSP container needs to compile a JSP page that uses one or more custom tag libraries, it first checks the syntax of the page's custom tags against the corresponding entries in the libraries' TLDs. Then, for TLDs that specify tag library validators, each validator is called to examine the entire contents of the JSP page and perform whatever checks are appropriate. (The validators are called in the same order as the corresponding `taglib` directives or `xmlns` attributes appear in the page.) The contents of the JSP page are provided to the validator using the XML representation. This allows the validator to parse the page's contents, so that it may find and examine the tags it is intended to validate.

Tag library validators are created as subclasses of the `javax.servlet.jsp.tagext.TagLibraryValidator` class. A validator is associated with a custom tag library by specifying the name of its `TagLibraryValidator` subclass in the `<validator-class>` element of its TLD. When the JSP container is compiling a page using the library, an instance of this class is obtained—either by retrieving it from a resource pool or by constructing a new one—and provided with access to the page's contents in order to validate them.

This is accomplished by calling the validator instance's `validate()` method, which is expected to perform the validation of JSP pages. The default implementation of this method, provided by the `TagLibraryValidator` base class, does nothing. In order to validate a JSP page, then, library-specific subclasses must provide their own implementations of this method, whose signature is as follows:

```
public ValidationMethod[] validate (String uri, String prefix,
                                    javax.servlet.jsp.tagext.PageData page)
```

As its signature indicates, the JSP container passes three arguments to the `validate()` method when it is called to validate a JSP page. The first two arguments are character strings identifying the URI of the tag library's TLD and the prefix used by the library's custom tags within the page, respectively. The values of these two arguments thus correspond directly to the values of the `taglib` directive or `xmlns` attributes that caused the validator to be called in the first place.

The final parameter of the `validate()` method is an instance of the `javax.servlet.jsp.tagext.PageData` class. It is this instance that exposes the contents of the JSP page to the validator. This class supports just a single method, `getInputStream()`, that returns an instance of `java.io.InputStream` for reading the XML representation of the page. The `validate()` method can then pass this input stream to an XML parser for extracting and validating the relevant custom tags.

Based on these three inputs, then, the `validate()` method knows how the tag library is being referenced by the page, and has full access to the contents of the page. Using this information, it is able to determine whether or not the use of the tag library by the page is valid. It is the `ValidationMessage` array returned by this method that conveys this determination to the JSP container. If the validator finds no problems with the contents of the JSP page, it is expected to return either null or an empty array. If the page is found to be invalid, however, the `validate()` method should return a populated array of `ValidationMessage` objects whose properties explain why the page's use of the tag library is invalid. These messages are then displayed by the JSP container to assist the page author in correcting whatever problems were detected.

Since a given tag library may be used by multiple JSP pages managed by the same container, there are efficiency benefits to be gained by reusing `TagLibraryValidator` instances. To that end, JSP containers are allowed to store these instances in a resource pool, from which they may be removed for use and returned for reuse.

Recall from the description in chapter 18, the TLD provides an `<init-parameter>` element for passing initialization parameters to a tag library validator. Each time the container removes a `TagLibraryValidator` instance from its resource pool, it will call the instance's `setInitParameters()` method, passing it a `java.utils.Map` instance which maps the names of those initialization parameters to the values supplied for them in the tag library's TLD. This mapping can be retrieved by the validator instance within its `validate()` method by calling the `getInitParameters()` method. This initialization must take place each time the validator is removed from the resource pool, since the same validator class can be shared by multiple tag libraries. Once removed from the resource pool, the container can apply the validator instance to multiple JSP pages before returning it to the resource pool. For example, if one JSP page uses the `<jsp:include>` action to include another JSP page, both of which make use of the same custom tag library, the container can use the same `TagLibraryValidator` instance to validate both pages. Furthermore, the JSP container is permitted to apply this instance to both pages simultaneously, so thread safety is an important consideration for tag library validators.

When returning the `TagLibraryValidator` instance to its resource pool, the JSP container is required to call `release()`. This method is provided so that developers can ensure that any resources the instance might have created or obtained while performing its validation are deallocated. The default implementation provided by the `TagLibraryValidator` base class does nothing; it must be overridden if any validator-specific resource management is required.

The life cycle of a tag library validator thus has three major phases. First, an instance of the appropriate `TagLibraryValidator` subclass is created and added to the JSP container's resource pool. Next, whenever its services are required to validate one or more JSP pages, the instance is removed from the pool and its `setInitParameters()` method is called. For each page to be validated, its `validate()` method is called. Once the validation sequence is complete, the validator's `release()` method is called, and the instance is returned to the resource pool. In the final phase of its life cycle, when the instance is no longer needed (perhaps because the container has no JSP pages that haven't been validated and compiled), it is removed from the resource pool and made available for garbage collection.

20.4 Example validators

To illustrate the use of these methods in implementing tag library validators, we will present three examples. The first, which is more of a debugging aid than an actual validator, uses the input stream exposed by the `PageData` object to make a copy of the XML representation of a JSP page for subsequent review. (When validating a JSP page using the standard representation, the XML view into which it is translated for validating and compiling is only temporary. The JSP container is free to discard it after generating the servlet code for the page.) The other examples, however, are true validators.

Two major types of XML parsers are currently in wide use, known by the acronyms SAX and DOM. SAX parsers use an event-based model, in which the parser sends events to an associated event handler by invoking callback routines as it encounters constructs within the page being parsed. DOM parsers have a more structural focus. As a DOM parser traverses an XML document, it constructs a tree of objects that models the document's contents and structure, using different classes of objects for the various categories of data (e.g., elements, attributes, body content) it encounters. DOM parsers are therefore very useful for examining the structure of XML documents and the relationships among their elements. Because the output of a DOM parser is a large tree structure representing the entire contents of the parsed document, however, use of this approach tends to be rather memory-intensive. SAX parsers, on the other hand, process a document's contents one element at a time. As a result, they can be used very efficiently for searching through XML documents without incurring significant overhead with respect to memory utilization. Their disadvantage is that, due to their event-driven nature, they are not as well-suited to global analysis of a document's contents.

The second example validator to be presented here demonstrates the use of a SAX parser, while the third employs a DOM parser. In both cases, JAXP version 1.1 is used to create, configure, and run the selected parser. JAXP is a set of generalized APIs for interacting with XML parsers that provides a set of standard abstractions for accessing parser functionality. JAXP provides hooks for plugging in third-party XML parsers and using them via the JAXP interfaces; many Java-based XML parsers available now include JAXP integration.

Other approaches to parsing XML documents for tag library validation are also possible. Those based on document schemas—such as XML Schema, Relax NG, and Schematron—hold particular promise for JSP validation because they enable the validation requirements to be specified declaratively via a schema specification, rather than via Java code. Since schema languages are design for expressing relationships and dependencies, validation requirements expressed in this manner should be much easier to create and maintain. In any event, the increasing popularity of XML for data representation ensures that we haven't heard the last word on XML parsing and validation; any new technologies developed for these purposes should be readily adaptable to JSP tag library validation.

20.4.1 Copying validator

As previously suggested, this first example tag library validator doesn't perform any validation. Instead, it simply takes advantage of the functionality provided by the validation API to make a copy of the XML representation of any JSP page to which it is applied.

As is the case for all tag library validators, the class implementing this validator is a subclass of `javax.servlet.jsp.tagext.TagLibraryValidator`:

```
public class CopyingTLV extends TagLibraryValidator {
  static private String DEST_FILE = "/tmp/ParsedPage.xml";
  ...
}
```

To simplify the implementation, the class defines a single static variable, `DEST_FILE`, which indicates where the XML representation should be stored.

As is the case for all tag library validators, `CopyingTLV` obtains access to the XML representation by means of its `validate()` method, defined as follows:

```
public ValidationMessage[] validate (String prefix, String uri, PageData page) {
  InputStream in = null;
  try {
     in = page.getInputStream();
     copyToFile(in, DEST_FILE);
  }
  catch (IOException e) {
    return new ValidateionMessage[1] {
      new ValidationMessage(null, e.getMessage() );
  }
  finally {
    if (in != null) try { in.close(); } catch (IOException e) {}
  }
  return null;
}
```

It is the third parameter, the `PageData` instance named `page`, that ultimately provides the access. This instance's `getInputStream()` method is called to obtain an input stream for reading the XML representation, which is then copied to the file name specified by the `DEST_FILE` static variable by means of the `copyToFile()` utility method.

As noted previously, a tag library validator indicates the success or failure of a page validation via the return value of its `validate()` method. In this case, validation only fails if some problem occurs while obtaining or copying the input stream, in the form of a `java.io.IOException` being thrown. Since the `validate()` method cannot itself throw an exception, it catches any exceptions raised within the method body, and uses the error message associated with that exception to construct its return value. Recall that a non-null return value indicates that validation has failed, and should be an array of `ValidationMessage` objects explaining why. The error message from the `IOException` is thus a fine source for this explanation. Only if all other operations succeed does the method return null, indicating successful validation of the JSP page.

If an `IOException` is raised, then the code in the `catch` block will be called upon to handle it. This block constructs a `ValidationMessage` array of length one, and populates it with a single new instance of the `ValidationMessage` class. The constructor for this message takes two arguments, an ID string and a message describing the validation error. The message argument is obtained from the `IOException` object. The ID string argument is an indication of which custom tag was responsible for the validation error, and will be described in detail later in the chapter. Since there is no individual custom tag being checked by this validator, a null value is supplied as the first argument to the constructor.

The code defining the `copyToFile()` utility method is a straightforward application of Java's built-in I/O classes:

```
private void copyToFile (InputStream stream, String filename)
  throws IOException {
  PrintWriter out = null;
  BufferedReader in = null;
  try {
    out = new PrintWriter(new FileWriter(filename));
    in = new BufferedReader(new InputStreamReader(stream));
    String line;
    while ((line = in.readLine()) != null) {
      out.println(line);
    }
  }
  finally {
    if (out != null) out.close();
```

```
    if (in != null) in.close();
  }
}
```

A `java.io.FileWriter` provides access to the named file, and is wrapped inside a `java.io.PrintWriter` in order to take advantage of the latter class's `println()` method. A `java.io.InputStreamReader` is wrapped around the input stream originally passed to the method, which is itself wrapped inside a `java.io.BufferedReader`. The `BufferedReader` class provides a `readLine()` method which is used to iterate through the input stream line-by-line, so that its contents may be written via the `println()` method. The `readLine()` method returns `null` once all available input is exhausted, providing a convenient termination condition for this iteration. A `try/finally` block is employed to make sure that all I/O streams are closed when the method is finished. It doesn't catch any exceptions, however. If an exception is raised in this utility method, it needs to be passed back up to the `validate()` method for further processing.

The full source code for the `CopyingTLV` validator is presented (in abbreviated form) in listing 20.3. With respect to seeing this validator in action, it turns out that we already have. The XML representation appearing in listing 20.2 was generated by applying the `CopyingTLV` validator to the (standard representation) JSP page presented in listing 20.1. The TLD entry for enabling this validator within a custom tag library is as follows:

```
<taglib>
  ...
  <validator>
    <validator-class>com.taglib.wdjsp.mut.CopyingTLV</validator-class>
    <description>
      Makes a copy of the most recently validated XML representation.
    </description>
  </validator>
  ...
</taglib>
```

Listing 20.3 The CopyingTLV tag library validator

```
package com.taglib.wdjsp.mut;

import javax.servlet.jsp.tagext.TagLibraryValidator;
import javax.servlet.jsp.tagext.ValidationMessage;
import javax.servlet.jsp.tagext.PageData;
import java.io.InputStream;
import java.io.FileWriter;
import java.io.PrintWriter;
import java.io.InputStreamReader;
```

```
import java.io.BufferedReader;

import java.io.IOException;

public class CopyingTLV extends TagLibraryValidator {
  static private String DEST_FILE = "/tmp/ParsedPage.xml";

  public ValidationMessage[] validate (String prefix, String uri, PageData
   page) {

    ...

  }
  private void copyToFile (InputStream stream, String filename)
      throws IOException {
    ...
  }
}
```

20.4.2 Script-prohibiting validator

In previous chapters, we have cautioned against excessive use of scripting elements within an application's JSP pages. While in practice it is very difficult to avoid them completely (particularly the use of expressions for specifying request-time attribute values), those wishing to take this advice to heart may find it encouraging to discover that the tag library validation API may be used to enforce restrictions on the use of JSP scripting elements.

This is the task of our next tag library validator, implemented via the `ScriptFreeTLV` class. Like the `CopyingTLV`, this validator does not, strictly speaking, validate a custom tag library. Because a tag library validator has complete access to the full XML representation of a page, however, it can be used to impose constraints on the built-in JSP tags, as well. The `ScriptFreeTLV` validator uses exactly this approach to ensure that a JSP page is free of `<jsp:declaration>`, `<jsp:scriptlet>`, and `<jsp:expression>` tags.

A SAX parser is employed to detect these tags. When applying a SAX parser to an XML document, it is necessary to provide a content handler (i.e., an instance of the `org.xml.sax.ContentHandler` interface) to receive the parsing events as the document is traversed. For the `ScriptFreeTLV` validator, the content handler will be implemented as an inner class named `MyContentHandler`. Each time the SAX parser detects a new element, it notifies the handler by calling one of its methods. If the detected element corresponds to one of the three JSP scripting elements, a tag-specific counter is incremented within the handler. After the parsing of the document is complete, if any of these counters is greater than zero, the validator reports the prohibited usage as an error.

Initialization parameters

To make this validator more flexible, it will support four initialization parameters, for individually controlling which of the four types of scripting elements are to be restricted. The TLD entry for specifying and configuring this validator would therefore take the following form:

```
<taglib>
  ...
  <validator>
    <validator-class>com.taglib.wdjsp.mut.ScriptFreeTLV</validator-class>
    <init-param>
      <param-name>allowDeclarations</param-name>
      <param-value>false</param-value>
     <description>Permit JSP declarations if true (default is false).</descrip-
  tion>
    </init-param>
    <init-param>
      <param-name>allowScriptlets</param-name>
      <param-value>false</param-value>
    <description>Permit JSP scriptlets if true (default is false).</description>
    </init-param>
    <init-param>
      <param-name>allowExpressions</param-name>
      <param-value>true</param-value>
      <description>Permit JSP expressions if true (default is false).</descrip-
  tion>
    </init-param>
    <init-param>
      <param-name>allowRTExpressions</param-name>
      <param-value>true</param-value>
      <description>
        Permit JSP expressions as request-time attributes if true
           (default is false).
      </description>
    </init-param>
<description>
      Enforces prohibitions against JSP scripting elements.
    </description>
  </validator>
  ...
</taglib>
```

As indicated by this TLD fragment, this validator has four initialization parameters, `allowDeclarations`, `allowScriptlets`, `allowExpressions`, and `allowRTExpressions`, for controlling which scripting elements are allowed, and which are forbidden.

These initialization parameters are modeled as instance variables of the class implementing the validator, as follows:

```
public class ScriptFreeTLV extends TagLibraryValidator {
  private boolean allowDeclarations = false;
  private boolean allowScriptlets = false;
  private boolean allowExpressions = false;
  private boolean allowRTExpressions = false;
  ...
}
```

These four boolean instance variables are set by overloading the `setInitParameters()` method, inherited from the `TagLibraryValidator` base class:

```
public void setInitParameters (Map initParms) {
  super.setInitParameters(initParms);
  String declarationsParm = (String) initParms.get("allowDeclarations");
  String scriptletsParm = (String) initParms.get("allowScriptlets");
  String expressionsParm = (String) initParms.get("allowExpressions");
  String rtExpressionsParm = (String) initParms.get("allowRTExpressions");

  allowDeclarations = "true".equalsIgnoreCase(declarationsParm);
  allowScriptlets = "true".equalsIgnoreCase(scriptletsParm);
  allowExpressions = "true".equalsIgnoreCase(expressionsParm);
  allowRTExpressions = "true".equalsIgnoreCase(rtExpressionsParm);
}
```

The first action taken by this method is to make sure that the superclass's `setInitParameters()` method is called, so that it can take care of any bookkeeping the superclass needs to do. Next, each of the four initialization parameters is retrieved from the `Map` (an abstraction of a hash table, introduced as part of Java 2's Collections API), using the names specified in the TLD entry. The values specified in the TLD take the form of text strings, so a series of string comparisons is performed to set the instance variables. Note that `Map`'s `get()` method will return `null` if there is no entry for the corresponding initialization parameter in the TLD. This is the reason behind the somewhat awkward practice of calling the `equalsIgnoreCase()` method on the `String` literal (i.e., `"true"`) and providing the retrieved value as that method's parameter. Doing so enables us to avoid the potential `NullPointerException` that might occur if the method were instead called on the (possibly `null`) retrieved value with the `String` literal as its argument.

Parsing

The initialization parameters provide added flexibility for potential users of this tag library validator. The primary functionality of the validator, however, is the parsing of JSP pages to detect specific tags. For the `ScriptFreeTLV` validator, this is accomplished by means of a SAX parser.

JAXP relies on factory objects to construct SAX parsers. In addition to its instance variables for supporting the initialization parameters, the validator needs an instance variable for its parser factory:

```
public class ScriptFreeTLV extends TagLibraryValidator {
  ...
  private SAXParserFactory factory;

  public ScriptFreeTLV () {
    factory = SAXParserFactory.newInstance();
    factory.setValidating(false);
    factory.setNamespaceAware(true);
  }
  ...
}
```

The factory is an instance of the `javax.xml.parsers.SAXParserFactory` class, and a constructor method is provided to create and configure this instance. The factory class provides a static `newInstance()` method for constructing factory instances, and the `setValidating()` and `setNamespaceAware()` methods tell the factory what types of parsers it should create. In this case, since there is typically no DTD associated with the XML representation of a JSP page, the factory is configured to produce nonvalidating parsers. Because JSP actions rely on XML namespaces, however, it is important that any parsers applied to a JSP page are compatible with and fully aware of XML namespace conventions.

Creating and applying a parser is the job of the `validate()` method, defined as follows:

```
public ValidationMessage[] validate (String prefix, String uri, PageData page)
  {
  ArrayList msgs = new ArrayList();
  InputStream in = null;
  SAXParser parser;
  MyContentHandler handler = new MyContentHandler(msgs);
  try {
    synchronized (factory) {
      parser = factory.newSAXParser();
    }
    in = page.getInputStream();
    parser.parse(in, handler);
  }
  catch (ParserConfigurationException e) {
    addMessage(msgs, null, e.getMessage());
  }
```

```
    catch (SAXException e) {
      addMessage(msgs, null, e.getMessage());
    }
    catch (IOException e) {
      addMessage(msgs, null, e.getMessage());
    }
    finally {
      if (in != null) try { in.close(); } catch (IOException e) {}
    }
    String results = handler.reportResults();
    if (results != null) addMessage(msgs, null, results, 0);
    return (ValidationMessage[]) msgs.toArray(new ValidationMessage[0]);
}
```

The first task here is to construct an `ArrayList` for storing validation messages, and to use it to instantiate a content handler. As previously mentioned, `ScriptFreeTLV` defines an inner class named `MyContentHandler` which fills this role. Next, the validator's parser factory is used to construct a parser, which will be an instance of JAXP's `javax.xml.parsers.SAXParser` class. Note that the construction of a parser by the parser factory is not guaranteed to be thread-safe, so a `synchronized` block has been introduced to protect this operation.

Next, an input stream is obtained from the method's `page` parameter, for accessing the XML representation of the page being validated. The input stream and the content handler are passed as arguments to the `SAXParser` instance's `parse()` method to simultaneously parse and validate the page. These steps have the possibility of throwing a variety of exceptions, as indicated in the `validate()` method body. As was the case for `CopyingTLV`, all exceptions are caught and their error messages are used to construct `ValidationMessage` instances indicating that validation was unsuccessful. A `finally` clause is provided to make sure the input stream for the XML representation is always closed.

The last step of `validate()` is to call on the content handler to report its results. If any prohibited scripting elements were found on the page, the content handler's `reportResults()` method is expected to return a `String` value summarizing such violations. If not, it should return `null`, indicating that validation was successful.

20.4.3 Error handling

A non-null result from the `reportResults()` method is treated similarly to the error messages associated with any caught exceptions: a corresponding `ValidationMessage` instance is created and added to a collection of such messages being maintained by the validator. A utility method, `addMessage()`, is employed to manage this collection, and is defined as follows:

```
private void addMessage (ArrayList messages,
                         String jspId, String msg, int index) {
    ValidationMessage vMessage = new ValidationMessage(jspId, msg);
    if (index < 0) {
      messages.add(vMessage);
    } else {
      messages.add(index, vMessage);
    }
  }
```

The first argument is the list of messages being maintained, while its second argument is the ID string mentioned previously. The third argument represents the message, and is combined with the second argument to construct the `ValidationMessage` instance.

The fourth and final argument indicates where in the list of messages this new instance should be inserted. As the method body indicates, if this index value is negative, the message will be added to the end of the list. Otherwise, it will be inserted at the specified location. This fourth argument is taken advantage of in the final call to `addMessage()` by the `validate()` message, in order to ensure that the final results from the content handler will be inserted at the beginning of the array of validation messages.

As a convenience to the developer, a second version of this method is provided which has no explicit index argument:

```
  private void addMessage (ArrayList messages, String jspId, String msg) {
    addMessage(messages, jspId, msg, -1);
  }
```

This version simply calls the original method, supplying –1 as the index. The net effect is that, if no index value is supplied, the default behavior is to append the new message to the end of the list.

Within the body of the `validate()` method in the example, only null values are provided for the ID string argument, `jspId`, of the `addMessage()` method. As indicated earlier, this argument is provided to allow the tag library developer to tie the error message to a specific tag within the page. This allows the JSP container to map the error to a specific location with the original JSP page, and thereby provide more meaningful feedback to the page author.

Where does this ID string come from? Since it is the JSP container that must map the IDs to file locations, it only makes sense that they be provided by the container in the first place. In fact, before the container passes the XML representation of the page to the validator via the `PageData` argument of its `validate()` method, it adds these ID strings as attributes to each JSP tag present on the page. As indicated in llisting 20.4, this attribute is named `jsp:id`, and a unique value for that attribute is added to every built-in or custom JSP tag included in the XML representation. As the validator processes the page looking for errors, it can extract the value of this attribute from any tag found to have problems. This value may then be passed to the `ValidationMessage` constructor to map the validation error back to that specific tag.

NOTE Support for incorporating `jsp:id` attributes into the XML representation of JSP pages provided for validation is an optional element of the JSP 1.2 specification. As such, `validate()` methods must be carefully written in order to work properly whether or not these attributes are present. As demonstrated earlier in the chapter, a null value can be provided to the `ValidationMessage` constructor to indicate the absence of an ID string. A JSP container that supports `jsp:id` attributes will produce results such as those in listing 20.4 when preparing the XML representation of the JSP page in listing 20.1. A JSP container that does not support `jsp:id` attributes will produce results similar to those in listing 20.2.

Listing 20.4 JSP page using the XML representation, including jsp:id attributes

```
<jsp:root version="1.2" xmlns:jsp="http://java.sun.com/JSP/Page"
          xmlns:mut="/mutlib" jsp:id="10001">
<jsp:directive.page session="false" jsp:id="10002"/>
<jsp:text jsp:id="10003"><![CDATA[

]]>
</jsp:text>
<jsp:text jsp:id="10004"><![CDATA[

]]>
</jsp:text>
<jsp:scriptlet jsp:id="10005"><![CDATA[
 String zone = request.getParameter("timezone");
   if (zone == null) zone="EST"; ]]>
</jsp:scriptlet>
<jsp:text jsp:id="10006"><![CDATA[

]]>
</jsp:text>
<mut:timeOfDay id="timeOfDay"
   timezone="%= (zone == null) ? &quot;EST&quot; : zone %"
   jsp:id="10007"></mut:timeOfDay>
<jsp:text jsp:id="10008"><![CDATA[

<html>
<head>
<title>Standard and XML Representations</title>
```

```
</head>
<body>

]]>
</jsp:text>
<mut:ifProperty name="timeOfDay" property="daytime" action="include"
   jsp:id="10009">
<jsp:text jsp:id="10010"><![CDATA[

<p align="center">Good Day!</p>
]]>
</jsp:text>
</mut:ifProperty>
<jsp:text jsp:id="10011"><![CDATA[

]]>
</jsp:text>
<mut:ifProperty name="timeOfDay" property="daytime" action="exclude"
   jsp:id="10012">
<jsp:text jsp:id="10013"><![CDATA[

<p align="center">Good Night!</p>
]]>
</jsp:text>
</mut:ifProperty>
<jsp:text jsp:id="10014"><![CDATA[

</body>
</html>
]]>
</jsp:text>
</jsp:root>
```

20.4.4 Content handler

It is the content handler, then, that plays the pivotal role in performing the actual validation. It receives the events from the SAX parser that are used to detect any scripting elements present on the page, and the return value from its `reportResults()` method makes the final determination as to whether or not the page is valid.

By implementing the content handler as an inner class of `ScriptFreeTLV`, it automatically has access to all of the validator object's instance variables. In particular, it has access to the instance variables representing the validator's initialization parameters. In addition, it defines five of its own instance variables:

```
public class ScriptFreeTLV extends TagLibraryValidator {
  ...
  private class MyContentHandler extends DefaultHandler {
    private int declarationCount = 0;
    private int scriptletCount = 0;
```

```
    private int expressionCount = 0;
    private int rtExpressionCount = 0;
    private ArrayList messages;

    MyContentHandler (ArrayList messages) { this.messages = messages; }

    ...
  }
}
```

As their names suggest, the first four of these instance variables are used to keep track of how many declarations, scriptlets, and expressions have been found in the page being validated. The fifth provides a reference to the `ArrayList` local variable created by the validator for keeping track of validation messages. It is passed to the content handler as the sole parameter of its constructor.

The values for the four counters are obtained by parsing the page. Note that the `MyContentHandler` inner class is a subclass of the `org.xml.sax.helpers.DefaultHandler` class. This class provides default implementations of all of the callback methods needed to handle SAX events. To be precise, this class provides default implementations that ignore all SAX events.

This is actually a good thing, because it makes it easy to create subclasses that are interested in only a subset of those events. The subclass need only provide handlers for the events it is interested in, and can rely on the inherited methods to ignore the rest. For `ScriptFreeTLV`'s content handler, in fact, only one event handler method is required. Since the validator is only interested in keeping track of the occurrence of particular elements and their attributes, this is readily accomplished by overriding the `startElement()` event handler method:

```
public void startElement (String namespaceUri, String localName,
                          String qualifiedName, Attributes atts) {
  if ((! allowDeclarations) && qualifiedName.equals("jsp:declaration")) {
    ++declarationCount;
    addMessage(messages, getJspId(atts), "Declaration found.");
  } else if ((! allowScriptlets) && qualifiedName.equals("jsp:scriptlet")) {
    ++scriptletCount;
    addMessage(messages, getJspId(atts), "Scriptlet found.");
  } else if ((! allowExpressions) && qualifiedName.equals("jsp:expression")) {
    ++expressionCount;
    addMessage(messages, getJspId(atts), "Expression found.");
  }
  if (! allowRTexpressions) countRTExpressions(atts);
}
```

This content handler method will be called whenever the SAX parser detects the start of an XML element. The method's first parameter indicates the URI for the element's namespace (if any), while the second argument holds the element's name, absent any namespace prefix. The method's third and fourth parameters, however, contain the name of the element (with its namespace prefix) and a representation of its attributes, and are therefore of most use to the purpose at hand.

For each type of scripting element, then, `startElement()` first checks the appropriate initialization parameter to see whether or not its presence has been allowed. If so, the method then checks the element's prefixed name, as represented by the `qualifiedName` parameter, against the corresponding scripting element's name. If there's a match, the associated counter is incremented. This check is performed against the XML names of all three JSP scripting elements, `jsp:declaration`, `jsp:scriptlet`, and `jsp:expression`. After the page has been fully parsed, then, the final values of the counters for these three elements should accurately reflect the number of scripting elements present on the page.

NOTE Although `ScriptFreeTLV` has been written to completely restrict the use of specific built-in tags, the underlying approach is applicable to custom tag libraries. It would not be very difficult, for example, to use the `ScriptFreeTLV` code as the foundation for a new tag library validator that enforces a uniqueness constraint on one or more custom tags. Such a validator would apply the same basic algorithm as `ScriptFreeTLV`: instantiate a SAX parser, pass it a content handler that counts the number of occurrences of the relevant tags, then report any violations based on those tags counts. For `ScriptFreeTLV`, tag counts greater than zero are invalid. For tags that must be unique, a count greater than one would signal a problem.

In order to detect expressions used as request-time attribute values, the content handler must check the attributes of all XML elements. (This turns out to be considerably more efficient than trying to figure out in advance which elements have attributes that support request-time attributes and only checking those. It also has an important side benefit of making the code considerably more understandable.) This is accomplished by means of the `countRTexpressions()` method:

```
public void countRTExpressions (Attributes atts) {
  int stop = atts.getLength();
  for (int i = 0; i < stop; ++i) {
    String attval = atts.getValue(i);
    if (attval.startsWith("%=") && attval.endsWith("%")) {
      ++rtExpressionCount;
      addMessage(messages, getJspId(atts),
                 "Request-time attribute value expression found.");
    }
```

```
  }
}
```

This method is passed an instance of the `org.xml.sax.Attributes` class, which is a data structure representing the full set of attributes associated with an XML element. Its `getLength()` method is used to determine the total number of attributes for the element, allowing `countRTExpressions()` to iterate through them all (via the `getValue()` method of `Attributes`) looking for request-time attribute values. These are recognized by their `%=` and `%` delimiters, as described earlier in the chapter, causing the corresponding counter to be incremented and an appropriate validation message to be constructed.

Note that both `startElement()` and `countRTExpressions()` take advantage of a utility method named `getJspId()`. This method is used to obtain the value of the `jsp:id` attribute (if any), as discussed in the preceding section. The `getJspId()` method is defined as follows:

```
private String getJspId (Attributes atts) {
  return atts.getValue("jsp:id");
}
```

This method uses an alternate form of the `Attributes` class's `getValue()` method, which retrieves the value of an attribute specified by its name, rather than by its index. In this case, we are specifically interested in the value of the attribute named `jsp:id`. If no such attribute is found, the method returns `null`.

The final method defined by `MyContentHandler` is `reportResults()`. This method examines the content handler's four counters to determine whether or not it should construct a `String` value indicating why the page is invalid, and is defined as follows:

```
public String reportResults () {
  if (declarationCount + scriptletCount + expressionCount
      + rtExpressionCount > 0) {
    StringBuffer results = new StringBuffer("JSP page contains ");
    boolean first = true;
    if (declarationCount > 0) {
      results.append(Integer.toString(declarationCount));
      results.append(" declaration");
      if (declarationCount > 1) results.append('s');
      first = false;
    }
    if (scriptletCount > 0) {
      if (! first) results.append(", ");
      results.append(Integer.toString(scriptletCount));
      results.append(" scriptlet");
      if (scriptletCount > 1) results.append('s');
      first = false;
    }
```

```
      if (expressionCount > 0) {
        if (! first) results.append(", ");
        results.append(Integer.toString(expressionCount));
        results.append(" expression");
        if (expressionCount > 1) results.append('s');
        first = false;
      }
      if (rtExpressionCount > 0) {
        if (! first) results.append(", ");
        results.append(Integer.toString(rtExpressionCount));
        results.append(" request-time attribute value");
        if (expressionCount > 1) results.append('s');
      }
      results.append(".");
      return results.toString();
    } else {
      return null;
    }
}
```

The basic intent of this method is simple. If there is at least one prohibited scripting element (as determined by checking whether the sum of the counters exceeds zero), construct a `String` and return it. Otherwise, return `null`, indicating that the page is compliant.

Considerable complexity is introduced, however, by trying to craft a nicely worded, well-punctuated error message when validation fails. Unraveling the details is left as an exercise for the reader, but it is perhaps worth mentioning explicitly that efficiency is the motivation for introducing an instance of the`java.util.StringBuffer` class. Concatenation of `String` instances is a rather expensive operation in Java, which `StringBuffer`'s various `append()` methods allow us to avoid.

The full source code for `ScriptFreeTLV` and its `MyContentHandler` inner class is presented (in abbreviated form) in listing 20.5.

Listing 20.5 The ScriptFreeTLV tag library validator

```
package com.taglib.wdjsp.mut;

import javax.servlet.jsp.tagext.TagLibraryValidator;
import javax.servlet.jsp.tagext.ValidationMessage;
import javax.servlet.jsp.tagext.PageData;
import javax.xml.parsers.SAXParserFactory;
import javax.xml.parsers.SAXParser;
import org.xml.sax.Attributes;
import org.xml.sax.helpers.DefaultHandler;
import java.io.InputStream;
import java.util.Map;
import java.util.ArrayList;
```

```
import java.io.IOException;
import org.xml.sax.SAXException;
import javax.xml.parsers.ParserConfigurationException;

public class ScriptFreeTLV extends TagLibraryValidator {
  private boolean allowDeclarations = false;
  private boolean allowScriptlets = false;
  private boolean allowExpressions = false;
  private boolean allowRTExpressions = false;
  private SAXParserFactory factory;

  public ScriptFreeTLV () { ... }
  public void setInitParameters (Map initParms) { ... }
  public ValidationMessage[] validate (String prefix, String uri, PageData page)
   {
     ...
  }
  private void addMessage (ArrayList messages, String jspId, String msg, int
   index) {
     ...
  }
  private void addMessage (ArrayList messages, String jspId, String msg) { ... }

  private class MyContentHandler extends DefaultHandler {
    private int declarationCount = 0;
    private int scriptletCount = 0;
    private int expressionCount = 0;
    private int rtExpressionCount = 0;

    public void startElement (String uri, String localName,
                              String qualifiedName, Attributes atts) {
      ...
    }
    public void countRTExpressions (Attributes atts) { ... }
    private String getJspId (Attributes atts) { ... }
    public String reportResults () { ... }
}
```

Sample application

Before we can see this validator in action, we first need a JSP page that includes one or more scripting elements. Such a page, based on an example from chapter 5, is presented in listing 20.6. A manual count indicates that this JSP page includes one declaration, four scriptlets, and two expressions.

Listing 20.6 The ScriptFreeTLV tag library validator example page

```
<html>
<body>

<h1>Scriptful Page</h1>

<% String xParm = request.getParameter("x");
   long x = 0;
   try { x = Long.parseLong(xParm); }
   catch (NumberFormatException e) {}

   if (x < 0) { %>
        <p>Sorry, can't compute the factorial of a negative number.</p>
<% } else if (x > 20) { %>
        <p>Sorry, arguments greater than 20 cause an overflow error.</p>
<% } else { %>
        <p align=center><%= x %>! = <%= fact(x) %></p>
<% } %>

<%! private long fact (long x) {
        if (x == 0) return 1;
        else return x * fact(x-1);
} %>

</body>
</html>
```

If this page were permitted to run as is, it would produce output such as that depicted in figure 20.2. If the `ScriptFreeTLV` validator were applied to this page, however, a different result would be obtained. If the TLD entry presented earlier in the chapter were in effect, with initialization parameters set to prohibit declarations and scriptlets but allow expressions and request-time attribute values, attempting to view this page in a browser would instead yield an error message, similar to the one in figure 20.3. Note that, as a result of the initialization parameter settings, the error message flags the declaration and scriptlets as violations, but has ignored the two expressions. Also note that by taking advantage of the `jsp:id` attributes, the error message generated by the JSP container is able to reference the line numbers corresponding to the occurrences of the prohibited scripting elements in the original JSP page.

20.4.5 Nesting validator

The third and final example validator, `NestingTLV`, enables a custom tag library to detect tags that are improperly nested. The mut library's `<mut:index>` tag, for example, is only valid within the body of a `<mut:forProperty>` tag. The `NestingTLV`

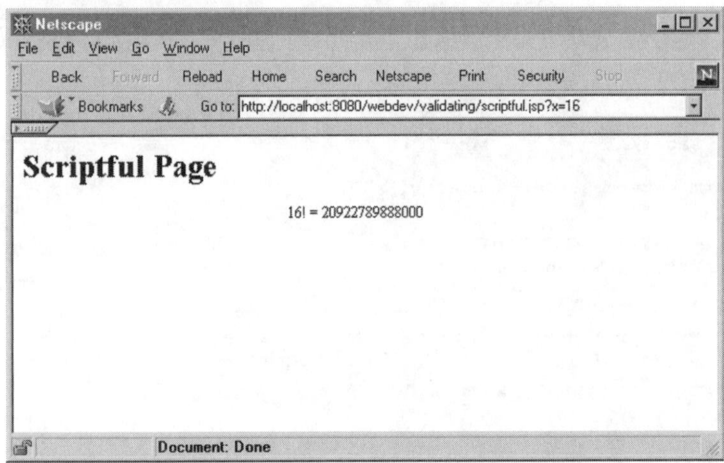

Figure 20.2 Normal output of the ScriptFreeTLV example page

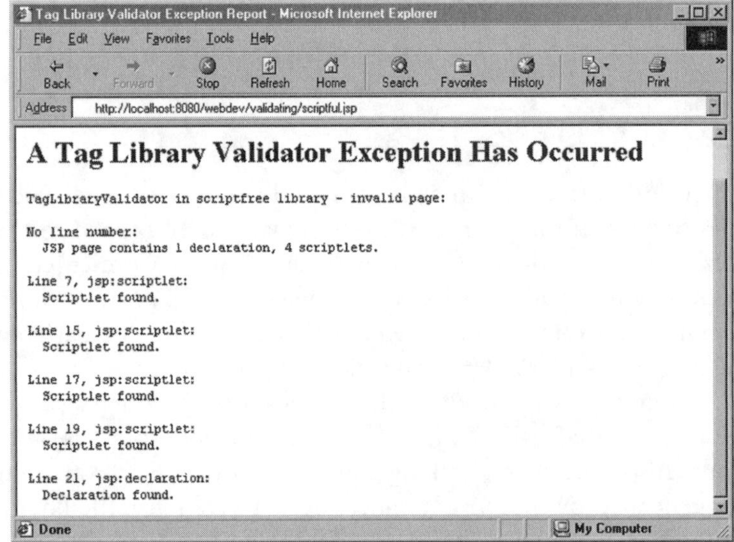

Figure 20.3 Output of the page compiler after validating the ScriptFreeTLV example page

validator provides a mechanism for enforcing relationships such as this during page compilation, by flagging tags that are not properly nested as invalid.

Since the nesting of tags is a property of the overall page structure, the use of a DOM parser to construct an object model of the page elements is preferable to SAX's event-driven approach. For this reason, `NestingTLV` relies on a DOM parser to extract the contents of a page's XML representation, and then examines the resulting object model for tags that are not properly nested.

Initialization parameters

For added flexibility, initialization parameters are provided for specifying the names of the two tags for which nesting is to be enforced. The TLD `<validator>` element for enforcing the mut library's nesting requirement is as follows:

```
<validator>
  <validator-class>com.taglib.wdjsp.mut.NestingTLV</validator-class>
  <init-param>
    <param-name>inner</param-name>
    <param-value>index</param-value>
    <description>Name of the inner tag.</description>
  </init-param>
  <init-param>
    <param-name>outer</param-name>
    <param-value>forProperty</param-value>
    <description>Name of the outer tag.</description>
  </init-param>
  <description>Validates tag nesting requirements.</description>
</validator>
```

The first initialization parameter, `inner`, names the inner tag in the nesting relationship. The inner tag may only appear within the body content of the relationship's outer tag, specified via the second initialization parameter, `outer`.

As was the case for the `ScriptFreeTLV` validator, instance variables are provided for storing the values of the initialization parameters, set via the class's `setInitParameters()` method.

```
public class NestingTLV extends TagLibraryValidator {
  private String inner, outer;

  public void setInitParameters (Map initParms) {
    super.setInitParameters(initParms);
    inner = (String) initParms.get("inner");
    outer = (String) initParms.get("outer");
  }
  ...
}
```

Note, however, that—as indicated in the example TLD—these instance variables store only the base names of the inner and outer tags, without any prefix. This is because the prefix with which a library's tags are used within a JSP page is set by the page itself. The prefix therefore cannot be specified in the TLD, and must be obtained by alternate means.

Parsing

As with SAX parsers, JAXP relies on factory objects to construct DOM parsers. `NestingTLV` therefore includes an instance variable named `factory` for storing its parser factory. The class's constructor is used to instantiate and configure this factory:

```
public class NestingTLV extends TagLibraryValidator {
  ...
  private DocumentBuilderFactory factory;

  public NestingTLV () {
    factory = DocumentBuilderFactory.newInstance();
    factory.setValidating(false);
    factory.setNamespaceAware(true);
  }
  ...
}
```

Once again, the factory—here, an instance of `javax.xml.parsers.DocumentBuilderFactory`—is configured to create parsers that do not validate against a DTD, but do support XML namespaces.

It is in `NestingTLV`'s `validate()` method that the actual parsing of JSP pages takes place. This method first makes sure that both of the validator's initialization parameters have been set, and then constructs a DOM parser to parse the XML representation of a page:

```
public ValidationMessage[] validate (String prefix, String uri, PageData page)
  {
  ArrayList messages = new ArrayList();
  if (inner == null)
    messages.add(new ValidationMessage(null, "No inner tag specified."));
  if (outer == null)
    messages.add(new ValidationMessage(null, "No outer tag specified."));
  if (! messages.isEmpty())
    return (ValidationMessage[]) messages.toArray(new ValidationMessage[0]);
  InputStream in = null;
  DocumentBuilder builder;
  try {
    synchronized (factory) {
      builder = factory.newDocumentBuilder();
    }
    in = page.getInputStream();
    Document doc = builder.parse(in);
    validateDocument(messages, doc, prefix + ":" + inner, prefix + ":" + outer);
  }
  catch (ParserConfigurationException e) {
    messages.add(new ValidationMessage(null, e.getMessage()));
  }
```

```
  catch (SAXException e) {
    messages.add(new ValidationMessage(null,e.getMessage()));
  }
  catch (IOException e) {
    messages.add(new ValidationMessage(null,e.getMessage()));
  }
  finally {
     if (in != null) try { in.close(); } catch (IOException e) {}
  }
  return (ValidationMessage[]) messages.toArray(new ValidationMessage[0]);
}
```

If either of the initialization parameters has not been set, a `ValidationMessage` is created indicating that validation failed. Otherwise, a new DOM parser in the form of a `javax.xml.parsers.DocumentBuilder` is created by calling the factory's `newDocumentBuilder()` method. Next, an input stream for reading the current page's XML representation is obtained from the `PageData` instance passed in as the method's third parameter. This input stream is then used to parse the XML representation, by supplying it as the argument to the `DocumentBuilder` instance's `parse()` method.

Unlike the SAX parser, no auxiliary content handler is required by the DOM parser. Instead of signaling events based on the contents of the parsed document, the DOM parser returns an object representing the complete contents of the page, in the form of a `org.w3c.dom.Document` instance. It is only after the document has been fully parsed that the page is validated by calling `NestingTLV`'s `validateDocument()` method, passing the `Document` object in as this method's second argument. Note that this method takes the qualified name of the inner and outer tags as its third and fourth parameters, respectively. Since the values of the `inner` and `outer` initialization parameters do not include the namespace prefix for the tag library, the prefix name supplied by the JSP container as the second argument to the `validate()` method is prepended to the values of the initialization parameters, along with a colon (the delimiter character for XML namespaces). Keep in mind that each custom tag library used by a JSP page, if it specifies a validator class, will independently validate that page. As such, each validator in turn will parse the entire contents of the page for itself. `NestingTLV` is only interested in the two tags named by its `inner` and `outer` initialization parameters, but it must search through the JSP page for all occurrences of these tags in order to validate the nesting relationship.

Finally, as was the case in the `validate()` method of the `ScriptFreeTLV` validator, any exceptions raised while constructing or running the parser are caught, and the associated error message is used to create a new `ValidationMessage` to indicate failure of the page validation.

Validation

Validation of the Document object returned by the parser is performed by searching for instances of the inner tag, and confirming whether or not they are enclosed by an instance of the outer tag. The Document object stores the page elements in a tree structure, consisting of nodes which may or may not have child nodes. The tree is searched for nodes whose names match that of the inner tag, and these are in turn examined to confirm whether or not they have a parent node whose name matches that of the outer tag.

The first step in this process takes place via the validateDocument() method, defined as follows:

```
private void validateDocument (ArrayList messages, Document doc,
                                String inner, String outer) {
  NodeList innerNodes = doc.getElementsByTagName(inner);
  int len = innerNodes.getLength();
   String errorString = null;
  for (int i = 0; i < len; ++i) {
    ValidationMesssage msg = validateInnerNode(innerNodes.item(i), outer);
     if (msg != null) messages.add(msg);
  }
}
```

First, a list of nodes (represented by an instance of org.w3c.dom.NodeList) whose names match that of the inner tag is generated by calling the Document object's getElementsByTagName() method. The validateDocument() method then iterates through that list of nodes, obtaining individual nodes (which are instances of the org.w3c.dom.Node class) by means of the list's item() method. The nesting of each node is then tested by calling the validateInnerNode() method, passing it the node and the name of the outer tag in which it is expected to be nested. (Recall that the tag names passed to this method have now been qualified by their namespace name.) If validateInnerNode() returns a ValidationMessage, it is added to the running list referenced by the messages parameter. When control passes back to the validate() method, this value will be included among those used to indicate to the JSP container that the page is invalid.

Inner nodes are validated by checking their ancestors (i.e., their parent node, their parent node's parent node, etc.) for occurrences of the outer tag. Here is the definition of validateInnerNode(), which performs this check.

```
private ValidationMessage validateInnerNode (Node innerNode,
                                            String outerName) {
  Node parent = findAncestor(innerNode, outerName);
  if (parent == null) {
    NamedNodeMap atts = innerNode.getAttributes();
```

```
    Attr idAttr = (Attr) atts.getNamedItem("jsp:id");
    String id = (idAttr == null) ? null : idAttr.getValue();
    return new ValidationMessage(id,
                                 "Improper nesting of " + innerName
                                 + " tag: must appear in body of "
                                 + outerName + " tag.");
  } else {
    return null;
  }
}
```

This method in turn relies on a utility method named `findAncestor()` to locate instances of the outer tag. If one is found, the `findAncestor()` method returns it, and the `validateInnerNode()` method returns null, indicating that `innerNode` is valid. If an instance of the outer tag is not found, `findAncestor()` returns null and `validateInnerNode()` returns a newly created instance of `ValidationMessage`. This validation message is ultimately returned to `NestingTLV`'s `validate()` method, which itself returns it to the JSP container as an indication that the page contains a tag that is not properly nested. Note that various objects and methods associated with JAXP's API for DOM parsing are called upon to retrieve the value of the `jsp:id` attribute of the improperly nested tag.

The final element of `NestingTLV` is the `findAncestor()` utility method, which is defined as follows:

```
private String findAncestor (Node child, String named) {
  Node parent = child.getParentNode();
  if (parent == null) {
    return null;
  }
  String parentName = parent.getNodeName();
  if (parentName.equals(named)) {
    return parent;
  } else {
    return findAncestor(parent, named);
  }
}
```

This method recursively walks through all of the ancestors of the supplied `child` node, checking the name of each parent—retrieved via the parent node's `getNode-Name()` method—to see if it matches the `named` parameter. If a matching node is found, it is returned. If not, the `findAncestor()` utility method is called recursively, with the current child's parent acting as the child for the next attempt. If the original inner tag node was not properly nested, eventually this method will reach the root element of the XML document, having checked each enclosing tag in turn and failing to find one whose name matches the sought-for outer tag. The root element has no parent, so in this case `findAncestor()` will return a null value to `validateInnerNode()`, resulting in the creation of a `ValidationMessage` for notifying the JSP container that the page is not valid.

The complete source code for the `NestingTVL` validator is presented in abbreviated form in listing 20.7.

Listing 20.7 The NestingTLV tag library validator

```
package com.taglib.wdjsp.mut;

import javax.servlet.jsp.tagext.TagLibraryValidator;
import javax.servlet.jsp.tagext.ValidationMessage;
import javax.servlet.jsp.tagext.PageData;
import javax.xml.parsers.DocumentBuilderFactory;
import javax.xml.parsers. DocumentBuilder;
import org.w3c.dom.Document;
import org.w3c.dom.NodeList;
import org.w3c.dom.Node;
import org.w3c.dom.NamedNodeMap;
import org.w3c.dom.Attr;
import java.io.InputStream;
import java.util.Map;
import java.util.ArrayList;

import java.io.IOException;
import org.xml.sax.SAXException;
import javax.xml.parsers.ParserConfigurationException;

public class NestingTLV extends TagLibraryValidator {
  private String inner, outer;
  private DocumentBuilderFactory factory;

  public NestingTLV () { ... }
  public void setInitParameters (Map initParms) { ... }

  public ValidationMessage[] validate (String prefix, String uri, PageData
   page) {
    ...
  }
  private void validateDocument (ArrayList messages, Document doc,
                                 String inner, String outer) {
    ...
  }
  private ValidationMessage validateInnerNode (Node innerNode,
                                      String innerName, String outerName) {
    ...
  }
  private String findAncestor (Node child, String named) { ... }
}
```

Sample application

Listing 20.8 presents a sample JSP page, based on the example page presented in listing 19.12, whose second occurrence of the `<mut:index>` tag is not properly nested. In this JSP page, the author has mistakenly assumed that the `<mut:index>` tag can be used to display the total number of iterations after the `<mut:forProperty>` tag has been closed. While this is not necessarily an unreasonable assumption, the implementation presented in chapter 19 does not support such a feature.

If the tag library is not configured to validate pages using the `NestingTLV` validator, then page compilation will be successful, but end users will see a run-time error when requesting the page, as depicted in figure 20.4. This exception is thrown by the custom tag's `doStartTag()` method, as presented in the previous chapter.

Listing 20.8 The NestingTLV tag library validator example page

```
<%@ taglib prefix="mut" uri="/mutlib" %>
<jsp:useBean id="plot" class="com.taglib.wdjsp.advtags.PlotBean">
  <jsp:setProperty name="plot" property="dataSize" value="12"/>
</jsp:useBean>
<html>
<head>
<title>Invalid Index Tag</title>
</head>
<body>
<h1>Invalid Index Tag</h1>
<center><table border=1>
<tr><th>i</th><th>X</th><th>Y</th></tr>
<mut:forProperty name="plot" property="data"
                 id="point" class="com.taglib.wdjsp.advtags.DataBean">
  <tr><td><mut:index start="1"/></td>
      <td><jsp:getProperty name="point" property="x"/></td>
      <td><jsp:getProperty name="point" property="y"/></td></tr>
</mut:forProperty>
</table></center>

<p align="center">
        There were <mut:index start="1"/> entries in the table.
</p>

</body>
</html>
```

When the custom tag library is configured to use this validator, however, a slightly different result is obtained. In this case, the error is generated during page compilation. If precompiling JSP pages (chapter 14) is a standard part of the development

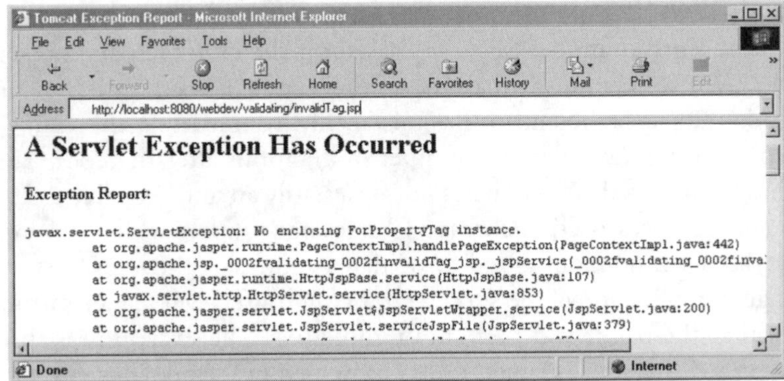

Figure 20.4 Request-time error for the NestingTLV example page when validation is not used

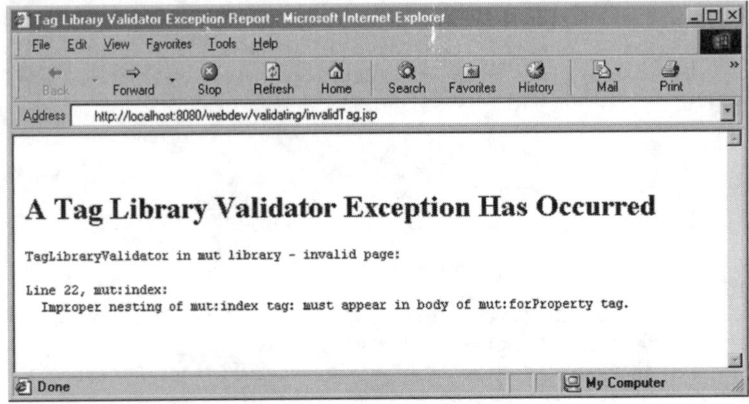

Figure 20.5 Compile-time error for the NestingTLV example page when validation is used.

process, then compilation errors such as this are likely to be noticed (and fixed) early in the development cycle. Run-time errors that can only be observed by submitting an appropriate HTTP request have a greater risk of being overlooked until later in the development process. Since the costs associated with fixing bugs tends to increase significantly as development progresses, it's always advantageous to find such problems earlier rather than later in the development cycle.

20.5 Packaging the tag library

In JSP 1.1, custom tag libraries must be packaged and deployed individually, as single-library JAR files. Version 1.2 adds the ability to package multiple custom tag libraries in the same JAR file. Single-library JAR files continue to work in JSP 1.2, but the new version of the specification also permits an individual JAR file to contain an arbitrary number of custom tag libraries, which may then be deployed *en masse* to a JSP 1.2 container.

20.5.1 Packaging a single library

As discussed in chapter 18, individual tag libraries are deployed in the form of JAR files containing both the tag handler classes and the TLD. The TLD appears in the META-INF directory of the JAR file, under the name `taglib.tld`. (See listing 18.1 for the basic outline of the TLD for the `mut` custom tag library.) The tag handler classes are organized into directories according to their package structure.

Any auxiliary classes upon which the tag handlers rely must also be present in the JAR file. This includes any application-specific base classes, inner classes, `BeanInfo` classes, or JavaBeans (such as our `TimeOfDayBean`) as well as any helper classes specified in the TLD's `<tei-class>` entries. The JAR file for deploying a JSP 1.2 tag library must also include any tag library validator or listener classes specified in its TLD. The full table of contents listing for the `mut` library's JAR file is presented in listing 20.9.

Listing 20.9 Contents of the JAR file for the mut tag library

```
META-INF/MANIFEST.MF
META-INF/taglib.tld
com/taglib/wdjsp/mut/DebugBufferTag.class
com/taglib/wdjsp/mut/DebugCookiesTag.class
com/taglib/wdjsp/mut/EncodeHtmlTag.class
com/taglib/wdjsp/mut/FailsafeTag.class
com/taglib/wdjsp/mut/ForPropertyTag.class
com/taglib/wdjsp/mut/ForPropertyTagBeanInfo.class
com/taglib/wdjsp/mut/ForPropertyTEI.class
com/taglib/wdjsp/mut/IfPropertyTag.class
com/taglib/wdjsp/mut/IndexTag.class
com/taglib/wdjsp/mut/NestingTLV.class
com/taglib/wdjsp/mut/TimeOfDayBean.class
com/taglib/wdjsp/mut/TimeOfDayTag.class
com/taglib/wdjsp/mut/UrlTag.class
```

As discussed in chapter 14, deploying the tag library to a JSP 1.1 container happens at the application level. The library's JAR file is added to the WEB-INF/lib directory associated with the application, and a copy of its TLD is added to the WEB-INF/tlds directory and assigned a library-specific name. A URI for accessing this TLD from the application's JSP pages is then created in the application's deployment descriptor, using a `<taglib>` entry such as the following:

```
<taglib>
  <taglib-uri>/mutlib</taglib-uri>
  <taglib-location>/WEB-INF/tlds/mut.tld</taglib-location>
</taglib>
```

As a result of including this entry in the application's web.xml file, JSP pages employing the `taglib` directive can reference this TLD via the specified URI. In this example, the URI /mutlib is mapped to the TLD for the `mut` custom tag library. This URI then serves as the value for the `uri` attribute in the `taglib` directive, as demonstrated in the sample pages presented in this and the previous two chapters.

20.5.2 Packaging multiple libraries

As of JSP 1.2, developers have the option of packaging multiple tag libraries together in the same JAR file. As when creating a JAR file for a single library, a JAR file containing multiple libraries must include all of the classes that implement those libraries' tag handlers, tag library validators, and listeners, arranged in a directory hierarchy matching the associated package structure. Other classes specific to those libraries, such as library-specific base classes, `TagExtraInfo` classes, and JavaBeans, should also be included in the JAR file.

The only difference from the single-library case, actually, is the handling of the TLD. Since there will be one TLD for each custom tag library contained in the JAR file, using the META-INF/taglib.tld file name won't work. Instead, each TLD file is placed in the META-INF directory of the JAR file using a library-specific file name, but preserving the .tld extension. Listing 20.10 depicts the contents of a JAR file containing three custom tag libraries: the `mut` library, with the `NestingTLV` validator, and two additional tag libraries based on the two other validators presented in this chapter.

Listing 20.10 Contents of the JAR file for the mut tag library

```
META-INF/MANIFEST.MF
META-INF/copyXML.tld
META-INF/mut.tld
META-INF/scriptfree.tld
com/taglib/wdjsp/mut/CopyingTLV.class
com/taglib/wdjsp/mut/DebugBufferTag.class
com/taglib/wdjsp/mut/DebugCookiesTag.class
com/taglib/wdjsp/mut/EncodeHtmlTag.class
com/taglib/wdjsp/mut/FailsafeTag.class
com/taglib/wdjsp/mut/ForPropertyTag.class
```

```
com/taglib/wdjsp/mut/ForPropertyTagBeanInfo.class
com/taglib/wdjsp/mut/ForPropertyTEI.class
com/taglib/wdjsp/mut/IfPropertyTag.class
com/taglib/wdjsp/mut/IndexTag.class
com/taglib/wdjsp/mut/NestingTLV.class
com/taglib/wdjsp/mut/ScriptFreeTLV$MyContentHandler.class
com/taglib/wdjsp/mut/ScriptFreeTLV.class
com/taglib/wdjsp/mut/TimeOfDayBean.class
com/taglib/wdjsp/mut/TimeOfDayTag.class
com/taglib/wdjsp/mut/UrlTag.class
```

This JAR file includes five additional files beyond those present in the single-library example presented previously: the two additional TLDs, the two tag library validator classes, and the inner class implementing `ScriptFreeTLV`'s content handler. The new TLDs are presented in listings 20.11 and 20.12.

Listing 20.11 Tag library descriptor for the copyXML custom tag library

```
<?xml version="1.0" encoding="ISO-8859-1" ?>
<!DOCTYPE taglib
        PUBLIC "-//Sun Microsystems, Inc.//DTD JSP Tag Library 1.2//EN"
        "http://java.sun.com/j2ee/dtds/web-jsptaglibrary_1_2.dtd">
<taglib>
    <tlib-version>1.0</tlib-version>
    <jsp-version>1.2</jsp-version>
    <short-name>copyXML</short-name>
    <uri>/copyXML</uri>
    <description>
        Validates JSP pages to make a copy of their XML representations.
    </description>

    <validator>
        <validator-class>com.taglib.wdjsp.mut.CopyingTLV</validator-class>
        <description>Copies XML representation.</description>
    </validator>

    <tag>
        <name>noop</name>
        <tag-class>javax.servlet.jsp.tagext.TagSupport</tag-class>
        <body-content>empty</body-content>
        <description>
            Does nothing.
        </description>
    </tag>
</taglib>
```

Listing 20.12 Tag library descriptor for the scriptfree custom tag library

```
<?xml version="1.0" encoding="ISO-8859-1" ?>
<!DOCTYPE taglib
      PUBLIC "-//Sun Microsystems, Inc.//DTD JSP Tag Library 1.2//EN"
      "http://java.sun.com/j2ee/dtds/web-jsptaglibrary_1_2.dtd">
<taglib>
    <tlib-version>1.0</tlib-version>
    <jsp-version>1.2</jsp-version>
    <short-name>scriptfree</short-name>
    <uri>/scriptfree</uri>
    <description>
        Validates JSP pages to prohibit use of scripting elements.
    </description>

    <validator>
        <validator-class>com.taglib.wdjsp.mut.ScriptFreeTLV</validator-class>
        <init-param>
                <param-name>allowDeclarations</param-name>
                <param-value>false</param-value>
                <description>
                    Controls whether or not declarations are considered valid.
                </description>
        </init-param>
        <init-param>
                <param-name>allowScriptlets</param-name>
                <param-value>false</param-value>
                <description>
                    Controls whether or not scriptlets are considered valid.
                </description>
        </init-param>
        <init-param>
                <param-name>allowExpressions</param-name>
                <param-value>true</param-value>
                <description>
                    Controls whether or not expressions are considered valid.
                </description>
        </init-param>
        <description>Validates page scripting requirements.</description>
    </validator>

    <tag>
        <name>noop</name>
        <tag-class>javax.servlet.jsp.tagext.TagSupport</tag-class>
        <body-content>empty</body-content>
        <description>
            Does nothing.
        </description>
    </tag>
</taglib>
```

As indicated by their TLDs, these are not really custom tag libraries, but simply take advantage of the custom tag library functionality to make their validators available for application to JSP pages. These TLDs include `<tag>` elements only because the DTD governing them requires the presence of at least one `<tag>` element. And the single tag that is specified, as the name selected for it suggests, doesn't actually do anything. In fact, the library doesn't even go through the trouble of defining a tag handler class, instead relying on the built-in `TagSupport` class. You may recall that the default implementation provided for this class's `doStartTag()` method is to simply return `Tag.SKIP_BODY`, while its `doEndTag()` method just returns `Tag.EVAL_PAGE`. As a result, the behavior of the aptly named `noop` tag defined in each of these TLDs is to ignore its body content (which its TLD entry prevents it from having in the first place) and continue processing the remainder of the page. (In programmer lingo, a *noop* is a function or method that does nothing: it performs *no op*erations.)

The utility of these two custom tag libraries, then, resides solely in their validators. Adding a `taglib` directive to a JSP page which references one of these two libraries does not have the effect of making new tags available (at least, not any particularly useful new tags). Instead, it has the sole effect of applying that library's validator to the page. Consider, for example, the following JSP page fragment:

```
<%@ taglib uri="/mutlib" prefix="mut" %>
<%@ taglib uri="/scriptfree" prefix="scriptfree" %>
...
<mut:timeOfDay id="time"/>
<mut:ifProperty name="time" property="morning">
  ...
</mut:ifProperty>
...
```

The first `taglib` directive makes all of the mut custom tags available from within the page, as well as ensuring that mut's `NestingTLV` validator is applied. The second `taglib` directive does not add any new tags (except for the dubious `noop` tag): its only purpose is to cause the `ScriptFreeTLV` validator to be applied.

In addition to support for multiple tag libraries within a single JAR file, JSP 1.2 also adds another feature to ease the deployment of custom tag libraries. As described in chapter 14, the URI specified in the `uri` attribute of a `taglib` directive must typically be manually mapped to the corresponding TLD file via the `web.xml` application deployment descriptor. In JSP 1.2, a default mapping between the URI and the TLD can be created automatically, based on the `<uri>` element in the TLD itself.

The JSP container creates this mapping by examining all of the JAR files deployed in an application (i.e., in its WEB-INF/lib subdirectory) to see if they contain any TLDs. Such TLDs are located by looking in the META-INF directory of the JAR file for any files with the .tld extension. The container then checks each such TLD for a `<uri>` element. If one is found, the URI specified as the value of that element is automatically mapped to the TLD in which it was found.

For the TLDs presented in listings 20.11 and 20.12, then, they will automatically be mapped to the URIs /copyXML and /scriptfree, respectively. The net effect of this behavior is that a page author can take a packaged tag library, drop it into his or her web application, and immediately start using the library, without having to reconfigure anything. The full control provided by the `web.xml` deployment descriptor is still available, of course, but the mechanism described here for automatically creating a default mapping for TLDs can be quite convenient, particularly when the web application developer is still in the early stages of a project and may be evaluating several alternative custom tag libraries for inclusion in the finished product.

20.6 For further information

Since their introduction in JSP 1.1, custom tags have proven themselves to be a powerful tool for expanding the scope and power of the base JSP technology. The range of potential applications for JSP custom tag libraries is vast, and we have only been able to scratch the surface of their capabilities in these three final chapters. For those readers wishing to take full advantage of them in their own web applications, here are some pointers to a number of important resources for custom tag users and developers.

Now that JSP has been widely adopted and significant practical experience with its application has been gained, steps are being taken to supplement the existing set of built-in JSP tags. The intent of this effort is to provide page authors with greater "out-of-the-box" functionality, hopefully reducing the need to resort to scripting elements. Rather than add more built-in tags, however, an alternate approach has been adopted. Via the Java Community Process, specification of a Standard Tag Library providing a core set of commonly used tags (e.g., iteration, conditionalization, etc.) is currently under way. Once the specification is complete, the resulting custom tag library will become a required feature of all JSP containers. At the time of this writing, finalization of the Standard Tag Library was not expected for several months yet, but early access to a reference implementation of the custom tags proposed for inclusion in this library is now available.

Table 20.1 A sampling of the custom tag libraries available from the Jakarta Taglibs project

Tag Library	Description
DBTags	Custom tags for accessing SQL databases via JDBC.
I18N	A library supporting the internationalization of JSP pages.
IO	A set of tags for accessing external web resources (via HTTP, FTP, SOAP, etc.) from within JSP pages.
Request	Tags for accessing the properties of a JSP page's HTTP request.
Response	Tags for accessing the properties of a JSP page's HTTP response.
Session	Tags for accessing the properties of a user's session.
XSL	A set of tags for performing XML extensible stylesheet transformations.
XTags	Custom tags for manipulating the contents of XML documents.

Beyond the general-purpose tags planned for the Standard Tag Library, however, several examples of more targeted custom tag libraries are now available through the Jakarta Taglibs project. A variety of custom tag libraries—some of which are listed in table 20.1—are available through the project's web site, http://jakarta.apache.org/taglibs/. In keeping with the project's sponsorship by the Apache Software Foundation, all of the code implementing these libraries is available as open source. It is thus a tremendous resource for developers wishing to implement their own custom tag libraries by learning from the work of others. In addition, the Jakarta Taglibs project is the home for the reference implementation of the JSP Standard Tag Library.

The Jakarta web site is also home to the Jakarta Struts project, which implements a complete web application framework in the form of a controller servlet and several associated JSP custom tag libraries and utility classes. All of these framework classes, in both binary and source code forms, can be downloaded from the Struts homepage at http://jakarta.apache.org/struts/.

Finally, we invite you to join us at the book's companion web site, http://www.taglib.com/. All of the source code examples from the text are there, along with other sample code and custom tag libraries written by the authors. And as JSP and its associated web development technologies continue to mature, we'll be highlighting the important developments there to keep you informed.

A Changes in the JSP 1.2 API

A.1 Introduction

We created the second edition of this book in part to bring it up to date with the changes and enhancements to JSP technology. Since the release of the first edition, Sun has updated JSP to release 1.2, and the underlying Servlet API to release 2.3. For the benefit of readers of the first edition, the terminally impatient, and those wanting a look at what's new we have included this appendix to hit the highlights. The changes to the JSP API focus on fixing some rough spots in the language, improving custom tags, and better preparing the technology for tool support. While it doesn't cover the changes in detail, it does highlight important changes and introduces new functionality.

A.2 Changes to the API

Sun has recently updated the JSP API to release 1.2 and published errata to the 1.1 specifications. Likewise the underlying Servlet API has been updated to release 2.3. Here are some of the important changes.

A.2.1 *Java 2, Version 1.2 now a requirement*

Previous versions of JSP were based on the 1.1 JDK, even though they worked fine under the Java 2 JDK versions 1.2 and 1.3. Starting with the latest release of the API however, Sun has firmly tied JSP to the Java 2 family by requiring JDK 1.2 or higher as the underlying technology.

A.2.2 *Servlet API 2.3 required*

Since JSP is, in essence, an extension of the Servlet API, it is linked to the new version, 2.3. However, an explicit requirement of the 2.3 API is that containers must maintain backward compatibility with the 2.2 API, as well as the 2.2 deployment descriptor for web applications. This assures that existing applications will continue to function under the newer containers.

A.2.3 *XML syntax now fully supported*

There has always been a close relationship between XML and JSP, and it was assumed since the beginning that a full XML syntax would be required to enable parsing and generation of JSP content by page authoring tools. With JSP 1.2, the XML syntax is now fully developed. There is an XML representation for all of the page elements, including the raw content. Here's a quick example of what the XML version of an HTML "Hello World" page is shown in listing A.1:

Listing A.1 A "Hello World" JSP Expressed As XML

```
<jsp:root
  xmlns:jsp"http://java.sun.com/JSP/Page"
  version="1.2">
<jsp:text><!-[CDATA[<html>
<title>My Page</title>
<body>
<jsp:include page="top_banner.jsp"/>
Hello World.
   </body>
]]</jsp:text>
```

The ability to express a JSP page fully in XML provides a number of capabilities. It allows a machine-friendly format for page authoring tools, automated validation of the document structure, and the ability to use technology like XSL to help convert data directly into a JSP form. This is a big step in allowing the tool vendors to take JSP into the mainstream.

A.2.4 Determining the real path

One inconsistency that arose with the WAR format was the concept of determining the path to a request file via the `getRealPath` method of the request object. This method doesn't mean anything if the web application is being run directly from a WAR file. The new specification says that in such a case it should now return `null` if unable to determine an actual path to the resource. All in all, you probably want to avoid this method if you can.

A.2.5 Redirects are not relative to the servlet context

A clarification to Servlet API 2.2 was made to indicate that the `sendRedirect` method of the `HttpServletResponse` class should operate relative to the context root of the web server ("/"), rather than the context root of the servlet as some container vendors had surmised. To redirect to a URL relative to your servlet context instead, simply prepend the context path.

A.2.6 Restricted names

There was some contention as to which prefixes were reserved words in JSP. JSP 1.2 clears this up, stating that the prefixes `jsp`, `_jsp`, `java`, and `sun` cannot be used as the prefix in `taglib` directives, as element names used in actions, as attribute names, or in request parameters. This entire namespace is reserved for internal usage, and should not be used by application developers.

A.2.7 Page encoding attribute

The 1.2 JSP API adds an attribute to the page directive called `pageEncoding`. This new attribute allows you to specify the page encoding separately from the content type of the page, improving readability. It defaults to the encoding specified in the `contentType` attribute, if present, otherwise, the default encoding of ISO8859-1 (Latin-1) is used.

A.2.8 Flush on include no longer required

Prior to JSP 1.2, the `<jsp:include>` tag required a flush attribute with a value of `true`. This meant that as soon as you attempt to perform an inclusion, the buffer would be flushed and your output committed, preventing you from setting any response headers (such as setting cookies or redirecting the request) via the included page. The attribute now defaults to a value of `false` and is optional.

A.3 Web application changes

JSPs are packaged into WARs as defined in the Servlet API. Therefore, changes made to the web application format as part of Servlet API 2.3 are likely to affect JSP developers.

A.3.1 New 2.3 web application DTD

Along with the new API comes a new DTD to specify in the deployment descriptor. This helps the container tell version 2.3 applications from 2.2 applications, and validate the descriptor appropriately.

A.3.2 Handling of white space

Servlet containers are now required to be more lenient of white space in the deployment descriptor. They must ignore any leading or trailing white space surrounding PCDATA.

A.3.3 Resolving path names in the web.xml file

Clarifications and additions were made to the specifications regarding the handling of path names in the deployment descriptor. All paths are considered to be in decoded form. Any references to resources stored within a WAR (for example, images or other data files) must be referenced absolutely, starting with a "/".

A.3.4 Request mappings

Prior to the 2.3 API, there was confusion surrounding several elements of the request mapping facilities that has since been clarified. If you map a servlet to an entire directory hierarchy, for example, `/private/*`, the specification now states explicitly that it should match a request to `/private`. Another clarification is that request matching is case sensitive, so a request for `/userInfo` is different than a request for `/userinfo`.

A.3.5 Dependency on installed extensions

The new JSP API recognizes the difficulty of managing the installed extensions required by a web application and addresses this issue with a series of recommendations to container developers. They recommend that containers support a facility for easily adding extensions (in the form of jar files) to all of the container's applications, as well as a method for validating required extensions through an optional manifest file in the WAR.

A.4 Custom tag improvements

The addition of custom tag capabilities in the 1.1 API has created excitement in the development community. Already well under way is an effort to define a standard set of tags that would be available in all containers. Several new capabilities made it into the new API to help proliferate custom tags.

A.4.1 Translation time validation

A new element, `<validator>`, has been added to support translation time validation. This element uses the `<validator-class>` element to define a class that can be used to validate proper use of the tags in a document. It allows you to enforce rules about which tags can appear where, and in what combinations.

A.4.2 New tag interfaces

A new custom tag interface, `IterationTag`, provides a convenient way to create looping related custom tags while the `TryCatchFinally` (which can be implemented by any tag) improves exception-handling capabilities.

A.4.3 Changes to the TLD

The TLD is an XML document that tells the JSP container about the custom tags you have written. Several important changes to the TLD DTD have been made in version 1.2 of the JSP API.

New <variable> element

A new `<variable>` element is available to specify any scripting variables defined by a custom tag. This tag obviates the need for a `TagExtraInfo` class in many cases, and improves translation time validation capabilities.

<jsp-version> element now required

The `<jsp-version>` element is used to specify the minimum version of the JSP API that the tag library supports. This element was optional in JSP 1.1, but is now required. This will prevent conflicts between tag libraries and their containers as the technology continues to progress. The TLD is not compatible with the version 1.1 TLD, but servlet containers are required to support both formats.

Improved documentation elements

In JSP 1.2 the TLD has been extended to allow more detailed documentation about the tags. A new optional element, `<example>`, has been added to the `<tag>` element. This element can be used to specify an intended usage of the tag, to give the user some clue about how to use it. The `<info>` element, which has always existed for the `<tag>` element, has been renamed `<description>` and can now be used on the `<variable>`, `<attribute>`, and `<validator>` elements as well. The TLD can be read by a page-authoring tool or translated directly into documentation via XSL, similar to how javadoc turns Java source into API documentation.

A.5 JavaBean changes

JavaBeans, the component model for JSP development has not changed much in the new API, but several important clarifications have been made.

A.5.1 Bean tags cannot implicitly access scriptlet objects

In some vendor's implementations the `<jsp:getProperty>` and `<jsp:setProperty>` tags could access variables defined by scriptlets and custom tags, while others could not because in some containers, the JSP tags interacted only with objects stored in the page context. The specification now clearly states that these tags should work with the page context exclusively. If custom tags or scriptlets wish to expose any objects they create to these tags they must explicitly do so by adding them to the page context.

A.5.2 Fully qualified class names required

Some early JSP implementations honored import statements in the `<jsp:useBean>` tag and allowed class names that were not fully qualified in this tag, but this has been clarified in version 1.2 and is no longer allowed. Even if your container supports this shortcut, you should always fully qualify your class names to keep your code compatible with other containers or updates to yours. Note that for scripting variables, imported packages are supported and fully qualified class names are not required.

A.6 New servlet features

Two new features of the Servlet API, servlet filters and application events, will prove especially useful in building JSP applications.

A.6.1 Servlet filters

This feature is based on a nonstandard feature seen in the early servlet container precursors called servlet chaining. With servlet filters you can define special filter classes that can interact with the request headers and content prior to the servlet or JSP receiving the request. Filters can also be applied to the response from a servlet or JSP to perform additional processing. You can apply multiple filters to given sets of requests at deployment time, without the underlying servlet or JSP having any knowledge of the filters presence. This will become *the* way to add authentication, logging, and encryption capabilities to web applications of the future.

A.6.2 Application events

Application level events provide a mechanism for responding to signals about the state of the servlet container and the servlet application life cycle. For example, your code can be informed just prior to a servlet context being initialized, any time attributes are added to the application scope, or a new session is created. It provides for a much more cohesive web application than was previously possible. A `<listener>` element has been added to the TLD, allowing custom tags to receive these events and react to them.

B Running the reference implementation

For most people, experimenting with programming languages is an integral part of learning them. JSP is no exception to this rule. To help developers get up and running quickly in cases where they have no JSP container to use, this appendix provides information about installing Tomcat.

Tomcat is a free servlet and JSP container that provides the official reference implementation of the Servlet and JSP standards. The standards are developed under the Java Community Process, but Tomcat is a product of the Jakarta Project, which exists under the umbrella of the Apache Software Foundation. The entire Tomcat distribution, including its source code, is available freely from Apache's web site.

Computers and televisions often come with "Quick Start" guides to help impatient consumers get started. If Tomcat were such a product, here is the guide it might come with. Of course, Tomcat comes with its own documentation; the guide here provides a roadmap to help you locate, download, and install the product. For more information, refer to the documentation on the http://jakarta.apache.org/tomcat site.

B.1 Prerequisites

Tomcat is written in Java, and like all Java programs, it requires a working Java environment in which to run. The most recent versions of Tomcat require a JDK of at least version 1.2. If you do not already have access to a suitable JDK on your system, you will need to download and install one. JDKs for many common platforms are freely available from Sun Microsystems's web site. (See appendix D for the relevant URLs.)

B.2 Downloading and installing Tomcat

Once you have located or installed a suitable JDK, you can download and install Tomcat. The most recent version of Tomcat is always available from http://jakarta.apache.org/tomcat. Compared to traditional commercial products, open source software is updated extremely frequently. Therefore, it is difficult for us to recommend a specific version of Tomcat for all purposes, but we can provide information on the various version trees available at the time of this writing.

Broadly speaking, there are currently two versions of Tomcat that might interest you, Tomcat 3 and Tomcat 4. At the time this appendix was written, Tomcat 3 was still a more mature product, with release-quality versions (e.g., Tomcat 3.2.2) having been subjected to widespread use and testing. Even the latest versions of Tomcat 3, however, do not support the Servlet 2.3 and JSP 1.2 standards, which this book covers. Therefore, for support of these standards, you will need to turn to Tomcat 4.

WARNING When this appendix was written, Tomcat 4 had just been officially released. Its initial versions will likely be suitable for your experimentation with JSP, but if you run into unexplained problems, you might wish to drop back to a more tried-and-true version.

Just as it is difficult for a book to document an actively changing open source product, it's hard for printed material to provide instructions on how to use a web site. Links can, of course, change, and sites can be restructured. However, for quite some time, the Jakarta Tomcat site has offered precompiled, binary releases under a link labeled Binaries. Following this link, you will typically see categories of versions, including Release Builds, Milestone Builds, and Nightly Builds. The Release Builds category contains stable, well-tested versions of products. Milestone Builds typically includes versions that are stable but known to be flawed or incomplete. Nightly Builds are simply snapshots of the current versions of products; as we've mentioned, open source software changes actively—often day-to-day—and each day's version can be different from the last. Such temporary, "nightly" versions are often unstable and should generally be avoided unless you either contribute your own code to the project or absolutely need a new feature that can't be found elsewhere.

TIP Experienced Java developers may prefer to download source code and build it themselves, instead of downloading precompiled binary releases. If you want to download the Tomcat source code, you should look for a Source Code line instead of Binaries. We can't guarantee that the link will be labeled identically in the future, but it shouldn't be too difficult to find. The installation instructions given in this appendix apply specifically to the precompiled binary releases.

Once you choose the version you wish to download, click its link. You will be presented with a list of files from which you can choose the individual distribution to download. Two popular formats that are typically offered on Jakarta's site are Zip (.zip) and compressed tar (.tar.Z). Zip files are typically more natural on Windows systems, while tar files are used more widely on UNIX. Both formats, however, are usable on most platforms. Separately from the files' formats, which are indicated by file extensions, you might see a variety of base file names as well. The Tomcat distributions will probably look like jakarta-tomcat-***<version>***.zip or jakarta-tomcat-***<version>***.tar.Z.

From here, you can pick an appropriate file and download it by following its hyperlink. Once you download the file, you will need to expand it. The exact procedure for expanding a file archive depends on the system you use and the type of file archive (Zip versus compressed tar, and so on). On Windows, you can typically load Zip files in a graphical package that expands them for you. On UNIX systems, you can usually expand a Tar.Z file using the command

```
% uncompress -c filename.tar.Z | tar xvf -
```

TIP Because JAR files use the same format as Zip files, you can use the `jar` utility that comes with the JDK to unpackage a Zip file on both Windows or UNIX platforms. The command for doing this is `jar xvf filename.zip`.

After you expand the archive, you can finally start Tomcat. First, change into the new directory you created by expanding the archive. This directory is typically called `jakarta-tomcat-`***`<version>`***. If you ran the `uncompress` or `jar` commands we suggested from the command line, this directory will be created underneath your current directory at the time you execute the command.

Once you have changed to the base directory of the Tomcat tree, you can start Tomcat by typing bin/startup.sh on UNIX systems or bin\startup on Windows. On UNIX systems, if you get an error related to file permissions, you will need to execute the command

```
% chmod u+x bin/*.sh
```

before running bin/startup.sh.

NOTE If you get an error related to the environment variable `JAVA_HOME` not being set, you will need to set this variable. If you know how to set environment variables from the shell or interface you typically use, you can simply set this variable to the base directory of your JDK's installation. This is the directory in the JDK distribution that contains such subdirectories as bin, jre, and lib.

If you want to modify your Tomcat installation so that it can find your JDK every time it runs, you can add an appropriate line to the file bin/catalina.sh (bin\catalina.bat on Windows) from the root of your Tomcat installation. This line should be added toward the top of the file—after the initial comments but prior to other commands—and should look like

```
JAVA_HOME=path to your JDK directory
```

and on UNIX systems and like

```
set JAVA_HOME=path to your JDK directory
```

on Windows machines. The path to your JDK directory might look like `/usr/local/jdk1.3` on UNIX systems or `c:\jdk1.3` on Windows, but it can be located anywhere that you, your system's administrator, or another user has installed it.

By default, Tomcat runs on port 8080. If you can run a web browser on the same machine on which you just started Tomcat, you can therefore access the running Tomcat process over the web by loading the following URL from your browser: http://localhost:8080/

If your web browser runs on a different machine from Tomcat, replace `localhost` with the name of Tomcat's machine.

WARNING If another server on your machine uses port 8080, Tomcat will not be able to start by default. You can change the port that Tomcat runs on by editing the conf/server.xml file inside Tomcat's root directory (conf\server.xml on Windows). Because the exact procedure for doing this varies across Tomcat's versions, the easiest general procedure to follow is simply to replace all occurrences of the number 8080 with a different number corresponding to the port of your choice. If you want to proceed more carefully—after all, the characters 8080 might appear in a future version of the default conf/server.xml file and not correspond to a port number—you can always read the documentation that comes with your version of Tomcat to determine how to configure it.

Another thing to note: on Unix machines, unprivileged programs cannot typically bind to ports with numbers less than 1024. You must run Tomcat as the superuser for it to bind to port numbers below 1024. If you do this, you should have a good understanding of the security ramifications, for running programs as the `root` user on a Unix machine can be extremely dangerous.

If Tomcat has started successfully, you will see Tomcat's introductory screen, which provides links to documentation and sample applications. At the time of this writing, the current Tomcat version's initial screen contained a link labeled `JSP Examples`; clicking this link allows you to run the example JSP pages that come with Tomcat. These JSP pages are found in the directory webapps/examples/jsp underneath the root of your Tomcat installation (webapps\examples\jsp on Windows), and you are free to modify them. Because of the back-end machinery of JSP that we described in chapter 4, your changes will take effect automatically: simply edit the file, and you can reload its URL in a browser to see the effects of your changes. In fact, if you add a JSP file underneath this directory, you will be able to run it right away; no formal installation is necessary. That is, if you create a file called my-own-example.jsp inside webapps/examples/jsp (webapps\examples\jsp on Windows), you would be able to access it by loading the following URL from your web browser: http://localhost:8080/examples/jsp/my-own-example.jsp

As before, if your web browser runs on a different machine from your Tomcat installation, replace `localhost` with the name of Tomcat's host.

B.3 Web applications and Tomcat

Adding individual JSP files to the `examples` application that comes with Tomcat is suitable for small-scale testing. For instance, if you want to experiment with any of the stand-alone JSP examples from chapter 3, you can add them to Tomcat's `examples` application and cause them to run by accessing the appropriate URL, as with my-own-example.jsp.

However, it requires more forethought to use Tomcat with some types of JSP pages. For instance, as we've seen, many pages use JavaBeans or custom tag libraries. These pages depend on the specific Java class files that represent bean implementations and tag-handler logic. Tomcat needs a mechanism to determine the location of such dependencies.

To facilitate portable deployment, the servlet specification outlines a recommended directory structure for web applications. This structure is very similar to that of a WAR file, as presented in chapter 13. See figure 14.1 for a graphical representation of this structure.

Deploying applications on Tomcat is straightforward. By default, current versions of Tomcat will automatically notice both expanded web applications and WAR files that are placed in the `webapps` directory under Tomcat's root directory. For instance, if the webdev.war file from chapter 14 (figure 14.1) were copied to Tomcat's webapps directory, Tomcat would automatically notice this file upon initialization and thus be able to serve the `webdev` application. Assuming you added the webdev.war file to the version of Tomcat you installed using the instructions in section B.2, you would be able to access the root of the `webdev` application using the URL http://localhost:8080/webdev/ or a similar URL containing the Tomcat server machine's name for cases where Tomcat runs on a different machine from your web browser.

It is worth highlighting the purpose of two particular directories in the hierarchy of a web application. One directory, WEB-INF/classes (WEB-INF\classes on Windows), is for expanded directories of Java .class files. In the `classes` directory, just as in a directory of a typical Java class path, Java packages correspond to levels in the directory hierarchy. For instance, the file representing the `com.manning.examples.Example` class would appear underneath `classes` as `com/manning/examples/Example.class` on UNIX and `com\manning\examples\Example.class` on Windows. Separately, the lib directory underneath WEB-INF stores .jar files that are made accessible to the web application.

Suppose you wanted to run the JSP page from chapter 3 that uses the `HelloBean` class presented in the same chapter. Noting that this class is in the `com.tag-`

`lib.wdjsp.firststeps` package, you would copy its class file to the directory WEB-INF/classes/com/taglib/wdjsp/firststeps (or the corresponding path on Windows) inside your web application. This would make this class accessible to the JSP files in that application.

C Incorporating Java applets

Java applets are small applications that run within the context of a web browser. Because they can take advantage of the powerful GUI classes provided by the standard Java AWT and Swing class libraries, applets can be used to implement much richer user interfaces than is typically possible using HTML alone.

Using the latest versions of Java for applet development, however, requires browser-specific code. To simplify the deployment of applets based on Java 2, JSP provides the `<jsp:plugin>` action for cross-platform specification of Java 2 applets.

C.1 Browser support for Java

When Java was released to the programming community in 1995, it was primarily positioned as a language for deploying interactive applications via the web in the form of Java applets. Sun Microsystems' formal announcement of Java at SunWorld '95 was accompanied by the announcement of the HotJava browser, which was written in Java and included support for a new HTML tag, `<applet>`. At this same conference, Netscape revealed that it would be adding support for applets to its own browser product, including built-in JVMs for all of its major platforms. In December of that same year, Microsoft announced support for Java applets in Internet Explorer, based on Microsoft's own JVM for Windows. Less than a year after its formal introduction in May 1995, it appeared that Java had firmly established itself as a standard feature of web browsers.

Supporting a brand new programming language across diverse platforms and operating systems, however, proved to be problematic. The web browser was still in its infancy as a mass-market, consumer-oriented product, and the fact that Java incorporates advanced features such as garbage collection and multithreading did not make the task of incorporating the language into the browser applications any easier. As a result, the early browser JVMs were plagued with incompatibilities and inconsistencies that undermined Java's value proposition as a cross-platform programming language. The fierce competition between Netscape and Microsoft in the browser marketplace, as well as Sun's legal battles with Microsoft over the latter's in-house extensions to the language, provided additional impediments to the ongoing improvement of the browser-based JVMs. As a result, support for Java in the browser has languished at Version 1.1 of the specification, years after the Java 2 platform was released by Sun Microsystems in 1998. In 2001, Java became yet another casualty of the browser wars, when Microsoft removed client-side Java support from the default installation of its market-leading Internet Explorer product.

As a result of the failure of the browser vendors to produce robust, fully compatible JVMs supporting the Java 2 platform, Sun Microsystems has chosen to develop its own browser plug-in for running Java 2 applets and JavaBeans. Instead of relying on HTML's standard `<applet>` tag, support for which is provided by the browser itself, Sun has taken advantage of the browser-extension APIs built into these products to implement an alternative mechanism for running Java applets. The Java plug-in relies on its own JVM instead of the one built into the browser (if any). By taking advantage of the plug-in mechanism, applet support becomes browser-independent.

As an added benefit, because the extension APIs have been available for several years, the Java plug-in is fully compatible with many older versions of the popular browsers. This means that users often need not upgrade their web browsers in order to take advantage of the new features made available through the Java plug-in. In particular, the Java plug-in is compatible with Versions 3 and later of both Communicator and Internet Explorer. In late 2001, implementations of the plug-in are available for the following operating systems: Solaris, Microsoft Windows, Hewlett-Packard's HPUX, SGI IRIX, Compaq's Tru64 Unix, and Linux.

C.2 The plug-in action

Unfortunately, the HTML for adding an applet to a page using the Java plug-in is browser-specific. In addition, the plug-in code is itself platform-specific, based on the hardware and operating system it will be running on. As a result, configuring a page to run an applet via the plug-in is not very straightforward using HTML alone.

NOTE Plug-ins for Internet Explorer are specified via the HTML <OBJECT> tag. Plug-ins for Communicator are specified via the HTML <EMBED> tag.

To simplify this task, JSP provides the <jsp:plugin> action, which gives developers a cross-platform mechanism for specifying the use of the Java plug-in. The syntax for this action is as follows:

```
<jsp:plugin type="type" code="objectCode" codebase="objectCodeBase"
       height="height" width="width"
       attribute1="value1" attribute2="value2" … >
    <jsp:params>
     <jsp:param name="parameterName1" value="parameterValue1"/>
     …
     <jsp:param name="parameterNameN" value="parameterValueN"/>
    </jsp:params>
    <jsp:fallback>fallback text</jsp:fallback>
</jsp:plugin>
```

There are four basic elements to this JSP action. First, there are three required attributes for the <jsp:plugin> tag itself. There are also several optional attributes, many of which are carried over from the <applet> tag in HTML. The third element of a <jsp:plugin> specification is a set of parameter values, which are indicated via multiple <jsp:param> tags within the body of a <jsp:params> element, which is itself part of the body of the <jsp:plugin> action. Finally, the body of the action can also specify text to be displayed if for some reason the Java plug-in cannot be used. This is accomplished via the <jsp:fallback> tag.

C.2.1 Required attributes

There are five required attributes for the <jsp:plugin> tag, as summarized in table C.1. All have the same meaning as the corresponding attributes of the HTML <applet> tag, with the exception of the type attribute, for which the <applet> tag has no equivalent.

The type attribute is used to specify the type of Java component which is to be loaded and run by the plug-in. In addition to applets, which are indicated by providing the keyword `applet` as the value for this attribute, the Java plug-in can be used to run JavaBeans components within the browser. This latter behavior is specified by supplying the keyword `bean` as the value of the `type` attribute. The two valid values for this attribute, then, are as follows:

```
<jsp:plugin type="applet" … >
<jsp:plugin type="bean" … >
```

The `code` attribute is used to specify the file containing the compiled Java code for the applet or bean to be run. For applets, its value takes the form of a class file, qualified with the package name—if any—and including the .class extension. Alternatively, for both applets and beans, a file containing a serialized object may be specified.

The `codebase` attribute indicates the directory on the web server in which the applet or bean code may be found. Its value takes the form of a URL directory specification. Either an absolute or a relative URL may be provided; if the URL is not absolute, it is assumed to be relative to the URL of the JSP page containing the `<jsp:plugin>` tag. In either case, the file name specified for the `code` attribute is required to be relative to the directory specified for the `codebase` attribute.

The `height` and `width` attributes are used to designate the dimensions of the applet or the bean. They effectively specify a rectangular region of the browser page which is to be set aside for the display of the applet or Bean.

In the following `<jsp:plugin>` tag, for example, an applet is to be loaded from a class file:

```
<jsp:plugin type="applet" codebase="plugins"
            code="com.taglib.wdjsp.applet.CountDown.class" … >
```

In this case, the applet code may be found in the file plugins/com/taglib/wdjsp/applet/CountDown.class, where the subdirectories are derived by combining the value of the `codebase` attribute with the package names appearing in the value of the `code` attribute. Here, the plugins directory should be a subdirectory of the directory which contains the JSP page.

This second example loads a Bean from a serialized object file:

```
<jsp:plugin type="bean" codebase="/resources/objects"
            code="MagicPizzaBean.ser" … >
```

Here, the serialized object is stored in the file /resources/objects/MagicPizzaBean.ser. In this case, an absolute URL has been specified for the `codebase` attribute, so the resources directory should be one of the web server's top-level document directories.

Table C.1 Required attributes of the `<jsp:plugin> tag`

Attribute	Value	Description
`type`	`applet` or `bean`	Type of Java component to be loaded into browser.
`code`	File name	File containing Java component, either a serialized object or a class file qualified with package name, relative to `codebase` value.
`codebase`	Directory URL	Directory on server containing file specified by `code` attribute.
`height`	Integer	Vertical dimension (in pixels) of the Java component within the browser window.
`width`	Integer	Horizontal dimension (in pixels) of the Java component within the browser window.

C.2.2 *Optional attributes*

Several optional attributes are also supported by the `<jsp:plugin>` action, as summarized in table C.2. Those which share the same name as attributes of the original HTML `<applet>` tag have corresponding behavior. Three of these attributes, however, are unique to the `<jsp:plugin>` tag: `jreversion`, `nspluginurl`, and `iepluginurl`.

The `jreversion` attribute is used to indicate which version of the JRE is required to run the applet or bean. The value of this attribute is used to determine whether or not the JRE being used by the plug-in is compatible with the component that is to be loaded and run. The default value of this attribute is `1.1`, indicating the component is compatible with JRE version 1.1 or higher. The JRE for Java 2 is JRE version 1.2, so for Java 2 applets and JavaBeans this attribute should be set to `1.2`.

The `nspluginurl` and `iepluginurl` attributes are used to indicate the URLs from which the plug-in code for the browsers can be downloaded. The `nspluginurl` attribute specifies the location of the plug-in for Communicator, while `iepluginurl` provides the location of the plug-in for Internet Explorer. Default values for these two URLs are implementation-specific. Because the code for the plug-in can be quite large (i.e., multiple megabytes), you may wish to install copies of the plug-in software on a local server, to improve download performance. In this case, these two attributes are used to point to the local copies so that, if the plug-in has not been installed when the browser encounters the HTML generated by the `<jsp:plugin>` action, it will look for the required software on that local server instead of attempting to load it from some default location on the Internet.

Table C.2 Optional attributes of the `<jsp:plugin>` tag

Attribute	Value	Default	Description
`align`	Text string	`baseline`	Alignment of the Java component relative to other page elements. Allowed values are `left`, `right`, `top`, `texttop`, `middle`, `absmiddle`, `baseline`, `bottom`, and `absbottom`.
`name`	Text string	None	Name by which other components on the same page can reference the Java component.
`archive`	File names	None	Comma-separated list of JAR files containing resources (classes, images, data files, etc.) to be preloaded.
`vspace`	Integer	0	Margin (in pixels) that should appear on the left and right sides of the Java component in the browser window.
`hspace`	Integer	0	Margin (in pixels) that should appear above and below the Java component in the browser window.
`title`	Text string	None	Descriptive title for the applet that may be optionally displayed by the browser (e.g., via the status bar or as a tool tip).
`jreversion`	Version	`1.2`	Version of the JRE required to run the Java component.
`nsplugin`	URL	Implementation-specific	Location from which the Java Plug-in for Netscape Communicator can be downloaded.
`ieplugin`	URL	Implementation-specific	Location from which the Java Plug-in for Microsoft Internet Explorer can be downloaded.

C.2.3 *Parameters*

Applets may be configured on a page-by-page basis by means of parameters passed in from the browser. When using the HTML `<applet>` tag, this is accomplished via the `<param>` tag. When the `<jsp:plugin>` tag is used to specify an applet or bean, parameter values are set by means of the `<jsp:param>` tag, which takes the following form:

```
<jsp:param name="parameterName" value="parameterValue"/>
```

The `name` attribute designates the name of the parameter to be set, and the `value` attribute specifies its value, which may take the form of a JSP expression representing a request-time attribute value. An applet accesses these parameters via the `getParameter()` method of the `java.applet.Applet` class, and all applet parameter values are interpreted as character strings. The applet itself is responsible for parsing parameter values that represent other data types, such as numeric values.

Multiple applet parameters can be set via multiple `<jsp:param>` tags. All `<jsp:param>` tags, however, must occur within the body of `<jsp:params>` tag, which itself occurs within the body of the `<jsp:plugin>` action. The overall syntax for specifying applet parameters, then, is as follows:

```
<jsp:plugin ... >
    ...
    <jsp:params>
     <jsp:param name="parameterName1" value="parameterValue1"/>
     ...
     <jsp:param name="parameterNameN" value="parameterValueN"/>
    </jsp:params>
    ...
</jsp:plugin>
```

Note that only one set of parameter values, as bounded by the `<jsp:params>` and `</jsp:params>` delimiter tags, should occur within the body of the `<jsp:plugin>` action.

In addition to applet parameter values, the `<jsp:param>` tag can also be used to configure beans loaded via the `<jsp:plugin>` action. In this case, the `name` attribute of each `<jsp:param>` tag is interpreted as the name of a bean property, and the `value` attribute indicates the value to which the property should be set. As for applet parameters, bean property values can be provided via JSP expressions by providing a request-time attribute `value` for the value attribute.

C.2.4 Fallback text

Successful use of the `<jsp:plugin>` action is dependent upon the end user being able to run the Java plug-in from their browser. As a result of this reliance on the installation and configuration of end-user software, it is convenient to be able to gracefully handle situations in which, for whatever reason, the Java plug-in cannot be run. This is the role of the `<jsp:fallback>` tag.

The `<jsp:fallback>` tag is used to specify content to be displayed in the output of the JSP page in the event the Java plug-in fails to be started by the browser. This content is delimited by matching `<jsp:fallback>` and `</jsp:fallback>` tags, as in the following example:

```
<jsp:plugin … >
    …
    <jsp:fallback>
    Sorry, unable to start <b>Java Plug-in</b> to run Java 2 applet.
    </jsp:fallback>
    …
</jsp:plugin>
```

Note that since the `<jsp:plugin>` action is used to load Java components into a web browser, its utility is generally limited to JSP pages used to construct HTML documents. As a result, it is perfectly acceptable for the fallback text in the body of the `<jsp:fallback>` tag to include HTML markup, as in this example.

The fallback text is only displayed when there are problems with the plug-in itself. If, instead, there is a problem with the applet or JavaBean to be loaded via the plug-in, the plug-in will display an error message to that effect. The exact contents and presentation of this error message are implementation-specific.

C.3 Example: applet configuration

One particular advantage of combining JSP with applets is that the applet can be configured at run time. This is made possible by the use of request-time attribute values when specifying the `value` attributes of one or more `<jsp:param>` tags. In this way, the values of the corresponding applet parameters are computed by the JSP page at the time the request for the page is processed.

Consider, for example, the Java class presented in listing C.3. This class, `com.taglib.wdjsp.applets.CountDown`, defines an applet that implements a timer, counting down to a date and time specified via applet parameters. Since this is a book on JSP rather than applet design, we will not consider the details of this code. In brief, then, the various components specifying the state of the timer are stored as an array of `String` elements, which are updated via a thread represented by the `countdown` instance variable. This thread updates the timer's state every tenth of a second, until the countdown expires. Two parameters, named `endTime` and `endDate`, are used to configure the applet.

To allow the user to set these configuration parameters, a form could be provided for selecting the desired date and time. One such form is presented in figure C.1, with the corresponding (abbreviated) HTML code presented in listing C.1. Note that the value of the `action` attribute for this document's `<form>` tag is set to a JSP page, specifically `/webdev/countdown.jsp`.

When this form is submitted, the values of its form fields are sent via a `POST` request to the specified page. This page, whose source code appears in listing C.2,

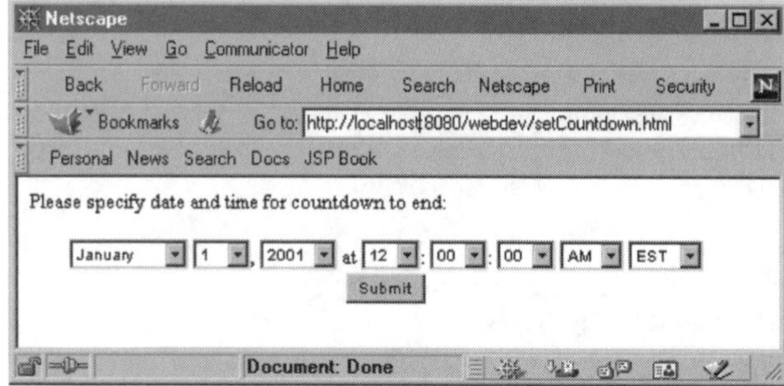

Figure C.1 Form for configuring countdown applet

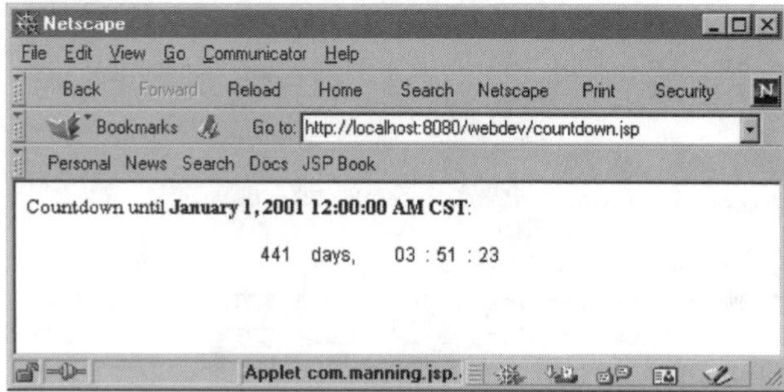

Figure C.2 Countdown applet running via `<jsp:plugin>` tag

uses those form values to construct a date string and a time string, using a scriptlet to retrieve those parameters from the `request` implicit object. These two strings are then supplied as parameters to the Java applet, via request-time attribute values. The result is presented in figure C.2

Listing C.1 Abbreviated HTML source code for applet configuration form

```
<html>
<body> Please specify date and time for countdown to end:<br>
<center><form action="/webdev/countdown.jsp" method="POST">
<select name="month" size="1">
  <option value="January" selected>January</option>
  <option value="February">February</option>
  ...
  <option value="December">December</option>
</select>
<select name="day" size="1">
  <option value="1" selected>1</option>
```

```
  <option value="2">2</option> ... <option value="31">31</option>
</select>,
<select name="year" size="1">
  <option value="2000" selected>2000</option>
  <option value="2001">2001</option> ... <option value="2005">2005</option>
</select>
at
<select name="hour" size="1">
  <option value="1">1</option> ... <option value="11">11</option>
  <option value="12" selected>12</option>
</select>:
<select name="minutes" size="1">
  <option value="00" selected>00</option>
  <option value="01">01</option> ... <option value="59">59</option>
</select>:
<select name="seconds" size="1">
  <option value="00" selected>00</option>
  <option value="01">01</option> ... <option value="59">59</option>
</select>
<select name="ampm" size="1">
  <option value="AM">AM</option><option value="PM">PM</option>
</select>
<select name="zone" size="1">
  <option value="EST">EST</option><option value="EDT">EDT</option>
  <option value="CST">CST</option><option value="CDT">CDT</option>
  <option value="MST">MST</option><option value="MDT">MDT</option>
  <option value="PST">PST</option><option value="PDT">PDT</option>
</select><br>
<input type="submit" value="Submit">
</form></center>
</body>
</html>
```

Listing C.2 JSP page for displaying applet via <jsp:plugin> tag

```
<html>
<body>
<% String month = request.getParameter("month");
   if (month == null) month = "January";
   String day = request.getParameter("day");
   if (day == null) day = "1";
   String year = request.getParameter("year");
   if (year == null) year = "2001";
   String hour = request.getParameter("hour");
   if (hour == null) hour = "12";
   String minutes = request.getParameter("minutes");
   if (minutes == null) minutes = "00";
   String seconds = request.getParameter("seconds");
   if (seconds == null) seconds = "00";
```

```
    String ampm = request.getParameter("ampm");
    if (ampm == null) ampm = "AM";
    String zone = request.getParameter("zone");
    if (zone == null) zone = "CST";
    String date = month + " " + day + ", " + year;
    String time =
     hour + ":" + minutes + ":" + seconds + " " + ampm + " " + zone;
 %>
Countdown until <b><%= date %> <%= time %></b>:<br>
<center>
<jsp:plugin type="applet" codebase="plugins"
            code="com.taglib.wdjsp.applets.CountDown"
            width="300" height="50"
            jreversion="1.2">
  <jsp:params>
    <jsp:param name="endDate" value="<%= date %>" />
    <jsp:param name="endTime" value="<%= time %>" />
  </jsp:params>
  <jsp:fallback>Unable to start Java Plug-in for applet.</jsp:fallback>
</jsp:plugin>
</center>
</body>
</html>
```

Listing C.3 com.taglib.wdjsp.applets.CountDown class

```
package com.taglib.wdjsp.applets;

import java.applet.*;
import java.awt.*;
import java.util.*;
import java.text.*;

public class CountDown extends Applet implements Runnable {
    private Thread countdown;
    private long ends;
    private int height, width;
    Image offscreen;
    private String[] text = new String[FIELDS];
    private int[] textWidth = new int[FIELDS];
    Font font;
    FontMetrics fontMetrics;
    private int fontHeight, ascent;

    static final int FIELDS = 7;
    static final int DAYS = 0;
    static final int HOURS = 2;
    static final int MINUTES = 4;
    static final int SECONDS = 6;
```

```
// Constructor
public CountDown () {
 ends = 0l;
 long now = new Date().getTime()/1000l;
 ends = now + 7l * 24l * 60l * 60l; // One week
 ends = now + 24l * 60l * 60l + 30; // One day
 text[HOURS+1] = ":";
 text[MINUTES+1] = ":";
 updateElements();
 width = 0;
 height = 0;
 font = new Font("Helvetica", Font.BOLD, 18);
 fontMetrics = this.getFontMetrics(font);
 fontHeight = fontMetrics.getHeight();
 ascent = fontMetrics.getAscent();
}

// Display code
public void paint (Graphics g) {
 g.setColor(Color.white);
 g.fillRect(0, 0, width, height);
 g.setColor(Color.black);
 int strWidth = 0;
 for (int i = 0; i < FIELDS; ++i) {
     textWidth[i] = fontMetrics.stringWidth(text[i]);
     strWidth += textWidth[i];
 }
 int x = (width - strWidth)/2;
 int y = (height + fontHeight - ascent)/2;
 for (int i = 0; i < FIELDS; ++i) {
     g.drawString(text[i], x, y);
     x += textWidth[i];
 }
}

// Thread code
public void run () {
 boolean updating = false;
 boolean counting = true;
 while (counting) {
     if (! updating) {
      updating = true;
      try {
          counting = updateElements();
          updateDisplay();
      }
      finally { updating = false; }
    }
    try { Thread.sleep(100); } catch (InterruptedException e) {};
 }
```

```
}

// Updating
final static long minuteSeconds = 60l;
final static long hourSeconds = 60l * minuteSeconds;
final static long daySeconds = 24l * hourSeconds;

private boolean updateElements () {
 long now = new Date().getTime()/1000l;
 if (now >= ends) {
     setDays(0);
     setElement(HOURS, 0);
     setElement(MINUTES, 0);
     setElement(SECONDS, 0);
     return false;
 } else {
     long remaining = ends - now;
     long days = remaining/daySeconds;
     setDays(days);
     remaining -= days*daySeconds;
     long hours = remaining/hourSeconds;
     setElement(HOURS, hours);
     remaining -= hours*hourSeconds;
     long minutes = remaining/minuteSeconds;
     setElement(MINUTES, minutes);
     remaining -= minutes*minuteSeconds;
     setElement(SECONDS, remaining);
     return true;
 }
}
private void setElement (int index, long t) {
 if (t < 10) {
     text[index] = "0" + Long.toString(t);
 } else {
     text[index] = Long.toString(t);
 }
}
private void setDays (long d) {
 text[DAYS] = Long.toString(d);
 text[DAYS + 1] = (d == 1l) ? " day, " : " days, ";
}

private void updateDisplay () {
 Dimension size = this.getSize();
 if ((offscreen == null)
     || (width != size.width)
     || (height != size.height)) {
     width = size.width;
     height = size.height;
     offscreen = this.createImage(width, height);
 }
```

```
    Graphics g = offscreen.getGraphics();
    paint(g);
    g = this.getGraphics();
    g.drawImage(offscreen, 0, 0, this);
  }

  // Applet Lifecycle
  public void init () {
    String endTime = getParameter("endTime");
    if (endTime == null) endTime = "12:00am";
    String endDate = getParameter("endDate");
    if (endDate == null) endDate = "January 1, 2001";
    DateFormat fmt = DateFormat.getDateTimeInstance(DateFormat.LONG,
                 DateFormat.LONG,
                 Locale.US);
    Date d;
    try {
        d = fmt.parse(endDate + " " + endTime);
    }
    catch (ParseException e) {
        System.err.println("Error while parsing date: " + e.getClass());
        System.err.println(e.getMessage());
        d = new Date();
    }
    ends = d.getTime()/1000l;
  }
  public void start () {
    countdown = new Thread(this);
    countdown.start();
  }
  public void stop () {
    if (countdown != null) countdown.stop();
    countdown = null;
  }
}
```

D JSP resources

D.1 Java implementations

http://java.sun.com/jdk
Sun Microsystem's implementations of the Java platform for the Solaris, Linux, and Windows operating systems.

http://www.developer.ibm.com/java/member/technical/jdk.html
IBM's implementations of the Java platform for the Windows, Linux, AIX, OS/2, AS/400, OS/390, and VM/ESA operating systems. Registration required.

http://www.sgi.com/developers/devtools/languages/java.html
SGI's implementation of the Java platform for the IRIX operating system.

http://www.hp.com/products1/unix/java/
Hewlett Packard's implementation of the Java platform for the HPUX operating system.

http://oss.software.ibm.com/developerworks/opensource/jikes/
Home page for Jikes, a high-speed Java compiler.

D.2 JSP-related web sites

http://java.sun.com/products/jsp
Sun Microsystem's official home page for JSP technology.

http://www.taglib.com/
Home page for this book, featuring source code and a collection of JSP custom tag libraries.

http://www.deepmagic.com/
Duane Fields' web site, with an archive of articles and presentations on JSP and Java development.

http://jakarta.apache.org/taglibs/
Jakarta open source tag libraries

http://www.ibazaar.com/jasp/index.htm
JaSP!, a web-based journal and newsletter focusing on JSP and related technologies.

http://www.serverpages.com/index.html
Online programmer resources for several server-side scripting technologies, including JSP.

http://us.imdb.com/Title?0084827
Critical resources for JSP book authors.

D.3 JSP FAQs and tutorials

http://java.sun.com/products/jsp/docs.html
A series of JSP tutorials and reference information from Sun Microsystems.

http://java.sun.com/products/jsp/faq.html
Sun's official online FAQ.

http://www.esperanto.org.nz/jsp/jspfaq.jsp
The unofficial online FAQ.

http://www.jguru.com/jguru/faq/faqpage.jsp?name=JSP
An interactive FAQ from jGuru, with visitor-submitted questions.

http://www2.software.ibm.com/developer/education.nsf/java-onlinecourse-bytitle
Online Java tutorials from IBM, including "Introduction to JavaServer Pages."

http://java.sun.com/products/jsp/tutorial/TagLibrariesTOC.html
A tutorial on writing tag libraries from Sun Microsystems.

D.4 JSP containers

http://jakarta.apache.org/tomcat/
Home page for Tomcat, the official reference implementation of the servlet and JSP specifications. Tomcat is available as source code and in compiled form.

http://www.caucho.com/
Web site for Resin, a servlet and JSP container supporting both Java and server-side JavaScript as its scripting languages.

http://www.klomp.org/gnujsp/
Home page for GNUJSP, an open source implementation of the JSP specification.

http://www.newatlanta.com/
Web site for New Atlanta, makers of ServletExec.

http://www.plenix.org/polyjsp/
An open source JSP container that supports multiple scripting languages.

D.5 Java application servers with JSP support

http://java.sun.com/j2ee
Sun Microsystem's home page for J2EE. The reference implementation of J2EE, available here, includes a JSP container.

http://www.orionserver.com/
Home page for the Orion application server.

http://www.allaire.com/Products/Jrun
Home page for JRun, from Allaire.

http://www.bea.com/java
Web site for BEA Systems, makers of the WebLogic application server.

http://www.bluestone.com/
Web site for the Bluestone/Sapphire web application server.

http://www.gemstone.com/
Web site for the GemStone application server.

http://www.ibm.com/software/webservers/
Home page for IBM's WebSphere application server.

http://www.inprise.com/appserver/
Web site for the Inprise application server from Borland.

http://www.iplanet.com/
Web site for the Sun-Netscape Alliance, makers of the iPlanet server.

http://www.oracle.com/java/
Web site for Oracle's 9i, with Java.

http://www.silverstream.com/
Web site for the SilverStream application server.

http://www.flashline.com/components/appservermatrix.jsp
A matrix comparing the features and platform support of all the major application servers (Java-based and otherwise), hosted by Flashline.com.

D.6 JSP development tools

http://www.allaire.com/Products/HomeSite
Home page for HomeSite, a web page authoring tool from Allaire with built-in support for JSP tags.

http://www.forte.com/
Forte is an integrated JSP development environment.

http://www-4.ibm.com/software/webservers/studio/index.html
Product information about IBM's Websphere Studio, which includes a tool for visually creating and editing JSP pages.

http://www.macromedia.com/software/ultradev/
Web site for Macromedia's UltraDev, a visual editor for authoring JSP pages.

D.7 Tools for performance testing

http://jakarta.apache.org/jmeter/
Like Tomcat, JMeter is a product of the Jakarta Project. JMeter is a tool for measuring servlet and JSP performance.

http://www.binevolve.com/velometer/velometer.vet
VeloMeter is a web server load tester from Binary Evolution, distributed as open source. A commercial version, VeloMeter Pro, is also available.

http://www.sitraka.com/
Sitraka Software's (formerly KL Group) JProbe ServerSide Suite bundles multiple tools for tuning the performance of server-side Java applications.

http://www.vmgear.com/
Optimize It!, from VMGear is a profiling tool for Java applications that can be integrated directly with a large number of JSP containers and Java Application Servers.

D.8 Mailing lists and newsgroups

JSP-INTEREST@java.sun.com
A mailing list for technical discussions among developers who are deploying JSP technology. To subscribe, use the archive site described next, or send an email

message to listserv@java.sun.com with the text subscribe JSP-INTEREST as the body of the message.

http://archives.java.sun.com/archives/jsp-interest.html
: These are the online archives for the `JSP-INTEREST` mailing list. Forms are available for searching past messages, as well as for subscribing or unsubscribing to the mailing list.

comp.lang.java.*
: This is the Usenet News hierarchy dedicated to discussion of the Java programming language. There are, as yet, no groups dedicated to either servlet or JSP development, but occasional discussions of these topics do appear on some of the existing Java newsgroups, such as comp.lang.java.programmer and comp.lang.java.misc. If you are relatively new to Java programming, you may find the discussions in the comp.lang.java.help and comp.lang.java.setup groups particularly helpful.

E JSP syntax reference

In this appendix we'll summarize the usage of all of the JSP tags discussed in this book. This listing is intended primarily as a quick reference to JSP, and repeats information presented elsewhere. If you're in a hurry, reading this appendix will get you started, but is no substitute for studying the thorough discussion and examples of each tag, especially the coverage provided in chapters 1 through 8.

E.1 Content comments

Content comments will be sent back to the browser as part of the response. Since they are comments, they do not produce any visible output, but they may be viewed by the end user via the browser's View Source menu item.

Syntax

XML: `<!-- comment -->`

Standard: `<!-- comment -->`

Description

Those familiar with HTML and XML will recognize that this is the standard comment syntax for the two markup languages. Thus, a JSP page that is generating either HTML or XML simply uses the native comment syntax for whichever form of content it is constructing. Content comments are part of the output from the page. You can, if you wish, include dynamic content in them. HTML and XML comments can, for example, include JSP expressions, and the output generated by these expressions will appear as part of the comment in the page's response.

Examples

```
<!-- begin dynamically generated content -->
<%= new java.util.Date() %>
<!-- end dynamically generated content -->

<!-- longs are 64 bits, so 20! = <%= fact(20) %> is the upper limit. -->
```

E.2 JSP comments

JSP comments are independent of the type of content being produced by the page. They are also independent of the scripting language used by the page. These comments can only be viewed by examining the original JSP file

Syntax

XML: same

Standard: `<%-- comment --%>`

Description

The body of a JSP comment is ignored by the JSP container. When the page is compiled into a servlet, anything appearing between these two delimiters is skipped while translating the page into servlet source code. For this reason, comments such as this are very useful for commenting out portions of a JSP page, as when debugging.

Examples

```
int y = 0;
int z = 3;
<%-- y = 2; --%>
z = 4;

<table width="150">
<%-- Really should make the width dynamic --%>
<tr><td>Hello There</td></tr>
</table>
```

E.3 <jsp:declaration>

Declarations define a variable or method for use on the current page, using the current page's designated scripting language.

Syntax

XML: `<jsp:declaration> declaration(s) </jsp:declaration>`

Standard: `<%! declaration(s) %>`

Description

Declarations are used to define variables and methods for use by other scripting elements on a specific JSP page. Multiple declarations may appear within a single tag, but each declaration must be a complete declarative statement in the designated scripting language. White space after the opening delimiter and before the closing delimiter is optional, but recommended to improve readability. Variables defined as declarations become instance variables of the servlet class into which the JSP page is translated and compiled. Since variables specified via JSP declarations are directly translated into variables of the corresponding servlet class, they may also be used to declare class variables, whose values are shared among all instances of a class rather than being specific to an individual instance. Methods defined via declarations become methods of the servlet class into which the JSP page is compiled. Class methods, also known as static methods, are associated with the class itself, rather than individual instances, and may be called without requiring access to an instance of the class. In fact, class methods are typically called simply by prepending the name of the class to the name of the method. Class methods may reference only class variables, not instance variables.

Examples

```
<%! private int x = 0, y = 0; %>

<jsp:declaration> String units = "ft"; </jsp:declaration>

<%!
  public long fact (long x) {
    if (x == 0)
      return 1;
    else
      return x * fact(x-1);
  }
%>
```

E.4 <jsp:directive.include>

The `include` directive enables page authors to include the contents of one file in another. The file to be included is identified via a local URL, and the directive has the effect of replacing itself with the contents of the indicated file.

Syntax

XML: `<jsp:directive.include file="localURL" />`

Standard: `<%@ include file="localURL" %>`

Description

There are no restrictions on the number of `include` directives that may appear in a single JSP page. There are also no restrictions on nesting; it is completely valid for a JSP page to include another JSP page, which itself includes one or more others. All included pages must use the same scripting language as the original page. The value of the `include` directive's `file` attribute can be specified as an absolute path on the local server, or relative to the current page, depending upon whether or not it starts with a forward slash character.

Examples

```
<%@ include file="includes/navigation.jsp" %>

<%@ include file="/shared/epilogue/copyright.html" %>
```

E.5 <jsp:directive.page>

The `page` directive is used to convey special processing information about the page to the JSP container. The `page` directive supports a wide range of attributes and associated functionality, as summarized in table E.1.

Syntax

XML: `<jsp:directive.page attribute1="value1" attribute2="value2" attribute3=… />`

Standard: `<%@ page attribute1="value1" attribute2="value2" attribute3=… %>`

Description

The `page` directive does not directly produce any output that is visible to end users when the page is requested; instead, it generates side effects that change the way the JSP container processes the page. The `page` directive supports a number of attributes. With the exception of the `import` attribute, however, no individual `page` directive attribute may be specified multiple times on the same page.

Table E.1 Attributes supported by the page directive

Attribute	Value	Default	Examples
`info`	Text string	None	`info="Registration form."`
`language`	Scripting language name	`"java"`	`language="java"`
`contentType`	MIME type, character set	See first example	`contentType="text/html;charset=ISO-8859-1"` `contentType="text/xml"`
`pageEncoding`	ISO character set	ISO-8859-1	`pageEncoding="ISO-8859-5"`
`extends`	Class name	None	`extends="com.taglib.wdjsp.MyJspPage"`
`import`	Class and/or package names	None	`import="java.net.URL"` `import="java.util.*, java.text.*"`
`session`	Boolean flag	`"true"`	`session="true"`
`buffer`	Buffer size, or `false`	`"8kb"`	`buffer="12kb"` `buffer="false"`
`autoFlush`	Boolean flag	`"true"`	`autoFlush="false"`
`isThreadSafe`	Boolean flag	`"true"`	`isThreadSafe="true"`
`errorPage`	Local URL	None	`errorPage="results/failed.jsp"`
`isErrorPage`	Boolean flag	`"false"`	`isErrorPage="false"`

Examples

```
<%@ page contentType="text/xml" %>

<%@ page import="java.util.*" %>

<%@ page info="This is a valid set of page directives." %>
<%@ page language="java" import="java.net.*" %>
<%@ page import="java.util.List, java.util.ArrayList" %>
```

E.6 <jsp:directive.taglib>

The `taglib` directive is used to notify the JSP container that a page relies on one or more custom tag libraries. A tag library is a collection of custom tags that can be used to extend the functionality of JSP on a page-by-page basis.

Syntax

XML: `<jsp:directive.taglib uri="tagLibraryURI" prefix="tagPrefix" />`

Standard: `<%@ taglib uri="tagLibraryURI" prefix="tagPrefix" %>`

Description

In both cases, the value of the `uri` attribute indicates the location of the TLD, and the `prefix` attribute specifies the XML namespace identifier that will be prepended to all occurrences of the library's tags on the page. Once this directive has been used to indicate the reliance of a page on a specific tag library, all of the custom tags defined in that library become available for use on that page. Because the tag prefix is specified external to the library itself, and on a page-specific basis, multiple libraries can be loaded by a single page without the risk of conflicts between tag names. If two libraries define tags with the same name, a JSP page would still be able to load and use both libraries since it can distinguish between those tags via their prefixes. As such, there are no restrictions on how many `taglib` directives may appear on a page, as long as each is assigned a unique prefix. If, however, the JSP container cannot find the TLD at the indicated location, or the page references a tag that is not actually defined in the library, an error will result when the JSP container tries to compile the page.

Examples

```
<jsp:directive.taglib uri="/localTags" prefix="my"/>

<%@ taglib uri="/EncomTags" prefix="mcp" %>
<mcp:showUser user="flynn">
  firstname, lastname, idnumber
</mcp:showUser>
```

E.7 <jsp:expression>

Expressions are code fragments evaluated at run time. The JSP expression element is explicitly intended for content generation, displaying the output of the code fragment's execution into the page content.

Syntax

XML: `<jsp:expression> expression </jsp:expression>`

Standard: `<%= expression %>`

Description

In both syntax cases, the *expression* should be a valid and complete scripting language expression, in whatever scripting language has been specified for the page. Note that no end-of-line marker (in Java, the ;) is present. The effect of this element is to evaluate the specified expression and substitute the resulting value into the output of the page, in place of the element itself. JSP expressions can be used to print out individual variables, or the result of some calculation or other operation. Any valid scripting language expression is allowed, so calls to methods are likewise permitted. Expressions can return Java primitive values, such as numbers, characters, and booleans, or full-fledged Java objects, such as `String` objects and JavaBeans. All expression results are converted to character strings before they are added to the page's output.

Examples

```
The value of PI is about <%= Math.PI %>

The time is <%= hours %> <%= (hours < 12) ? "AM" : "PM" %>

Hello <%= request.getRemoteUser() %>
```

E.8 <jsp:forward>

The `<jsp:forward>` action is used to permanently transfer control from a JSP page to another location on the local server.

Syntax

XML: `<jsp:forward page="localURL" />`

or

```
<jsp:forward page="localURL">
  <jsp:param name="parameterName1" value="parameterValue1"/>
  ...
  <jsp:param name="parameterNameN" value="parameterValueN"/>
</jsp:forward>
```

Standard: `same`

Description

The `page` attribute of the `<jsp:forward>` action is used to specify this alternate location to which control should be transferred, which may be a static document, a CGI, a servlet, or another JSP page. Since the `request` object is common to both the original page and the forwarded page, any request parameters that were available on the original page will also be accessible from the forwarded page. If additional parameters are supplied, they are passed to the receiving page.

The browser from which the request was submitted is not notified when the request is transferred to this alternate URL. In particular, the location field at the top of the browser window will continue to display the URL that was originally requested. Any content generated by the current page is discarded, and processing of the request begins anew at the alternate location. For added flexibility, the `<jsp:forward>` action supports the use of request-time attribute values. In addition, the `<jsp:param>` tag may be used to specify additional request parameters.

For the specific case when control is transferred to another JSP page, the JSP container will automatically assign a new `pageContext` object to the forwarded page. The `request` object and the `session` object, though, will be the same for both the original page and the forwarded page. Sharing of the `application` object depends upon whether or not the two pages are both part of the same application. Thus, some, but not all, of the attribute values accessible from the original page will be accessible on the forwarded page, depending upon their scope: page attributes are not shared, request and session attributes are, and application attributes may or may not be.

Examples

```
<jsp:forward page="showresults.jsp">
  <jsp:param name="header" value="Results of Query"/>
  <jsp:param name="color" value="blue"/>
</jsp:forward>

<% if (! database.isAvailable()) { %>
   // Notify the user about routine maintenance.
   <jsp:forward page="db-maintenance.html"/>
<% } %>
<%-- Database is up, proceeed as usual... --%>
```

E.9 <jsp:getProperty>

The `<jsp:getProperty>` action is the primary way to access a bean's properties in JSP.

Syntax

XML: `<jsp:getProperty name="`*`bean name`*`" property="`*`property name`*`"/>`

Standard: same

Description

Unlike the `<jsp:useBean>` action which performs some work behind the scenes but doesn't produce any output, the `<jsp:getProperty>` action produces content that we can see in the HTML generated by the page. The `name` attribute specifies the bean we are accessing, and should correspond to the identifier we selected for the bean in the `<jsp:useBean>` tag's `id` attribute. In the resulting HTML that is displayed at run time, this tag is replaced with the value of the property of the bean being requested. Of course, since we are creating an HTML document, the property is first converted into text by the JSP container. You can use as many `<jsp:getProperty>` tags in your page as you need. You can intersperse them with HTML to not only dynamically generate individual values and blocks of text, but to control attributes of the HTML as well. It is perfectly legal to nest JSP tags inside HTML attribute values. For example, a bean property could be used to control the page's background color, the width of a table, or the source of an image.

Examples

```
<jsp:getProperty name="user" property="department"/>

<jsp:useBean id="myclock" class="ClockBean"/>
<html>
<body>
```

```
The Bean says that the time is now:
<jsp:getProperty name="myclock" property="time"/>
</body>
</html>
```

E.10 <jsp:include>

The `<jsp:include>` action enables page authors to incorporate the content generated by another local document into the output of the current page.

Syntax

XML: `<jsp:include page="localURL" flush="boolean" />`

or

```
<jsp:include page="localURL" flush="true">
  <jsp:param name="parameterName1" value="parameterValue1"/>
  ...
  <jsp:param name="parameterNameN" value="parameterValueN"/>
</jsp:include>
```

Standard: same

Description

The output from the included document is inserted into the original page's output in place of the `<jsp:include>` tag, after which processing of the original page resumes. In contrast to the `<jsp:forward>` tag, this action is used to *temporarily* transfer control from a JSP page to another location on the local server. The `page` attribute of the `<jsp:include>` action is used to identify the document whose output is to be inserted into the current page, and is specified as a URL on the local server. The included page can be a static document, a CGI, a servlet, or another JSP page. As with the `<jsp:forward>` action, the `page` attribute of the `<jsp:include>` action supports request-time attribute values. The `<jsp:param>` tag may be used to specify additional request parameters.

The `flush` attribute of the `<jsp:include>` action controls whether or not the output buffer for the current page is flushed prior to including the content from the included page. As of version 1.2 of the JSP specification the `flush` attribute is optional, defaulting to `false`. In version 1.1 of the JSP specification this attribute is not only required, it has only one legal value, `true`. If enabled, the output buffer is flushed as the first step in performing the `<jsp:include>` action, forwarding to another page—including an error page—is not possible. Likewise, setting cookies or other HTTP headers will not succeed if attempted after processing a

`<jsp:include>` tag with buffer flushing enabled. Keep in mind however that even with this attribute disabled the page buffer may fill up as a result of the included content, causing an automatic flush.

If the included page changes, its changes will be reflected immediately. In contrast, the JSP `include` directive does not automatically update the including page when the included file is modified. This is because the `include` directive takes effect when the including page is translated into a servlet, effectively merging the base contents of the included page into those of the original. The `<jsp:include>` action takes effect when processing requests, and merges the output from the included page, rather than its original text.

Examples

```
<jsp:include page="/headers/support_header.jsp" flush="true"/>

<jsp:include page="topten.jsp" flush="true">
  <jsp:param name="category" value="books"/>
</jsp:include>
```

E.11 <jsp:plugin>

The `<jsp:plugin>` action provides a cross-platform mechanism for incorporating applets based on the Java 2 platform into JSP pages.

Syntax

XML:

```
<jsp:plugin type="type" code="objectCode" codebase="objectCodeBase"
            attribute1="value1" attribute2="value2" … />
```

or

```
<jsp:plugin type="type" code="objectCode" codebase="objectCodeBase"
            attribute1="value1" attribute2="value2" … >
  <jsp:params>
    <jsp:param name="parameterName1" value="parameterValue1"/>
    …
    <jsp:param name="parameterNameN" value="parameterValueN"/>
  </jsp:params>
  <jsp:fallback>fallback text</jsp:fallback>
</jsp:plugin>
```

Standard: same

Description

The `<jsp:plugin>` action uses Sun Microsystem's Java plug-in to run an applet or JavaBean in the end user's browser. Browser-specific code is inserted into the output of the JSP page for loading the Java plug-in, which is based on the Java 2 JVM, and running the specified code. The `code` attribute indicates the Java class to be run, while the `codebase` attribute indicates where this class is located on the server. If value of the `type` attribute is `"applet"`, the specified class is presumed to be an applet. If this attribute's value is `"bean"`, a JavaBean is assumed. The `<jsp:plugin>` action also supports all of the attributes supported by HTML's `<applet>` tag, of which the `height` and `width` attributes are required.

Applet parameters are specified via the `<jsp:param>` tag, and must be delimited as a group in the body of a `<jsp:params>` tag. The `<jsp:fallback>` tag is used to specify the content that should be displayed if the Java plug-in is not available in the end user's browser.

Examples

```
<jsp:plugin type="bean" code="timer.ser" width="100" height="50"/>

<jsp:plugin type="applet" codebase="plugins"
            code="com.taglib.wdjsp.applets.CountDown"
            width="300" height="50"
            jreversion="1.2">
  <jsp:params>
    <jsp:param name="endDate" value="<%= date %>" />
    <jsp:param name="endTime" value="<%= time %>" />
  </jsp:params>
  <jsp:fallback>Unable to start Java Plug-in for applet.</jsp:fallback>
</jsp:plugin>
```

E.12 *<jsp:scriptlet>*

Scriptlets are the primary way to include fragments of code, typically Java, into a JSP page. Scriptlets can contain arbitrary scripting language statements, which—like declarations—are evaluated for side effect only. Scriptlets do not automatically add content to a JSP page's output.

Syntax

XML: `<jsp:scriptlet>` *`scriptlet`* `</jsp:scriptlet>`

Standard: `<%` *`scriptlet`* `%>`

Description

For either tag style, the scriptlet should be one or more valid and complete statements in the JSP page's scripting language. Alternatively, a scriptlet can leave open one or more statement blocks, which must be closed by subsequent scriptlets in the same page. In the (default) case where the JSP scripting language is Java, statement blocks are opened using the left brace character (i.e., {) and closed using the right brace character (i.e., }). If a scriptlet opens a new block without also closing it, then the Java statements corresponding to any subsequent static content or JSP elements simply become part of this new block. The block must ultimately be closed by another scriptlet, or else compilation will fail due to a Java syntax error. A page's scriptlets will be run for each request received by the page—any variables introduced in a scriptlet are available for use in subsequent scriptlets and expressions on the same page (subject to variable scoping rules).

Examples

```
<jsp:sriptlet>
Date now = new java.util.Date();
out.println("The time is: " + now);
</jsp:scriptlet>

<table>
<% for (int j=0; j < 11; ++j) { %>
<tr><td><%= j %></td></tr>
<% } %>
</table>
```

E.13 <jsp:setProperty>

The `<jsp:setProperty>` action is used to modify the properties of beans used in the page.

Syntax

XML:

```
<jsp:setProperty name="bean name" property="property name" value="value"/>
```

or

```
<jsp:setProperty name="bean name" property="property name" param="param"/>
```

or

```
<jsp:setProperty name="bean name" property="*"/>
```

Standard: same

Description

The `<jsp:setProperty>` action can be used anywhere within the page to modify a bean's properties, as long as it appears after the `<jsp:useBean>` action used to define that bean. The bean is identified via the action's `name` attribute, which should correspond to the identifier originally assigned to a bean via the `id` attribute of its `<jsp:useBean>` tag. Only properties that have public setter methods can be modified via the `<jsp:setProperty>` action. The property to be set is specified via the tag's `property` attribute.

The `value` attribute is used to specify the value to be assigned to the indicated property, and may be a JSP expression representing a request-time attribute value. Alternatively, the `param` attribute can be used to specify the name of a request parameter whose value is to be copied to the bean property. As a special case, if the value of the `property` attribute is `"*"`, the JSP container will identify all of the request parameters whose names match those of bean properties, and make the corresponding assignments from the request parameter values to those matching properties. In all cases, the JSP container will attempt to coerce values specified by the `value` attribute or obtained from request parameters into the appropriate type for the specified property.

At run time the JSP container evaluates the tags in a page in the order they appear, from top to bottom. Any property values that you set will only be reflected in JSP elements that follow the `<jsp:setProperty>` tag within the page.

Examples

```
<jsp:setProperty name="user" property="daysLeft" value="30"/>

<jsp:setProperty name="user" property="daysLeft" value="<%= 15 * 2 %>"/>

<jsp:useBean id="clock" class="com.taglib.wdjsp.ClockBean">
  <jsp:setProperty name="clock" property="timezone" value="CST"/>
</jsp:useBean>
```

E.14 <jsp:useBean>

The `<jsp:useBean>` action tells the page that we want to make a bean available to the page. The tag is used to create a bean or fetch one from the server.

Syntax

XML: `<jsp:useBean id="bean name" class="class name"/>`

or

```
<jsp:useBean id="bean name" class="class name">
    initialization code
</jsp:useBean>
```

Standard: same

Description

The attributes of this tag specify the type of bean you wish to use and assign it a name that can later be used to refer to it. The `<jsp:useBean>` action comes in two forms, a single empty tag and a matching pair of start and end tags that contain the body of the tag, which can be used to specify initialization code. In its simplest and most straightforward form, the `<jsp:useBean>` tag requires only two attributes, `id` and `class`. The attributes of this tag are summarized in table E.2.

Table E.2 Attributes of the `<jsp:useBean>` tag

Attribute	Value	Default	Example Value
`id`	Java identifier	none	`myBean`
`scope`	`page`, `request`, `session`, `application`	page	`session`
`class`	Fully qualified Java class name	none	`java.util.Date`
`type`	Fully qualified Java class name	class value	`com.taglib.wdjsp.AbstractPerson`
`beanName`	Fully qualified Java class or serialized bean	none	`com.taglib.wdjsp.USCurrency.ser`

The `<jsp:useBean>` action creates or retrieves an instance of the bean and associates it with the identifier specified by the `id` attribute. This identifier can be used to access the bean from scripting elements, or in subsequent `<jsp:setProperty>` or `<jsp:getProperty>` tags. If a bean is not located in the scope specified by the `scope` attribute, a bean instance is created using the bean class's default constructor, and any content specified in the body of the `<jsp:useBean>` tag is processed. Otherwise, the bean is simply retrieved from the corresponding scope and the tag's body content is ignored.

Examples

```
<jsp:useBean id="now" class="java.util.Date"/>

<% @page import="com.taglib.wdjsp.*" %>
<jsp:useBean id="user" class="RegisteredUserBean"/>

<jsp:useBean id="user" class="RegisteredUser" scope="session"/>

<jsp:useBean id="news" class="NewsReports" scope="request">
  <jsp:setProperty name="news" property="category" value="financial"/>
  <jsp:setProperty name="news" property="maxItems" value="5"/>
</jsp:useBean>
```

F JSP API reference

This appendix provides summary information on the Java classes and interfaces defined by the Servlet 2.3 and JSP 1.2 specifications. It is intended as a quick reference for JSP application developers. Information about inheritance, variables, and methods is provided for each class and interface, where applicable. Note that deprecated methods have been omitted. In addition, changes introduced by these specifications relative to their 2.2 and 1.1 predecessors are marked with a dagger (†). For certain classes that are managed by the JSP container and do not provide public constructors (e.g., `javax.servlet.RequestDispatcher`), any alternative methods for obtaining instances of these classes, referred to as *factory methods*, are listed. For convenience, table 6.1, summarizing the JSP implicit objects and their types, is repeated here as well (see table F.1).

DEFINITION In the parlance of design patterns, the use of one type of object to abstract the instantiation of other types of objects is the *factory pattern*. Hence, methods for obtaining instances of a class without calling a constructor are described as *factory methods*.

F.1 JSP implicit objects

Table F.1 Implicit objects and their corresponding types

Object	Class or *Interface*	Attributes?
`page`[a]	*javax.servlet.jsp.HttpJspPage*	No
`config`	*javax.servlet.ServletConfig*	No
`request`	*javax.servlet.http.HttpServletRequest*	Yes
`response`	*javax.servlet.http.HttpServletResponse*	No
`out`	`javax.servlet.jsp.JspWriter`	No
`session`[b]	*javax.servlet.http.HttpSession*	Yes
`application`	*javax.servlet.ServletContext*	Yes
`pageContext`	`javax.servlet.jsp.PageContext`	Yes
`exception`[c]	`java.lang.Throwable`	No

a. The default type for accessing the page implicit object is java.lang.Object.

b. The session implicit object is only available on JSP pages that participate in session tracking. The default behavior is for all pages to partake in session tracking, but this can be overridden by specifying a value of `false` for the session attribute of the page directive.

c. The exception implicit object is only available on JSP pages that are designated as error pages by setting the `isErrorPage` attribute of the `page` directive to true.

F.2 Package javax.servlet

F.2.1 Interface Filter†

Constructors

No public constructors or factory methods.

```
Methodspublic void destroy ()
public void doFilter (ServletRequest request, ServletResponse response,
                      FilterChain chain)
    throws java.io.IOException, ServletException
public void init (FilterConfig config) throws ServletException
```

F.2.2 Interface FilterChain†

Constructors

No public constructors or factory methods.

Methods

```
public void doFilter (ServletRequest request, ServletResponse response)
    throws java.io.IOException, ServletException
```

F.2.3 Interface FilterConfig†

Constructors

No public constructors or factory methods.

Methods

```
public String getFilterName ()
public String getInitParameter (String name)
public java.util.Enumeration getInitParameterNames ()
public ServletContext getServletContext ()
```

F.2.4 Class GenericServlet

Inheritance

This is an abstract class.
Implements `Servlet`, `ServletConfig`, and `java.io.Serializable`.

Constructors

```
public GenericServlet ()
```

Methods

```
public void destroy ()
public String getInitParameter (String name)
public java.util.Enumeration getInitParameterNames ()
public ServletConfig getServletConfig ()
public ServletContext getServletContext ()
public String getServletInfo ()
public void init ()throws ServletException
public void init (ServletConfig config) throws ServletException
public void log (String message)
public void log (String message, Throwable t)
public void service (ServletRequest request, ServletResponse response)
     throws ServletException, java.io.IOException
```

F.2.5 Interface RequestDispatcher

Factory methods

```
ServletContext.getRequestDispatcher(String URL)
ServletContext.getNamedDispatcher(String URL)
ServletRequest.getRequestDispatcher(String URL)
```

Methods

```
public void forward (ServletRequest request, ServletResponse response)
     throws ServletException,
          java.io.IOException, java.lang.IllegalStateException
public void include (ServletRequest request, ServletResponse response)
     throws ServletException, java.io.IOException
```

F.2.6 Interface servlet

Constructors

No public constructors or factory methods.

Methods

```
public void destroy ()
public ServletConfig getServletConfig ()
public String getServletInfo ()
public void init (ServletConfig config) throws ServletException
public void service (ServletRequest request, ServletResponse response)
     throws ServletException, java.io.IOException
```

F.2.7 Interface ServletConfig

Factory methods

```
Servlet.getServletConfig()
```

Methods

```
public String getInitParameter (String name)
public java.util.Enumeration getInitParameterNames ()
public ServletContext getServletContext ()
public String getServletName ()
```

F.2.8 Interface ServletContext

Factory methods

```
Servlet.getServletContext()
ServletConfig.getServletContext()
```

Methods

```
public String getAttribute (String name)
public Java.util.Enumeration getAttributeNames ()
public ServletContext getContext (String uripath)
public String getInitParameter (String name)
public Java.util.Enumeration getInitParameterNames ()
public int getMajorVersion ()
public String getMimeType (String file)
public int getMinorVersion ()
```

```
public RequestDispatcher getNamedDispatcher (String URL)
public String getRealPath (String URL)
public RequestDispatcher getRequestDispatcher (String URL)
public java.net.URL getResource (String path)
     throws java.net.MalformedURLException
public java.io.InputStream getResourceAsStream (String path)
public java.util.Set getResourcePaths (String path)†
public String getServletContextName ()†
public String getServerInfo ()
public void log (String message)
public void log (String message, Throwable throwable)
public void removeAttribute (String name)
public void setAttribute (String name, Object value)
```

F.2.9 Interface ServletContextAttributeEvent†

Inheritance

Extends `ServletContextEvent`.

Constructors

```
public ServletContextAttributeEvent (ServletContext source,
                                     String name, String value)
```

Methods

```
public String getName ()
public String getValue ()
```

F.2.10 Interface ServletContextAttributeListener†

Inheritance

Extends `java.util.EventListener`.

Constructors

No public constructors or factory methods.

Methods

```
public void attributeAdded (ServletContextAttributeEvent event)
public void attributeRemoved (ServletContextAttributeEvent event)
public void attributeReplaced (ServletContextAttributeEvent event)
```

F.2.11 Interface ServletContextEvent†

Inheritance

Extends `java.util.EventObject`.

Constructors

```
public ServletContextEvent (ServletContext source)
```

Methods

```
public ServletContext getServletContext ()
```

F.2.12 Interface ServletContextListener†

Inheritance

Extends `java.util.EventListener`.

Constructors

No public constructors or factory methods.

Methods

```
public void contextDestroyed (ServletContextEvent event)
public void contextInitialized (ServletContextEvent event)
```

F.2.13 Class ServletException

Inheritance

Extends `Exception`.

Constructors

```
public ServletException ()
public ServletException (String message)
public ServletException (String message, Throwable rootCause)
public ServletException (Throwable rootCause)
```

Methods

```
public Throwable getRootCause ()
```

F.2.14 Class ServletInputStream

Inheritance

This is an abstract class.
Extends `java.io.InputStream`.

Factory methods

```
ServletRequest.getInputStream()
    throws IllegalStateException, java.io.IOException
```

Methods

```
public int readLine (byte[] b, int offset, int length)
     throws java.io.IOException
```

F.2.15 Class ServletOutputStream

Inheritance

This is an abstract class.

Extends `java.io.OutputStream`.

Factory methods

```
ServletResponse.getOutputStream()
     throws IllegalStateException, java.io.IOException
```

Methods

```
public void print (boolean b) throws java.io.IOException
public void print (char c) throws java.io.IOException
public void print (double d) throws java.io.IOException
public void print (float f) throws java.io.IOException
public void print (int i) throws java.io.IOException
public void print (long l) throws java.io.IOException
public void print (String s) throws java.io.IOException
public void println () throws java.io.IOException
public void println (boolean b) throws java.io.IOException
public void println (char c) throws java.io.IOException
public void println (double d) throws java.io.IOException
public void println (float f) throws java.io.IOException
public void println (int i) throws java.io.IOException
public void println (long l) throws java.io.IOException
public void println (String s) throws java.io.IOException
```

F.2.16 Interface ServletRequest

Constructors

No public constructors or factory methods.

Methods

```
public String getAttribute (String name)
public java.util.Enumeration getAttributeNames ()
public String getCharacterEncoding ()
public int getContentLength ()
public String getContentType ()
public ServletInputStream getInputStream ()
     throws IllegalStateException, java.io.IOException
public java.util.Locale getLocale ()
public java.util.Enumeration getLocales ()
```

```
public String getParameter (String name)
public String[] getParameterMap (String name)†public java.util.Enumeration get-
   ParameterNames ()
public String[] getParameterValues (String name)
public String getProtocol ()
public java.io.BufferedReader getReader ()
     throws IllegalStateException,
          java.io.IOException, java.io.UnsupportedEncodingException
public String getRemoteAddr ()
public String getRemoteHost ()
public RequestDispatcher getRequestDispatcher (String URL)
public String getScheme ()
public String getServerName ()
public int getServerPort ()
public boolean isSecure ()
public void removeAttribute (String name)
public void setAttribute (String name, Object value)
public void setCharacterEncoding (String encoding)
     throws java.io.UnsupportedEncodingException†
```

F.2.17 Class ServletRequestWrapper†

Inheritance

Implements `ServletRequest`.

Constructors

```
public ServletRequestWrapper (ServletRequest request)
```

Methods

```
public String getAttribute (String name)
public java.util.Enumeration getAttributeNames ()
public String getCharacterEncoding ()
public int getContentLength ()
public String getContentType ()
public ServletInputStream getInputStream ()
     throws IllegalStateException, java.io.IOException
public java.util.Locale getLocale ()
public java.util.Enumeration getLocales ()
public String getParameter (String name)
public String[] getParameterMap (String name)†
public java.util.Enumeration getParameterNames ()
public String[] getParameterValues (String name)
public String getProtocol ()
public java.io.BufferedReader getReader ()
     throws IllegalStateException,
          java.io.IOException, java.io.UnsupportedEncodingException
public String getRemoteAddr ()
public String getRemoteHost ()
```

```
public ServletRequest getRequest ()
public RequestDispatcher getRequestDispatcher (String URL)
public String getScheme ()
public String getServerName ()
public int getServerPort ()
public boolean isSecure ()
public void removeAttribute (String name)
public void setAttribute (String name, Object value)
public void setCharacterEncoding (String encoding)
    throws java.io.UnsupportedEncodingException
public void setRequest (ServletRequest request) throws IllegalArgumentException
```

F.2.18 Interface ServletResponse

Constructors

No public constructors or factory methods.

Methods

```
public void flushBuffer ()throws java.io.IOException
public int getBufferSize ()
public String getCharacterEncoding ()
public java.util.Locale getLocale ()
public ServletOutputStream getOutputStream ()
     throws IllegalStateException, java.io.IOException
public java.io.PrintWriter getWriter ()
     throws IllegalStateException,
          java.io.IOException, java.io.UnsupportedEncodingException
public boolean isCommitted ()
public void reset () throws IllegalStateException
pbulic void resetBuffer () throws IllegalStateException†
public void setBufferSize (int size) throws IllegalStateException
public void setContentLength (int length)
public void setContentType (String type)
public void setLocale (java.util.Locale locale)
```

F.2.19 Class ServletResponseWrapper†

Inheritance

Implements `ServletResponse`.

Constructors

```
public ServletResponseWrapper (ServletResponse request)
```

Methods

```
public void flushBuffer ()throws java.io.IOException
public int getBufferSize ()
```

```
public String getCharacterEncoding ()
public java.util.Locale getLocale ()
public ServletOutputStream getOutputStream ()
     throws IllegalStateException, java.io.IOException
public ServletResponse getResponse ()
public java.io.PrintWriter getWriter ()
     throws IllegalStateException,
          java.io.IOException, java.io.UnsupportedEncodingException
public boolean isCommitted ()
public void reset () throws IllegalStateException
pbulic void resetBuffer () throws IllegalStateException†
public void setBufferSize (int size) throws IllegalStateException
public void setContentLength (int length)
public void setContentType (String type)
public void setLocale (java.util.Locale locale)
public void setResponse (ServletResponse response)
     throws IllegalArgumentException
```

F.2.20 Interface SingleThreadModel

This interface defines no variables or methods.

F.2.21 Class UnavailableException

Inheritance

Extends `ServletException`.

Constructors

```
public UnavailableException (String message)
public UnavailableException (String message, int seconds)
```

Methods

```
public int getUnavailableSeconds ()
public boolean isPermanent ()
```

F.3 Package javax.servlet.http

F.3.1 Class cookie

Inheritance

Implements `Cloneable`.

Constructors

```
public Cookie (String name, String value) throws IllegalArgumentException
```

Methods

```
public Object clone ()
public String getComment ()
public String getDomain ()
public int getMaxAge ()
public String getName ()
public String getPath ()
public boolean getSecure ()
public String getValue ()
public int getVersion ()
public void setComment (String comment)
public void setDomain (String domain)
public void setMaxAge (int seconds)
public void setPath (String url)
public void setSecure (boolean flag)
public void setValue (String value)
public void setVersion (int version)
```

F.3.2 Class HttpServlet

Inheritance

This is an abstract class.

Extends `javax.servlet.GenericServlet`.

Implements `java.io.Serializable`, `javax.servlet.Servlet`, `javax.servlet.ServletConfig`.

Constructors

```
public HttpServlet ()
```

Methods

```
protected void doDelete (HttpServletRequest request,
                         HttpServletResponse response)
     throws javax.servlet.ServletException, java.io.IOException
protected void doGet (HttpServletRequest request,
                      HttpServletResponse response)
     throws javax.servlet.ServletException, java.io.IOException
protected void doHead (HttpServletRequest request,
                       HttpServletResponse response)
     throws javax.servlet.ServletException, java.io.IOException
protected void doOptions (HttpServletRequest request,
                          HttpServletResponse response)
     throws javax.servlet.ServletException, java.io.IOException
protected void doPost (HttpServletRequest request,
                       HttpServletResponse response)
     throws javax.servlet.ServletException, java.io.IOException
protected void doPut (HttpServletRequest request,
```

```
                        HttpServletResponse response)
     throws javax.servlet.ServletException, java.io.IOException
protected void doTrace (HttpServletRequest request,
                        HttpServletResponse response)
     throws javax.servlet.ServletException, java.io.IOException
protected long getLastModified (HttpServletRequest request)
protected void service (HttpServletRequest request,
                        HttpServletResponse response)
     throws javax.servlet.ServletException, java.io.IOException
public void service (HttpServletRequest request,
                     HttpServletResponse response)
     throws javax.servlet.ServletException, java.io.IOException
```

F.3.3 Interface HttpServletRequest

Inheritance

Extends `javax.servlet.ServletRequest`.

Constructors

No public constructors or factory methods.

Class variables

```
public static final String BASIC_AUTH = "BASIC";†
public static final String CLIENT_CERT_AUTH = "CLIENT_CERT";†
public static final String DIGEST_AUTH = "DIGEST";†
public static final String FORM_AUTH = "FORM";†
```

Methods

```
public String getAuthType ()
public String getContextPath ()
public Cookie[] getCookies ()
public long getDateHeader (String name)
public String getHeader (String name) throws IllegalArgumentException
public java.util.Enumeration getHeaderNames ()
public java.util.Enumeration getHeaders (String name)
public int getIntHeader (String name) throws NumberFormatException
public String getMethod ()
public String getPathInfo ()
public String getPathTranslated()
public String getQueryString ()
public String getRemoteUser ()
public String getRequestedSessionId ()
public String getRequestURI ()
public StringBuffer getRequestURL ()†
public String getServletPath ()
public HttpSession getSession ()
public HttpSession getSession (boolean create)
```

```
public java.security.Principal getUserPrincipal ()
public boolean isRequestedSessionIdFromCookie ()
public boolean isRequestedSessionIdFromURL ()
public boolean isRequestedSessionIdValid ()
public boolean isUserInRole (String role)
```

F.3.4 Class HttpServletRequestWrapper†

Inheritance

Extends `javax.servlet.ServletRequestWrapper`.
Implements `HttpServletRequest`, `javax.servlet.ServletRequest`.

Constructors

```
public HttpServletRequestWrapper (HttpServletRequest request)
    throws IllegalArgumentException
```

Methods

```
public String getAuthType ()
public String getContextPath ()
public Cookie[] getCookies ()
public long getDateHeader (String name)
public String getHeader (String name) throws IllegalArgumentException
public java.util.Enumeration getHeaderNames ()
public java.util.Enumeration getHeaders (String name)
public int getIntHeader (String name) throws NumberFormatException
public String getMethod ()
public String getPathInfo ()
public String getPathTranslated()
public String getQueryString ()
public String getRemoteUser ()
public String getRequestedSessionId ()
public String getRequestURI ()
public StringBuffer getRequestURL ()
public String getServletPath ()
public HttpSession getSession ()
public HttpSession getSession (boolean create)
public java.security.Principal getUserPrincipal ()
public boolean isRequestedSessionIdFromCookie ()
public boolean isRequestedSessionIdFromURL ()
public boolean isRequestedSessionIdValid ()
public boolean isUserInRole (String role)
```

F.3.5 Interface HttpServletResponse

Inheritance

Extends `javax.servlet.ServletResponse`.

Constructors

No public constructors or factory methods.

Class variables

```
public static final int SC_ACCEPTED = 202;
public static final int SC_BAD_GATEWAY = 502;
public static final int SC_BAD_REQUEST = 400;
public static final int SC_CONFLICT = 409;
public static final int SC_CONTINUE = 100;
public static final int SC_CREATED = 201;
public static final int SC_EXPECTATION_FAILED = 417;
public static final int SC_FORBIDDEN = 403;
public static final int SC_GATEWAY_TIMEOUT = 504;
public static final int SC_GONE = 410;
public static final int SC_HTTP_VERSION_NOT_SUPPORTED = 505;
public static final int SC_INTERNAL_SERVER_ERROR = 500;
public static final int SC_LENGTH_REQUIRED = 411;
public static final int SC_METHOD_NOT_ALLOWED = 405;
public static final int SC_MOVED_PERMANENTLY = 301;
public static final int SC_MOVED_TEMPORARILY = 302;
public static final int SC_MULTIPLE_CHOICES = 300;
public static final int SC_NO_CONTENT = 204;
public static final int SC_NON_AUTHORITATIVE_INFORMATION = 203;
public static final int SC_NOT_ACCEPTABLE = 406;
public static final int SC_NOT_FOUND = 404;
public static final int SC_NOT_IMPLEMENTED = 501;
public static final int SC_NOT_MODIFIED = 304;
public static final int SC_OK = 200;
public static final int SC_PARTIAL_CONTENT = 206;
public static final int SC_PAYMENT_REQUIRED = 402;
public static final int SC_PRECONDITION_FAILED = 412;
public static final int SC_PROXY_AUTHENTICATION_REQUIRED = 407;
public static final int SC_REQUEST_ENTITY_TOO_LARGE = 413;
public static final int SC_REQUEST_TIMEOUT = 408;
public static final int SC_REQUEST_URI_TOO_LONG = 414;
public static final int SC_REQUEST_RANGE_NOT_SATISFIABLE = 416;
public static final int SC_RESET_CONTENT = 205;
public static final int SC_SEE_OTHER = 303;
public static final int SC_SERVICE_UNAVAILABLE = 503;
public static final int SC_SWITCHING_PROTOCOLS = 101;
public static final int SC_UNAUTHORIZED = 401;
public static final int SC_UNSUPPORTED_MEDIA_TYPE = 415;
public static final int SC_USE_PROXY = 305;
```

Methods

```
public void addCookie (Cookie)
public void addDateHeader (String name, long date)
public void addHeader (String name, String value)
```

```
public void addIntHeader (String name, int value)
public boolean containsHeader (String name)
public String encodeRedirectURL (String url)
public String encodeURL (String url)
public void sendError (int statusCode)
     throws java.io.IOException, IllegalStateException
public void sendError (int statusCode, String message)
     throws java.io.IOException, IllegalStateException
public void sendRedirect (String location)
     throws java.io.IOException, IllegalStateException
public void setDateHeader (String name, long date)
public void setHeader (String name, String value)
public void setIntHeader (String name, int value)
public void setStatus (int statusCode)
```

F.3.6 Class HttpServletResponseWrapper†

Inheritance

Extends `javax.servlet.ServletResponseWrapper`.
Implements `HttpServletResponse`, `javax.servlet.ServletResponse`.

Constructors

```
public HttpServletResponseWrapper (HttpServletResponse response)
```

Methods

```
public void addCookie (Cookie)
public void addDateHeader (String name, long date)
public void addHeader (String name, String value)
public void addIntHeader (String name, int value)
public boolean containsHeader (String name)
public String encodeRedirectURL (String url)
public String encodeURL (String url)
public void sendError (int statusCode)
     throws java.io.IOException, IllegalStateException
public void sendError (int statusCode, String message)
     throws java.io.IOException, IllegalStateException
public void sendRedirect (String location)
     throws java.io.IOException, IllegalStateException
public void setDateHeader (String name, long date)
public void setHeader (String name, String value)
public void setIntHeader (String name, int value)
public void setStatus (int statusCode)
```

F.3.7 Interface HttpSession

Constructors

No public constructors or factory methods.

Methods

```
public Object getAttribute (String name) throws IllegalStateException
public java.util.Enumeration getAttributeNames ()
     throws IllegalStateException
public long getCreationTime () throws IllegalStateException
public String getId ()
public long getLastAccessedTime ()
public int getMaxInactiveInterval ()
public javax.servlet.ServletContext getServletContext ()†
public void invalidate () throws IllegalStateException
public boolean isNew () throws IllegalStateException
public void removeAttribute (String name) throws IllegalStateException
public void setAttribute (String name, Object value)
     throws IllegalStateException
public void setMaxInactiveInterval (int seconds)
```

F.3.8 Interface HttpSessionActivationListener†

Inheritance

Extends `java.util.EventListener`.

Constructors

No public constructors or factory methods.

Methods

```
public void sessionDidActivate (HttpSessionEvent event)
public void sessionWillPassivate (HttpSessionEvent event)
```

F.3.9 Interface HttpSessionAttributeListener†

Inheritance

Extends `java.util.EventListener`.

Constructors

No public constructors or factory methods.

Methods

```
public void attributeAdded (HttpSessionBindingEvent event)
public void attributeRemoved (HttpSessionBindingEvent event)
public void attributeReplaced (HttpSessionBindingEvent event)
```

F.3.10 Class HttpSessionBindingEvent

Inheritance

Extends `java.util.EventObject`.
Implements `java.io.Serializable`.

Constructors

```
public HttpSessionBindingEvent (HttpSession session, String name)
public HttpSessionBindingEvent (HttpSession session,
                                String name, Object value)†
```

Methods

```
public String getName ()
public HttpSession getSession ()
public Object getValue ()†
```

F.3.11 Interface HttpSessionBindingListener

Inheritance

Implements `java.util.EventListener`.

Constructors

No public constructors or factory methods.

Methods

```
public void valueBound (HttpSessionBindingEvent event)
public void valueUnbound (HttpSessionBindingEvent event)
```

F.3.12 Class HttpSessionEvent†

Inheritance

Extends `java.util.EventObject`.
Implements `java.io.Serializable`.

Constructors

```
public HttpSessionEvent (HttpSession session)
```

Methods

```
public HttpSession getSession ()
```

F.3.13 Interface HttpSessionListener†

Inheritance

Extends `java.util.EventListener`.

Constructors

No public constructors or factory methods.

Methods

```
public void sessionCreated (HttpSessionEvent event)
public void sessionDestroyed (HttpSessionEvent event)
```

F.3.14 Class HttpUtils

Deprecation

This class has been deprecated as of Servlet 2.3. Equivalent functionality is available via the `javax.servlet.ServletRequest` and `javax.servlet.http.HttpServletRequest` interfaces.

Constructors

```
public HttpUtils ()
```

Class methods

```
public static StringBuffer getRequestURL (HttpServletRequest request)
public static java.util.Hashtable parsePostData (int length,
                                                  ServletInputStream in)
   throws IllegalArgumentException
public static java.util.Hashtable parseQueryString (String queryString)
   throws IllegalArgumentException
```

F.4 Package javax.servlet.jsp

F.4.1 Interface HttpJspPage

Inheritance

Extends `JspPage`.

Constructors

No public constructors or factory methods.

Methods

```
public void _jspService (HttpServletRequest request,
                         HttpServletResponse response)
     throws ServletException java.io.IOException
```

F.4.2 Class JspEngineInfo

Inheritance

This is an abstract class.

Factory methods

```
JspFactory.getEngineInfo()
```

Methods

```
public String getSpecificationVersion ()
```

F.4.3 Class JspException

Inheritance

Extends `Exception`.
Implements `java.io.Serializable`.

Constructors

```
public JspException ()
public JspException (String message)
public JspException (String message, Throwable rootCause)†
public JspException (Throwable rootCause)†
```

Methods

```
public Throwable getRootCause ()
```

F.4.4 Class JspFactory

Inheritance

This is an abstract class.

Factory methods

```
JspFactory.getDefaultFactory()
```

Class methods

```
public static JspFactory getDefaultFactory()
public static void setDefaultFactory (JspFactory defaultFactory)
```

Methods

```
public JspEngineInfo getEngineInfo ()
public PageContext getPageContext (javax.servlet.Servlet servlet,
                                   javax.servlet.ServletRequest request,
                                   javax.servlet.ServletResponse response,
                                   String errorPageURL,
                                   boolean needsSession, int bufferSize,
                                   boolean autoFlush)
public void releasePageContext (PageContext context)
```

F.4.5 Interface JspPage

Inheritance

Extends `javax.servlet.Servlet`.

Constructors

No public constructors or factory methods.

Methods

```
public void jspDestroy ()
public void jspInit ()
```

F.4.6 Class JspTagException

Inheritance

Extends `JspException`.

Constructors

```
public JspTagException ()
public JspTagException (String message)
```

F.4.7 Class JspWriter

Inheritance

This is an abstract class.

Extends `java.io.Writer`.

Constructors

```
protected JspWriter (int bufferSize, boolean autoFlush)
```

Class variables

```
public static final int DEFAULT_BUFFER;
public static final int NO_BUFFER;
public static final int UNBOUNDED_BUFFER;
```

Instance variables

```
protected boolean autoFlush;
protected int bufferSize;
```

Methods

```
public void clear () throws java.io.IOException
public void clearBuffer () throws java.io.IOException
public void close () throws java.io.IOException
public void flush () throws java.io.IOException
public int getBufferSize ()
public int getRemaining ()
public boolean isAutoFlush ()
public void newLine () throws java.io.IOException
public void print (boolean b) throws java.io.IOException
public void print (char c) throws java.io.IOException
public void print (char[] s) throws java.io.IOException
public void print (double d) throws java.io.IOException
public void print (float f) throws java.io.IOException
public void print (int i) throws java.io.IOException
public void print (long l) throws java.io.IOException
public void print (Object o) throws java.io.IOException
public void print (String s) throws java.io.IOException
public void println ()throws java.io.IOException
public void println (boolean b) throws java.io.IOException
public void println (char c) throws java.io.IOException
public void println (char[] s) throws java.io.IOException
public void println (double d) throws java.io.IOException
public void println (float f) throws java.io.IOException
public void println (int i) throws java.io.IOException
public void println (long l) throws java.io.IOException
public void println (Object o) throws java.io.IOException
public void println (String s) throws java.io.IOException
```

F.4.8 Class PageContext

Inheritance

This is an abstract class.

Factory methods

```
JspFactory.getPageContext(...)
```

Class variables

```
public static final String APPLICATION;
public static final int APPLICATION_SCOPE;
public static final String CONFIG;
public static final String EXCEPTION;
public static final String OUT;
```

```
public static final String PAGE;
public static final int PAGE_SCOPE;
public static final String PAGECONTEXT;
public static final String REQUEST;
public static final int REQUEST_SCOPE;
public static final String RESPONSE;
public static final String SESSION;
public static final int SESSION_SCOPE;
```

Methods

```
public Object findAttribute (String name)
public void forward (String localURL)
     throws javax.servlet.ServletException,
          java.io.IOException, IllegalArgumentException,
          IllegalStateException, SecurityException
public Object getAttribute (String name)
     throws NullPointerException, IllegalArgumentException
public Object getAttribute (String name, int scope)
     throws NullPointerException, IllegalArgumentException
public java.util.Enumeration getAttributeNamesInScope (int scope)
public int getAttributesScope (String name)
public Exception getException ()
public JspWriter getOut ()
public Object getPage ()
public javax.servlet.ServletRequest getRequest ()
public javax.servlet.ServletResponse getResponse ()
public javax.servlet.ServletConfig getServletConfig ()
public javax.servlet.ServletContext getServletContext ()
public javax.servlet.http.HttpSession getSession ()
public void handlePageException (Throwable t)
     throws javax.servlet.ServletException, java.io.IOException,
          NullPointerException, SecurityException
public void include (String localURL)
     throws javax.servlet.ServletException, java.io.IOException,
          IllegalArgumentException, SecurityException
public void initialize (javax.servlet.Servlet servlet,
                        javax.servlet.ServletRequest request,
                        javax.servlet.ServletResponse response,
                        String errorPageURL, boolean needsSession,
                        int bufferSize, boolean autoFlush)
     throws java.io.IOException,
          IllegalStateException, IllegalArgumentException
public JspWriter popBody ()
public BodyContent pushBody ()
public void release ()
public void removeAttribute (String name)
public void removeAttribute (String name, int scope)
public void setAttribute (String name, Object value)
     throws NullPointerException
```

```
public void setAttribute (String name, Object value, int scope)
    throws NullPointerException, IllegalArgumentException
```

F.5 Package javax.servlet.jsp.tagext

F.5.1 Class BodyContent

Inheritance

This is an abstract class.

Extends `javax.servlet.jsp.JspWriter`.

Constructors

```
protected BodyContent (javax.servlet.jsp.JspWriter writer)
```

Methods

```
public void clearBody ()
public void flush () throws java.io.IOException
public javax.servlet.jsp.JspWriter getEnclosingWriter ()
public java.io.Reader getReader ()
public String getString ()
public void writeOut (java.io.Writer writer) throws java.io.IOException
```

F.5.2 Interface BodyTag

Inheritance

Extends `Tag`. As of JSP 1.2, also extends `IterationTag`.

Constructors

No public constructors or factory methods.

Class variables

```
public static final int EVAL_BODY_BUFFERED;†
```

Methods

```
public void doInitBody () throws javax.servlet.jsp.JspException
public void setBodyContent (BodyContent content)
```

F.5.3 Class BodyTagSupport

Inheritance

Extends `TagSupport`.

Implements `BodyTag`, `Tag`, `java.io.Serializable`. As of JSP 1.2, also implements `IterationTag`.

Constructors

```
public BodyTagSupport ()
```

Methods

```
public int doAfterBody ()throws javax.servlet.jsp.JspException
public int doEndTag () throws javax.servlet.jsp.JspException
public void doInitBody () throws javax.servlet.jsp.JspException
public int doStartTag () throws javax.servlet.jsp.JspException
public BodyContent getBodyContent ()
public javax.servlet.jsp.JspWriter getPreviousOut ()
public void release ()
public void setBodyContent (BodyContent content)
```

F.5.4 Interface IterationTag†

Inheritance

Extends `Tag`.

Constructors

No public constructors or factory methods.

Class variables

```
public static final int EVAL_BODY_AGAIN;
```

Methods

```
public void doAfterBody () throws javax.servlet.jsp.JspException
```

F.5.5 Class PageData†

Constructors

```
public PageData ()
```

Methods

```
public java.io.InputStream getInputStream ()
```

F.5.6 Interface Tag

Constructors

No public constructors or factory methods.

Class variables

```
public static final int EVAL_BODY_INCLUDE;
public static final int EVAL_PAGE;
public static final int SKIP_BODY;
public static final int SKIP_PAGE;
```

Methods

```
public int doEndTag ()throws javax.servlet.jsp.JspException
public int doStartTag () throws javax.servlet.jsp.JspException
public Tag getParent ()
public void release ()
public void setPageContext (javax.servlet.jsp.PageContext context)
public void setParent (Tag parent)
```

F.5.7 Class TagAttributeInfo

Constructors

```
public TagAttributeInfo (String name, boolean required,
                         String type, boolean requestTime)
```

Class methods

```
public static TagAttributeInfo getIdAttribute (TagAttributeInfo[] array)
```

Methods

```
public boolean canBeRequestTime ()
public String getName ()
public String getTypeName ()
public boolean isRequired ()
```

F.5.8 Class TagData

Inheritance

Implements `Cloneable`.

Constructors

```
public TagData (Object[][] attributes)
public TagData (java.util.Hashtable attributes)
```

Class variables

```
public static final Object REQUEST_TIME_VALUE;
```

Methods

```
public Object clone ()
public Object getAttribute (String name)
public String getAttributeString (String name)
```

```
public String getId ()
public void setAttribute (String name, Object value)
```

F.5.9 Class TagExtraInfo

Constructors

```
public TagExtraInfo ()
```

Methods

```
public TagInfo getTagInfo ()
public VariableInfo[] getVariableInfo (TagData data)
public boolean isValid (TagData data)
public void setTagInfo (TagInfo info)
```

F.5.10 Class TagInfo

Constructors

```
public TagInfo (String tagName, String tagClassName, String bodyContent,
                String infoString, TagLibraryInfo taglib,
                TagExtraInfo tei, TagAttributeInfo[] attributeInfo)
public TagInfo (String tagName, String tagClassName, String bodyContent,
                String infoString, TagLibraryInfo taglib,
                TagExtraInfo tei, TagAttributeInfo[] attributeInfo,
                String displayName, String smallIcon, String largeIcon,
                TagVariableInfo[] tagVariableInfo)†
```

Class variables

```
public static String BODY_CONTENT_EMPTY;
public static String BODY_CONTENT_JSP;
public static String BODY_CONTENT_TAG_DEPENDENT;
```

Methods

```
public TagAttributeInfo[] getAttributes ()
public String getBodyContent ()
public String getDisplayName ()†
public String getInfoString ()
public String getLargeIcon ()†
public String getSmallIcon ()†
public String getTagClassName ()
public TagExtraInfo getTagExtraInfo ()
public TagLibraryInfo getTagLibrary ()
public String getTagName ()
public VariableInfo getVariableInfo (TagData data)
public boolean isValid (TagData data)
public void setTagExtraInfo (TagExtraInfo tei)†
public void setTagLibrary (TagLibrary library)†
```

F.5.11 Class TagLibraryInfo

Inheritance

This is an abstract class.

Constructors

No public constructors or factory methods.

Methods

```
public String getInfoString ()
public String getPrefixString ()
public String getReliableURN ()
public String getRequiredVersion ()
public String getShortname ()
public TagInfo getTag (String shortname)
public TagInfo[] getTags ()
public String getURI ()
```

F.5.12 Class TagLibraryValidator†

Inheritance

This is an abstract class.

Constructors

```
public TagLibraryValidator ()
```

Methods

```
public java.util.Map getInitParameters ()
public void release ()
public void setInitParameters (java.util.Map map)
public String validate (String prefix, String uri, PageData page)
```

F.5.13 Class TagSupport

Inheritance

Implements `Tag`, `java.io.Serializable`. As of JSP 1.2, also implements `IterationTag`.

Constructors

```
public TagSupport ()
```

Class methods

```
public static final Tag findAncestorWithClass (Tag from, Class klass)
```

Methods

```
public int doAfterBody () throws javax.servlet.jsp.JspException
public int doEndTag () throws javax.servlet.jsp.JspException
public int doStartTag () throws javax.servlet.jsp.JspException
public String getId ()
public Tag getParent ()
public Object getValue (String name)
public java.util.Enumeration getValues ()
public void release ()
public void removeValue (String name)
public void setId (String id)
public void setPageContext (javax.servlet.jsp.PageContext context)
public void setParent (Tag parent)
public void setValue (String name, Object value)
```

F.5.14 Class TagVariableInfo†

Constructors

```
public TagVariableInfo (String nameGive, String nameFromAttribute,
                        String className, boolean declare, int scope)
```

Methods

```
public String getClassName ()
public boolean getDeclare ()
public String getNameFromAttribute ()
public String getNameGiven ()
public int getScope ()
```

F.5.15 Interface TryCatchFinally†

Constructors

No public constructors or factory methods.

Methods

```
public void doCatch (Throwable t) throws Throwable
public void doFinally ()
```

F.5.16 Class VariableInfo

Constructors

```
public VariableInfo (String variableName, String className,
                     boolean declare, int scope)
```

Class variables

```
public static int AT_BEGIN;
public static int AT_END;
```

```
public static int NESTED;
```

Methods

```
public String getClassName ()
public boolean getDeclare ()
public int getScope ()
public String getVarName ()
```

index

Symbols

.CVS file 488
.NET 7
:getProperty 609, 613
:setProperty 588, 609, 612
:useBean 588
<% and %> delimiters 32, 33
  in JSP 10
  origins in ASP 7
<%= delimeter 36
<%@ include %>. *See* include directive
<%@ page %> 53
<%@ taglib %> directive 50
<applet> 683, 685, 713
<attribute> 541, 563
<BASE> 393
<body-content> 539, 568
<context-param> 412, 413
<declare> 540, 558
<description> 397, 406, 537, 540, 541, 543
<display-nam> 540
<display-name> 397, 406, 536
<distributable> 397
<EMBED> 685
<error-page> 413
<example> 543
<filter> 406
<filter-class> 407
<filter-mapping> 406, 407
<filter-name> 407
<icon> 397, 406
<init-param> 399, 406, 537
<init-parameter> 633
<input> 446, 447–449
<jsp:declaration> 84, 627, 638
<jsp:directive.include> 80
<jsp:directive.page> 69
<jsp:expression> 88, 627, 638
<jsp:fallback> 685, 689
<jsp:forward> 75, 106, 117, 122, 125, 126, 158–159, 427, 709
<jsp:getProperty> 43, 128, 146–147, 179, 588, 596, 597, 710
<jsp:include> 82, 106, 117, 124, 125, 158–159, 238, 240, 421, 633, 711
<jsp:param> 123, 124, 688, 690, 709, 711, 713
<jsp:params> 689, 713
<jsp:plugin> 73, 128, 685, 712
<jsp:root> 625
<jsp:scriptlet> 91, 627, 638
<jsp:setProperty> 43, 128, 148–149, 154, 157, 179, 542, 596, 613, 714
  form support 64
  wild card 154, 515
<jsp:text> 626
<jsp:useBean> 43, 128, 142, 145, 151, 192, 584, 589, 597, 609, 612, 613, 710, 715
  type attribute 164
<jsp-file> 402
<jsp-version> 536
<large-icon> 397, 536, 540
<listener> 538
<listener-class> 538
<load-on-startup> 399, 403
<mime-mapping> 411
<mut:ifProperty> 44
<name> 539, 542
<name-from-attribute> 541, 558
<name-given> 540, 558
<OBJECT> 685
<option> 448
<param> 688
<param-name> 399, 407, 537

<param-value> 399, 407, 537
<required> 542
<rtexprvalue> 542, 543
<scope> 540, 558
<select> 448
<servlet> 397, 400
<servlet-class> 398
<servlet-mapping> 400, 475
<servlet-name> 398, 400, 407
<session-config> 412
<session-timeout> 412
<short-name> 536
<small-icon> 397, 536, 540
<table> 35
<tag> 535, 538
<tag-class> 539
<taglib> 405, 535, 662
<taglib-location> 405
<taglib-uri> 405
<tei-class> 539, 556, 583, 588
<textarea> 447
<tlib-version> 536
<type> 543
<url-pattern> 400, 407
<validator> 537
<validator-class> 537
<variable> 540, 558, 583
<variable-class> 540, 558, 588
<welcome-file-list> 397
_jspService() 53, 93

A

absolute URLs 393
abstraction 130
  and JavaBeans 13
accept header 473
access control 361
accessor methods 168–169, 171
  getter method 168, 171
  setter method 168, 171
actions 41, 50, 68, 102, 629
  custom 48
  standard 48
Active Server Pages 7, 36, 47
ActiveX components 7
addCookie() 419, 421
Allaire ColdFusion. *See* ColdFusion
Apache
  Server 24
  Server. *See also* web server
  Software Foundation 8, 12, 676
API for XML Processing 12
applets 8, 683, 689
application beans 163
application flow 231–232, 247
application implicit object 114, 123, 385, 467
application initialization parameters 413
application logic 230–231, 265, 287
application scope 120, 163
application server 264, 699
architecture 233
  multitier 263
  page-centric 233, 270
  requirements 268
  servlet-centric 233, 265
architecture multitier 266
ASCII text 475
ASP
  See also Active Server Pages
  similarities to JSP 11
ASP.NET 7
attribute scope 119
attributes 118
authentication 195, 247, 335, 337, 361
AuthenticationFilter 361, 408
autocommit 216, 223
autoFlush attribute 77, 79, 421
availability 269
AWT 683

B

back button 232, 251, 291
BannerBean 494
base name, Java classes 73
BeanInfo 189, 546, 590, 597, 603, 606
beanName attribute 190
beans. *See* JavaBeans
Blue Cookie Page 423
BodyContent 548, 570, 588, 596, 740
BodyTag 544, 547, 569, 575, 596, 616, 740
BodyTagSupport 544, 562, 570, 573, 596, 616, 740
bookmarking 233
boolean properties 178, 180
bound properties 192
browser 472

buffer 58
buffer attribute 75, 77
buffered output 75, 76
  See also output buffering
BufferedReader 469
ByteArrayInputStream 377
ByteArrayOutputStream 377
bytecodes 8

C

C language
  as programming language 5
C preprocessor 81
C sharp 7
C++ 6
CachedRowSet 212
caching 161, 163, 481
  prevention 109
Calendar 586
CDATA 626, 627, 629
CGI. *See* Common Gateway Interface
character set 71, 72
checked keyword 448
class methods 87
class path 394, 395
class variables 85
clearBody() 569
client/server protocol 19
Cocoon 12
code generation 489
coin flips 33–35, 40–41
Colburn, Rafe 235
ColdFusion 6–7, 199, 200
  similarities to JSP 11
color bars 523
COM 6
command pattern 249, 265, 287
CommandToken 292
comments 68, 97, 98, 702
commit() 216
Common Gateway Interface 4–5
  contrast with template systems 6
  scripting 468
compilation 7
  in ASP.NET 7
  into Java bytecodes 8
  of JSP into servlets 52
  of PHP 7
compilation error 92, 100, 114, 561
component 13
component-centric design 130
components
  architecture 13, 130–131, 240
  development 131, 140
  model 130
  persistence 160
composite pages 238
compound interest calculator 152
CompoundInterestBean 184, 187
conditionalization 93, 97, 587
  example 33
  tenary operator 90
conference booking tool 217
config implicit object 104, 116
configuring beans 181
connection pool 209
ConnectionBean 209, 219
constrained properties 192
container. *See* servlet, container, JSP container
content comments 98, 702
content handler 638, 645
content type 20, 71, 410, 411, 433, 471, 472
contentType attribute 71, 411, 525
control layer 230–232
cookies 26, 59–61, 67, 76, 106, 126, 128, 419, 431, 441, 563, 565, 568, 571, 727
  restrictions 425
CopyingTLV 635
CORBA 6
CountDown applet 690
CSS-1 483
custom tags 15, 44, 57, 66, 68, 82, 97, 121, 141, 174, 395, 468, 530, 531, 559, 583, 707
  API 544
  attributes 533
  body content 548
  descriptor 82, 405, 531, 535, 556, 559, 567, 587, 608, 609, 661, 707
  hierarchy 614
  interaction 614
  libraries 405, 698
  nested 570
  validation 556
  versioning 536

D

data beans 139, 271
data sources 200

databases 87, 254, 264
  access 217
  database-driven JSPs 202
  handling large sets of results 211
  handling nulls 207
  java.sql package 199
  persistent connections 208
  persistent ResultSet 211
  prepared statements 201, 283–284
  type conversion 205
DataBean 610
dates and times
  from a database 206
DebugBufferTag 561
declarations 84, 609, 704
  method 86
  variable 84
declare flag 557
DefaultHandler 646
deployment descriptor 105, 114, 116, 386, 387, 390, 396, 475
deprecated methods 718
destroy() 25
directives 68
  JSP 47
distributed
  architectures 263
  transactions 269
  web applications 397
division of labor 132, 134, 270
DMZ 267, 268, 275
doAfterBody() 549, 569, 573, 577, 600
doCatch() 554, 577
Document Object Model 12, 634, 652
Document Type Definition 11, 396, 623, 665
DocumentBuilder 655
DocumentBuilderFactory 654
doEndTag() 546, 549, 563, 564
doFinally() 554, 578
doGet() 57
doInitBody() 549
DOM. *See* Document Object Model
doPost() 25, 57
doStartTag() 546, 561, 564, 577, 585, 589, 598, 617
Drumbeat 2000 700
DTD. *See* Document Type Definition
dynamic content 470–492
  definition 3
  history 2–8
  justification 3–4
  simple JSP examples 32–44
dynamic HTML 441
dynamically generating property values 170

E

EJBs. *See* Enterprise JavaBeans
electronic mail 432–433, 501
  JavaMail 426, 432, 503, 531
Element Construction Set 10
email. *See* electronic mail
encodeHTML 572
EncodeHtmlTag 573
encodeURL() 570
Encom 335
Enterprise JavaBeans 263, 270
  and ColdFusion 6
  and Javabeans 264
  EJB container 264, 412
Ericsson R320 38
error handling 63, 94, 227, 252
  run time 56
  tag library validation 632
  translation-time 55
error page 79, 120, 126, 425
errorPage attribute 76, 79, 80, 94, 426
EVAL_BODY_AGAIN 549, 600
EVAL_BODY_BUFFERED 577
event listeners 409, 538
example tag library 559
Excel 488
Excel spread sheets 488
exception 63
exception implicit object 80, 120, 426, 427, 435, 719
expressions 84, 88
extends attribute 53, 72, 104
Extensible Markup Language. *See* XML
eXtensible Server Pages 12
Extensible Stylesheet Language Transformations 12
external content 482
extranet 267

F

fact() 86, 89, 93, 94, 98, 99, 106
factorial 86
factory method 718

factory pattern 718
failsafe 575
FailsafeTag 576
FAQ 698
FaqBean 276
FaqRepository 279
FaqRepositoryException 285
FaqServlet 312
FetchEmployeeServlet 258
file extension 52, 474
Filter 327, 330, 719
FilterChain 327, 331, 409, 719
FilterConfig 330, 362, 374, 407, 720
filters 327, 406
findAncestorWithClass() 615
firewall 267
flow control 93, 241, 247, 288
Flynn, Kevin 70, 91, 708
for loop 94
form processing
  persistent interfaces 447
FormBean 454
forms
  and HTTP methods 23
  handling 152, 155, 296, 441, 452
  persistent interfaces 446–447, 516
  submission 155
  support in JSP for 64
forProperty 588, 595, 616
  tag 596, 618
ForPropertyTagBeanInfo 606
ForPropertyTEI 608
freeMemory() 62

G

GameGrid 91
GET 21
  and servlets 25
getAttribute() 243, 246, 249
getAttributeString() 609
getClass() 597
getContextPath() 393
getCookies() 419, 421
getHeaders()
  as HTTP-specific method 26
getId() 609
getIndexedReader() 602
getInitParameter() 413
getInitParameters() 633
getInputStream() 632
getLastAccessedTime() 163
getMaxInactiveInterval() 163
getMimeType() 524
getPageContext() 524
getParam() 442
getParameter() 26, 38, 39, 64, 689
getParamValues() 442
getParent() 614, 615
getPathInfo() 249, 401
getPreviousOut() 570, 578
getReader() 602
getRemoteAddr() 27, 39
getRequestDispatcher() 107, 244
getRequestURL() 216, 246, 429
getResource() 394
getResourceAsStream() 394
getServletPath() 246
getString() 569
getter method 168, 171
getVariableInfo() 556, 608, 609
Gregg, Preston 253

H

headers 76, 128
  HTTP 20
Hello, world! 31
HelloBean 43, 681
helper class 533, 534, 556, 595, 600, 608
  naming convention 608
Hewlett Packard 697
hidden form elements 249, 446
HomeSite 700
HTML
  embedding code within 5
  encoding 572
  entity 447, 572
  printed by servlets 10
  production by JavaBeans 15
  tags 393
HTML. *See* Hypertext Markup Language
HTTP 72, 419, 422, 441
  cookies. *See* cookies
  GET 429
  GET method 347
  headers 106, 126
  POST method 347
  protocol 232
  status code 414

HTTP GET. *See* GET
HTTP POST. *See* POST
HTTP. *See* Hypertext Transfer Protocol 18
HttpJspPage 104, 735
HttpResponseWrapper 374
HTTPS 422
HttpServlet 25
HttpServletRequest 25, 39, 64, 106, 393, 419, 429, 729
HttpServletRequestWrapper 329, 332, 730
HttpServletResponse 25, 108, 419, 730
HttpServletResponseWrapper 329, 333, 376, 732
HttpSession 112, 163, 733
HttpSessionActivationListener 410, 733
HttpSessionAttributeListener 369, 410, 538, 733
HttpSessionBindingEvent 191
HttpSessionBindingListener 114, 190, 210–211, 734
HttpSessionEvent 734
HttpSessionListener 369, 410, 538, 735
HttpUtils 216, 429
Hypertext Markup Language 18
Hypertext Transfer Protocol 18–23, 57

I

IBM 697
if statement 93
ifProperty 588
IfPropertyTag 588
IIS. *See* Internet Information Server
IllegalArgumentException 95
IllegalStateException 125
implicit object 38, 64, 103, 196, 524, 562
  attributes 103, 106, 112, 115, 117, 123
import attribute 69, 72, 435, 706
import statement 73
include directive 71, 80, 81, 84, 116, 127, 238, 239, 629, 705, 712
index 616
index generator 517
indexed properties 137, 150, 172–174, 176, 194, 510, 600, 610
  accessing through bean tags 175
IndexTag 616
industry standards 16
InetAddress 440
info attribute 70
inheritance 718
initialization parameters 104, 114, 116
initializing beans 150
  from request 151
  properties 156
instance variables 85, 170, 185
Internet Assigned Numbers Authority (IANA) 71, 411
Internet Information Server. *See* web server
intranet 267–268
intranet example 335
introspection 167, 590, 595, 599, 602, 610
IntrospectionException 592, 603
introspector 590, 606
invoke() 605
IP address 28, 39, 437
iPlanet 699
isChecked() 443
isErrorPage attribute 79, 120, 435, 719
isNew() 41
ISO-8859-1 character set 71, 72
isSelected() 443
isThreadSafe attribute 85
isValid() 556, 608, 609
iteration 93, 94, 97, 587, 595
  example 34
IterationTag 546, 596, 741

J

J2EE. *See* Java 2 Platform, Enterprise Edition
J2ME. *See* Java 2 Platform, Micro Edition
J2SE. *See* Java 2 Platform, Standard Edition
Jakarta Tomcat 31, 405, 698
  and JSP 1.2 677
  and web applications 681
  builds 678
  downloading 677
  installation and use 676–682
  version 3 677
  version 4 677
JARs 532, 661
  jar command 395
  JAR files 385, 395
Java
  bytecodes 8
  CGI programs in 5
  ColdFusion extensions in 6
  generating with JSP 489
  history 683
  on the web 8–11

Java 2 683
  Enterprise Edition (J2EE) 396, 536, 539, 699
Java 2 Platform
  Enterprise Edition 15
    BluePrints 16
  Micro Edition 15
  Standard Edition 15
Java APIs for XML Processing 634
Java applets. *See* applets
Java Community Process 8, 10, 57, 676
Java Development Kit 677, 697
Java plug-in 128, 684
Java Server Pages
  application 163
  as a template system 10
  Bean tags 140
  comments 98
  components 202
  container 68, 70, 72, 390, 392, 399, 698
    version information 116
  future outlook 16
  history 10
  JSP 1.1 126, 535, 536, 539, 549
  JSP 1.2 72, 126, 319, 406, 530, 533, 535, 537, 538, 541, 543, 558, 623, 660, 718
  life-cycle methods 87
Java servlet technology. *See* servlets
Java servlet. *See* servlet
Java Virtual Machine 8, 684
Java Web Server 10
java.io.Serializable 62
java.sql package 199
JAVA_HOME 679
JavaBeans 13–15, 42–44, 66, 68, 89, 93, 128, 130, 135, 203, 530, 531, 545, 603
  accessibility 157
  and EJBs 264
  API 135, 166, 191
  bean containers 135
  configuring 164, 181
  constructors 181
  containers 135, 137, 166
  conventions 166
  creating 165
  data beans 139
  data types 137
  defining properties 168
  event model 191
  from a database 202
  indexed property 595
  initializing 150, 151, 155
  initializing from the request 151
  interfaces 189
  life span 157, 195
  persisting 202–205
  properties 135
  property sheets 138
  removing from scope 195
  scope 157
  self populating from a database 204
  serialized 190
  service beans 139
  support in JSP for 64
  visual 139
JavaMail 426, 432, 503, 531
  See also electronic mail 531
JavaScript 7, 19, 67, 133, 296, 298, 437, 451, 485, 528, 699
  cross-frame 439
  generating with JSP 437
  onChange() handler 439
  onKeyPress() handler 440
  onSubmit() handler 451
javax.servlet package 25
javax.servlet.Servlet interface 53
javax.sql 199
JAXP. *See* Java APIs for XML Processing
JCP. *See* Java Community Process
JDBC 199, 216, 254, 531, 540
  data types 205
  JDBC 2.0 200, 211, 212
JDBC Data Access API 14
JDK. *See* Java Deveopment Kit
Jedi training 234
JMeter 700
JNDI 200, 283
JRE 687
JRun 699
JScript 7
JSP
  contents of pages 47
  JSP 1.2 543
  standard tag library. *See* JSPTL
JSP container 31, 52, 53
  See also Jakarrta Tomcat
JSP style sheets 483
JspException 253, 551, 562, 599, 736
JSP-INTEREST 700
JspPage 104, 404, 737
JspTagException 562, 603, 605, 618

JSPTL (JSP Standard Tag Library) 57
JspWriter 109, 548, 618, 737
JVM. *See* Java Virtual Machine

L

latin-1 character set 72
life span 157
life-cycle events 87, 538
linked properties 136–137
Linux 697
LISP 5
load balancing 62
log files 114
LoginServlet 344
LogoutServlet 358
Lora 446

M

Macromedia ColdFusion. *See* ColdFusion
mail merge 6
mail. *See* electronic mail 531
maintenance 269
makeErrorReport() 427
MANIFEST.MF 532
Manning utility tags 560
Math.random() 33
Matryoshka dolls 327
MD5 292
mediator pattern 242, 286
message digest 252
META-INF directory 532
methods
  HTTP 21
Microsoft
  Internet Explorer 684, 687
  Windows 82, 437, 697
Microsoft Windows 7
  ColdFusion on 6
MIME 471
MIME types 71, 410, 411, 433, 471
  setContentType() 411
  text/html 410
modification date 467
multiformat applications 473
multipage transaction processing 217
multiplication table 35
multithreading 78
  See also isThreadSafe attribute
  thread safety 77, 85
multitier architectures 263, 266
multivalued properties. *See* indexed properties

N

NamedRequestDispatcher 246
namespaces
  XML 49
NestingTLV 651
Netscape
  Application Server 264
  Communicator 437, 684, 687
Node 656
NodeList 656
non-HTML content 37, 470–492
null values 180
NumberFormat 562

O

Object 104, 116, 597, 606
onChange() handler 439
onKeyPress() handler 440
onSubmit() handler 451
open source 7, 667, 699
out implicit object 109, 549
out.println() 27, 33, 53
output buffer 76, 125, 128, 421
  buffer size 76
  clearing 111
  default size 75
  error pages 79
  flushing 111, 125, 126
  size parameters 111

P

packages 72, 75, 143
page beans 158
page compiler 401
page compiler servlet 403, 533
page directive 68, 70, 85, 94, 104, 114, 120, 411, 421, 426, 427, 435, 613, 629, 706, 719
page implicit object 104, 719
page scope 120
page-centric design 233, 270
  limitations 241

PageContext 557, 738
implicit object 117, 123, 303
instance variable 562, 565, 570, 583, 589, 598, 600, 614
PageData 632, 741
pageEncoding attribute 72
page-to-page communication 294
performance 269
JSP performance 54
persistence 265
long term 190
persistent connections 208
persistent ResultSet 211
PHP 7, 199
plain text output 475
PlotBean 610
ports
TCP 680
POST 21, 429
and servlets 25
precompilation 54, 659
precompiling JSP pages 386, 403, 404
prepared statements 201, 283–284
presentation layer 230–231
PrintWriter 109, 428
process
definition 5
properties 135, 168
data types 137
handling null values 180
indexed 137
linked 136
name conventions 171
read-only, write-only 136
property
JavaBeans 42
property descriptors 603
property sheets 138
PropertyDescriptor 591, 607
PropertyVetoException 192
protocol
client/server 19
definition 18
request/response 19
protocols
bidrectional 19
proxies. *See* web proxies
public web 267

Q

quote generator 497

R

radio buttons 447
read-only property 171
Recognizer 91
Red Cookie Page 421
reference implementation
reflection 167, 590, 591, 595, 599, 600, 604
relative URL 393
release() 553, 564, 565, 571, 584, 589, 592, 601, 617, 633
reloading a page 232, 251, 291
removing a bean 195
reportCookies() 431
reportException() 428
reportHeaders() 430
reporting system problems 437
reportParameters() 429
reportRequest() 428
request 24, 448
attributes 103, 106, 159, 243–246, 248, 253, 446, 720
beans 159
headers 419, 430
HTTP 18
implicit object 38, 64, 105, 123, 196, 419, 423, 427, 442, 446, 467
parameters 67, 106, 123, 124, 126, 152, 155–157, 249, 430, 442, 447–449, 451, 453
scope 120
spoofing 156
request parameters 38
request phase 54
request/response model 19, 24, 52
requestContains() 443
RequestDispatcher 243–245, 247, 253, 446, 720
forward() 244
include() 245
request-time attribute expressions 52
request-time attribute values 52, 122, 124, 126, 542, 689, 690, 709, 711, 715
XML representation 627
Resin 67, 699
resource pooling 534, 544, 556

response 24
headers 77, 112, 419, 421
HTTP 18
implicit object 38, 64, 107, 419, 421
ResponseWrapper 374
ResultSet 203, 212
persistent 211
reusability 130–131
and JavaBeans 13
risk factors 269
role-based pages 233
role-based security 336
RoleFilter 364, 408
rollback() 216
rotating banner ad 494
run time
of JSP page 54
run-time errors 76

S

SAX. *See* Simple API for XML
SAXParser 642
SAXParserFactory 641
scalability 269
scope 92, 119, 164, 195, 557
application 120
of JavaBeans 157
page 158
request 159
session 120
screen mapper 248
ScriptFreeTLV 638
scripting
elements 66, 68, 71, 102
language 66, 80, 84, 89, 104, 601
comments 99
variables 533, 538, 557, 559, 583, 595, 599, 600, 608, 609
scripting elements 47
scripting language
and JavaBeans 14
in template systems 6
scriptlets 84, 91, 93, 99, 713
and JavaBeans 192
search engine 3
security 156, 195
selected keyword 448
self-populating Beans 204
sendEmail() 432
sending mail. *See* electronic mail
separation
of presentation and implementation 2, 14, 41–44
serialization 269
serializable interface 190
server control. *See* ASP.NET
Server Side JavaScript 199
server.xml 680
service beans 139
service() 25, 53
servlet 9, 98, 104, 122, 124, 126, 128, 159, 233, 242–249, 253, 265, 270, 386, 397, 402, 446, 718, 720
and web servers 24
comparison with applets 9
comparison with CGI 9–10
compilation of JSP to 52, 56
container
definition 24
version information 116
drawbacks 10
errors 426
example code 26
history 10
mapping 400
request attributes 247, 253, 446, 720
RequestDispatcher 246
Servlet 2.3 319
Servlet API 2.1 244
Servlet API 2.2 159, 244
Servlet API 2.3 126, 538
servlet interface 25
structure 24
technical overview 23–29
with JSP 242, 287
servlet chaining 326
servlet container
See also Jakarta Tomcat
servlet engine. *See* servlet container
servlet JSP standards
See Jakarta Tomcat
servlet-centric design 233, 265
ServletConfig 105
ServletContext 114, 244, 385, 413, 721
ServletContextAttributeEvent 722
ServletContextAttributeListener 410, 538, 722
ServletContextEvent 722
ServletContextListener 410, 538, 723
ServletExec 699

ServletRequest 25, 105, 724
ServletRequestWrapper 329, 332, 725
ServletResponse 25, 107, 726
ServletResponseWrapper 329, 332, 726
session 39, 59–63, 269, 413
  attribute 70, 75, 114, 719
  beans 160
  events 190
  ID 568, 570, 571
  implicit object 38, 39, 64, 75, 112, 120, 123
  management 67, 75, 112, 114, 120, 123, 160, 567, 568
  migration 63
  scope 120
  timeout 113
session identifier 59
session management 19, 39, 59
  special considerations 61
setAttribute() 39, 246, 583, 585
setBodyContent() 548
setContentType() 411
setInitParameters() 633, 640
setMaxAge() 421
setMaxInactiveInterval() 163, 412
setPageContext() 545, 562
setParent() 545, 614
setStatus() 414
setter method 168, 171
shopping cart 161, 190
Simple API for XML 12, 634, 638
SimpleBeanInfo 607
SimpleUserBase 339
SimpleUserDataManager 340
singleton pattern 279, 283
SMTP 432–433
socket connections 507
Solaris 697
source
  viewing HTML 35
spawned
  definition 5
spread sheets 488
SQL 201, 216, 254, 540
SQLException 285, 414
stack trace 425, 428, 436
standard action
  definition 50
startsWithVowel() 86
state
  HTTP as not preserving 19
stateful
  HTTP as not 19
stateless
  HTTP as 19
  protocols, implecations of 59
static content 3
  example 31
static methods 87
static variables 85
status line
  HTTP 20
sticker 499
sticky widgets 441, 515
StringBuffer 428, 574
StringReplaceFilter 372
StringReplaceResponse 375
StringWriter 428
style sheets 483
Submit buttons 449
Sun Microsystems 697
superclass 72
Swing 683
synchronized keyword 78, 284
syntax 48–50
system commands 468

T

table
  HTML 35
  multiplication 35
tag 544, 561, 615, 741
tag constants
  EVAL_BODY_AGAIN 547
  EVAL_BODY_BUFFERED 548, 577
  EVAL_BODY_INCLUDE 546, 548, 589
  EVAL_PAGE 547, 563
  REQUEST_TIME_VALUE 556
  SKIP_BODY 549, 577, 585, 589, 599, 600, 618
  SKIP_PAGE 547
tag handler 534, 544, 661
  naming convention 561
  resource management 556
  reuse 534, 550
tag libraries. *See* custom tags
tag library validator 631
  sequencing 632
TagAttributeInfo 559, 742
TagData 556, 609

TagExtraInfo 539, 556, 558, 608, 743
TagInfo 559, 743
taglib directive 82, 405, 530, 531, 625, 662, 665, 707
taglib.tld 532, 661
TagLibraryInfo 559, 744
TagLibraryValidator 632, 744
TagSupport 544, 561, 562, 615, 744
TagVariableInfo 559
team size 270
TEI 608
  See also TagExtraInfo
Tell a Friend! sticker 499
Telnet
  comparison with HTTP 19
template systems 5–8
testing 404
text areas 447, 516
text field 446
throwable 56, 120, 435
timeOfDay 583, 594
TimeOfDayBean 584, 594
TimeOfDayTag 584
TimerBean 161
timestamp 206, 285
TimeZone 586
TLD. See tag library, descriptor 83
TmpServletOutputStream 376
Tomcat. *See* Jakarta Tomcat
toString() 89
touch 82
transaction 216, 218, 232
  integrity 251, 269, 291
  management 263
  monitors 264
  processing 216–217
  support 265
  token 251, 252
transferring control 117, 122, 125
transformation
  XSLT 12
translation 52–56
  errors 55
  versus execution 54
trigger properties 136, 205
try block 94, 96, 426, 435
TryCatchFinally 554, 575
tutorial 698
type conversion 137, 179

U

Unicode 628
UNIX 82, 109, 468, 680
  time 109
UnknownFaqException 285
Uniform Resource Locator. *See* URL
URL 22, 567
  absolute 393
  mapping 386, 392, 400
  parameters 28, 38
  relative 393
  rewriting 567, 568
URLDecoder 424
user authentication 195, 335, 337
user-agent 472
UserBean 337
UserDataManager 338
UserSessionManager 341

V

validate() 632
validating
  custom tag libraries 533
validation 533
  client-side 451
  custom tag libraries 537
  of JSP pages 12
  of XML documents 11
  server-side 452
ValidationMessage 632
valueBound() 191
valueUnbound() 191
VariableInfo 557, 609
VariableInfo constants
  AT_BEGIN 558
  AT_END 558
  NESTED 558, 609
velocity 8
View Source 35, 98, 525
virtual private networks 267
visibility 557
visual component Beans 138–139
VPN. *See* Virtual Private Network
VXML 479

W

WAR. *See* web archive

wasNull() 207
WDDX and XML 11
WDDX. *See* Web Distributed Data Exchange
web application deployment descriptor. *See* deployment descriptor
web applications 230
  from component 133
web archive 385
  <context-param> 412
  <description> 397
  <display-name> 397
  <distributable> 397
  <icon> 397
  <init-param> 399
  <large-icon> 397
  <load-on-startup> 399
  <param-name> 399
  <param-value> 399
  <servlet> 400
  <servlet-class> 398
  <servlet-mapping> 400
  <servlet-name> 398, 400
  <session-config> 412
  <session-timeout> 412
  <small-icon> 397
  <url-pattern> 400
  <web-app> 397
  <welcome-file-list> 397
  classes directory 394
  creating 395
  deployment descriptor 386
  expanded 415, 417
  files 390, 392
  lib directory 395
  registering with JSP container 386
web browser 19–23
Web Distributed Data Exchange 6, 8
web server
  communication with external process 4
  definition 18
web server clustering 269
web teams 132
web.xml 386, 389, 532, 662
WEB-INF 681
WEB-INF directory 386, 394
  classes directory 394, 405
  lib directory 395, 405, 661
  tlds directory 395, 405, 532
WebLogic 699
WebSphere 160, 264, 699, 700
while loop 94
white space 148
Whois 505
Windows. *See* Microsoft Windows
Wireless Markup Language 37, 474
withArticle() 86
WML 474
worker beans 139
write-only property 171
WYGIWYG 478, 489
WYGIWYG output 476

X

XML 11–13, 47, 71, 82, 98, 121, 386, 387, 396, 531, 622
  and JSP 12
  empty tags 49
  entities 629
  generating 477
  namespace 49, 625, 655, 707
  overview 48–50
  page translation 69
  syntax 51
  view of JSP pages 50
XML Path Language 12
XML representation 623
  root element 625
xmlns attribute 625
XPath. *See* XML Path Language
XSLT. *See* Extensible Stylesheet Language Transformations 12
XSP. *See* eXtensible Server Pages

Z

Zip files 678